ROYAL HISTORICAL SOCIETY

STUDIES IN HISTORY

New Series

GEORGE CHASTELAIN AND
THE SHAPING OF VALOIS BURGUNDY

Studies in History New Series

Editorial Board

Professor Martin Daunton (*Convenor*)
Professor David Eastwood
Dr Steven Gunn
Professor Colin Jones
Dr Peter Mandler
Professor Pat Thane
Dr Simon Walker
Professor Kathleen Burk (*Honorary Treasurer*)

GEORGE CHASTELAIN
AND THE SHAPING
OF VALOIS BURGUNDY

POLITICAL AND HISTORICAL CULTURE AT COURT
IN THE FIFTEENTH CENTURY

Graeme Small

THE ROYAL HISTORICAL SOCIETY
THE BOYDELL PRESS

© Graeme Small 1997

All rights reserved. Except as permitted under current legislation no part of this work may be photocopied, stored in a retrieval system, published, performed in public, adapted, broadcast, transmitted, recorded or reproduced in any form or by any means, without the prior permission of the copyright owner

The right of Graeme Small to be identified as the author of this work has been asserted in accordance with sections 77 and 78 of the Copyright, Designs and Patents Act 1988

First published 1997
The Royal Historical Society, London
in association with
The Boydell Press, Woodbridge
Reprinted in paperback and transferred to digital printing 2011
The Boydell Press, Woodbridge

ISBN 97 0 86193 237 5 hardback
ISBN 978 1 84383 634 6 paperback

The Boydell Press is an imprint of Boydell & Brewer Ltd
PO Box 9, Woodbridge, Suffolk IP12 3DF, UK
and of Boydell & Brewer Inc,
668 Mt Hope Avenue, Rochester, NY 14620, USA
website: www.boydellandbrewer.com

A CIP catalogue record for this book is available
from the British Library

Library of Congress Catalog Card Number 97–16769

This publication is printed on acid-free paper

Contents

	Page
Acknowledgements	vii
Abbreviations	ix
Introduction	1
1 Origins and Early Career (c. 1414–1446)	9
2 The Courtier (1446–1475)	51
3 The Chronicler and *Indiciaire*	91
4 The Making of the Chronicle	128
5 Reading the Chronicle	162
6 The Audience of the Chronicle	197
Conclusion	228
Appendices	
1. The manuscripts: a codicological survey	231
2. An anomalous work and its context	245
Bibliography	249
Index	293

For my parents

Acknowledgements

I have incurred a great number of debts while working on this book. I would like to express my gratitude in the first instance to the various bodies which provided funding or other assistance for my research: the Scottish Education Department, the British Academy, the Travel and Research Committee of the University of Edinburgh, the Small Grants Committee of the University of Newcastle upon Tyne, the Research Committee of the Department of History at Keele University and the Faculty of Arts Research Support Sub-Committee at the University of Glasgow. The French Department of the University of Edinburgh kindly provided me with accommodation in Paris through an agreement with the École normale supérieure. At a later stage the University of Glasgow Publications Fund provided a generous grant in aid of publication for which I am most grateful.

I am glad to thank all those who have supplied me at some point or other with information which has contributed to the writing of this book, although naturally I would not wish to burden them with any responsibility for the way I have used it: Christopher Allmand, Jean-Pierre Aniel, Tôru Araki, the late John Armstrong, Peter Arnade, Janet Backhouse, Mark Ballard, Eric Balthau, Philip Bennett, Susanna Bliggenstorfer, Lorne Campbell, Pierre Cockshaw, Frank Daelemans, Kathleen Daly, Edward De Maesschalck, Alain Derville, Jean Devaux, Paul De Win, Jean Dumoulin, Claude Gauvard, Bernard Guenée, Margaret Harvey, Tony Holden, Michael Jones, Anne-Françoise Labie, Marie-Christine Laleman, Eric Lecomte, Alistair Millar, David Morgan, Pierre Mouriau de Meulenacker, Guy Muraille, Jacques Paviot, Graham Runnalls, René Stuip, Claude Thiry, Malcolm Vale, Michel Vangheluwe, Cyriel Vleeschouwers, Anne Wanono and Rob Wegman. Many gaps remain in my knowledge of Chastelain and his world; without such patient and often very generous help, however, the gaps would have been far greater.

I owe a particular debt of gratitude to four friends who provided me with invaluable assistance and who, along with their families, made my research trips both happy and memorable. Daniel Lievois guided me through the archives of Ghent and provided me with precious information and advice for the first chapter, to which Marc Boone added his own contribution. Ludovic Nys pursued references and was always willing to discuss ideas, while Laurence Vanderstraeten furnished me with material from the Archives départementales du Nord. Without them my experience in Belgium and France – and this book – would have been altogether different.

I wish to thank Peter Lewis, Tony Goodman, John Stephens, Peter Jackson, David Laven, Philip Morgan, Mark Galeotti and Stuart Airlie for helping untangle some of my ideas and arguments, and Michael Jones, Steve Gunn and

Christine Linehan for all their efforts at the publication stage. Malcolm Gaskill was a greater help than even he knows during the writing of this book, and Paul Nugent generously (though recklessly, as it turned out) gave freely of his time and personal possessions. Ken Fowler introduced me to George Chastelain and his work over twelve years ago and supervised the doctoral thesis upon which this study is based. He has been a constant source of encouragement and guidance ever since.

Last but not least, I would like to thank my wife Philippa and my family for their unstinting support.

Graeme Small
Glasgow
May 1997

Abbreviations

AB	*Annales de Bourgogne*
ABSHF	*Annuaire-bulletin de la Société de l'histoire de France*
ACO	Archives de la Côte d'Or
ADN	Archives départementales du Nord
AEM	Archives de l'État à Mons
AGR	Archives générales du royaume
AMV	Archives municipales de Valenciennes
Barrois, Bibliothèque	J. Barrois, *Bibliothèque protypographique, ou librairies des fils du roi Jehan, Charles V, Jean de Berri, Philippe de Bourgogne et les siens*, Paris 1830
Bartier, Légistes	J. Bartier, *Légistes et gens de finance au XVe siècle*, Brussels 1952
BCRH	*Bulletin de la Commission royale d'histoire*
Beaucourt, Histoire	G. du Fresne de Beaucourt, *Histoire de Charles VII*, 6 vols, Paris 1881–91
BEC	*Bibliothèque de l'École des chartes*
BL	British Library
BM	Bibliothèque municipale
BMGN	*Bijdragen en Mededelingen betreffende de Geschiedenis der Nederlanden*
BML	Biblioteca Medicea-Laurenziana
BN	Bibliothèque nationale de France
BNB	*Biographie nationale de Belgique*
BR	Bibliothèque royale Albert 1er
BSHAG	*Bulletin de la Société d'histoire et d'archéologie de Gand*
CCABN	*Cinq-centième anniversaire de la bataille de Nancy (1477)*, Nancy 1979
Chartier, Chronique	Jean Chartier, *Chronique de Charles VII, roi de France*, ed. A. Vallet de Viriville, 3 vols, Paris 1858
Commynes, Mémoires	Philippe de Commynes, *Mémoires*, ed. J. Calmette and G. Durville, 3 vols, Paris 1924–5, repr. 1981
CTO	R. De Smedt (ed.), *Les chevaliers de la Toison d'Or*, Frankfurt am Main 1994
d'Escouchy, Chronique	Mathieu d'Escouchy, *Chronique*, ed. G. du Fresne de Beaucourt, 3 vols, Paris 1863–4
Doutrepont, Littérature	G. Doutrepont, *La littérature française à la cour des ducs de Bourgogne*, Paris 1909

du Clercq, Mémoires	Jacques du Clercq, Mémoires, ed. J. A. C. Buchon, in Collection des chroniques nationales françaises: Chroniques d'Enguerrand de Monstrelet, xii–xv, Paris 1826–7
FA	La 'France anglaise' au moyen âge, Paris 1988
FFQS	B. Chevalier and P. Contamine (eds), La France de la fin du XVe siècle, Paris 1985
HMGOG	Handelingen der Maatschappij voor Geschiedenis en Oudheidkunde te Gent
IRHT	Institut de recherche et d'histoire des textes (Paris)
Itinéraires	H. Vander Linden, Itinéraires de Philippe le Bon, duc de Bourgogne (1419–1467) et de Charles, comte de Charolais (1433–1467), Brussels 1940
JMH	Journal of Medieval History
La Marche, Mémoires	Olivier de La Marche, Mémoires, ed. H. Beaune and J. d'Arbaumont, 4 vols, Paris 1883–8
Lefèvre, Chronique	Jean Lefèvre de St Rémy, Chronique, ed. F. Morand, 2 vols, Paris 1876–81
MA	Le Moyen Age
Molinet, Chroniques	Jean Molinet, Chroniques, ed. G. Doutrepont and O. Jodogne, 3 vols, Brussels 1935–7
Monstrelet, Chronique	Enguerran de Monstrelet, Chronique, ed. L. Douët-d'Arcq, 6 vols, Paris 1857–62
PCEEBM	Publications du Centre européen d'études burgundo-médianes (1958–83)
PCEEB	Publications du Centre européen d'études bourguignonnes (XIVe–XVIe siècles) (1984–)
Plancher, Histoire	U. Plancher, Histoire générale et particulière de Bourgogne, 4 vols, Dijon 1739–81
PTSEC	Positions des thèses soutenues à l'École des chartes
RBPH	Revue belge de philologie et d'histoire
RH	Revue historique
RN	Revue du Nord
SAG	Stadsarchief Gent
UBG	Universiteitsbibliotheek Gent
Vaughan, CTB	R. Vaughan, Charles the Bold, London 1973
Vaughan, PTG	R. Vaughan, Philip the Good, London 1970

All references in the text are to Kervyn de Lettenhove's edition of Chastelain's Chronicle (1863–6), supplemented by that of Delclos (1991) for previously unknown fragments in BL, Add. MS 54156. Full references are given in the bibliography. Kervyn's edition is denoted by Roman numerals indicating the volume, followed by a comma and Arabic numerals for the page reference. Delclos's edition is denoted by the name of the editor, followed by a comma and the page reference in Arabic numerals. Unless otherwise stated, sums of money are in pounds of Flanders.

Introduction

Some time after the publication in 1930 of his important article, 'L'État bourguignon, ses rapports avec la France et les origines d'une nationalité néerlandaise', Johan Huizinga received a letter from Henri Pirenne.[1] Huizinga had dedicated his study to the great Belgian historian, but Pirenne's response was more than an act of courtesy. The article had highlighted the rather different views on Valois Burgundy which the two men held. A response of sorts was required.

Nearly thirty years earlier, in the second volume of his government-sponsored *Histoire de Belgique*, Pirenne had attributed a special place to the Valois dukes in the history of his relatively young nation.[2] Philip the Bold (1363–1404) and John the Fearless (1404–19), although they had acquired dominions and aspirations in the Low Countries which outweighed in importance the lands (if not the titles) granted by the crown in eastern France, remained heavily involved in the political life of the realm. So great was John's embroilment that eventually he would be murdered at Montereau by the supporters of one of his opponents, the future Charles VII. Famously, Pirenne thought that the impact of this one event was enough to bring about decisive change in the political history and political culture of Valois Burgundy under John's son, Philip the Good (1419–67): 'Désormais ce n'est plus en France ni par la France, c'est hors de France et contre la France que la maison de Bourgogne poursuivra l'accomplissement de ses desseins.'[3] The English alliance (1420–35) freed Philip's hands to pursue a policy of dynastic expansion within the Low Countries and towards the Rhine – a policy which achieved relatively quick and dramatic results.[4] As his dominions expanded, he presided over

---

[1] Huizinga first treated the subject in 1911, but it only appeared fully as 'Uit de voorgeschiedenis van ons nationaal besef', in *Tien Studiën*, Haarlem 1926. A much-changed French version, delivered at the Sorbonne, was published in three parts in MA xl (1930), 171–93; xli (1931), 11–35, 83–96. See also idem, *Verzamelde Werken*, Haarlem 1948–53, ii. 161–215, and cf. A. G. Jongkees, 'Une génération d'historiens devant le phénomène bourguignon', BMGN lxxxviii (1973), 215–32 (repr. with slight alterations in idem, *Burgundica et varia*, Hilversum 1990, 131–49).
[2] H. Pirenne, *Histoire de Belgique*, ii, Brussels 1902 (all references hereinafter to the revised third edition of 1922); B. Lyon, *Henri Pirenne*, Ghent 1974, 151ff.; N. F. Cantor, *Inventing the Middle Ages*, Cambridge 1992, 128.
[3] Pirenne, *Histoire de Belgique*, ii. 238. Political history is concerned with events; political culture is concerned more with the attitudes and values which shape and respond to those events.
[4] The most important acquisitions – by diplomacy, purchase and less often conquest – were as follows: the counties of Namur (1421–9), Holland, Zeeland and Hainaut (1428–33),

1

nothing less than the 'formation and constitution of the Burgundian state'.[5] The third duke's achievement was pursued by his son, Charles the Bold (1467–77), under whom 'la maison de Bourgogne dépouille ... les dernières traces de son origine'.[6] However, it was Philip, not Charles, who had laid the foundations of Belgium: 'Son intérêt s'est confondu avec l'intérêt national, et c'est avec raison que Juste Lipse a décerné à Philippe le Bon le titre de *conditor Belgii*.'[7] The strains of *La Muette de Portici* are almost audible behind the remark.[8]

The tinge of patriotism in Pirenne's scholarly masterpiece was not rejected out of hand.[9] Soon after the work's publication, Georges Doutrepont signalled changes in the historical culture of the Burgundian court under Philip the Good which he clearly linked to the perception of political developments discussed above.[10] Other historians were less impressed by Pirenne's seemingly nationalist agenda, but his central thesis concerning the emergence of a Burgundian state proved to be influential. The three most important syntheses this century on the history of Valois Burgundy elaborate this theme, albeit in different ways and to differing degrees.[11] The influence has perhaps been most apparent in the substantial work of Richard Vaughan, for whom 'the formation of the Burgundian state' and its severance from France occurred even earlier than Pirenne had suggested – during the reign of Philip the Bold. Philip's grandson had simply overseen its 'apogee'.[12] In his own day, of course, the influence of Pirenne's views was all the greater. By the time Huizinga's article appeared, the *Histoire de Belgique* had already entered its fifth edition.

Despite the use of the term 'État bourguignon' in the title of his study,

and the duchies of Brabant, Limbourg (1430) and Luxembourg (1441–3). In several of these cases the ground had been prepared for Philip by his father and grandfather.
[5] H. Pirenne, 'The formation and constitution of the Burgundian state', *American Historical Review* xiv (1908–9), 477–502.
[6] Idem, *Histoire de Belgique*, ii. 321.
[7] Ibid. ii. 173.
[8] On the events of the revolution of 1830 see F. Van Calken, *Histoire de Belgique des origines à nos jours*, Brussels 1944, 491.
[9] Pirenne denied the work had a patriotic slant: *Henri Pirenne*, i, Brussels 1938, 48, 122.
[10] See table of abbreviations. Doutrepont's work discussed historical literature and, by extension, the sense of the past – two facets of any elite's historical culture – at the Burgundian court. Despite his chosen title, he detected the emergence of an autonomous Burgundian historical culture. His views are discussed more fully in ch. 3 below.
[11] These, in chronological order, are the five-volume study by R. Vaughan (*Philip the Bold*, London 1962; *John the Fearless*, London 1966; PTG; CTB; and *Valois Burgundy*, London 1975); the *Algemene Geschiedenis der Nederlanden*, iv–v, Haarlem 1980; and W. Prevenier and W. Blockmans, *The Burgundian Netherlands*, trans. P. King and Y. Mead, Cambridge 1986.
[12] Professor Vaughan began to revise his position in an article which did not achieve the prominence of his multi-volume study: 'Hue de Lannoy and the question of the Burgundian state', in R. Schneider (ed.), *Das spätmittelalterliche Königtum im Europäischen Vergleich*, Sigmaringen 1987, 335–45.

Huizinga was at odds with his friend.[13] He did not believe that the Valois dukes had ruled over a state by any modern or even contemporary definition of the concept. Although the ambitions of Philip and Charles increasingly confronted the interests and rights of the crown, they never made a complete break from the kingdom, politically or emotionally.[14] This typically bold argument was rooted less in an analysis of events than in a study of the sentiments and attitudes of those who participated in them.[15] Typically too, Huizinga drew heavily upon one major source: the Chronicle of George Chastelain (c. 1414–75), official historian to the last two dukes.[16] At the time, Chastelain's text provided virgin terrain for Huizinga to read off meanings and arguments. The chronicler's life and work had been recovered from obscurity by forty years of pioneering research in the previous century, but only one other monograph had attempted to fathom his thinking.[17] Like the butterfly he modestly claimed to be, Huizinga alighted upon passages of the Chronicle to reveal Chastelain as an 'idéaliste', an 'esprit simple d'une bonté naturelle' who lived uneasily between, on the one hand, the genuine belief that his master was a loyal French prince, and, on the other, an inchoate awareness of the fact that a new and different political power was coalescing around the ducal dynasty.[18] His was a troubled but undoubtedly Francocentric outlook. Huizinga worked outwards from such 'conceptions' – or, as he also calls them, 'illusions'

---

[13] For their friendship see Lyon, *Henri Pirenne*, 185–6.
[14] The break began to emerge after 1461, and it came from France, not Burgundy (p. 32): 'Louis XI a compris qu'il fallait avant tout tracer une démarcation nette séparant ses sujets fidèles de ceux du duc. La zone large qui permettait de se nommer loyal Français et bon Bourguignon à la fois devait cesser d'exister.'
[15] One contemporary, Lucien Febvre, was also keen to downplay the idea of a Burgundian state: 'Les ducs Valois de Bourgogne et les idées politiques de leur temps', *Revue bourguignonne* xxiii (1913), 27–50. Jacob Burckhardt († 1897), who influenced Huizinga in other ways, expressed strikingly similar views: *Judgements on history and historians*, trans. H. Zohn, London 1959, 90–3.
[16] I have chosen to respect Chastelain's own spelling of his name, as recorded in ADN B17698, although I agree with Delclos that the chronicler may not have written his name in a uniform way. I am less inclined to accept the manuscript evidence he cites, since the volumes in question were written by scribes after the chronicler's death: J.-C. Delclos, ' "Je doncques George Chastellain . . . " ', *Revue des langues romanes* xcvii (1993), 75–92 at p. 92 n. 55. For criticisms of Huizinga's reliance upon a limited source base in *The waning of the Middle Ages*, London 1924 (first publ. 1919) see F. W. N. Hugenholtz, 'The fame of a masterwork', in W. R. H. Koops, E. H. Kossmann and G. van der Plaat (eds), *Johan Huizinga, 1872–1972*, The Hague 1973, 91–103.
[17] G. Pérouse, *Georges Chastellain*, Paris 1910. In the words of one commentator, this study 'côtoie souvent le bavardage'. The first pioneering wave of scholarship may be located between the edition of a Chronicle fragment by J. A. C. Buchon (1827) and onwards, through the discovery of all but one of the principal manuscripts and the biographical research of A. Pinchart (1862), to Kervyn's edition of 1863–6. In that last year the recovery of Chastelain and his work could be described as 'l'une des conquêtes de l'érudition moderne': G. du Fresne de Beaucourt, 'Le chroniqueur Georges Chastellain', *Revue bibliographique et littéraire* ii (1866), 57–65 at p. 57.
[18] Huizinga, *Verzamelde Werken*, i. 41.

– to explain the actions of the duke and those who surrounded him.[19] A reading of Chastelain's Chronicle revealed why there could be no Burgundian state before 1477: how could these dukes, 'issus de la souche royale depuis un demi-siècle seulement', easily shed the lilied mantle?

Just as Pirenne's vision had an influence upon the work of Richard Vaughan, so too did Huizinga's upon that of Paul Bonenfant.[20] For the latter, Philip's state had come about more by chance than design, and was in many respects little more than the fulfilment of aspirations which earlier princes in the Low Countries had held. It lacked cohesion and a centre. Bonenfant was not alone in extrapolating the essential idea which lies at the heart of Huizinga's thesis, but it was he who took it the furthest.[21] In the process, he raised a seemingly sterile – because irresolvable – debate as to whether the Burgundian dukes thought and behaved primarily as French princes (Bonenfant) or autonomous rulers (Vaughan).[22] Although successors may have polarised their views, Pirenne and Huizinga did not wish to go so far. The former had shaped the *facts* of Burgundian history as they appeared to him. The latter had shaped the *ideas* of Burgundian contemporaries and arrived at conclusions of his own. Hence this comment in Pirenne's letter to Huizinga:

> Je dirais volontiers qu'étant donné votre point de vue, vous avez raison. Mais, en envisageant le sujet d'une manière plus concrète, dans les faits plutôt que dans les idées, dans ce que les ducs ont fait sans peut-être avoir voulu le faire,

---

[19] 'Parce qu'au fonds ce sont les illusions qui dominent les actions politiques du moyen âge bien plus que n'ont fait la raison, le calcul, l'intérêt bien compris' (p. 179).

[20] P. Bonenfant, 'Les traits essentiels du règne de Philippe le Bon', *Bijdragen en mededelingen van het historisch Genootschap te Utrecht* lxxiv (1960), 10–29. Bonenfant did however acknowledge the existence of a Burgundian 'state' and a connection – albeit a distant one – between it and Belgium: 'L'État bourguignon', in *La Monocratie*, Brussels 1969, 429–46; and 'Du *Belgium* de César à la Belgique de 1830', *Annales de la Société royale d'archéologie de Bruxelles* l (1956–61), 31–58 esp. p. 58.

[21] André Leguai comes to similar conclusions but from a different perspective. He carried some of the valuable ideas arising from his early research on the dukes of Bourbon into a Burgundian context: *Les ducs de Bourbon pendant la crise monarchique du XVe siècle*, Paris 1962, esp. pp. 183–9. His views on Burgundy are best encapsulated in three important articles: 'Les "États" princiers en France à la fin du moyen âge', *Annali della Fondazione italiana per la storia amministrativa* iv (1967), 133–67; 'La "France bourguignonne" dans le conflit entre la "France française" et la "France anglaise" (1420–1435)', in *FA*, 41–52; and 'Royauté française et État bourguignon de 1435 à 1477', *PCEEB* xxxii (1992), 65–75.

[22] Hence, for example, an opinion on the work of Marianne Awerbuch, who attempted to argue from Huizinga's perspective that none of the dukes aimed at the foundation of a state, but simply pursued factional or dynastic objectives: 'Über die Motivation der burgundischen Politik im 14. und 15. Jahrhundert', unpubl. Ph.D. diss. Berlin 1970. One reviewer was led to ask whether there were not 'andere, präzisere, nützlichere Themen aus dem weiten Feld der burgundischen Geschichte': W. Paravicini, 'Sechs Neuerscheinungen zur burgundisch-französischen Geschichte im 15. Jahrhunderts', *Francia* ii (1974), 665–91 at p. 672. Cf. Prevenier and Blockmans, *Burgundian Netherlands*, 209: 'It would serve no purpose to establish whether Philip the Bold and John the Fearless were French, Burgundian or Flemish rulers; they were either all three or none at all.'

on le voit apparaître, me semble-t-il, d'une manière un peu différente. Il y a en somme plusieurs vérités pour une même chose: c'est un peu, comme en peinture, une question d'éclairage. L'essentiel est de faire réfléchir.[23]

Pirenne agreed to disagree.

Somewhere in this compromise between ideas and facts the voice of George Chastelain has been lost. It is interesting to note that Pirenne did not express an opinion on the chronicler, preferring instead to cite Gaston Paris's estimation of Chastelain's literary qualities.[24] By implication, the official historian stood on the sidelines as the 'Burgundian state' took shape.[25] Huizinga, for all his endeavours to enter the minds of contemporaries, ultimately marginalised the chronicler too. If his remarks are taken at face value, it would seem that Chastelain dimly perceived but attempted to resist the inevitable: the gap which was gradually emerging between Valois Burgundy and Valois France. The remarks of 'le grave Chastellain' (an 'esprit lourd et prolixe, mais sérieux et sincère'), although reflective of the time and place of their formulation, smacked of 'naïveté'. Huizinga was certainly a pioneer in the field of cultural history, but the 'enormous condescension of posterity' can be sensed in these judgements.[26]

It is not entirely clear that Chastelain has yet been rescued. Three subsequent monographs placed him and his work between two obvious stools: between the certainty that a Burgundian state existed (Pirenne) and the chronicler's apparently keen sentiment that the umbilical cord to France remained intact (Huizinga).[27] Chastelain's commentators explained – at times, it seems, excused – this sentiment by a single fact which is thought to have shaped his ideas. He had spent a formative period of ten years in royal service before entering the Burgundian court. If he was especially sensitive to the ties between his past and present masters, and less receptive to the idea of an autonomous Burgundian state, then this peculiarly *personal* experience was the explanation. Like an historiographical Canute he fought the tide of history by advocating an outmoded ideal of Franco-Burgundian union. For Urwin, the Chronicle was 'un effort de propagande . . . pour la réunion de ces deux maisons'; for Hommel, 'l'axe de la politique du Grand George . . . est l'entente entre les deux branches des Valois'.[28] Delclos believed that Chastelain remained 'attaché à l'union entre le roi de France et le duc de Bourgogne', although his illusions gradually disappeared as his life wore on. The chronicler

---

[23] Huizinga, *Verzamelde Werken*, vi. 504.
[24] Pirenne, *Histoire de Belgique*, ii. 468–9.
[25] A similar opinion informs Vaughan's comments on the value of Burgundian chronicles which 'tend to concentrate unduly on one thing or another': *The Valois dukes of Burgundy*, Hull 1965, 9 (reprinted with some alterations in his *Valois Burgundy*, ch. iii).
[26] E. P. Thompson, *The making of the English working classes*, Harmondsworth 1968, 13.
[27] K. Urwin, *Georges Chastelain*, Paris 1937; L. Hommel, *Chastellain 1415–1474*, Brussels 1946; J.-C. Delclos, *Le témoignage de Georges Chastellain*, Geneva 1980.
[28] Urwin, *Georges Chastelain*, 31; Hommel, *Chastellain*, 52.

remained 'immobile dans un monde en mouvement'.²⁹ To his sympathetic commentators, the official historian's greatness resided in his adherence to his principles. His was a personal drama, and his work bore witness to it. In adopting this admirable position, however, all three commentators acquiesce in the marginalisation of Chastelain's views which is implicit in the work of Pirenne and explicit in that of Huizinga. He is still viewed through the gap which separates the two models of historical development.

Any attempt to understand Chastelain's views in their own right must reconcile more effectively the ideas he expressed with a fuller range of facts from his experience. His 'témoignage' can only be explained if it is contextualised. This does not simply mean that Chastelain's life and work should be juxtaposed in the hope that, by a process of osmosis, the contemporary meaning of the latter will become apparent. We must move from the immediate foreground occupied by the text to the dynamic forces which conditioned its conception, elaboration and reception. In other words, the commentator must look behind, within and beyond the text to understand its meaning.³⁰

Behind the text, the profile of the historian should be delineated – not in isolation, but in relation to his public and peers. Before the age of print (and no doubt for long thereafter, albeit for different reasons), the historian and his public were closely connected due to such practical considerations as the limitations of literacy, the cost of manuscript production and the nature of the patronage nexus.³¹ It is therefore not enough to locate the historian in time and place. We are encouraged to track him – so far as we can – as he moves through his milieu, and to explore his changing position, status and connections within it in the hope of elucidating the view of the past, distant or near, which he was led to formulate in that context. Despite the importance attached to his sojourn in France, George Chastelain's career has not been contextualised in this way.

In the second instance, the author's intentions should be traced within the text. These were naturally determined by personal interests, but also by factors that were often beyond his control: the availability of sources, the practical

---

²⁹ Delclos, *Le témoignage*, 359; cf. the titles to chs ii–v of the same book.
³⁰ These approaches are expounded with clarity in the work of Bernard Guenée: *Histoire et culture historique dans l'Occident médiéval*, Paris 1980, and *Politique et histoire au moyen âge*, Paris 1981.
³¹ Fellow monks, from the same house or from sister houses, thus often constituted the first and perhaps the densest circle of the monastic chronicler's audience. The latter radiated outwards in increasingly ill-defined circles through other clerics and onwards – although by this stage diffusion could be more sporadic – to literate members of the laity. Most lay chroniclers writing in the vernacular wrote first and foremost for an aristocratic audience whose households they may have frequented or belonged to, and whose patronage helped to provide them with a living and to spread knowledge of their work in related (or even politically opposed) circles. Other social groups – townsmen 'aping their betters', clerics in search of *exempla* or perhaps nostalgic for their roots – may have come into contact with the work, but they were not targeted as its primary audience.

conditions under which he worked and the expectations of others, whether patrons or peers. The more reflective historian was confronted at each stage in his task with a variety of choices, sometimes dilemmas. What could or should be included in the work? What form would it take? Upon the choice (or the patron's stipulation) of genre depended a further range of considerations: content, obviously, but also structure, language, style and tone. In considering these matters the modern commentator is led to break with earlier, often dismissive attitudes towards chronicles and to view medieval historical narratives for what, very often, they were: the products of considerable research and reflection undertaken within a framework of constraints. It is inadvisable to read off opinions or views from such a work and to interpret them as incogitant utterances. The author's intentions should be understood through his knowledge of his audience, his methods and conditions of work.

Finally, the text should not simply be considered as the product of a political and/or historical culture, but as an agent within it. Here we must look beyond the narrative to its diffusion and impact. Who were its readers? Where and when did they live? What did they make of it? The importance of this approach is highlighted by Guenée in a passage which deserves to be quoted in full:

> En effet, l'étude de l'histoire politique m'a persuadé qu'en définitive la vie et la solidité des États dépend moins de leurs institutions que des idées, des sentiments et des croyances des gouvernés. Mais ces mentalités politiques elles-mêmes ne sont-elles pas largement façonnées par le passé que chacun se croit? Un groupe social, une société politique, une civilisation se définissent d'abord par leur mémoire, c'est-à-dire par leur histoire, non pas l'histoire qu'ils eurent vraiment, mais celle que les historiens leur firent.[32]

By examining a work's diffusion within an elite we may therefore reflect upon the latter's historical culture. This in turn points to an understanding of the elite's sense of its own past. These limited objectives are more attainable than the loftier (if related) questions addressed in Huizinga's analysis of the sense of identity which prevailed within the Burgundian governing classes. As Pirenne rightly perceived, the analysis of 'idées' alone is problematic. By lowering our sights we might begin to trace the ideas of contemporaries to the *facts* which shaped their own experience. The study of the diffusion and reception of historical narratives through manuscript survival and ownership constitutes a first step in this direction. In Chastelain's case that step has not yet been taken, and this despite Vallet de Viriville's call, as long ago as 1867, for a description ('précise, technique et comparée') of the manuscripts.[33]

With these problems and methods in mind, this study begins with an examination of the political culture which Chastelain lived and breathed. The first chapter is concerned with his origins and early career until his entry to

---

[32] Guenée, *Histoire et culture historique*, 16.
[33] Review of Kervyn's edition, *Journal des Savants* (1867), 49–63, 183–99, 385–93 at pp. 386–7.

the Burgundian court in 1446. Although this period included his royal service, there are good reasons to believe that his time in France was not the formative experience it has been taken for. The second chapter considers Chastelain's career as a ducal servant until his death in 1475. We will explore his changing position and connections within the Burgundian elite, thereby evaluating his proximity to the centre and his ability to grasp and reflect its lineaments. The views he expressed in his Chronicle will be linked at this stage to his experience at the ducal court, rather than its royal counterpart. The third chapter moves from the question of political culture to its closely related historical pendant. Here we will examine the reasons for his nomination as chronicler in 1455 (to which the grander title of *indiciaire* was added in 1473), the nature of the patronage nexus (the ultimate cause of his text's existence, we should not forget), and the audience that he was addressing. The historical culture from which the work emerged determined its content and characteristics quite as much as Chastelain's political experience. At this point it should be possible to see how the two combined by attempting a reading of the work. Before doing so, a major problem in interpreting the Chronicle must be addressed; namely, the fragmentary survival of the text. Chapter four is concerned with the extent of and reasons for this feature of the work. By examining the making of the Chronicle – its sources, redaction and the question of the original archetype – we may compensate, at least in part, for the work's incomplete state. The fifth chapter will then consider the ideas which Chastelain sought to convey to his public in the light of the contextual factors described in the first three chapters. Here it will be argued that his text was less a disillusioned and highly personal 'témoignage' than a structured and layered response to the historical events which affected the Burgundian political community. Since historians are now accustomed 'à ne plus considérer une oeuvre simplement à sa naissance, mais tout au long de sa vie et de son succès',[34] the sixth and final chapter is concerned with the Chronicle's audience. In the course of that discussion it will be possible to resolve some of the outstanding problems relating to the work's fragmentary survival as discussed in chapter four.

If, in the process, this book also says something about the models which still influence our understanding of the phenomenon of Valois Burgundy, then that is not entirely coincidental. 'Small facts speak to large issues.'[35] The connection is inevitable for, despite the (rarely conscious) marginalisation of his ideas by posterity, George Chastelain and his work were central to the political and historical culture of the Burgundian court. The chronicler's views were shaped by his experiences; in turn, he shaped Burgundian history. As we have seen and will see again in this study, the reshaping of Valois Burgundy by later historians has not always been to Chastelain's benefit.

---

[34] Guenée, *Histoire et culture historique*, 15.
[35] C. Geertz, 'Thick description: toward an interpretive theory of culture', in his *The interpretation of cultures*, New York 1973, repr. London 1993, 3–30 at p. 23.

1

Origins and Early Career (c. 1414–1446)

If we define the background of an individual in terms of his family, social standing, education, training or experience, then our knowledge of George Chastelain's background before his retainment in ducal service in 1446 is limited indeed. His most recent biographer is able to cite a funerary inscription which can be used to date the chronicler's birth to 1414 or 1415, two documents attesting to his studies at the University of Louvain between 1430 and 1432, and four financial records which place him in ducal service in 1434 and in royal service ten years later.[1] Compared to what we know of the backgrounds of court colleagues such as Olivier de La Marche or Philippe de Commynes, this is a fairly meagre harvest.[2] Since the first studies of Chastelain's work emerged, however, the early period of the chronicler's life has been viewed as a crucial phase in the formation of his outlook. Chastelain undoubtedly encouraged his readers in this line of thought, and it is his comments on the matter which have informed the judgements of most historians. We may begin by following their lead.

---

[1] Hommel, *Chastellain*, 25–37 (without references). The funerary inscription in fact suggests Chastelain was born in 1404 or 1405: *Histoire ecclésiastique de la ville et comté de Valentienne par Simon Le Boucq*, ed. A. Dinaux, Valenciennes 1844, 48; T. Leuridan, 'Épigraphie de Valenciennes', *Mémoires de la Société d'études de la province de Cambrai* xxv (1932), 113. Hommel points out contradictions between the evidence of the epitaph and remarks in the Chronicle to which we shall return. He argues that Chastelain was in fact born in 1415, and that the reference to his 'lxx ans' in Mar. 1475 was a scribal error: 'lx ans' is indeed much more likely. We might add that the term 'lx ans' indicates that he died in his sixtieth year: he may have been born at some point after Mar. 1414, as we shall see. Reviewing Hommel, O. Jodogne pointed out that Chastelain had attended Louvain University: *Revue d'histoire ecclésiastique* xli (1946), 141–2. Hommel acknowledged the omission in his *Pages choisies de Chastellain*, Paris 1949, 17. The original matriculation records of Louvain were destroyed, but see *Matricule de l'Université de Louvain*, I, ed. E. Reusens, Brussels 1903, 48: 'Gregorius (sic) Casteleyn de Gandavo. Determinavit 14 novembris 1430'; 'Georgius Casteleyn. Bac. art. 16 martii 1432: Georgius'. Since the first of these procedures normally took place in the first term of the second year, Chastelain probably enrolled at Louvain in 1429 (see *Matricule*, pp. xix–xx). For the payments made to Chastelain by the ducal administration (discussed further below) see ADN, Série B (hereinafter, ADN B) 1951, fo. 119v; B1982, fo. 201; B1988, fos 188v, 196.

[2] J. Dufournet, *La vie de Philippe de Commynes*, Paris 1969; J.-M. Duvosquel, 'Bourgeoisie ou noblesse?', in J.-C. Aubailly and others (eds), *'Et c'est la fin pour quoy sommes ensemble'*, Paris 1993, ii. 535–48; H. Stein, *Étude biographique, littéraire et bibliographique sur Olivier de La Marche*, Brussels 1888.

The chronicler's account

Chastelain's references to his background, scattered throughout his surviving works, all relate to one significant passage situated towards the end of the prologue of the Chronicle. After mentioning to the reader his present position as pantler to Philip the Good, he writes that he was

> fils Jehan, né en l'impériale conté d'Alost en Flandres, extrait de la maison de Gavre et de Mammynes, sobrement instruit ès lettres, nourry en fleur de jeunesse ès armes, et en la hantise des cours royales et nobles hommes, souverainement des François, enaigri durement ès armes et exercité sous longues annuyeuses contraires fortunes. (i, 11)

This statement conforms to a generic formula commonly found at an early stage in the text of later medieval vernacular chronicles. Originating, it has been suggested, in juridical practice, the function of such passages was simple: the chronicler's identity, his social position and geographical origins were recorded at the outset as a means of establishing his bona fides within a community of shared values. This was intended to guarantee the credibility of his text.[3] Chastelain's subsequent elaboration on these points may be read in a similar light.

In one of his *opuscula*, the *Exposition sur vérité mal prise*, Chastelain qualified the aristocratic credentials mentioned in his prologue by stating that 'clair assez [suis] de génération, et que moult noble et vertueux ventre me répandi en main de matrone' (vi, 435). Like Mathieu d'Escouchy, he suggests that his noble status derived in particular from the maternal line.[4] Although no further clarification is given in the chronicler's surviving works, this lineage almost certainly had a prestigious ring to it for a contemporary audience. In the later 1450s, as at least some in Chastelain's court public would have been aware, a prose romance, epic in proportion and tone, was circulating in Burgundian circles. This was the *Histoire des Seigneurs de Gavre*.[5] The chronicler indicated in the *Exposition* that he could have come from better stock, but the fashionable family background he claimed in the Chronicle may well have compensated for this.[6]

The chronicler's account of his geographical origins also calls for some

---

[3] C. Marchello-Nizia, 'L'historien et son prologue', in D. Poirion (ed.), *La chronique et l'histoire au Moyen Age*, Paris 1984, 13–24.
[4] d'Escouchy, *Chronique*, i. 2.
[5] *Histoire des Seigneurs de Gavre*, ed. R. Stuip, Paris 1993.
[6] The *Histoire des Seigneurs de Gavre* was first presented to Philip the Good by Jean de Wavrin in 1456: C. Thiry, 'Une rédaction du XVIe siècle de l'*Histoire des Seigneurs de Gavre*', in *Mélanges offerts à Pierre Le Gentil*, Paris 1973, 839–50 at p. 839 n. 2. On the popularity of the work and other mentions of the Gavres in contemporary literature see R. Stuip, 'L'*Histoire des Seigneurs de Gavre*', in Q. Mok, I. Spiele and P. Verhuyck (eds), *Mélanges Smeets*, Leiden 1982, 281–92, and 'Le public de l'*Histoire des Seigneurs de Gavre*', in K. Busby and E. Cooper (eds), *Courtly literature*, Amsterdam–Philadelphia 1990, 531–7.

comment. Chastelain claimed the county of Aalst (Alost), situated immediately to the south and south-east of the city of Ghent beyond the River Scheldt, as his birthplace.[7] His, apparently, was a rural background, quite distinct from the urbanised milieux of fifteenth-century Flanders. Chastelain returned to this theme in the modish, pastoral style affected by many of his literary contemporaries – and appreciated by aristocratic audiences in the more peaceful climate of the middle of the fifteenth century – when he wrote, around 1463, of his 'rudesse champestre'.[8] The image of the country squire clearly formed part of the public *persona* he wished to present to his public.

Equally significant is Chastelain's indication that he was born in imperial, rather than French royal, Flanders. Several commentators regard this as an anomaly: as a native of the county of Aalst, it has seemed strange that he could describe himself as French, either by allegiance or by language.[9] Yet Chastelain clearly did not feel he was presenting an inconsistency to his audience here. At a later stage in his work he included Aalst, along with Brabant, Hainaut and the county of Burgundy, among the 'pays que le duc tenoit en l'Empire ayans affinité audit royamme [de France]' (Delclos, 125).[10] Affinities between some ducal territories and those ruled directly by the king were clearly linked in the prologue to those sentiments which led the type of aristocratic Burgundian servant he claimed to be to take up royal service at some stage in their careers.

The prologue's version of the chronicler's youth then progresses to educational matters, although most of our information on this point is conveyed, once again, in the *Exposition*.[11] Chastelain states that he was 'mis à puérile escole' (vi, 265) at the age of seven. His early schooling may have taken place in Ghent where, we are told, he witnessed as a 'jeusne enfant' (ii, 16) Philip the Good's entry into the city with Isabella of Portugal in 1430. Chastelain also states that he was an 'escolier' at Louvain in the same year (ii, 76).[12]

---

7 F. De Smedt, *Description de la ville et du comté d'Alost*, Aalst 1852; D. Nicholas, *Medieval Flanders*, London–New York 1992, 446–7.
8 The citation given is from Chastelain's *Douze dames de rhétorique* (vii, 179). On the genre see D. Poirion, *Le poète et le prince*, Paris 1965, 89, 488–94.
9 On language see C. A. J. Armstrong, 'The language question in the Low Countries', in J. Hale, R. Highfield and B. Smalley (eds), *Europe in the late Middle Ages*, London 1965, 386–409, repr. in Armstrong's *England, France and Burgundy in the fifteenth century*, London 1983, 189–212.
10 The overlapping of royal and ducal interests in Aalst and these other regions was still apparent in 1464, when Louis XI was obliged to ask the *Parlement* and his *baillis* in the North not to interfere – 'pour occasion des limites d'entre notre Royaume et les païs de l'Empire' – in the affairs of the county of Aalst: Plancher, *Histoire*, iv. p. ccxlviii.
11 Chastelain's literary baggage is discussed in ch. iv below.
12 These are the two references which contradict Chastelain's epitaph mentioned above. Had Chastelain been born in 1405, he is unlikely to have described himself as a 'jeusne enfant' in 1430. Most university undergraduates began their studies around the age of fifteen – Chastelain's probable age in 1429 or 1430: L. Moulin, *La vie des étudiants au moyen âge*, Paris 1991, 23, 31.

Although nothing more is said in the Chronicle on the nature of his intellectual training or qualifications, Chastelain later discussed his studies in the *Exposition*. He placed them in three categories: those which were 'nécessaires', concerning the articles of faith; those which were 'utiles', the 'sciences et disciplines' which gave him the intellectual apparatus to 'discerner... entre vérité et mensonge'; and finally those which were 'glorieuses et louables à l'homme', namely the study of history, philosophy and poetry, and what they could teach him in particular about emperors, kings, dukes, barons and nobles 'dès le principe du monde jusqu'au présent' (vi, 280-1). Chastelain, like his contemporaries, was sensitive to historical culture from an early stage. He places far greater emphasis here on the exemplary value of history than he does on 'sciences et disciplines', the dialectical skills which the arts curriculum sought to convey through the reading of such works. Despite his relatively advanced studies, then, he did not seek to present himself as a dry scholar learned in 'clergie'.

In part at least, this representation of his studies relates to his earlier statements on his lineage. For Jean Miélot, the anonymous author of the *Enseignements de vraie noblesse* and certain other literati at the Burgundian court, nobility was as much a function of virtue and contemplation as it was a birthright.[13] Chastelain's noble credentials, however fashionable they might have appeared, were none the less imperfect. By partaking to some extent of the modish view that certain intellectual qualities amounted to moral attributes, he reminded a public well-versed in the concept of true nobility that a modicum of learning made good the flaws in one's lineage. The bridge which was clearly being built between author and audience was strengthened in another way by these remarks. In effect, Chastelain seems to have been presenting himself as the type of noble preceptor which Christine de Pisan had counselled the prince to seek out. Through his studies he was more a 'discret pruedomme bien morigin é et amant Dieu' than one of those 'soubtilz philiosophiens' whose minds were cluttered up with less practical or morally useful learning.[14] It is interesting to note that although he had clearly enjoyed a university training, Chastelain also shared (in his text, at least) the low esteem in which Philippe de Commynes held 'clercs et gens de robbe longue' who 'a tous propos ont une loy au bec ou une hystoire'.[15] Learning was an attribute, but only certain types of learning could be flaunted. Chastelain's was thus a functional education, proper to the true aristocrat destined for an active life. His audience was left in no doubt that he was, to employ a modern phrase, 'one of us'.

'Distrait des écoles', the *Exposition* then portrays his progression from

---

[13] C. Willard, 'The concept of true nobility at the Burgundian court', *Studies in the Renaissance* xiv (1967), 33–48; A. Vanderjagt, *Qui sa vertu anoblist*, Groningen 1981.
[14] Christine de Pisan, *Le Livre du corps de policie*, ed. R. H. Lucas, Geneva 1967, 6.
[15] Commynes, *Mémoires*, i. 129. On Chastelain's similar attitude towards clerics in government, cf. J. Bartier, *Charles le Téméraire*, Brussels 1944, 71–2.

learning to the 'affections mondaines' of travel, love and arms (vi, 265). Although he claims to have visited many regions, Chastelain repeatedly associates his experiences with a sojourn in the kingdom of France. 'Cuidant prospérer [s]on chemin', he sought the 'périlleuses habitations de dame court' and the 'hantises des princes', by which means he hoped to 'grandir... sourdre et monter' (vi, 265). The chronicler uses the term 'nourriture' (vi, 433) of his stay in the kingdom to imply that he was successful in finding a place in the service of the king or one of his principal servants. There is no specific indication as to who this might have been. On two separate occasions, however, he does imply that his sojourn was lengthy.[16] It is also suggested that this period of his life included service in a military capacity, for Chastelain had been the 'mainteneur de querelle des... François, tant à l'espée comme à la plume' (vi, 300). Most importantly, he indicates to his reader that he had moved in the highest of royal circles. In one passage we are told that he had attended mass in the presence of Charles VII (ii, 53). At the royal court or other 'conventions royales' (ii, 169-70) he had seen Jean IV and Jean V, counts of Armagnac, Bernard, count of Pardiac, and Charles's mistress, Agnès Sorel, 'la quelle je vis et cognus' (iv, 365). Among his acquaintances and confidants he includes the later queen of England, Marguerite d'Anjou, Charles VII's half-sister, Marguerite de Valois, and two men who, in their day, figured among the most influential advisers to the king, Georges de La Trémoille and Pierre de Brézé.[17] One imagines that French readers would have been impressed.

By contrast with the detail on his French sojourn which Chastelain provides for his reader, the account of his entry into Burgundian service is brief. This, we are given to believe, was because the transition from royal to ducal service had been easy. His only comment on the subject is found in the *Exposition*, where we learn that Philip the Good had raised him from humble status to lodge him with 'les princes de son peuple' (vi, 435). The reader is left to surmise that the chronicler's reputable aristocratic stock, the education and experience which befitted his station, and his sojourn in French royal service together constituted suitable credentials for his entry into Philip's service.

In the light of these comments it is not surprising that past commentators have considered Chastelain's sojourn in France as the key to the formation of his outlook. After all, this seems to have been the chronicler's intention. In drawing upon his testimony, however, the modern reader must bear in mind that the value of his remarks is circumscribed by such factors as the conventions of his chosen genre or his awareness of the audience to whom those remarks were addressed.

It is clear, for example, that the background Chastelain delineates in the

---

[16] Addressing Charles VII, Chastelain notes he had had 'longue habitude avec ta chevalerie' (vi, 433). See also *Le temple de Bocace*, ed. S. Bliggenstorfer, Bern 1988, 3-5.
[17] Ibid. 3-4; Delclos, 311. Chastelain remained in contact with Brézé after he had entered Burgundian court service: iv, 231, 357; v, 93. For La Trémoille see i, 337-41.

Exposition and prologue to his Chronicle conforms in essence to a recognisable pattern found in contemporary fictional or pseudo-historical accounts of the rise of the young courtier. In two works written within a few years of Chastelain's appointment, Anthoine de La Sale's *Le Petit Jehan de Saintré* and the anonymous *Livre des faits de Jacques de Lalaing*, the idealised account of the protagonist's background has the following central elements: the aristocratic credentials which mark the young man out for court service, education befitting his station, frequentation of the princely court and the experience in arms which completed his training.[18] These clear parallels should not lead us to disregard Chastelain's accounts of his background as pure fiction, but they do remind us that he slotted his experience into moulds which were predetermined by his own, and by his audience's, historical culture.

His comments on his background were also shaped in part by the particular functions of the text in which they appeared. Chastelain's *Temple de Bocace* was finished in 1465 as a work of consolation for Marguerite d'Anjou after her recent traumas in England. A distant, impersonal tone would hardly have been appropriate here. Chastelain thus had good reason to underscore the personal relationship between the court chronicler and the miserable queen. The *Exposition sur vérité mal prise*, which conveys more information on Chastelain's background than any of his other texts, should be read in the light of similar considerations. In the tense political climate of the late 1450s, the chronicler had taken the French to task in his *Dit de vérité* (vi, 219–42) for their hostility towards Philip the Good. The backlash which followed the circulation of this piece – including, according to Chastelain, the issuing of threats upon his life (vi, 244) – led him to write the *Exposition* as a justification of the earlier work, as an exercise in self-criticism and as something of an *apologia pro vita sua*.[19] If, as it would appear, the *Exposition* was directed at a hostile royalist audience, it is reasonable to suggest that the chronicler had good reason to emphasise the time he had spent as a loyal servant of the French king.

When reading Chastelain's account of his social origins and early career, we are thus confronted with experiences which were refracted, and almost certainly distorted, through a complex prism made up of textual needs, authorial

---

[18] Saintré is described as the 'aisné filz au seigneur de Saintré en Thoraine': Antoine de La Sale, *Jehan de Saintré*, ed. J. Misrahi and C. Knudson, Geneva 1978, 2. In his youth he was counselled not to follow the 'estudes des tres prudentes et saintes sciences de theologie' – which, of course, were university subjects – but to learn the 'belles doctrines' (ibid. 29, 34) appropriate to the knight. Saintré 'vint en grace au roy' (ibid. 2) after he had been presented at court. Much of the remaining narrative of his life is taken up by his exploits in arms. Lalaing's lineage was equally well-attested (all references to Kervyn's publication of the work in vol. vii of his edition of Chastelain: here, 78). His schooling, like Chastelain's, began at the age of seven when he was 'baillé à un clerc' to teach him to read and write in Latin and French. Like Saintré he was presented at court (ibid. 26–7) and was shown in the remainder of the text to be a well-travelled and accomplished combatant.

[19] C. Thiry, 'Stylistique et auto-critique', in *Actes du VIe colloque international sur le moyen français*, III: *Recherches sur la littérature du XVe siècle*, Milan 1991, 101–35.

perceptions of audience response and a range of personal considerations of which only some may now be apparent. These observations inevitably lead us to re-examine such record evidence as we have.

Joris Castelain's background

With two notable exceptions to which we shall return, every discussion of Chastelain's family is based upon the record evidence first put forward by Alexandre Pinchart.[20] He suggested that the chronicler descended from a cadet branch of the Tollin family, hereditary castellans of the town of Aalst since the middle of the fourteenth century. His view was based on several premises. A full list of the fiefs and *arrière-fiefs* held in the county of Aalst, composed by the comital *sous-bailli* in 1406, does not contain any reference to a family by the name of Chastelain.[21] Noting that cadet lines of major families occasionally appropriated some element of the name of the main line, Pinchart concluded that the Chastelains may have been connected to the Tollins on the grounds that they employed an alias, *Borchgrave* or *Chastelain*, which stemmed from their hereditary office. In support of this argument, the arms reputedly engraved on Chastelain's tomb at Valenciennes were interpreted as a variation upon those of the main line of the Tollin family.[22] Pinchart emphasised the hypothetical nature of his research, and it is of course no easy matter to establish a cast-iron case in this type of inquiry. However, in the absence of any record of a noble family by the name of Chastelain in the relatively good documentation for the fiefs of the county of Aalst at the time, and in view of the fact that the chronicler claimed affiliation to the Gavre and Masmines families rather than the Tollins, it is surprising that his deliberately tentative conclusions should have achieved such unanimity among subsequent commentators.[23]

By focusing on the chronicler's claim that he was 'extrait de la maison de Gavre', however, Pinchart's research could have been taken a little further. This line of argument must be explored before any definitive judgement on

---

[20] A. Pinchart, 'Historiographes, indiciaires, écrivains', in *Messager des sciences historiques* (1862), 301–21.
[21] Pinchart used two copies of this list, now AGR CC1064, 1067. His findings are accurate.
[22] According to Leboucq, Chastelain's tomb bore arms of 'sable à une fasce d'argent': *Histoire ecclésiastique*, 47. Those of the Tollin family were 'composées d'un écu de sable à la fasce d'argent à trois merlettes de même en chief': Pinchart, 'Historiographes', 304; BM Besançon, Collection Chifflet MS 186, fo. 228; BM Arras, MS 926, fo. 48v. Pinchart explained the difference between the two by the fact that cadet branches often suppressed (or added) detail in the arms of the main line.
[23] The Flemish version of *Masmines* is *Massemen*. However, since the spelling can vary considerably in contemporary documents in French or Flemish (Massemine, Massyminen, Mammynes etc.), I will use the former unless I am citing an original source where it is written in another way.

the value of his thesis can be made. There are in fact clear connections between the Gavres and the Tollins, from whom Pinchart believed the chronicler to be descended. It is known that Marguerite de Gavre, sister of Jean de Gavre, bishop of Cambrai, married Jean IV de Gand, a.k.a. Vilain, lord of Huysse and Sint-Jansteen.[24] A daughter of this union, Marie Vilain, later became the second wife of Philippe Tollin, hereditary castellan of Aalst.[25] Here, perhaps, is the missing connection in Pinchart's research between the Gavres and the Tollins. If Chastelain was connected to the latter as Pinchart suggested, his extraction from the Gavres, mentioned in his prologue, could be attested. To this genealogical link we might add the fact that on two occasions in his Chronicle, Chastelain highlights the deeds of certain members of these families: the role of Jean de Gavre, bishop of Cambrai, as godfather to Philip the Good's short-lived son Anthony is mentioned, and the chronicler dwells at length upon the martial virtues of the sons of Jean Vilain at the battle of Mons-en-Vimeu in 1421.[26] Moreover, it has been claimed that the arms depicted on Chastelain's tomb were not a variant on those of the Tollins (as Pinchart suggested), but were in fact those of the Vilain family through whom the Tollins, and consequently their cadet line from which Chastelain is thought to descend, were linked to the Gavres.[27]

Despite these connections, the evidence is simply too fragmentary to shore up Pinchart's analysis of the chronicler's background. It would be hazardous to read too much into Chastelain's positive treatment of certain noblemen of his region or, for that matter, to lay too great an emphasis upon the evidence of a tomb which was probably made, and was certainly altered, after his death.[28] Most importantly, the hypothesis falls down on the progeny of the marriage of

---

[24] R. de Liedekerke, *La maison de Gavre et de Liedekerke*, Brussels 1969, ii, genealogical tables, nos i, iv.

[25] Pinchart mentions the marriage himself without noticing that Marie's mother belonged to the Gavre family: 'Historiographes', 302 n. 2. Cf. Brussels, BR MS 18204–8, fo. 176: 'Le premier chastelain ou viscomte d'Alost que je trouve avoir esté un nommé Philippe Tollin chastellain de Alost qui se allia avec Marie de Vilain, fille de Jan de Vilain.'

[26] ii, 147; i, 268–70. It may be significant that Chastelain adds these details to his principal source for the early parts of his work, the Chronicle of Enguerran de Monstrelet. Chastelain's debt to Monstrelet is discussed in ch. iv below.

[27] F. van den Bemden, 'Renseignements généalogiques inédits sur Georges Chastelain, historien gantois', *BSHAG* viii–ix (1901), 319–24 at p. 321; substantiated by a depiction of the Vilain arms in an unfoliated heraldic appendix in J. Huyttens, *Recherches sur les corporations gantoises*, Ghent 1861.

[28] At least one of the tombs of the collegiate church of La Salle-le-Comte, where the chronicler was buried, survived the destruction of the building in the middle of the seventeenth century: L. Nys, 'La sculpture funéraire médiévale à Valenciennes', in P. Beaussart and L. Nys (eds), *Richesses des anciennes églises de Valenciennes*, Valenciennes 1987, 31–65. Even if Chastelain's tomb had also survived, its reliability would have been undermined by the fact that he died intestate and therefore probably did not leave instructions relating to it. The epitaph which eventually appeared on the tomb contained an error as to his age, and the tomb was altered early in the sixteenth century by the addition of an inscription by Jean Lemaire de Belges (see ch. 6 below).

Philippe Tollin (alias le *Chastelain*) and Marie Vilain. Returning once again to the evidence adduced by Pinchart, it appears unlikely that a cadet branch that stemmed from any younger son of this union could have been established much before the fourth decade of the fifteenth century.[29] The chronicler, as we have seen, was already an 'escolier' at Louvain by this stage. In short, it is not possible to concur with the long-held belief that Chastelain descended from the hereditary castellans of Aalst, despite the proven affiliations of this family to the Gavres from whom the chronicler claimed descent. In reality, his claimed links to the noble families he mentions were far more tenuous. To establish the chronicler's family group we must turn our attention from Pinchart's hypotheses to the chronicler's statement that he was 'extrait . . . de la maison de Mammynes'. Here the record evidence is more substantial.[30]

The earliest evidence to substantiate this claim came in the form of two documents discovered in the city records of Ghent. These concerned the commercial transactions of a certain Marie van Masmines and her husband, Jan Castelain, which took place in 1425 and 1432.[31] Although this material did not reveal any offspring the couple might have had, later documentation establishes that they were the parents of four children named Joris, Lisbette, Lodekine (Louis) and Mergriete.[32] The couple's marriage took place some time

---

[29] Pinchart, 'Historiographes', 302–4. He noted the lack of information on younger sons and cadet lines of the Tollin family.

[30] I became aware of the existence of the material discussed in the following pages through the research of two scholars who, although near contemporaries, were unaware of each other's work, and whose findings have passed virtually unnoticed: T. de Limburg-Stirum, 'Notes sur la famille de Georges Chastelain', *Annales de la Société d'émulation pour l'étude de l'histoire et des antiquités de la Flandre* 3rd ser. vi (1871), 1–6; Van den Bemden, 'Renseignements généalogiques'. Van den Bemden's work may have been passed over because of an ill-informed remark on its value made after his death by N. de Pauw: see V. Fris, *Bibliographie de l'histoire de Gand depuis les origines jusqu'à la fin du XVe siècle*, Ghent 1907, 196. Van den Bemden's extensive notes are conserved in UBG HS 2693. I am grateful to Daniel Lievois for his generous assistance with this material. For an earlier redaction and selected editions of some of the material which follows see G. Small and D. Lievois, 'Les origines gantoises du chroniqueur bourguignon George Chastelain', HMGOG ns xlviii (1994), 121–77.

[31] Limburg-Stirum, 'Notes', 5–6. In the first document, dated 7 July 1425, Marie van Masmines, acting on behalf of 'haaren man' Jan Castelain, acknowledged a debt to Gillis Lambrechts. Three instalments for the repayment were scheduled, with a boat ('scip') owned by Marie, along with its cargo of cloth, provided as surety: SAG 301 (series)/ 28 (volume)/ 1424–5 (year), fo. 114v (not 115v, as Limburg-Stirum indicates). In the second document, dated 22 Sept. 1432, Marie, 'Jan Kasteleins wettelick wyf', acted once more on her husband's behalf in the matter of a debt he owed to Ghiselbrecht Martins 'vanden coepe van lynwade' (fine linen): ibid. 32/1432–3, fo. 12v.

[32] Proven by Van den Bemden, although he did not publish or summarise the contents of the three main documents which attest to the composition of the family unit. On 26 Nov. 1439, Joris Castelain and his sister Lisbette were named as the heirs in a settlement arising from their grandmother's inheritance. Both had reached the age of majority, unlike their brother and sister, Lodekine and Grielkine, who were explicitly named as the children of Jan Castelain and his wife Marie van Masmines: SAG 330/22/1439–40, fo. 39v. Exactly the same relationship is given in a document dated 16 Apr. 1440 which concerns the same

between May 1405 and April 1409.[33] This Joris (or George) Castelain had a father by the name of Jan and a mother who was a van Masmines. Like the 'Georgius' who graduated from the University of Louvain in 1432, and like the 'jeusne enfant' who witnessed the entry of Philip the Good into the principal city of Flanders in 1430, he lived in Ghent. Like the chronicler who was later buried in Valenciennes, he appears to have been born in the second decade of the fifteenth century. Joris Castelain was George Chastelain.

The chronicler's family group can be reconstructed in some detail. His mother, Marie, was the daughter of Gheerart van Masmines, who met with a violent death in Ghent in 1405, and Sophie van Culsbrouc, who died in 1439.[34] The blood money which was paid for the killing of Gheerart, which amounted to the substantial sum of 400*l.p.*, may be taken as an indication of the relative importance of Chastelain's unfortunate grandfather and the family he came from.[35] This finds some confirmation in what we know of Gheerart's own father, Gillis van Masmines. Described as a bastard of the family, Gillis served in 1400 as the comital *bailli* of Eke, a town to the south of Ghent.[36] The lordship of Eke belonged to one branch of the Masmines clan, suggesting that the chronicler's great-grandfather had some small share in the political influence which his better-known relatives enjoyed in Flanders.[37] The connections of Marie's mother, Sophie van Culsbrouc, also indicate a relatively elevated

---

inheritance: 22/1439–40, fo. 84v. Later that year, on 22 Nov., 'Lodewyc Castelain en Mergriete Castelains, kinderen van Jan Kastelain bij jfr. Marie van Massemen' were still not of an age to act on their own behalf: 22/1440–1, fo. 17v.

[33] On 20 May 1405, Marie, 'dochter van . . . Gheeraert van Masmine', was still under the guardianship of her grandfather: ibid. 330/13/1404–5, fo. 44. By 11 Apr. 1409, however, 'Marye van Masmine, dochter van . . . Gheeraert' was mentioned as the wife of Jan Castelain: 14/1408–9, fo. 37. This suggests that Chastelain, whose legitimacy is never in doubt in the surviving documentation, is unlikely to have been born in 1405 as his epitaph suggested.

[34] The date of Sophie van Culsbrouc's marriage to Gheerart van Masmines is not known, but the union is attested ibid. 13/1404–5 fo. 11v, where she is described on 20 Oct. 1405 as the 'weduwe van Gheeraerd van Masmine'. The inheritance discussed above which passed to George Chastelain and his family was Sophie's. Her will is dated 19 Oct. 1439: 22/1439–40, fo. 32.

[35] This sum, plus a further 60*l.p.* to pay for masses for the soul of the deceased, is mentioned in the settlement of the murder, dated 22 Oct. 1405: ibid. 330/13/1404–5, fo. 66v. 400*l.p.* represented roughly 33 pounds of Flanders: D. Nicholas, *The metamorphosis of a medieval city*, Lincoln, Nebr.–London 1987, p. xi. It is thought that a family of four could live in the later fourteenth century on an annual rent of 7*l.*: idem, *The domestic life of a medieval city*, London–Lincoln, Nebr. 1983, 134. See p. 181 for the question of blood money.

[36] *Regesten op de Jaarregisters van de Keure: schepenjaar 1400–1401*, ed. M. Houbrechts, Ghent, 1969, 8 (no. 39). It is unlikely that this is the same 'Gilles de Masmines' mentioned in the records of the comital administration of Ypres and its region in 1434: J. Van Rompaey, *Het grafelijk baljuwsambt in Vlaanderen tijdens de Bourgondische periode*, Brussels 1967, 652.

[37] The lord of Eke until his death in 1393 was Philip van Masmines, also lord of Hundelgem. In 1389 Philip arbitrated in a dispute involving Gillis: SAG, Fonds Lanchals, no. 693 (8 Mar. 1389). I am most grateful to Mr Eric Balthau for this and other information. He is currently working on a study of the van Zottegem/van Ressegem/van Massemen family.

social position. Sophie's immediate family included three brothers, one of whom held the office of provost of the church of St Veerle (St Pharaïlde) in Ghent.[38] The family held property in Ghent, at Lede and Haaltert (near Aalst), and at Idegem, Schendelbeke and Moerbeke in the south-east of the county of Flanders.[39] After the murder of Gheerart, Sophie van Culsbrouc became the third wife of Jan van Munte, an office-holder of some distinction within the civic administration of Ghent.[40] The career of this man – to which, along with several of these matters, we shall return – was no doubt assisted by the fact that he belonged to one of the more important families of later medieval Ghent.[41]

When we turn to Chastelain's descent on his father's side, it becomes clear why he placed so much emphasis in his writings upon the maternal lineage described above. The family name itself did not necessarily imply a noble background, for the office of castellan was not a noble preserve in the fifteenth century, nor was this office the unique etymological root of the family name.[42] Jan Castelain was in fact a commoner who appears in the city records of Ghent as a 'scipman' (shipper).[43] The eventful business careers of Jan and his relatives in this line of work during the first few decades of the fifteenth century merit closer examination, not least for what they reveal of the day-to-day activities and preoccupations of the chronicler's closest relatives.

The business which Jan Castelain and Marie van Masmines participated in was effectively a family affair: it involved Jan's parents and his brother, and would later involve some of his own children. Jan's father, also named Jan,

---

[38] Sophie's brothers were Jan, Ghisbrecht and Gheerart: SAG 330/13/1404–5, fo. 11v; 19/1427–8, fo. 4v. The last of these references mentions Jan's office as provost (to which we shall return). As a cleric, Jan had no progeny. Ghisbrecht had at least one daughter by the name of Mergriete, mentioned in the second of these references. Chastelain's other relations, all alive in the 1430s and 1440s, included five children born to Gheerart van Culsbrouc: Jan, Anthonis, Lievine, Gheerart and Mergriete: 22/1439–40, fo. 32; 301/37/1443–4, fo. 35; and 330/23/1445–6, fo. 57.

[39] J. Van den Bruelle, *Geschiedenis van Haaltert*, n.p. 1975, i. 65, 67. For Idegem, Schendelbeke and Moerbeke, see SAG 330/13/1404–5, fo. 11v.

[40] This was also Sophie's third spouse – after Gheerart, she had been married to Heinric van de Voerde: 'Armorial et généalogie de la maison de Munte', in the *Généalogie de la famille de Bracle*, SAG, unnumbered series (heraldic and genealogical manuscripts), fos 688–717 at fo. 705 (described in J. Decavele and J. Vannieuwenhuyse, *Stadsarchief van Gent*, Ghent 1983, 253).

[41] See also P. de l'Espinoy, *Recherches des antiquitez et noblesse de Flandres*, Douai 1631, 277–8; J. de Herckenrode, *Nobiliaire des Pays-Bas et du comté de Bourgogne*, Ghent 1865, ii. 1399–1401.

[42] In the duchy of Burgundy at least, *châtelains* were as likely to come from the mercantile classes as they were from the lesser nobility: Bartier, *Légistes*, 56–61. See under 'C(h)astel(l)ain' in E. Vroonen, *Les noms de famille en Belgique*, Brussels s.d.; A. Dauzat, *Dictionnaire étymologique des noms de famille et des prénoms de France*, 3rd edn, Paris 1951; E. Verwijs and J. Verdam, *Middelnederlandsch Woordenboek*, iii, The Hague 1894.

[43] SAG 301/19/1407–8, fo. 24v (7 Mar. 1408), recording Jan's debt of 2l. to Willem van Eeken for the final instalment 'van eenen scheepe'.

seems to have sold at least one boat before his death in 1405.[44] His mother, Lisbette van Erpe (a.k.a. Castelain), bought a craft in April 1401.[45] Her business transactions over the next ten years or so, in conjunction with her sons or in her own right, reveal that the Castelains were not consistently successful at this early stage.[46] By the end of the decade Lisbette was unable to provide her own collateral for a loan to buy a boat, and soon fell further into debt.[47] Around the same time she was ordered to pay a series of creditors and had to pledge another of her boats as a guarantee of repayment for monies she owed.[48] In these difficult circumstances it is apparent that the affairs of the entire family were compromised. Two of Lisbette's sons were active at this time, but neither Jan nor Pieter seem to have reached a position which might have enabled them to put the family's fortunes in the shipping industry on a firmer footing. Jan, the future chronicler's father, was the more enterprising of the two.[49] He appears as a guarantor, debtor and purchaser in a variety of transactions concerning (among other things) cloth, a diamond and a boat.[50] In April 1409 he successfully fought a legal action against his wife's grandfather, Gillis van Masmines.[51] The money the couple received from this case must have brought some welcome relief, but it was only temporary. Jan's financial

---

[44] Jan Castelain 'daude' appears in the company of his son, Jan Castelain 'de jonghe', as a witness to an act in Feb. 1405: ibid. 18/1404–5, fo. 28v. This would appear to be the same Jan Castelain who sold a boat to Jan Lammins in July 1401: 16/1400–1, fo. 77. The wife of Jan Castelain 'daude', Lisbette van Erpe, is mentioned as his widow in another document of that year: 330/13/1404–5, fo. 65v.

[45] Ibid. 301/16/1400–1, fo. 61. She was old Jan's second wife. Mergriete Scaepdrivers, by whom he had three daughters, died in 1384: ibid. 330/7/1383–4, fo. 76v; L. Wynant, *Regesten van de Gentse staten van goed*, Brussels 1979, ii. 177. By 1382 Jan already had sons by Lisbette and so raised two families: Nicholas, *The domestic life*, 167.

[46] Two early documents reveal the Castelains working as a family unit. In 1405 Lisbette provided surety for Jan when he gave his boat in part exchange for another: ibid. 301/18/1405–6, fo. 62v. The following year her other son, Pieter, acted as her guarantor when she bought a boat for 5l. 10s.: ibid. 18/1406–7, fo. 44v.

[47] The boat was bought in Mar. 1408: ibid. 301/19/1407–8, fo. 9. Within a few weeks Lisbette had borrowed the substantial sum of 3l. from Gillis de Clerc: ibid. fo. 68.

[48] Ibid. 301/20/1408–9, fos 18, 66, 67, 76v, 78v.

[49] For Pieter's activities see ibid. 301/19/1406–7, fo. 72 (condemned to pay a debt); 20/1408–9, fo. 15, and 20/1409–10, fo. 46 (agreements to purchase two boats which remained in the vendor's hands until full payment was made); 20/1408–9, fo. 1v, and 20/1409–10, fos 27, 29v (purchase of linen cloth and two lots of armour).

[50] Ibid. 301/18/1404–5, fo. 24v (guarantor for Lievin Dhane for the sum of 16l.p.); 330/13/1404–5, 'Soendinc bouc', fo. 68 (debt of 100l. owed to Mergriete vander Haghen); 301/19/1406–7, fos 50, 59v (purchase of cloth to the value of 16s.; instructed to pay debt of 5s. 4d. to Jacop de Meys); 19/1407–8, fos 6, 8, 11v, 24v, 29, 37, 42, 45, 51, 52 (ordered to repay three further debts; purchase of a diamond from Willem de Vremde; purchase of a larger boat from Wouter Callen; acknowledgement of four further debts, the greatest of which was for 3l.).

[51] The couple demanded payment from Gillis of sums he owed them from the blood money received for the murder of Gheerart. Despite Gillis's objections, the aldermen ordered him to pay 30l.p. to his granddaughter and her new husband: ibid. 330/14/1408–9, fo. 37.

commitments were onerous enough, but he seems to have had to subsidise those of his mother as well.[52] With Lisbette and his brother Pieter, Jan was obliged in September 1409 to acknowledge a substantial debt which his mother owed for a boat she had bought over two years earlier.[53] Towards the end of the year he appears to have assumed responsibility for another of his mother's transactions, this time for the purchase of beer.[54] With no end to their mother's debts in sight, Pieter and Jan Castelain faded for a time from the records of the Ghenter business world at the start of the second decade of the fifteenth century.[55] They were soon followed by Lisbette herself.[56] The fact that Jan's eldest child was born in the county of Aalst in that same decade, rather than in Ghent where these early transactions took place, bolsters the impression that the Castelains left to pursue their fortunes outside the city. As we shall see at a later stage, it is possible to suggest more precisely where this might have been.

In the years leading up to his birth, the financial circumstances of Chastelain's immediate family were, to say the least, variable. Gradually, Jan Castelain and his industrious wife began to turn their fortunes around. Their reappearance in the city records in the middle of the second decade of the fifteenth century marks the beginning of a period of considerable commercial activity.[57] Acting in her husband's name, Marie was involved in purchases of furs and woollen cloth.[58] Jan bought a boat, presumably to ship these and other commodities.[59] The couple seem to have had some difficulty in 1425 in repaying an instalment of a debt of 100*l.p.*, but their finances did not remain in this precarious state for long. Marie pledged a boat as security against the debt and later sold some land she had inherited in the *pays* of Aalst, in and around the village of Ottergem.[60] By 1430 Jan was sufficiently confident in his

---

[52] For Jan's activity in this period, see ibid. 301/20/1408–9, fos 7v (debt of 4s.), 43 (debt of 5s.); 20/1409–10, fo. 15 (purchase of a boat from Pieter Sleyman, for which the sum of 3*l*. 6s. was still owed).
[53] Ibid. fo. 4.
[54] In July 1409 Lisbette acknowledged a debt of 29s. to Clais Nymhagen for beer. By the end of the year it was Jan who owed the same sum to the same man: ibid. fo. 6.
[55] Pieter acknowledged a debt to Lisbette vander Pale in Feb. 1410: ibid. fo. 40.
[56] In Aug. 1410 Lisbette owed 43s. 11d. for planks she had bought to effect repairs on a boat: ibid. 301/21/1410–11, fo. 1. In Sept. 1411 her four-year-old debt to Marie Clobbaerts for the boat she had bought was still not paid, and a clause in the agreement permitted Clobbaerts to reclaim her property if payment had not been made by the following year: 21/1411–12, fo. 14.
[57] At an unspecified date in 1415 or 1416, Beatryce van der Hellen demanded payment of the large sum of 100*l.p.* which the couple owed her for unknown reasons: ibid. 330/16/1415–6, 'Soendinc bouc', fo. 6v.
[58] Ibid. 301/25/1419–20, fos 40v, 73, 82v.
[59] Ibid. 301/26/1420–1, fo. 14.
[60] Gillis Lambrechts, who had acted as a guarantor for Jan and Marie and who had had to pay out on their behalf, demanded this sum from the couple: ibid. 301/28/1424–5, fo. 114v (the document discovered by Limburg-Stirum). The sale of land is recorded at 28/1425–6, fo. 116v.

affairs to disburse the enormous sum of 21*l*. for a new boat while his son was attending Louvain University.[61] The couple continued to trade in the 1430s in fine linen and other commodities, and towards the end of the decade Jan had sufficient surplus capital to invest in a house that was almost certainly not the family home.[62] Their daughter Lisbette now began to figure in the business.[63] The Castelains' climb to relative prosperity and commercial respectability is confirmed by documents from the end of the decade, where we learn that Jan Castelain was chosen by several people to act as a personal agent in their affairs.[64] We may conclude that the chronicler's father had succeeded in imposing himself as a trusted member of the business community.

Whatever his maternal lineage, whatever the pretensions he expressed in his writings, it is clear that Joris Castelain's immediate family background was firmly rooted, not in the rural estates of the Flemish nobility, but in the urban world of the shipping industry and commerce. In his shift over thirty years from his Ghent origins to the Burgundian court, this man rose to a different station in life. In the process, he apparently assimilated the cultural traits of another social group. His ability – stemming from his need – to do so makes him a particularly useful source for the study of values and attitudes within the environment to which he acclimatised. It should also be pointed out that individual advancement and acculturation rarely happen unless the individual in question, or those about him, want them to do so. Joris Castelain was an aspirant; so too, perhaps, were members of his family. Although this observation runs like a thread throughout the following interpretation of his life, we would do well at this stage not to draw too sharp a distinction between Joris and George. The horizons of this son of a Ghent shipper – geographical, linguistic, social or political horizons – were not so narrow as they might appear at first glance. His transition from city to court is explained by the multi-faceted relationship between two milieux which are often considered to be quite separate.

The shippers constituted an economically important group in later fourteenth- and early fifteenth-century Flanders.[65] As Ghent's place in the international wool industry declined in this period, they emerged as a vital force in the reorientation of the city's economy.[66] Ghent became the major redistributive centre for basic goods which were needed to house, heat, clothe and feed

---

[61] Ibid. 31/1431–2, fo. 4v.
[62] For their commercial activities, see ibid. 30/1430–1, fos 79v, 81; 32/1432–3, fo. 12v; 34/1436–7, fo. 70. The house was bought from Anthone de Jonghe. To judge by its cost (5*l*. 10s.) it was probably too small to serve as the main family residence: 34/1437–8, fo. 68v.
[63] Ibid. fo. 167v (acknowledgement of a debt of 26s. to Kateline van der Donct).
[64] Ibid. 301/35/1439–40, fo. 40v; 36/1440–1, fos 71v, 79v, 122v.
[65] F. de Potter, *Gent van den oudsten tijd tot heden*, Ghent 1883–1901, viii. 93–7.
[66] T. Lloyd, *The English wool trade in the Middle Ages*, Cambridge 1977; D. Nicholas, *Town and countryside*, Bruges 1971, and 'Economic reorientation and social change in fourteenth-century Flanders', *Past and Present* lxx (1976), 3–29.

the largely urbanised populations of the region.[67] Much of this trade was carried in the *pleiten* or the less capacious *duermen* which the shippers used on the fluvial and canal networks around Ghent.[68] As a result of their activities many shippers plied their trade in northern France, where the food supply of Ghent so often had to be bought. Some kept houses there, others maintained boats in the region for reasons of business. Among the latter were members of Chastelain's family. In 1409, his uncle, Pieter, bought a boat in Tournai. Two years later his grandmother, Lisbette, retained a boat at Béthune.[69] The shippers were certainly among the least parochial of Ghent's tradesmen.

The interchange which resulted from the grain trade and other commercial activities naturally encouraged bilingualism within socio-professional groups predominantly made up of native Flemish speakers, from the measurers and money-changers to the merchants and shippers themselves. Schooling in French existed within Ghent itself for this purpose, and often younger children were sent to a Francophone region to learn or improve their grasp of the language.[70] Whether Joris benefited in these ways can only be a matter for conjecture. However, the business interests of his immediate family were not the only encouragement he may have received to become proficient in French. Among the more well-to-do families – families like the van Muntes and the van Culsbroucs, to which he was related – bilingualism was also considered to be a desirable attribute.[71] It may be a long way from such humble beginnings to the polished French of the chronicler, 'le grand George' who looked down, with the condescension of the parvenu, upon the 'thiois' of the Flemish townsfolk, but at least we can see why and where his first steps in that direction might have been taken.[72] The geographical and linguistic horizons of Joris were not as limited as we might think.

---

[67] G. Bigwood, 'Gand et la circulation des grains en Flandre, du XIVe siècle au XVIIIe siècle', *Vierteljahrsschrift für Sozial- und Wirtschaftsgeschichte* iv (1906), 397–460; Nicholas, *Metamorphosis*, 224–67. Unless otherwise indicated, the following remarks are based on Nicholas.

[68] F. Corryn, 'Het Schippersambacht te Gent (1302–1492)', HMGOG ns i (1944), 165–204 at pp. 178–83. Chastelain's family used *pleiten*, which were capable of carrying up to 63,000 kg of cargo; the smaller *sei*, which measured around 20 metres in length and carried roughly a third of the *pleite*'s capacity; and the *durmeschip*, which was comparable in size to the *sei*. These craft do not appear to have been designed for the open sea.

[69] SAG 301/20/1409–10, fo. 46; 21/1411–12, fo. 14.

[70] M. Heins, *Les écoles au moyen âge à Gand*, Ghent 1885; Nicholas, *The domestic life*, 127.

[71] Not least because the ruling elite with which they associated was predominantly francophone, and because the more advanced levels of study which could give access to that elite often had to be followed at Paris or Orléans: P. Rogghé, 'De Gentse klerken in de XIVe en XVe eeuw', *Appeltjes van het Meetjesland* xi (1960), 5–142 at pp. 125–6. As we shall see, two members of Chastelain's extended family studied at Paris.

[72] There is no doubt that Chastelain considered language as a function of, and a reflection upon, social background. Flemish and even poor French were remarked upon in disparaging terms in his work: iii, 104 (Friesian ambassadors who 'n'entendoient françois ne que bestes brutes'); iii, 258 (the Brabantine woodsman and 'son povre rude patois'); iv, 263 (Jean Coustain and his 'grosse naturelle langue bourguinotte, la plus grosse et rude qu'oncques on

The same might be said of his social horizons. Although they did not start out well, the Castelains were no poor relations in their socio-professional milieu – a milieu which, more than most in fifteenth-century Ghent, included prosperous and aspiring families. Their property interests in the city are still not well known, but the sums they spent on boats suggest that, when pressed, they could mobilise substantial financial resources.[73] To judge from the types of goods which the family bought and sold, it would also appear that they often traded at the luxury end of the market, or, more simply, that they acquired luxury goods for themselves.[74] Items of armour figured among these possessions – objects that might not normally be associated with middling townsmen, but which some clearly bought. To Gillis van Masmines, acting for his granddaughter after the death of Gheerart, it may have seemed that Jan Castelain was a husband with decent prospects. For Jan, like many of his background and standing, the possibility of marrying into the lesser local nobility must also have seemed an attractive option.[75] In effect, Chastelain, his brother and his sisters thus came from that grey area where successful townsfolk and minor nobles merged, and where the strictest definitions of nobility were blurred.[76] There

---

l'avoit oy'). Those with refined French were inevitably praised, such as Pierre de Brézé or Philippe Pot. There is little doubt that such remarks stemmed from the community of values which the author sought to share with his audience. However, they surely stemmed more fundamentally from Chastelain's aspirations. As a fourteenth-century English speaker observed of language and class, 'oplondysch men wol lykne hamsylff to gentil men, and fondeth with gret bysynes for to speke Freynch for to be more ytold of': P. Burke and R. Porter (eds), *The social history of language*, Cambridge 1987, 7–8.

[73] The chronicler's grandmother paid out 5l. 10s. and 6l. 15s. for two craft: SAG 301/18/1406–7, fo. 44v; 19/1407–8, fo. 9. Pieter, the chronicler's uncle, is recorded as having spent 24l. of Tournai in 1410 for a 'scip': 20/1409–10, fo. 46. The chronicler's father, the most dispendious member of the family, is recorded in similar transactions as having laid out between 3l. 6d. and 21l. in the period from 1408 to 1430 on a series of different vessels: 19/1407–8, fos 24v, 37, 45; 20/1409–10, fo. 15; 31/1431–2, fo. 4v. These transactions indicate a respectable degree of liquidity at a time when a guild master's income amounted to roughly 12l. per annum: M. Boone, '*Plus dueil que joie*', *Bulletin trimestriel du Crédit communal de Belgique* clxxvi (1991–2), 3–25 at p. 8.

[74] For wool cloth and fine linen see SAG 301/19/1407–8, fo. 52; 20/1408–9, fo. 1v; 25/1419–20, fos 73, 82v. For wood, furs and a diamond see 21/1410–1, fo. 1; 25/1419–20, fo. 40v; 19/1407–8, fo. 29. For the next sentence on armour see 19/1406–7, fo. 70v; 20/1409–10, fos 27, 29v. Arms and armour had to be bought directly from the armourers for the use of private citizens. The armourers did not normally allow them to be bought for resale: Nicholas, *Metamorphosis*, 269–70.

[75] Chastelain's awareness of the value of a good marriage emerges in his observation that Jean de la Driesche, a commoner, was 'richement marié à une noble femme en Bruges, avecques laquelle il monta en estat': v, 221.

[76] Cf. P. De Win, 'The lesser nobility of the Burgundian Netherlands', in M. Jones (ed.), *Gentry and lesser nobility in late medieval Europe*, Gloucester 1986, 95–118. For the strictest definition of nobility which prevailed at the time – noble birth (or ennoblement), the avoidance of commercial or manual activities in maintaining oneself and a lifestyle which befitted the noble's rank in society – see P. De Win, 'Queeste naar de rechtspositie van de edelman in de Bourgondische Nederlanden', *Tijdschrift voor Rechtsgeschiedenis* liii (1985),

is no doubt that Chastelain stretched those definitions to the limit in his own account of his background; but then again, was this not true of many others who, when obliged by circumstance or by law to justify their lineage, did so in flattering or even fallacious terms?[77] His noble credentials were no weaker than those of Jean Ryolet, a minor noble from Burgundy whose legal defence of his aristocratic privileges in 1455 was upheld on the strength of his maternal descent and the evidence of those who attested to his service in arms.[78] Much like his acquaintance, Jean Lefèvre (who affected the nobiliary particle 'de St Rémy'), Chastelain clung a little anxiously to his noble credentials once he had entered Burgundian court service.[79] In 1461, he made himself known to the duke's financial officers as 'George Chastellain, *dit de Mamines*'.[80]

One way of locating the political orientations of Chastelain and his immediate family would be to look at the interests and predispositions of the shippers as a whole.[81] Because of their economic importance, their primary concern lay with the government of Ghent itself. The shippers figured prominently among the fifty-three *kleine neringen* (small guilds) whose elected representatives constituted the second of the three groups behind the regime of the Three Members, the means by which Ghent was governed from c. 1370 to 1453. The first group consisted of the *poorterij* families, an urban elite of certain well-established families, the third of the representatives of the textile trades.[82] Although they were concerned with maintaining this status quo within the city and the comparatively significant political role which it afforded them, the shippers also had loyalties and interests further afield. During the later fourteenth and fifteenth centuries the majority of them exchanged their diffidence or hostility towards the Flemish counts for a far more supportive attitude towards their new rulers, the dukes of Burgundy. This made increasing sense as more and more of the regions they dealt with outside Flanders came

223–74, and Olivier de La Marche's *Livre de l'advis de gaige de bataille*, in *Traités du duel judiciaire*, ed. B. Prost, Paris 1872.

[77] The lesser noble with non-noble blood in his veins 'was all the more insistent on his noble status'; the latter was recognised, in part at least, 'simply by the consensus of public opinion and the tacit recognition of (his) new peers': E. Perroy, 'Social mobility among the French *noblesse* in the later Middle Ages', *Past and Present* xxi (1962), 25–8 at pp. 29, 35.

[78] J. Richard, 'Les états de service d'un noble bourguignon au temps de Philippe le Bon', AB xxix (1957), 113–24; M.-T. Caron, *La noblesse dans le duché de Bourgogne 1315–1477*, Lille 1987, 39–41.

[79] According to his editor, Lefèvre was not of noble birth but was ennobled later in life. He obtained the fief of St Rémy by marriage, and preferred to be known by that name: Lefèvre, *Chronique*, i. pp. xi–xiv.

[80] ADN B2040, fo. 234; italics mine.

[81] Marc Boone has shown that among the shippers of Ghent the political outlook of the socio-professional grouping was formed in large part by family solidarities within what, by the early fifteenth century, had become a hereditary profession: M. Boone, *Gent en de Bourgondische hertogen, ca. 1384–ca. 1453*, Brussels 1990, 122–3.

[82] The regime of the Three Members is described in some detail in ibid. 27–123. See also M. Boone and W. Prevenier, '1300–1500', in J. Decavele (ed.), *Ghent*, Antwerp 1989, 81–104 esp. pp. 93–8.

under the umbrella of ducal rule. The stance adopted by the shippers in moments of crisis between the city and central authority reveals their loyalties. As early as 1385, the dean of the guild, Rogier Everwijn, played a significant role in negotiating the peace of Tournai between Philip the Bold and Ghent.[83] Philip the Good renewed the guild's privileges in November 1436, perhaps in response to the role the shippers had played earlier that year in transporting the Ghent militia to the ill-fated siege of Calais, but perhaps also to bolster the loyalties of known sympathisers within the city.[84] Months later, after the rebellion of Bruges and under the threat of an uprising in Ghent, Philip the Good enjoyed the full backing of the shippers who, with certain other conservative guilds, effectively prevented the escalation of an ugly situation.[85] In the early stages of the conflict over the town's resistance to the *gabelle* of 1447 – which would eventually lead to the city's attempts to involve the French monarchy and the outbreak of the Ghent war – the shippers were once more behind the duke. In 1451 some of their number figured among the conspirators who attempted to de-stabilise the increasingly radical authorities of the city.[86] Sixteen years later, when Charles the Bold was confronted on the Friday Market by an angry crowd during his first visit to the city as duke, he found himself surrounded and protected by members of the more conservative guilds, 'les navieurs, bouchers et poissonniers et aucuns autres qui là se vinrent joindre avecques luy atout leurs bannières'.[87] In view of their actions on these critical occasions, the shippers could justifiably be described as collaborators of the ducal regime within Ghent.[88] Despite his background in a city which had a long history of troubled relations with the Burgundian elite, Chastelain's family thus belonged to a relatively powerful group which strongly supported the dukes and which was courted by them.

Beyond his immediate family and the question of loyalties within their milieu, Chastelain's political horizons opened out onto the elite in other ways. The influence of the extended family upon an individual's outlook and standing could be considerable in Ghent as elsewhere in late medieval society.[89] Relatives in positions of authority or influence could serve as patrons, advisers or at least as role models. Among his Masmines connections, two of Chastelain's known relatives may have been in a position to fulfil one or more of

---

[83] Boone, *Gent*, 203.
[84] Nicholas, *Metamorphosis*, 237; SAG series 180, no. 2, fos 37–8v (a copy of the privileges); M.-R. Thielemans, *Bourgogne et Angleterre*, Brussels 1966, 90–107. Good relations with those who plied the waterways with large craft were potentially useful to central authorities: cf. G. Fourquin, 'La batellerie à Paris au temps des Anglo-Bourguignons (1418–1436)', MA lxix (1963), 707–25 at pp. 721–4.
[85] Boone and Prevenier, '1300–1500', 99.
[86] V. Fris, *Histoire de Gand*, Brussels 1913, 125–36, and 'La conspiration de Pierre Tyncke, à Gand, en 1451', BSHAG xiii (1905), 121–6. On the role of the French monarchy see M. Boone, 'Diplomatie et violence d'état', BCRH clvi (1990), 1–54.
[87] The observation is from Chastelain himself: v, 269.
[88] Boone, *Gent*, 79, 179, 240, 246.
[89] Nicholas, *The domestic life*, 175–81.

these functions. It has been suggested that Chastelain's great-grandfather, Gillis van Masmines, was the illegitimate son of a major member of the Masmines family, either Gheerart van Ressegem, lord of Laarne and Kalken, or his brother, Philip van Masmines, lord of Eke.[90] A more distant relative of the future chronicler, Louis van Masmines, lord of Hollebeke, was certainly linked to these major figures. Louis was the husband of Sophie van Culsbrouc's step-daughter, Katheline van Munte.[91] The son of Jan van Masmines, lord of Kalken, Overmere and Uitbergen, he was also the grandson of Gheerart van Ressegem and the great-nephew of Philippe van Masmines mentioned above.[92] At the very least, one imagines, connections like these entitled Chastelain to think that the world of the old, landed Flemish nobility, sometimes seen in opposition to the towns, was not so very far from his own.

One other Masmines link indicates that the even more exclusive milieu of the court elite did not seem so distant either. When Joris bought a horse in 1440 for the substantial sum of 10l., it was a bastard of the Masmines family, Hector, who served as his guarantor.[93] Chastelain and Hector were almost certainly close associates, perhaps even distant relatives: it is otherwise difficult to explain why Hector undertook such a potentially onerous commitment on Joris's behalf. We know from other sources that Hector was the son of Waleran, lord of Masmines, Westrem and Beerlegem, and therefore the half-brother of Waleran's legitimate heir, Robert van Masmines.[94] In Robert we reach a figure of considerable stature within the Burgundian elite, a man whom Chastelain himself, once he became official chronicler, admired as a 'moult vaillant chevalier flandrois' (ii, 63).[95] Robert's illustrious career under John the Fearless and Philip the Good was predominantly military in nature, from his involvement in the military campaigns of John the Fearless around Paris in 1417 to the siege of Compiègne a few months before his death in September 1430.[96] Between these dates he was *bailli des bois* for Hainaut, a ducal *conseiller et*

---

[90] I am grateful once again to Eric Balthau for this information.
[91] SAG 330/15/1414–5, fo. 51; 20/1432–3, fos 18, 31v, 75v, 86v, 101v; 21/1435–6, fos 68, 108.
[92] Louis is mentioned as the son of Jean: ibid. 330/11/1398–9, fo. 64v. His relationship to the other Masmines is also explained in 13/1406–7, fo. 29v.
[93] Ibid. 301/35/1439–40, fo. 119v. We will return to this document at a later stage.
[94] In Apr. 1431, Hector formally acknowledged that he was satisfied by his late brother Robert's handling of the estate of their dead father, Waleran, 'heer van massemin': ibid. 31/1431–2, fo. 67v.
[95] As already mentioned, and as we shall see in greater detail in ch. 4 below, Chastelain closely followed the Chronicle of Enguerran de Monstrelet for the surviving fragments of his first two books. In retelling Monstrelet's account of the battle of Mons-en-Vimeu, however, Chastelain altered his source to insert Robert's name among those knighted before the engagement: cf. i, 257; Monstrelet, *Chronique*, iv. 67.
[96] E. Balthau, 'Robert de Masmines', in *CTO*, 54–5; repr. with footnotes as 'Robrecht van Massemen, heer van Massemen, Westrem, Hemelveerdegem, Beerlegem, Sint-Martens-Lierde, Sint-Maria-Lierde, Parike, Leeuwergem en Elene (1385/1390–Sept. 1430)', *Handelingen der Zottegems Genootschap voor Geschiedenis en Oudheidkunde* vii (1995), 153–8.

chambellan and – surely his greatest honour – one of the first knights of the Order of the Golden Fleece, the collar of which he can be seen wearing in one of two surviving portraits.[97] It is clear that Hector was also acquainted with other members of the wider family, one of whom, Cornelius van Blaesvelt, was prepared to act as his own guarantor.[98] Cornelius enjoyed a career in Burgundian service as *bailli* of Flobecq, Lessines and Tielt.[99] His brother, Louis van Blaesvelt 'dit de Masmines', lord of Gestel and Bierges, was a man of even greater importance.[100] He is recorded as an *écuyer tranchant* to Philip the Good in the 1430s and 1440s, and was knighted in 1452 or 1453.[101] He went on to become a *conseiller et chambellan* to the duke, but was better known as Philip's master falconer until his death in the early 1460s.[102] If it could give him access to men of this standing, Chastelain's association with Hector van Masmines was potentially very fruitful indeed. Through this figure the worlds of city and court came together.

In addition to these connections within the old Flemish nobility and among the ranks of trusted ducal servants, the well-documented careers of two other members of Chastelain's extended family group reveal that Joris had relatives in high places within the urban elite and the Church. Both of these men belonged to the upper bourgeoisie of Ghent who, like the shippers, often had more to gain from the ducal regime than they did from any marriage of convenience with the textile guilds. One came from a family with a history of ducal service, the other served the dukes himself. These men were Jan van Munte, the third husband of Chastelain's grandmother, and Jan van Culsbrouc, her brother.

---

[97] The portraits, one a drawing in the *Recueil d'Arras*, the other attributed to the Master of Flémalle, are published together ibid. 155.
[98] SAG 330/20/1433–4, fo. 33 (9 Nov. 1433).
[99] ADN B2037, no. 62.710; van Rompaey, *Het grafelijk baljuwsambt*, 647; M. Vleeschouwers-Van Melkebeek, 'Het archief van de bisschoppen van Doornik', *BCRH* cxlix (1983), 121–376 at p. 304.
[100] The relationship is attested in C. Vleeschouwers, *Het archief van de Abdij van Boudelo te Sinaai-Waas en te Gent*, ii, Brussels 1983, 663–4 (no. 922). I am grateful to Dr Vleeschouwers for sending me a copy of the document. Louis van Blaesvelt 'dit de Masmines' is not to be confused with his homonym Louis van Masmines, lord of Hollebeke, mentioned earlier as a distant relative of Chastelain. The latter died in 1451: SAG series LXXXIV, no. 1, p. 164. Louis van Blaesvelt 'dit de Masmines' died around ten years later: ADN B2045bis, fos 34, 207v; B2051, fo. 183. Louis and Cornelius van Blaesvelt were bastard sons of Robert Tincke, alias de Maarschalck, lord of Blaesvelt: SAG 330/13/1404–5, fo. 37v; 14/1408–9, fo. 41. Tincke was the father-in-law of Waleran van Masmines: Balthau, 'Robrecht van Massemen', 153. I would also like to thank Dr Paul De Win for his information on the Blaesvelt family.
[101] ADN B1954, fo. 135; B1982, fos 169r–v; B3659, fo. 70v; W. Paravicini, 'Soziale Schichtung und soziale Mobilität am Hof der Herzöge von Burgund', *Francia* v (1977), 127–82 at p. 167; ADN B2012, fos 17, 277r–v, 278v; B2017, fos 36v, 166v–7, 244; B2020, fos 156–7; B8042, fo. 40v; B2030, fos 16v, 23v; B2034, fos 25v, 57v. I have found no evidence to suggest that Chastelain had any dealings with Louis or Cornelius once his own court career was underway, but this obviously does not mean that none existed.
[102] ADN B1988, fo. 10v; B2012, fo. 34; B1607, fo. 15; B2026, fo. 243.

The van Muntes were one of the wealthier families of later medieval Ghent, and as such they figured among those elite clans which contributed loans to their native city in 1436.[103] Their lineage, sufficiently prestigious for the lives of some members of the family to be commemorated in the church of St Baafs, included a pantler of the count of Flanders.[104] This last point marks the van Muntes out as a family which tended to support the ruling dynasty, and there is evidence that this was still the case in the middle of the fifteenth century. Among those compromised in 1451 or 1452 as a result of their perceived support of Philip the Good was Willem Quillette, son-in-law and heir of Jan van Munte.[105] Jan himself held office within the city's administration on at least three occasions, once as an alderman of the lower bench of magistrates and twice as an elector of the prince.[106] Inevitably, he figured in the membership of the more select 'clubs' of Ghent which served as a means of gaining influence and favour among the powerful. A portrait of him survives in a contemporary depiction of the four masters of the Table of the Holy Ghost, originally a charitable organisation which had become the preserve of the city's social elite.[107] Even more revealing, perhaps, is a reference to Jan van Munte as a knight of the Order of St John.[108] The author of the most recent study of the Order's activities in Flanders is inclined to believe – but unable to show – that this reference concerned Jan's relative, Willem van Munte.[109] Although the possibility of a mistaken identity is important in itself, we should not let it obscure the point in the present context. The Order of St John was one of several points of contact between urban elites and the knights of the Burgundian court. Through his connections to the van Muntes, whether Jan or

---

[103] M. Boone, 'De Gentse lening van 1436', *Appeltjes van het Meetjesland* xxxix (1988), 87–99 at p. 96.

[104] UBG HS G11478 ('Recueil des épitaphes de la ville de Gand'), i, fos 77, 82–3; iv, fos 53, 165; F. de Potter and J. Broeckaert, *Geschiedenis van de gemeenten der Provincie Oost-Vlaanderen*, Ghent 1864–70, v. 8–11.

[105] Quillette's marriage to Jan's daughter, Johanne van Munte, is attested in SAG 330/20/1432–3, fos 18, 31v, 86v, 101v; 21/1435–6, fos 68, 108. He is mentioned in connection with a banning from Ghent during the city's conflict with Philip the Good: 'Bewijsstukken betreffende den opstand van Gent tegen Philips den Goede', ed. V. Fris, HMGOG xxii (1914), 333–453 at p. 367.

[106] *Memorieboek der stadt Ghendt*, ed. P. Van Der Meersch, Ghent 1859–61, i. 166 (1417), 181 (1426), 184 (1428). During his service in 1417, Jan was accorded an allowance for clothing to process as one of the city's aldermen: SAG, series 400, no. 12 (1417–18), fo. 204.

[107] Decavele, *Ghent*, 88.

[108] UBG HS G11478, iv. fo. 197: 'Mer Jan van Munte, Rudder van St Jans Ordre, oude Commandeur in Vlaanderen'.

[109] M. Vander Stichele, 'De Hospitaalbroeders van St.-Jan van Jeruzalem in de balije en commanderij Vlaanderen tot 1550', unpubl. *mém. de licence*, Leuven 1982, 48 n. 4. Willem was undoubtedly a knight of the Order, but no conclusive evidence on Jan has yet come to light. On Willem, see *Handelingen van de leden en van de staten van Vlaanderen (1384–1405)*, ed. W. Prevenier, Brussels 1959, 465.

Willem, Joris Castelain had another window onto the governing classes which his immediate background did not obviously offer him.

The aspirations of Joris or his immediate family were even more likely to have been encouraged by the example of Jan van Culsbrouc.[110] Jan's training took place in Paris, where he obtained the degree of Master of Arts and his *licence* in canon law.[111] Thereafter he accumulated an impressive series of benefices which no doubt helped to launch his career at a higher level.[112] In November 1413 he rose to the office of provost of the collegiate church of St Veerle in Ghent, and at a later stage he is thought to have served as a ducal ambassador to the papal curia.[113] Although Jan was inevitably active in the affairs of the Church, he was not restricted to this sphere alone. The dukes of Burgundy were in the habit of placing trusted servants in influential ecclesiastical posts, but St Veerle itself already had a long association with the ruling dynasty as the comital church for Flanders.[114] Indeed, during van Culsbrouc's time as provost the church was adorned with a stained glass window depicting the Crucifixion, St John the Evangelist and the ducal couple.[115] As the occupant of the most senior ecclesiastical office at St Veerle until his death, Jan was well qualified for a parallel career in secular politics.

It is in this connection that we find him, in 1416, in the city of his *alma mater* with deputies of the Four Members of Flanders. Jan, apparently the senior member of this deputation to Charles VI, played his part in winning royal consent to a year-long truce between Flanders and England.[116] His experience as a negotiator was later called upon by Philip the Good, who entrusted van Culsbrouc and the ducal secretary Thierry Gherbode at the very start of his reign with the highly sensitive matter of negotiating an extension of the

---

[110] Although Jan was Joris's great-uncle, it will become apparent that relations between the two were in fact much closer than this distant blood link implies.

[111] Jan was described in 1403 as 'magistro in artibus et licentiato in jure canonico Parisius': *Documents relatifs au Grand Schisme*, VI, ed. P. Briegleb and A. Laret-Kayser, i, Brussels–Rome 1973, 664 (no. 3096).

[112] *Documents relatifs au Grand Schisme*, V, ed. M.-J. Tits-Dieuaide, ii, Brussels–Rome 1960, 120–1 (no. 283).

[113] L.-A. Canivez, 'Collégiale de Ste-Pharaïlde à Gand', *Annales de la Société royale des beaux-arts et de la littérature de Gand* iv (1851–2), 195–233 at pp. 203–4. A copy of the document recording Jan's installation at St Pharaïlde (Veerle) exists in UBG HS 567, fo. 2. For some of Jan's dealings with the lesser clergy of the Low Countries in his capacity as provost see Vleeschouwers, *Het archief van de Abdij van Boudelo*, ii. 619–20 (nos 844, 845). Jan is also described as a 'conseiller des ducs de Bourgogne et leur ambassadeur vers le St-Siège' and as a 'juge et commissaire apostolique': J. F. Foppens, *Histoire du conseil de Flandre*, ed. A. O'Kelly de Galway, Brussels 1869, 101.

[114] E. de Moreau, 'Les familiers des ducs de Bourgogne dans les canonicats des anciens Pays-Bas', in *Miscellanea historica in honorem L. Van der Essen*, Brussels 1947, 429–37.

[115] The window was commissioned in 1433: J. C. Smith, 'The artistic patronage of Philip the Good, duke of Burgundy (1418–67)', unpubl. Ph.D. diss. Columbia 1979, 307.

[116] *Handelingen van de leden en van de staten van Vlaanderen (1405–1419)*, ed. A. Zoete, Brussels 1981–2, ii. 1051–2.

commercial treaty between England and Flanders.[117] Their success in this difficult area contributed to the signing, within a few weeks, of Philip the Good's alliance with Henry V.[118] The chronicler's great-uncle was the instrument of policies which stemmed from a temporary union between the duke's immediate interests and the deeper-rooted Anglophile tendencies of some of his subjects, particularly among the textile sector in Ghent.[119] Although Chastelain came from a city whose nominal overlord was the French king, it is worth remembering that many of its inhabitants were not naturally well-disposed towards the monarchy.

In the course of these activities van Culsbrouc inevitably came into close personal contact with senior Burgundian servants. In his correspondence with Thierry Gherbode, for example, we learn that the son of this ducal secretary was kept under van Culsbrouc's watchful eye at the school of St Veerle in Ghent.[120] He also met and knew such men through his activities in the *Conseil de Flandres*, the principal judicial institution of the county and one of the means by which the dukes sought to check Ghent's particularism.[121] In 1424, for example, he was part of a deputation from the *Conseil* which conducted negotiations with representatives of the duke of Brabant at Mechelen over a dispute between that city and Brussels. Among his colleagues on this occasion were such prominent former servants of John the Fearless as Roland d'Uutkerke, Simon de Fourmelles, Louis de Moerkerke and, perhaps most interestingly, Colart II de La Clyte, lord of Commynes.[122] Chastelain's great-uncle was an associate of the memorialist's father. There can be little doubt that van Culsbrouc was firmly established in the highest political circles – ecclesiastical, urban and ducal – in fifteenth-century Flanders. It is not surpris-

---

[117] F. de Coussemaker, 'Thierry Gherbode, secrétaire et conseiller des ducs de Bourgogne et comtes de Flandre', *Annales du Comité flamand de France* xxvi (1901–2), 175–385 esp. p. 368; *Le Cotton manuscrit Galba B. 1.*, ed. E. Scott and L. Gilliodts van Severen, Brussels 1896, 391–410; ADN B569, no. 15418; B570, no. 15423; and *Comptes généraux de l'état bourguignon entre 1416 et 1420*, ed. M. Mollat and R. Favreau, Paris 1965–76, i. 314, 318. Jan's reluctance to attend these negotiations is evinced in a choice piece of special pleading, dated Dec. 1419, in which he claimed that 'il n'avoit argent, ne robes, ne ne savoit rien de la matiere par ce que onques mais n'en avoit oy parler': AGR CC 21797, fo. 38v. I am grateful to Marc Boone for this last reference.

[118] E. Varenbergh, *Histoire des relations diplomatiques entre le comté de Flandre et l'Angleterre au moyen âge*, Brussels 1874, 509–10.

[119] M. Haegeman, *De Anglofilie in het graafschap Vlaanderen tussen 1379 en 1435*, Courtrai–Heule 1988.

[120] Van Culsbrouc wrote to Gherbode on 30 Mar. 1419 on the subject of the clothing of his son: ADN B570, no. 15423. The existence of a school attached to St Veerle naturally raises the possibility that Chastelain may have received his early education there.

[121] Van Culsbrouc served on the *Conseil* for at least two years, from 1424 to 1426: ibid. B4093, fo. 42; B4094, fo. 50; B4095, fo. 89. On the role of the council see Boone, *Gent*, 188–91.

[122] ADN B4092, fos 83v–4. For the broader context of these activities and the nature of the work of members of the *Conseil* see M. Boone, 'Une famille au service de l'État bourguignon naissant', *RN* lxxvii (1995), 233–55.

ing, then, that in his last recorded mission, in 1435, he was given the prestigious task of receiving the main papal negotiator behind the treaty of Arras, Cardinal Nicolò Albergati.[123] Eight years later, van Culsbrouc was laid to rest in the choir of the comital church of St Veerle where a plaque was fixed to commemorate his years in the service of Church and State.[124]

Joris Castelain was not born with the advantages and aspirations of the landed Flemish nobleman; yet through men like Jan van Culsbrouc, Jan van Munte and Hector van Masmines, through the political loyalties of his milieu, the standing of his family and the nature of their trade, he was none the less able to look beyond the world of the shipping industry in Ghent towards other things. Even in this highly particularist city, the links between middling people like the Castelains and the ducal elite could be very numerous indeed. If his aspirations led anywhere, they led less to the distant French court, as George Chastelain would have his (French) audience believe, than to the Burgundian court, where the shippers found allies and where some of Joris Castelain's relatives procured advancement for themselves. The journey from Ghent to ducal service – a journey begun by Joris, but completed by George – can be followed in an account of our subject's early career.

Early career

The means of gaining access to a position at the Burgundian court have received surprisingly little attention. If there was an established pattern in such matters, it began with the securing of a place for the aspirant in the retinue of an established courtier. The two may already have been connected by ties of kinship, lordship or regional association, all of which perpetuated the presence of certain families in court service (and made access to posts which were in the court's gift more difficult for those who did not have such advantages).[125] Through the good offices of his patron, the young nobleman could subsequently gain a foothold in the aulic hierarchy.[126]

---

[123] Ghent, Rijksarchief, Fonds van het Sint-Veerlekapittel te Gent, no. 157, fo. 50 (copied in UBG HS 572, fos 189–91). On Albergati's role see J. Dickinson, *The Congress of Arras 1435*, Oxford 1955, passim.

[124] UBG HS G11478, iv ('Église de St Pharaïlde'), fos 369, 375: 'Hic jacet Joa.es de Culsbrouck, in Artibus Magister et in Decretis Licentiatus, quondam huius ecclesiae praepositus et excellentissimi Dni. Principis Phli. Ducis Burgundiae et Comitis Flandriae Consiliarius, qui obijt Ao Dni. 1443 die 18 Julij. Orate pro eo.'

[125] Among the household officers, for example, certain Brabantine families maintained their influence in this way: W. Paravicini, 'Expansion et intégration', *BMGN* xcv (1980), 298–314 at p. 307. A similar phenomenon existed among those Burgundian families which held several administrative posts in their grasp: Bartier, *Légistes*, 83–92.

[126] J. Bartier, 'De Bourgondische adel', *Flandria Nostria* iv (1959), 319–44 at p. 321; Paravicini, 'Soziale Schichtung', 137–8. Cf. A. Schoonheere, 'Les premiers pas de Philippe de Commynes à la cour et sous les armes de Bourgogne', *Mémoires de la Société d'histoire de Comines-Warneton et de la région* (hereinafter cited as *MSHCW*), xxiii (1993), 51–84.

This fast-track to court office was certainly taken by the likes of La Marche or Commynes, but we should not assume that it was the norm. Significant numbers of less privileged men may not have been in a position to follow their lead. Quite how such men attained their rank is more difficult to assess, and for good reason. At a court where the *roturier*, whatever his office or wealth, was always second-best to the noble born-and-bred, lesser social origins were an embarrassment which one did not seek to expose or explain at length.[127] Chastelain, a prime example of this himself, reflects the values of the milieu which had adopted him in his aloof treatment of those who climbed the social ladder: witness his attitude to Pierre Bladelin, receiver-general of Philip the Good's finances, who 'n'estoit que un bourgeois de Bruges, venu et fait tel, moi voyant et vivant' (v, 44).[128] Like Odot Molain, whose rise from merchant to ducal counsellor is well documented, these men made the most of such personal qualities, family connections and material advantages as they had.[129] Social ascension was achieved through ambition and a sense of opportunity; it was maintained by the ability to acculturate. The story of Chastelain's early career, where it can be pieced together, is dominated by these strands.

The earliest indication of this dates to the decision that he should attend university. Shipping, by the early fifteenth century, was a hereditary profession, yet the Castelains were prepared to forego the services of their eldest son and meet the expense of his education.[130] Such decisions were apparently taken more readily by bourgeois families or even those of the lesser nobility than they were by guildsmen.[131] It would appear that the Castelains, now with a toehold on the social ladder, were looking to their son to bear the family name in higher places. They may also have been encouraged in this line of thinking by their associates. Traditions of university study were already becoming established within close or extended families, and in Jan van Culsbrouc the Castelains had

---

[127] The inferiority of the *roturier* could be illustrated in a number of ways, but perhaps it is best seen in *Les honneurs de la cour* by Alienor de Poitiers, where a Burgundian hierarchy of nobility between individuals 'du mesme degré et d'une mesme noblesse' is clearly articulated: *Mémoires sur l'ancienne chevalerie*, ed. J. B. de Lacurne de St-Palaye, Paris 1759, ii. 169–282 at p. 262.

[128] Cf. his comments on Giovanni Arnolfini, Jean Coustain and Roland Pipe: iv, 33, 191, 234–5.

[129] J. Bartier, 'L'ascension d'un marchand bourguignon au XVe siècle', AB xv (1943), 185–206.

[130] On the hereditary nature of the shipper's guild see Boone, *Gent*, 246. For evidence of the costs of study at Louvain see J. Wils, 'Documents relatifs à l'histoire de l'Université de Louvain', *Analectes pour servir à l'histoire ecclésiastique de la Belgique* 3rd ser. ii (1906), 489–507.

[131] A study of the social origins of Brabantine students in the fifteenth century reveals that very few came from guild backgrounds, and the vast majority from more well-to-do, bourgeois milieux: H. de Ridder-Symoens, 'Possibilités de carrière et de mobilité sociale des intellectuels-universitaires au moyen âge', in N. Bulst and J.-P. Genet (eds), *Medieval lives and the historian*, Kalamazoo 1986, 343–57 at p. 346.

before them an example of the potential benefits of a more rigorous education.[132]

Quite where Joris's training would take him was in large part a function of his place and degree of study. Here, contrary to Hexter's view, it would appear that 'Georgius Casteleyn' was indeed 'aspiring to preferment in the church or to a place in the ducal bureaucracy'.[133] At the very least, these were the obvious prospects for a young man of his background and qualifications. The University of Louvain was emerging after its foundation in 1425 as a focal point for the formation of secular and ecclesiastical cadres within its immediate region. It provided an affordable alternative to the universities of Paris and Orléans which, in any case, were more difficult to reach in these years because of military operations in northern France.[134] This localisation of talent was reinforced by the university's inevitable dealings with political authorities in the Burgundian Netherlands, and was fuelled by the numerical preponderance of men from the six dioceses of the Low Countries within the student body.[135] As a result, graduates of the university figured increasingly among the occupants of posts within the Burgundian court, or posts which lay in its gift within the secular and ecclesiastical hierarchies of the ducal dominions.[136] One of the more striking examples of a Louvain man who made a brilliant career for himself at court is Antoine Haneron, originally from the diocese of Arras, a Paris graduate who came to Louvain around 1429 and who, as a regent in the Faculty of Arts, probably taught Chastelain and/or rented him lodgings in one of the boarding schools or *pedagogia* run by the regents.[137] He certainly

---

[132] J. Verger, 'Noblesse et savoir', in P. Contamine (ed.), *La noblesse au moyen âge, XIe–XVe siècles*, Paris 1976, 289–313 at pp. 299–300.
[133] J. Hexter, 'The education of the aristocracy in the Renaissance', in his *Reappraisals in History*, London 1961, 45–70 at p. 60. Cf. F. Rapp, 'Universités et principautés', PCEEB xxviii (1988), 115–31.
[134] The University of Paris was a pro-Burgundian institution at this time: J. Verger, 'The University of Paris at the end of the Hundred Years' War', in J. Baldwin and R. Goldthwaite (eds), *Universities in politics*, Baltimore–London 1973, 47–78 at pp. 52–3, 55; G. L. Thompson, *Paris and its people under English rule*, Oxford 1991, 158, 196. It was not the foundation of Louvain itself which staunched the flow of students from the Low Countries to Paris, but rather the dangers of travel in northern France: A. van Belle, 'La faculté des arts de Louvain: quelques aspects de son organisation au XVe siècle', in J. Ijsewijn and J. Paquet (eds), *The universities in the late Middle Ages*, Louvain 1978, 29–41 at p. 47; A. L. Gabriel, 'Intellectual relations between the University of Louvain and the University of Paris in the fifteenth century', ibid. 82–132 at p. 83. Chastelain himself appears to have had a high opinion of the University of Paris: see vii, 9.
[135] J. Paquet, 'Bourgeois et universitaires à la fin du moyen âge: à propos du cas de Louvain', MA lxvii (1961), 325–40; A. Derville, 'Les étudiants morins à l'Université de Louvain au XVe siècle', *Bulletin de la Société des antiquaires de la Morinie* xviii (1955), 365–84. I am grateful to Professor Derville for providing me with a copy of his article.
[136] R. de Keyser, 'Chanoines séculiers et universités', in Ijsewijn and Paquet, *Universities in the late Middle Ages*, 584–95 at p. 592; Bartier, *Légistes*, 51, 388 n. 1, 400 and n. 2, 405 and n. 4.
[137] For Haneron at Louvain see Gabriel, 'Intellectual relations', 86, 91. His works are dealt with in J. Ijsewijn-Jacobs, 'Magistri Anthonii Haneron (ca. 1400–1490)', *Humanistica*

examined Chastelain for his degree in February 1432.[138] Haneron went on to become a regular ducal ambassador, but entered court service as a tutor of the count of Charolais in 1441: in other words, the teacher who certainly examined the shipper's son at Louvain was the first to shape the mind of the future Charles the Bold.[139] For Joris and his family, the University of Louvain, rather than the more cosmopolitan (and, of course, French) *alma mater* of his great-uncle, was a logical choice. The life of the bureaucrat or the lure of a benefice may well have figured prominently in Joris's view of his own future at this stage.

In view of his family associations, the pursuit of such goals was understandable. At least two of his relatives had carved out careers for themselves in the ducal administration and in the Church. One of them, Jan van Culsbrouc, was clearly prepared to offer patronage to men of his connection. In addition to his supervision of the studies of Thierry Gherbode's son, he was himself succeeded in the office of provost of St Veerle by his nephew, also named Jan, who would later become chaplain to the chapel of the Holy Cross at the castle of Menen, and a canon and cantor of the cathedral church of Our Lady of Tournai.[140] Joris thus had possibilities of advancement beyond Louvain – greater possibilities, perhaps, than a young man of a more privileged background. Whatever these opportunities might have brought him, however, it would appear that he did not take either of the paths suggested by his training.

One possible explanation for this may lie in the fact that the arts degree was an insufficient qualification for the more lucrative positions which Chastelain's great-uncle and his mother's cousin had acquired. The study of theology, medicine and, above all, law were the most appropriate disciplines for men of lesser backgrounds who sought to translate specialised learning into material benefit.[141] In this context it is revealing to note that the dukes of Burgundy and members of the ducal family, themselves generous patrons of students, were

---

Lovaniensia xxiv (1975), 29–59; xxv (1976), 1–83. For the teaching role of regents in the Faculty of Arts see Van Belle, 'La faculté des arts', 45. Their role in running the *pedagogia* is discussed in E. De Maesschalck, 'The relationship between the university and the city of Louvain in the fifteenth century', History of Universities ix (1990), 45–71 at p. 48. I am grateful to this last author for his advice on Chastelain's studies at Louvain.

[138] *Promotions de la faculté des arts de l'Université de Louvain (1428–1797)*, ed. E. Reusens, Louvain 1869, 25–7. Students who took this exam were normally eighteen years of age – another reason for suggesting Chastelain was born in 1414, rather than in 1415.

[139] H. Stein, 'Un diplomate bourguignon du XVe siècle', BEC xcviii (1937), 283–348. We will return to Haneron's relationship with Chastelain in ch. ii below.

[140] On young Jan see SAG 301/39/1446–7, fo. 191v; 49/1466–7, fo. 121v; 54/1477–8, fo. 52v; and J. de Vos, *Les dignités et les fonctions de l'ancien chapitre de Notre-Dame de Tournai*, Bruges 1898, ii. 28–30. I am grateful to Canon Jean Dumoulin for supplying me with the last of these references. Nepotism like that practised within the van Culsbrouc family was naturally widespread among the cadres: P. Kauch, 'L'apparition d'un nouveau groupe social aux Pays-Bas bourguignons', *Revue de l'Institut de sociologie Solvay* xv (1935), 122–9 at p. 128.

[141] W. Prevenier, 'Officials in town and countryside in the Low Countries', *Acta historiae Neerlandicae* vii (1974), 1–17 at pp. 7–8.

inclined to sponsor studies in the advanced, vocational fields which lay beyond the basic grounding offered by the arts degree.[142] Joris's qualifications could only have taken him so far.[143]

A second explanation can be suggested. A career in the Church or ducal bureaucracy, however obvious a choice, was of course not the only option for the graduate with pretensions to noble status. Learning, if not the learning of the bookish cleric, was one way for the lesser noble to catch the eye of the prince or the highly-placed courtier, but there were also more traditional means of gaining recognition and advancement. Service in arms was perhaps the most obvious of these, and this was the path which Chastelain, with his eyes on the main chance, took.

No attempt has been made to explain or to set in its proper context the document which proves this point. It takes the form of a payment which was made at Lille on 30 April 1434 to 'George Chastellain, escuier, auquel mondit seigneur pour les bons et agréables services qu'il lui a faiz en ses armées et autres manieres [et] espere qu'il fera encores a donné de sa grace especial pour une foiz la somme de quatre vins dix frans monnoie roial'.[144] The ducal army referred to here was the large contingent that accompanied Philip the Good in his uncharacteristically energetic and successful campaigns in and around the duchy of Burgundy between July and November 1433.[145] In view of his substantial remuneration, we may surmise that Chastelain was either among the original force from Flanders and Picardy which accompanied Philip in his journey south in July, or among the reinforcements raised in those same regions in August by one of the duke's main captains, Philippe, lord of Ternant.[146] The dating of Chastelain's retrospective payment indicates that he also figured in the reduced contingent which remained with the duke up to the time of his

---

[142] Among the many examples which could be cited see ADN B1991, fos 161v–2 (Jean de Brabant, student in law, sponsored by Isabella of Portugal at Paris, 1446); B2012, fo. 65 (Guy de Douzy, student in theology, sponsored by Philip the Good at Paris, 1453); B2040, fo. 209 (Antoine Paternostre, son of a ducal *huissier de salle* and a student in medicine, sponsored by Philip the Good at Louvain, 1461).

[143] On the limitations of the basic arts degree see J. Verger, *Histoire des universités de France*, Paris 1986, 97.

[144] ADN B1951, fo. 119 v.

[145] Vaughan, *PTG*, 66–7; Beaucourt, *Histoire*, ii. 46–8.

[146] Useful comparisons for rates of pay are provided by a Burgundian document published in A. Tuetey, *Les écorcheurs sous Charles VII*, Montbéliard 1874, ii. 5–7. 'Une paye d'hommes d'armes' was worth 12 francs per month (a 'paye' comprised two combatants, one of whom was the man-at-arms who received the greater share of the salary). To judge from French royal evidence from the same period, a man-at-arms received less, although only 25% less, than a noble *écuyer*: P. Contamine, *Guerre, état et société à la fin du moyen âge*, Paris–The Hague 1972, 630–1. At these rates, and even allowing for such differences, Chastelain may have served for up to eight or nine months. For the use of Flemish men-at-arms in July and Aug. see A. Bossuat, *Perrinet Gressart et François de Surienne, agents de l'Angleterre*, Paris 1936, 208; and ADN B1951, fos 96v–7. Some documents relating to the campaign survive in Dijon but do not concern the troops raised in the North: ACO B11805–6.

return to the Low Countries in the spring of 1434.[147] Quite how Chastelain managed to involve himself in this expedition cannot be known, although once again we may strongly suspect that the family connections of Gillis or Hector van Masmines were instrumental in bringing him to wider attention. One known link may well have been decisive here. Philippe de Ternant's wife, Isabeau de Roye, was the step-sister of Robert van Masmines's wife, Elizabeth van Leeuwergem.[148] The two knights of the Golden Fleece were effectively brothers-in-law. As we shall see later in this chapter and more fully in the next, Chastelain's connections with Ternant were a feature of his career at the Burgundian court. We may legitimately wonder whether the association between the two men began at this stage and through these affiliations. The spider's web of connections which bound members of the political elite together could also serve the function of drawing lesser men like Chastelain towards the centre. Within eighteen months of leaving Louvain, Joris had succeeded in inserting himself by means of the ennobling profession of arms among the ranks of the *écuyers* of the predominantly Francophone elite; in other words, at the lower end of the aristocratic scale.[149] George Chastelain, from a family of townsmen who thought armour was worth owning, had made a name for himself in the military world of the Burgundian elite. Since the fact has been overlooked by those who emphasise the chronicler's account of an early career in French arms, it is also worth underlining that at this stage he appears to have spent several months in continuous ducal service. During this time he presumably began to integrate, establishing contacts with potential patrons and acquaintanceships among his peers. Was his outlook formed more by his contact with Charles VII's 'chevalerie' as he informed the (French) audience of the *Exposition*, or by his nascent associations among those who served Philip the Good?

There are other reasons for doubting the chronicler's testimony on this crucial point. It is usually suggested that following his spell in Philip the Good's armies, Chastelain, like others among the soldiery whose services were no longer in such demand after the treaty of Arras, made a virtue of necessity: he left for the kingdom to seek his fortune in the service of the French crown.

---

[147] *Itinéraires*, 110–20. For others who remained with Philip and were paid at the same time as Chastelain see ADN B1951, fos 120–1.

[148] Margareta van Gistel was the mother of Robert van Masmines's wife, Elisabeth van Leeuwergem. After the death of her husband she married Mathieu de Roye. This couple had two children, Guy de Roye (made a knight of the Golden Fleece in 1461) and Isabeau de Roye. The latter married Philippe de Ternant: Balthau, 'Robrecht van Massemen', 156 n. 6.

[149] By this time the title of *écuyer* constituted 'la dernière catégorie de la hiérarchie nobiliaire, les simples bourgeois et autre "canaille" n'en ayant jamais fait partie, si ce n'est à titre d'usurpation': H. Dubled, 'L'écuyer en Alsace au moyen âge', *Revue d'Alsace* xcii (1953), 47–56 at p. 51; cf. A. de Barthélemy, 'De la qualification d'écuyer', *Revue nobiliaire* iii (1865), 33–40. For an apposite discussion of arms as an ennobling profession see M. Keen, 'Chivalry, nobility and the man-at-arms', in C. T. Allmand (ed.), *War, literature and politics in the late Middle Ages*, Liverpool 1976, 32–45.

This, it is thought, is when George Chastelain developed the views which he would retain for life. Arras may well have made a profound impression upon a young man who, although an experienced campaigner, had only just emerged from his teenage years. However, new evidence suggests that if he was affected by such sentiments, he did not (or was not in a position to) act upon them.

After his spell in ducal service, and at a time when he is thought to have been spending 'longs ans' in France, Chastelain was in fact back in Ghent. This first becomes apparent in three transactions he was involved in during May 1439. Early in the month he acknowledged a large debt to Perrin van der Kerke for the purchase of furs.[150] Little over a week later another substantial debt was contracted, this time to his father in part payment for a boat and its contents.[151] At the end of the month, George 'ende joncfrouwe Lisbette zyn zuster' made arrangements to buy a large quantity of cloth from Jan van Ghent.[152] Together, these documents indicate that Chastelain was making a determined effort to establish himself in commerce. This was no flying visit to the city on his part. Later that summer, the *vinders* of the parish of St Jacob – justices of the peace whose task it was to arbitrate in disputes between private individuals – ordered him to make good a debt of 16s., plus costs, to Simon Utenhove.[153] This is an early sign that Chastelain may have been stretching his resources a little too far. By the end of the year, however, he was able to buy wood to the value of 8*l*.[154] Heavy investments of this sort were common among shippers who traded in the commodity or used it for the building of boats. The outlay and his other transactions are consonant with the type of commitment required in a new business venture. For all his training, his aspirations and his early fortunes in ducal service, George Chastelain had fallen back on the family business.

Before considering his progress, it is worth noting that this turn of events in Chastelain's life finds a parallel – a somewhat uncanny parallel, in view of the historiographical lineage connecting the two men – in the career of Jean Froissart. The latter, who was every bit as discreet on the subject of his bourgeois origins (and quite as much the parvenu in later life), returned to the family business in Valenciennes after his first flirtation with aristocratic society.[155] Yet perhaps we should not be surprised that their fate was so similar.

---

[150] SAG 301/35/1438–9, fo. 106v, published in Small and Lievois, 'Les origines gantoises', 164 (app. i).
[151] SAG 301/35/1438–9, fos 177v–8, published in Small and Lievois, 'Les origines gantoises', 164 (app. ii). The sum involved was 3*l*.
[152] SAG 301/35/1438–9, fo. 174v, published in Small and Lievois, 'Les origines gantoises', 164 (app. iii). The amount of cloth George bought with his sister is suggested by the large sum involved (2*l*. 19s.). Lisbette still owed 13s. 4*d*. of this sum in Sept. 1439: 35/1439–40, fo. 11v.
[153] Ibid. fo. 39v, published in Small and Lievois, 'Les origines gantoises', 166 (app. vii). On the role of the *vinders* in Ghent see M. Heins, *Gand*, Ghent 1912–15, i. 517–18.
[154] SAG 301/35/1439–40, fo. 61, published in Small and Lievois, 'Les origines gantoises', 165 (app. v).
[155] After the death in 1369 of his patron, Philippa of Hainaut, Froissart – who was then in

The social slope could prove slippery for those who were lacking in pedigree or patronage. Chastelain's change of direction may be explained by this comparison, but its implications should also be emphasised. His 'formative' years in France, commonly thought to have stretched from 1435 to 1444, now appear far fewer in number.

Nor, indeed, are there grounds for believing that Chastelain had spent any of the years prior to 1439 in France. He may still have been in Ghent. The age of majority in that city marked the point at which one could act independently in business transactions.[156] This was normally attained at the age of fifteen. Due to problems caused by teenagers unable to conduct their affairs, however, the age of twenty-five was often informally accepted, and later legally imposed, as the point at which one became a free agent in the Ghenter business world.[157] This may well explain why George appears in the city records when he does. If, as other evidence indicates, he was born *around* (although not necessarily *in*) 1415, it is more than plausible that Chastelain attained the age of twenty-five in April or May 1439. The silence of the sources from 1434 until that year would be explained, not by Chastelain's sojourn in France, but by the likelihood that he was simply biding his time and engaged in other activities in his family's native city.

Soon after these developments, the dispendious shipper received a timely windfall. His grandmother, Sophie van Culsbrouc, died in late October or early November 1439. George, his brother Louis and his sisters, Lisbette and Mergriete, were named as the main beneficiaries of her substantial estate.[158] When the division of the legacy finally took place in April 1440, George's siblings received Sophie's immovable goods at Wetteren, but the bulk of her property passed to the eldest grandson.[159] The most significant element of this

---

his early thirties – returned to Valenciennes where, he tells his reader, 'je me suis mis dans la marchandise': G. Coulton, *The chronicler of European chivalry*, London 1930, 39; F. S. Shears, *Froissart, chronicler and poet*, London 1930, 33.
156 Nicholas, *The domestic life*, 136.
157 Cf. *Coutume de la ville de Gand*, ed. A. E. Gheldof and others, Brussels 1868–87, i. 666–7; J. van Houtte, *De voogdij over de minderjarigen in het Oud-Belgisch recht*, Ghent 1930; P. Godding, *Le droit privé dans les Pays-Bas méridionaux du 12e au 18e siècle*, Brussels 1987, 72–3.
158 Sophie died between the date of her will (18 Oct.: SAG 330/22/1439–40, fo. 32) and 26 Nov., when George and his siblings appear as her heirs: ibid. fo. 39v. This last document is published in Small and Lievois, 'Les origines gantoises', 164–5 (app. iv). The first document is itself revealing of Sophie's status. She requested to be buried in the Church of St Peter at Ghent beside her husband, Jan van Munte; alternatively, if she died at Lede, she would be buried in the Church of Our Lady in the family tomb. Provision was made for her soul to be remembered in her favourite churches (St John's at Ghent, the monastery of Tussenbeke and in the parish churches of Lede, Wetteren, Kalken and Uitbergen). Money and 1,500 white loaves were to be distributed among the poor on the day of her burial, and the priest Jan Gaffelkin, mentioned elsewhere as the guardian of George Chastelain's younger brother Louis and his sister Mergriete, was paid for masses.
159 SAG 330/22/1439–40, fo. 84v, published in Small and Lievois, 'Les origines gantoises', 167–8 (app. x).

inheritance was Sophie's fief of Ghinderop, situated at the very centre of the village of Lede in the county of Aalst.[160]

Chastelain's association with Ghinderop sheds new light on some of the more puzzling aspects of his background, notably the question of his birthplace and his claimed relationship with the Gavre family. In the aftermath of the financial difficulties of Lisbette van Erpe, Jan Castelain and Marie van Masmines appear to have made their living outside Ghent between c. 1410 and 1415. Nothing would have been more natural than for the couple to withdraw to Lede in these circumstances, where Marie's mother was in a position to offer them lodgings. A lengthy sojourn at Lede would explain why the Castelains, rather than Sophie's other relatives among the van Culsbroucs, were so favoured in the will. The 'main de matrone' into which Chastelain was delivered from the 'moult noble et vertueux ventre' of his mother may thus have been Sophie van Culsbrouc's. The fief she left to her grandson was attached to the feudal court of Oordegem, within the jurisdiction of the lords of Gavere (Gavre).[161] We can therefore be certain that an association of sorts existed between Chastelain and this family – although whether the association really did extend beyond this seigneurial bond, or whether its importance was exaggerated by the parvenu and writer, is impossible to say. If the latter is true, then Chastelain made more of Ghinderop through literary licence than he did in real life.

The fief, estimated in 1440 at more than twenty hectares, represented a useful piece of capital.[162] By this stage Chastelain was very much in need of it. Between February and April 1440 he was condemned by the *vinders* of the parish of St John to repay debts on no fewer than five occasions.[163] His inheritance left him feeling sufficiently flush to buy an expensive horse in April, and in the following month he looked to capitalise on his good fortune by selling a large number of timber trees which were on his land at Ghinderop.[164] It was stipulated in this agreement that the trees were to remain on

---

[160] J. de Brouwer, *Geschiedenis van Lede*, Lede 1963, 22–3.
[161] Ibid. 22.
[162] Sophie had acquired the fief by 8 Feb. 1400, when she sold a part of it (situated behind the *Hof te Culsbrouc*) to Pieter van Doerne. This, the size of the fief and other information relating to Ghinderop can still be found in documents which are kept in a house on the spot where Chastelain's fief lay. I am grateful to the Cooreman-Van den Haute family (Hoogstraat 12, Lede) who presently own the house and its documents; to the De Monie family, the former owners, who pointed out the existence of the documents; and above all to Daniel Lievois, who helped me obtain this information and see the documents.
[163] SAG 301/35/1439–40, fo. 131 (condemnation 4 Feb., registered 22 July, 2l. 12d.); fo. 43v (condemnation 23 Feb., registered 14 Aug., 17s. 4d.); fo. 43 (condemnation 27 Feb., registered 12 Mar., 5s. 1d.; condemnation 6 Apr., registered 10 May, 24s. for the purchase of armour plus a further 2s. 6d.; condemnation 16 Apr., registered 3 June, 20s.). All documents published in Small and Lievois, 'Les origines gantoises', apps xiv, xix, vi, xi, xii.
[164] The purchase of this horse was mentioned earlier in connection with Hector van Masmines. For the sale of 195 timber trees to Gillis de Knijf see SAG 301/36/1440–1, fo. 5v, published in Small and Lievois, 'Les origines gantoises', 173 (app. xxi).

Chastelain's land for a year, an arrangement which suggests that he was planning some way ahead in his business affairs. As spring turned into summer, however, Chastelain's debts continued to mount, along with the judgements of the *vinders* against him.[165] Between April 1439 and August 1440 his recorded expenditure amounted to more than 38*l*.: a remarkable amount in view of his family's earlier business dealings. In these circumstances it is perhaps not surprising to find that on 9 July, just a few months after inheriting it, Chastelain seems to have been obliged to sell a half-share of his fief at Ghinderop for an unspecified sum to his great-uncle, Jan van Culsbrouc.[166] This may well have eased his financial worries, but by liquidating part of his assets he was also adding to his problems. Chastelain's earlier agreement relating to timber on his land was now annulled. The trees were no longer his to sell.[167] In October he sold the remaining half of 'tgoed te Ghinderop' to his great-uncle.[168] The sale could not have endeared him to his father who, faced with George's wasted opportunities, was obliged to intervene himself. On 15 February 1441 Jan Castelain attempted to make Jan van Culsbrouc honour a large debt of 25*l*. which his son had incurred in his dealings, and for which Chastelain had pledged all or part of Ghinderop as surety. The legal action was unsuccessful.[169]

Chastelain's career in commerce had ended disastrously. For once he accurately described the events of his youth when he wrote, many years later, that he had been 'exercité sous longues annuyeuses contraires fortunes' (i, 11). Jan took over his son's business and personal affairs.[170] George's brother Louis, who reached the age of majority in November 1440, became the active shipper of the family.[171] By early 1441 Chastelain's assets were depleted and relations between his immediate family and his influential great-uncle were soured.

---

[165] SAG 301/35/1439–40, fo. 43v (condemnation 7 June, registered 19 July, 14s. 6d.; condemnation 21 June, registered 19 July, 21s. 3d.; condemnation 27 May, registered 19 July, 20d.); fo. 132v (condemnation 30 July, registered 14 Aug., 10s. 8d.). Chastelain also acknowledged a debt of 29s. 11d. for the purchase of wool cloth on 7 July: fo. 146v. All documents published in Small and Lievois, 'Les origines gantoises', apps xvi, xviii, xvii, xx, xiii.
[166] The sale is recorded in a document (9 July 1440) owned by Dr Cooreman and published in Small and Lievois, 'Les origines gantoises', 169–71 (app. xv).
[167] SAG 301/36/1440–1, fo. 5v, published in Small and Lievois, 'Les origines gantoises', 173 (app. xxi).
[168] The sale is recorded in a third document (20 Oct. 1440) owned by Dr Cooreman and published in Small and Lievois, 'Les origines gantoises', 173–6 (app. xxii).
[169] SAG 301/36/1440–1, fo. 76.
[170] On 15 Feb. 1441, Jan, acting in his own name and in that of George, acknowledged receipt from his daughter Mergriete of sums owed to them for jewels and movable goods in her possession: ibid. fo. 78, published in Small and Lievois, 'Les origines gantoises', 176 (app. xxiii). Three days later Jan gave full legal powers to his other daughter, Lisbette, to act in his name and in that of George in the dispute with Jan van Culsbrouc: 301/36/1440–1, fo. 103v, published in Small and Lievois, 'Les origines gantoises', 176 (app. xxiv).
[171] SAG 330/22/1440–1, fo. 17v; his guardian had been the priest Jan Gaffelkin who figured in Sophie van Culsbrouc's will. By 12 Dec. 1440, Louis was in business acknowledging a

When Jan van Culsbrouc died two years later, the once-promising nephew was either not around to be a beneficiary of his will or was no longer considered sufficiently close to figure in it.[172] Sometime in 1441, it would appear, Chastelain left Ghent under a cloud.[173]

Such were the events behind the departure for France. Nothing in Chastelain's background suggested this course of action in 1435. Early in 1441, by contrast, a change of direction was desirable, even necessary, if the aspirant were to salvage anything from the wreckage of his career. From this point until his appearance at the Burgundian court in the autumn of 1444 – a period of three and a half years, and not ten as was once thought – it seems likely that he was to be found in the kingdom.

Quite where in the kingdom, and in what capacity, remains a matter for conjecture. The task of tracing an individual in fifteenth-century Ghent or in ducal service at this time is as nothing by comparison with the problem of locating him in the armies of an itinerant king or among the retinues of the many who served him. Chastelain certainly became attached at some point in these years to Pierre II de Brézé, and it is through him that we might expect to trace the chronicler's movements.[174]

Brézé's growing influence at the royal court in the period from 1441 to 1444 is well-attested, as are the many offices which he acquired.[175] His itinerary, although much better known for his later years, can occasionally be traced.[176]

---

debt of 3l. to Rombout Mueleneere: 301/36/1440–1, fo. 29v. At the end of Jan. 1441 he purchased some armour, and on 5 Apr. he bought a piece of land: fos 69v, 93v.

[172] Jan van Culsbrouc's heirs appear in a document dated 20 Aug. 1443: ibid. 37/1443–4, fo. 35.

[173] The Castelains seem to have been represented in Ghent after the departure of George, and the apparent disappearance from the records of his father, by three main family members: Louis and Mergriete (George's brother and sister), and another Jan Castelain, son of Pieter Castelain, who was probably George's cousin. References to their activities can be found ibid. fo. 185; 330/23/1445–6, fo. 6; 301/38/1445–6, fo. 175v; 39/1447–8, fo. 112; 40/1448–9, fo. 31; 40/1449–50, fo. 84v. In another document, Jan Castelain rented a brothel: 38/1445–6, fo. 164v. My research went as far as 1453, the end of the Ghent war, but Van den Bemden – who followed both series 301 and 330 into the sixteenth century – did not find any more references to either George or his father.

[174] In Oct. 1444 he is mentioned in the Burgundian accounts as 'Georges le Chastelain escuier serviteur de monsr. le seneschal de Poitou': ADN B1982, fo. 201.

[175] P. Bernus, 'Essai sur la vie de Pierre de Brézé (vers 1410–65)', PTSEC 1906, 7–17; R. Favreau, 'Pierre de Brézé (vers 1410–1465)', Société des lettres, sciences et arts du Saumurois cxvii (Feb. 1968), 25–38. P. Méchineau, Les chevaliers de la victoire: Pierre de Brézé, ministre de Charles VII, Cholet 1986, is much less well informed. On the subject of his emerging influence and offices see Beaucourt, Histoire, vi. 291–3, and G. Dupont-Ferrier, Gallia Regia ou état des officiers royaux des bailliages et des sénéchaussées de 1328 à 1515, Paris, 1942–61, i. 355–6; iii. 350; iv. 254–5, 477–8, 527–8, 530; v. 226. On his role as seneschal of Poitou see P. Guerin, 'Recueil de documents concernant le Poitou dans les registres de la chancellerie de France', Archives historiques du Poitou xxix (1898), 178 n. 2. Only five men appear to have attended more sessions of Charles VII's council than Brézé: P.-R. Gaussin, 'Les conseillers de Charles VII (1418–1461)', Francia x (1982: publ. 1983), 67–130 at pp. 70–5.

[176] On Brézé's later career see P. Bernus, 'Le rôle politique de Pierre de Brézé au cours des

What eludes us is the composition of his entourage, while his affinity, revealed more fully in the documents after 1450, is also obscured in the years that concern us owing to the absence of the type of information which is more readily available for his son.[177] In the absence of such information we cannot rule out the possibility that Chastelain, with his known Burgundian connections, was simply seconded to Brézé's service in 1444 as a potentially useful member of the seneschal's embassy to the ducal court. Although he may well have been included for this reason, several of his remarks and at least three of his works suggest that his association with Brézé was of longer standing.

Brézé's Angevin connections had brought him to prominence in royal service, and it is interesting to note that Chastelain has particular knowledge of developments associated with that circle from 1442 to 1444 – years in which Angevin influence at court was still marked.[178] This may explain why Chastelain claimed that he had made the acquaintance of Marguerite d'Anjou; that he had heard of the counsel given to René d'Anjou to maintain good relations with the duke of Burgundy; or that he had met Agnès Sorel who, after all, came to the king's attention early in 1443 from an Angevin background.[179] Yet it is difficult to escape the conclusion that Chastelain's familiarity with this milieu stemmed, not from his entry into the Angevin orbit, but more specifically from an association with Brézé. It is only from the chronicler, for example, that we learn of Brézé's hand in the king's decision to obstruct the marriage proposed early in 1443 between Charles, count of Nevers, and Marguerite d'Anjou.[180] Chastelain is also able to reveal that the rise to prominence at the royal court in 1442 of Gaston, count of Foix, owed much to Brézé's influence.[181] His knowledge of the banishment of the lord of Pons in January 1442 may also be

---

dix dernières années du règne de Charles VII (1451–61)', BEC lxix (1906), 303–47, and 'Louis XI et Pierre de Brézé (1440–65)', *Revue de l'Anjou* ns lxiii (1911), 241–89, 355–71. His movements in the years from 1441 to 1444 included participation in the siege of Pontoise and Creil in the second half of 1441 (Beaucourt, *Histoire*, iii. 183–4); the protection of the frontiers with English Normandy in the company of Dunois in the spring of 1442 (ibid. 237 n. 5); his trip to the Midi later that year, and until mid-1443, in the company of the king (Bernus, 'Essai', 10); his presence at court in Saumur in the autumn of 1443 (Beaucourt, *Histoire*, iv. 20); and his role in the negotiations, at Tours, for the marriage of Henry VI and Marguerite d'Anjou in May 1444 (ibid. iii. 275).

[177] Gareth Prosser has studied Brézé's affinity in the period 1450–65, but the earlier period is less well known. The Brézé family papers contain some information on Pierre II, but much more on Jacques and his household. There is nothing on Pierre II's household here: Chantilly, Musée Condé, Cabinet des titres, carton 37 'Brézé'. See also Paris, BN, Pièces originales, no. 509, 'Brézé'; ibid. Dossiers bleus, no. 134, 'Brézé'.

[178] On Angevin influence at court (Duke René, Charles of Maine and the king's wife, Marie d'Anjou) see M. G. A. Vale, *Charles VII*, London 1974, 86–114.

[179] Chastelain's claimed associations with Marguerite d'Anjou and Agnès Sorel are discussed above. For the advice given to René d'Anjou see ii, 43. On Sorel's first meeting with Charles VII while in the entourage of Isabelle, wife of Duke René, see A. Lecoy de La Marche, *Le roi René*, Paris 1875, i. 228.

[180] v, 18; cf. Beaucourt, *Histoire*, iii. 260.

[181] vii, 47; cf. Beaucourt, *Histoire*, iv. 90–1.

related to the fact that Brézé was then seneschal of Poitou, the region most affected by the acts of rebellion which brought Pons his punishment.[182] More telling, however, is the fact that almost twenty years after his time in France, Chastelain wrote an eloquent defence of Brézé in his hour of need; four years after that, he penned a stirring lament on the subject of Brézé's death at Montlhéry.[183] The connection between the two men was clearly not a fleeting one. This is confirmed for the earlier period by Chastelain's first known work, *L'oultré d'amour*.[184] Vallet de Viriville argued persuasively that this piece was written during Chastelain's time in France, and that it was destined for Brézé.[185] The seneschal was something of a wordsmith himself.[186] In writing for him, Chastelain had alighted upon another of the means by which the aspirant could endear himself to a patron: not service in arms, not bookish learning and the ability to counsel, but poetry, the pastime of the great and the good. The process of Chastelain's acculturation to aristocratic ways, hinted at in his background but first begun in earnest in 1433-4, had developed still further. It should also be noted that his first foray into poetry took place within the context of a French literary culture.

The importance of Chastelain's sojourn in France thus should not be under-estimated. Yet neither should it be exaggerated, as previous commentators have been tempted to do. It is possible that his (clearly successful) years in France instilled in him a sense of loyalty to the Crown which, as a Ghent shipper, he might not otherwise have felt. He did have much to be grateful for. Yet if such sentiments were in any way related to the amount of time he spent in the kingdom, we must surely revise our perception of them as the inevitable product of a decade in royal service. When looked at from another perspective, indeed, Chastelain's shorter stay in France may appear, not as the all-important, formative influence in the moulding of his outlook, but as a phase – perhaps even an interruption – in that process which led from Ghent to the Burgundian court. If he were destined to enjoy a political career, then his background, training and family connections all pointed in the direction of

---

[182] iii, 214; cf. Tuetey, *Les écorcheurs*, i. 127 n. 1. For Brézé's nomination to the post of seneschal early in 1441 see Bernus, 'Essai', 9. Another Poitevin connection is provided by Chastelain's report of a conversation he had with Marguerite de Valois, the illegitimate sister of Charles VII, who was 'mariee en Poitou' to a major landholder in the region, the lord of Belleville (Delclos, 311-12).

[183] *Déprécation pour messire Pierre de Brézé* and *Épitaphe de messire Pierre de Brézé*: vii, 37-73.

[184] vi, 67-128.

[185] A. Vallet de Viriville, 'Oeuvres de Georges Chastellain', *Journal des Savants* (1867), 49-63, 183-99, 385-93 at p. 197; cf. J. Lemaire, 'L'oultré d'amour de George Chastelain: un exemple ancien de construction en abyme', *Revue romane* xi (1976), 306-16.

[186] For Brézé's verse see Charles d'Orléans, *Poésies*, ed. P. Champion, Paris 1923-7, ii. 498, 525; *Rondeaux et autres poésies du XVe siècle*, ed. G. Raynaud, Paris 1889, 80, 111, 112. Brézé's literary standing was high in the eyes of René d'Anjou, who included an epitaph to the seneschal in his *Livre du cuer d'amour épris: oeuvres complètes du roi René, duc d'Anjou*, ed. T. de Quatrebarbes, Angers 1844-6, iii. 118.

the ducal elite rather than its royal counterpart; and it was to the former, not the latter, that he eventually gravitated.

However, the idea that Chastelain's sojourn in France constituted an interruption is an unhelpful, even misleading, way of looking at his career. It implies that service in the kingdom was somehow a deviation from the norm among aspiring or established Burgundian servants. The activities of several Burgundian servants in the 1430s and 1440s show that this was not the case. The recovery of Paris was achieved with the assistance of several hundred Burgundian men-at-arms under the command of Philippe de Ternant, the ducal captain who had raised the Flemish contingents to which Chastelain may have been attached in 1433, and Jean de Villiers, lord of l'Isle-Adam.[187] Five years later – in fact, in the same year that Chastelain himself appears to have left for France – Louis de Luxembourg led 600 combatants southwards to join the French siege of Pontoise.[188] As we saw at an earlier stage, one of the royal captains at that siege was Pierre de Brézé, who very probably met members of the Burgundian contingent of men-at-arms.[189] Although some are inclined to view the 1440s as a period which saw mounting tension and an increasing distance between the duke and the king, Philip the Good was clearly not troubled by the fact that some of his men received royal pay. The Burgundians who participated in the reconquest of Normandy at the end of the decade left with his blessing.[190] The road to royal service was a well-travelled one for Chastelain's superiors and those he could now claim as his peers in the Burgundian Netherlands.

Without these connections between the French and Burgundian elites, indeed, Chastelain's entry into royal service is hard to understand. Owing to the increasing unwillingness of the French nobility to turn out or volunteer for royal armies, Charles VII and his captains may well have been prepared to accept 'sans formalité' those who presented themselves for military service in the early 1440s.[191] Yet how many seriously entertained the possibility of being retained in France without some credible backing which vouched for their abilities? Where could Chastelain himself expect to find such support? Surely his best hopes for a recommendation lay with members of that social group which he had only just begun to edge his way into, the court nobility of the Burgundian Netherlands – for some of whom, at least, service in France was a recognised means of advancement. Although his first contacts with the ducal elite may not have been sustained, there is no reason to suppose that access to

---

[187] E. Cosneau, *Le connétable de Richemont, Artur de Bretagne (1393–1458)*, Paris 1886, 242–9; Thompson, *Paris*, 234–6.

[188] Beaucourt, *Histoire*, iii. 179.

[189] This is obviously an occasion when Chastelain might have encountered Brézé, but there is no evidence to substantiate the possibility.

[190] Bossuat, *Perrinet Gressart*, 340–1; Cosneau, *Le connétable*, 396. For a more pessimistic reading of Franco-Burgundian relations in the 1440s see Vaughan, *PTG*, 113–22.

[191] On the 'carence de la noblesse française' prior to the creation of the *armées de l'ordonnance* see Contamine, *Guerre, état et société*, 253–73. The quotation is at p. 268.

it was denied him after 1434. His brother Louis and his associate or distant relative, Hector van Masmines, are both listed among the members of the guild of St George in Ghent. This was an archery guild for the crossbow which served as an extension of the civic militia, but which was also an important social and political institution in Ghent with its club for the under-eighteens, its own charitable organisation, a wide membership, including members of conservative guilds like the shippers and the butchers, and – last but not least – a substantial number of honorary members including Adolf of Cleves and members of the Luxembourg family. Antoine Haneron, Chastelain's former regent at Louvain, also figured in the membership list. The guild of St George thus brought Ghenters into contact with men of the Burgundian court.[192] In June 1440, at precisely the time when Chastelain may have been looking for a way out of his personal difficulties, the guild staged a great archery contest between contingents, each made up of ten men, from over fifty towns in northern France and the Low Countries. The duke was represented on this important occasion by some of his more experienced captains. Two of these men, Simon de Lalaing and Jean de Créquy, the lord of Canaples, were seasoned campaigners from the wars in France. It is naturally impossible to say whether, at the contest of June 1440, Chastelain made or renewed those contacts which would soon bring him into royal service. What matters is that such contacts could still be made between city and court, and that they could lead in the direction which the aspirant took.

Those who emphasise the apparent singularity of Chastelain's more royalist remarks – and who explain them away by the years he spent in France – may thus be missing a point of deeper significance. Chastelain's brief career in France was not unusual among Burgundian servants. Others had passed through a phase of royal service. Perhaps, then, Chastelain's outlook was not so unusual either. After all, Burgundian political culture was not formed in a vacuum. Between the royal and ducal courts, between the French and Burgundian 'states' – so often seen in isolation from, and in opposition to, one another – there existed a more nuanced interplay resulting from the personal interests, experiences and values of men like Lalaing, Villiers, Ternant and, of course, Chastelain himself. This interplay is of considerable importance in the rest of this study. In the present context it helps to explain the final matter for discussion: the question of Chastelain's return to ducal service in 1446.

This point in Chastelain's life has been portrayed in dramatic terms. In the mounting tension between duke and king, it has been written, Chastelain felt

---

[192] The membership of Louis, Hector, Haneron and the others mentioned here is attested in the records of the guild: Ghent, Bijlokemuseum, MS 1101, fos 22, 31, 36, 232v (the manuscript is on permanent loan to the museum from the SAG). On relations between the Sint-Jorisgilde and the ducal elite see Boone, *Gent*, 114–18. On the guild itself and the remarks which follow see UBG HS G6112 (containing an account of the archery competiton of 1440); J. Moulin-Coppens, *De geschiedenis van het oude Sint-Jorisgilde te Gent*, Ghent 1982, esp. pp. 84–106; and F. de Potter, *Jaarboeken der Sint-Jorisgilde van Gent*, Ghent 1866, 61–98.

obliged to choose between his royal benefactor and his natural lord.[193] His integrity in opting for the latter is emphasised to distinguish his apparent change of allegiance from that of Philippe de Commynes twenty-six years later.[194] Commynes – in the language of the Cold War, during which the last major study of him was completed – has been seen as a defector.[195] We are entitled to ask whether Chastelain really needs to be saved from this comparison. Commynes did not 'defect'; he left Charles the Bold for the duke's royal overlord, however displeasing this might have been to the former.[196] It would appear that Chastelain's reversion to ducal service in 1446 also stemmed from practical considerations, even if they were of a rather different order.

Philip the Good must have noted with interest the presence of one of his former servants in the entourage which accompanied Pierre de Brézé to court in 1444. Chastelain was clearly not in the same league as his diplomatic superiors, but he had probably gained in stature by his association with them – not just Brézé, but also Jean Rabateau, royal counsellor and president of the *Parlement* of Paris, or Étienne Chevalier, treasurer to Charles VII and a counsellor himself.[197] This was dazzling company for a man who, little more than three years earlier, had been struggling to make ends meet in Ghent. The matters with which Chastelain was conversant, albeit as a secondary member of the embassy, may also have revived ducal interest in him. In these negotiations Philip the Good was most concerned with the activities of the *écorcheurs* on the frontiers of the duchy of Burgundy, and with the long-standing problem of royal enclaves in ducal territories.[198] The French agenda included the annulment of the ransom owed to Philip by René d'Anjou and the jurisdiction of the *Parlement* in the county of Flanders. These matters were among the most contentious issues in Franco-Burgundian relations in the years following the treaty of Arras. The Brussels conference which addressed them inaugurated a longer phase of negotiations which were held in Rheims, Châlons and Paris between 1445 and 1448.[199] Perhaps in the expectation of drawn-out

---

193 Hommel, *Chastellain*, 30.
194 Pérouse, *Georges Chastellain*, 16.
195 This is a central theme in J. Dufournet, *La destruction des mythes dans les Mémoires de Philippe de Commynes*, Geneva 1966.
196 Professor Michael Jones makes this trenchant observation on Dufournet's understanding of the memoirist's change of camp: Philippe de Commynes, *Memoirs*, ed. M. Jones, Harmondsworth 1972, 43–4.
197 ADN B1982, fos 64v, 126r–v, 132r–v, 133, 188v–9, 200. On Rabateau and Chevalier see Vale, *Charles VII*, 87, 99, 166, 171 n. 4, 205, 208, 222–3. For what follows on the embassy itself see Beaucourt, *Histoire*, iv. 122–4.
198 On the problem of the *écorcheurs* see Tuetey, *Les écorcheurs*, i. 15–60. Philip the Good's grievances are listed in two documents, now ACO B11906, B11908, the first of which is published in Plancher, *Histoire*, iv. pp. clxxii–clxxv. On the problem of the enclaves see J. Richard, ' "Enclaves" royales et limites des provinces: les élections bourguignonnes', AB xx (1948), 89–113 esp. pp. 100–2, and 'Les débats entre le roi de France et le duc de Bourgogne sur la frontière du royaume à l'ouest de la Saône', *Bulletin historique et philologique du comité des travaux historiques* (1964), 113–32 esp. pp. 118–23.
199 Beaucourt, *Histoire*, iv. 128–37.

discussions, Philip paid particular attention to the diplomatic protocol of bestowing gifts upon the ambassadors. Brézé, Charles VII's favourite, received a gift of plate and the huge sum of 1,000 écus.[200] Well-targeted largesse, the great lubricant in the machinery of princely politics, was also directed at Brézé's useful servant. Chastelain received 48*l*. from the duke 'pour avoir et acheter ung cheval quant il a esté devers lui avec sondit maistre'.[201]

Brézé was almost certainly unperturbed by the special attention paid to his servant. Chastelain was well-qualified to become an 'expert fixer' in his master's dealings with Philip the Good, and any favours shown to him by the duke were promising.[202] In the context of the wider issues which publicly separated Burgundy from France, men like Chastelain, whose experience enabled them to move easily between the two, were clearly valuable. Brézé was prepared to go to far greater lengths than this in order to manipulate political situations. As his complicated dealings with Guillaume Mariette reveal, he excelled in the gathering of information and the spreading of disinformation.[203] The real truth behind Brézé's relationship with Mariette, who first appears as a Burgundian servant around 1446, is no doubt irrecoverable.[204] From documents which were later found in Mariette's possession, however, at least two relevant points emerge: first, that Brézé was prepared to use men with Burgundian contacts to achieve his ends; and second, that a number of individuals around Philip the Good – including Pierre de Bauffremont and, perhaps not surprisingly, Philippe de Ternant – were considered to be susceptible to royal influence.[205]

---

[200] ADN B1982, fos 126r–v; B3659, fo. 75. This last folio reveals that the costs incurred by the French ambassadors, amounting to 595*l*., were also defrayed by the duke.

[201] ADN B1982, fo. 201. On the practice and wisdom of gift-giving see A. Derville, 'Pots-de-vin, cadeaux, racket, patronage', *RN* lvi (1974), 341–64; and M. Boone, 'Dons et pots-de-vin, aspects de la sociabilité urbaine au bas moyen âge', *RN* lxx (1988), 471–87.

[202] The term 'expert fixer' is borrowed from P. S. Lewis, 'The centre, the periphery and the problem of power distribution in later medieval France', in J. R. L. Highfield and R. Jeffs (eds), *The crown and local communities in England and France in the fifteenth century*, Gloucester 1981, 33–50 at p. 40 (repr. in P. S. Lewis, *Essays in later medieval French history*, London 1985, 3–29). For another of Brézé's fixers see the role of his secretary, Jean Doucereau, as described in Bernus, 'Le rôle politique', 333, 343–6.

[203] It is interesting to note that Chastelain puts the following pleasantry into Brézé's mouth in a passage where the seneschal is addressing Philip the Good (1463): 'Mon très redoubté seigneur, jà-soit-il que peu coustumier soye de vray dire, et, qu'en manière d'un mondain parler, mes propres amis mesmes ne me croient pas tousjours, toutesvoies présentement, contraire de mon usage, me voy et treuve contraint de dire vray': iv, 289. Chastelain evidently remembered his former master's habits well.

[204] The Mariette affair, which nearly brought Brézé his comeuppance in 1447–8, is revealed in the depositions published in d'Escouchy, *Chronique*, iii. 265–341. For interpretations see Bernus, 'Louis XI et Pierre de Brézé', 247–54; Beaucourt, *Histoire*, iv. 202–19; and Vale, *Charles VII*, 106–14.

[205] In a memorandum supposedly sent by Mariette to Philip the Good, it is reported that 'ledit sen(eschal) dit qu'il scet bien estre bien à lui et à son commandement Ter(nant) et Cher(ny), par especial Ter(nant)': see the depositions cited above, p. 270. On the career of Bauffremont see M.-T. Caron, 'Pierre de Bauffremont', in *CTO*, 58–9.

Chastelain may not have been another Guillaume Mariette, but it is possible to see the value which Brézé attached to him. He used his versatile servant repeatedly in his subsequent dealings with Philip the Good. In the summer of 1445, as the Burgundian and French parties hammered out their differences at Châlons, Chastelain arrived at the ducal court in Ghent to discuss 'certaines choses et matières secrètes'.[206] He was back once more in his home town in December that year where 'il a sé[j]ourné par aucun temps en attendant la response de certain[e]s affaires'.[207] These visits had no doubt made him a familiar figure at court; so familiar, in fact, that when he reappeared in the following April, Philip the Good granted him 8l. to attend a tourney at Arras.[208] The royal servant's easy familiarity with Burgundian courtiers is clear. For some of them at least, he may have seemed a kindred spirit: indeed, the jousts which Chastelain was given a special grant to attend were those of Philippe de Ternant whom Brézé considered an amenable sort, and to whom Chastelain himself may already have been connected. Sometime after this, and almost imperceptibly, Chastelain slipped back into Burgundian service. By the autumn, after spending a 'grande espace de temps ... en la ville de Bruxelles et ailleurs', Chastelain was known to the ducal administration as an 'escuier pannetier de mondit seigneur'.[209] This small transfusion of talent from one part of the French body politic to another attracted no opprobrium from Chastelain's former masters. In the same document, indeed, we learn that he was already preparing his return to them to deal with familiar business: not, this time, as Brézé's servant, but as the emissary of Philip the Good.

The chronicler was clearly accurate in suggesting that his shift from royal to ducal service was easy, even natural. As much of this chapter has shown, however, this is one of the few points of contact between his roseate account of his early years and such record evidence of them as survives. George, the aspirant, arrived thanks to the many connections – themselves rather more profound and intricate than is commonly recognised – between city and court. It is understandable that once he had acculturated to his new surroundings, however, he was inclined to obscure or overlook Joris's background. In a century preoccupied with status, respect for blue blood and hierarchy were particular obsessions at the Burgundian court. Instead of emphasising his time as a shipper and his origins as a shipper's son, he chose to reinterpret his past creatively by playing upon his years in France and, in the process, reconstructed his *persona* in the image of the type of nobleman his audience and his court peers might easily have recognised and found worthy of credence and/or preferment. French service, it now transpires, was simply a phase in his passage

---

[206] ADN B1988, fo. 188v. The payment (60l.) is recorded under the rubric for the months of June and July.
[207] Ibid. fo. 196, repeated in B3659, fo. 79. The payment was for 40l.
[208] ADN B1991, fo. 186v.
[209] Ibid. fo. 192.

from Ghent to the Burgundian court, rather than the formative influence it has seemed to previous commentators. Crucially, however, it was a phase which other Burgundian servants had passed through. His experience was not unique. In the desire to see the chronicler's outlook as the product of a singular career, another possibility has therefore been overlooked. Perhaps there were more like him within the ducal elite: men for whom the political cultures of Valois France and Valois Burgundy – despite Montereau, Troyes and the expansion of the 1430s (which, after all, were then recent events) – could still seem intertwined. A discussion of Chastelain's career at the Burgundian court is necessary if we are to explore this theme further.

2

The Courtier (1446–1475)

The second half of Chastelain's life, spent entirely in ducal service, has for long been better documented than the first. We may assume that many aspects of his career did not find their way into the bountiful records of the *Chambre des comptes*, but at least these were trawled thoroughly by Pinchart; so much so, in fact, that little has been discovered since.[1] Unfortunately, no attempt has been made to address the simple but fundamental question which Pinchart's bare documents naturally give rise to, and which we must pose at the outset: just how close did Chastelain come to the heart of the Burgundian elite?[2]

This problem gains in importance when we remember that the resolution of another depends upon it. Without a more rounded understanding of the extent and quality of Chastelain's changing experience at the political centre, we cannot assess how representative – or otherwise – his views upon it might have been. Indeed, this deficiency, like the previous paucity of sources on his early life, has had the effect of augmenting the importance attached to his time in France. Without more detailed knowledge of the frequency and duration of his sojourns at court, his evolving functions and status within its hierarchy and, last but not least, the personal circles in which he moved, it has been easier to trace the controlling framework of his thought to that formative period he claimed to have spent in royal service, rather than to the much longer time he undoubtedly spent at the Burgundian court. Hence our concentration upon this first set of issues in the present chapter. The discussion will move through

---

[1] Pinchart, 'Historiographes'. He relied almost exclusively on the records kept by the financial officers of the northern ducal territories. The method is logical: Chastelain's career was spent almost exclusively in these regions. His few journeys to the southern territories made no impression on the relevant records of the Burgundian receiver-general: ACO B1706, B1712, B1713 (1447–9); B1728, B1729 (1453–5). Kervyn de Lettenhove, Pérouse and Hommel were all content to repeat Pinchart's findings. Urwin drew some benefit from A. Le Glay and others, *Inventaire sommaire des archives départementales du Nord*, Lille 1863–1906, but did not uncover material beyond what is conveyed there. Hence P. Muret's call for further biographical research: 'Chastelain parmi nous', *RBPH* lxi (1983), 367–72 at p. 371. In addition to Le Glay on the ADN see R.-H. Bautier and others (eds), *Les sources de l'histoire économique et sociale du moyen âge*, Paris 1984.

[2] An issue raised by Delclos when he called for a 'volume pour étudier sa vie, encore mal connue, et surtout pour déterminer le rôle – apparamment assez important – qu'il a pu jouer auprès de ses maîtres ... en tant que conseiller et en tant qu'ambassadeur': 'Le témoignage de Georges Chastellain', partially publ. Ph.D. diss. Sorbonne 1977, i. 1.

three chronological phases, each with its own characteristics and each roughly a decade in length. The first is the story of Chastelain's gradual integration within the Burgundian elite.

Integration (1446–54)

Although the chronicler's emergence into the foreground of ducal politics is the main concern here, we should not forget that the developments we are concerned with remain part of a broader canvas dominated by Franco-Burgundian relations. Chastelain, who had ended his days in royal service as an ambassador to Burgundy, was now sent by the duke on two lengthy missions 'par devers le roy', from 27 September to 15 November 1446, and from 20 January to 22 March 1447.[3] The significance of these embassies is two-fold.

In the first instance, and particularly by their timing and duration, they are indicative of that continuing interplay between royal and ducal elites in which Chastelain himself was now an old hand. Alongside the wider diplomatic process set in motion at Brussels in 1444 and culminating, four years later, at Paris, it made good sense to maintain less formal channels of communication. While Chastelain was in France, Philip the Good's envoys were with the duke of Orléans and the dauphin.[4] Contact was maintained with Pierre de Brézé, and both he and Rolin Renault, a royal equerry whom Chastelain appears to have known, were the beneficiaries of ducal largesse.[5] At the same time, Philip the Good deployed men whom Charles 'réputoit beaucoup' (iii, 19) in his dealings with the king. One such man – well known to Brézé, the dominant figure in the royal entourage – was Bertrandon de la Broquière, who spent no less than six months with the king between March and October 1446.[6] The length of this sojourn stemmed partly from the nature of Bertrandon's mission, but partly also from an awareness that advantages might accrue from the

---

[3] Sometime in Sept. Chastelain received 32l. for his services in Brussels and in anticipation of his mission to France: ADN B1991, fo. 192. Later he was granted a retrospective payment of 98l. for the forty-nine-day embassy (the dates of which are given), and a further 10l. 52s. 'pour le salaire des secretaires et aussi le droit de seaulx de certaines lettres royaulx qu'il obtint': ibid. fos 77v–8. The following Jan. he received a prospective payment of 24l. to travel from Ghent to the king 'pour . . . affaires secrez': ibid. fo. 196v. After his return, and on 21 Apr., he received 99l. 4s. for his sixty-two-day trip (again, the dates of which are given: B1994, fo. 78v).

[4] The ducal secretary Louis Dommessent was with Charles d'Orléans in Nov. 1446; Oudart Chapperel, a *maître des requêtes*, was with the dauphin slightly earlier: ADN B1991, fos 78, 191v.

[5] Letters were sent to the king and Brézé in the summer of 1446: ibid. fo. 99v. Brézé had received a horse from the duke earlier that year: B1988, fo. 212. In the next, Renault received 120l. 'pour aucunes causes et matieres secretes': B1994, fo. 159v. Chastelain did not think much of Renault's character or abilities: iii, 388–9.

[6] ADN B1991, fos 77, 82v, 99v. According to Guillaume Mariette, Brézé cultivated relations with Bertrandon: d'Escouchy, *Chronique*, iii. 269–70.

placement of servants for prolonged periods at the royal court in times of intense diplomatic activity. The well-connected emissary was in an excellent position to act as the eyes and ears of his principal.[7] Hence, no doubt, a major mission to the French court in the following April for a further period of three months, this time jointly directed by Pierre de Goux and another Burgundian whom Brézé thought – perhaps presumptuously, but that is not the point – to be 'bien à lui et à son commandement', Pierre de Bauffremont.[8] In addition to these men, whose familiarity with the royal milieu was clearly of value to the duke, one further Burgundian emissary featured heavily in Philip's plans. His remuneration marked him out as a 'grand ambassadeur', and he was the only ducal agent to effect prolonged visits to the royal court between the two main missions. This, of course, was Chastelain, Brézé's former servant.[9] It was clearly thought that he, like some others in Burgundian service, could steer a path through royal networks of influence and favour.

In view of the complex web of rights and interests which bound together Philip the Good and his royal 'souverain', the ability of servants like Chastelain to work with certain elements within the royal elite was essential. In turn, these missions afforded the pantler a hard-headed understanding of his master's position in relation to the crown – a point overlooked by those who consider him an idealist in matters of Franco-Burgundian affairs. Although the purpose of the second embassy was deliberately kept secret in the ducal accounts, the first concerned 'certaines choses touchans le fait de la terre de Cousy et conté de Tonnoire, et aussy le adiournement d'aucuns ses [Philip's] vassaulx et féaulx de Picardie qui avoient esté adiournez en personne a la court de parlement a Paris contre ung appellé Dimanche de Court'. The matter of Cousy and Tonnerre was part of the wider quarrel over royal enclaves in the duchy of Burgundy which loomed large after 1435.[10] Despite the terms of the treaty of Arras, which gave Philip the Good the right to raise revenue and appoint officials in these lands, the obstructive policies of royal officers in Tonnerre continued to undermine ducal authority. The second part of this remit, although it concerned jurisdictional rather than territorial issues, also revealed the extent to which the duke was limited in his powers by the rights of the crown. The charges brought before the *Parlement* by the royal captain,

---

[7] D. Queller, *The office of ambassador in the Middle Ages*, Princeton 1967, 88. Permanent ambassadors in the Italian style were not deployed by rulers of the Low Countries until the end of the fifteenth century: C. de Borchgrave, 'Diplomates et diplomatie sous le duc de Bourgogne Jean sans Peur', PCEEB xxxii (1992), 31–47 at pp. 43–4.

[8] Beaucourt, *Histoire*, iv. 337–8. For Brézé's reported attitude to Bauffremont see d'Escouchy, *Chronique*, iii. 269–70.

[9] Chastelain's remuneration of 2 francs per day, revealed in the documents relating to his embassy cited above, was at the lower end of the pay scale for 'grands ambassadeurs': D. Hillard-Villard, 'Les relations diplomatiques entre Charles VII et Philippe le Bon de 1435 à 1445', PTSEC (1963), 81–5 at p. 83.

[10] See ch. 1 above.

Dimanche de Court, were trivial in themselves, but this did not prevent the *Parlement* from exploiting them to the full.¹¹ In an apparently calculated move, one of its *huissiers* was sent to interrupt the festivities of the Ghent chapter of the Order of the Golden Fleece with personal summonses for the Burgundian perpetrators of the attack and, more significantly, for the duke himself.¹² Arras may have given Philip the Good personal exemption from 'tout cas, de subjeccion, hommage, ressor, souveraineté et autres', but cases such as this were a constant reminder of the fact that the *Parlement*'s writ still ran in many of the lands he held of the crown.¹³ Because of their direct experience in such matters, Chastelain and some of his court colleagues almost certainly did not share our modern perception of a Burgundian state which was successfully extricating itself from its ties to the kingdom. Royal rights might be circumvented and the most damaging effects of the king's power might be palliated, but neither could be easily removed or wished away.

It was against this wider backdrop of Franco-Burgundian relations, and no doubt through the prestige he derived from his role in it, that Chastelain began to integrate within the Burgundian elite. The first indication of this is found in his new office within the household: known as a simple *écuyer* before his first mission, he appears in the accounts after September 1446 as an *écuyer panetier*.¹⁴ This was undoubtedly a step forward. The office required the swearing of an oath to a ducal *maître d'hôtel* 'au bien et à l'honneur de la maison' (v, 156), and with it came a series of unspecified 'drois, prerogatives, libertez, franchises, prouffiz et emolumens'.¹⁵ Since the duties of court officers were often 'personal and variable' rather than 'technical and official', there is little point in attempting a precise definition of the functions which were attached

---

[11] In Aug. 1445, Dimanche de Court received royal letters of remission for his excesses while leading his troops through Picardy two years earlier. At the time, revenge was exacted when he was ambushed by a force sent from Philip the Good under the orders of Étampes. The dispute was subsequently perpetuated by the intervention of the *Parlement*. The affair dragged on until the Paris settlement of 1448 and the grant of royal letters of remission to one of the Burgundian captains involved in the attack on Dimanche de Court: Tuetey, *Les écorcheurs*, ii. 435–7; ADN B1991, fos 141v–2 (dispatch of Burgundian letters to the *Parlement* on the case, Mar. 1447); Paris, BN, Collection de Bourgogne no. 95, fo. 1039 (resolution of the matter in the 'Appointements de Paris', 1448).
[12] See Chastelain's comments: vi, 289.
[13] E. Cosneau, *Les grands traités de la guerre de cent ans*, Paris 1889, 143–4. Comparable instances of the use of the powers of the *Parlement* are discussed in W. P. Blockmans, 'La position du comté de Flandre dans le royaume à la fin du XVe siècle', in *FFQS*, 71–89.
[14] ADN B1991, fo. 192. The household records are quite specific as to office, not least because different rates of pay applied to different offices.
[15] U. Schwarzkopf, *Die Rechnungslegung des Humbert de Plaine über die Jahre 1448 bis 1452*, Göttingen 1970, 40–2. Examples of the oath sworn by pantlers are to be found in H. Nélis, *Chambre des comptes de Lille*, Brussels 1915, 32 (nos 391 and 397). Some efforts have been made to analyse the nature of the 'drois, prerogatives ... et emolumens' enjoyed by ducal secretaries, legists and financial officers, but those of the pantlers and other household offices remain comparatively obscure: cf. Bartier, *Légistes*, 93–189; P. Cockshaw, *Le personnel de la chancellerie de Bourgogne-Flandre*, Courtrai–Heule 1982, 21–31, 104–58.

to the title.¹⁶ As a pantler, however, it can be said that Chastelain belonged to one of the four household services which also comprised the *eschansons*, *escuyers tranchants* and *escuyers d'escurie*. These offices appear to have been equal in rank, and the number of men in each category increased from twelve under Philip the Good in 1426 to fifty under Charles the Bold in 1473.¹⁷ Above them in the aulic hierarchy were more select groups, the *chevaliers et chambellans* and the *maîtres d'hôtel*; below them came the mass of lesser household servants, from the ducal heralds to the domestic servants. As a member of a substantial middling group at court, then, Chastelain enjoyed a relatively, but not markedly, privileged position. In a hierarchy where precedence was determined by proximity to the person of the prince, the pantler could be called upon to manage, through his subordinates, the service and even the tasting of the duke's food. Largely a ceremonial role, this none the less reflected well upon the value and trust which was publicly placed upon the office holder.¹⁸

The extent of Chastelain's integration at court was also dictated by the frequency and duration of his sojourns with the elite. The household ordinances stipulated that individual *panetiers* should serve on a rota basis by term, the latter usually three months in duration in any given year.¹⁹ Salaries were recorded on the daily rolls of household expenditure known as the *escroes*.²⁰ It has been stated that Chastelain appears in these documents from 1448, but the 'Georget' in question is almost certainly a *souffleur de cuisine* appointed at an earlier stage.²¹ However, the fact that Chastelain's name is absent in the *escroes* does not imply that he was absent from the court; it simply indicates that he

---

¹⁶ D. A. L. Morgan, 'The king's affinity in the polity of Yorkist England', *Transactions of the Royal Historical Society* (hereinafter cited as *TRHS*) 5th ser. xxiii (1973), 1–25 at p. 4. For an attempt to describe the pantler's role at the Burgundian court see U. Schwarzkopf, 'Studien zur Hoforganisation der Herzöge von Burgund aus dem Hause Valois', unpubl. Ph.D. diss. Göttingen 1955, 78–83. Unless otherwise stated, what follows is based on this work and on Olivier de la Marche's *Estat de la maison du duc Charles de Bourgoingne*, in La Marche, *Mémoires*, iv. 1–189.

¹⁷ E. Lameere, 'La cour de Philippe le Bon', *Annales de la Société d'archéologie de Bruxelles* xiv (1900), 159–72; W. Paravicini, 'Die Hofordnungen Herzog Philipps des Guten von Burgund: Edition', I, *Francia* x (1982), 131–66; II, ibid. xi (1983), 257–301; III, ibid. xiii (1985), 191–211; IV, ibid. xv (1987, publ. 1989), 183–231; V, ibid. xviii (1991), 111–23.

¹⁸ On the hierarchy surrounding the service of food see A. Lafortune-Martel, *Fête noble en Bourgogne au XVe siècle*, Montreal–Paris 1984, 102–3.

¹⁹ W. Paravicini, 'The court of Burgundy', in R. G. Asch and A. M. Birke (eds), *Princes, patronage and the nobility*, Oxford 1991, 70–102 at pp. 78–9, 87. One advantage of the scheme was that it brought large numbers of the nobility into contact with the court elite on a regular basis: C. A. J. Armstrong, 'Had the Burgundian government a policy for the nobility?', in J. S. Bromley and E. H. Kossman (eds), *Britain and the Netherlands*, Groningen 1964, ii. 9–32 (repr. in Armstrong, *England, France and Burgundy*, 213–36), and 'The golden age of Burgundy', in A. G. Dickens (ed.), *The courts of Europe*, London 1977, 55–75.

²⁰ W. Paravicini, '*Ordonnances de l'hôtel* und *escroes des gaiges*', in Bulst and Genet, *Medieval lives*, 243–66.

²¹ According to Hommel, Chastelain was receiving 'un traitement fixe de sept sous par jour' from 1448 onwards: *Chastellain*, 31. There is indeed a 'Georget' in these records who is paid at this rate, but he figures much lower down the ranks than we would expect for an

served as a *panetier* in an extraordinary capacity.[22] His position may not have been as well-established as that of other ducal pantlers, but we should not conclude that he was a marginal figure by comparison. Indeed, in the years 1446–8 Chastelain was regularly defrayed for the expenses he incurred in following the court's movements throughout the Low Countries. In the autumn of 1446, as we have seen, he is described as having served Philip the Good 'par grant espace de temps'. In the following spring he accompanied the court from Bruges to Ghent, and was in attendance once more in October when Philip decamped to Brussels.[23] In the first few months of 1448 he was with the court once more, first at Brussels and then at Lille.[24] Such evidence indicates that at least in this early period of his career, Chastelain may even have been a more regular attender at court than any of his colleagues who served 'par terme'. It is perhaps no coincidence that his attendance corresponds to a continuing period of Franco-Burgundian dialogue in which his personal qualities and experience may well have proven useful.

Alongside the official hierarchy of service there existed a parallel network of influence and favour based upon the principal courtiers and their servants. This network also fashioned the personal experience and fortunes of individuals.[25] Leading figures at court sat at the apex of pyramidal structures consisting of lesser men who, by their loyalty and service, could hope for advancement through their patron's good offices.[26] Chastelain's integration at the level of these more obscure but fundamentally important networks is revealed in his repeated associations throughout his early years with Philippe, lord of Ternant.[27]

écuyer panetier. The 'Georget' in question was probably a *souffleur de cuisine* appointed as a ducal 'afforeur de vin' in 1440: Nélis, *Chambre des comptes*, 9.

[22] An inspection of the surviving *escroes* for the years 1446–56 does not throw up any reference to Chastelain: see the very full records conserved as ADN B3411–3420. The only possible figure who might be confused with him is the herald Chasteaubelin, whose name is occasionally written in a similar way. This was 'Engherant Aliemart dit Chasteaubelin, roi d'armes de Hainaut', who lived in Valenciennes: ibid. 62H 73 (1465), fo. 69. Those who served in an extraordinary capacity, like Chastelain, were described as being 'sans ordonnance'. They received one-off payments according to the time they spent at court, as in the case of a pantler, paid in 1453, who 'n'a point esté a gaiges, ne n'a livrée par les escroes de la despense ordinaire de l'ostel d'icellui seigneur': ibid. B2012, fo. 141. This group of court servants deserves as much attention as individuals who appear in the 'ordonnances' of the household.

[23] Ibid. B1994, fos 166v, 170v. The court moved from Bruges to Ghent at the end of May, and was in Brussels by the second half of Sept.: *Itinéraires*, 250–3.

[24] ADN B1998, fos 124v–5, 131. The court was at Brussels until early Apr., and at Lille by the nineteenth of that month: *Itinéraires*, 254–7.

[25] Cf. P. S. Lewis, *Later medieval France*, London 1968, 153–7.

[26] Chastelain was alive to this in his own Chronicle, as illustrated in his account of the rise of Guillaume Fillastre who 'voloit de la main du seigneur de Croy et du mareschal de Bourgongne'. 'Par la promotion' of the former, Fillastre became head of the ducal council in 1457, '(et) aprièmes ne fait que monter en l'eschelle': iii, 332–4.

[27] M.-T. Caron, 'Philippe de Ternant', in *CTO*, 59–60.

We have already seen that Chastelain may have been connected with Ternant in 1433, perhaps as a result of the latter's known relationship with the Masmines family, and that he certainly attended Ternant's *pas d'armes* at Arras in April 1446.[28] In August 1447 he left Bruges 'en la compagnie de Monseigneur de Ternant' and another figure from his past, Antoine Haneron, for a two-month embassy to the Rhenish town of Moers.[29] This mission was sent in support of John of Cleves in his long-standing dispute over the town of Soest with the archbishop of Cologne and the powerful Moers family from which he came.[30] Chastelain does not appear to have had any experience in this area of ducal diplomacy, and his knowledge of German was at best slight: two factors which suggest the former Louvain student was not sent as a specialist to assist Haneron, the former Louvain regent and Chastelain's degree examiner, who was an expert in these areas.[31] The only other satisfactory explanation for Chastelain's presence here – namely, that it stemmed from a pre-existing connection with Ternant in whose retinue he would have come – is further suggested by Olivier de La Marche's rise under the protection of this influential courtier. Like Chastelain, La Marche attended Ternant's jousts in 1446; like Chastelain, too, he participated in the mission to Moers, despite not having any known aptitude for the task. He did so at Ternant's personal request.[32] His presence is to be explained by the fact that he, like Philibert de Jaucourt and Alardin de La Gazelle, moved in Ternant's orbit: indeed, La Marche later rose to the office of *écuyer panetier* with Ternant's backing.[33] If the shadowy world of patronage between greater and lesser courtiers is revealed in this type of information, then Chastelain, quite as much as La Marche, came from Ternant's stable. The point finds confirmation in a hitherto unexplained mission

---

[28] See ch. 1 above.
[29] ADN B1994, fo. 168. Ternant, and presumably Chastelain, were at first sent by Haneron to Louis de Luxembourg and Cornille, the bastard of Burgundy, who were then preparing a military force to support John of Cleves in his dispute with the archbishop of Cologne. Thereafter he (and certainly Chastelain) accompanied Haneron to Moers for negotiations relating to the dispute. Haneron, Ternant and Chastelain were involved in these duties from 4 Aug. to 30 Sept.: ibid. fos 84v–5v.
[30] F. Petri, 'Nordwestdeutschland in der Politik der Burgunderherzöge', *Westfälische Forschungen* vii (1953–4), 80–100 at pp. 87–90; Y. Lacaze, 'Philippe le Bon et l'Empire', *Francia* ix (1981), 133–75; x (1982), 167–227 at ix. 165–6; W. Paravicini, 'Moers, Croy, Burgund', *Annalen des historischen Vereins für den Niederrhein* clxxix (1978), 7–113.
[31] Recounting the visit of an imperial ambassador in 1463, Chastelain notes that the envoy 'fit les salutations de par l'empereur au duc en gros haut allemant, tellement qu'à peine nul ne le savoit entendre, fors que mot çi, mot là': iv, 424. There is no record in the full accounts of ducal embassies before this point of any trip Chastelain might have made within the German-speaking world. On Haneron's expertise see Stein, 'Un diplomate bourguignon'. The article does not mention this embassy, but it does refer to Haneron's other trips within the empire.
[32] Stein, *Étude biographique*, 25.
[33] La Marche, *Mémoires*, ii. 113. On Alardin de la Gazelle, 'serviteur du seigneur de Ternant' see ADN B1954, fo. 278. On Ternant's relations with Philibert de Jaucourt see ibid. B2002, fos 50v–1.

which Chastelain was paid for in October 1448. In that month he accompanied Ternant to the duchy of Burgundy.[34] The purpose of this trip was not related to official business but to Ternant's private interests, the latter having been allowed to raise an *aide* on barrels of wine exported from the duchy in part payment of the sum of 5,000 *saluts* which was owed to him by Philip the Good.[35] Chastelain, we may conclude, was assisting his master in his personal affairs.[36]

Ternant was certainly well-placed to advance Chastelain's career.[37] A member of the select group of *chevaliers, conseillers et chambellans*, he figured (with Robert van Masmines) in the first batch of knights to be elected to the Order of the Golden Fleece. He was also one of Philip the Good's most trusted military commanders – in the French campaigns before 1435, or in Luxembourg in 1443 – and, apparently, a natural choice as an emissary to France.[38] With the exception of a temporary fall from grace to which we shall return, his influence at court remained considerable into the 1450s.

For our purposes, there is one aspect of this illustrious career which deserves particular emphasis. Like Chastelain himself, Ternant had marked French connections. In 1435 he was one of an inner circle of ducal counsellors including Nicolas Rolin, Pierre de Bauffremont and Antoine de Croy who proved amenable to the inducements of Charles VII in the latter's attempts to ensure ducal approval for the treaty of Arras.[39] Following the withdrawal of the duke from his English alliance, Ternant, as we have seen, participated with Simon de Lalaing in the French recapture of Paris. For his efforts he was rewarded for a brief spell with the *prévôté* of the city, where he remained popular thanks to an earlier expedition to protect it in 1431.[40] Ternant was of that school of Burgundian courtiers who had tasted the benefits of office and favour in the kingdom in the course of their careers; additionally, as we shall see, he had family connections there. The emphasis upon the formative influence of

---

[34] Ibid. B2000, fo. 120r–v.

[35] Ternant had gone to Burgundy to raise the *aide* ('de viij s. pour querir sur tous les vins qui partiront hors dudit pays') in Oct.: ADN B2000, fo. 101v. On 4 Nov., he received a lump sum of 2,000 *saluts* 'en deduction de la somme de cinq mille salus . . . dont mondit seigneur est tenu devers luy': ibid. fo. 20. It was common practice for the duke to borrow from his courtiers.

[36] One further connection between Chastelain's career and that of Ternant will be discussed below. It should also be noted that Chastelain reserves special treatment for Ternant in his Chronicle by including a glowing account of his first major outing in arms: ii, 30–1. This is borrowed, not from his usual source, Monstrelet, but from Lefèvre: *Chronique*, ii. 176–7.

[37] In addition to Caron's article mentioned above see V. Fris, 'Philippe de Ternant', *BNB* xxiii, Brussels 1921–4, c. 705–8.

[38] Cf. Beaucourt, *Histoire*, iii. 100 (1438), 129 n. 1 (1440), 271 n. 2 (1444); iv. 116, 118, 120 (1444); ADN B1988, fo. 123 (1445), B2017, fo. 152v (1454).

[39] Only Bauffremont and Rolin received more than the 8,000 *saluts* which Ternant was given: M.-R. Thielemans, 'Les Croÿ, conseillers des ducs de Bourgogne', *BCRH* cxxiv (1959), 1–141 at p. 72.

[40] For the 1431 expedition see above; on the *prévôté* see Caron, 'Ternant' and Fris, 'Ternant'.

Chastelain's time in France seems even less justified when we note that he associated for a longer period at the Burgundian court with men of this experience.

It was during his time with Ternant that Chastelain produced a work – his second surviving piece, it would appear – which his master, with his known interests, no doubt appreciated.[41] This was *Le throsne azuré*, written to celebrate the French reconquest of Normandy in August 1450.[42] With the benefit of hindsight, the commemoration of this event at the Burgundian court may appear curious, even eccentric.[43] However, for men like Ternant or for those ducal servants who served in Normandy under the cross of St Andrew and a royal banner, the sense of achievement which this work reflected was widely shared. The progress of French arms was followed with keen interest at the Burgundian court. In the period from April to June 1450, an equerry of the count of Eu was handsomely rewarded for bringing 'les premieres nouvelles' of a royal victory to Brussels, just pipping the poursuivants of Brézé and the lord of Croy, who arrived in the company of a royal messenger with news of the fall of Caen. In August, the poursuivant of the count of St Pol and a royal sergeant brought details of the 'recouvrance et conqueste', while three months later a servant of Jacques Coeur, the king's principal financier, rushed to Lille with news of royal victories in the Bordelais. In this atmosphere of mounting excitement, the tone of *Le throsne azuré* is readily understood.[44] With this evidence we return once more to the theme adumbrated at the end of the preceding chapter and repeated in the context of Chastelain's missions to France. It is clearly not enough to state that the chronicler's outlook was the product of his short spell in royal service. Instead, it may be related to his experience and acculturation within an elite which recognised the

---

[41] T. Sankovitch argues that *Le miroir de mort* is Chastelain's second surviving work and identifies it with a 'histoire et moralité sur le fait de la danse macabre' performed at Bruges in 1449. Chastelain would have drawn upon his experience in Paris (?) – where he would have seen the 'danse macabre' of the Holy Innocents – to write it: 'Death and the mole: two fifteenth-century dances of death', *Fifteenth century studies* ii (1978–80), 211–17. The argument cannot be substantiated. C. Martineau-Génieys discusses the work but does not raise the question of its date: *Le thème de la mort dans la poésie française de 1450 à 1550*, Paris 1978, 191–219. Another commentator and editor suggests a date between 1435 and 1461, but only the latter date is explained in any detail: T. van Hemelryck, 'Villon, lecteur de Chastelain?', *Les lettres romanes* xlviii (1994), 3–15, and George Chastelain, *Le miroir de mort*, Louvain-la-Neuve 1995.

[42] vi, 133–8. The royalist tone of this work is unadulterated by irony or faint praise. Its dating is suggested by a reference to the fall of Normandy ('Bien a paru à ceste oeuvre *présente* ... En ramenant Normandie dolente': p. 136, italics mine) and by an indication that the struggle continued, no doubt in Gascony ('Poursieu ton coup, tout Anglois s'espoente/ Devant ton bras qui fait trembler le monde': p. 137).

[43] In a famous passage written some time after 1470, it appeared to another former Louvain University figure, Thomas Basin, that the 1450s was a period in which the king, with his hands now free of the English problem, could at last bring the house of Burgundy to its knees: *Histoire de Charles VII*, ed. C. Samaran, Paris 1964–5, ii. 246.

[44] ADN B2004, fos 306, 307–9v, 310v–11.

interpenetration of Valois Burgundy and royal France: not simply by dint of the inescapable jurisdictional or territorial realities discussed earlier, but also, and more profoundly, through personal interest or inclination.

One last indication of Chastelain's integration in these years is to be found in his apparent disaffiliation from his former milieu, the Flemish city of Ghent. Although considered in the early 1440s as a potential base of Burgundian power, Ghent had become much less pliant to ducal authority by the time George was making his way at court.[45] Tensions between the city and the ducal elite increased after Ghent's refusal to contribute to the *gabelle* levied in 1447. They finally erupted into open hostilities with the Ghent War of 1452–3.[46] A previously unnoticed entry in the receipt-general reveals that Chastelain himself played a role in the early stages of this conflict, and that in the widening gulf between city and court, he associated himself with his Burgundian master and peers.

At some point in November 1449, Chastelain was sent from the court at Bruges to the city of Ghent to 'besongner en aucunes matieres secretes'.[47] The mission, although it lasted only four days, occurred at a crucial stage in relations. Three months earlier Philip had attempted to put a brake on Ghent's mounting particularism by intervening in the electoral process of its council. His attempts to secure the election of more malleable men figured prominently in a list of grievances presented to him in November by a civic deputation.[48] Philip the Good's actions reveal that his tolerance had been sorely tested by this protest and the obduracy of which it seemed symptomatic. On 16 November, and again nine days later 'bij zijnen mandemente', he communicated his displeasure to the Ghenter authorities.[49] On 29 November, and perhaps in the expectation of trouble, 'lettres closes touchans la ville de Gand' were sent to ducal *baillis* in the towns of the surrounding region.[50] One week after that, a deputation from the Members of Flanders arrived in the city on the first of several conciliatory missions which were to contribute to the uneasy *status quo*

---

[45] The restoration of the comital castle at Ghent, the purchase of residences there by leading ducal officers and the 'charmepolitiek' of Philip the Good with regard to the city, all in the early 1440s, have led some to conclude that Ghent was then figuring in ducal plans for the future: Boone, *Gent*, 224–5; Fris, *Histoire de Gand*, 124; M. Boone, M.-C. Laleman and D. Lievois, 'Van Simon sRijkensteen tot Hof van Ryhove', *HMGOG* ns xliv (1990), 47–85 esp. pp. 66–8. The events described below brought this brief honeymoon period to a dramatic close.
[46] M. Populer, 'Le conflit de 1447 à 1453 entre Gand et Philippe le Bon', *HMGOG* ns xliv (1990), 99–123.
[47] ADN B2002, fo. 141. The exact date of the mission is not recorded, but the payment is listed at an early stage in a rubric entitled 'parties de menuz voyaiges et messageries sur les mois de novembre et decembre l'an mil iiijc xlix': fo. 139v. Chastelain received 6l. 8s. for the trip.
[48] *Dagboek van Gent van 1447 tot 1470*, ed. V. Fris, Ghent 1901–4, i. 70–80.
[49] *Memorieboek*, i. 228–9. Philip's 'mandemente' was issued on the Feast of St Catherine (25 Nov.).
[50] ADN B2002, fo. 144.

that lasted until 1451.[51] Due to the tight-lipped nature of our source, the precise details of Chastelain's duties in all of this cannot be ascertained. However, it is clear that his mission – because of its timing, the level of his remuneration, and the fact that he was sent 'par le commandement et ordonnance' of the duke to deal with matters 'à l'intention de [s]ondit seigneur' – was considered a highly sensitive one. He had returned to Ghent as the representative of an increasingly resented external authority. Although open hostilities had for now been averted, the city was to become a dangerous place for men of his allegiance.[52] In fact, it was not until 1458, fully five years after the end of hostilities, that the duke solemnly granted his full pardon to Ghent on the occasion of his entry into the city.[53] Having thrown in his lot with the ducal elite, Chastelain may not have found it easy to maintain links with his Ghent past after 1449.

Such considerations may explain why, the following year, he appears to have been establishing connections elsewhere – a second facet of his disaffiliation from Ghent. With the aid of a gift of 24*l*. from Philip the Good, he left the court at Lille to go 'ès pais et conté de Haynnau'. The trip concerned 'aucunes choses touchans son bien [et] avancement'.[54] Personal grants of this kind are not uncommon in the accounts of the receiver-general, and were generally made to assist servants in such domestic matters as the contracting of marriages or visits to their families.[55] It is impossible to say whether Chastelain himself had acquired land or a bride which would specifically explain his visit to Hainaut, or whether known Masmines connections in the county encouraged him to take up residence there.[56] Four and a half years later, however, his

---

[51] *Memorieboek*, i. 229.
[52] By 1451 Burgundian supporters and servants were no longer guaranteed fair treatment from the authorities: *Bewijsstukken betreffende den opstand van Gent tegen Philips den Goede*, ed. V. Fris, Ghent 1914, 26. As we saw in ch. 1 above, at least one member of Chastelain's extended family was compromised in these events.
[53] J. C. Smith, 'Venit nobis pacificus Dominus', in *'All the world's a stage'*, i, Pennsylvania 1990, 259–90.
[54] The payment is recorded under the rubric for Nov. 1450, and refers to a journey which Chastelain 'a nagaire fait de la ville de Lille': ADN B2004, fos 305v–6.
[55] Further examples from the same register include the marriages of Robert de La Harpe, Jean Coustain or Josse de Halluin, and a gift to Olivier de La Marche 'pour aler en Bourgogne ou il tient son mesnaige': ibid. fos 272v, 275v, 279v, 308; cf. U. Schwarzkopf, 'Zum höfischen Dienstrecht im 15. Jahrhundert', in *Festschrift für Hermann Heimpel*, Göttingen 1972, ii. 422–42 at pp. 435–6.
[56] Chastelain does not appear as a fief-holder in Hainaut in this period, although he may well have acquired some other landed interest: A. Scufflaire, *Les fiefs directs des comtes de Hainaut de 1349 à 1504*, Brussels 1978–84. His only known child was a bastard son, Gonthier, discussed in ch. 6 below. When Gonthier was legitimised in 1530, he did not provide the authorities with his mother's name – the document simply notes that both George Chastelain and Gonthier's mother were unmarried when he was born: ADN B1741, fos 201v–2. As we saw in ch. 1 above, Robert van Masmines had been *bailli des bois* for Hainaut, and Cornelius van Blaesvelt was a *bailli* in the county. One further Masmines connection exists in the form of a debt contracted by Waleran de Masmines, father of

personal interests in the region were confirmed by a grant of lodgings at the Salle-le-Comte, the ducal palace in the second town of Hainaut, Valenciennes.[57] We may conclude that Chastelain had begun to lay down new roots with ducal assistance in 1450, and that by 1455 the process was complete.

Despite his presence among the elite and his integration within the formal and informal hierarchies that operated at that level, it is far from clear that Chastelain enjoyed regular access to, let alone close familiarity with, the decision-taking circles at the centre of the Burgundian polity in these early years. He had been of value to the duke in his dealings with the king, but the thawing of Franco-Burgundian relations which preceded and accompanied the royal campaigns against the English (1449–51) may well have lessened the duke's immediate need for the expertise he could offer. In these circumstances Chastelain's status as an extraordinary servant, rather than one who served regularly 'par terme', placed him at a disadvantage. To judge from the accounts of the receiver-general, he was still active in Burgundian service between 1449 and 1451. He accompanied the duke from Bruges to Brussels in January 1450; later, apparently between April and June, he left the principal city of Brabant for an unknown destination.[58] In the autumn we find him once again with the court as it moved from Arras to Hesdin early in September, then on to Lille in October. In that same month he left to go to Brussels.[59] As we enter 1451, however, the references become even thinner on the ground. On 17 March he left the court at Brussels for 'certains lieux' on a secret mission lasting four days, and in May he attended the Mons chapter of the Order of the Golden Fleece.[60] Even allowing for missions which may have escaped the otherwise close scrutiny of the duke's financial officers, the declining frequency of references would suggest a slackening in his activities.[61] The rewards he received for his

---

Hector, in Valenciennes in 1414: AMV J2/358, fo. 45. I am grateful to Dr Ludovic Nys and Professor Albert Châtelet for the reference, although unfortunately it does not reveal any particular implantation of the Masmines in the town. In the year before Chastelain's first visit to Hainaut, Antoine Haneron was *prévôt des églises de Mons*, the capital of the county: J.-M. Cauchies, *La législation princière pour le comté de Hainaut: ducs de Bourgogne et premiers Habsbourg (1427–1506)*, Brussels 1982, 531.

[57] Discussed more fully below.

[58] ADN B2004, fos 299, 309v. The court decamped from Bruges to Brussels for a brief period from 14 to 16 Jan. before moving on to Mechelen for the second half of the month. Philip was back in Brussels by 5 Feb., and remained there until mid-July: *Itinéraires*, 271–4.

[59] ADN B2004, fos 311v, 312. The court moved from Arras to Hesdin sometime between 6 and 10 Sept., then from Hesdin to Lille around 7 Oct.: *Itinéraires*, 275–6. The reasons for Chastelain's departure for Brussels 'ou mois d'octobre' – while the court remained at Lille – are not known.

[60] ADN B2008, fos 127v, 309. The secret mission in Mar. may be related to the arrival, two days earlier, of a royal embassy: Beaucourt, *Histoire*, v. 227–8. The fact that Chastelain was paid in 'royale monnoie' may indicate that his mission involved a trip to the kingdom. It was accepted practice for the emissary to be paid 'a la monnoye des lieux ou il seroit': ADN B2017, fo. 110v (concerning Waleran de Soissons).

[61] Some of Chastelain's activities may well have escaped record. In the Chronicle, for example, he describes a natural phenomenon with apparently supernatural significance 'vers

diplomatic and household duties in the eighteen months to May 1451 amounted to little more than one third of those granted for the equivalent period following his entry into Burgundian service.[62] From this date until September 1454, a period of nearly three and a half years, Chastelain is entirely absent from the records.[63]

It would be possible to dwell on a number of factors which might explain Chastelain's evanescence in the accounts.[64] Behind them all, however, lies a general, explanatory fact: he had not yet made himself indispensable at court. One possible illustration of this point is to be found in a further revealing (and not coincidental?) linkage between his career and that of Philippe de Ternant. Late in 1449, the point at which Chastelain's court attendance and the missions with which he was entrusted became less frequent, his patron suffered a temporary but dramatic fall from grace.[65] Ternant's initial error was to arrest an English merchant during a period of truce; he compounded the misdemeanour by sending the prisoner for safekeeping to his brother-in-law in France. This may well have been an opportunity for other calumnies or genuine grievances to be raised by those who did not wish him well at court.[66] On 22 November 1449, apparently at the insistence of Isabella of Portugal (whose Anglophile tendencies Chastelain repeatedly noted with disdain), Ternant was confined to Courtrai castle. He was still there on 30 June 1450.[67] The following

---

l'an XLVIII, sur les marches de Bretagne'. He implies (though does not state) that he had witnessed this event 'de mon sçu': iii, 361. There is nothing relating to this in the records of the *Chambre des comptes*.

[62] A total of 337*l*. granted between Apr. 1446 and Oct. 1447, compared to 124*l*. granted between Nov. 1449 and May 1451. These figures are based on references cited above. They only provide a crude indication of the extent of Chastelain's integration.

[63] The accounts examined for these years are as follows: ADN B2009 (*pièces comptables*, 1451), B2010 (*pièces comptables*, 1452), B2011 (*pièces comptables*, 1452), AGR CC1921 (register, 1452), ADN B2012 (register, 1453), B2013–6 (*pièces comptables*, 1453). The absence of documentation from May 1451 until Sept. 1454 stands in sharp contrast to its availability either before or after, and this at a time when our sources are of comparable quality and quantity.

[64] During the Ghent war of 1452–3, for example, Chastelain may have melted into the anonymous soldiery, if he was not too old by this stage. His disappearance from the records before that point may have resulted from his domestic circumstances in Hainaut, from his retention in the retinue of a court patron like Ternant, or from a period of sustained writing in which many of his lost works, listed at vi, 268, might have been completed. This last point could explain why Chastelain was held in such high regard for his 'choses nouvelles et moralles' at the time of his appointment – after all, the vast majority of his surviving lesser works postdate his appointment in 1455.

[65] Fris, 'Philippe de Ternant'; F. de Reiffenberg, *Histoire de la Toison d'Or*, Brussels 1830, 33.

[66] Ternant was also accused of having embezzled monies destined to pay for Burgundian troops and to buy off the mercenaries under the command of the dauphin. For this last mission see AGR *Acquits de Lille*, no. 1159, box (c): Ternant's receipt for 10,000 *écus* destined for the dauphin, 28 Feb. 1445.

[67] Cf. the payment to Maillart de Flechin, a ducal equerry appointed 'a la garde du seigneur de Ternant': ADN B2020, fo. 178v. Other guards and a cook were paid for their services

year he was ordered by the Mons chapter of the Golden Fleece to atone by means of a pilgrimage to Santiago de Compostela, and did not reappear in ducal service until the hostilities against Ghent in 1452. As we have seen, the last reference to Chastelain's movements also dates to this chapter of the Golden Fleece.

The connection is suggestive, but we can say no more than that. Whatever the true nature of the difficulties he faced in the early 1450s, whether from changes in the political climate, personal circumstance, the fortunes of his patron or indeed a combination of such factors, it would appear that Chastelain was simply not well enough established to weather them. He may have integrated within the court society, but his progress there was erratic, his proximity to the political centre as yet intermittent. From 1454, however, this was to change.

The corridors of power (1454–c. 1464)

Chastelain reappears in the ducal accounts in September 1454. From this point, and for at least the following decade, his career entered a new phase characterised by regular sojourns at court, a much greater degree of preferment and closer relations, as a senior ducal servant himself, with a variety of men at the core of the Burgundian elite. To employ a hackneyed but appropriate phrase, he now gained access to the corridors of power. This change in Chastelain's fortunes requires some explanation. It was only after several months that he was once more referred to in the accounts by his familar household title.[68] He had not simply returned to court: he had been re-established there. Moreover, this comeback took place in special circumstances. In September 1454, Philip the Good was not minded to augment his household by welcoming old servants back to the fold. He had just returned from his trip to the Empire where discussions were held on the matter of the projected crusade.[69] Two days before leaving for Germany, he had disbanded his ordinary retinue and cut or abolished daily provision for his servants in an attempt to save money for the business of the cross. These

---

between 1 Feb. and 31 Mar.: B4101, fo. 121. On 2 Jan. 1452, Maillart, and six archers received final payment for their service and costs 'ou fait de la despense de monsieur de Ternant en le menant prisonnier . . . de la ville de Bruges au chastel de Courtray': AGR CC1921, fos 363v–4. According to La Marche, Ternant was kept confined for over a year: *Mémoires*, ii. 142. For Chastelain's more disparaging comments on Isabella of Portugal see iii, 7, 21–3, 426, 444; iv, 345; v, 208, 311.

[68] 'Ecuyer panetier': ADN B2020, fo. 329v. His status is indeterminate in the records to that point, just as it had been in 1433–4.

[69] Philip left for Germany with only thirty companions on 24 Mar. and was back in the lands of the prince of Orange at Nozeroy by 25 July: d'Escouchy, *Chronique*, ii. 243; *Itinéraires*, 330. On the wider context see N. Housley, *The later crusades: from Lyons to Alcazar, 1274–1580*, Oxford 1992, 101.

drastic measures were to remain in force until at least 1 January 1455.[70] The uncharacteristic bout of ducal parsimony was clearly relaxed in Chastelain's case for a particular reason. This, it transpires, was his proven ability to write. Chastelain's career after 1454 was built on a skill which the aspirant – an adept, of necessity, in the art of pleasing the prince – had gleaned from his new court peers and nurtured as his pastime.

Although the subject of Chastelain's historico-literary skills belongs more properly to later chapters, it deserves attention here for its role in the revival and reorientation of his flagging career. *Le throsne azuré*, probably more than *L'oultré d'amour*, had already brought his abilities to the duke's attention. It was therefore fairly natural that Philip the Good should have turned to Chastelain when seeking to enliven, with an appropriate display of rhetorical fireworks, the negotiations at Nevers for the marriage of his son to Isabelle de Bourbon. Chastelain's *Complainte d'Hector*, performed with the assistance of La Marche and others, fitted the occasion admirably.[71] The content of the work is significant in itself, but more important at this stage is the nature of the audience which saw the performance.[72] In addition to Philip the Good, his sister and members of the Burgundian and Bourbon courts, the piece was seen by Charles d'Orléans, the leading prince-poet of the day.[73] This arbiter of taste, to whom Philip the Good had himself addressed his modest forays into poetry, was clearly impressed. Both Chastelain and La Marche were thought worthy of contributing to a collection Charles kept of his own verse and that of other eminent literati.[74] Thanks to the impact of his work and this princely sanction of his abilities, Chastelain was marked out as the type of man that dukes should cultivate and keep. For the next nine months he was a constant presence at court.[75] This period of good fortune culminated, on 25 June 1455, in his appointment as the duke's official historian.[76]

---

[70] Vaughan, *PTG*, 266–7; U. Schwarzkopf, 'La cour de Bourgogne et la Toison d'Or', *PCEEBM* v (1963), 91–104 at p. 99.
[71] ADN B2017, fos 237v–8; cf. L. de Laborde, *Les ducs de Bourgogne*, Paris 1849–52, i. 417–18.
[72] The work is discussed in ch. 3 below.
[73] In addition to the references cited above which reveal the presence of 'monseigneur d'Orleans, madame son espeuse et madame de Bourbon', there is a further payment to Orléans for attending: ADN B2017, fo. 231v.
[74] A. T. Harrison, 'Orléans and Burgundy', *Stanford French Review* iv (1980), 475–84. On the contributions of Chastelain and La Marche to Orléans's *recueil* see *Rondeaux et autres poésies*, nos 105–6. La Marche had known Orléans since at least 1447: *Mémoires*, ii. 115.
[75] Chastelain's itinerary matches that of the court, first in the duchy of Burgundy in the autumn and winter of 1454, then in the Low Countries in the first half of 1455: cf. ADN B2017 fos 238r–v, 239, 240v, 241; B2020, fos 329v, 331, 340v; *Itinéraires*, 332–43. The rewards he received in these nine months totalled around 106*l*., almost as much as he had received in the eighteen months to May 1451 when his fortunes were waning.
[76] The most significant record of this appointment is that kept by the *audiencier*: Nélis, *Chambre des comptes*, 49. This and three other references from the ducal accounts for Hainaut and Valenciennes are published in Urwin, *Georges Chastelain*, 164–5. The documents themselves will be referred to below.

Purely in terms of his personal status, Chastelain's nomination placed him on a par with courtiers he had previously frequented as an inferior. The grant which was made to him of permanent lodgings in a ducal residence was almost a unique privilege.[77] His remuneration is no less revealing of his standing. The daily allowance which servants received from the duke was often a small part of their income, but rates were fixed to reflect the importance of the office and its incumbent in the aulic hierarchy. Chastelain's allowance of 36s., paid in one annual instalment of 657L, was equivalent or superior to that of the ducal *conseillers et chambellans*.[78] Although he was still known as a *panetier*, his allowance was in fact twice that of the household *écuyers*.[79] Exceptional individuals warranted exceptional treatment, a complete package of 'entretenement . . . et provision' (vii, 227). In this regard it is worth noting that similar, if less impressive, incentives were accorded by Philip the Good to Jan van Eyck. The painter and the poet-historian were placed directly under the duke's patronage 'tant qu'il lui plaira'; both owed their rise to 'leurs vertus' (in the sense of their merits) and not to 'la maison dont ils sont'.[80] Writing had thus freed Chastelain from the vicissitudes which could beset minor courtiers, reliant as they were upon less-coveted talents and the patronage of the great. Comparisons between van Eyck and the chronicler end there, however. Chastelain, unlike the famous embellisher of St Baafs where the lives of his own distant relatives were commemorated, did not remain on the periphery.[81] The aspirant, now the established servant, rode his success to the centre of the elite. This point is crucial to the understanding of his Chronicle. As he worked on the text, the once-expendable equerry was emerging as a politically active and privileged insider.

At least part of this journey took place against a backdrop of Franco-Burgundian relations, the familiar frame of reference for Chastelain's political experience. In the summer of 1457, Philip the Good was harbouring Louis, dauphin and future king of France, in his dominions.[82] The duke could

---

[77] It also suggests that Chastelain did not have much in the way of personal resources to fall back on. One is led to wonder how radically his financial circumstances had improved since he left Ghent.

[78] Cf. ADN B2030, fos 128 (Philippe de Croy), 129r–v (Jean de Poitiers), 130 (Philippe Pot), 131r–v (Claude de Rochebaron), 133v (Chrestien de Digoine). It should be noted that each of these men was only paid by ducal command 'par jour quant il est par devers luy et en son service pour le service et estas et office de conseiller et chambellan'. Chastelain was paid throughout the year.

[79] Ibid. fos 148v (Philippe de Poitiers), 150v–1 (Pierre de Hagenbach).

[80] The phrase is borrowed from La Marche, *Mémoires*, iv. 26. Van Eyck's 'abilité et souffisance' led to his nomination as a ducal *valet de chambre*, the grant of an annual allowance of one hundred pounds of Flanders and a house in Lille: W. H. J. Weale, *The Van Eycks and their art*, 2nd edn, London 1913, 9.

[81] I refer to van Eyck's Adoration of the Mystic Lamb, made for Joos Vijd to adorn his chapel in the church. Chastelain may well have seen the work, since it was completed in 1432: E. Dhanens, *Van Eyck*, London 1973, 13.

[82] P.-R. Gaussin, *Louis XI*, Paris 1976, 41–3; F. de Reiffenberg, *Mémoire sur le séjour que*

realistically envisage a long-term *rapprochement* with the monarchy as a result of this benevolence; he may even have entertained the possibility of a return to the heyday of Burgundian influence in the kingdom.[83] In the interim, however, he had to contend with the dauphin's father, exasperated by Louis and egged on by royal counsellors who had good reason to fear the dauphin's accession. In such circumstances Chastelain's services were at a premium. Despite his main obligation to write (an activity which almost certainly accounted for the intervening two years), he was now called upon three times in as many months to serve as a ducal emissary.[84]

The most significant point to emerge from two of these missions is that Chastelain still had his finger on the pulse of the French body politic. The purpose of the first is not mentioned in the accounts, where we are simply told that he was sent from Bruges 'a Paris et a Rouan' between 7 June and 4 July. In the Chronicle, however, Chastelain indicates that 'conventions secrètes' were being held by royal captains 'à Paris et ailleurs' (iii, 362) at precisely this time. 'En ce mesme mois de juillet' (iii, 326), he had also witnessed the mounting impatience of the French for himself, 'non par oïr dire, mais par vraye congnoissance du cas, hantant les divers lieux du monde' (iii, 326). It would appear that the chronicler's remit in France included a watching brief.

This also seems to have been part of the second mission, from 16 August to 4 September, when he accompanied Philippe Pot from Amiens 'en aucuns lieux ou mondit seigneur leur avoit ordonné'. Philip the Good was sufficiently wary of Charles VII's intentions at this point in time to effect a morale-boosting tour of the Somme towns, a region which he considered to be 'l'escu' (iv, 402) of his dominions.[85] Men like Chastelain were useful outriders in such situations. With his known contacts at the heart of the French elite, he was in a position to sound out those who were charged with executing royal plans. While this may only be inferred in the case of his mission with Pot, we are on firmer ground in suggesting that his trip to Rouen had precisely that purpose.[86] At the time of his mission a royal fleet was assembling off the coast of Normandy. The ships would eventually be deployed against the English at

---

Louis, dauphin de Viennois, depuis roi sous le nom de Louis XI, fit aux Pays-Bas de l'an 1456 à l'an 1461, Brussels 1829.
[83] P. Bonenfant, *Philippe-le-Bon*, Brussels 1943, 88–9; Vaughan, PTG, 354. The matter is discussed further in ch. 5 below.
[84] Urwin, *Georges Chastelain*, 166, and Hommel, *Chastellain*, 34, mistakenly assert that these missions – which they also amalgamate into one – occurred in 1459. Chastelain's payments are recorded in the accounts for that year, but are explicitly described as having taken place in 'l'an cccc lvij': ADN B2034, fos 10v, 257v. Unless otherwise stated, the following paragraphs are based on the information found in these references. Because he deemed that Chastelain's daily allowance was sufficient to meet his costs, the receiver-general did not pay out on this occasion. However, the chronicler did manage to prise 55*l.* 4s. from the receiver of Flanders: B4105, fo. 144.
[85] Beaucourt, *Histoire*, vi. 125–6; *Itinéraires*, 374–5.
[86] Chastelain alludes to this trip in the Chronicle, but says only that he was there 'en aucuns affaires de mon maistre le duc de Bourgongne': iii, 359.

Sandwich, but it was initially feared in Burgundian circles that they would be used to harry the Flemish ports 'pour cause du dauphin' (iii, 349–50).[87] Chastelain's trip to Rouen could at least verify the true extent of the danger, particularly since the commander of the French fleet, who was also the captain of the city, was then based there. Chastelain was no stranger to this man – the *grand sénéchal* of Normandy, his old master and personal friend, Pierre de Brézé.[88] As so often in the chronicler's experience, personal contacts could cut across those affairs of state which we, in our desire to trace the severance of Valois Burgundy from Valois France, are more inclined to highlight.

These missions suggest that Chastelain, at the very least, was as significant a figure in ducal diplomacy now as he had been ten years earlier. His third and final task that summer reveals more clearly an increase in his stature and a greater familiarity with the principal concerns of his master.

On 21 September, a high-level deputation from France, led by the bishop of Coutances, finally entered Brussels. The duke had been kept on tenterhooks since July, when news of their imminent arrival had first reached the court. His anxieties could hardly have been eased by the knowledge that the envoys were concerned primarily with the thorny question of the dauphin.[89] Embassies of this nature were often met *en route* by a welcoming party of sufficient stature and competence to deal with any preliminary business. According to Philippe de Commynes, who was well-versed in Burgundian diplomatic practice, the choice of representatives for such sensitive tasks was critical:

> l'on les doit bien traicter et honorablement recueillir, comme envoyer au devant d'eulx, les faire bien loger et ordonner gens seürs et saiges pour les accompaigner ... : car, par là, on scet ceulx qui vont vers eulx et garde-l'on les gens malcontent de leur aller porter nouvelles; car en nulle maison tout n'est content.[90]

The men selected by the duke – the bishops of Amiens and Arras, and Jean de Clugny, a ducal *maître des requêtes* – conformed to these requirements of protocol and practicality.[91] Philip took the added precaution of intercepting Coutances and his colleagues at the earliest opportunity. Baudouin d'Oignies, one of the select group of *chevaliers, conseillers et chambellans* and an old hand in such matters, seems at first to have been chosen for this onerous but prestigious task.[92] He returned empty-handed to the court on 28 August. One

---

87 Beaucourt, *Histoire*, vi. 144–6.
88 Brézé's expedition is described in the work cited immediately above. It is unfortunate that the 'comptes de Jean le Prince pour les navires de Pierre de Brézé, 1455–7', mentioned in the inventory of the Chantilly archives, now appear to be lost: *Chantilly, les archives*, Paris 1926–9, i. 7.
89 Beaucourt, *Histoire*, vi. 149–52; C. Duclos, *Histoire de Louis XI*, Paris 1745–6, iii. 185–91; A. de Barante, *Histoire des ducs de Bourgogne*, 5th edn, Paris 1837–8, vii. 343–52.
90 Commynes, *Mémoires*, i. 219.
91 These men were ordered on 8–9 Sept. to gather at Tournai: ADN B2026, fos 281v–2.
92 Baudouin travelled from Hesdin to the frontier regions of Péronne, St Quentin and Cambrai between 26 July and 28 Aug.: ibid. fos 187v–8. His experience as a ducal

week later he was replaced by Chastelain. The official chronicler left the court at Nivelles with a ducal messenger at his disposal. The latter he sent back to the court within days 'pour faire rapport que les diz ambassadeurs estoient passez parmy Cambrai'.[93] Chastelain, for his part, did not return to Brussels until 21 September: the point at which Coutances made his entry into the city. Not only was he the first ducal servant to come into contact with the royal representatives, he had also remained with them, and the duke's other eminent envoys, as they engaged in the initial business of this highly sensitive embassy. At this stage in his career, of course, Chastelain had the necessary *gravitas* for the role: scholars and poets were as acceptable as men of higher social rank in such lofty diplomatic contexts.[94]

These events suggest that in the summer of 1457, Chastelain entered the ranks of the 'gens seürs et saiges' whom Philip could entrust with his most pressing business. In reality, he had already moved towards the centre of the decision-taking elite by this time. Several months earlier he had been made a ducal *conseiller*.[95] The formulaic statement in his letters of nomination seems at first to say little or nothing on the reasons for his promotion. No single skill or attribute qualified a courtier to be an adviser to the duke.[96] In Chastelain's case, however, the nominee's 'sens, prudence, discretion, souffisance . . . et bonne diligence' may have been especially telling. In a famous letter written not much later, the counsellor Jean de Lannoy advised his son to keep his nose in his books; all too often, he wrote, he had been embarrassed in the duke's council by his inability to better the advice of the eloquent and learned '*ystoryens*' who had spoken before him.[97] *Bons mots* and historical exempla

---

representative on sensitive missions went at least as far back as 1428, when he was part of the embassy sent to Portugal to vet Philip the Good's future bride: *Collection de documents inédits concernant l'histoire de la Belgique*, ed. L. P. Gachard, Brussels 1833–5, ii. 63–91.

[93] In a previously unnoticed entry we learn that Chastelain awaited the ambassadors at Cambrai, whence he dispatched the messenger – Rogerin de Pontiga – 'es villes de St Quentin, Peronne et en autres passaiges . . . pour savoir et enquerir de la venue desdis ambassadeurs': ADN B2026, fos 287v–8. On how the Burgundian messenger system operated, albeit at an earlier stage, see T. Kanao, 'L'organisation et l'enregistrement des messageries du duc de Bourgogne dans les années 1420', *RN* lxxvi (1994), 275–98, and 'Les messagers du duc de Bourgogne au début du XVe siècle', *JMH* xxi (1995), 195–226.

[94] Men of 'lesser estate' could be sent on diplomatic missions where 'the ceremonial requirement was not controlling'. This was the case for Chastelain's missions to France in 1446 or 1447. In the mission discussed here, however, it was important that the social status of the envoy was appropriate, rendering him 'personally acceptable to the recipient'. Men of letters entered this category: Queller, *Office of ambassador*, 152–3, 173–4.

[95] Chastelain's nomination on 14 Jan. 1457 is recorded in a ducal letter patent: Nélis, *Chambre des comptes*, 151. The following quotation is from this source.

[96] 'Toutes les personnes capables de servir le duc étaient appelées conseillers. Leur nombre variait suivant les circonstances': M. Jollant, 'Philippe le Bon et les officiers ducaux', *AB* lv (1983), 137–9.

[97] Italics mine. For this quote and related comments see the 'Coppie des lettres envoyées par Jehan seigneur de Lannoy à Loys son filz' in B. de Lannoy and G. Dansaert, *Jean de Lannoy le bâtisseur, 1410–1492*, Paris 1937, 119–210 esp. pp. 119–21, 138–40, 147–8.

commanded respect (if not from Commynes); political and historical culture combined in the council chambers. There was a place here for an official historian.

Chastelain's experience as a *conseiller* naturally had certain limitations which ought to be defined. The *grand conseil* to which he belonged consisted of 'gens sages [et] experts, preudommes et féables'; they dealt with matters of justice, finance 'et autres grandes et pesans matieres qui journellement ... surviennent et peut survénir'.[98] Within such a broad organisation there was considerable scope for specialisation. In turn, this placed some matters beyond the ken of the ordinary *conseiller*. It is no surprise, therefore, that Chastelain's grasp of financial reforms can occasionally leave the institutional historian unimpressed. Such matters were reserved for experts.[99] Nor should we expect the chronicler to lead us infallibly through the decisions of the innermost sanctum of the *conseil*, consisting as it did of largely informal gatherings of a handful of the duke's closest advisers. If the chronicler, in common with the vast majority of *conseillers*, was not closely involved in the debates of the 'conseil privé' (iii, 80), this did not prevent him from observing such occasions or from speculating on (or indeed, from having certain knowledge of) decisions taken at that level.[100] This awareness stems from the fact that the *grand conseil* provided the forum and personnel for all manner of business concerning the duke. If some matters passed into the hands of specialists or a select few, all *conseillers* were none the less subject to the orders of the duke's chancellor and could be summoned by him for 'la consultation et expédition de nos besongnes et affaires touchant nous et nos pays et seigneuries' so that these might be 'veues, advisées et digérées'.[101] It is clearly the breadth, and not the

---

[98] Quotations from a document recording Philip's reorganisation of his council in Aug. 1446: G. Aubrée, *Mémoires pour servir à l'histoire de France et de Bourgogne*, Paris 1729, ii. 172–7. For what follows see J. Van Rompaey, 'De Bourgondische staatsinstellingen', in *Nieuwe Algemene Geschiedenis der Nederlanden*, Haarlem 1980, iv. 136–54, and *De Grote Raad van de hertogen van Bourgondië en het Parlement van Mechelen*, Brussels 1973; E. Lameere, *Le grand conseil des ducs de Bourgogne de la maison de Valois*, Brussels 1900.

[99] For example, Chastelain's interpretation of the financial reforms of 1457 as an attempt to unseat the chancellor Nicolas Rolin has been criticised: J. Bartier, 'Une crise de l'état bourguignon', in *Hommage au Professeur Paul Bonenfant (1899–1965)*, Brussels 1965, 501–11. Perhaps the reforms did strike some contemporaries in that light; at the very least, it seems excessive – and is certainly misguided as regards the functions of the Chronicle – to conclude from this one example that Chastelain revealed an 'absence d'intérêt pour tout ce qui concerne le fonctionnement de l'état bourguignon': ibid. 502. Elsewhere in financial matters, Chastelain's 'errors' (in the eyes of twentieth-century positivists) have turned out to be accurate reflections of events: cf. (for example) G. Bigwood, *Le régime juridique et économique du commerce de l'argent dans la Belgique au moyen âge*, Brussels 1921–2, i. 385; corrected in Cauchies, *La législation princière*, 477 n. 25. A comment on the historicity of Froissart's chronicles ('peut-être nos critères modernes de la véracité historique s'appliquent-ils mal au récit') is equally valid for Chastelain: G. Diller, 'Robert d'Artois et l'historicité des *Chroniques* de Froissart', MA lxxxvi (1980), 217–31 at p. 221.

[100] Cf. iii, 80, 204, 391, 424–5; iv, 157.

[101] Aubrée, *Mémoires*, ii. 173.

limitations, of Chastelain's experience at the centre which should be underlined here.

Although a few depositions and memoranda can still be consulted, minutes for the meetings of ducal councils, unlike those for some of their royal counterparts, have not survived.[102] In their absence we must rely upon the Chronicle for some understanding of Chastelain's experience of the council and its business. Perhaps not surprisingly, his accounts become more frequent and detailed in nature in those passages relating to the council's activities after January 1457.[103] Although he rarely mentions his own presence on such occasions, Chastelain does employ the pronoun 'on' in his accounts of certain council meetings, thereby suggesting the taking of a collective decision to which he himself was party. In his text for August 1457, for example, he gives a full description of negotiations between ducal emissaries and the English of Calais concerning recent border clashes, and of the subsequent report by the Burgundian deputies on the matter to the duke at Hesdin:

> Quant donques cestes difficultés droit-cy furent mises en la digestion du conseil, là où *on* considéroit que ceste rumeur ne dépendoit que de débas entre privées personnes . . . fut conclu certes estre plus utile d'appointer avecques rudes méchans gens à leur avantage, qu'en tenant son coeur et son poing fermé entrer en inconvénient à leur cause. (iii, 338–9)[104]

Similar remarks are made in his narrative of a council meeting in September 1464. On this occasion, upon hearing of the death of Pope Pius II, the council decided to shelve the crusading expedition of Anthony, bastard son of the duke:

> En fin des longs argumens, *on* s'arresta à ce, et s'y consenti le duc, qu'*on* remanderoit l'armée, et envoieroit-*on* à Marseille et en Avignon homme propre pour recevoir l'artillerie qui estoit dedens la navire, et la mettroit-*on* en Avignon sous la garde de la ville jusques au mars prochain. (v, 59)

It is possible, of course, that Chastelain framed his narrative in this way to heighten the effect, but in both cases we can be almost certain that he was present. *Conseillers* were eligible to attend meetings of the *grand conseil* during their sojourns with the duke, and we know from other sources that Chastelain was at court when these councils were called.[105] Indeed, his attendance in the

---

[102] Lameere comments on the problems of describing the precise workings of the institution: *Le grand conseil*, 101. The historian of the royal council is fortunate to dispose of a fragment of the register for business conducted in 1455: N. Valois, *Le conseil du roi aux XIVe, XVe et XVIe siècles*, Paris 1888, repr. Geneva 1975, 231–323.
[103] For a rare example of council business before this date in the Chronicle see iii, 220. At iii, 139, Chastelain reveals that he had not seen the contents of the duke's treaty with the Brederode family in 1456; we may wonder whether this stemmed from his non-inclusion at this point in the council's affairs.
[104] Italics mine, in this quotation and the next.
[105] In the first case, Chastelain had newly returned from his mission with Pot, discussed above, and was about to intercept the French ambassadors. Around this time too, he was

years 1455–64 appears to have been more frequent and sustained than at any earlier stage in his career – we have seen that he was based at court throughout much of 1457, and he was regularly with Philip the Good's entourage in 1461, 1463 and 1464.[106] We may surmise that accounts of meetings of the council which occurred at these times were probably written by an eye-witness and participant. While Philip the Good toured the Somme towns in September 1457, for example, the lord of Fontaines 'estoit venu à conseil' (iii, 366) to report that the city of Liège was on the point of rebellion. Chastelain, who was with the duke on this trip and was therefore eligible to attend his council, is able to relate the precise nature of the ducal response. In his narrative for the summer of 1463, a whole chapter is devoted to the impasse reached by the royal and ducal councils at Hesdin in their re-negotiation of matters agreed at Paris in 1448. Again, Chastelain was with the court when the council was called.[107] There are further, often very full, accounts of council meetings and decisions in the Chronicle after 1457 for which the evidence is less clear. These include councils which dealt with the royal embassy led by Rolin Renault (whom Philip had cultivated in the previous decade) in 1458; the royal summons to attend the trial of Alençon in September 1458; Louis XI's proposals to undermine Burgundian salt production early in 1462; Philip the Good's crusading plans in December 1463; the dispute over the succession of Louis de Chalon in 1464; or Charles the Bold's intentions to make his solemn entry into Ghent in June 1467.[108] Even if Chastelain was not in attendance on each and every one of these occasions, his detailed knowledge of the council's decisions clearly indicates that he had the means to keep abreast of its business. In these years, comparatively few men – dozens, not hundreds – were better placed than the official chronicler to understand the political culture of the Burgundian elite.

His experience at the centre was further widened in this period through the contacts and personal circle he established there. Some of the individuals he mentions in the Chronicle were certainly no more than interlocutors encountered at court: the herald of the king of Castile who visited in 1457, for example;

---

with the court at Hesdin where he spoke to a herald of the king of Castile: iii, 343. In the second case Chastelain tells us shortly before his narrative of the council meeting that the role of the Venetians in the crusade had been discussed at the court at Hesdin, 'moi présent': v, 47.

[106] Delclos, 164 (1458); ADN B2040, fo. 234 and iv, 39, 52 (all 1461); iv, 398–9 (1462); iv, 313, 355, 357, 398–9 (all 1463); v, 47, 91, 103, 123, 154 (all 1464). As we shall see in ch. 3 below, Chastelain's historiographical appointment was closely modelled on the post of royal *chroniqueur*. Jean Chartier, the occupant of that office, was obliged by his remit to follow the king's court in its peregrinations. Although we have no evidence that the same applied to Chastelain, his frequent sojourns with the court suggest that this was probably the case, at least in the first years of his appointment.

[107] iv, 420–1. Chastelain's presence at Hesdin that summer is attested by a conversation he had had there with his old master, Brézé, then visiting the court in the company of Marguerite d'Anjou; with Philippe Pot, 'conférant avec moy'; and with the lord of Lannoy: iv, 357, 355, 398–9.

[108] iii, 391, 424–5; iv, 223, 438; v, 69, 249.

or the German knight passing through Valenciennes in 1458; or certain 'courtisiens de Romme en l'hostel du duc' with whom he had contact in the same year.[109] His relations with Jean II, duke of Bourbon, or Giovanni Arnolfini, the Lucca merchant immortalised by van Eyck, were probably of a similar nature.[110] Although brief, encounters such as these were none the less a useful source of information. It was the privilege of the court chronicler to see, and be seen by, prestigious or exotic visitors.[111]

Chastelain also associated with a wide variety of ducal servants within the court itself. Among the minor court officials he seems to have known on this basis were Philippe Martin, a *valet de chambre*, and Jean Caron, a *sommelier* and later a *clerc* of the ducal chapel.[112] Further up the social scale, Chastelain conversed easily with members of some of the more significant families of the ducal dominions. These men included Charles de Chalon, who had attained the rank of *chevalier, conseiller et chambellan* by 1452, and the lord of Biévène, of the well-connected and influential Rubempré family, who personally relayed his fears to Chastelain after the arrest of his bastard brother in suspicious circumstances late in 1464.[113] There is nothing in the Chronicle to suggest that these were anything more than acquaintanceships. However, the differing status of the men in question suggests that Chastelain was able to range freely among the personnel of the court, and could thus keep track of, and later reflect in his writing, the gamut and nuance of opinion within different sectors of the elite.

By contrast, several of Chastelain's contacts clearly stand out as closer acquaintances, some even as personal friends. Together they constitute the personal circle through which his experience of Burgundian political life, in part at least, was mediated. Jean Lefèvre de St Rémy, although around twenty

---

[109] iii, 343; Delclos, 96, 164.
[110] iv, 39, 356–7.
[111] See also Chastelain's apparently deliberate attempt to see some of the refugees from Constantinople during their visit to the Low Countries in 1461: Delclos, 287. The question of Chastelain's sources, touched upon here, is discussed in ch. 4 below. There is unfortunately no parallel in his work for the insights which Froissart gives on his questioning of interlocutors, such as the Bascot de Mauléon: cf. P. Tucoo-Chala, 'Froissart dans le Midi pyrénéen', in J. J. N. Palmer (ed.), *Froissart: historian*, Woodbridge 1981, 118–31.
[112] It is only from Philippe Martin that Chastelain could have gleaned a piece of information regarding the duke in 1464: v, 102–3. The same is true of information Chastelain received from Caron regarding Philip's altercation with his son in 1457: iii, 232. On Caron's career see J. Marix, *Les musiciens de la cour de Bourgogne au XVe siècle*, Paris 1937, 196–7. The suggestion made there that Caron was the author of the twenty-second story in the *Cent nouvelles nouvelles* is interesting. Philippe Martin's brother, who also served in the duke's private chambers, has been attributed with the seventy-eighth story. The official chronicler's association with these men may thus have stemmed from their common literary interests. This is certainly apparent in some of the other relationships discussed below. See *Les cent nouvelles nouvelles*, ed. F. P. Sweetser, Geneva–Paris 1966, 145–9, 461–6. On the Martin brothers see Caron, *La noblesse*, 395–6.
[113] On Chalon see iv, 451–2. His official title in 1452 is recorded in AGR CC1921, fo. 127v. On Biévène see v, 90–1.

years Chastelain's senior, certainly entered this category. The chronicler counted himself among the 'privés amis' of the king-at-arms of the Order of the Golden Fleece. To judge from Lefèvre's deference to Chastelain in his own memoirs, the sentiment was reciprocal.[114] The connection between the two men may have originated in their shared historical interests, but their conversations were not limited to that topic alone.[115] Lefèvre was prepared to share his knowledge of and opinions on more recent political developments with the official chronicler.[116] This, too, was a feature of Chastelain's relationship with Michel de Chaugy.[117] These men may have known each other through their respective positions as *écuyer panetier* and *maître d'hôtel*, since pantlers took their orders from these officers. In the Chronicle we learn that Chastelain served Philip the Good at table under Chaugy's direction.[118] Although his subordinate, he was Chaugy's near contemporary in age and in length of service at court, and both seem to have shared a common interest in literary matters.[119] Olivier de La Marche, another of the chronicler's close associates, also indulged in this pastime. These two had known each other since 1446, as we have seen, and they later combined their talents in the staging of the *Complainte d'Hector*. Since *maîtres d'hôtel* were usually entrusted with the organisation of court festivities, it is perhaps not surprising that Chastelain, so often the poet on such occasions, developed a working relationship with both.[120] In the case of La Marche at least, a friendship was also struck up: in his *Mémoires* he fondly remembered Chastelain as 'mon singulier ami'.[121]

Chastelain's considerable experience at the centre of the ducal elite could only be enhanced by his relations with these three men. The Golden Fleece, of which Lefèvre was the principal officer, was a central plank of ducal power. Philip the Good used the institution as a means of lending cohesion to his disparate dominions, by recruiting to it members of the most influential families under his lordship, and of cementing relations with other principalities and kingdoms, by offering the collar to his peers and superiors among Europe's ruling elite. Lefèvre himself did far more than officiate at the chapters of the order consisting of these influential individuals or their representatives. He maintained its records, kept track of the activities of its members at home and

---

[114] Cf. iv, 398–9 and Lefèvre, *Chronique*, i. 2, 7.
[115] On the historiographical relationship between the two see ch. 4 below and J.-C. Delclos, 'Jean Lefèvre', *Rencontres médiévales en Bourgogne (XIVe–XVe siècles)*, i (1991), 7–18.
[116] iii, 90, 373; iv, 398–9.
[117] It was almost certainly from Chaugy that Chastelain heard of Charles VII's deathbed repentance for his treatment of Philip the Good: Delclos, 297, 303.
[118] iii, 157.
[119] Chaugy is thought to have entered court service in 1442: M. Martens, 'Bruxelles, capitale', in P. Bonenfant and others, *Bruxelles au XVe siècle*, Brussels 1953, 48. He is credited with five of the stories in the *Cent nouvelles nouvelles*.
[120] O. Cartellieri, *The court of Burgundy*, London 1929, repr. New York 1970, 147, 157. Chaugy was one of the 'souverains conduiseurs' of an elaborate feast held by the duke in Paris in 1461: iv, 140.
[121] La Marche, *Mémoires*, i. 184.

further afield and in its service became one of the most widely-travelled and high-ranking diplomats at Philip the Good's disposal.[122] A survey of his activity in the later 1450s and early 1460s, when his friendship with Chastelain was well-established, reveals that his ambassadorial expertise was also geared towards Franco-Burgundian relations. Between 1456 and 1462, Toison d'or was deployed in every major embassy which the duke sent to France, visiting Charles VII or Louis XI on more than a dozen occasions, alone or in the company of leading ducal advisers and sometimes for several months at a time.[123] In Lefèvre, Chastelain thus had a friend whose seasoned understanding of the finer details of ducal policy with regard to the king of France, and of the workings and membership of the Order the Golden Fleece, few – if any – could match.[124]

Chaugy and La Marche were perhaps even closer to the centre, albeit in other ways. Both were members of the council, but as *chevaliers* they enjoyed a higher status within the aulic hierarchy than Lefèvre or Chastelain.[125] Both also served as ducal ambassadors, with Chaugy to some extent sharing Lefèvre's specialisation in Franco-Burgundian affairs.[126] Where the herald's office gave him particular insight into the elite membership of the Golden Fleece, Chaugy and La Marche played a key role as *maîtres d'hôtel* in the organisation of the Burgundian court.[127] Among their many duties, the *maîtres d'hôtel* appointed and directed household officers, organised and kept account of the daily service of food and were responsible for discipline within the ducal entourage. They were also expected to chaperone and cater for the many visitors and ambassadors who sojourned with the duke.[128] Responsibilities such as these placed La Marche and Chaugy at the hub of court life. Again, it would appear, Chastelain had friends in high places: men in vantage points which enabled them to know, understand and digress upon developments at court which might otherwise have escaped his attention.

In an age of personal government, however, the greatest influence lay with men who were closest to the duke himself. Chastelain certainly had access to Philip the Good, but the Chronicle does not provide any clear evidence of the

---

[122] F. Koller, *Au service de la Toison d'Or*, Dison 1971, 137–40.
[123] ADN B2026, fos 193–4v, 221r–v (1456); 194v, 260v, 305, 308 (1456–7); B2030, fos 180v–1 (1457–8), 198v–9, 227v, 318v (1458); B2034, fos 94v, 97v, 132v–3, 134 (1459); B2040, fos 139v, 151v (1460); B2045 bis, fos 145–6, 149 (1461), 170 (1462).
[124] As we shall see in ch. 5 below, Chastelain clearly reflected the opinions of the knights of the Golden Fleece in key passages of his Chronicle.
[125] Unless otherwise stated, the information on La Marche is from Stein, *Étude biographique*. I was unable to consult l'Abbé Reure, 'Michel de Chaugy et les autres personnages peints sur les volets du triptyque d'Ambierle', *Bulletin de la Diana* ix (1896–7). For Chaugy's status as a *chevalier et conseiller*, however, see ADN B2020, fo. 346.
[126] Ibid. B2012, fo. 243 (1453); B2017, fos 22v, 132v–3 (1453–54); B2040, fos 155v–6, 178; B2045 bis, fos 145–6, 147v–8 (1461).
[127] The earliest reference I have found to Chaugy in this office occurs ibid. B2017, fo. 26 (1454). La Marche held the post by 1461.
[128] La Marche, *Mémoires*, iv. 13–15.

sort of intimacy between the two which Commynes claimed in his relationship with Louis XI.[129] Several of their reported conversations related to mundane political business rather than personal matters.[130] Chastelain famously took the liberty of telling Philip that his good fortunes in this life could prejudice his fate in the next (v, 246). Philip, 'la larme en l'oeil', was prepared to share the same confidence with Guillaume Fillastre.[131] For the most part the duke's confessions to Chastelain were of a similarly public, formal nature – the type of comment which a great man might want his official historian to hear and record for posterity.[132] There were exceptions to this. On one occasion Philip asked Chastelain's opinion on a matter of protocol; on another, he took pleasure in making a little joke to his pantler on the occasion of his sixtieth birthday.[133] The duke of Cleves, 'qui n'y entendoit riens, ne savoit à quoy tourner ses paroles' (iii, 134), looked on bemused as this more intimate exchange took place. Elsewhere, however, it was Chastelain, an adept in 'the courtly art of observation', who watched from afar.[134] As Philip supped, the pantler noted 'comment en parlant avec luy beaucoup en disnant et que je regarday taisamment ses manières, me sambloit lors qu'onques prince de meilleur samblant n'avoie vu en armes, ne qui tant fist à redouter, à le voir comme il estoit là assis' (iii, 157). Later, he would write of Philip that 'en ses vieux jours s'esseuloit fort en closture, et venoit-on à luy à danger' (iv, 237). Chastelain managed to get close to the duke, but not as close as he would have liked.

Happily, however, there were some among his personal circle who did – perhaps not so much Lefèvre or La Marche, but certainly Philippe Pot, lord of La Roche.[135] Although a younger man, Pot already held the rank of *écuyer tranchant* by the time Chastelain entered court service in a similar capacity.[136] Pot's rise through the aulic hierarchy was rapid. By 1454, when he took the vows of the Pheasant, he had entered the select group of *chevaliers, conseillers et chambellans*.[137] Throughout the later years of Philip the Good's reign he was involved in a wide range of governmental affairs, including diplomatic missions

---

[129] Commynes, of course, was capable of error and falsification: K. Bittmann, *Ludwig XI. und Karl der Kühne*, Göttingen 1964–70.

[130] In 1455, for example, Chastelain warned the duke of discontent in Valenciennes: iii, 40–1. In 1461, Philip complained to Chastelain that he had had no reward for the kindness shown to Louis XI: iv, 143. For Chastelain's personal affection for the duke see ch. 5 below.

[131] Guillaume Fillastre, *Le premier volume de la Toison d'Or*, Paris 1516, fo. 130. Philip also told Fillastre how much he wished he had been at Agincourt with the other princes of France: fo. 124.

[132] On two occasions, for example, Philip announced, either directly to Chastelain or in his company, his pious intent with regard to the crusade: iv, 298, 458.

[133] For the protocol scene see iv, 313.

[134] On the courtly art of observation see N. Elias, *The court society*, Oxford 1983, 104–6.

[135] H. Bouchard, 'Philippe Pot, grand-sénéchal de Bourgogne (1428–1493)', *PTSEC* (1949), 23–7.

[136] Pot was an *écuyer tranchant* in 1444: ADN B1982, fo. 183. He still held that office in 1450: B2004, fo. 317v.

[137] Ibid. B2017, fo. 35v.

to the kingdom, the financial reforms of the later 1450s, and assemblies of the estates of the duchies of Burgundy and Brabant in 1457 and 1463.[138] The highpoint of his influence was reached at the very end of the reign, by which time Pot had attained the rank of *premier chambellan*.[139] For those not related to the duke by blood, this represented the pinnacle of a career at court. The *premier chambellan* headed the four household services, guarded the duke's great seal, controlled access to the ducal chambers and was served with his prince at table. He received acts of homage on the duke's behalf, and in times of war he was expected to serve as his lieutenant and standard-bearer.[140] These trappings of influence and authority were firmly underpinned by Pot's proximity to Philip the Good – the latter, after all, was his godfather.[141] In the many disputes between Philip and his son – arising from the latter's second marriage in 1454, their violent quarrel of 1457 or the dominant role of the Croy family towards the end of the reign – Pot was the duke's confidant or mediator.[142] He was seen by others as a man who could bend the duke's ear.[143] This influential and eloquent man, known to his court peers as 'bouche de Cicéron' for his rhetorical powers and literary interests, was also close to the duke's chronicler.[144] Relations between the two certainly dated to the joint mission of 1457 discussed above, but may have gone back to their shared status as household equerries after 1446. Pot provided information to Chastelain on developments at court, substantiating the chronicler's claim that 'j'estoie privé à celuy de La Roche et fiable' (v, 155).[145] On occasion, the Chronicle affords a glimpse of relations between himself and this 'sage homme'. In an account of a court scene at Hesdin in 1463, Chastelain describes Pot 'conférant avec moy' (iv, 355) on matters relating to the Croy family. A more intimate scene is recorded in 1464, when he communed alone with Pot 'à son coucher, . . . assis en banc devant le feu' (v, 155) on the same subject. The chronicler thus had access to the chamberlain's private space, signifying a considerable degree of familiarity within the hierarchical and protocol-laden environment of the court.

---

[138] Ibid. B2030, fo. 161v (1457); B2034, fos 108r–v (1459); B2040, fos 155r–v (1461); B2051, fos 198v–9v (1463).
[139] Caron, *La noblesse*, 134–5.
[140] La Marche, *Mémoires*, iv. 12–13; G. Huydts, 'Le premier chambellan des ducs de Bourgogne', in *Mélanges d'histoire offerts à Henri Pirenne*, Brussels 1926, i. 263–70.
[141] Caron, *La noblesse*, 511. Pot represented Philip the Good at at least two baptisms in order to 'donner son nom', suggesting still further the close relationship between master and this servant: ADN B2017, fos 217v–18, 237.
[142] iii, 19–22, 275–85; v, 154–74.
[143] v, 69; iv, 116.
[144] On Pot 'bouche de Cicéron' see R. Walsh, 'The coming of humanism to the Low Countries', *Humanistica Lovaniensia* xxv (1976), 146–97 at p. 189. His rhetorical powers were most famously deployed at the meeting of the Estates General in 1484: H. Bouchard, 'Philippe Pot et la démocratie aux États généraux de 1484', AB xxii (1950), 33–40. On Pot's literary interests – which may also have brought him into contact with Chastelain – see Doutrepont, *Littérature*, 311, 337–8, 498.
[145] Cf. iii, 279.

Among Philip the Good's personal confidants, the few individuals who could equal Pot's intimacy with the ageing duke belonged for the most part to the Croy family: Antoine, lord of Croy and count of Porcien; his brother Jean, lord of Chimay and Tours-sur-Marne; the latter's son Philippe, lord of Sempy and Quiévrain; and Jean de Lannoy, nephew to the first two.[146] The rise and fall of the Croy was recounted by Chastelain from his standpoint as a personal acquaintance or friend of some of these men.[147] His closest contacts were with Philippe, a younger man who occasionally acted as *premier chambellan* in his uncle's absence. Chastelain described him as his 'très-accointé et ami privé' (v, 178) in 1464, and their association was still intact eleven years later when they engaged in a friendly correspondence at the time of the siege of Neuss.[148] Chastelain was also privy to the thoughts of Jean de Lannoy, the counsellor who, as we have seen, thought so highly of 'ystoryens' like himself. Not long after his appointment the official chronicler had the benefit of Lannoy's expert opinion (as *stadhouder* of Holland) on the subject of the rebellion of the Brederode family.[149] Seven years later, when Lannoy (then governor of Lille) was on the point of disgrace, Chastelain was party to his fears in a far more personal matter, namely the duke's mounting suspicions with regard to himself and his family.[150] This evidence suggests that the chronicler had achieved a fair degree of familiarity with some of the Croys. The most senior members of the family were not distant figures for him either. In September 1464 Antoine de Croy disclosed to the chronicler the personal and, in the context of his imminent fall from grace, potentially damaging news that Louis XI had offered to make him *grand sénéchal* of Normandy.[151] Just two months later he was to be found in the company of Pot, Lannoy and Quiévrain 'en la chambre dudit Croy, . . . là où avoit plusieurs chevaliers et escuyers, gens de bien, devisans ensemble l'un ça, l'autre là, assis sur banc et sur couche, comme de costume est en court' (v, 154). Chastelain was not simply hobnobbing with the great and the good here, as was Froissart, for example, in his second visit to England. The official chronicler mixed with such men on an entirely different basis: his career had developed with theirs, he had served under them or in their company on domestic and diplomatic duty, and he entered the council

---

[146] The influence of the Croy family has been studied in great detail and requires little comment here: see Thielemans, 'Les Croÿ'; R. Born, *Les Croy*, Brussels 1981 (unfortunately and inaccurately blames the bad press accorded to the Croy family on Chastelain); L. Régibeau, 'Le rôle politique des Croy à la fin du règne de Philippe le Bon, 1456–1465', unpubl. *mém. de licence*, Brussels 1956. I am grateful to the librarian of the Brynmor Jones library, University of Hull, for allowing me to consult a microfilm of this last work. For the first and third of these men see P. De Win, 'Anthoine de Croy', in CTO, 49–53; W. Ossoba, 'Philippe de Croy', ibid. 149–50. See also CTO, 60–2, 109–10.

[147] C. Thiry, 'Les Croy face aux indiciaires bourguignons: George Chastelain, Jean Molinet', in Aubailly and others, '*Et c'est la fin*', iii. 1363–80.

[148] viii, 261–8.

[149] iii, 79–80.

[150] iv, 398.

[151] v, 88.

chamber with them on an equal footing, perhaps more confidently than some. With these men and through them, Chastelain moved into the sphere of the politically powerful.

Of course, not all of Chastelain's acquaintances or friends were such leading lights within the court environment. Jacques de Fallerans was an equerry like himself, as was Hervé de Meriadec.[152] Bartier regrets that Chastelain devoted as much space to the latter as he did to the ducal chancellor Nicolas Rolin, but this is simply a reflection of the circles in which he moved.[153] By the same token, his predilection for lesser members of the Luxembourg family may seem curious by comparison with his treatment of its most important representative, Louis, count of St Pol. Unlike Louis, however, Jacques (his brother, lord of Richebourg and Fiennes) and Jean (a bastard of the Luxembourg family, lord of Haubourdin) were among Chastelain's 'bien accointé[s] et très-privé[s]' associates, as indeed was Jacques's servant, the Picard equerry Antoine de Lamet.[154]

These men may have been less important than some of Chastelain's other friends at court, but we under-estimate his connections with them at our peril. Through them, too, he formed his understanding of the Burgundian court – a court which, like that of the king and certain other princes, was as much a 'power-complex of influence and favour' as it was an institution of government.[155] It is important to note that each of these men, like Chastelain and Ternant, had connections beyond the Burgundian elite which led into a wider French polity. Meriadec – a Breton himself, and therefore an illustration of the transferability of men from one court to another – belonged to a family which had produced participants in the French reconquest between 1435 and 1450.[156] In 1461 he was granted the significant royal office of *bailli* of Tournai.[157] The Luxembourg family had territorial possessions in both France and Burgundy.[158] Jacques de Luxembourg's brother-in-law was Arthur de Richemont, constable of France under Charles VII and later duke of Brittany

---

[152] It was from Fallerans that Chastelain learned, among other things, of the count of Armagnac's passion for his sister: Delclos, 257–9; iv, 110–12. Chastelain may have known this servant of the marshal of Burgundy through La Marche, his childhood friend and court companion: Stein, *Étude biographique*, 15. Meriadec – 'escuyer de bon los, dont ay fait d'autre part mention assez' (iv, 33) – is never explicitly cited, but Chastelain is well informed on his diplomatic missions, conversations with the duke and connections at court: iii, 11–12, 208; iv, 351.
[153] Bartier, *Légistes*, 6.
[154] v, 15. From Haubourdin, for example, Chastelain learned of an anecdote recounted by Charles VII's widow: iv, 368–70. For Fiennes and Lamet see v, 13–16, 492. On the careers of these men see P. De Win, 'Jean de Luxembourg', in CTO, 80–2; and J. Paviot, 'Jacques de Luxembourg', ibid. 138–40.
[155] Lewis, *Later medieval France*, 121–2.
[156] Guillaume Gruel, *Chronique d'Arthur de Richemont, connétable de France, duc de Bretagne (1393–1458)*, ed. A. Le Vavasseur, Paris 1890, 105, 206.
[157] iv, 33.
[158] Vaughan, CTB, 250.

in his own right.[159] This may explain why Jacques was made *gouverneur* of Rennes, where he was seconded by his Picard servant and fellow Burgundian courtier, Antoine de Lamet.[160] It may also explain why, later in his career, he was prepared to abandon his office as a *conseiller et chambellan* to Charles the Bold to take the road to royal service.[161] The careers, family traditions and landed interests of these men were not unusual at the Burgundian court, at least among those who, like Chastelain, had risen to prominence under Philip the Good. Even Jean Lefèvre de St Rémy, with his relatively humble background, could apparently count among his relatives the de Reilhac family, whose lands lay in France and whose members included a royal counsellor, a royal secretary and a royal servant at the *Parlement*.[162] The backgrounds and careers of Chastelain's other principal associates conform to a similar pattern. Michel de Chaugy, Philippe Pot and the members of the Croy family are particular cases in point.

Chaugy belonged to a family whose territorial possessions spanned the Franco-Burgundian divide. Upon the death of his father, his elder brother inherited the family estates in the Bourbonnais while Chaugy himself received the lands held in the duchy of Burgundy.[163] By these means, the Chaugys – and certain others who acted in like fashion, notably the Chalons, the La Trémoilles and the Luxembourgs discussed above – sought to protect the family patrimony from the vagaries of princes.[164] The danger posed by the latter was revealed in the case of the Chaugy family in 1473, when Charles the Bold stipulated that Michel's relatives 'qui sont et demeurent en France' were to be excluded from any provision he might make in his will for the lands he held in ducal territory.[165] It is therefore unsurprising that on the death of the duke, Chaugy, like some other important men from the duchy, entered royal service as a *conseiller et chambellan*.

Philippe Pot also took this route after 1477, and was rewarded with his appointment as *grand-sénéchal* of Burgundy by Louis XI. Vaughan is surely right in his view that Pot, Chaugy and others like them cannot be judged too harshly

---

[159] B.-A. Pocquet du Haut-Jussé, *Deux féodaux*, Paris 1935, 91.
[160] H. Morice, *Mémoires pour servir de preuves à l'histoire ecclésiastique et civile de Bretagne*, Paris 1742–46, iii. 1722, 1724, 1757–8.
[161] This he did after his capture in a military engagement just a few months after the death of his friend, the official chronicler: Jean de Haynin, *Mémoires 1465–77*, ed. D. D. Brouwers, Liège 1905–6, ii. 200–2.
[162] According to A. de Reilhac, *Jean de Reilhac*, Paris 1886–87, i. 10. The suggestion that another Burgundian memoirist, Jacques du Clercq, also had close connections in the kingdom (some of them with marked Armagnac leanings) deserves more attention than it has received: cf. A. Vallet de Viriville, 'Duclercq, Jacques', in *Nouvelle biographie générale*, xv, Paris 1852, 16–17; N. Pons, review of G. Barner, *Jacques Du Clercq und seine* Mémoires, Düsseldorf 1989, in *Francia* xviii (1991), 319–20.
[163] Caron, *La noblesse*, 387.
[164] On the Chalon family see Vaughan, *CTB*, 232. On the La Trémoilles see W. A. Weary, 'La maison de La Trémoille pendant la renaissance', in *FFQS*, 197–212.
[165] Caron, *La noblesse*, 78–9, 275, 280–1.

for their abandonment of Mary of Burgundy.[166] However, to say that their landed interests in the duchy gave them no alternative but to join the king is to overlook an equally significant point. These men often came from families in which royal service had for long been a natural choice.[167] Until their acquisition of lands in Burgundy around 1360, indeed, the patrimony of the Pot family lay in royal France.[168] Thereafter, some led careers in both the kingdom and the duchy, the most successful being Philippe's grandfather Regnier, servant of Charles VI and the first three dukes of Burgundy.[169] In Philippe's own lifetime, his brother Guyot served at the Burgundian court as an *escuier d'escuierie*, and was involved in the financial reforms of 1457.[170] As early as 1454, however, he was also mentioned in the Burgundian accounts as an 'escuier, conseiller et chambellan' of the duke of Orléans.[171] By 1468, when he was at the meeting of Charles the Bold and Louis XI at Péronne, Guyot had entered royal service. The following year he became the royal *bailli* of Vermandois and an ambassador of considerable stature.[172] In these circumstances we can see why, for his brother Philippe, boundaries that might seem to exist between Valois France and Valois Burgundy were less an obstacle than a permeable membrane.

By comparison with the Pots and the Chaugys, however, the Croys provide the most dramatic and best-known example of a family with interests in both the Burgundian dominions and the kingdom of France. The effective founder of the family's fortunes, Jean de Croy, served John the Fearless in France and received considerable favour from Charles VI.[173] His son Antoine was considered by Charles VII to be a worthy (or simply useful) beneficiary of his largesse as early as 1435.[174] He later served for three months under the king during the reconquest of Normandy with a Burgundian contingent of 200 horse, all paid for by the duke himself.[175] However, it was during the early years of the reign of Louis XI that the Croys were to enjoy their greatest favours from the king.

---

166 Vaughan, *CTB*, 233. The others we might include here are Guillaume de Rochefort, Jean de Neuchâtel or Philippe de Crèvecoeur, the last two knights of the Order of the Golden Fleece.
167 Despite his extensive landed interests in the south La Marche remained with Mary and her Habsburg husband. He may have been wary of Louis XI, who had cause to resent his involvement in the scandal of the bastard of Rubempré. It has been pointed out that Commynes's grandfather took the road to royal service long before Philippe himself: Duvosquel, 'Bourgeoisie ou noblesse?', 546–7.
168 Caron, *La noblesse*, 15, 379, 389, 508.
169 J. Pot, *Histoire de Regnier Pot*, Paris 1929.
170 ADN B2017, fo. 294v; B2026, fo. 300; and see ch. 5 below.
171 ADN B2017, fo. 251.
172 P.-R. Gaussin, 'Les conseillers de Louis XI (1461–1483)', in *FFQS*, 105–34 at p. 112; see also ch. 5 below.
173 Cf. Thielemans, 'Les Croÿ', 7–8, and R. C. Famiglietti, *Royal intrigue*, New York 1986, 136 n. 21.
174 Thielemans, 'Les Croÿ', 7–8.
175 ADN B2020, fo. 319–20v. The huge payment of 3,600*l*. which Croy received was for a series of military actions against the English dating back to 1436. It was made, curiously,

In 1461, Antoine de Croy was appointed as *conseiller* and *grand maître d'hôtel*. This last office, it should be stressed, gave a Burgundian servant the right to nominate royal officers himself. Jean and his son Philippe became royal *conseillers et chambellans* in the following year. In addition to these key posts at the royal court, the family was granted land and other offices in the north of the kingdom.

In the long run, of course, the dual allegiance of the Croys proved to be their undoing. This was not because their ducal master resented their involvement in the affairs of the kingdom *per se*. Philip the Good appears to have condoned and encouraged their developing influence in France, even if others on both sides of the frontier, most notably the count of Charolais and certain advisers to Louis XI, found it intolerable.[176] The real reason for their loss of ducal favour and their temporary exile in the kingdom lay in the Croys' abuse of their privileged status, in particular their involvement in the sale of the Somme towns to Louis XI in 1463 and their refusal to mend their fences with Charolais. These matters earned them universal disapproval at the Burgundian court, to which the chronicler, despite his friendship with members of the family, felt obliged to add his own voice.[177]

Through his close knowledge of the Croys' fate, his dealings with the other ducal servants discussed above and his own advancement as a ducal chronicler, diplomat and counsellor, Chastelain clearly attained the centre in the years after 1454. But the centre of what? It is tempting to say that he had reached the centre of the Burgundian state, yet it is not clear from the preceding analysis that Chastelain, his friends or acquaintances would have shared our understanding of what that term meant. The corridors of power through which they moved were many and varied. They led in different directions. Most ended in great halls where these men congregated and attempted to make themselves useful to the king or prince who commanded that space. They were drawn to particular centres by accident of birth, by following in the footsteps of their ancestors, by unalloyed self-interest or by combinations of these factors. Malcontents like Commynes moved on, but so too did others, albeit less dramatically or with less compromising results for themselves. Chastelain

---

in 1455. Further royal grants to Antoine de Croy are discussed in L. P. Gachard, *Études et notices historiques concernant les Pays-Bas*, Brussels 1890, iii. 548–52.

[176] In a choice passage of reported speech, Chastelain noted the hostility in some royalist quarters to the Croy in 1463: 'Vous autres, les Bourgongnons, il vous semble bien que vous gouvernez le roy et ce royaume, et que tout vous est entre mains parce que le seigneur de Croy gouverne le roy ... Tant que le roy aura affaire du seigneur de Croy, il s'en servira et aidera, jusques à estre venu à ses fins. Mais là venu, par Dieu! il lui baillera de la pelle sur cul': iv, 422. Charolais's hostility to the Croy is well documented in Régibeau, 'Le rôle politique'; cf. A. Grunzweig, 'Namur et le début de la guerre du bien public', in *Études d'histoire et d'archéologie namuroises dédiées à Ferdinand Courtoy*, Namur 1952, 531–64 esp. pp. 531–41; and P. Bonenfant and J. Stenghers, 'Le rôle de Charles le Téméraire dans le gouvernement de l'état bourguignon en 1465–1467', AB xxv (1953), 7–29, 118–33 esp. pp. 9–12.

[177] See, for example, v, 108.

himself is a case in point: like Guillaume Fillastre (whom he knew, but who occupied a loftier position as chancellor of the Golden Fleece), he had shifted from the Angevin orbit to the Burgundian.[178] Indeed, some were obliged by force of circumstance to move to and fro between these centres. The lord of Antoing, Philip the Good's *souverain* in Hainaut, is an example of this.[179] Antoing 'avoit moult à perdre au royaume; sy avoit-il ès pays du duc auquel il estoit frère d'ordre' (iii, 84). No wonder, then, that he was 'tout perplex' (iii, 85) in 1456 when a royal officer from the *Parlement* demanded that he release a girl whom the duke had placed in his charge. Luckily, Philip understood and resolved his predicament – perhaps because, as Chastelain knew from his own diplomatic experience, the third Valois duke remained acutely aware of the long reach of royal sovereignty.

Other than obstructionism or outright revolt, an effective counter to this was a policy which, not coincidentally, would also have severely curtailed the movement of servants from one princely orbit to another and the accumulation by these men of lands and offices from more than one master. This policy was the practical enforcement of *princely* sovereignty.[180] Philip the Good was certainly conscious of the latter's importance, but with regard to his own servants he took no great steps towards it until late in his reign.[181] Even then, Jean Coustain was executed for *lèse-majesté* because of his plot against the life of the count of Charolais, not for any treasonous activity involving another prince.[182] So long as the duke's hand remained light, the small, select centre which Chastelain knew would open out onto a wider polity. The later 1460s would see a narrowing of these horizons. Louis XI, more than any previous king, rigorously prosecuted for treason those servants who strayed from the

---

[178] J. Du Teil, *Un amateur d'art au XVe siècle*, Paris 1920, 6–9. Fillastre gave Chastelain information on events in Hungary: Delclos, 85.

[179] For the following see iii, 81–9; R. C. Van Caeneghem, *Les arrêts et jugés du Parlement de Paris sur appels flamands conservés dans les registres du Parlement 1320–1521*, Brussels 1966–77, ii. 84–7; Paris, BN, MS fr. 5044, fo. 35 (royal correspondence on the case). A current research project in Belgium and Holland is exploring the role of ducal counsellors, their connections and landed interests in 'la construction bourguignonne' in the Low Countries, from Philip the Good to Mary of Burgundy. However, landed interests like those discussed here, not to mention the family traditions and political and historical cultures discussed elsewhere in this chapter, also had a determining role to play in the formation of outlooks within the Burgundian elite.

[180] M. Jones, 'Bons Bretons et bons François', *TRHS* 5th ser. xxxii (1982), 91–112, repr. in his *The creation of Brittany*, London 1988, no. xiv. Similar problems suggested similar (but not necessarily more practicable) solutions in the relationship, from 1259 onwards, between Plantagenet and Capetian/Valois: M. G. A. Vale, *The Angevin legacy and the Hundred Years' War*, Oxford 1990.

[181] On the evidence for Burgundian treason trials, I follow the view of Jones ('Bons Bretons', 349 and n. 101) rather than that of Armstrong, who argued for an earlier deployment of the notion of *lèse-majesté* by Burgundian dukes. Jones argues convincingly that the precise use of the term does not occur until the 1460s.

[182] Chastelain uses this term of Coustain's crime: iv, 260. Coustain is also referred to as 'le traistre': v, 263.

royal circle.[183] Charles the Bold also broke with the policies of his predecessors in that matter.[184] With this development the Burgundian elite which Chastelain had grown to know would change in important ways. As we shall see in the last section, however, these were changes which the chronicler was to observe at a distance.

Valenciennes (c. 1464–1475)

In a letter he wrote from Valenciennes on 9 August 1465, Chastelain told his correspondents at the *Chambre des comptes* that he would shortly be travelling 'devers les seigneurs', provided he could 'trouver voie de seurté' through the roads of northern France made dangerous by the war of the Public Weal.[185] The official chronicler was clearly keen to garner first-hand news of the battle of Montlhéry. The letter is unusual, not simply as a rare piece of Chastelain's correspondence, but as one of the few indications in the last decade of his life that he still travelled and lived with the court elite. Otherwise, the evidence reveals that he was making far greater use of his residence at Valenciennes in these years.[186] The text of the Chronicle for 1466–7, 1468 and 1470 contains only one mention of his presence at court.[187] Six such references occur in the shorter text for 1464 alone.[188] The chronicler's citation of opinions expressed to him by his contacts at court, regular until 1464, is limited in the reign of Charles the Bold to a single comment relayed to him by an anonymous ducal servant.[189] Similarly, his accounts of council meetings, an index of his continuing political role after 1457, dry up in the later sections of the Chronicle.

His withdrawal was not the result of any eclipse in his fortunes. In the inevitable reshuffling of offices which followed the new duke's accession in 1467, Chastelain retained both his post and his income.[190] In 1470 he received

---

[183] S. Cuttler, *The law of treason and treason trials in later medieval France*, Cambridge 1981, 213–37.
[184] Jones, 'Bons Bretons', 349. Further useful comment on the subject is to be found in W. Paravicini, 'Peur, pratiques, intelligences', in FFQS, 183–96 at pp. 192–3.
[185] ADN B17698 (alphabetical order).
[186] Chastelain's correspondence with Philippe de Croy in 1475 (discussed above) was sent from Valenciennes. The works he addressed to Charles the Bold in this period (see ch. 3 below) were also sent from there. An earlier version of the material that follows appeared as G. P. Small, 'George Chastelain à Valenciennes', *Valentiana* iv (1989), 26–31.
[187] v, 491 (1470). Chastelain takes the trouble to mention explicitly his attendance when he had never bothered to do so in the past: 'J'estoie en court à ceste heure'. This may suggest that the event was exceptional.
[188] v, 47, 91, 93, 108, 123, 154.
[189] v, 312: Charles the Bold had revealed his intention 'à tel qui le me révéla depuis'. Delclos is right to be cautious about the absence in the Chronicle of any reference to direct personal contact between Charles the Bold and his official chronicler, but the omission is certainly striking by comparison with passages relating to Philip the Good: Delclos, *Le témoignage*, 41–2. Chastelain does once refer to a comment he had heard Charolais make: iv, 477.
[190] See app. 2 below. On Charles the Bold's new 'équipe personnelle' see Bartier, *Charles*

a clear mark of favour when he was exempted by order of the duke from payment of the *maltôte*, a tax levied on wine and beer and a major source of revenue for the municipal authorities of Valenciennes.[191] This was a greater privilege than it might at first appear. Seven years earlier, Jean de Croy had arbitrarily announced at Valenciennes 'en pleine congrégation du peuple' (iv, 347) that he would not be paying the *maltôte*. The decision angered a populace and an urban magistrature who had recently shown themselves to be extremely sensitive to Burgundian attempts to over-ride their privileges.[192] The fact that only Chastelain and the armourers' guild (inevitably a favoured group) were exempted in 1470 reveals the significance of Charles the Bold's concession. To this privilege was added, three years later, a far greater acknowledgement of

---

le Téméraire, 68–70. Chastelain's salary was recorded at first between the accounts of the receiver of Hainaut and that of the Salle-le-Comte at Valenciennes. Perhaps as a result of this administrative problem, perhaps as a result of his continued presence at court in these years, the payments he received between 1457 and 1463 were erratic (although he did receive full payment eventually): ADN B8043, fo. 77v; B9882, fo. 35v; B8044, fo. 36; B8045, fo. 62v; B2044, no. 63236; B9886, fo. 28. Thereafter, Chastelain's annual salary was drawn regularly at Valenciennes. This may suggest a stabilisation of his position in the town after 1463, a point also suggested by the evidence of the Chronicle as discussed in the previous paragraph: B9887, fo. 28v; B9888, fo. 33; B9889, fo. 30; B9890, fo. 28v; B9891, fo. 28v; B9892, fo. 32v; B9893, fo. 35v; B9894, fo. 38; B9895, fo. 38; B9896, fos 40r–v; B9897, fos 41r–v; B9898, fos 39r–v. With cool efficiency, Chastelain's salary was stopped on 13 Feb. 1475 – almost certainly the date of his death: B9899, fos 35v–6. His salary was a heavy burden on the local receipt, amounting to 16% of the average annual income in the 1460s: V. Delsart, 'Les finances de la prévôté de Valenciennes sous les maisons de Bavière et de Bourgogne (1389–1477)', in L. Nys and A. Salamagne (eds), *Valenciennes aux XIVe et XVe siècles*, Valenciennes 1996, 37–53 at p. 42.

[191] Chastelain's exemption (and that of the armourers, discussed below) is revealed in AMV BB 202, and in a copy of Jean Cocquiau's manuscript history of the town: AEM MS 89, fo. 295. Cocquiau's unfoliated introduction notes that 'les principales ressources de la ville derivent des maltotes', a point that is further suggested by the number of ducal *ordonnances* on the matter: J.-M. Cauchies, 'Liste chronologique provisoire des ordonnances de Philippe le Bon, duc de Bourgogne, pour le comté de Hainaut', *Bulletin de la Commission royale pour la publication des anciennes lois et ordonnances de Belgique* xxvi (1973–4), 35–146 at pp. 61, 82, 94, 101, 108, 117, 121, 133, 138.

[192] In 1455 the duke eventually permitted the Valenciennois to exercise their ancient right to stage judicial duels in the case of murderers accused by members of the victim's family. Chastelain recounts the town's jealous defence of this right in the face of ducal discontent: iii, 38–49. The grotesque encounter which resulted on this occasion was witnessed and described by Chastelain himself (see the previous passage, completed in Delclos, 325–7). The passage was first published in H. Kondo, 'Le chapitre IX du livre IV de la *Chronique* de Georges Chastellain dont la dernière partie est jusqu'ici inconnue', *ICU Comparative Culture* vi (1983), 24–31. Cf. O. Cartellieri, 'Ein Zweikampf in Valenciennes im Jahre 1455', in *Festschrift Johannes Hoops*, Heidelberg 1925, 169–76, and F. Manetti, 'Giudizio di dio a Valenciennes nel 1455', *PCEEBM* xix (1978), 47–53. On Valenciennes's readiness to defend its privileges see L. Cellier, 'Une commune flamande', *Mémoires historiques sur l'arrondissement de Valenciennes* iii (1873), 27–387, at pp. 201–35; J.-M. Cauchies, 'Valenciennes et les comtes de Hainaut (milieu XIIIe–milieu XVe siècle): des relations politiques mouvementées', in Nys and Salamagne, *Valenciennes aux XIVe et XVe siècles*, 67–88. The latter also deals with the duel of 1455 at pp. 82–4.

the chronicler's shining reputation within court circles. At the Valenciennes chapter of the Order of the Golden Fleece, Charles conferred on him the rather pretentious title of *indiciaire* and, perhaps most importantly, a knighthood in recognition of his services.[193] His friend Lefèvre had received this last honour in 1468 'pour toutes ses labeurs passées' (v, 384). The stock of the one-time Ghent shipper was at its highest in these later years of his life.

Chastelain's withdrawal to Valenciennes thus appears to have been a personal choice. It can be suggested that this was informed by the nature of his work and his personal circumstances. On the first point, Walter Map's aphorism that 'the muses are fugitives from all courts' was as true of fifteenth-century Burgundy as it was of twelfth-century England.[194] Ducal translators and scribes were most often based in towns such as Lille, Hesdin or Ghent, where they enjoyed the time and the facilities to get on with the writing and production of their texts.[195] Chastelain may have been under an obligation to attend court, but it is clear from certain passages in his Chronicle that he did occasionally return to Valenciennes to write in the years before 1463.[196] The town itself could provide for his needs. There were *parcheminiers* and paper sellers in Valenciennes.[197] Although there were manuscript *ateliers* there too, the evidence suggests that the copying of Chastelain's work was an in-house operation or, at the very least, a process which was carried out under his close supervision.[198] This laborious task tied the chronicler to a defined place of work and

---

[193] But not membership of the Order or the office of king-at-arms: cf. P. Bonenfant, 'Chastellain fut-il chevalier de la Toison d'or?', RBPH xxv (1946–47), 143–4; C. Gaier, 'Technique des combats singuliers d'après les auteurs bourguignons', MA xci (1985), 415–57; xcii (1986), 5–40 at p. 420. Molinet (ii. 594) thought he was ennobled.

[194] Map cited in R. F. Green, *Poets and princepleasers*, Toronto 1980, 12.

[195] Doutrepont, *Littérature*, 456–9.

[196] This is suggested by his references to fairly insignificant events which had occurred in the town: see iii, 98 (drowning of a man in a cauldron), 315 (the flight of some Lombards to the town); Delclos, 106 (death of a young money changer); Delclos, 159–61 (a joust), 256 (short stay of the count of Armagnac); iv, 30 (the making of 'brodures' and other accoutrements there for Louis XI's coronation), 170 (suicide of a cobbler).

[197] D. Vanwynsberghe, 'La miniature à Valenciennes: état des sources et aperçu chronologique de la production (fin XIVe–1480)', in Nys and Salamagne, *Valenciennes aux XIVe et XVe siècles*, 181–200; H. Servant, 'Culture, art et société à Valenciennes dans la deuxième moitié du XVe siècle', unpubl. *École des chartes* diss. 1989, i. 126–7, 151–9, 286–319. This last author does not think Chastelain's sojourns in Valenciennes were regular (i. 262–6) – a view neither she, nor P. Lefrancq who shares it, substantiates: P. Lefrancq, 'Les Valenciennois devant leur histoire et devant leurs historiens', *Histoire des mentalités dans le nord de la France*, Lille 1979, 29–35. At least someone in Valenciennes thinks otherwise: it is to my knowledge the only town in the world which has a street named after him! See A. Gauvin, *Petite histoire des rues de Valenciennes*, Valenciennes 1974, 107.

[198] One of the Chronicle manuscripts, Brussels, BR, MS 15843, was emended by Chastelain himself. It is written on the same paper, and in places by the same hand, as the only manuscript of his *Exposition sur vérité mal prise*, now Brussels, BR, MS 11101. The latter figured in the inventory of Philip the Good's library in 1467: Barrois, *Bibliothèque*, 153, no. 969. The relationship between these two manuscripts – the one emended by Chastelain, the other presented to the duke by the chronicler, both made of the same materials and

created the need for a competent staff under his direction. It has long been accepted that Jean Molinet was part of this team.[199] Although only one other member of his entourage is known to us by name, there are good reasons for believing that others worked with or under the chronicler.[200] Chastelain's exemption from the *maltôte* in 1470 noted his personal requirement of eight *muids* of wine per annum – in other words, over 1,800 litres.[201] Unless he was an exceptionally thirsty historian, the implication here must be that Chastelain had a larger household and occasional visitors to cater for.

This evidence also reveals something of Chastelain's standard of living in Valenciennes.[202] It was clearly not only work which kept him at the Salle-le-Comte. The mere fact that his residence had a leaky roof in 1461 ('qui lui tourne a grant dommaige') did not make the Salle-le-Comte the dilapidated palace it is sometimes taken to be.[203] The municipal authorities of Valenciennes were less forthcoming than those of Lille or Brussels when Philip the Good asked them to fund the rebuilding of his residence in 1458, but the 4,000*l.t.*

---

written in places in the same hand – indicates that Chastelain had close control of the production of his manuscripts. Those of the Chronicle are discussed in detail in ch. vi and app. I below. Chastelain may have used vellum in his presentation works, as suggested by the inaccurately entitled copy of his *Advertissement au duc Charles* which his master possessed: Barrois, *Bibliothèque*, 314, no. 2213.

[199] Molinet's relationship with Chastelain before he replaced him as official chronicler is suggested by his well-known remark that he had been 'nourri en son école plusieurs ans'. Dupire is inclined to date the association to 1465, but without evidence: *Jean Molinet*, Paris 1932, 13. Jean Devaux has suggested that Chastelain and Molinet may have met in Paris in 1461 during the chronicler's visit to the capital for the coronation of Louis XI. He notes that the earliest mention of Molinet at Valenciennes dates to 1471. I am grateful to Jean Devaux for the paginated proofs of sections of his study of Molinet which he sent in advance of publication: *Jean Molinet, indiciaire bourguignon*, Paris 1996, 123–7.

[200] Jean Chenebaut 'serviteur de George Chastellain' received 60s. for bringing a presentation copy of the *Déclaration de tous les hauts faits* to Charles some time before 19 July 1467: ADN B2064, fo. 202. On 12 July 1465, his correspondents at the *Chambre des comptes* received his letter 'baillées par son vallet': B17698.

[201] I am inclined to accept Sivéry's quantification of the *muid* (227.2 litres) over that of Sommé (130.4 litres), since the former is concerned primarily with Hainaut: cf. G. Sivéry, *Les comtes de Hainaut et le commerce de vin au XIVe siècle et au début du XVe siècle*, Lille 1969, 196; M. Sommé, 'Étude comparative des mesures à vin dans les états bourguignons au XVe siècle', *RN* lviii (1976), 171–83.

[202] My attempts to find evidence for any family or property interests Chastelain might have had outside the confines of the Salle-le-Comte were no more successful than those mentioned in M. Caffiaux, 'Archives communales de Valenciennes', *Bulletin de la Commission historique du Département du Nord* x (1868), 175–91 at p. 188. I concentrated my research on Series J (*Embriévures et criées* and *Bordereaux des Werps*) and Series W (*Greffe des Werps*) of this collection from 1455 to 1483. The absence of the chronicler from the town records may be due to the fact that the municipal authorities had no jurisdiction over the Salle-le-Comte: M. Bauchond, *La justice criminelle du magistrat de Valenciennes au moyen âge*, Paris 1904, 48; H. D'Oultreman, *Histoire de la ville et comté de Valenciennes*, Douai 1639, 284.

[203] ADN B17687 (alphabetical order). On the palace generally see V. Maliet, 'Valenciennes: La Salle-le-Comte', in P. Beaussart and A. Salamagne (eds), *Châteaux-chevaliers en Hainaut au moyen âge*, Brussels 1995, 134–7.

they voted to this end were none the less put to good use.[204] In 1465 at least, one of the rooms in Chastelain's home there was suitable for the count of Charolais himself 'qui y couche dedens quant il y est'.[205] This glimpse of Chastelain's material surroundings in the later 1460s is deepened and widened in the accounts.[206] There we learn that 'le logis Jorge' was situated in close proximity to the 'grant salle', the house of the receiver and, less grandly, a loft for storing oats. To the rear it looked out onto the Escaut; to the front, a courtyard. There was also a well. The house had a chapel, a cellar and a ground floor consisting of 'l'estable des cheveux dudit George', a kitchen and, close by, 'la place qu'on dist [la] tuerie dudit hostel'. From the ground floor one gained access to the living quarters by means of a stairway (with its own locked doors) and the 'ghalleries' it climbed to. The windows of the gallery let in the cold: 'seize aulnes de grosse toille' had to be fitted to wooden frames and hung there 'pour esconser le vent'. Off this draughty passage lay several rooms, one of which may have been the spot where Chastelain stood, night after night, peering above the rooftops of Valenciennes to see a comet which apparently presaged great events for 1468.[207] Among these rooms were 'le grant chambre de George Chastelain' and one further, private room which is of particular interest. It gave on to the stairway on one side and the gallery on the other. Built at Chastelain's request, this was his 'comptoir' – the same 'contoir' where he sat, on the morning of 11 July 1465, to pen a letter to his correspondents at the *Chambre des comptes*, but where he was normally to be found writing his Chronicle.[208] In his advancing years, Chastelain might well have felt that the new surroundings provided for him by the duke more than made up for the lost opportunity of his fief at Ghinderop.

What was the significance of Chastelain's withdrawal to Valenciennes? On

---

[204] AEM MS 89, fo. 217: 'Accord faict au duc pour faire ung logis à la salle, après qu'en personne en eut faict demande. C'est au Conseil du XXIX decembre qu'on promist s'efforcer pour cela, le plus que on polroit. Et le XIXe de janvier, appert que le duc fit ladite requête en personne. Et fut accordé la somme de IIII m. livres tournois. Et se trouve la description du lieu à faire au registre des consaux. Mais ne fut ledict accord accepté, attendu que ceulx de Bruxelles ly faisoient ung logiz de XL m. escus, et ceulx de Lille X m. Et aussy qu'entant ledict lieu achevé, il si tiendroit pour estre plus près de ses pays d'arthois et picardie, et pour sa santé et bonne réception qu'on luy avoit faict dernièrement. Sur quoy accordé IIII m. escus. Et au XXVIIIe de may LXII, se voit que l'ouvraige s'advanchoit ... Apriesmes fut l'ouvraige achevé loing temps après; car les comptes [furent] acceptés au Conseil du 18 d'apvril LXVI.'

[205] ADN B17698 (alphabetical order).

[206] What follows is drawn from the many, detailed descriptions of the repairs or improvements effected in Chastelain's residence between 1457 and 1474: ibid. B9881, fo. 29; B9882, fos 38v, 40v, 41, 47, 49v, 51; B9883, fos 26v, 32, 36v, 37; B9884, fos 33, 39v; B9885, fos 29v, 32; B9886, fos 31, 34; B9887, fos 32r–v; B9889, fo. 42; B9890, fos 36r–v, 37; B9891, fo. 37v; B9893, fos 42v, 43v, 46r–v; B9894, fos 44v, 45v–6v, 47v, 49v–50, 50v–1; B9895, fo. 49; B9897, fo. 53v; B9898, fos 46v, 49v.

[207] For the comet scene see v, 432–4.

[208] ADN B17698: 'De vostre grace resservez moy ce qui vous en samble bon et au surplus commandez sur George. A ce matin XIe juillet en mon contoir.'

one level, it certainly did not mean that he was now cut off from that flow of news which was necessary for his work. The town itself, then comparatively large and commercially vibrant, was well connected by road and river to all the major urban centres of the Low Countries.[209] Royal France lay less than two days' ride to the south; the royal enclave of Tournai, separated from Valenciennes by the forest of St Amand, was closer still.[210] Any notion of a geographical boundary between royal France and the Valois Burgundian dominions may have been particularly difficult to formulate here. The Salle-le-Comte was an important administrative centre for local ducal government, and as such it was a hive of activity where news may have passed even more quickly than through the town itself.[211] It was regularly used as a base by the most senior comital officers or those who acted on their behalf, notably the *grand-bailli* of Hainaut and the *prévôt-le-comte*. Antoine Rolin and Jean de Rubempré held the first of these offices during Chastelain's time at Valenciennes, as did two other servants who were equally important in their own right but who were better known to him: Jean de Croy and his son Philippe, the chronicler's personal friend.[212] Among the *prévôts-le-comte* at Valenciennes were Simon de Lalaing and Pierre de Hennin, lord of Boussu.[213] The latter, at least, was an associate of Chastelain's, as was another office holder based at Valenciennes, Jacques de Harchies, *bailli des bois* of Hainaut.[214]

If Chastelain was well placed to follow events from Valenciennes, there is no escaping the fact that he knew the court less well in these later years of his life. On several earlier occasions the core of the ducal entourage had descended upon the Salle-le-Comte with its train of household officers, the staff of the

---

[209] G. Sivéry, 'Commerce et marchands à Valenciennes à la fin du moyen âge', in *Valenciennes et les anciens Pays-Bas*, Valenciennes 1976, 71–81; M. Sommé, 'Les déplacements d'Isabelle de Portugal et la circulation dans les Pays-Bas bourguignons au milieu du XVe siècle', *RN* lii (1970), 183–97.
[210] Which may well explain Chastelain's particular knowledge of developments at Tournai, the nearest royal town: iii, 300; Delclos, 226, 263–71; iv, 172, 192–3, 358–9, 478–80; v, 150, 491. For a valuable guide to the matter of boundaries raised in the next sentence see C. Gauvard, 'L'opinion publique aux confins des états et des principautés au début du XVe siècle', in *Les principautés au moyen âge: actes du Ive congrès de la Société des historiens médiévistes de l'enseignement supérieur public*, Bordeaux 1973, 127–59 at pp. 128–32. I am grateful to Professor Gauvard for sending me a copy of her article.
[211] With regard to information which could be gleaned from the town, it is interesting to note that Chastelain was aware of the records of the *prévôt* of the city and the ways in which they were used: iii, 41. On the office see L. Cellier, 'Les prévôts de Valenciennes', *Mémoires historiques sur l'arrondissement de Valenciennes* iv (1876), 129–347.
[212] G.-H. Gondry, *Mémoire historique sur les grands baillis de Hainaut*, Mons 1888, 99–111.
[213] See, for example, ADN B9889, fo. 28v; B9891, fo. 28, and the other registers under the rubric relating to the ducal officers. It could only have been from Boussu that Chastelain garnered certain pieces of information: iv, 413–14. Elsewhere he is well informed on his activities: iv, 268, 351; v, 319–20, 331–4.
[214] Chastelain seems to have had information from Harchies on two matters: iii, 367; v, 402–3. The first of these references mentions his office at Valenciennes.

chapel and the chancery.[215] The count of Charolais had also been a regular visitor to Valenciennes.[216] By the time Chastelain had established himself in the mid 1460s, however, the town rarely figured on the court's itinerary. Charles visited it only three times as duke, twice for a night and once for little more than two weeks.[217] Herein, no doubt, lies the most significant aspect of Chastelain's withdrawal to Valenciennes. It was not so much that the chronicler was distanced from the Burgundian court in his old age. (Although this he certainly was, not just physically, but mentally – a series of vituperative attacks on court life are proof enough of his disaffiliation from the mores of the elite.)[218] More specifically, he was distanced from the court of Charles the Bold. The new duke's ways, as we shall see at a later stage, were not always to his liking. Chastelain, who died on or shortly before 13 February 1475, remained to the last a creature of Philip the Good.[219]

The previous chapter ended with a problem. The official chronicler's concentration upon a wider political culture connecting both Valois France and Valois Burgundy could not easily be explained by that 'formative' period he was once thought to have spent in France. Did it then stem from his twenty-eight years in Burgundian service, as Huizinga instinctively believed but did not explain? This chapter has responded to that question in the affirmative, at least so far as Chastelain's years under Philip the Good are concerned. Because of his need to assimilate and advance within an elite upon which he depended for his 'recongnoissance et provision' (vii, 227), Chastelain was more sensitive than most to its fundamental characteristics. The centre he found was rather more fluid than some commentators, with their concern for the emergence of a Burgundian state distinct from France, are inclined to believe. Royal and ducal interests could certainly collide, sometimes with ominous repercussions as Chastelain knew. Below the surface of events, however, the political culture of the Valois Burgundian elite did not abut on or exclude that of the French: in the experience of the chronicler and many of his friends, the two intermingled. The Chronicle was the product of such underlying mentalities. To this set of perceptions, grounded in personal interests, family traditions or accepted legal realities, a second may now be added: not the political culture of the Burgundian court, but its historical counterpart.

---

[215] L. Devillers, 'Les séjours des ducs de Bourgogne en Hainaut, 1427–1482', BCRH vi (1879), 323–468 at pp. 356–60
[216] Itinéraires, 430, 437, 448, 452, 457, 458.
[217] H. Vander Linden, Itinéraires de Charles, duc de Bourgogne, Marguerite d'York et Marie de Bourgogne, Brussels 1936, 7, 51; Devillers, 'Les séjours', 368.
[218] v, 250–1, 276, 287, 367–8, 418.
[219] Before his death Chastelain thought to pave his way in the next life. According to a later historian of Valenciennes he founded 'a leglize de n(ost)re dame de la salle en vallenciennes (ou il gisi) la solemnite de St George': BM Valenciennes, MS 670–1, fo. 287.

3

The Chronicler and Indiciaire

Although Chastelain took with him into his *comptoir* at Valenciennes his formative and continuing experiences of the Burgundian elite, the Chronicle was clearly not influenced by these factors alone. Three others form the subject matter of the present chapter. They have more to do with Burgundian historical culture than its closely-related political counterpart.

The impetus behind official history came, not from the writer himself, but from his patron, Philip the Good.[1] At the outset, therefore, some attempt must be made to elucidate the circumstances in which it was thought desirable or even necessary to appoint an official chronicler, for it was in response to this precise historical moment that the nature of his task was defined. While a sense of the past in any community is in part a function of contemporary circumstances, it is also moulded by existing historiographical traditions. It follows that Chastelain's Chronicle should be considered in a second context, namely the nature and development of historical culture at the Burgundian court. Finally, Chastelain was naturally conscious as he composed his text that he was contributing to that historical culture himself. An official historian did not merely commune with himself or posterity. Chastelain's perception of his public, its identity and interests, clearly had a bearing upon the work he was to produce.

The Chronicle was an official history in the most precise sense of the term: not only was it commissioned and sanctioned by a higher authority, the writing of it was the principal justification of the author's remunerated office.[2] We might therefore expect that the historical moment which inspired the creation of the post had particular if not exclusive relevance to the Burgundian political community; that the historical culture from which it sprang had evolved primarily in that milieu; and that the work was intended to address and

---

[1] The decision to appoint an official chronicler differed from less formal examples of ducal patronage: it was taken at the highest possible level, by the duke in his council. Comparisons with the patronage afforded to other writers is discussed more fully below. For art patronage, cf. Smith, 'The artistic patronage', 152, 249, 336; L. Campbell, 'The art market in the southern Netherlands in the fifteenth century', *Burlington Magazine* cxviii (1976), 188–98.
[2] J. Krynen has argued that any writer drawn to a court was 'official' in the sense that s/he wrote for a patron: *Idéal du prince et pouvoir royal en France à la fin du moyen âge*, Paris 1981, 197. This does not help us distinguish between different individuals in a milieu which, after all, attracted the lion's share of authors writing in the vernacular. More apposite is Antonia Gransden's view that 'an official history can be defined as one commissioned by a person exercising authority to represent the point of view of his office': 'Propaganda in English medieval historiography', *JMH* i (1975), 363–81 at p. 363.

contribute to this community's emerging sense of its own past. For some at least, Philip the Good's reign witnessed the evolution of a specifically Burgundian sense of the past along the lines suggested – or dictated? – by the apparent political ambitions of the duke and those around him. Hence, for example, the view that

> la littérature de Bourgogne, considérée dans ses grandes lignes, dessine une courbe analogue à celle de la politique. Plus elle progresse, plus elle se donne une physionomie spéciale. De française et parisienne qu'elle est à ses débuts, elle tend à devenir régionale et particulariste. Commencée par les Christine de Pisan et les Eustache Deschamps qui sont de France, elle s'achève dans l'oeuvre des Olivier de La Marche et des Georges Chastellain qui sont de Belgique.[3]

The line connecting Doutrepont to Pirenne, suggested in the introduction to this study, is clear. Just as there is good reason to question such determinism in matters of Burgundian political culture, so too should we be wary of applying comparable views to its historical pendant.

The historical moment

If the impulse to write or commission history came at times from the most banal or personal of circumstances, it also arose from great events – the First Crusade, for example, or the Italian Wars – which instilled in contemporaries a sense of historical moment and the desire to have the latter enshrined in writing.[4] In the early sixteenth century the Venetian authorities appointed Andrea Navagero as their official historian because, in their opinion, recent years had witnessed greater accomplishments than at any time since the city's foundation.[5] Charles VII made Jean Chartier the first ever remunerated 'chroniqueur du roy' on 18 November 1437, just six days after his solemn entry into Paris which had been recovered from the English in the previous year.[6] In one fell swoop the king sought to erase the memory of the dual monarchy, just as he was seeking to untangle its complex legacy of mixed loyalties and divided interests in the political sphere.[7] There is little doubt that the creation of

---

[3] Doutrepont, *Littérature*, 511.
[4] B. Lacroix, *L'historien au moyen âge*, Montreal–Paris 1971, 27 n. 37; M. A. Fitzsimons and others (eds), *The development of historiography*, Harrisburg 1954, 43; E. Cochrane, *Historians and historiography in the Italian Renaissance*, Chicago 1981, 163–71.
[5] F. Gilbert, 'Biondo, Sabellico and the beginnings of Venetian official historiography', in J. G. Rowe and W. H. Stockdale (eds), *Florilegium Historiale: essays presented to Wallace K. Ferguson*, Toronto 1971, 275–93 at p. 286.
[6] S. M. Farley, 'French historiography in the later Middle Ages, with special reference to the *Grandes chroniques de France*', unpubl. Ph.D. diss. Edinburgh 1969, 109; Beaucourt, *Histoire*, iii. 51.
[7] A. Bossuat, 'Le rétablissement de la paix sociale sous le règne de Charles VII', MA lx (1954), 137–62, trans. in P. S. Lewis (ed.), *The recovery of France in the fifteenth century*, London 1971, 60–82.

Chastelain's official post arose from a sense of historical moment. The prologue to the Chronicle is imbued with a strong sense of eventful times. In the following pages an attempt will be made to define the nature of the historical developments which inspired Philip the Good and his counsellors to establish, at this point, that 'direct connection between action and the recording of action' which is a 'necessity of government'.[8]

In this respect it may be no coincidence that the official post emerged in a period considered by some historians to have been the pinnacle of Burgundian achievement. For Pirenne, 1454 represented 'le point culminant' of the reign of Philip the Good.[9] Vaughan echoed the point: in the years 1454–5, 'Philip was perhaps at the height of his power and prestige'.[10] Yvon Lacaze went further: '1454–5 marquent – nous n'hésitons pas à l'affirmer – l'apogée de la dynastie'; the success of ducal policies in these years 'le prouve surabondamment'.[11] It might be argued that Philip the Good and his advisers consciously decided to glorify the Burgundian achievement by employing an official historian.

Such an argument could be based on a number of grounds. In the first instance, the core of the ducal dominions, the centre-piece of any Burgundian sense of achievement, had been in place for over two decades. Philip's victory over Ghent in 1453, achieved with the concerted deployment of the resources and manpower of many of his lands, neutered the last remaining centre of urban revolt against his rule.[12] Peace, meanwhile, had brought prosperity under the duke; Commynes's later description of Philip's lands as 'terres de promission', and this in a period marked by economic contraction, may well have held some truth.[13] In particular, economic well-being was enhanced in the years that concern us by two developments: the success of Philip's commercial policies towards England, ensuring a greatly increased monetary supply in his dominions which peaked in 1455; and the return of the Hanseatic *kontor* to Bruges, thereby re-establishing mercantile relations disrupted in 1451.[14] The popularity of the duke in his own lands reached a high point in 1454 through a series of entries into major cities.[15]

These indices of success at home were matched by achievement on the wider European stage. The territorial integrity of Philip's dominions was

---

[8] D. Hay, 'The Historiographers Royal in England and Scotland', *Scottish Historical Review* xxx–xxxi (1951–2), 15–30 at p. 15.
[9] Pirenne, *Histoire de Belgique* ii. 256.
[10] Vaughan, *PTG*, 334.
[11] Y. Lacaze, 'Philippe le Bon et les terres d'Empire', AB xxxvi (1964), 81–121 at p. 119.
[12] I exclude the nominally independent bishopric of Liège from this observation.
[13] R. Van Uytven, 'La Flandre et le Brabant, "terres de promission" sous les ducs de Bourgogne?', RN xliii (1961), 281–317. See also ch. 6 below.
[14] J. H. A. Munro, *Wool, cloth and gold*, Brussels-Toronto 1972, 129, 150–1; Y. Lacaze, 'Contribution à l'histoire économique et politique des pays de "par-deça"', MA lxxv (1969), 95–119, 291–320.
[15] Cf. iii, 32–5, and du Clercq, *Mémoires*, xiii. 173.

bolstered in 1454–5 by negotiations in the Empire over the status of Luxembourg, just as Burgundian diplomacy was offering the prospect of consolidating and expanding ducal influence in the key bishoprics of Liège and Utrecht and deeper into the Rhineland.[16] The duke's crusading ambitions and policies enabled him to gain practical advantage and to occupy the moral high ground in Christendom. Here, his visit to Germany in 1454 to discuss the matter at Regensburg enhanced his status as the leading prince of the Empire. His crusading zeal also made him a favoured son of the papacy.[17] 1454–5 was indeed a period of achievement. The central characteristic of its many components is an impression of specifically Burgundian glory, quite independent of, indeed partly at the expense of, French royal or imperial prestige. For Philip the Good and his counsellors, as for the authorities of Venice looking back on the accomplishments of their city, it may have seemed that an historical moment was upon them.

Of course, the apogee of Philip's reign is appreciable with the benefit of hindsight. The modern historian is aware of the disruptions of the second half of the decade when internecine strife at court and worsening relations with France would put a very different complexion on the possibilities of Burgundian development. This aside, it is equally true that the *Zeitgeist* stemming from any Burgundian sense of achievement may well have been obscured for contemporaries by the concatenation of two epochal events in 1453: the fall of Constantinople, news of which probably reached the Burgundian court in July or August, and the recapture of Bordeaux by the French in October.[18] These great watersheds were the only specific developments in the immediate past which Chastelain mentioned in his prologue. The French, he writes, were delivered

> hors de la main de Pharaon et de la captivité en Babilonne, par ceux mesmes qui longuement discors ensemble, parens prochains, mus de charité, se sont rejoints en amour sous divine cremeur: Charles roy de France, septiesme de ce nom, et Philippe duc de Bourgongne, contemporains et en égalité d'âge, régnans glorieusement tous deux en ce royaume et dehors, à la dure confusion de leurs ennemis et à la grant joye et félicité de leurs subjets. (i, 9)

Further on, reiterating the classic themes of crusade *excitatoria*, he writes of developments in the East:

> Et dernièrement . . . s'est eslevé en mes jours l'ennemy cruel de Dieu, le grand Turc, un nouveau Mahomet, violeur du crucifix et de son Eglise, despiteur de sa loy, prince de l'armée de Satan, lequel levant sa corne d'orgueil, par

---

[16] Lacaze, 'La diplomatie bourguignonne', 81.
[17] See, for example, Calixtus III's extravagant praise of Philip in this regard in 1455: A. G. Jongkees, *Staat en kerk in Holland en Zeeland onder de Bourgondische hertogen, 1425–1477*, Groningen 1942, 37.
[18] Beaucourt, *Histoire*, v. 283–5; H. Müller, *Kreuzzugspläne und Kreuzzugspolitik des Herzogs Philipp des Guten von Burgund*, Göttingen 1993, 59–93.

présomption de sa terrienne puissance en quoy se confie, a osté aux chrestiens leur bastille de Constantinople et soumise à sa dition en confuse et douloureuse attente cy-après. (i, 11)

These events had a pan-European or French significance; neither was particularist in any exclusively Burgundian sense, even if the official chronicler sought to link Philip the Good to both.

But the two events were not simply connected by their contemporaneity. Peace within Christendom was a precondition of crusade. The fall of Bordeaux and Constantinople heightened, respectively, the prospect of the former and the need for the latter. The link between the recovery of French fortunes and the launching of a crusade against the Turks had been made as early as 1446 by Charles VII himself, who informed the future Constantine XI of his desire to follow in the footsteps of his ancestors once the English had been expelled.[19] Similar thoughts were entertained at the Burgundian court. Chastelain addressed Charles in his *Throsne azuré* as the

> Bras renforchié de grâce espéciale
> Pour envaïr mescréance paienne. (vi, 133)

Not much later, in an embassy to the king in the summer of 1451, Jean Germain, the chancellor of the Golden Fleece, suggested – with reference to a shared historical culture – that the victorious monarch, like a new David or Charlemagne, could now apply himself with his loyal Burgundian duke to the rescue of the Church.[20] The connection was later echoed in an anecdote told to Jean de Haubourdin by none other than Charles VII's widow, Marie d'Anjou. According to this story, a holy man had predicted that the king, 'par oeuvre miraculeuse', could achieve the 'glorieuse recouvrance' of the kingdom on condition that he later fulfil his Christian duties against the Turk.[21] The momentous events of 1453 were thus connected in the minds of contemporaries. In what follows it will be argued that the historical moment which inspired the creation of Chastelain's post was not a self-referential sense of the achievement of the Burgundian state, but a point in time when Franco-Burgundian relations seemed to offer an opportunity to carry out Christ's work in the East.

To make this case we must first establish the seriousness with which Philip the Good took his crusading plans and the significance of Chastelain's appointment in relation to them. As many have pointed out, a solicitous attitude towards the crusade could certainly give the duke a means of rivalling the prestige of greater princes. It might even have given rise to thoughts of an

---

[19] Beaucourt, *Histoire*, v. 190–1.
[20] C. Schefer, 'Le discours du voyage d'oultremer au très victorieux roi Charles VII, prononcé en 1452 [sic] par Jean Germain, évêque de Chalon', *Revue de l'Orient latin* iii (1895), 302–42. Germain had already addressed crusading issues in his *Débat du Chrétien et du Sarrazin*: F. Berriot, 'Images de l'Islam dans le *Débat* manuscrit de Jean Germain (1450)', *Réforme, humanisme et renaissance* xiii (1981), 1–14.
[21] iv, 368–70.

untouchably prestigious crown: that of the duke's ancestor, Baldwin IX of Flanders, Latin emperor of Constantinople, or that of Jerusalem itself.[22] If the spiritual and the political did combine in such a heady mix in Philip's case, we cannot judge his commitment unfavourably on the strength of any worldly ambitions he – like so many prospective crusading princes before him – might have entertained.[23] After the promulgation of Nicholas V's crusading bull on 30 September 1453, he quickly made clear his crusading intentions by dispatching a small naval force to the pope (November 1453) and by securing the support of his followers at that great court occasion, the Vows of the Pheasant (Lille, February 1454).[24] Although the departure, planned for 1455, had to be postponed to 1 March 1456, preparations continued apace.[25] Abroad, Philip's diplomatic activity was above all geared to the need of the departing crusader to resolve outstanding disputes. At home, the careful deployment of ducal propaganda served to remind Philip's subjects of his intentions, while his administration concerned itself with logistical matters and the raising of manpower and finance.[26] The extent of these preparations left few untouched by the duke's great purpose in 1454–5, least of all those who enjoyed his artistic or literary patronage and whose talents were mobilised to assist in its promotion. Court artists were heavily employed in the Feast of the Pheasant and other crusade preparations.[27] In this atmosphere the appointment of an official

---

[22] Febvre, 'Les ducs Valois'; J. C. Kervyn de Lettenhove, *Histoire de Flandre*, Brussels 1847–50, v. 47.

[23] What follows is further borne out by Richard's short but powerful analysis of the importance of the crusade to Philip, emphasising – with the insight of an historian well-acquainted with crusader mentalities – that the duke's initiative was not the extravagant propaganda ploy it is often made out to be: J. Richard, 'La croisade bourguignonne dans la politique européenne', PCEEBM x (1968), 41–4.

[24] For the papal bull, *Etsi ecclesia Christi*, see Housley, *The later crusades*, 100–1. For the naval force of four galleys see Jean de Wavrin, *Recueil des croniques et anchiennes histoires de la Grant Bretaigne*, ed. W. Hardy, London 1864–91, v. 240. On the Feast of the Pheasant see A. Grunzweig, 'Philippe le Bon et Constantinople', *Byzantion* xxiv (1954), 47–61 at pp. 54–5.

[25] Y. Lacaze, 'Politique "méditerranéenne" et projets de croisade chez Philippe le Bon', AB xli (1969), 5–42, 81–132; C. Marinesco, 'Philippe le Bon, duc de Bourgogne, et la croisade, i. 1419–1453', *Actes du VIe congrès international des études byzantines*, Paris 1950, 149–68, and 'Philippe le Bon, duc de Bourgogne, et la croisade, ii. 1453–1467', *Bulletin des études portugaises* ns xiii (1949), 3–28.

[26] Propaganda included the display of Turkish prisoners and Greek refugees throughout 1455: ADN B2020, fos 338v–9, 346v, 355v. Philip commissioned immensely detailed reports such as that published in J. Finot, 'Projet d'expédition contre les Turcs préparé par les conseillers du duc de Bourgogne Philippe le Bon', *Mémoires de la Société des sciences de Lille* xxi (1895), 161–206. War materials were bought up and Burgundian supporters were reminded of their vows: ADN B2020, fos 85v, 210, 196, 212, 244v–5, 372v. Finance in the form of *aides* was raised throughout the duke's territories: ibid. fos 205v–6, 216, 221; Plancher, *Histoire*, iv. 286.

[27] Lafortune-Martel, *Fête noble en Bourgogne*, 111ff.; G. Doutrepont, 'À la cour de Bourgogne', *Revue générale* (1899), 787–806; (1900), 99–118; P. Perdrizet, 'Jean Miélot, l'un des traducteurs de Philippe le Bon', *Revue d'histoire littéraire de la France* xiv (1907), 472–82 at p. 476.

chronicler was a natural and perhaps even necessary step. Chastelain's brief for the Chronicle from the duke and his council was to recount notable deeds worthy of memory which had happened, which were happening and which could come to pass in the future. In June 1455, the most important event in the last two categories was undoubtedly the crusade.

Relations with France were central to the achievement of this aim. Lacaze has argued that practical difficulties ruled out any real co-operation between duke and king, and that this problem, combined with imperial inertia, led Philip to evolve an independent policy centred on relations with Mediterranean powers to further his crusading aims.[28] Without disputing the tenor of this argument, we should not underplay the fact that the French king had a pivotal role to play in the duke's ambitions.

Contemporary perceptions were important here. These were inevitably shaped in part by the fact that the royal and ducal houses partook of a common crusading tradition which was preserved in the history books. Baldwin IX may have been a peculiarly Flemish crusading hero, but among the non-fictional crusading characters associated with the court there were other figures whose exploits pointed to a linked crusading past.[29] Louis IX was a more significant figure in the ducal library than the Flemish count.[30] Indeed, in Roger van der Weyden's Beaune altarpiece of the Last Judgement, Philip the Good is said to be represented among the elect in the garb of the saintly crusader king himself.[31] This representation seems natural when we recall, as Jean Miélot reminded his Burgundian court audience in 1455, that the French were traditionally the true champions of the faith.[32] When, in the following year, the dauphin sought to justify his flight to Burgundy to his father, he could find no more plausible justification than his expressed intention to participate in Philip's crusade.[33] Perhaps most importantly, the linked crusading tradition was conserved in the memory of John the Fearless's leadership, under a royal

---

[28] Lacaze, 'Politique "méditerranéenne" ', passim.
[29] Philip II and Louis IX were accompanied to the East by Burgundian dukes, Hugh III and Hugh IV respectively. The Barons' Crusade of 1239 to 1241 saw Hugh IV leave France under a royal banner: J. Riley-Smith, *The crusades*, London 1987, 116; J. Richard, *St Louis*, ed. S. D. Lloyd, trans. J. Birrell, Cambridge 1992, 91–3, 108.
[30] Cf. Doutrepont, *Littérature*, 264; G. Dogaer, 'Handschriften over de kruistochten in de librije der hertogen van Bourgondië', *Spiegel Historiael* ii (1967), 457–65 at p. 459.
[31] Smith, 'The artistic patronage', 35, 245; N. Veronée-Verhaegen, *Les primitifs flamands. Corpus de la peinture des anciens Pays-Bas méridionaux au XVe siècle, XIII: L'Hôtel-Dieu de Beaune*, Brussels 1973, pl. xxix and text. I am grateful to Dr Lorne Campbell for his comments on the work.
[32] In his translation of a *Directorium ad passagium faciendum* (1332), rendered as an *Advis directif pour faire le voyage d'oultremer*: A. G. Heron, '*Il fault faire guerre pour paix avoir*: crusading propaganda at the court of Duke Philippe le Bon of Burgundy', unpubl. Ph.D. diss. Cambridge 1992, 86.
[33] *Lettres de Louis XI, roi de France*, ed. J. Vaesen and E. Charavay, Paris 1883–1909, i. 77. The previous year, Louis had (more honestly?) expressed his reservations on the subject of Philip's plans: *Dispatches with related documents of Milanese ambassadors in France and Burgundy, 1450–1483*, ed. P. M. Kendall and V. Ilardi, Athens, Oh. 1970–1, i. 156.

banner, of the Franco-Burgundian contingent on the Nicopolis expedition. The memory was so vital in Philip's mind that he seems to have conflated his father's captor with the 'Grand Turc' of his own day.[34]

Connected to these perceptions were certain hard realities which made the king a central figure in Philip's plans. The duke could not hope to fulfil his vows without the leave or at least the blessing of his royal overlord. Relations with rulers in other lands might further the attainment of the crusading goal, but without royal approval Philip could not even guarantee his own commitment. The ducal crusader had to be sure of the security of his lands, family and interests during his absence. He had to raise men and money for his venture from the territories he held of the king. Franco-Burgundian relations in the immediate wake of the fall of Constantinople and the French reconquest were dictated by these needs which, in turn, contextualise the official chronicler's appointment.

Upon receiving news of the papal bull, Philip placed his plans to take the cross before the king.[35] Within a few weeks of the favourable response he had organised and held the Feast of the Pheasant. It is significant that the opening remarks of the crusade vow he took on that occasion envisaged its fulfilment within a crusading army led by the king in person, or by a royal deputy, princely or otherwise. Only if neither proved possible would Philip leave for the East in the company of other western princes, 'pourveu que ce soit du bon plésir et congié de mondit seigneur le Roy'.[36] Philip's subsequent announcement to Charles that he would be attending the crusading congress of Regensburg in April 1454, at the request of Frederick III, was in keeping with the king's stated policy.[37] Charles himself had been invited to send a deputation, and he had declared that he would not contemplate going on crusade unless the Germans did likewise.[38] Before setting out, however, Philip found it expedient to reaffirm his French princely credentials in March by preparing the ground for the marriage of the count of Charolais to Isabelle de Bourbon.[39] According to Chastelain he thereby quashed any thoughts Charles and his mother might have been harbouring for the arrangement, in Philip's absence in the East, of

---

[34] Grunzweig, 'Philippe le Bon', 54–5. Vaughan argues that Philip the Bold took care to stress the 'Burgundian character' of the Nicopolis expedition, but also notes that John took his leave of the king at Paris and visited St Denis, that most royal of holy places, before moving on to Dijon: *Philip the Bold*, 68.

[35] Dec. 1453: Lacaze, 'Politique "méditerrannéenne" ', 91; Beaucourt, *Histoire*, v. 394.

[36] A contemporary copy of Philip's vow is in ADN B854, no. 15.907 (published in Finot, 'Projet d'expédition', 179–80). It was only later, when the king's lukewarm attitude became fully apparent, that Philip offered to serve under the emperor or an imperial delegate: A. G. Jongkees, 'Pie II et Philipe le Bon, deux protagonistes de l'union chrétienne', *PCEEBM* xx (1980), 103–15, revised and annotated in his *Burgundica et varia*, 172–90 (see the latter version, p. 182).

[37] J. D. Hintzen, *De kruistochtplannen van Philips den Goede*, Rotterdam 1918, 87–8.

[38] Beaucourt, *Histoire*, v. 395.

[39] d'Escouchy, *Chronique*, ii. 241–2.

an English alliance.⁴⁰ This the duke could scarcely countenance. Henry VI reportedly described him around this time as 'the man in the world whom he would most willingly fight'.⁴¹ The treaty of Arras still had a bitter aftertaste. If Philip did not have direct knowledge of these alleged remarks, he none the less felt it necessary in 1454 to strengthen his defences against a possible English attack, just as Charles VII was then doing.⁴² The crusade was not the only incentive Philip had to maintain good relations with the king.

This community of interests received further expression at the festivities organised by the duke at Nevers in September 1454 to settle the details of his son's marriage. This, as we have seen, was the occasion for the staging of Chastelain's *Complainte d'Hector*.⁴³ A brief analysis of its central message reveals that the author himself was in tune with the thrust of ducal policy which would later lead to his appointment.

The *mystère* dramatised a reconciliation. Following the prologue, the opening scene finds Alexander before the tombs of Hector and Achilles, mortal enemies in life, musing on their past glories. He accords Achilles the greater honour, since it was he who had overcome Hector. Hector himself then appears on stage to chastise Alexander for this judgement: his death had been procured

> Vilainement par derrière enferrée
> Par main encor de royaulté vestue. (vi, 177)

Alexander seeks to reason with Hector, but Hector remains reticent:

> Vint Achiles remply de félonnie
> Et me férit par derrière le dos,
> Dont mort souffris et lui honteux deslos.
> Mais si cela se peut nommer victoire,
> C'est donc grand los que de vil oeuvre voire. (vi, 185)

Failing to placate Hector, Alexander invites Achilles to justify his crime, advising him that in doing so 'tu mettras fin éternelle à un débat jà trop longuement duré entre vous deux' (vi, 194). Achilles in turn expresses regret at the killing of Hector, which has become a slight on his honour. He explains

---

⁴⁰ iii, 19–29. Philip also put paid to earlier plans to contract a marriage for Charles in the Empire: W. Lippert, 'La Bourgogne et la Saxe, 1451-4', *Mémoires de la Société Éduenne* ns xxv (1897), 1–44. On the Bourbon marriage alliance see Leguai, *Les ducs de Bourbon*, 176. Armstrong emphasises that in this, the second marriage contracted for Charles, the duke again chose a French princess to be the bride of his sole heir. The decision is revealing of Philip's dynastic objectives: 'La politique matrimoniale des ducs de Bourgogne de la maison de Valois', AB xl (1968), 5–58, 89–139, repr. in his *England, France and Burgundy*, 237–342 (see the latter version, p. 246).
⁴¹ Vale, *Charles VII*, 161 and n. 4.
⁴² Beaucourt notes Charles VII's defensive precautions at this time, but not those which were taken by Philip the Good: *Histoire*, v. 405–6; cf. ADN B2017, fos 158v, 160v, 161, 163v, 164, 165; B2020, fos 213v, 215v–16.
⁴³ See ch. 2 above.

his actions as revenge for Hector's murder of 'Patroclus, mon très-aimé cousin, et mon très-cher et cordial et très-cher parent' (vi, 197). Since Hector himself admits that murder at an earlier stage in the work, the forgiveness Achilles seeks is duly given and honour is restored.

Beneath the allegory and the poetic licence, the play communicates and commemorates many of Philip's aspirations at this precise time. Alexander, one of the Nine Worthies, was regarded as the conqueror of Greece, Tyre, Jerusalem and the whole of the East.[44] Such was his popularity in contemporary chivalric literature that elements of his adventures found their way into other texts, notably the *Voeux du Paon* which had served as an inspiration for Philip the Good's Feast of the Pheasant earlier that year. Philip, on the eve of his crusade, was clearly being equated with Alexander the Great.[45] This character advocates and achieves the reconciliation of Hector and Achilles. Hector, the murderer of Patroclus, was himself 'occis sur aguet' (vi, 195). Here was a thinly disguised John the Fearless, guilty of the death of Louis d'Orléans, and murdered in turn at Montereau in 1419. The identity of Achilles, who exacted revenge for his 'cher parent et amy' Patroclus, would thus have been clear to the audience: Charles VII, tainted in Burgundian eyes by his involvement at Montereau. Had Charles observed the treaty of Arras to the letter, this 35-year-old crime might have faded more from men's thoughts. In the matter of John's assassins, however, he had not done so. As late as 1448 Philip the Good was still raising the grievance.[46] By presenting Alexander as the agent of reconciliation between Hector and Achilles, the play formulated the generous view that bygones could now be bygones.[47] The marriage which eventually ensued from the negotiations at Nevers, consummated on 30 October 1454, confirmed the reconciliatory thrust of a policy geared towards stable relations within the kingdom – stable relations which were then of vital importance to the prospective crusader.[48]

From this time until Chastelain's official appointment, the duke and his leading advisers were careful to build upon the prevailing climate of Franco-

---

[44] P. Meyer, *Alexandre le Grand dans la littérature française du moyen âge*, Paris 1886, ii. 133–210, 267–8.

[45] In a forged letter from Mehmed II to Philip the Good thought to have been written in the following year, the 'Grand Turc' himself claimed to be the 'True heir to King Alexander and Hector of Troy' and promised that Philip's army would meet the same fate as his father's: Vanderjagt, *Qui sa vertu anoblist*, 24–5; Vaughan, PTG, 366–7.

[46] A. Mirot, 'Charles VII et ses conseillers assassins présumés de Jean sans Peur', AB xiv (1942), 197–210 at pp. 206–8.

[47] As we shall see in ch. 5 below, Chastelain was later prepared to castigate the king in his Chronicle for the murder of John the Fearless. The latter was not produced, like the *Complainte*, for a specific occasion.

[48] Another reading of this text, while identifying the main characters in the way I propose, suggests an alternative message. It strikes me that this reading misunderstands the context in which the work was written: not in a period of 'guerre froide' between Philip the Good and Charles VII, but in fact in a period of *entente*: G. Collard, 'Georges Chastellain (1415–1475)', unpubl. mém. de licence, Liège 1978, 77–84.

Burgundian *entente*. In December 1454 Simon de Lalaing was sent to Charles VII to inform the king of developments at Regensburg.[49] The Burgundian counsellor was to seek royal approval for the raising of money and men within the lands which the duke held of the crown, and to request that other royal subjects might join Philip if they so wished in taking the cross. Lalaing was also instructed to offer Charles the protection of Philip's dominions and the safekeeping of his son while he was in the East. By seeking this level of consensus in his preparations for the crusade, Philip was prepared to make concessions which would have compromised a more independent ruler – indeed, the type of independent ruler he is so often thought to have been. It was now becoming clear that Charles was too preoccupied with the 'affaires du royaume' to take the cross himself, a point he expressed with apparent regret to the Burgundian knights Jean de Croy and the bastard of St Pol when they visited him informally early in 1455.[50] This left Philip free to follow in his father's footsteps as the leader of a Franco-Burgundian crusade. After further negotiations at La Charité (February 1455), Charles VII gave letters of credence to Jean le Boursier on 6 March to present a formal reply to Philip's requests.[51] One day earlier, the Milanese ambassador Raimondo de Marliano wrote to his master that 'lo Re mostra havere in amore Monsegnore de Burgogna, e para essere bona intelligentia fra loro'.[52] This was confirmed when Boursier reached Bruges at the end of April. Despite certain reservations, he announced that Charles would accord many of Philip's requests. Chastelain's account of the embassy conveys a considerable sense of optimism at this stage in Franco-Burgundian relations, a sentiment apparently shared by Philip's chancellor Nicolas Rolin.[53] In a letter arriving at the end of May, the latter described his master as being 'tant content que plus ne pourroit' at the position the king was taking. Rolin was himself dispatched by Philip in the company of Antoine de Croy to the French court at the end of May. There they were welcomed by Charles d'Orléans, who had witnessed for himself the sentiments which Chastelain had dramatised in his *Complainte d'Hector*.[54] According to Mathieu d'Escouchy, one of their duties was to convey a request from Philip that he might be accorded the use of the French royal banner for his crusade. This was symptomatic of the extent to which the crusade and Franco-Burgundian relations were interwoven in Philip the Good's mind at this time. Had the request been granted, Philip would have set out, not as the Great Duke of the West, but, like John the Fearless before him, as the crusading representative of the French kingdom.

---

[49] Beaucourt, *Histoire*, v. 406–7.
[50] Information conveyed by Chastelain: iii, 14–15.
[51] Plancher, *Histoire*, iv, pp. ccxvii–ccxix.
[52] *Dispatches*, i. 163.
[53] iii, 36–7; R. Berger, *Nikolas Rolin*, Fribourg 1971, 194.
[54] ADN B2020, fos 261v, 283v; d'Escouchy, *Chronique*, ii. 312–13. The king did not respond as Philip might have hoped; the point for us is that the duke had thought – or felt it necessary – to ask.

It was at precisely this juncture that the duke and his council took the decision to appoint Chastelain. The need for an official record of events arose from a sense of the historical moment in June 1455, just as the French crown and the Venetian republic were moved to make similar appointments themselves. With the benefit of hindsight, that historical moment might appear to have been one of Burgundian achievement, a high point in the development of ducal status and authority. However, for contemporaries at the Burgundian court, including Chastelain, it is apparent that any such perspective was subsumed within a much grander scheme of things. His task was formulated in response to these circumstances. Hence the definition of his subject matter which placed Christendom first, France second and Burgundy third as one of the latter's constituent parts: 'la très-ressongnable charge d'escrire tous les haulx et grans faits de la chrestienté, souverainement de ce noble royaume et de ses dépendances' (vi, 268). A curiously deferential view of history from the pen of an official Burgundian chronicler, perhaps, but one which is consonant with the historical moment that led to his appointment.

Historical culture

If the historical moment of Chastelain's nomination was not exclusively Burgundian, there are strong reasons for arguing that the historical culture from which it sprang was. The latter has long been interpreted as the product of a fledgling – in some eyes, well-developed – Burgundian state. To paraphrase Pocock, ducal historiography could thus be seen as both the record and instrument of that process whereby the political centre consciously fostered the coalescence of a wider political community around itself.[55] The earliest expression of the view may be found in Michelet's famous aphorism that 'l'histoire s'est faite bourguignonne' in the fifteenth century. Auguste Molinier based his analysis of the historiographical production of northern France and the Low Countries on this premiss.[56] A political community does indeed define itself in part by its history, or rather, to paraphrase Guenée, that which is attributed to it by its historians.[57] The latter were at least as numerous at the Valois Burgundian court as they had been in many of its lesser predecessors throughout northern France and Flanders.[58] A discussion of the historical culture to which they contributed is clearly required.

---

[55] J. G. A. Pocock, 'The limits and divisions of British history', *American Historical Review* lxxxvii (1982), 311–36 at p. 321.
[56] A. Molinier, *Les sources de l'histoire de France*, Paris 1904, iv. 186–206.
[57] For Guenée see introduction. Molinier's views on an alien historical culture imposed on the kingdom from the north may well be linked to the recent experience of the Franco-Prussian war, as D. Hay suggests in his 'History and historians in France and England during the fifteenth century', *Bulletin of the Institute of Historical Research* (hereinafter cited as *BIHR*) xxxv (1962), 111–27.
[58] M.-A. Arnould, *Historiographie de la Belgique*, Brussels 1947, 13–22; F. Quicke, *Les*

There is no doubt that the chronicler's appointment took place at a time of growing interest on the duke's part in the history of the different lands he governed. During the second half of the reign, with the territorial base of Valois Burgundy established, Philip acquired individual histories of almost all his major dominions. Despite the fact that the oldest of these, the duchy of Burgundy, was held of the French crown, Philip apparently sought an autonomous account of its past. In 1461 Hugues de Tolins was sent to the duchy to gather material for a chronicle of the deeds of the 'rois et ducs qui ont esté en Bourgogne le temps passé'.[59] Histories of the county of Flanders had been accruing in the collection for some time, and in this period Philip's continuing interest is witnessed by further commissions from one of his favourite scribes, David Aubert.[60] The history of the most important of Philip's acquisitions, Brabant, was covered in a Latin chronicle he ordered from Emond de Dynter, and a French translation was requested from Jean Wauquelin after its presentation in 1447.[61] One year earlier Wauquelin had been called upon to fill another gap when he was asked to prepare a translation of the *Annales historiae illustrium principum Hannoniae* of Jacques de Guise.[62] With Hainaut thus provided for, the only remaining major territories not to have inspired some form of historiographical treatment were the counties of Holland and Zeeland. The lacuna was addressed by an anonymous translation of Jean de Beka's *Chronicon continens res gestas episcoporum sedis Ultrajectanae et comitum Hollandiae*.[63] The French version was presented to the duke and can be dated to the years 1453–7, a period in which Philip was attempting to place his bastard son David in the episcopal see of Utrecht and to extend his influence over Friesland.

chroniqueurs des fastes bourguignons, Brussels 1943, 6–8. The origins of the phenomenon have been traced to a shared sense of identity within the aristocracy in the face of royal pressure and the emergence of rivals in the form of urban elites: G. M. Spiegel, 'Pseudo-Turpin, the crisis of the aristocracy and the beginnings of vernacular historiography in France', *JMH* xii (1982), 207–23, and *Romancing the past*, Berkeley–Oxford 1993. The nurturing of these talents is discussed in M. D. Stanger, 'Literary patronage at the medieval court of Flanders', *French Studies* xi (1957), 214–29. Further relevant comment in G. P. Small, 'Chroniqueurs et culture historique', in Nys and Salamagne, *Valenciennes aux XIVe et XVe siècles*, 271–96.

[59] G. Peignot, *Catalogue d'une partie des livres composant l'ancienne bibliothèque des ducs de Bourgogne de la dernière race*, Paris 1830, 37; Laborde, *Les ducs de Bourgogne*, i. 473. The fate of Tolins's work is unknown, but it may well be closely connected to a later text discussed in ch. 6 below.

[60] Doutrepont, *Littérature*, 419–24.

[61] Edmond de Dynter, *Chronique des ducs de Brabant*, in *Chroniques belges inédites*, ed. P. F. X. de Ram, Brussels 1854–60. For a stimulating study of the work in the context of Brabantine historiography (and in which the revised spelling of Dynter's Christian name is established) see R. Stein, *Politiek en historiografie*, Leuven 1994, esp. pp. 59–99.

[62] E. Matthieu, 'Un artiste picard à l'étranger', *Mémoires de la Société des antiquaires de Picardie* xix (1889), 333–56 at pp. 339–45.

[63] W. Noomen, *La traduction française de la Chronographia Johannis de Beka*, The Hague 1954, esp. pp. 60–5.

From this evidence a case can be made for the emergence, in the years immediately preceding Chastelain's appointment, of a dynastic Burgundian historiography which sought to situate Philip's rule over a wide variety of territories within a legitimate historical context. From this first level of historical awareness the pattern extended to a second in the form of works which provided a more integrative historical view of Burgundian rule in the present.

Philip the Bold had been the subject of near contemporary reportage in a work which he possessed, the Chronicles of Jean Froissart.[64] Philip the Good was not to enjoy this privilege until 1447, when the first major work to do so was presented to him by Enguerran de Monstrelet, *prévôt* of Cambrai.[65] Monstrelet described himself in his prologue as the continuator of Froissart, and consequently took up his account of events in 1400. Although the work was mentioned in the inventory of the ducal library as 'parlant des histoires de France', it included coverage of the major episodes of the first half of Philip the Good's reign.[66] Here, the treaties of Troyes and Arras, the foundation of the Order of the Golden Fleece, as well as Philip's acquisition of Holland, Zeeland, Hainaut, Brabant and Luxembourg were dignified as matters of historical record for the first time. Perhaps not surprisingly the work made an immediate impression upon the historical culture of the Burgundian court. The subject of an anonymous continuation from 1444 to 1467, it was employed in contemporary histories written by courtiers or ducal officers such as Jacques du Clercq (who began writing in 1448), Jean de Wavrin (1455), Jean Lefèvre de St Rémy (c. 1460) and Chastelain himself.[67] In this way the reign of Philip the Good entered into an overlapping historical tradition which stretched back from Burgundian historians through Monstrelet and on to Froissart. By the second third of the fifteenth century the contemporary deeds of the Valois dynasty, as well as the lands over which it ruled, had begun to find their own niche in works of history.

A third type of narrative extended the Burgundian sense of the past even further back: historical fiction. Prose renderings of earlier verse epics and romances were carried out for the ducal court. As part of the wide range of narratives which contemporaries could call history, they too occupied a place in Burgundian historical culture.[68] Many of these works recounted the exploits

---

[64] Philip the Good had at least four Froissart manuscripts: Barrois, *Bibliothèque*, 207–8, nos 1425–8.
[65] ADN B1991, fo. 184v; D. Boucquey, 'Enguerran de Monstrelet, historien trop longtemps oublié', *PCEEB* xxxi (1991), 113–25.
[66] Barrois, *Bibliothèque*, 123, no. 705.
[67] J. Stenghers, 'Sur trois chroniqueurs', *AB* xviii (1946), 122–30; P. Bonenfant, *Du meurtre de Montereau au traité de Troyes*, Brussels 1958, pp. vi–vii.
[68] G. Doutrepont, *Les mises en proses des épopées et des romans chevaleresques du XIVe au XVIe siècle*, Brussels 1939, 414–66; R. Morse, 'Historical fiction in fifteenth-century Burgundy', *Modern Language Review* (hereinafter cited as *MLR*) lxxv (1980), 48–64. On the breadth of genres which were considered to be historical see D. B Tyson, 'French vernacular

of literary heroes – such as Auberi le Bourguignon or Gilles de Chin – who had real or imagined links with the Valois Burgundian dynasty or the lands over which they ruled. For Yvon Lacaze, the one common strand which ran through such works was their intention to furnish the Burgundian lands with an integrated set of legendary traditions.[69] Jean Wauquelin's *Girart de Roussillon* (1447) is the clearest case in point. Wauquelin based his work upon a fourteenth-century poem and certain other texts recounting the life of the ninth-century Burgundian hero. Philip may have had good reason for identifying himself with Girart. Both were vassals of the king of France, and both clashed with their royal suzerain throughout their eventful careers. The legendary Girart was portrayed as exemplary in his dealings with the Church, and his expeditions against non-Christians had more than a ring of contemporary relevance for Philip the Good. Perhaps the most important feature of Girart's story was the fact that many of his lands were, by the fifteenth century, in the hands of Philip the Good himself. The various settings of the legend were thus familiar to a contemporary Burgundian audience, a fact which might have enabled them to project ducal rule into a distant and heroic past.[70] Hence Lacaze's belief that the ducal scribes engaged in this work were conducting a 'vaste mouvement de propagande', the principal function of which was to promote cultural and political cohesion within an heterogenous 'État bourguignon'. This set of legendary traditions, integrative in intent, may have combined with the more recent deeds of the dynasty and the history of its individual dominions to form the principal elements of an emerging, multi-layered Burgundian sense of the past.

Taken together, these themes in Burgundian historical culture compare with the 'overall tendency' which Gabrielle Spiegel has detected in the Dionysian tradition of French royal historiography: 'to assimilate past and present into a continuous stream of tradition, and to see in this very continuity a form of legitimation'.[71] Neither the king of France nor the Valois duke of Burgundy were unique in this respect. Several fifteenth-century princes, within the kingdom or on its periphery, felt and acted upon the need for some form of dynastic historiography.[72] Among these, the closest parallel to the

---

history writers and their patrons in the fourteenth century', *Medievalia et Humanistica* xiv (1986), 103–24 at p. 104.

[69] Y. Lacaze, 'Le rôle des traditions dans la genèse d'un sentiment national au XVe siècle', BEC cxxix (1971), 303–85.

[70] A similar process can be seen at work in a text Lacaze mentions but does not integrate within his argument, the *Roman de Buscalus*: cf. G. P. Small, 'Les origines de la ville de Tournai dans les chroniques légendaires du bas moyen âge', in *Les grands siècles de Tournai*, Tournai–Louvain-la-Neuve 1993, 81–113 esp. pp. 104–13.

[71] G. M. Spiegel, 'Political utility in medieval historiography', *History and Theory* xiv (1975), 314–25 at p. 316.

[72] K. Daly, 'Some seigneurial archives and chronicles in fifteenth-century France', *Peritia* ii (1983), 59–73; A. Perret, 'Chroniqueurs et historiographes de la maison de Savoie aux XVe et XVIe siècles', in *Culture et pouvoir au temps de l'humanisme et de la renaissance*, Paris 1978, 123–34.

Burgundian example thus far described was ducal Brittany, where the Montfortist dynasty is commonly attributed with political motives to match those detected within its Valois counterpart in Burgundy: 'la volonté de soustraire le duché à la tutelle française, d'en faire un État souverain, égal en droit à son voisin français'.[73] Breton historiography, while not as striking in its depth as that of Valois Burgundy, bore the imprint of such concerns. The major Breton historians from Guillaume de St André to Alain Bouchart had for the most part some association with the ducal court or administration, even if none had the status of official historian enjoyed by Chastelain. Within this corpus, many themes suggest a wish to 'bretonniser' the past, such as, for example, the emphasis upon the origins and ancient royal status of Brittany, the renown of its constituent geographical parts and people and the denigration of the foreigner, particularly the French.

However, just as Montfortist Brittany may be adjudged to have gone further and earlier in the direction of autonomy and a separate sense of identity than Valois Burgundy, its historiography presented a more coherent and sustained image of a specifically Breton past.[74] The legendary traditions of Burgundian historical fiction appear eclectic by comparison with those of Brittany. As Lacaze rightly points out, this was 'une littérature aux multiples aspects', a 'véritable salmigondis' consisting of numerous traditions which were not always easily reconciled with one another.[75] The author also notes that interest in such traditions was closely linked to specific political circumstances.[76] The individual histories of Burgundian ducal dominions remained just that, and as such could not convey to the same extent the teleological import of those

---

[73] J. Kerhervé, 'Aux origines d'un sentiment national', *Bulletin de la Société archéologique du Finistère* cviii (1980), 165–206 at p. 201.

[74] On the first point see M. Jones, 'Brittany in the Middle Ages', in his *The creation of Brittany*, London 1988, 1–12 at p. 9; A. Leguai, 'Les "états" princiers', at p. 147, and 'Royauté et principautés en France aux XIVe et XVe siècles', MA ci (1995), 121–36 at pp. 123, 127–8; J. Kerhervé, 'Taxation and ducal power in late medieval Brittany', *French History* vi (1992), 1–23. On the second, cf. idem, 'Aux origines d'un sentiment national'.

[75] Lacaze, 'Le rôle des traditions', 304, 319. The author also rightly notes (p. 316) that certain historiographical traditions in the duke's northern territories reflected earlier rivalries or even conflicts between principalities – such as Hainaut or Brabant – which later came under Burgundian rule. It is difficult to see how a sense of unity could emerge from such diversity: cf. Small, 'Chroniqueurs et culture historique', 286–7.

[76] Ibid. 380: 'En fait, la propagande bourguignonne par le canal de l'épopée nous paraît, du moins dans ses manifestations les plus importantes, singulièrement restreinte dans le temps.' The majority of texts he cites congregate around the years 1446–48, a period when Philip the Good was negotiating the status of his lands in the empire and examining the possibility that some might be raised to the status of a kingdom. The close link between these texts and circumstances in the 1440s is demonstrated and emphasised in A. Hagopian-van Buren, 'Philip the Good's manuscripts as documents of his relations with the empire', *PCEEB* xxxvi (1996), 49–69. Lacaze also points out that the importance of the figure of Girart de Roussillon was limited in time ('Le role des traditions', 316), and that Charles the Bold's tastes were not the same as his father's (pp. 363–4), thereby implying that the continuity so vital to the establishment of Burgundian traditions was impaired.

elements of Breton historiography which tied the people and the land to one ruler and a common destiny.[77] Certain characteristics of this Breton historiography differed markedly from those we can trace in the official Burgundian Chronicle of George Chastelain. Pierre Le Baud wrote so that his Breton reader might be aware of the 'longue extraction et progression de son pays et toutes les choses qui au temps passé y sont advenues'.[78] For the anonymous of St Brieuc, this focus was a necessary corrective to the damage done by the *Grandes Chroniques de France* which, in his view, had deliberately obscured Breton history in favour of that of the French crown.[79] We have already seen that Chastelain had a far less exclusive understanding of his geographical remit. Where the particularist Bretons sought to break with French royal tradition, Chastelain seems to align himself to it.[80] In view of his official status and the Burgundian sense of the past which was emerging in the years surrounding his appointment, it is possible to see why, once again, his outlook has long been attributed to a peculiarly personal, even marginal, experience of political life.

Yet such views are only surprising if we insist on the dominance of particularist aspirations at the heart of a distinct Burgundian state. We have already suggested that such sentiments should not be over-emphasised, at least with regard to the personnel of the court whom Chastelain knew. If 'l'histoire s'est faite bourguignonne' in the respects discussed above, there existed at the Burgundian court a parallel and pervasive set of historiographical traditions which, although often overlooked, presents another picture. These traditions indicate that, in several profound respects, 'l'histoire bourguignonne est restée française'.

The controlling framework of Burgundian historical culture in this period, provided by Philip the Good's impressive patronage and library, derived in fact from a peculiarly Valois tradition of princely bibliophism.[81] His great-uncles and his grandfather, the founder of the ducal library, had all been patrons and readers on the grand scale.[82] The collections of the third Valois duke of Burgundy represented a continuation of this tradition, since little of his collection appears to have been inherited from his non-Valois dynastic predecessors in Burgundy or Flanders. Within the library the history of France

---

[77] Unless, of course, one argues that there was 'unité dans la diversité' (p. 376), a 'patriotisme' which was effectively a 'synthèse de patriotismes régionaux' (p. 379), and that this sentiment was propagated by a process of osmosis (p. 377). This argument, and a comparative neglect of the Francocentric elements of Burgundian historical culture discussed below, strike me as the least convincing elements of Lacaze's study.

[78] Pierre le Baud, *Histoire de Bretagne, avec les chroniques des maisons de Vitré et de Laval*, ed. C. d'Hozier, Paris 1638, 1.

[79] *Cronicon Briocense, chronique de St-Brieuc*, ed. G. Le Duc and C. Sterckx, Rennes–Paris 1972, 60–2.

[80] See ch. 4 below for further comment.

[81] F. Salet, 'Mécénat royal et princier au moyen âge', *Comptes-rendus de l'Académie des inscriptions et belles-lettres* (1985), 620–9.

[82] M. J. Hughes, 'The library of Philip the Bold and Margaret of Flanders, first Valois duke and duchess of Burgundy', *JMH* iv (1978), 145–88.

enjoyed a dominant position. The only rubric in the inventory of 1467 to specifically mention historical works was given the title 'Croniques de France'.[83] Under this heading chronicles relating to Brabant, Hainaut, and Flanders were listed without the slightest hint of incongruity. Moreover, these works were greatly outnumbered by others which took France as their subject matter. The representation of French history in the Burgundian library far outshone the place it occupied in libraries of other princes of the realm, such as Charles d'Orléans or René d'Anjou, whose interests were far more closely associated with those of the king.[84] Francocentric historiography was a commonplace of Burgundian historical culture – the mainstream, not the exception.

This was not simply because Philip the Good had inherited a substantial corpus of French history works from the time when his immediate predecessors visited Paris and promoted their interests there. Philip maintained the tradition himself. To take only French royal chronicles as an illustration, the duke inherited four, bought others, was given one by Guillaume Fillastre and acquired separate French royal genealogies.[85] In 1461 he went to the bother of sending an envoy to St Denis to check on protocol for French coronations.[86] Even David Aubert, one of the scribes thought to have been busily engaged in constructing an autonomous Burgundian sense of the past on the duke's behalf, deferred to the authority of the Dionysian sources and referred his reader to them.[87] This seemed a natural thing to do in Burgundian circles. The anonymous Burgundian author of a chronicle fragment concerned with Louis XI's reign omitted to recount the details of Louis's dispute with his father because 'on la trouvera par escript es croniques de sondit père Charles VIIe roy de France'.[88] The indigenous dynastic literature in circulation at court did not displace earlier, co-existing, and perhaps even more long-lived traditions of French historical culture which held a natural appeal for the double peer of the realm and the political community for which he was the focus.[89] The

---

[83] Barrois, Bibliothèque, 205–6.
[84] P. Champion, La librairie de Charles d'Orléans, Paris 1910; Lecoy de La Marche, Le roi René, ii. 187–90.
[85] Doutrepont, Littérature, 420–4. Even Charles the Bold commissioned an ornate 'Croniques de France' from Louis Liédet: A. Pinchart, 'Miniaturistes, enlumineurs et calligraphes employés par Philippe le Bon et Charles le Téméraire et leurs oeuvres', Bulletin des Commissions royales d'art et d'archéologie iv (1865), 473–510 at p. 479.
[86] ADN B2040, fo. 250r–v.
[87] R. Guiette, 'Chanson de geste, chronique et mise en prose', Cahiers de civilisation médiévale vi (1963), 423–40 at p. 426; J. M. G. Schobben, La part du Pseudo-Turpin dans les Croniques et conquestes de Charlemaine de David Aubert, The Hague 1969, 11.
[88] A. Coulon, 'Fragment d'une chronique du règne de Louis XI', Mélanges d'archéologie et d'histoire de l'École française de Rome (hereinafter cited as MAHEFR) xv (1895), 103–40 at p. 114.
[89] For this reason I cannot agree with Lacaze's conclusion that the ducal court was 'le creuset par excellence de l'unification spirituelle de l'État bourguignon': 'Le rôle des traditions', 380. Although he implicitly acknowledges the existence of a Francocentric

influence of this strand in the historical culture of the court is clearly evinced in the patronage of the official chronicler. The argument here must pass through an analysis of the forms of patronage which furnished the duke and his court with works of history.

Chastelain's place in this context can be located in relation to the plethora of historiographical talent described by David Aubert in a famous passage written around 1462:

> Très renommé et très vertueux prince Philippe, duc de Bourgogne a des longtemps accoustumé de journellement faire devant lui lire les anciennes histoires; et pour estre garni d'une librairie non pareille a toutes autres il a des son jeune eaige eu a ses gaiges pluseurs translateurs, grans clers, experts orateurs, historiens et escripvains et en diverses contrees en gros nombre diligemment labourans.[90]

This contemporary perception of an impressive group of historians in Philip's pay seems at first glance to bolster the views of Lacaze. However, closer inspection of the patronage network which connected these writers to the duke suggests instead a far more heterogenous body of individuals and texts. At the risk of imposing artificial distinctions upon them, we might detect three categories among the writers of historical works who benefited in some way from ducal sponsorship.

In the first instance, there were officials at court whose 'gaiges' were regulated by the household or administrative hierarchy of service and who wrote history of their own volition or as a sideline to their other activities. These men would include Jean Lefèvre, Jean de Wavrin, *conseiller et chambellan*, or Jean Mansel, ducal receiver for Hesdin.[91] In one respect at least Chastelain seems to approximate to this category of historian. Like them he retained the status of a household officer, for in all but one of the documents relating to his services after 1455 he is described as an *écuyer panetier*.[92] As we have seen, however, Chastelain's remuneration did not conform to the norms which applied elsewhere at court: it was paid in one annual instalment, not 'par termes', and was twice the normal salary for an *écuyer*. Like Chaucer, therefore, he appears to have retained a title of convenience which no longer reflected

---

historical culture at the Burgundian court (cf. ibid. 309, 338, 375, 382), its relative weight in the minds of contemporaries is not considered. It will be argued in ch. 6 below that the widespread success of a specifically Burgundian historical culture was much more a post-Valois phenomenon.

[90] P. Cockshaw, 'Mentions d'auteurs, de copistes, d'enlumineurs et de libraires dans les comptes généraux de l'état bourguignon (1384–1419)', *Scriptorium* xxiii (1969), 122–44 at p. 122 n. 1.

[91] See ch. 2 above; M. Yans, 'Jean de Wavrin', BNB xxvii–viii, Brussels 1938, c. 129–32; L. Delisle, 'L'oeuvre de Jean Mansel', *Journal des Savants* (1900), 16–26, 106–17, 196–7.

[92] Chastelain's salary payments are discussed in ch. 2 above. On one occasion only he is referred to as the 'croniqueur de mondit seigneur': ADN B2040, fo. 234.

his main occupation.[93] By the same token, he was not simply another courtier who wrote history in his spare time. There is no evidence that the works written by men in this category were directly solicited by Philip the Good, or that they derived any financial reward from them.[94] Ducal patronage was limited in such cases to the fact that the court provided a cultural climate in which the writing of history was regarded as a worthwhile pursuit – although this may be considered important in itself.[95]

Chastelain might also be compared with those who were expressly commissioned or invited by the duke to present a work to him: Emond de Dynter, for example, or Hugues de Tolins, known as the duke's 'chroniqueur' or 'maistre chroniqueur'.[96] Here again, the singularity of Chastelain's position is evident. These men acted upon individual commissions and received piece rate payments. Emond de Dynter was given 200 Rhine florins for his work, while Tolins received the lesser sum of 50 francs.[97] Even Enguerran de Monstrelet's vast and influential chronicle was rewarded with a single payment of 50 *éscus*.[98] It is impossible to know in such cases whether the reward was solely intended for the writing of history, for the cost of preparing the presentation volume, or even for services rendered by the author in another capacity.[99] By comparison with the permanently established, regularly remunerated official chronicler, these men may have found the rewards of writing history fairly meagre. They were nevertheless luckier than some other writers who worked for the court.[100]

Closer comparisons with Chastelain's position seem to exist among those creative individuals who were offered a salaried position at court, and with it the leisure to pursue literary or artistic activities on a regular basis. Jean Froissart's post as 'clerc lisant' at the court of Edward III is an example of this

---

[93] J. R. Hubert, *Chaucer's official life*, Menasha 1912, 58.
[94] Nor, for that matter, is it clear that the duke saw copies of the works of Lefèvre or Wavrin. The latter presented his *Recueil* to Edward IV, but apparently not to his own master: Doutrepont, *Littérature*, 445. Such factors are rarely mentioned in discussions of the so-called 'école bourguignonne': see L. Hommel, 'Les chroniqueurs bourguignons', in G. Charlier and J. Hanse (eds), *Histoire illustrée des lettres françaises de Belgique*, Brussels 1958, 105–18.
[95] The absence of specific commissions or financial rewards does not mean that these men drew no benefit from their work; we simply cannot say what it was: see W. C. McDonald and U. Goebel, *German medieval literary patronage from Charlemagne to Maximilian I*, Amsterdam 1973, 5.
[96] A. Pinchart, 'De Tolins, Hugues', *Messager des sciences historiques* (1884), 169–70; Paris, BN, Collection de Bourgogne, no. 22, fo. 83.
[97] ADN B2040, fo. 251v; B1994, fo. 155v.
[98] Ibid. B1991, fo. 184v.
[99] D. B. Tyson, 'Patronage of French vernacular history writers in the twelfth and thirteenth centuries', *Romania* c (1979), 180–222 at p. 184.
[100] Martin Le Franc, for example, whose *Champion des dames* did not meet with the approval he expected from Philip the Good in 1442. He took the unusual step of writing a plea for the work's recognition, and covered himself by addressing his next production to both Philip and Charles VII: G. Paris, 'Un poème inédit de Martin Le Franc', *Romania* xvi (1887), 383–437.

more inclusive form of patronage, the so-called 'household system'.[101] Among those retained in this way at the Burgundian court were the principal writers discussed by Lacaze: David Aubert (the duke's 'escripvain de livres'), Jean Miélot ('secrétaire aux honneurs'), or Jean Wauquelin ('translateur et valet de chambre'). To judge from the number and variety of its occupants, the duke used the office of *valet de chambre* as a quasi-institutional mechanism of patronage for those who fulfilled a role in the cultural life of the court. Among them were the keepers of the ducal library and tapestries, the principal repositories of Burgundian historical culture.[102] Other ducal *valets* included poets and scribes, painters and manuscript illuminators, musicians, tailors and embroiderers, as well as goldsmiths and experts in the making of mechanical *entremets*.

The activities of some *valets* corresponded to the duties incumbent upon Chastelain. Michaut Taillevent is a case in point. Many of the earlier, reflective works which Chastelain claimed to have written (but which no longer survive) bear comparison, in their titles at least, with Taillevent's literary production.[103] Taillevent also wrote occasional poems and theatrical works which, like many of Chastelain's *opuscula*, were intended to commemorate great events in the life of the Burgundian political community: *Le songe de la Toison d'Or*, for example, written shortly after the Order's foundation, or the *Poèmes sur la prise de Luxembourg* (1443).[104] His position as an occasional poet, like Chastelain's, had something of an institutional nature: he had a fixed salary within the household and a successor, appointed in 1458, in the person of Jean de Ponceau du Poncelet.[105] Chastelain knew something of the latter, 'en son vivant varlet

---

[101] On Froissart's post in England see J. Vale, *Edward III and chivalry*, Woodbridge 1982, 46. He later occupied a similar post at the court of Guy de Blois: M.-T. Medeiros, 'Le pacte encomiastique', MA xciv (1988), 237–55 at p. 240. I first came across the 'household system' in R. Boase, *The troubadour revival*, London 1978, 73; it appears to have been first used in P. Burke, *Tradition and innovation in Renaissance Italy*, London 1974, 97, 374–5.

[102] On *valets* see Laborde, *Les ducs de Bourgogne*, i. 388, 402, 428, 432, 434, 438, 444, 466, 469, 507; ii. 210, 213, 219; J. Paviot, 'Jacques de Brégilles, garde-joyaux des ducs de Bourgogne Philippe le Bon et Charles le Téméraire', RN lxxvii (1995), 313–20; T. Walton, 'Amé de Montgesoie, poète bourguignon du XVe siècle', AB ii (1930), 134–58, and 'Les poèmes d'Amé de Montgesoie', *Medium Aevum* ii (1933), 1–33.

[103] Chastelain lists these works at vi, 268: *La tractation des deux félicités, Le livre de trois divers nobles, Le livre des humaines grâces, Le livre des périls du monde, Le livre du père à son fils, Le livre du faux amoureux, Le livre de la condition de fortune, Le livre de la cause des infortunes, Le livre des abusemens de court, Le livre de la tranquillité des courages* 'et plusieurs autres'. Although it is impossible to know the contents of these works, the conventional themes they lay claim to by their titles compare with Taillevent's *La destrousse, Le passe temps, Le débat du coeur et de l'oeil, Le régime de fortune*, or *Le congé d'amour*. For this and what follows see R. Deschaux, *Un poète bourguignon du XVe siècle, Michault Taillevent*, Geneva 1975.

[104] Ibid. 309–19.

[105] Ibid. 25 n. 64, 26 n. 68, 27 nn. 70, 74, 28 n. 77. For additions and corrections see ADN B1942, fos 37, 160; B1945, fo. 107v. On Ponceau see P. Champion, *Histoire poétique du XVe siècle*, Paris 1923, i. 289. He is attributed with several stories in the *Cent nouvelles nouvelles*: J. H. Watkins, 'A note on the *Cent nouvelles nouvelles*', MLR xxxvi (1941), 396–7. The latter

de chambre et rhetoricien', whom he described as 'un povre vallet clergeant' (iv, 259).

The terms he uses to describe Poncelet are redolent of the gulf which separated such beneficiaries of the existing 'household system' of patronage from the new post of official chronicler.[106] Despite some similarities in what was expected of them, the official chronicler-cum-occasional poet stood head and shoulders above his contemporaries in Burgundian service. Once again, the level of his remuneration may be taken as an illustration of this. The latter was considerably superior to the norms which applied in this sphere of ducal patronage. Taillevent and Poncelet, for example, were retained at a daily rate of 6s., or one-sixth of the chronicler's income. Jean Miélot received 12s. per day. Jean Wauquelin, for his part, was accorded an annual salary of 120l. for his services as *valet* (compared to Chastelain's 657l.).[107] We have no evidence that these men were handed so specific a brief as that given to Chastelain, and it is certainly true that none was engaged in his appointed task on such a permanent basis as the official chronicler. Such comparisons suggest that Chastelain came as close as one could get in the fifteenth century to the professional writer. Some, inevitably, are cautious of using this term in a medieval context.[108] Their reticence may be explained by the long-held belief that the writing of history was 'nobody's *business*' in the Middle Ages, that it was an 'avocation rather than a vocation'.[109] Only with the advent of the printing press, it is thought, was the writer more clearly freed from the patronage bond.[110] When the latter was as complete and lavish as it clearly was in Chastelain's case, we may wonder whether such provisos are necessary.

A second indication of Chastelain's superiority in the Burgundian milieu is found in the scale of public recognition accorded to him and his office. The fact that he was expressly asked in 1455 to write a chronicle rather than any other historical genre was itself an early indication of the primacy of his task in a Burgundian court context.[111] Chronicles were high history. According to

---

cites the document whereby 'Monseigneur le duc retint . . . Poncelet . . . ou lieu de feu Michault Taillvent, aux gaiges de six sols par jour.'

[106] Cf. the description of Taillevent as a 'joueur de farce': ADN B1938, fo. 171; A. de La Fons Melicocq, 'Les rois de la fève, les fous en titre d'office et de la chapelle, les joueurs de farce et les mommeurs de l'hôtel de Philippe le Bon, duc de Bourgogne', *Messager des sciences historiques de Belgique* (1857), 393–400.

[107] These figures are given in the works cited earlier relating to these men.

[108] J. Holzknecht, *Literary patronage in the Middle Ages*, Philadelphia 1923, 55–61, 102–3.

[109] V. H. Galbraith, *Historical research in medieval England*, London 1951, 11; T. F. Tout, 'Literature and learning in the English civil service in the fourteenth century', *Speculum* iv (1929), 365–89 at p. 381; B. Guenée, 'Y a-t-il une historiographie médiévale?', *RH* cclviii (1977), 261–75 (repr. in his *Politique et histoire*).

[110] J. Van Dorsten, 'Literary patronage in the Elizabethan age', in G. F. Lytle and S. Orgel (eds), *Patronage in the Renaissance*, Princeton 1981, 191–206; J. Lough, *Writer and public in France*, Oxford 1978, 7–30.

[111] On recognised differences between genres see B. Guenée, 'Histoire, annales, chroniques', *Annales E. S. C.* (1973), 997–1016 (repr. in his *Politique et histoire*), and

Alain Bouchart, 'il n'est permis à personne composer cronique, s'il n'y a pas esté ordonné'.[112] Jean de Roye and Commynes echoed these sentiments, albeit in different ways.[113] In 1473, as we have seen, Chastelain's renown was carried to new heights by the bestowal upon him of the title of *indiciaire* at the festivities surrounding the Valenciennes chapter of the Golden Fleece.[114] The term itself has aroused some interest, partly because of its subsequent history, partly because of its meaning.[115] On the latter point, there is no reason to believe that it implied any change of function for Chastelain.[116] However, it did reflect Charles the Bold's high esteem of his father's chronicler – a sentiment which he may also have revealed when, one year earlier, he went against his Italophile instincts and turned down the offer of Stephanus Surigonus' services as a panegyrist.[117] It was customary to recognise the pre-eminence of the duke's chronicler in Burgundian literary circles. Pierre Michault, Olivier de La Marche and Jean Lefèvre de St Rémy all sang his praises, while Jean de Haynin considered even the correspondence of 'Monsieur l'Indiciaire' to be worthy of inclusion in the autograph manuscript of his *Mémoires*.[118] Chastelain was a

---

'Histoire et chronique: nouvelles réflexions sur les genres historiques au moyen âge', in Poirion, *La chronique et l'histoire*, 3–12.

112 Alain Bouchart, *Grandes croniques de Bretaigne*, ed. M.-L. Auger and G. Jeanneau, Paris 1986, i. 77.

113 Jean de Roye would not call his work a chronicle for this reason (although posterity did not respect his wishes). Characteristically, Commynes accused chroniclers of writing only what would please their masters: Jean de Roye, *Journal, connu sous le nom de Chronique scandaleuse*, ed. B. de Mandrot, Paris 1894–6, i. p. ix; Commynes, *Mémoires*, ii. 172–3.

114 See ch. 2 above.

115 H. Naïs, 'Grand temps et longs jours sont, monsieur l'indiciaire', in *Mélanges de linguistique française et de philologie et littérature médiévales offerts à Paul Imbs*, Strasbourg 1973, 207–18; B. A. Vermaseren, 'Het ambt van historiograaf in de Bourgondische Nederlanden', *Tijdschrift voor Geschiedenis* lvi (1941), 258–73.

116 The only possible confusion here is Molinet's later reference to the duty of the 'indiciaire' to record 'par escripture authentique les admirables gestes des chevaliers et confrères de l'ordre': *Chroniques*, ii. 594. This implied connection with the Golden Fleece has led some to believe that Chastelain was – or had become – the historiographer of the order in particular: M. Keen, 'Chivalry, heralds and history', in R. H. C. Davis and J. M. Wallace-Hadrill (eds), *The writing of history in the Middle Ages*, Oxford 1981, 393–415 at p. 406. Less understandably it has been suggested that Lefèvre was Chastelain's successor: M. Krabusch, 'Georges Chastellain als Geschichtsschreiber und Betrachter des politischen Lebens seiner Zeit', unpubl. Ph.D. diss. Heidelberg 1950, 14. In fact, the Order had always had some form of historiographical record: P. Gorissen, 'De historiographie van het Gulden Vlies', *Bijdragen voor de geschiedenis der Nederlanden* vi (1951–2), 218–24. Moreover, Guillaume Fillastre had been asked five years earlier to provide a fuller history of the Order by the duke himself. Molinet's reference is thus to be explained by the context in which Chastelain was given the title – i.e. during a chapter of the Golden Fleece.

117 Walsh, 'The coming of humanism', 162–3. It is equally possible that Charles felt that he was well served in this domain by other indigenous talent described in P. C. Boeren, *Twee Maaslandse dichters in dienst van Karel de Stoute*, The Hague 1968.

118 The views of La Marche and Lefèvre on Chastelain are given in ch. 2 above. For Michault's view see Doutrepont, *Littérature*, 321; for Haynin see J. Van den Gheyn, 'Le manuscrit original des *Mémoires* du sire de Haynin', *BCRH* lxx (1901), 44–59; A. Bayot,

paragon among those who wrote history at court, whether of their own volition, on an occasional basis at the duke's request, or in a more permanent capacity by means of the 'household system'.

These remarks lead to two conclusions: the official chronicler was regarded by his peers and his patron as the centre-piece of Burgundian historical culture; and the patronage model used in his appointment did not come from existing structures within the court. That is not to say that Chastelain's patronage and duties were without precedent. The inspiration behind this flagship of ducal historiography – the mainstream representative, not one of the peripheral figures of Burgundian history writing – came from the continuing influence of French historical culture at Philip the Good's court.

For most of Chastelain's lifetime and for long before, royal history was written at the abbey of St Denis.[119] This historiographical connection dated back to the twelfth century, but it was not until the fifteenth that it assumed a formal, institutional nature.[120] The first signs of change came in 1410, when the monks of St Denis affirmed that their chronicler, Michel Pintoin, was a royal officer, and this because he was appointed 'par l'autorité du roy' and because '(il) fait serement au roy et a livrée à l'ostel du roy'.[121] By the time of Jean Chartier's nomination in 1437, the integration of the official chronicler within the aulic hierarchy was more thorough. Chartier reveals this himself in his description of his post.[122] Like Pintoin, he took an oath as a servant of the king, and in return for his work he was to receive an annual salary of 250l.t. This figure, the first recorded salary for a 'chroniqueur du roy', was not arbitrarily chosen. It was based on the rate accorded to an officer of the court, the *maître d'hôtel*. The right to wear the king's livery was now supplemented by an equivalence in status to a senior post in the royal household. It was intended

---

'Notice du manuscrit original des *Mémoires* de Jean de Haynin', *Revue des bibliothèques et archives de Belgique* (1908), 109–44. Haynin also copied Chastelain's verse on Philip the Good's death: vii, 281–4. Chastelain's influence upon some of these memorialists is discussed in ch. 6 below.

[119] In 1461 Louis XI appointed Jean Castel as his historiographer, taking the tradition away from St Denis: iv, 100. Another 'ystorien du roy', Guillaume Danicot, was in place between 1466 and 1472. The post may have returned to St Denis with the appointment of Mathieu Levrien towards the end of the reign: A. Bossuat, 'Jean Castel, chroniqueur de France', *MA* lxiv (1958), 285–304, 499–538; J. Lesellier, 'Un historiographe de Louis XI demeuré inconnu, Guillaume Danicot', *MAHEFR* xliii (1926), 1–42; C. Samaran, 'Un ouvrage de Guillaume Danicot, historiographe de Louis XI', *MAHEFR* xlv (1928), 8–20; and idem, 'Mathieu Levrien, chroniqueur de St Denis à la fin du règne de Louis XI', *BEC* xcix (1938), 125–31.

[120] G. Spiegel, *The chronicle tradition of St Denis*, Brookline, Mass.– Leyden 1978, 122–3.

[121] H.-F. Delaborde, 'La vraie chronique du Religieux de St-Denis', *BEC* li (1890), 93–110 at p. 96. The *Religieux* was identified as Michel Pintoin in N. Grévy-Pons and E. Ornato, 'Qui est l'auteur de la chronique latine de Charles VI dite du Religieux de St Denis?', *BEC* cxxxiv (1976), 85–102.

[122] C. Samaran, 'La chronique latine de Jean Chartier (1422-1450)', *ABSHF* (1926), 183–273; repr. in his *Une longue vie d'érudit*, Paris 1978, i. 285–375 at pp. 351–2; Chartier, *Chronique*, i. 2–3.

that the chronicler, despite his monastic status, should follow the itinerant court in carrying out his duties.

Chastelain's appointment did not simply parallel that of the royal chronicler; it mirrored it in almost every respect. Like Chartier, Chastelain was commissioned to write a chronicle, the princely genre of history. Chartier was asked to enlarge upon the mainly Latin Dionysian tradition by producing a fuller vernacular version of his work.[123] Chastelain, for his part, wrote in French from the outset. There is no conclusive proof that the Burgundian chronicler swore a distinct oath of loyalty to his master as his French counterpart was required to do, but in any case he had already done so as an *écuyer* of the household.[124] Moreover, we can be certain that the practice was associated with the Burgundian post, since Chastelain's successor swore to 'faire bien, deuement et lealment, toutes et singulieres, les choses que bon et leal historiographe et chronicqueur dessys dit poelt et doit faire et qui audit estat compete et appertient'.[125] Chartier and Chastelain both received salaries which were based on existing rates of pay within the household, those of a *maître d'hôtel* and a *conseiller* respectively. Unlike conventional servants, however, both men were paid annually for their services. The reason for this appears to have been purely practical since, as a later official historian of the French monarchy wrote, 'la fonction des historiographes ne peut pas estre divisée par quartiers, semestres, (ou) saisons, . . . leur tasche estant continue'.[126] It is no coincidence that Burgundian official history corresponded to its royal counterpart in each of these key aspects. The enormous success and prestige of the Dionysian tradition encouraged emulation.[127] Finally, as we have attempted to show in this section, the historiographical product of St Denis was, at the very least, as integral a part of Burgundian historical culture as it was in any other area of the Francophone world.

In the final analysis, of course, it is hardly surprising that this should have been the case. The significance of the commonplace has been played down in favour of the new and the emergent which, perhaps inevitably, excite more attention. If the tender shoots of a specifically Burgundian historical culture were pushing through, they were doing so in ground which was still permeated by a deeper French sense of the past.[128] In appointing an official chronicler in

---

[123] C. Samaran, 'La chronique latine inédite de Jean Chartier (1422–1450) et les derniers livres du Religieux de St-Denis', BEC lxxxvii (1926), 142–63.
[124] See ch. 2 above.
[125] Molinet, *Chroniques*, iii. 20.
[126] Charles Barnard, cited in F. Fossier, 'La charge d'historiographe du 16e au 19e siècle', RH cclviii (1977), 73–92 at p. 91.
[127] On the success and geographical presence of the French royal chronicles see Guenée, *Histoire et culture historique*, 320–3, and 'Les Grandes chroniques de France: le Roman aux roys (1274–1518)', in P. Nora (ed.), *Les lieux de mémoire*, II: *La nation*, Paris 1986, i. 189–213.
[128] In this regard Lacaze's argument is weakened by the absence of any thorough examination of the success and geographical presence of the works he cites: cf. J. Richard, 'Un sentiment "national" bourguignon?', AB xlv (1973), 182–4.

the French royal style, Philip the Good was simply doing what came naturally to later medieval princes of the realm – meeting a perceived need by the appropriation of royal institutions.[129]

However, royal institutions, once transplanted into the princely environment, took on a life of their own. They served the prince's ends. The duke now had at his disposal an official historian who was well-placed to address and reflect the historical identity of the elite to which he belonged. Chastelain's personal awareness of that wider public was in turn a further influence upon the writing of his Chronicle. In the final section, therefore, some attempt must be made to identify Chastelain's perception of where his audience lay.

History and poetry

As we shall see in a later chapter, the diffusion of the Chronicle only occurred after the death of its author.[130] During his lifetime, however, Chastelain was afforded a clear idea of the eventual audience for the work by the reception of his *opuscula*, those 'choses nouvelles et moralles' which Philip the Good had also requested him to write in 1455.[131] Poetry was a recognised part of the historian's repertoire: here, Chastelain differed little from his precursor, Jean Froissart, his contemporary royal counterpart, Jean Castel, or his official Burgundian successor, Jean Molinet.[132] Charles the Bold himself seems to have blurred any hard and fast distinction which we might care to draw between the poet and the historian when he gave Chastelain the single, all-embracing title of *indiciaire*: 'celuy qui demonstroit par escripture authentique les

---

[129] Cf. idem, 'Les institutions ducales dans le duché de Bourgogne', in F. Lot and R. Fawtier (eds), *Histoire des institutions françaises au moyen âge*, Paris 1957, i. 209–48.

[130] The actual – rather than the intended – audience of the Chronicle is the subject of ch. 6 below.

[131] Chastelain was already deemed to be 'expert et congnoissant' in the writing of 'choses nouvelles et moralles': the duke was clearly thinking here of works like *La complainte d'Hector* or *Le throsne azuré*. The adjective 'nouvelle' had very general connotations of fashionableness and creative merit, and was thus commonly used in the titles of contemporary theatrical productions as a means of generating interest: *Recueil de farces françaises inédites du XVe siècle*, ed. G. Cohen, Cambridge, Mass. 1949, pp. xi–xviii; *Recueil général des sotties*, ed. E. Picot, Paris 1902–12, i. 175, 199; iii. 79, 99, 121, 205, 321. The adjective 'morale' implied didactic intent, as in Jean Miélot's 'moralités' of 1456, 'contenant aucuns des bons mots des anciens philosophes': Doutrepont, *Littérature*, 141, 492. It is employed in a similar sense in the contemporary genre of the morality play. Such representations were fictional in nature and most often employed allegorical characters, but could also draw their lesson from contemporary political events and act as vehicles for commenting on them: A. E. Knight, *Aspects of genre in late medieval French drama*, Manchester 1983, 17–38, 42–7; W. Helmich, *Die Allegorie im französischen Theater des 15. und 16. Jahrhunderts*, Tübingen 1976, 19–27.

[132] B. J. Whiting, 'Froissart as poet', *Medieval studies* viii (1946), 189–216; J. Quicherat, 'Recherches sur le chroniqueur Jean Castel', BEC ii (1841), 461–77; G. A. Brunelli, 'Jean Castel et le *Mirouer des dames*', MA lxii (1956), 93–117; Jean Molinet, *Faictz et dictz*, ed. N. Dupire, Paris 1936–39.

admirables gestes'. This view was echoed in Jean Lemaire's remark that 'ce terme d'Indiciaire vault autant à dire comme démonstrateur'.[133] The occasional work enabled the *indiciaire* to reflect various dimensions of the historical moment which presented itself, to demonstrate its significance and to fix an interpretation of it within the consciousness of a contemporary audience.[134] The Chronicle on the other hand connected the flow of events in a continuous historical narrative. To this extent the works differed in form and function; they do not necessarily lend themselves to the same type of analysis.[135] In terms of their subject matter and reception, however, it is clear that the two types of activity may be compared. Chastelain justifies this approach himself. He had a unitary conception of his *oeuvre*, as witnessed by the incidence of direct or indirect cross-reference between the Chronicle and certain *opuscula*, and the transfer and elaboration of ideas, themes and even forms of words from one to the other.[136] If the former was history, the latter might be called 'history-in-the-making'.[137]

The *opuscula* have been the subject of increased attention since the last biographies of Chastelain were written.[138] Despite surveys of the survival of the manuscripts, however, the success and geographical presence of these works, not to mention the manner in which these were achieved, have excited

---

[133] Lemaire develops the gloss in his epitaph to Chastelain and Molinet: 'Pourquoi se firent-ilz indiciaires lors? Pour ce qu'ils nous ont monstré d'histoire les trésors': Naïs, 'Grands temps et longs jours', 209, 214–15.

[134] P. Zumthor, *Le masque et la lumière*, Paris 1978, 52–3.

[135] Hence the primary focus in this study upon the Chronicle. The *opuscula* concentrated upon a point in time, albeit one which was tied more or less loosely to a wider conception of the course of events. The Chronicle was in intention a sustained attempt to elucidate history in its broad sweep. The one sought immediate impact in specific circumstances, the other provided a coherent frame of reference.

[136] When recounting the death of Philip the Good in the Chronicle, Chastelain refers his reader to 'un livret à part' on the subject, his *Déclaration de tous les hauts faits*: v, 243. Passages from his *Advertissement au duc Charles* were inserted *verbatim* in the Chronicle, a fact obscured by Kervyn's curious removal of them in his edition.

[137] C. J. Brown, *The shaping of history and poetry in late medieval France*, Birmingham, Al. 1985. Alternatively, H. Wolff has pointed out how often the Chronicle contains set piece passages which could be freestanding works on a specific theme. She calls them 'hors d'oeuvres': 'Prose historique et rhétorique', in *Actes du VIe colloque international sur le moyen français*, II: *Rhétorique et mise en prose*, Milan 1991, 87–104.

[138] In addition to the works cited to this point or subsequently see C. de Rosanbo, 'Notice sur les *Douze dames de rhétorique*', *Bulletin de la Société française de reproduction de manuscrits à peintures* xii (1929), 5–16; M. Maurin, 'La poétique de Chastellain et la *Grande rhétorique*', *Publications of the Modern Language Association of America* (hereinafter cited as *PMLAA*) lxxiv (1959), 482–4; K. Hemmer, *Georges Chastellain (1405–75)*, Münster 1937; C. Lambert, 'Louenge à la trèsglorieuse Vierge de Georges Chastelain: étude et édition', unpubl. mém. de licence, Liège 1983; C. Thiry, 'Le vieux renard et le jeune loup', MA xc (1984), 455–85; J. Devaux, 'George Chastelain rhétoriqueur', ibid. xcix (1993), 516–32; D. Cowling, 'Text and building', in D. Maddox and S. Sturm-Maddox (eds), *Literary aspects of courtly culture*, Cambridge 1994, 123–32.

little interest.[139] On this last point we may assume that the manuscript was not the only means of dissemination, particularly in Burgundian court circles. Several contemporary references describe Chastelain as an 'orateur', a term which (outside the diplomatic context) was used to designate men-of-letters who produced occasional pieces to be declaimed 'de vive voix' at court.[140] Chastelain indicates as much in his description of Charles the Bold holding forth 'en beau parler . . . comme un orateur' before his assembled nobility at court 'là où il leur fit diverses remonstrances selon les divers temps et causes' (v, 368–9). This understanding of the word suggests that elements of the chronicler's work were intended in the first instance to be aired orally on formal court occasions.

Le dit de vérité (late 1450s) is one text which may have received this treatment. The title of the work, its use of verse and relative brevity all constitute the hallmarks of the contemporary genre of the dramatic monologue.[141] *Le lyon bandé* (1456) affords a clearer illustration. The poem is written as an address to Philip the Good and employs the second person singular and verbs such as 'entendre', 'réciter', and 'dire' to frame the discourse. Each of the duke's exploits to the time of writing is placed in chronological order, with pride of place accorded to his 'oeuvres nouvelles', the submission of Utrecht and his triumphant entry into the city on 5 August 1456. The official chronicler had been with the duke five days earlier as he prepared to make his entry, and was thus on hand to magnify the solemnity of the occasion:

> Ne me loist-il que je die et déclaire
> Ton fier arroy, ta triomphante entrée

---

[139] Cf. i, pp. xlviii–lxiv, and Urwin, *Georges Chastelain*, 23–9. Much work remains to be done on the success of these lesser works, not least because the surveys are far from complete. For other manuscripts see Chantilly, Musée Condé, MS 687 and BM Besançon, MS 554 (both *L'oultré d'Amour*); Edinburgh, National Library of Scotland, MS 19.1.4 (*La mort du roi Charles VII*); L. Mourin, 'Un manuscrit inconnu de l'*Advertissement au duc Charles* de Georges Chastellain', *Scriptorium* ii (1948), 119–21; O. Pächt and D. Thoss, *Die illuminierten Handschriften und Inkunabeln der österreichischen Nationalbibliothek, französische Schule II*, Vienna 1977, 13–14 (unspecified work by Chastelain). There is also a manuscript of the *Miroir de Mort* at Aberystwyth: A. H. Diverres, 'Le miroir de mort by Georges Chastellain', *The National Library of Wales Journal* i (1940), 218–19. A systematic examination of library catalogues would no doubt reveal many more – a task which lies beyond the aims of the present study. The bibliography reflects my initial work in Parisian libraries to this end.

[140] Chastelain was described during his lifetime or very shortly after as a 'très cler orateur' (Pierre Michault); the 'noble orateur' (Jean Lefèvre); 'le clair orateur' (Jean Robertet); and the 'très expert orateur' (Jean Molinet): Doutrepont, *Littérature*, 321; Lefèvre, *Chronique*, i. p. xlix; Jean Robertet, *Oeuvres*, ed. M. Zsuppan, Geneva–Paris 1970, 159; Molinet, *Chroniques*, ii. 593. Little more than twenty years after his death he was remembered in Habsburg circles as an 'orateur et historiographe': ADN B2160, no. 71.117. On the diplomatic functions of the 'orateur' see D. E. Queller, *Early Venetian legislation on ambassadors*, Geneva 1966, 50, and *The office of ambassador*, 63. On men-of-letters as 'orateurs' see R. Weiss, *Humanism in England in the fifteenth century*, Oxford 1951, 122–6; Green, *Poets and princepleasers*, 174–5; Holzknecht, *Literary patronage*, 183–4.

[141] D. Poirion (ed.), *Précis de littérature française au moyen âge*, Paris 1983, 306–9.

> Qui *aujourd'huy*, sans à nulluy desplaire,
> Porte lueur, resplendit et esclaire
> Comme un soleil sur umbreuse contrée. (vi, 161)[142]

Three further mentions of the word 'aujourd'huy' in rapid succession fix the purpose of the work to a specific time and place (vi, 162–3), perhaps even to a formal assembly at some point in the ducal entry when Philip was surrounded by the splendid array of courtiers mentioned in the Chronicle account:

> N'as-tu o toy le plus bel présentage
> De chevaliers de ce monde présent,
> Et là où gist si ample et grant partage
> D'honneur, de sens et de tout haut fruitage. (vi, 162)[143]

Bearing in mind that 'readers were few and hearers were numerous' before the age of print, and considering the functions attributed to 'orateurs' by contemporaries, we may suspect that public orations like this one probably performed at Utrecht were a significant outlet for Chastelain's production.[144] They had the basic function of magnifying the person of the prince within the confines of his own court, or at most within a restricted circle associated with the ducal elite. On such occasions Chastelain was addressing the privileged few as an interpreter and/or shaper of their collective consciousness.

Through another set of works the chronicler was able to envisage a wider audience for his literary production. Chastelain's plays are distinguished from the dramatic monologue by the provision of spoken and sung verse for named characters and by the inclusion of rudimentary stage directions within the text. *La mort du duc Philippe* (1468) and *La paix de Péronne* (1468) certainly enter this category.[145] Of the two, the performance of *La mort du duc Philippe* is more easily situated.[146] The internal evidence indicates that the occasion for the work was (once again) a ducal entry, and the concluding lines make a clear connection between the performance and Valenciennes.[147] Doutrepont suggests – but is unable to prove – that the work was performed in the town in April 1468.[148] On 27 March, however, Charles had formally taken possession of the county of Hainaut at Mons.[149] There, a gift of 20*l*. was made to 'six

---

[142] Italics mine. Chastelain was with the duke as he prepared his entry: iii, 134.
[143] For the splendour of Philip's entourage on this occasion see iii, 141–54.
[144] H. J. Chaytor, *From script to print*, Cambridge 1945, esp. pp. 115–38.
[145] vii, 237–80, 423–52.
[146] It has been suggested that the *Paix de Péronne* was performed at Aire before Charles and Louis: Doutrepont, *Littérature*, 363–4. Whether Chastelain was able to produce the work in so short a time is at least debatable; cf. the caution of C. Thiry, 'Un panégyrique pessimiste', *Marche romane* xxvi (1976), 31–55 esp. pp. 36–7.
[147] 'Les anges' describe 'Nos coeurs, nos âmes, nos racines/ Clamans à vostre *entrée* à gorge': vii, 279 (italics mine). The work ends with the following lines: 'Ce dit vostre humble Valenchines/ Par la bouche de vostre George': vii, 280.
[148] Doutrepont, *Littérature*, 364–5.
[149] Devillers, 'Les séjours', 364–8.

compaignons, joueurs de Valenciennes . . . quant ils ont joué devant luy . . . ung jeu de personnaige'.[150] Five or six actors would have been necessary for the performance of Chastelain's work.[151] If he were to have any control over the performance, it made sense to employ a local troupe. We may conclude that this was Chastelain's play.

The urban setting of the performance is particularly noteworthy. The text places repeated expressions of communal grief and expectation in the mouth of 'les hommes'. This was very probably a concession to a wider audience of Hainaulter noblemen, urban dignitaries and lesser townsmen who witnessed the performance. A work he produced not long after was certainly seen by such a public. In July 1469, one of Chastelain's servants received payment from the civic authorities of Ghent for having brought from his master a written version of the 'mysteres' which were performed when Charles the Bold entered the city in May.[152] The festivities which accompanied ducal entries into Ghent were normally stage-managed by the *rederijkkamers* of the city, but there was a degree of communication and cooperation between these circles and the court.[153] The text which Chastelain wrote for this occasion cannot now be identified with certainty, although it is at least possible, as Kervyn once thought, that this was in fact the *Louenge au duc Charles* (vii, 453–5). The reference to the work in the town accounts is none the less sufficient proof that through his plays, Chastelain was able on occasion to reach beyond the Burgundian court, thereby embracing a more heterogenous, urban audience in the collective experience of theatre.

The close association between the works of the 'orateur'/ playwright and the formal occasion for which they were written did not mean that their impact was transitory. Many went on to enjoy a second life in manuscript form.[154] Inventories of the ducal library reveal that several of Chastelain's 'livrets' were destined in the first instance for the ducal patron: the *Exposition sur vérité mal prise* (c. 1460–1), the *Advertissement au duc Charles* (c. 1468) and the *Louenge à la très-glorieuse vierge* (s.d.) found their way into his collection. Philip the Good may also have had copies of *La mort du roy Charles VII* and the *Recollection*

---

[150] Laborde, *Les ducs de Bourgogne*, i. 499.
[151] The play opens with four characters on stage: *le ciel, la terre, les anges, les hommes*. At a later stage there appears 'un nouvel personnage sans nom et clos dedens le ciel sans estre vu': vii, 277. The number of characters on stage at any one time, in addition to the implications of this stage direction, suggest that five 'joueurs' were required at the very least.
[152] V. Fris, 'La restriction de Gand (13 juillet 1468)', BSHAG xxx (1922), 57–142 at p. 138. The context of the entry is discussed in P. J. Arnade, 'Secular charisma, sacred power: rites of rebellion in the Ghent entry of 1467', HMGOG ns xlv (1991), 69–94.
[153] Olivier de La Marche, for example, was himself a member of a Brussels guild of rhetoricians, and had assisted in the production of Chastelain's *Complainte d'Hector*. I am grateful to Dr Arnade for the first piece of information on La Marche. The link is discussed in greater detail in a forthcoming article by Alistair Millar, 'Olivier de La Marche and the urban culture of late medieval Brussels', delivered as a paper to the Centre de recherches francophones belges at Edinburgh, May 1996.
[154] Barrois, *Bibliothèque*, 153, 178, 210, 211, 314.

des merveilleuses advenues (c. 1464–6). These works were either dispatched from Valenciennes to the court, as in the case of the *Louenge au duc Charles* (c. 1469), or were presented to the duke by the author in person.

The act of presentation in such cases marked a beginning, rather than an endpoint, in the life of the work.[155] From here a process of vertical dissemination took place; the text passed down through the court to individual readers who, emulating the duke or genuinely interested themselves in the latest offering from *le grand George*, desired to have their own copies of his work. The sporadic evidence of the *ex-libris* and other inscriptions indicate that these included highly placed courtiers such as Philippe de Lannoy, son-in-law of Chastelain's acquaintance, Jean; Adolf of Cleves, lord of Ravenstein; his wife Beatrice, a close associate of the countess of Charolais until her early death in 1462; and Louis de Bruges, whose library may have been second only to that of the duke himself.[156] Lesser nobles at court procured copies of Chastelain's work, including two *valets de chambre*, Jean Machefoing and Jean Martin (whose brother Philippe was an acquaintance of Chastelain's); and possibly Philippe Bouton, one of the duke's equerries, who may have been the original owner of the largest single collection of Chastelain's *opuscula*, now MS Med. Pal. 120 of the Biblioteca Medicea Laurenziana in Florence.[157] It is interesting to note that Chastelain's writings also seem to have been of interest to the 'clercs' of the court, and this despite the different cultural tastes commonly attributed to that milieu. Among the readers in this category were Jean Cueillette, one of Charles the Bold's legal officers, and Antoine de Vergy, tutor to Jacques de Bourbon.[158] The *indiciaire* clearly had broad appeal.

So broad, indeed, that the presentation and dissemination of his *opuscula* did not always begin with the ducal patron himself. Chastelain's growing reputation and the impact of specific orations or performances encouraged others to approach him directly with suggestions for work. In 1465 the officers of the *Chambre des comptes* took it upon themselves to commission a verse work on the Last Judgement from Chastelain. This was required for insertion in the

---

[155] R. K. Root, 'Publication before printing', PMLAA xxviii (1913), 417–31.

[156] Philippe de Lannoy owned a composite manuscript (now Brussels, BR, MS 21.521-31) containing *Le miroir de mort* and other works by Chastelain. Adolf of Cleves owned a copy of *Le prince*, now Brussels, BR, MS 11.020-33. Louis de Bruges owned a copy of *Le temple de Bocace* (now Paris, BN, MS fr. 1226), as did Beatrice of Cleves (now Brussels, BR, MS 10.485). On the last two see Bliggenstorfer, *Le temple de Bocace*, 50, 75. Louis also possessed a copy of Chastelain's *Douze dames de rhétorique*: J. Van Praet, *Recherches sur Louis de Bruges*, Paris 1881, 170–1.

[157] On Jean Martin see Bliggenstorfer, *Le temple de Bocace*, 67–8. Machefoing owned a copy of the *Déclaration de tous les hauts faits* (now Paris, Bibliothèque St-Geneviève, MS 1999). On Bouton (who is discussed in more detail in ch. 6 below) see S. Bliggenstorfer, 'Castellani Georgii, Opera poetica gallice', Vox romanica xliii (1984), 123–53.

[158] On Cueillette see idem, *George Chastelain*, 61; on Vergy see J.-C. Muhlethaler, 'Un manifeste poétique de 1463: les Enseignes des *Douze dames de rhétorique*', in *Actes du Ve colloque international sur le moyen français*, i, Milan 1985, 83–101.

new murals adorning their palace at Lille.[159] The genesis and success of the *Temple de Bocace* also owed little to the intervention of the duke. The work was apparently suggested to Chastelain by Agnès de Bourbon, Philip's sister, and was intended for the consolation of Marguerite d'Anjou. Philip the Good does not seem to have been given a copy, but the text did enjoy a considerable vogue at his court.[160] In cases such as these the professional writer clearly knew himself to be addressing a much wider audience than the prince at the centre of the elite: he spoke to (and for) members of the court, as well as those who were associated with it. The idea that Chastelain could voice collective Burgundian sentiments which were not necessarily those of the ruler, or of all within the elite, will be taken further at a later stage.

By means of the public oration, performance or the presentation and circulation of manuscripts, Chastelain's work thus percolated the Burgundian political community, overflowing on specific occasions into associated milieux such as the urban elites of the ducal dominions. The means by which his work was disseminated are perhaps more varied than has been suggested in the past, but the extent of its reception, so far as we can follow it, comes as no surprise. We would naturally expect Chastelain to have been read or heard by a primarily Burgundian audience, and that his work should therefore have reflected concerns which were prevalent in such circles.

The possibilities of reaching an even wider audience – specifically, one which lay beyond the ducal dominions – were restricted by certain obvious limitations. The *orateur* or playwright had a captive audience at the Burgundian court, but only rarely was Chastelain able to address a French public in either capacity. The *Complainte d'Hector*, as we have seen, was an exception to this. The *Mort du roy Charles VII* may have had a similar public at some point during Philip the Good's visit to Rheims and Paris for the coronation of Louis XI in 1461, although this cannot be confirmed by documentary evidence.[161] On top of these constraints, Chastelain did not benefit from the appearance of the printing press in the Low Countries during his lifetime. The new technology was not known in Valenciennes before Jean Molinet's day, and it was only in the early sixteenth century that works such as the *Miroir de mort*, *La complainte d'Hector* or *Le temple de Bocace* were printed.[162]

---

[159] Chastelain's correspondence is printed in Urwin, *Georges Chastelain*, 228–31. The mural was commissioned from a Lille painter, Jean Pillot, in 1462: J. Houdoy, *Études artistiques: artistes inconnus des XIVe, XVe et XVIe siècles*, Paris 1877, 28–32; Le Glay and others, *Inventaire*, i. 116. In 1465 Chastelain was called in to write his verse to adorn Pillot's work: H. Platelle, 'La vie religieuse à Lille', in *Histoire de Lille*, Lille 1970, i. 304–417 at pp. 416–17.

[160] Bliggenstorfer, *Le temple de Bocace*, passim.

[161] Cf. B. Guenée and F. Lehoux, *Les entrées royales françaises de 1328 à 1515*, Paris 1968, 26.

[162] See ch. 6 below; E. Droz and C. Dalbanne, 'Le *Miroir de mort* de Georges Chastellain', *Gutenberg Jahrbuch* (1928), 89–92; B. Moreau, *Inventaire chronologique des éditions parisiennes du XVIe siècle*, II: *(1511–20)*, Paris 1977, no. 1571; *Catalogue des livres composant la*

Despite these limitations we should not under-estimate the manuscript as an effective instrument for the dissemination of Chastelain's work beyond the Burgundian court. According to Molinet, indeed, the *opuscula* 'sont devoléz par divers pays et contrées' (ii, 594). Some indication of this is afforded by *Les paroles de trois puissants princes*, written around the time of the trial of Alençon in 1458.[163] Chastelain resorted to the ploys of the pamphleteer to circulate this work. The text was left anonymously and on public view at the residence of the duke in the knowledge that it would be brought to the attention of a wider audience. To judge from the provenance of four surviving versions, Chastelain's expectations were not misplaced. The text seems first to have been copied at the court itself where it found its way into the collection linked with the ducal equerry mentioned earlier, Philippe Bouton, and the autograph manuscript of Jean de Haynin's memoirs.[164] Evidence that the work then circulated more widely within the ducal dominions is provided by Jacques du Clercq. Although he lived in Arras and did not hold office at court, the memoirist was able to reproduce its exact contents.[165] A fourth contemporary manuscript containing the work belonged not to some Burgundian courtier or provincial noble in the Low Countries, but to two readers who moved in quite different circles: Jean de Derval, lord of Malestroit, and his wife Hélène.[166] The latter's godmother was Yolande d'Anjou, and she was herself a sister-in-law to Duke René. Quite how Chastelain's work should have reached these particular readers will be suggested below. For the moment, however, we should stress that this instance of the reception of his writing in France was not an isolated case.

Most of Chastelain's *opuscula* are now to be found in composite manuscripts of the fifteenth century whose contents provide clues as to the geographical origins of their owners. BN, MS fr. 12788 contains Chastelain's *Lyon rampant*, along with a smattering of verse by Pierre Michault and Jean Molinet. BR, MS 21521-31, with its copies of *Le temple de Bocace* and *Le miroir de mort*, also incorporates the *Voyages et ambassades* of Guillebert de Lannoy, the anonymous *Lyon couronné* and two works by Molinet. In cases such as these we may assume a Burgundian provenance for the manuscript, since each consists in the main of works which were produced at or for the court. But many of Chastelain's works are also to be found in volumes consisting of the work of mainstream French poets, such as Christine de Pisan, Charles d'Orléans or François Villon.[167] Copies of *La complainte d'Hector*, the *Épistre à Jean Castel*, *L'oultré*

---

bibliothèque de feu Monsieur le Baron James de Rothschild, Paris 1884–1920, i. no. 487; *De la lecture des livres françois, considérée comme amusement: première partie*, Paris 1780, 295–316.
[163] vi, 217-18.
[164] Bliggenstorfer, 'Castellani Georgii', 132-3; BR, MS II 2545, fo. 4v.
[165] As Kervyn points out in a footnote to his publication of the *Paroles*.
[166] BM Rouen, MS 1234; A. Coville, *Recherches sur quelques écrivains du XIVe et du XVe siècle*, Paris 1935, 164-7; J. Dupic, 'Un bibliophile breton au XVe siècle, Jean de Derval', *Trésors des bibliothèques de France* xix (1935), 157-62.
[167] Cf. BN, MSS fr. 1104, 2264, 2861, 25434.

d'amour, Le miroir de mort and *La mort de Charles VII* are preserved in contemporary manuscripts which are largely devoted to the work of the dominant French literary figure of the fifteenth century, Alain Chartier.[168] Here it would seem that Chastelain had attracted the attention of a less parochial audience.

The likelihood that this readership included subjects of the French crown with marked royalist sympathies is suggested by the reception of a work mentioned earlier, *Le dit de vérité*. This poem survives in a complete state in only one manuscript, but Chastelain was later to claim that it had been 'divulgué en diverses mains' within the kingdom. As a result, he claimed, he had been 'durement mesvolu, jusques à estre menacé de grief de corps' (vi, 244), and was led to take the unusual step of writing a lengthy justification which was presented to Philip the Good.[169] It may seem suspicious that Chastelain is our only source on this scandal, but the reaction to his *Lyon rampant* (1467) suggests that he was not exaggerating the breadth of the reception of his work in the kingdom.[170] This poem, commemorating the achievements of his ducal master, was first circulated at the Burgundian court. It was imitated there by Jean Molinet. Over time, however, the *Lyon rampant* elicited no fewer than five replies from different parts of France.[171] One is an anonymous 'responce à Georges', but the others are attributed in the manuscripts to specific authors: 'Petit Dare de Rouen', apparently of Norman extraction but otherwise unknown; Gilles des Ormes, who was based at Blois in the service of Charles d'Orléans's widow, Mary of Cleves; René Tardif, described as a servant of Charles d'Anjou, count of Maine; and Jean Robertet, who by this stage in his career was associated with the courts of Jean II de Bourbon and Louis XI.[172] These responses to the *Lyon rampant*, combined with the reaction to *Le dit de vérité* and the manuscript survival of other *opuscula*, all point to the conclusion that Chastelain's work attained a significant degree of penetration within the wider Francophone world during his lifetime. The point is significant for our purposes and must be explained.

The dissemination of Chastelain's work owed much to the existence of an informal network of communication which linked the articulate of later medieval France. Poets and writers sought each other out to exchange verse and engage in debate, and it was by means of this literary grapevine that works were circulated and reputations made or broken. If Gilles des Ormes knew of Chastelain's *Lyon rampant*, this was probably because Chastelain, as we have

---

[168] J. C. Laidlaw, *The poetical works of Alain Chartier*, Cambridge 1974, 62, 104–6, 109–10, 115–16, 119–20.

[169] See ch. 1 above; Thiry, 'Stylistique et auto-critique', esp. pp. 101–21.

[170] vii, 207–12.

[171] Paris, BN, MS fr. 1717, fos 2v–5; MS fr. 12788, fo. 129. Kervyn does not print that of René Tardif, and implies that these works from French sources were replies to Molinet's poem, rather than Chastelain's. This is not the implication in the manuscripts.

[172] Poirion, *Le poète et le prince*, 179, 182–3; Charles d'Orléans, *Poésies*, i. 617–18; Paris, BN, MS fr. 1717, fo. 4; L. Turlin, 'Notes sur Jean Robertet, grand rhétoriqueur, secrétaire de Jean II de Bourbon', *Bulletin de la Société d'émulation du Bourbonnais* lix (1976), 231–47.

seen, had already made a name for himself in Orleanist circles: in 1454 he had participated in an exchange of verse with Charles d'Orléans (whom he had impressed), Olivier de La Marche and Pierre Chastellain, the poet of René d'Anjou.[173] Exchanges such as this, or the correspondence which Chastelain conducted with Jean Castel at the French royal court, were rather more than innocent pastimes.[174] They provided the means by which an author's work could be relayed to a wider audience. The correspondence with Castel, for example, survives in at least three contemporary manuscripts, none of which appears to have belonged to either author. If, as has been suggested, Chastelain's work did indeed influence that of Guillaume Gaudoul at the court of René d'Anjou, then we may suspect that it was through these or similar channels.[175]

We are able to illustrate this process more fully with two particular cases, the first of which is provided by *Les douze dames de rhétorique*.[176] The exchange was instigated by Jean Robertet, then secretary, counsellor and poet to Jean II de Bourbon. In his epistles Robertet displays an impressive and revealing familiarity with Chastelain's early work by making reference to *Le lyon bandé*, *L'oultré d'amour*, *Le miroir des nobles hommes de France* and *Le throsne azuré*. Within just eight years of his appointment Chastelain's *opuscula* had already begun to circulate among the literati of France. Robertet sought the honour of receiving a piece of verse from the great man, and to this end enlisted the support of two nobles with connections at the courts of Burgundy and Bourbon, Antoine de Vergy and André de Vitri-La Rière. From this point the correspondence between the two poets became a matter of public attention. After much prompting from his three supplicants Chastelain seems to have been pressurised by the Burgundian court into picking up the challenge. When it finally came his reply to Robertet was considered a public event in itself. Chastelain's verse was formally presented to the duke of Bourbon at a court banquet by (for some unknown reason) a chamberlain of Charles VII. Robertet records that the work was 'prise en gré de lui, (et) louée de tous', and afterwards 'recueillie en tel honneur et vénérence qu'il appertient à si haut et riche envoy'. He even felt it necessary to address to de Vergy 'une petite épistre testificative de la réception' accorded to the text (vii, 183). The exchange of verse between Chastelain and Robertet thus drew in a much wider audience – Bourbon, Burgundian and possibly even royal – which took a lively and active interest in the work of the poets.

---

[173] See ch. 2 above.
[174] For this and what follows on Castel see vi, 139–45.
[175] G. Gros, '*Querant l'un oeil envers les cieulx estendre*', MA xcviii (1992), 429–45 at pp. 444–5. It has even been suggested that Chastelain's work may have been an influence on Villon: van Hemelryck, 'Villon'.
[176] In addition to the studies of Muhlethaler and Zsuppan cited above see *Les douze dames de rhétorique*, ed. L. Batissier, Moulins 1838; M.-R. Jung, 'Les *Douze dames de rhétorique*', *Actes du IIIe colloque international sur le moyen français*, Tübingen 1982, 229–40; C. J. Brown, 'Du nouveau sur le "mistere" des *Douze dames de rhétorique*', BCRH cliii (1987), 181–221.

A similar pattern can be detected in the reception of Chastelain's work in Breton circles, where Chastelain's correspondent was Jean Meschinot, 'gentil homme de la garde' and poet to François II and his ally, Gui XIV, count of Laval.[177] Like Robertet, Meschinot appears to have been acquainted with Chastelain's work, for the influence of the former's *Lay de Nostre Dame de Boulogne* and some of his *Ballades* has been detected in the poetry of his Breton counterpart.[178] Relations between the two men developed further around the time of the war of the Public Weal or shortly after when Chastelain sent Meschinot a copy of *Le prince*.[179] The work was a thinly veiled attack on Louis XI. Meschinot warmed to its themes in his own *Vingt-cinq ballades*.[180] In the wake of this correspondence and no doubt as a result of it, both Meschinot and Chastelain were to attract attention at the courts of Burgundy and Brittany respectively. Jean de Croy, chamberlain to Charles the Bold and a personal friend of Chastelain's, commissioned Meschinot to write a *Complainte* on the death of Isabella of Portugal in 1472.[181] In turn Chastelain's work gained currency in Meschinot's circles. As we have seen, Meschinot enjoyed the protection of Count Gui XIV of Laval. Gui's daughter was none other than Hélène de Derval, mentioned above in connection with *Les paroles de trois puissants princes*.[182] This work was part of a composite manuscript which she and her husband had made for them, now MS 1234 of the Bibliothèque municipale in Rouen. The volume is in fact the second largest contemporary collection of Chastelain's *opuscula*. Just as Robertet had acted as a conduit through which Chastelain's work was channelled to a Bourbon audience, Meschinot seems to have fulfilled a similar function in Breton circles.

From this brief survey of the diffusion and reception of the *opuscula* it is apparent that Chastelain was able to formulate a clear idea of the intended audience for his Chronicle as he worked on the text. Part of his task entailed the fashioning of an historical consciousness within the court elite and associated urban elites which centred upon the person of the prince and his deeds. Hence, for example, the texts he produced to commemorate the death of Philip the Good and the accession of Charles the Bold, or those which were probably performed or read on the occasion of ducal entries into Utrecht, Mons and Ghent. At the same time, Chastelain was aware that his work was known at

---

[177] A. de La Borderie, 'Jean Meschinot, sa vie et ses oeuvres', BEC lvi (1895), 99–140, 274–317, 601–33.

[178] Jean Meschinot, *Lunettes des princes*, ed. C. Martineau-Genieys, Geneva 1972, pp. xxxv, xxxviii.

[179] vii, 457–86. The work was once thought to have been written around 1453 as a general attack on all princes: A. Piaget, '*Les princes* de Georges Chastellain', Romania xlvii (1921), 161–206. This view has been rejected – the work was directed instead against Louis XI: J.-C. Delclos, '*Le prince* ou *les princes* de Georges Chastellain: un poème dirigé contre Louis XI', Romania cii (1981), 46–74. For a revision see L. W. Johnson, 'Prince or princes? Fifteenth-century politics and poetry', The French Review lxviii (1995), 421–30.

[180] Meschinot, *Lunettes*, xlii–liii.

[181] Ibid. xxxii–iii.

[182] Coville, *Recherches*, 164–7; Bliggenstorfer, *Le temple de Bocace*, 84.

the courts of the king, the dukes of Brittany, Orléans, Bourbon and Anjou, as well as at those of the counts of Maine and Laval. Here, the historical issues which he defined and commented upon had a broader resonance: the reconquest of France, the death, accession and conduct of kings, or the good government of the realm. Just as his post was born of an historical moment of Franco-Burgundian dialogue, so it perpetuated that dialogue through the lines of communication which naturally linked the courts of France. His was a Burgundian voice which was heard in the kingdom. Crucially, Chastelain carried that knowledge into the writing of his Chronicle.

As we saw in in the first two chapters, it is hazardous to isolate the political culture of a distinct Burgundian state from that of other elites within the kingdom. Chastelain and his friends at court illustrate this problem at one level; the political interests and inclinations of his first ducal master at another. It is clear that similar difficulties arise in defining an autonomous Burgundian historical culture. The nature of Chastelain's appointment as the mainstream representative of Burgundian historiography provides strong evidence of the continuing cultural influence of the Dionysian tradition, just as the ducal library itself reveals the persistence and vitality of Francocentric traditions in court circles. When 'Norman' is supplanted by 'Burgundian' and 'French' substituted for 'English' in the following passage, a comment on the historiography of an earlier period becomes relevant to our own: 'The truth of the matter was that it was impossible for the Normans to suppress the English tradition. England . . . had a much longer history which was bound to capture the imagination of anyone with a historical turn of mind.'[183] These observations will be carried into a reading of the Chronicle, the subject of the next chapter but one. Before we can broach such a reading, however, a major impediment to our understanding of Chastelain's intentions must be addressed – the fragmentary survival of the text itself.

---

[183] R. H. C Davis, *The Normans and their myth*, London 1976, 130.

4

The Making of the Chronicle

Few historians – if any – have considered Chastelain's Chronicle to be a failure. When the work is approached from the perspective of the patronage nexus discussed in the previous chapter, that conclusion seems inescapable. Instead of the sustained, coherent, accessible narrative which Philip the Good or his son might have hoped for, the Chronicle survives in a series of disjointed fragments.[1] Some or all of the intervening passages may have been lost in the course of the work's *Nachleben*.[2] Within those that remain, lacunae of greater or lesser length – incomplete sentences, missing chapters or series of chapters – impair the text's coherence. This has been taken as an indication that the work was never finished.[3] If so, the official Burgundian chronicle clearly did not measure up to its Dionysian counterpart as an 'auxiliaire du pouvoir'.[4] Political and historical cultures might seem to converge once more, this time

---

[1] The surviving text may be divided into seven sections of unequal length and varying internal coherence. Each is published by Kervyn, with the exception of new material in London, BL, Add. MS 54156 for the years 1455, 1457 and 1458–61. This material was first edited (but not in its entirety) in H. Kondo, 'Étude de la *Chronique* de Georges Chastelain: le texte inédit du IVe livre de *Chronique* d'après le manuscrit de la British Library Add. MS 54156 (folios 309r–426r)', unpubl. Ph.D. diss. International Christian University, Tokyo 1988. A fuller, more accessible edition was published by Delclos in 1991 (see table of abbreviations). The seven sections of text may be divided in the following manner: (a) 1419–22 (i, 1–348): from the news of John's murder at Montereau to the burial of Charles VI; (b) 1430–31 (ii, 5–220): from the foundation of the Order of the Golden Fleece, ending (despite two prolongations on the subject of the Hussites and the Council of Basel) with a French attack on Corbie, shortly after the burning of Joan at Rouen. Kervyn's publication of an account of the Ghent war at this point (ii, 221–390) is based on a mistaken attribution discussed more fully below; (c) 1454–62 (iii, 5–49; Delclos, 325–7; iii, 50–229; Delclos, 29–111; iii, 230–445; Delclos, 329–30; iii, 445–90; Delclos, 121–323; iv, 5–276): from Philip the Good's return from the empire to an English raid on Brittany in Aug.–Sept. 1462; (d) 1463–4 (iv, 277–498; v, 5–212): from the arrival of Marie d'Anjou at Sluis to an account of the French embassy sent to Lille on the affair of the bastard of Rubempré; (e) Aug. 1466 (v, 212–27): a brief passage mainly concerned with the marriage and political difficulties of Louis de Luxembourg; (f) 1467–8 (v, 227–445): from the death of Philip the Good, ending shortly before the conference at Péronne; (g) 1470 (v, 447–508): from an account of the royal embassy to Charles at St Omer, ending shortly before Edward IV's flight to the Low Countries. In these divisions of the work I have avoided referring to the distinct books which, although sometimes mentioned in the text, were ultimately imposed by Kervyn. They will be discussed more fully at a later stage.

[2] Discussed in ch. 6 below.

[3] Cf. Kervyn's comment at i, p. xliii.

[4] Guenée, *Histoire et culture historique*, 345.

to ironic effect: the discrete fragments of Chastelain's Chronicle mirror the disparate dominions of the dukes themselves.

This is not to over-politicise or demean what others have often considered to be a work of considerable literary merit in its present condition. Historiography, particularly of the official variety, served political ends; it furnished (or was intended to furnish) the dynasty with a cohesive, rational and viable view of the past. The present chapter seeks to establish the reasons for and extent of these apparent shortcomings in advance of our reading of the work. Was the enterprise flawed in conception and/or execution? Was it sufficiently encouraged and sustained by the dynasty which was its intended beneficiary? To answer these questions we must consider the making of the Chronicle: its written sources, their nature and provenance; the manner and speed of its redaction; and the extent of any archetype in Chastelain's possession. The aim is to evaluate the gap which appears to separate the Chronicle in its present state from the aspirations and model that lay behind it. Only then can a reading of the surviving fragments be attempted.

Written sources

Some attempt to identify Chastelain's sources is necessary, not least because they, and the channels through which they passed, reveal the extent of the assistance given by his sponsor. Diligent patrons concerned themselves with such matters. St Denis was a natural locale for royal historiography thanks to the abbey's substantial library.[5] Patrons could provide writers with access to libraries other than their own, as Anne of Brittany did for her official chronicler in 1498; or access to archival documentation, as Charles VII did for Jean Juvenal des Ursins in 1444.[6] Some took this logic further by commissioning histories from bureaucrats who were already familiar with their archival repositories, or by instructing the administration – as happened in Hungary and Milan – to supply historians with material on a regular basis.[7] Burgundian official history may have been sustained in comparable ways.

Before this possibility is examined, however, two important obstacles to the identification of Chastelain's sources deserve emphasis. First, it is often

---

[5] J. W. Thompson, *The medieval library*, Chicago 1939, 308.
[6] Guenée, *Histoire et culture historique*, 99; P. S. Lewis, 'War propaganda and historiography in fifteenth-century France and England', *TRHS* 5th ser. xv (1965), 1–21 at p. 16 (repr. in his *Essays*).
[7] H. Courteault, 'Un archiviste des comtes de Foix au XVe siècle', *Annales du Midi* vi (1894), 272–300. The Hungarian royal chancery provided charters for János Küküllei's biography of Louis I: E. Mályusz, 'La chancellerie royale et la rédaction des chroniques dans la Hongrie médiévale', *MA* lxxv (1969), 51–86, 219–54. In the duchy of Milan, ready-made collections of documents – prepared by the chancery for the use of Crivelli and Simonetta – were sufficiently sophisticated for one commentator to describe them as 'blueprints for history': G. Ianziti, *Humanistic historiography under the Sforzas*, Oxford 1988, esp. pp. 61–174.

impossible to tell whether the chronicler derived his information from a text that had come into his possession, or from an oral source which conveyed much the same news.[8] We know that his account of the crusading exploits of Jean de Rebremettes was based upon the testimony of a herald of the king of Castile.[9] Chastelain met and conversed with this herald, yet he may also have seen the latter's written account.[10] He was well-informed on the ambassadorial addresses by Jean le Boursier (1455) and George Neville (1463), and was probably in the audience on both occasions.[11] But written versions of these discourses were also available, and it is impossible to know whether Chastelain used these, his own recollections or even both.[12] Such cases may reveal the chronicler's access to material or the wisdom of appointing an official historian who was often resident at court, but they do little to ease the task which has been set here.

A second problem lies in the fact that Chastelain was more concerned with producing a work of high history than he was with revealing its constituent parts, let alone their provenance. In places he does provide a glimpse of his working practices and the care he took over his material. News of Louis XI's close escape when sailing on the Gironde in 1462 was very probably conveyed to the Burgundian court in a letter. Chastelain carefully noted that the source did not reveal whether the English who had pursued the king's ship were aware of the identity of its precious passenger.[13] News of John Hunyadi's great victory at Belgrade in July 1456 came to the official chronicler in two slightly different forms. Chastelain gave both, 'pour satisfaire à toutes deux et à ceux qui les ont envoiées' (iii, 113).[14] These examples aside, however, he – like the majority of his contemporaries, it must be said – did not share Matthew Paris's predilection for the *pièce justificative* or the explicit reference.[15] The value of a work of history was measured less by any modern standards of accuracy than by its acceptability to a contemporary audience. The standing of the patron or the

---

[8] Delclos also makes this point, citing the chronicler's use of both written and oral sources on the coronation of Louis XI (iv, 45): *Le témoignage*, 47. For some of the texts Chastelain might have used see Paris, BN, MS fr. 5739, fos 238–44; L. P. Gachard (ed.), *La Bibliothèque nationale à Paris*, Brussels 1875–7, i. 90–1.

[9] Delclos, 77–9.

[10] BM Besançon, Collection Chifflet MS 208, fos 58–9.

[11] iii, 36–7 (Boursier); iv, 374–5 (Neville). On the practice of reading letters aloud at court see *Dispatches*, i. 348.

[12] Plancher, *Histoire*, iv. no. clxx; Paris, BN, MS fr. 1278, fos 64–5v. Another example is to be found in Chastelain's account of the curiously excessive hospitality Philip showed to the queen in 1464: cf. v, 27–31 and the duke's letter to Louis XI on the matter, published in Philippe de Commynes, *Mémoires*, ed. D. Godefroy and Lenglet du Fresnoy, Paris 1747, iv. 422–6. Chastelain's text accurately reflects the letter's description of the episode, but it may equally have been recounted to him by friends at court.

[13] iv, 198. See also iv, 220: the 'sobre record des choses' prevented him from placing too much interpretation on news from the East.

[14] In contrast to this diligence, however, Chastelain admits that 'n'ai point fait fortes enquestes' into Warwick's 1470 coup against Edward IV: v, 489.

[15] R. Vaughan, *Matthew Paris*, London 1958 repr. 1979, 5.

author carried more weight than any carefully constructed critical apparatus. Official chroniclers naturally had an authority which few historians could match – and Chastelain, as we have seen, took particular care to emphasise his own.[16]

These problems should be borne in mind, but they are not insurmountable. This is particularly true of Chastelain's use of narrative sources rather than official information. Most medieval chroniclers looked first to an existing body of literature for their material. Chastelain's cultural baggage was impressive – or at least it was made to appear so, particularly in the *opuscula*. Citations, references or mere allusions hinting at a vaster literary substructure (rather than an information-gathering network) naturally lent credence to the author's *oeuvre* and drew the prospective reader or listener into an orbit of assent – a consideration of great importance to any writer who wished to convey his message. Not surprisingly, therefore, Chastelain reveals an easy familiarity with Scripture and patristic writings.[17] In the same vein there are many references to specific classical authors or, more generally, to 'les nobles historiographes romains' (iii, 359).[18] These were more or less stock references to the formative traditions of western historiography.[19] More interestingly, perhaps, we may also infer that he had some familiarity with the work of authors as diverse as Gregory of Tours,[20] Geoffrey of Monmouth,[21] Galbert of Bruges,[22] Alan of Lille[23] and Giovanni Boccaccio.[24] He appears to have read Christine de Pisan (on Charles V at least),[25] as well as anonymous histories or epics

---

[16] See ch. 1 above, and B. Guenée, '*Authentique at approuvé*', in *La lexicographie du latin médiéval*, Paris 1981, 215–29.

[17] Cf. i, 2–4, 45; ii, 115; iii, 43, 413, 449; Delclos, 99, 252, 317, 320; iv, 19–20, 309; vi, 62, 64, 82, 132; vii, 5, 19ff., 110, 111, 128, 139, 276, 295–7, 363, 384–92.

[18] Cf. i, 4–6, 45; ii, 151–2, 181; iii, 349; iv, 227–8, 296, 356; v, 168, 356; vi, 53–4, 79, 150, 152, 164, 167ff., 171; vii, 43, 54, 169, 174–7, 316, 330, 365–6, 370–2, 379, 424–6.

[19] This is not to dismiss the importance of Chastelain's literary sources – the topic is simply too vast for full consideration here.

[20] This is suggested by C. Thiry with regard to Chastelain's cryptic reference to 'la vision de Méronnée' in his *Exposition* (vi, 413–14): 'Stylistique et auto-critique', 111 n. 17. Thiry suggests this may be a misreading, and in fact a reference to the vision of Mérouvée in Gregory of Tours, *History of the Franks*, v, ch. xiv, where Mérouvée's chances of inheriting the Frankish kingdom are discussed. To these observations it is worth adding that the application of Salic law in the kingdom of the Franks is dated in some texts to the start of Mérouvée's reign, enabling him to succeed from Clodion le Chevelu: C. Beaune, *Naissance de la nation France*, Paris 1985, 53, 234, 277, 283. Philip the Good's library contained an (unidentified) 'croniques de France, nommées Merouée': Barrois, *Bibliothèque*, 205, no. 1418. Chastelain's reference may well have come from this source.

[21] See vii, 381–2.

[22] Chastelain does not mention Galbert, but digresses upon the subject matter of his work on the murder of Charles the Good, count of Flanders (i, 26).

[23] See vi, 332.

[24] In addition to *Le temple de Bocace* see v, 40; vi, 80.

[25] His digression (vii, 325–8) on Charles V in the *Advertissement au duc Charles* is most likely to have come from the principal work on the subject, Christine's *Livre des fais et bonnes meurs du sage roy Charles Quint*.

concerning the Arthurian legends,[26] Richard II of England,[27] Ogier le Danois, Doon de Mayence or Girart de Roussillon.[28] This is almost certainly the tip of the iceberg. As we shall see in the next chapter, the true extent of the author's learning seems to have been far greater.

How was the chronicler to feed such an eclectic reading habit? Whatever the extent of his reading in his youth, it is clear that Chastelain continued to digest a wide variety of work throughout his life.[29] There is no surviving indication that he had his own library at the Salle-le-Comte. If he did, however, the evidence relating to the libraries of his colleagues at court, avid readers but wealthier individuals in their own right, suggests that his personal collection, however impressive by contemporary standards, was unlikely to have met his needs.[30] Nor was Valenciennes a particularly promising source.[31] It would seem, therefore, that the chronicler was indebted to his patron in the first instance for the use of his well-stocked library. Two other further strands of evidence point to this conclusion. First, other court literati (Jean Mansel, Jean d'Enghien, Jean de Wavrin and Guillaume Fillastre, among others) were able to consult or borrow books from the duke's collection. William Caxton had the same privilege.[32] It is scarcely conceivable that the official chronicler was any less fortunate than the dilettante or the interested outsider. Secondly, a high proportion of the texts which Chastelain cites or alludes to were kept in the library.[33] They were looked after by Jean Martin, a ducal *garde des joyaux* who thought sufficiently highly of Chastelain's work to possess a copy of the *Temple de Bocace*, and Jacques de Brégilles, another *garde des joyaux* whose

---

[26] iii, 279; vi, 53.
[27] i, 26; v, 501.
[28] vii, 425.
[29] Chastelain's education is discussed in ch. 1 above.
[30] Cf. Bartier, *Légistes*, 276–7; A. Boinet, 'Un bibliophile du XVe siècle', BEC lxvii (1906), 255–69; C. C. Willard, 'Isabel of Portugal, patroness of humanism?', in *Miscellanea di studi e ricerche sul quattrocento Francese a cura di Franco Simone*, Turin 1967, 517–45; A. Naber, 'Les manuscrits d'un bibliophile bourguignon du XVe siècle, Jean de Wavrin', RN lxxii (1990), 23–48; Van Praet, *Louis de Bruges*, 181–3.
[31] The first evidence of a bookseller in the town dates to 1486. For this and the question of libraries in Valenciennes see Servant, 'Culture, art et société', i. 286–319.
[32] P. Saintenoy, *Les arts et les artistes à la cour de Bruxelles*, Brussels 1934, 91–122; Doutrepont, *Littérature*, 465–8; D. Bornstein, 'William Caxton's chivalric romances and the Burgundian renaissance in England', *English Studies* lvii (1976), 1–10.
[33] Many of the classical sources were translated and abridged in Jean Mansel's monumental and highly successful *Fleur des histoires* which was in the ducal library: Barrois, *Bibliothèque*, nos 714–19. Chastelain's reference (v, 168) to Aristotle's 'enseignemens' to Alexander almost certainly came from 'Les enseignemens que Aristote fist a Alixandre' (no. 955). For Boccaccio in the ducal library see ibid. nos 875, 878, 880, 881, 883; for Geoffrey of Monmouth, no. 1927; for Richard II, no. 1456; for Christine de Pisan on Charles V, nos 917, 984; for Arthurian romances, nos 1234, 1239, 1245, 1263; for Girart de Roussillon, no. 1446; and for Ogier le Danois, nos 1317–18.

probity Chastelain admired.[34] The Chronicle was thus the product of Burgundian historical culture as it was conserved in the ducal library.

Due deference to appropriate historical authorities was naturally more impressive in a chronicle than a dazzling array of literary references.[35] Here, Chastelain set forth his credentials by claiming to have used 'les escrits des historiographes nouveaux de mon temps' (i, 12). In reality he seems to have drawn on one work in particular, the Chronicle of Enguerran de Monstrelet (another text from the ducal library).[36] As the earliest sustained narrative of the initial stages of Philip's reign, Monstrelet's Chronicle provided a full, convenient and authoritative source for Chastelain's redaction of events in his first and second surviving fragments. The following passage is fairly typical of the tinkering he carried out on his predecessor's work (Monstrelet first, Chastelain second with principal alterations in italics):

> Or est vérité que après ce que le duc Phelippe de Bourgongne eut célébré la feste de la Purificacion de Nostre Dame, délaissant ilec [Arras] la duchesse sa femme, s'en ala en son chastel de Bapaumes et puis à Oissy en Cambrésis, devers sa tante, la contesse de Haynnau, avecques laquelle eut parlement.[37]

> Philippe doncques, le duc bourgongnon, se partit d'Arras tantost après *la Chandeleur*, laissa la duchesse sa femme audit lieu, et mut en noble et bel arroy de seigneurie et de belles gens d'armes. La nuit prit son premier gist à Bapaumes, et lendemain à Oisy en Cambresis, vers *la douagière de Haynaut*, sa tante, pour aucuns certains affaires, dont ils prirent advis ensemble. (i, 106)

With the exception of certain chapters which were omitted or abridged and a limited number (containing few substantive additions) which were added, Chastelain's first fragment is extremely close to the corresponding text in Monstrelet.[38] His second fragment displays greater independence, as witnessed by the continuing practice of omission or abridgement and the addition of substantively new chapters.[39] Some of these additions may be explained by the chronicler's increasing willingness to include his personal experiences or

---

[34] Jean's ownership of this manuscript is discussed in ch. 3 above; as we saw in ch. 2 above, Chastelain knew Jean's brother, Philippe. For Brégilles see v, 230–2, and Paviot, 'Jacques de Brégilles'.
[35] Which may explain why the *opuscula* are more heavily laden with literary references than the Chronicle.
[36] Barrois, *Bibliothèque*, no. 705.
[37] Monstrelet, *Chronique*, iii. 374.
[38] Chastelain's debt to Monstrelet has long been recognised, but was first fully examined in Delclos, 'Le témoignage', i. 30–147. It is not necessary to repeat the detail found there. It is possible that variations between Chastelain's account of events surrounding the death of Michelle de France at Ghent in 1422 and that of Monstrelet, detected by Delclos, stem from Chastelain drawing upon his own recollections or, more likely, upon views he might have heard later within his family: Delclos, 'Le témoignage', 89.
[39] Relating, for example, the 1430 entry of Philip the Good into Ghent, his succession as duke of Brabant in the same year and Chastelain's famous gallery of princely portraits.

knowledge of events, but others appear to have originated in a second source of written material to which we shall return.

Monstrelet's Chronicle was often supplemented in Burgundian texts by those other potential mines of information for this period, French royal histories. This fact is further proof, if any were needed, that the Dionysian tradition loomed large in the Burgundian historical consciousness.[40] Chastelain himself acknowledged a debt to 'toutes les choses escrites à Saint-Denys' in his prologue (i, 12), and we have seen that the ducal library was well-stocked with the different recensions of the *Grandes Chroniques*. Delclos found no evidence for any such borrowings.[41] The omission is curious in view of the Dionysian influence on Chastelain's appointment. Mindful of the Breton attitude to French royal history, we may even find it suspicious: did the official chronicler deliberately eschew the pervasive influence of the abbey of St Denis when writing ducal history?

There are a number of reasons to think not. In reality the royal chronicles were of limited use to Chastelain in his first two surviving fragments, the only sections of his text in which he was reliant upon other histories. There was little in the corresponding passages of Pintoin's work to retain his attention. By comparison with Monstrelet's accounts of the sieges of Roye or Melun, for example, Pintoin's are perfunctory in the extreme. The same can be said of Jean Chartier's narrative for 1430 and 1431, the subject matter of Chastelain's second fragment. The royal chronicler's account of these years runs to a mere ten printed pages. It follows from these observations that Chastelain may well have used the work of his French counterpart where it seemed more suited to his task. The surviving fragments of his Chronicle do not reveal this, but we should not assume that the same holds true of any intervening passages he might have written.

It is also difficult to reconcile the apparent omission of Dionysian sources with Chastelain's references elsewhere to 'les choses escrites à Saint-Denys'. Pierre de Brézé's exploits, he reminded his reader, were recorded 'ès croniques du roy aussi' (iii, 347). He abbreviated his account of the coronation of Louis XI in 1461 because 'ce se peut trouver ès registres divers qui tousjours s'entretiennent et s'en vont d'un train' (iv, 62). This knowledge of the French 'kalendes' (vi, 238) is further confirmed by his account of how, in 1461, Louis XI 'prist indignation contre ceux de Saint-Denis et par courroux tira hors des mains l'autorité de chroniquer, et [la] mist en la main d'un religieux de Clugny, lequel il manda venir devers luy, appelé maistre Jehan' (iv, 100). The 'Maistre Jehan' in question was none other than Jean Castel, whom Chastelain was quick to engage in a mutually appreciative literary correspondence. Contact between the royal and ducal traditions was direct and personal in this case.

---

[40] On the systematic use of Jean Chartier's Chronicle by the anonymous Burgundian continuator of Monstrelet, Jacques du Clercq and Jean de Wavrin see Stenghers, 'Sur trois chroniqueurs'.

[41] Delclos, *Le témoignage*, 33.

Moreover, Chastelain did not simply show an interest in the royal chronicles. In certain passages he clearly borrowed from them. Chartier may have been of limited use, but he did incorporate some detail from the royal historian's account of the battle of Mons-en-Vimeu.[42] In a passage concerning a banquet in honour of the recently crowned king in 1461, Chastelain mentioned the last time – according to 'ce que on en trouve par escript' (iv, 85) – the 'table de marbre' had been used. This occurred during the visit of Emperor Charles IV to Paris in 1378, an event described in detail by Pierre d'Orgemont in his recension of the *Grandes Chroniques*.[43]

Chastelain also mimicked the Dionysian habit of creating epithets for kings of France.[44] His rationale for choosing the epithet 'l'Auguste' for Philip the Good provides a clear example of a borrowing from the traditions of St Denis. Philip was august because his fortunes were forever augmenting, he was august in bearing and – to milk the point to the full – because he was born in the month of August (ii, 150-1). The fact that Philip was born in July was clearly irrelevant.[45] The point here was to establish a credible and hopefully durable epithet: and where better to look than in the royal chronicles? Hence the direct correspondence between Chastelain's justification and that advanced more than two centuries earlier on behalf of Philip II by the Dionysian monk Rigord.[46] The chronicler had clearly used the work of his French counterparts; not slavishly, however, but creatively, for royal memories were here used to Burgundian ends. The passage testifies to a process of selective appropriation rather than one of unthinking acculturation. A common historical culture certainly linked the two official traditions, the one well established, the other nascent. They did not necessarily arrive at the same conclusions.[47]

To judge from Froissart's extensive use of Le Bel and other texts, the availability of such authoritative, ready-made sources could greatly accelerate the redaction process.[48] In this respect Monstrelet's Chronicle was a boon to

---

[42] Relating Philip the Good's first military engagement with the supporters of the dauphin, Chastelain mentions that one of the duke's captains wore his master's arms in order to shield him from being singled out by the enemy: i, 260. This piece of information, absent in Monstrelet and other accounts of the battle, is mentioned in Chartier, *Chronique*, i. 20.
[43] *Les Grandes Chroniques de France*, ed. P. Paris, Paris 1836-8, vi. 381-98. This was a particularly famous episode in royal historical culture – Charles V of France had used the occasion to give the emperor a lesson on the history of his kingdom.
[44] After considering the epithets attributed to previous kings of France by their Dionysian chroniclers, Chastelain alights on the epithet 'vertu' for Charles VII (Delclos, 315-22).
[45] 31 July 1396: Bonenfant, *Philippe*, 7.
[46] *Oeuvres de Rigord et de Guillaume le Breton*, ed. H.-F. Delaborde, Paris 1882-85, i. 6.
[47] This theme will be taken further in ch. 5 below. In the *Exposition sur vérité mal prise*, Chastelain upbraids his French audience and refers them to truths which 'les histoires françoises récitent et recordent': vi, 344. The reader is also told to look in the chronicles 'faites et escrites de ceux de vostre parti, de ceux qui vous faveurent et magnifient, et qui vivent de vos gages et bienfaits': vi, 401. This attitude is challenging, not deferential.
[48] P. Philippeau, 'Froissart et Jean Le Bel', *RN* xxii (1936), 81-111; J. J. N. Palmer, 'Froissart et le héraut Chandos', *MA* lxxxviii (1982), 271-92.

Chastelain: the subject matter of the two men coincided as far as 1444. As he drew nearer to the period in which he was writing, however, it is clear that Chastelain ceased to rely upon earlier chronicles. The task of recording 'par ordre' the 'grands et difficiles affaires' of history was not quite so easy now, as he admitted himself: 'pour en faire la narration, sans chanceler, ne varier çà, ne là, *ne faire d'autrui estoffe ouvrage d'emprunt*, il y a chose haute et de grand effet' (v, 243).[49] These problems were eased by the availability and, it will be shown, the provision of a wide variety of source materials including private correspondence, newsletters, memoranda and diplomatic instruments.

Apart from his exchanges of verse and letters to the *Chambre des comptes*, all that survives of the chronicler's correspondence is his letter to Philippe de Croy at the siege of Neuss and a reply which, rather ironically, arrived at Valenciennes a short time after his death.[50] Croy's letter is revealing none the less. We learn that this was not an isolated occurrence; the two men were in the habit of writing to one another.[51] To judge from the contents of his reply Croy clearly believed that it was incumbent upon him to provide 'Monsieur l'indiciaire' with news. He digressed upon the duke's movements, the composition of his army, the nature of the Burgundian fortifications and the ambassadors who had visited the camp. Most revealing of all is Croy's final reference to a description of the imperial army and its defensive measures which, he reminds Chastelain, 'vous sont toutes connues, pour quoy je me passe de vous en escrire' (viii, 268). Croy had not sent these 'nouvelles' himself. The implication is that the official chronicler was receiving news by other channels: channels which were sufficiently well-known for the courtier to mention them as a matter of course. This view finds support in Olivier de La Marche's near contemporary description of Chastelain poring over 'rapportz, opinions, advis et ramentevances à luy rapportées, dictes et envoyées'.[52] It would seem that someone, somewhere, was looking after the chronicler's needs.

In reality, however, it is likely that a good deal of this material reached Chastelain from a variety of sources – or, as La Marche puts it, 'de toutes pars'. His correspondence with Croy is again suggestive here. The exchange was effectively public in nature, as witnessed by the rather self-conscious tone of the letters and the fact that they were copied by third parties.[53] Contemporary chroniclers with links to the governing classes must have found material of this nature relatively easy to come by. Mathieu d'Escouchy was able to describe Philip the Good's trip to the Empire in 1454 thanks to the circulation of a letter on the subject, originally addressed to several Burgundian bureaucrats

---

[49] Italics mine.
[50] viii, 261–8. The letter refers to events which occurred early in Mar. 1475. As we have seen, evidence from the financial accounts indicates that Chastelain died on or before 13 Feb.
[51] viii, 266.
[52] La Marche, *Mémoires*, i. 184–5. The passage was written when the memorialist was 45 years old – in other words in the early 1470s, during Chastelain's lifetime.
[53] See ch. 2 above.

by the clerc of Jean de Scoenhove.⁵⁴ We may suspect that Chastelain had seen the letter himself.⁵⁵ The two chroniclers certainly used a common source in the form of a previously unknown newsletter for their accounts of the visit of John of Cleves to the congress of Mantua.⁵⁶ Chastelain's description of the earthquake which devastated Naples in 1456 was also based on a contemporary newsletter of which other chroniclers were aware.⁵⁷ In these and other cases he drew upon a body of material which was available, more or less readily, in the public domain.⁵⁸

His advantage – and it was not inconsiderable – lay in the fact that such correspondence was more accessible at the centre than it was on the periphery. The description by an anonymous Burgundian servant of Louis XI's preparations for his coronation was known to Chastelain, for example, as was an account of the reversal of Edward IV's fortunes in 1470.⁵⁹ This last piece of news was conveyed in a letter from the *bailli* of Dijon, then in Flanders, to 'Monsieur le president du Parlement en Bourgogne'. It is unlikely that Chastelain saw this version, but he had clearly seen a copy just like it – an indication that within the Burgundian administration there existed a network of communication which benefited court personnel.⁶⁰ The centre naturally took a hand in relaying such news further afield.⁶¹ In view of the channels which were open to him, however, we may doubt whether Chastelain had to wait for the formal

---

54 d'Escouchy, *Chronique*, ii. 246–59; iii. 444–8.
55 Chastelain begins his fourth book with a summary of the Regensburg conference which compares in several respects to d'Escouchy's.
56 Delclos, 241–52; d'Escouchy, *Chronique*, ii. 376–93. A substantial fragment of this newsletter is to be found in BM Besançon, MS 1516, fos 9–14v. Writer and addressee are unidentified.
57 Delclos, 95–100; d'Escouchy, *Chronique*, ii. 344–50; Chartier, *Chronique*, iii. 70–2. For copies of the newsletter which conveyed this information see Courtrai, Bibliothèque publique MS 358 (not consulted); and Brussels, BR, MS 19684.
58 For further examples see the 'briefvets' (iv, 150) which were posted at royal command on the churches of Paris instructing the populace to process in honour of the king and duke in 1461; or the letters from Greek ambassadors to Philip the Good which Chastelain refers to (Delclos, 288), and which appear to have been more widely available: G. Brom, *Archivalia in Italië*, The Hague 1908–14, ii. 270.
59 Cf. iv, 55, and *Collection de documents inédits*, ed. Gachard, ii, no. 18, particularly p. 168. For what follows, cf. v, 501–8, and Paris, BN, MS fr. 3887, fos 85r–v: 'la trayson faicte en angleterre au roy Edouard dangleterre comme la escript monsr. le bailli de dijon'.
60 'It is this intimacy of the governing class, its limited size, its inter-connectedness (by kinship and through the ties binding patron and client), and its openness, which make the circulation of news within it easy': C. F. Richmond, 'Hand and mouth', *Journal of Historical Sociology* i (1988), 233–52 at p. 242.
61 Twice in 1453, for example, Philip the Good sent out messengers to the towns around Ghent 'afin de faire crier et publier de par mondit seigneur', first, his reasons for declaring war on Ghent, and second, the truce he had granted to the city: AGR CC1921, fos 236v, 254. In France, the royal administration under Louis XI decided the text of circulars destined for the *bonnes villes* containing news or instructions and even the timing of their dissemination: B. Chevalier, 'The *bonnes villes* and the king's council in fifteenth-century France', in Highfield and Jeffs, *The crown and local communities*, 110–28 at p. 119.

proclamation of ducal letters on matters of public concern.[62] It is conceivable that the count of Charolais's letters to the 'bonnes villes' on the subject of his father's illness in 1462 reached Chastelain in the form of the copy sent to Valenciennes; likewise, Charles's manifesto against the Croy family in 1465, or the widely-circulated letters on the conspiracy of Jean de Chassa in 1470.[63] Elsewhere, however, it is clear that Chastelain did not pick up such information second-hand. Unless we posit the existence of some formal channel of communication, it is difficult to explain his detailed knowledge of the royal letters sent to Tournai in 1460 on the subject of the election of the new bishop, or those which were sent to Bruges in 1463 by Philip the Good to express his discontent at the town's decision to send deputies to a meeting of the estates called by his son.[64]

These cases naturally lead us to ask whether Chastelain was the beneficiary, as Crivelli was in Milan, of some established link between the ducal administration and the post of official historian. The evidence does not reveal the existence of any formal mechanism here, but it does suggest that Chastelain had useful connections with those who recorded the duke's business. In addition to their financial role, the officers of the *Chambres des comptes* provided a relatively sophisticated ancillary service. They were well-versed in the collection, ordering and dissemination of factual information relating to the activities, past and present, of the duke's government.[65] Thanks to their

---

[62] On the dissemination of news see K. A. Fowler, 'News from the front: letters and despatches of the fourteenth century', in P. Contamine, C. Giry-Deloison and M. Keen (eds), *Guerre et société en France, Angleterre et en Bourgogne*, Lille 1991, 63–92; C. A. J. Armstrong, 'Politics and the battle of St Albans', *BIHR* xxxiii (1960), 1–72, and 'Some examples of the distribution and speed of news at the time of the Wars of the Roses', in R. W. Hunt, W. A. Pantin and R. W. Southern (eds), *Studies in medieval history presented to F. M. Powicke*, Oxford 1948, 429–54 (this and the preceding item repr. in his *England, France and Burgundy*, 1–72, 97–122); P. Seguin, 'L'information à la fin du XVe siècle en France: pièces d'actualité imprimées sous le règne de Charles VIII', *Arts et traditions populaires* (1956), 309–30; (1957), 46–74.

[63] Chastelain summarises the 1462 letters at iv, 200–1. An account of their contents and an indication of the recipients (including the municipal authorities at Valenciennes) is to be found in ADN B2045, fos 185v–6v. On the manifesto against the Croy and the letters relating to Chassa see v, 111–12, 472–83. Delclos cites Jacques du Clercq's version of the manifesto against the Croy family: *Le témoignage*, 51 n. 113. The original is published in Gachard, *Collection de documents*, i. 132–43. For the 1470 letter see Duclos, *Histoire de Louis XI*, iii. 360–5. On the 1462 letters and the 1465 manifesto see also *Der Briefwechsel Karls des Kühnen (1433–1477)*, ed. W. Paravicini, Frankfurt am Main 1995, i. 70–1; ii. 111–14.

[64] Delclos, 266; iv, 466–7. Chastelain's use of the written version of the king's wishes as expressed to the Tournaisiens is clearly indicated by the exact reproduction of Charles's view that Toul 'ne lui estoit seur ne féable ne agréable': A. de La Grange, 'Extraits des registres des consaulx de la ville de Tournai, 1431–76', publ. as *Mémoires de la Société historique de Tournai* xxiii (1893), 250–1. The original of Philip's letter to Bruges (31 Dec. 1463) is published in Lettenhove, *Histoire de Flandre*, v. 513–14.

[65] J. Richard, 'Les archives et les archivistes des ducs de Bourgogne', *BEC* cv (1944), 123–69.

inventories, the staff of the *Chambre* were able to refer back to much earlier records in order to retrieve, for specific purposes, a dossier of material or a single document.[66] These could be collated around a theme, such as the debts owed to earlier dukes of Brabant by the French crown, or even rendered into French for ducal ambassadors, as in the case of certain letters 'translatees de hault aleman' in 1455.[67] Archival records served a similar purpose to chronicles; indeed, both were used in the sphere of ducal diplomacy.[68]

The establishment of relations between the official chronicler and the personnel of the *Chambre* would have been a natural step. Unfortunately, Chastelain's unwillingness to clutter his narrative with explicit references, in addition to the problem of conflated oral and written sources in his work, make it virtually impossible to adduce clear examples. Any number of facts mentioned in the Chronicle could have been communicated to Chastelain by the administration. However, there is one piece of evidence which suggests that the step may have been taken. Chastelain was not beholden to the *Chambre des comptes* at Lille for the payment of his salary. He even refused payment from them for his work on their new mural in 1465, which he had travelled the short distance to Lille to inspect.[69] In his letter to this effect, Chastelain stated that

> je ne veul point vendre mon service fait as gens de bien a pris d'argent et par especial a vous autres, lesquelz je veul servir gratis et pour nient et en attente d'avoir bien plus grande retribucion que d'argent. Cele heure poroit venir, veu que souvent ay et puis avoir a faire de vous.[70]

The official historian was thus accustomed to receiving nonpecuniary services from his friends among the personnel of the *Chambre*, and he fully expected to go on receiving such services in the future.

---

[66] Inventories are discussed ibid. 156–9. In 1441 a ducal secretary and the keeper of the charters for Hainaut were paid for the four months they spent at Le Quesnoy putting the charters left by the dowager countess of Hainaut in order and for creating an inventory: AGR CC1921, fos 182v–3. For examples of the retrieval of old documents see ADN B2030, fo. 282v (a copy of the treaty of Arras, sent for in 1458); B2064, fo. 275 (Charles the Bold's request in 1467 for a copy of the act of homage performed by his ancestors for the county of Artois).
[67] Ibid. B2045, fos 199v–200; B2020, fos 280, 281v. For other thematic compilations of documents see B2034, fos 79v–80v (the consultation in 1449 at the 'tresor des chartes de flandres' of documents relating to the Paris conferences of the previous year); B2002, fo. 181v (payment to a royal clerc in 1449 for 'pluseurs extraits et autres copies contenant grandes escriptures touchans tant aux fais de mds. le duc comme de feu mds. son pere').
[68] Cf. O. Cartellieri, 'Über eine burgundische Gesandtschaft an den kaiserlichen und päpstlichen Hof im Jahre 1460', *Mitteilungen des Instituts für Österreichische Geschichtsforchung* (hereinafter cited as *MIOG*) xxviii (1907), 448–64 at pp. 459–60; P. Bonenfant, 'La persistance des souvenirs lotharingiens', *Bulletin de l'Institut historique belge de Rome* xxvii (1952), 53–64 at p. 63, and 'Etat bourguignon et Lotharingie', *Bulletin de l'Académie royale de Belgique* xli (1955), 266–82 at p. 274; A. Leguai, 'Charles le Téméraire et l'histoire', *PCEEBM* xxi (1981), 47–53.
[69] See ch. 3 above.
[70] ADN B17698; Urwin, *Georges Chastelain*, 228–31.

Close links certainly existed between the official chronicler and other elements of the ducal administration. Chastelain derived particular benefit from his relations with Jean Lefèvre de St Rémy, king-at-arms of the Order of the Golden Fleece.[71] Second only to Monstrelet, indeed, Lefèvre was Chastelain's principal source for the redaction of his second fragment. It was from him, for example, that the chronicler lifted an account of the first exploits in arms of his own former patron, Philippe de Ternant (ii, 30–1). He also found Lefèvre useful on the subject of Joan of Arc (ii, 46–7). At times he could not resist the conflation of his two main sources, as in his account of the rout by the French in 1430 of a Burgundian contingent which was too busy hunting to notice the proximity of the enemy. Monstrelet had the Burgundians chasing hares. For Lefèvre, the quarry was a fox.[72] Keen not to miss the dramatic potential of the episode, Chastelain first describes 'le malheureux déduit de lièvres'; then, as the excitement mounted, the appearance of 'un renard, par lequel ils se remirent à la cryée et à la huée' (ii, 127). His use of Lefèvre was more prosaic elsewhere in the second fragment. Rather than adduce further detail, it is more important to note Chastelain's continuing awareness of the value of Toison d'Or's testimony later in his work. The account of the Hungarian embassy to Charles VII in December 1457 is based upon a written source by Lefèvre, for example (iii, 373). In describing the 1461 chapter of the Golden Fleece which took place at St Omer, Chastelain mentioned (but eventually decided not to use) a fuller account of the festivities which was almost certainly written by the king-at-arms.[73]

The chronicler was clearly not using Lefèvre's memoirs in the form that we now know them, but a series of shorter narratives or reports which the herald would later fashion himself into a consecutive narrative.[74] The writing of such reports was part of Toison d'Or's job. From the inception of the Order, the chief herald had the task of providing material for the *greffier*, who was expected to record the business of the Golden Fleece and matters pertaining to its members.[75] He did not only provide material for the men who held this office, the

---

[71] See in general Delclos, 'Jean Lefèvre'.

[72] Monstrelet, *Chronique*, iv. 422; Lefèvre, *Chronique*, ii. 192. Delclos points out another instance where Chastelain conflates the two: cf. ii, 130–4; Monstrelet, *Chronique*, iv. 425–6; Lefèvre, *Chronique*, ii. 193–4.

[73] Chastelain notes that the 'magnificence d'estat et de noble arroy' of the occasion is discussed more fully elsewhere; he will not repeat this information 'sur le recours a ycelui lieu la ou tout au long se treuve declairé': Delclos, 275.

[74] Delclos, 'Jean Lefèvre', 14–15. In a forthcoming paper, Claude Thiry suggests that Jean de Haynin may also have written his memoirs for the official chronicler. His lands were not far from Valenciennes and it is possible that the two men knew each other. The connection is plausible (see also ch. 6 below on the matter), but cannot be proven due to the loss of those parts of Chastelain's text which correspond to de Haynin's work. There is no documented link between the two.

[75] P. Gorissen, 'De historiographie van het Gulden Vlies', *Bijdragen voor Geschiedenis der Nederlanden* vi (1951–2), 218–24.

ducal secretaries Jean Hibert or Martin Steenberghe. Lefèvre considered himself to be obliged by his oath 'contenu ès capittre dudit ordre' to

> rédigier et mettre par escript aucunnes petites récordacions et mémores, esquelles sont contenues, en chéefz, pluiseurs choses advenues, desquelles j'ay poeu avoir congnoissance; et, ce fait, les ay envoyés au noble orateur, George Chastelain, pour aucunnement, à son bon plaisir et selonc sa discrétion, les employer ès nobles histoires et cronicques par luy faictes.[76]

History continued to be an offshoot of heraldry, just as it had been in the work of Froissart. Yet there is an important distinction to be made here. History emerged not simply from the friendship of two men, the one a herald, the other a chronicler. More precisely, it emerged from an established practice of collaboration between the incumbents of offices created and defined by the duke as part of the patronage of Burgundian official history. Chastelain put a personal interpretation on his material, but the latter was clearly provided for him on some occasions.

The chronicler was privileged in one final respect. There is clear evidence that he received written information on some formal basis from those who, unlike himself, were still involved in ducal diplomacy. Embassies generated a great deal of documentation in the form of letters of credence or instruction given to envoys, the *pièces justificatives* they used and the reports they filed with their principals. The end-products of the diplomatic process – treaties, alliances and the like – could enter the public domain and contemporary chronicles in the form of circulars or *criées*. However, the documentation employed to achieve these ends was less likely to filter down to a wider audience. Chastelain enjoyed greater access to this type of information than any of his contemporaries.

The flight of the dauphin to Burgundian territory, for example, was a portentous matter which occasioned a flurry of diplomatic activity in the years 1456–7. When he came to write up these events, Olivier de La Marche simply noted that 'se passoit le temps en embassades'.[77] Like Jacques du Clercq, he makes no reference to the finer details of these embassies or the documentation to which they gave rise.[78] The *chroniqueur du roy*, as we might expect, was better informed: Chartier was able to summarise the diplomatic exchange between Charles VII and Burgundian ambassadors which occurred in December 1456.[79] Mathieu d'Escouchy had access to the same report.[80] He also claimed knowledge of the contents of an earlier letter sent by Charles VII to Philip the Good

---

[76] Lefèvre, *Chronique*, ii. 2.
[77] La Marche, *Mémoires*, ii. 412.
[78] du Clercq, *Mémoires*, xiii. 195–6.
[79] Chartier, *Chronique*, iii. 57–65.
[80] d'Escouchy, *Chronique*, ii. 335–43. For the next sentence cf. d'Escouchy's account of the letter Charles sent to Philip: 'lui rescripvit qu'il en (Louis) fist comme il voudroit que le Roy eust fait, si samblablement fust tiré devers lui' (ibid. ii. 331); and the rather different sentiments the king actually expressed as recorded *verbatim* by Chastelain (iii, 201–3).

on the matter, but his version is a complete misrepresentation of the king's views. Between them, then, these chroniclers were able to adduce one piece of diplomatic correspondence. Chastelain, by contrast, had close knowledge of the dauphin's requests and the king's response shortly before Louis's flight to the Low Countries, and went on to provide his reader with full transcripts of no less than six letters.[81]

This is not an isolated occurrence. Early in 1459 a major Burgundian embassy was dispatched to Charles VII's court at Montbazon and Tours to put the ducal and delphinal cases. Noting the gravity of the situation, Jacques du Clercq knew that the 'notables remontrances' of the ducal party had received a 'rigoureuse response'.[82] Mathieu d'Escouchy's account is much more thorough.[83] This is to be explained by the fact that many of the exchanges which took place were recorded at Charles VII's command 'afin que la teneur en fust divulguee . . . et portee par toutes les parties de son royamme et ailleurs' (Delclos, 190).[84] Hence d'Escouchy's ability to quote in full the chancellor's response (7 March 1459) to Jean de Croy's earlier oration, a 'cédule' from the Burgundian ambassadors requesting more information (8 March) and the royal reply which they received (11 March). Yet Chastelain was again better informed than his contemporaries. In addition to the three documents circulated by the king and cited by d'Escouchy, he conveys further material which could only have come from the Burgundian administration: letters of instruction given to the ambassadors by the dauphin (22 December 1458) and the duke (8 January), the full contents of Jean de Croy's oration (9 February) and a clarification of the dauphin's requests which the ducal envoys were asked to provide (13 February).[85] It has been suggested that Chastelain resorted to the extensive citation of diplomatic instruments as a way of impressing his impartiality upon the reader.[86] The chronicler certainly had every reason to create such an impression. However, we should bear in mind that this information was only available at the discretion of the authorities. It is surely the provision of such material for the official chronicler, rather than the question of his impartiality, which deserves to be noted here. Although he was not always privy to the contents of the diplomatic bag, on certain sensitive issues

---

[81] iii, 56, 59–60, 178–9, 201–3, 216–18, 222–5. The first three letters are published in *Lettres de Louis XI*, i. 72–3, 75, 77–8. The last is published in Duclos, *Histoire*, iii. 135–7. Chastelain's detailed account of the mission of the dauphin's ambassadors to Charles VII is to be found at iii, 56–68, 161–6. Duclos publishes the original letters of credence and the royal reply: ibid. iii. 100–1, 104–17.

[82] du Clercq, *Mémoires*, xiii. 301.

[83] d'Escouchy, *Chronique*, ii. 395–416.

[84] The replies were also known to a Tournaisien historian for this reason: *Chronique des Pays-Bas, de France, d'Angleterre et de Tournai*, ed. J. J. de Smet, in *Recueil des chroniques de Flandre*, Brussels 1856, iii. 115–569 at pp. 537–53.

[85] Delclos, 172, 178–87, 188–9, 191–209, 209–10, 210–11; cf. Beaucourt, *Histoire*, vi. 209–25.

[86] Delclos, *Le témoignage*, 47.

Chastelain was granted access to relatively full dossiers which had been used in another context to argue the ducal case.[87]

Considerable care was thus taken to flesh out the official Chronicle with a variety of sources: narrative histories, personal and public correspondence, memoirs and other documents generated by ducal government. Chastelain could rely upon the help of others to fulfil his 'très-ressongnable charge' (vi, 268). The surviving fragments of his work are naturally better informed than the chronicles of many, if not all, of his contemporaries. It should also be emphasised that the Chronicle was all the more reflective of the range of opinion within the Burgundian political elite. The text, like its author, was closely linked to the centre: a point which is easily forgotten when the emphasis is placed only on his 'témoignage' or, less kindly, upon his naivety. By the same token his failure to produce a sustained, coherent, legitimating narrative now appears all the more surprising. If the enterprise was well supported by its patron, it follows that it may have been flawed in other ways.

Redaction

By the terms of his remit Chastelain found himself obliged to interrupt the redaction of his Chronicle to meet his patron's additional need for 'choses nouvelles et moralles'. Few contemporary official historians faced such pressing demands on their time. Burgundian official history may thus have collapsed and splintered under the weight of expectations placed upon it by its intended beneficiary. It is clear from this comment that an attempt must be made to evaluate the nature of Chastelain's other writing commitments in relation to the speed and manner of his redaction of the Chronicle.

Jean-Claude Delclos has proposed a chronology for the composition of the Chronicle.[88] He starts from the premiss that Chastelain was not in the habit of reworking his text 'dans la grande majorité des cas' – otherwise, as he admits, the exercise would not have a point. From the internal evidence of the Chronicle he concludes that the writing of the first fragment (1419–22), underway before August 1456, was finished by late 1458.[89] At least three quarters of the second fragment (1430–1) and probably more had been set down by the end of 1459.[90] If Chastelain wrote up his account of events in

---

[87] For the only clear example of Chastelain's inability to see diplomatic material see iii, 139 (on the treaty Philip accorded to the Brederode family).
[88] Delclos, Le témoignage, 53–82.
[89] Delclos takes Chastelain's comment that Charles VII and Philip 'se sont rejoints en amour sous divine cremeur' as a sign that the troubles occasioned by the flight of the dauphin in Aug. 1456 were not yet apparent: ibid. 54. Whether this type of reference is as reliable as he suggests will be examined at a later stage. He takes the first clear indications of a date for the redaction of 'Book II' as proof that the first fragment was finished by this stage – i.e. late 1458 or early 1459: ibid. 54–61; for the references he cites see ii, 153, 164.
[90] Delclos argues for late 1459 on the strength of Chastelain's reference to Jean V count

their chronological order, one may doubt whether he had sufficient time to narrate in full the developments of the intervening years (1422–30). The same doubt arises in more striking terms for that vast lacuna, twenty-three years in length, which separates the second fragment from the third. Delclos finds that Chastelain had reached the seventeenth chapter of this fragment by May 1461, or, at the very latest, by July.[91] The chronicler is thought to have continued to work on this third fragment of the text in 1461 and beyond.[92] If this was the case, Chastelain had little over a year (from late 1459 to early 1461) in which to write his account of events from 1430 to 1454: a tall order for a writer who apparently took over two years to write up events from 1419 to 1422.

The lacuna could only have been made good if Chastelain had worked simultaneously on different sections of his text. Delclos cites some evidence for this but does not find it substantial enough to alter his belief that Chastelain pursued a sequential redaction of events. The example he gives is the interruption of the account of the later 1450s by the redaction of the 'proesme' to the so-called 'Livre VI' commemorating Louis XI's accession in 1461.[93] The chronicler seems to have advanced on two fronts during the latter half of that year.[94] He does not appear to have returned to his 'Livre VI' until late 1463 or early 1464.[95] This raises the possibility – which Delclos does not mention –

---

of Armagnac who, 'longuement tenu en prison, à grant dur parvint à la franchise de son premier estat': ibid. 59; cf. ii, 168. He takes this as a reference to Jean V's flight in Nov. 1459 from the imprisonment imposed on him by Charles VII, rather than to the later restitution of Jean V's position and lands by Louis XI. This assumption is based on an earlier reference in the fragment which indicates that Charles VII was alive when that particular passage was written: ii, 62.

[91] Delclos, Le témoignage, 61. This view is based on two passages. In the first, writing of the arrest and imprisonment of the duke of Alençon in May 1456, Chastelain notes that 'de cinc ans après il ne vuida de prison': iii, 101. At a later stage Chastelain indicates that at the time of writing Charles VII was still alive: iii, 165. Charles died in July.

[92] The clearest piece of evidence adduced here is a passage in which Chastelain attributes the dauphin's favourable attitude to the marshal of Burgundy in 1456 to information given him by the bastard of Armagnac. The latter, it is noted, 'depuis devint marissal de France': iii, 180. This occurred in 1461.

[93] Delclos, Le témoignage, 66. Although there is no specific passage which proves that the 'proesme' was written in Aug. 1461, Delclos argues that the positive attitude which Chastelain displays towards the new king was only possible at the very beginning of the reign. To this end he quotes Chastelain's optimism at iv, 5–6.

[94] Not long after the 'proesme', Chastelain seems to be aware of two events which occurred in Oct. 1461 (the banishment of Pierre de Brézé and the visit of the count of Charolais to Tours: iv, 27, 69). By Dec. 1461, 'le cincquiesme mois de sa (Louis's) régnation', the chronicler had reached ch. xxxv: iv, 129. Delclos suggests that, as he worked on these passages, Chastelain was also working up his account of the later 1450s. He bases this view on Chastelain's increasingly hostile attitude to the dauphin in those earlier passages. This, he believes, was the work of a man who had experienced the deceptions of the early part of Louis's reign. For examples of Chastelain's apparently changed attitude, cf. iii, 392–3, 446–8.

[95] For example, Delclos cites Chastelain's account of the death of the countess of St Pol in Mar. 1462 and his reference to the dispute over her legacy which was only resolved 'au bout de deux ans': iv, 219. The chronicler also seems to be aware of information which

that Chastelain used the intervening two years to build up his unwritten or unfinished accounts of earlier periods. From the end of 1463 and at least until 1465, however, he is thought to have reverted to a more or less sequential redaction of events.[96] The chronicler, it is argued, was now unlikely to have returned to earlier, unfinished accounts. Delclos suggests that a further lacuna in 'Livre VI', from September 1462 to August 1463, may never have been filled as a result.[97] The remaining sections of the work, occupying the last 300 pages of Kervyn de Lettenhove's edition, do not substantially alter these findings.[98] The last surviving fragment of the Chronicle is thought to have been written by April 1471, a little less than four years before Chastelain's death.

Delclos's dating of the composition of the Chronicle forms one of the central supports for his subsequent reading of the text. He argues that Chastelain's Chronicle was not, like the *Mémoires* of Philippe de Commynes, a 'reconstruction des faits à la lumière de toute une vie'.[99] Confirmation of this view is sought in the related argument that Chastelain was not in the habit of returning, with hindsight, to passages he had finished. Written at the most within two years of events, on occasion only a few days, the Chronicle reflected instead 'la spontanéité de ses réactions' to recent developments and enabled his reader, through the recounting of relatively fresh news, to follow 'la disparition progressive de ses illusions'. One inevitable corollary of this argument is the conclusion that many, perhaps most, perhaps even all of the missing fragments of the Chronicle were simply never written.[100] Chastelain's Chronicle may thus have succumbed to the burden of repeated deadlines for 'choses nouvelles' which were written in response to great events that required rapid (if not immediate) commemoration.

This gloomy hypothesis can be tempered by a number of more positive facts. The first of these concerns Chastelain's *opuscula* and, in particular, the demands they placed upon his time. In his *Exposition sur vérité mal prise*, most probably written in 1460 or early 1461, Chastelain refers to ten lesser works and 'plusieurs autres' which he claimed to have completed by this stage in his career.[101] With the exception of four works which were written shortly before

---

Pierre de Brézé could not have given him before Aug. 1463: cf. Delclos, *Le témoignage*, 71; iv, 231.
[96] The chronicler's only explicit references to dates of redaction are at iv, 460–1 and v, 65. For Delclos's analysis see *Le témoignage*, 71–7.
[97] Ibid. 71.
[98] Ibid. 78–81. For the only explicit authorial reference to a date of redaction see v, 371.
[99] For this and what follows see Delclos, *Le témoignage*, 82.
[100] Cf. ibid. 61: 'Rien ne prouve qu'il ait effectivement écrit le troisième (livre), que nous ne possédons plus aujourd'hui'; ibid. 71: 'Nous savons que le fils de Chastellain présenta ... à la reine de Hongrie (*sic*) une copie complète des oeuvres historiques de son père, mais rien ne prouve que cette copie ait contenu une version intégrale ... et qu'elle ait rassemblé autre chose que les divers fragments existants.'
[101] For the list of these works see ch. 3 above. The *Exposition* cannot be dated precisely. Since it ends on an address to Charles VII, the work appears to have been written before his death in July 1461: vi, 420–36. The last event it mentions is the condemnation of the

or shortly after the accession of Louis XI, a further eleven *opuscula*, published in volume six of Kervyn's edition, also pre-date the *Exposition*.[102] Chastelain had thus devoted a good deal of energy to his 'choses nouvelles et morales' by the end of 1461. They are noticeably less numerous from that point on. Sixteen *opuscula* survive for the much longer period to Chastelain's death.[103] One of these may originally have been an extract from the Chronicle. Eight were written in an intense but relatively short burst of activity in 1467 and 1468.[104] Moreover, none of Chastelain's surviving works for this period approximates in length to the *Exposition*: his *Temple de Bocace* (1465), the longest piece in prose or verse for this later period, is considerably less than half its length. Crude quantitative measures are imperfect indications of Chastelain's productivity and his ability to find time for his Chronicle after 1461. Whatever the problems posed by the writing of verse or by the inherent difficulties of certain subject matters (issues we can mention but not analyse), there is none the less a good deal of evidence to suggest that he was not overwhelmed by the need to write *opuscula*, at least not after 1461. He consequently had greater leisure to write the Chronicle.

Moreover, it is quite clear that Chastelain reconciled his various commitments with impressive efficiency. His literary activity in the second half of 1461 and the first of 1462 may serve as an example. This seems to have been a busy period in the redaction of the Chronicle: Chastelain is thought to have made

---

duke of Alençon at Vendôme in Oct. 1458: vi, 385. At the time of writing, however, war between Charles and Philip seemed imminent: vi, 314. This may have seemed possible to a perceptive contemporary observer at any point after the failure of the diplomatic discussions of Feb.–Mar. 1459, but it was certainly a clearer prospect in the course of 1460 and particularly in 1461 when the king began military preparations. On this point see Emanuele de Iacopo's letter of Aug. 1460 in which the outbreak of hostilities within days is predicted: *Dispatches*, i. 370. When we take into account the fact that the *Exposition* followed on from *Le dit de vérité* – which set down virtually every theme taken up in the later work – it seems highly unlikely that the *Exposition* could have been written any earlier than in the course of 1460.

[102] The *Mystère* on the subject of Charles VII's death, the *Entrée du roy Loys en nouveau règne* and the *Déprécation pour messire Pierre de Brézé* related to events which occurred in 1461. The *Épistre à Jean Castel* could have been written any time after Castel's appointment in 1461, but we may assume that it was written sooner rather than later: the official chronicler was out to impress his new French counterpart. I do not include two other works published in volume six among these works, *Le miroir de vie* (by Molinet) and the *Concile de Basle* (wrongly attributed to Chastelain): J. Beck, *Le Concile de Basle (1434)*, Leiden 1979, 13; K. Urwin, 'Date of the *Mystère du Concile de Basle* attributed to Georges Chastelain', *MLR* xxx (1935), 508–10.

[103] These are published in the seventh and eighth volumes of Kervyn's edition. I do not include Chastelain's correspondence with Philippe de Croy in this total, or the *ballades*, the attribution of which is far from certain in many cases: V. L. Saulnier, 'Sur George Chastelain poète et les rondeaux qu'on lui attribua', in *Mélanges offerts à Jean Frappier*, Geneva 1970, ii. 987–1000.

[104] The *Advertissement au duc Charles*, as we saw in ch. 3 above, may well have been associated with the text of the Chronicle. For this and the other works written in 1467 or 1468 see vii, 207–452.

headway on two of his books, and certainly gathered further material for the work in the company of the ducal party which went in August and September to Rheims and Paris for Louis XI's coronation.[105] In addition he certainly found time to write the *Mystère de la mort de Charles VII* and a substantial prose work, the *Traité par forme d'allégorie mystique sur l'entrée du roy Loys en nouveau règne*. But his labours in these few months were not over yet. One of Louis's first actions was the shunning then banishment of Charles VII's principal adviser and Chastelain's former master, Pierre de Brézé. By October Brézé was in a royal prison.[106] He would not be released until the following May. At some point in the intervening period Chastelain urged for the former seneschal's release in his third text in less than nine months, the *Déprécation pour Messire Pierre de Brézé*.

This period of activity, like that from 1467 to 1468, would suggest that the chronicler was able to produce work quickly. The point is confirmed by the speed of redaction of individual *opuscula* and certain passages of the Chronicle. The *Déclaration* was written within a month, at the very most, of Philip the Good's death.[107] The chronicler allowed himself just a few days for the verse commissioned by the officers of the *Chambre des comptes* in 1465.[108] Delclos too has found evidence of Chastelain's impressive work rate within the Chronicle. Chapters lvii to lxii of the second fragment of 'Livre VI', which occupy nearly nineteen pages in Kervyn's edition, appear to have been written in less than a week.[109] This is all the more creditable when we note that the chronicler also seems to have been in Bruges that week to gather information. Chastelain's 'comédices' thus need not have been a major obstacle to the continuing redaction of what, significantly, he considered to be his most important task, 'la très-ressongnable charge' of the Chronicle. Like Jean Froissart, who produced a substantial number of *opuscula* in addition to a monumental chronicle, he was a prolific writer.

Such was Froissart's productivity, indeed, that he found time to draft several versions of large parts of his own chronicle.[110] In this he took to extremes what historians of any generation have recognised as a natural feature of the historiographical process: the writing and re-writing of the narrative, the insertion of new material or perspectives, the removal of infelicitous phrases or redundant passages.[111] The author lived with his text then as now, moving backwards and forwards with a mixture of purpose and trepidation through this small world of his own making. This comparison between Froissart and Chastelain – not of how much they actually wrote, but of how quickly they knew they could write and revise – naturally leads us back to the problem of

---

[105] iv, 39, 52.
[106] Bernus, 'Louis XI et Pierre de Brézé', 260–5.
[107] See app. 2 below.
[108] This work is discussed in ch. 3 above.
[109] Delclos, *Le témoignage*, 71–3. The passage in question is to be found at iv, 442–61.
[110] J. J. N. Palmer, 'Book I (1325–1378) and its sources', in his *Froissart: historian*, 7–24.
[111] Guenée, *Histoire et culture historique*, 200.

the incomplete state of our text. Delclos is prepared to admit that the work resembled, to some extent at least, 'un perpétuel chantier'.[112] However, he also holds with a chronology of composition that left little or no time for Chastelain to fill out, touch up or even (like Froissart) rebuild older parts of the edifice. In reality, of course, it is extremely difficult to construct a safe chronology for the composition of the work.

This point can be made in a number of ways. Explicit redaction dates in passages of the text may seem to provide solid indicators of when they were first written, but it is inadvisable to assume that the dating of chapters and perhaps even sentences on either side of that passage is guaranteed by the same evidence. To be certain of the relationship in time between the formulation of one comment or idea and another, we would need to know far more than we do about the author's working practices. Some reference to the manuscripts is essential for this task, and even then they may be deceptive. BR, MS 15843, for example, is the only manuscript of the Chronicle to date from Chastelain's lifetime. It is not a first draft nor (to judge by the numerous authorial and scribal changes) the finished version. In this manuscript a reference to the dating of a particular passage ('leure de ce chappitre') has been emended with an interlinear addition by a scribe. The addition may have been made to respect Chastelain's original draft, but it may equally have been inserted at the scribe's initiative or by mistake.[113] Similar uncertainties arise in other cases. The emended Arras volumes, long thought to have formed part of Chastelain's original copy, are in fact rather more recent.[114] The 'authorial' alterations which are incorporated within Kervyn's edition, including one particularly happy phrase cited by a modern commentator as proof of Chastelain's literary abilities, were thus the work of a later scribe or reader.[115]

The value of the internal evidence of the printed text for the purposes of dating the work is clearly undermined by these facts. If this is true in passages where redaction dates are clearly mentioned, there is even greater cause for scepticism in cases where the textual evidence is less direct. One example may suffice to illustrate this point. Delclos advances the hypothesis that Chastelain's critical attitude towards the dauphin in his narrative for the early months of 1458 resulted from the chronicler's experience of Louis's actions as king.[116] He argues that the passages in question were likely to have been

---

[112] Delclos, *Le témoignage*, 65–6.
[113] Cf. iii, 165; Brussels, BR, MS 15843, fo. 66v.
[114] See app. 1 below for Quicherat, Kervyn and the dating of the Arras manuscripts in question.
[115] For the phrase in question see ii, 47: Joan of Arc's banner is described as 'haut eslevé et volitant en l'air du vent'. A. Rousseaux was inspired by precisely this phrase to write 'voilà quatre ou cinq mots où la riche langue de son (Chastelain's) siècle donne l'envol aux plus légères beautés': *Le monde classique*, Paris 1941–56, iii. 92. When we turn to the manuscript, we find that the original, prosaic 'haut esleve en air' was fashioned by a later hand into this finer phrase: BM Arras, MS 256 (406), fo. 29.
[116] Delclos, *Le témoignage*, 62–3; see also his edition at p. 19, where he detects 'un

written during or after the year of the coronation, 1461. Yet there are three further scenarios here which, because they are equally possible, militate against the attribution of any particular redaction date. First, it is clear that Burgundian courtiers did not have to wait until the coronation to get a measure of the dauphin's personality.[117] Chastelain's comments may therefore have been written at an earlier date. Secondly, it is conceivable that these remarks were added with hindsight – not in the manuscript we now have, but in an earlier draft.[118] Finally, we should bear in mind the likelihood that Chastelain's comments on the dauphin were informed not by any specific turn of events that needs to be dated, but more simply by his desire to implant a negative image of the dauphin in the mind of his audience at that particular point in the text. The latter had an inner dynamic in which the author's views, experience and awareness of his audience were quite as important as the impact at a specific point in time of any particular extra-textual circumstance. In fact, the passages cited and dated by Delclos might have been written (and re-written) at a number of different stages.

Such observations naturally lead us to doubt whether Chastelain habitually wrote his surviving narrative of events in sequential order or tended to leave it unchanged once he had done so. Although Kervyn mentions them only infrequently, emendations and additions are encountered on more than one-third of the folios of BR, MS 15843.[119] A good number of these corrections were carried out by Chastelain himself: clear proof, in other words, that the author combed through his work, updating or altering earlier comments on later occasions and in different circumstances.[120] If the reader of BR, MS 15843

---

changement d'attitude, une sévérité qui ne peuvent se comprendre qu'à partir de septembre 1461', moment où Chastellain commence à perdre ses illusions sur le nouveau roi'.
[117] Prospero da Camogli learned from his visits to Brussels and Genappe in Mar. 1461 that the dauphin was regarded with suspicion by servants at the court of Burgundy: *Dispatches*, ii. 188. Before the coronation the ambassador thought Louis had had quite enough of Philip, and reported that the dauphin even suspected the count of Charolais of harbouring a secret desire to hand him over to the king: *Dépêches des ambassadeurs milanais en France sous Louis XI et François Sforza*, ed. B. de Mandrot, Paris 1916–23, i. 13. On the value of this testimony see G. Soldi Rondinini, 'Aspects de la vie des cours de France et de Bourgogne par les dépêches des ambassadeurs milanais (seconde moitié du XVe siècle)', in *Adelige Sachkultur des Spätmittelalters*, publ. in Österreichische Akademie der Wissenschaften ccclii, Vienna 1982, 195–214.
[118] After all, who (save Chastelain himself) is to say how many versions particular texts or passages went through before reaching the state they are presently in?
[119] For this and what follows see ch. 6 and app. 1 below.
[120] None of these changes constitutes a dramatic rewriting of the original text, but more substantial alterations may well have been carried out in the holograph. In describing how he had served Philip the Good a hearty breakfast on 10 Aug. 1456, Chastelain improved his text and heightened the subjective impression of his master which it conveyed (excised words in parentheses, additions in italics): 'Sy me recorde comment en parlant avec luy beaucoup en disnant et que je regarday taisamment ses manieres *me sambloit lors* qu'onques (ce croy je) prince de meilleur samblant (n'avoit esté veu) *n'avoie veu* en armes': fo. 100. Elsewhere he toned down or enhanced the original. Philip the Good's entry into Utrecht

finds himself at one remove (at least) from Chastelain's first 'réactions' to events, we may legitimately doubt the text's capacity to reveal unerringly the 'spontanéité' of the author's sentiments.[121] This conclusion highlights the need for a reading of the work that is built on firmer ground than any progression of Chastelain's thought suggested by the chronology of its composition – in fact, a reading which considers his work as a reconstruction of events based upon experiences garnered during his lifetime.

Leaving that broader point aside until the following chapter, another requires emphasis here. There are now no pressing reasons to believe that great tracts of the Chronicle were left unwritten because of the author's relentless schedule. Chastelain worked fast. He had a ready-made source for much of the period he intended to cover, and he even found the time to go over his material.[122] Blanks were certainly left in the manuscript, but then Antoine de La Sale also left blanks (with the intention of coming back to them) in what is usually considered to be a finished work.[123] Many of the larger lacunae in BR, MS 15843 are to be explained not by the author's failure to write certain passages, but by the loss of certain quires before the intervention of the binder.[124] The discovery of BL, Add. MS 54156 revealed that Chastelain's narrative for the years from 1454 to 1458 was in fact much fuller. None of these

---

in 1456, originally 'paisible et victorieuse la plus que oncques avoit esté veue', became simply 'paisible et victorieuse': fo. 108. Guillaume Bische, Louis XI's servant, was an 'homme subtil et ingénieux' and, upon later reflection, also 'de grant sens et de conduite': fo. 212. It was enough to accuse Arnold van Egmond of 'lacheté' without levelling the charge of 'malice' as well: fo. 119.

[121] Even from the internal evidence of the published version of the Chronicle it is possible to adduce further instances where a later reworking is conceivable. The fragment of the first book, thought to have been finished by 1458, contains a passage which may be read as an allusion to a turn of events that was only apparent in 1461: on his deathbed, Henry V was told that his son would not reign in France, and Chastelain adds that the same came true of his reign in England: i, 340. It is difficult to believe such a view could have been held before the Battle of Towton in 1461: A. J. Pollard, *The Wars of the Roses*, London 1988, 27. Two passages in the second fragment, thought to have been finished by 1459, might be taken as references to events which did not occur until rather later. Here, Chastelain describes Philip the Good as 'le Grand duc du Ponant', an epithet which is thought to have been coined in 1461: cf. ii, 150; A. Grunzweig, 'Le Grand duc du Ponant', MA lxii (1956), 119–65. Likewise, Chastelain's reference to the crusading victories of Henry IV of Castile might well concern the achievements of 1462, rather than the lesser victories of the 1450s which Delclos believes to have been in the chronicler's mind: cf. ii, 153; Delclos, *Le témoignage*, 59. In his edition (at p. 19), Delclos himself found one passage which 'laisse place à l'hypothèse de fragments écrits à des moments différents et tardivement réunis'.

[122] Indeed, the emendations in BR, MS 15843 may be revealing of his own view of just how far he had come with his work: none was particularly elaborate, perhaps because the author felt that fine-tuning, rather than extensive alteration, was more appropriate at this stage.

[123] F. Desonay, 'Comment un écrivain se corrigeait au XVe siècle', *RBPH* vi (1927), 81–121 at p. 111.

[124] Critically, this intervention occurred after Chastelain's death. On this and the other points pertaining to the manuscripts here see ch. 6 and app. 1 below.

remarks permits us to conclude that the Chronicle was ever a finished work, but they do point to the existence, during Chastelain's lifetime, of a more complete archetype of the official chronicle of the dukes of Burgundy. Our concern must now be to establish its extent.

The archetype

Throughout his lengthy narrative the chronicler took care to contextualise his writings with signposts back and forward to other relevant sections of the work. Such passages could only have been written by the author himself for the simple reason that no-one else knew what had (or had not) been recounted at an earlier stage. He attached particular value to these cross-references as a means of avoiding repetition, since 'raconter une chose deux fois seroit vice' (v, 243). Hence his comment that 'quand cela sera escript ou devant ou derrière, en ceste présente oeuvre, je me repose assez seurement de avoir collement sans réitération nouvelle' (v, 243). These references are of course distinct from simple allusions to historical events which are not explicitly mentioned as part of a previous narrative. Sigismund's crusades against the Hussites (1420-31) are discussed in the second fragment, for example, but Chastelain does not imply that he had accorded them fuller treatment in an earlier passage, now lost.[125] Here the chronicler made positive assumptions as to his audience's historical culture, just as he did when mentioning events which preceded the period covered in his own work.[126]

By contrast, several of Chastelain's references to previous passages can be traced within the surviving fragments. Recounting a conspiracy against Charles the Bold in which the king was implicated in 1470, for example, Chastelain thought it expedient to remind his reader of the blame Louis XI had incurred in an earlier episode:

> se procura un grand blasme, jà-soit-ce que autrefois, sept ans par avant, avoit procuré tout le semblable, par le bastard de Rubenpré, qui en fut pris et rattaint du vivant du père, le duc Philippe, comme le conte en a esté fait en son lieu, et par quoy maintenant je m'en déporte. (v, 480)

The text relating to Rubempré does indeed survive in an earlier fragment.[127] When he came to describe William Neville's raid on Brittany in the late summer of 1462, Chastelain again sought to place the event in its context by explaining the English action in the following terms: 'ce firent en revenge de ce que les Bretons, du temps du roy Charles, avoient fait le pareil en Angleterre

---

[125] ii, 213.
[126] Chastelain's sensitivity to (and ability to play upon) his audience's historical culture will be discussed from another perspective in the following chapter.
[127] v, 76ff, esp. pp. 81–7.

sous messire Pierre de Brézé, comme a esté conté en son lieu' (iv, 276). These events, which occurred in 1457, are recounted in the so-called 'Livre IV'.[128]

It would be fastidious to recite each and every instance of this working practice; we are more concerned here with the analytical possibilities it offers. As Chastelain used such references in a regular and accurate way we may reasonably assume that references to missing sections of his work provide a fair idea of their contents. Although some commentators have noted this compositional technique, none has used it systematically to this end.[129] In view of the various hypotheses relating to Froissart's 'lost chronicle' (based on rather less evidence than we propose to use here), this appears a missed opportunity.[130] Some caution and restraint must inevitably be exercised. Only explicit references can be given credence, and for brevity's sake we may concentrate our attention on the many occasions when the author refers his reader to an earlier passage.

Despite the availability of Monstrelet's account and Lefèvre's 'récordations' for the earlier part of his work, Chastelain's Chronicle presents a considerable lacuna for the years between 1422 and 1430. The evidence indicates not only that he had a fuller text for these years, but that he very probably used familiar sources when writing it. The first indications come early in the second fragment, where Chastelain reminds his reader that 'avez ouy par cy-devant assez comment le duc présent avoit donné en mariage sa soeur Anne au duc de Bethfort, régent soy-disant de France' (ii, 9). Two chapters later, describing a Franco-Burgundian joust at Arras in 1430, he recalled an earlier occasion in which one of the French participants, Poton de Saintrailles, 'avoit fait autrefois armes en ladite ville à l'encontre de Lyonnet de Vandomme devant ce duc mesmes, comme il a esté traité dessus en mon autre livre devant cestuy-cy' (ii, 18–19). These events occurred in the spring of 1423. The only earlier text to accord any significant treatment to both is Monstrelet's Chronicle, where they form the subject matter of two consecutive chapters.[131] At a later stage in the second fragment, Chastelain wrote of further events which had occurred in these years but for which there is no surviving account. The manner of Philip the Good's acquisition of Brabant in 1430 at the expense of his aunt Margaret, countess of Hainaut, was to be praised. Chastelain linked this to Philip's earlier victory in Holland over Margaret's daughter, Jacqueline of Bavaria, 'comme plus à plein sera déclaré cy-après, en tant qu'il touche ceste duché, et comme amplement est assez remonstré par ci-devant en tant que toucher peut la conqueste de Hollande et les pays de [l]a fille' (ii, 85). The reference to the conquest of Holland, achieved in a series of campaigns between 1425 and 1428,

---

[128] iii, 347–53.
[129] Delclos listed some of these references in 'Le témoignage', i. 4, noting that they permit us 'dans une faible mesure' to establish the contents of missing fragments. Kervyn seems to have used at least two of these references: i, p. l.
[130] N. Cartier, 'The lost chronicle', Speculum xxxvi (1961), 424–34.
[131] Monstrelet, Chronique, ii. 147–54.

is not unique in the Chronicle. Writing of the fire which devastated Dordrecht in 1457, Chastelain notes that 'de ceste ville se pourroient dire beaucoup de hautes besongnes, mais assez en y a escrit du temps que le duc conquist Hollande en son moyen et à tant m'en déporte droit-cy, car droit-là s'en treuve la description toute' (iii, 322). These references are unfortunately too vague to permit close correlations with the detailed coverage of Monstrelet and Lefèvre.[132] By contrast, Chastelain seems to have used one or other (and perhaps even both) in a lost chapter concerning Philip the Good's return to Paris in September 1429 after his long campaigns in Holland. The existence of this passage is indicated early in the second fragment:

> vous qui avez lu mon premier livre ycy-devant, il vous peut bien souvenir comment, vers la fin d'iceluy, je traite, comment ce jeusne duc Philippe, tirant atout son armée vers Paris, passa par devant la cité de Senlis, là où ses ennemis en grant nombre estoient dedens, et comment, à la requeste d'aucuns nobles hommes dudit lieu, . . . furent emprises et accordées à faire certaines armes à cheval dedens un jour pris. (ii, 17–18)

Monstrelet describes Philip's journey in some detail but makes no mention of a prospective tournament.[133] Lefèvre does, however, and in terms which are strikingly reminiscent of those employed by Chastelain.[134] Finally, both of the chronicler's main sources devote several chapters to two significant events in January 1430: Philip's marriage to Isabella of Portugal and the foundation of the Order of the Golden Fleece which took place during the festivities. Chastelain's second fragment begins with an account of the latter. Although the former is not described, it is clear from the following remark that he had dealt with it: 'Vous avez ouy les hautes solempnités des noces de ce duc qui furent faites dedens la riche ville de Bruges, dont les haulx et grans estats des dames et seigneurs, ensemble les manières et somptueuses décorations de la feste, ont esté déclarées pleinement par articles' (ii, 5–6). Monstrelet abbreviated his account of the festivities on the grounds that they would be 'trop longz à déclairer'.[135] Lefèvre, by contrast, profited from having attended the event and indulged ('pleinement', as Chastelain put it) his customary prolixity in the description.[136] Once again, he appears to have used familiar sources in a chapter which, although lost, he clearly believed his reader could consult. We have no evidence that his archetype contained any more material. The fact that these passages dealt with a chronological span of events – in 1423, 1425–8, 1429 and 1430 – may be revealing here. The lacuna from 1422 to 1430 is more apparent to the modern reader than it was to the author, writing (and re-writing) in the 1450s, '60s and '70s.

---

132 Or, for that matter, Emond de Dynter's account: *Chronique des ducs de Brabant*, iii. 472–3.
133 Monstrelet, *Chronique*, iv. 359–61.
134 Lefèvre, *Chronique*, ii. 175–6.
135 Monstrelet, *Chronique*, iv. 371.
136 Lefèvre, *Chronique*, ii. 158–72.

More striking than this lacuna is a second which stretches from 1431 to 1454. This was a critical period in French and Burgundian history; it was also one in which Chastelain himself had played an active role. Moreover, the lacuna here is even greater than Kervyn's edition would suggest. His attribution of the Ghent war account was made in error. The editor himself suspected as much, for towards the end of his mammoth task he recognised that the account may in fact have been the work of Jean Lefèvre.[137] A recent close stylistic analysis confirmed the mistake.[138]

Despite this, it is clear that Chastelain considered his archetype to include coverage of at least some of the events between the death of Joan of Arc and the return of Philip the Good from the empire twenty-three years later. For more than half of the period he still had Monstrelet's narrative to fall back on. He may have used this work in an account of the conspiracy of Gilles de Postelles against Philip the Good in 1433 or in his description of the negotiations for the treaty of Arras (1435).[139] Chastelain's explicit mention of the 'pacification honorable et méritoire en la ville d'Arras, à haulx et grans mistères solennels, déclarés souffisamment en mon second volume, par quoy je les trespasse' (iv, 7), leaves little doubt that he considered the congress and treaty as part of an earlier text. If he did continue to hang his narrative around that of his predecessor, Chastelain seems also to have incorporated some of his own experiences. These had already begun to figure in his second fragment. The first indication of this comes in a description of the retinue which accompanied the dauphin Louis to the Burgundian court in 1456. Chastelain noted in particular the presence of 'le seigneur de La Barde, neveu au seigneur de Pons, banny et chassé de France, comme en mon second livre icy-devant a esté déclaré comment et pourquoy' (iii, 214). The lord of Pons, who held lands in Poitou, was banished in January 1442 as a result of his insurrection against Charles VII.[140] The seneschal of Poitou at the time was Pierre de Brézé. In view of Chastelain's proven connections with the latter we may suspect that

---

[137] viii, p. ix. The attribution originated in Jules Chifflet's unsubstantiated assumption that Chastelain was the author of the *Chronique de Jacques de Lalaing*: see *Histoire du bon chevalier Jacques de Lalaing escrite par messire Georges Chastellain*, ed. J. Chifflet, Brussels 1634, 1–2. B. Renard later noted that the work on Lalaing drew heavily upon Brussels, BR, MS 16881 – that is to say, the Ghent war narrative – concluding from this link that the author of the Lalaing biography and BR, MS 16881 were one and the same, i.e. Chastelain: B. Renard, 'Quelques observations à propos de quatorze chapitres inédits de Georges Chastellain', *Trésor national* i (1842), 91–9. The weak premiss at the root of this argument renders it dubious to say the least.

[138] Delclos's persuasive argument and supporting evidence are set out in 'Le témoignage', i. 325–49.

[139] Chastelain at least intended to write a narrative on the conspiracy of Postelles, although whether he did so is another matter: ii, 85. Monstrelet devoted a whole chapter to the event: *Chronique*, v. 67. In addition to the clear reference to a passage on the treaty of Arras which is cited on this page, Chastelain also refers to the episode ('comme avez oÿ ailleurs') in his account of events in 1458: Delclos, 223–4.

[140] This matter and the two which follow are discussed, with references, in ch. 2 above.

this putative passage had some basis in his personal experience. Brézé also figures in a second, almost contemporaneous episode which Chastelain claimed to have described. The reference arises in the context of the 1458 marriage of the count of Nevers to a daughter of the lord of Albret. At this stage Chastelain recalled an earlier plan proposed by Philip the Good for a marriage between Nevers and Marguerite d'Anjou 'comme ailleurs a esté narré en son lieu' (iii, 452). The plan foundered, as we have seen elsewhere, upon the intervention of Chastelain's former master, Pierre de Brézé, early in 1443. This apparent focus on French affairs in the years 1442 and 1443 is sustained in a third reference which occurs in the narrative for 1464. There we are reminded that Isabelle d'Armagnac 'avoit esté pourparlée, comme a esté conté en autre lieu, pour le roy Henry d'Angleterre, avant que le mariage de luy fust traité de la fille au roy de Cécile' (v, 18). The proposal, first mooted in May 1442, was finally shelved in January 1443. This event and the two others which form a cluster around that period did not make an impact upon the royal chronicle.[141] We are left to infer that Chastelain had not only written some form of narrative for these years, but that he may even have incorporated his experiences in France within it.

The chronicler's concern in this missing section with developments in the kingdom does not appear to have been limited to the years 1442–3.[142] In the so-called 'Livre VI' Chastelain recounts an anecdote in which it was revealed to Charles VII by 'un saint homme' that he was destined to recover the kingdom:

> De quoy, comme il a esté sçu et cognu par le monde, et par ce que moy et autres en ont escrit, la vérité en ensievy tantost; ... Et furent Normandie et Guienne reconquises sur les Anglois, et les habitans anciens ennemis tous expuls et chassés, dissipés et occis à peu de perte des Francs. (iv, 368)

Two further references leave little doubt that episodes in the reconquest of Normandy formed part of this putative text. Describing the exploits of François de Surienne, Chastelain mentions the famous mercenary's resignation from the Order of the Garter 'comme il appert par les contes qui en sont faits, là où ils duisent' (iv, 233). This event occurred during the reconquest.[143] The reader

---

[141] It is conceivable that Chastelain could have gleaned some of this information from Berry herald, but it would appear that the latter's *Chroniques* did not begin to circulate until after his death around 1455. There is no record of a copy of this work in the ducal library. For the date of the work see Gilles le Bouvier, *Les chroniques du roi Charles VII*, ed. H. Courteault, L. Celier and M.-H. Jullien de Pommerol, Paris 1979, p. ix.
[142] In addition to the examples which follow, Chastelain's account of events in 1457 suggests the existence of an earlier text for 1448. He was reminded during his trip to Normandy in 1457 of a curious aerial battle between jays and magpies which had occurred nine years earlier on the frontiers of Brittany. This had not been included in his Chronicle because circumstances 'ne se peuvent toutes réciter en leurs propres lieux et heures, quant elles eschéent, pour ce que mémoire est là vile': iii, 361.
[143] Beaucourt, *Histoire*, v. 424–5.

is also referred to an earlier passage ('comme vous avez bien oy': iii, 348) in which Pierre de Brézé became captain of Rouen and seneschal of Normandy – rewards which were granted by Charles VII after the fall of the Norman city in 1449. Chastelain did not participate in these events and he had not yet been appointed as official chronicler. The period would thus have been difficult to recount without the aid of a written source. As we have seen, however, other Burgundian court writers drew upon the eyewitness account provided by the *chroniqueur du roy* to describe these events. Chastelain may well have followed this logical course himself. The details of Surienne's change of camp and Brézé's rewards were there for the borrowing in Chartier's unique account.[144] The latter's frank chapter on 'la belle Agnès' also presented a ready-made source for a further putative narrative concerning her death in February 1450.[145] With these comments we return to a theme adumbrated at an earlier stage. It would appear that the official Burgundian chronicler had indeed used a Dionysian source where he found it expedient to do so.

This point underlines one of the more striking aspects of those passages which Chastelain believed his reader could consult in the missing account of the years from 1431 to 1454. He certainly cast his net wide, incorporating comments in some form or other on the murder of the earl of Douglas by James II in 1452, 'conté par cy devant en ung autre volume' (Delclos, 253); the fall of Constantinople in 1453, 'parce que ailleurs je vous en ay fait reccort' (iii, 109); or Philip the Good's visit to the congress of Regensburg, recounted 'en un précédent volume' (v, 60).[146] In particular, however, it is clear that many of the official Burgundian chronicler's lost passages were concerned with developments in France. Even in those parts of the Chronicle which now appear to be lost, the continuing interplay between French and Burgundian historical cultures is evident; so much so, in fact, that we are entitled to believe that Chastelain did not stray far from his original intention to write the history of 'ce très-chrestien royaume, clarifié par battures et souffrances' (i, 11). *How* he described those events may never be known, of course, although his approach was surely little different from that which will be outlined in the following chapter with regard to the surviving passages.

Until further manuscripts are discovered it is impossible to say whether Chastelain's putative narrative contained anything other than the developments discussed above between 1431 and 1454. The evidence presented thus far none the less belies the fragmentary state of the work as it stands in the manuscripts. Again, it is revealing that we are confronted with a broad chronological span of events: 1433, 1435, 1442–3, 1448, 1449, 1450, 1452, 1453 and 1454. Further evidence of a more complete archetype is to be found within the surviving fragments themselves. The extra material in BL, Add. MS

---

[144] Chartier, *Chronique*, ii. 172–3.
[145] iv, 366: 'comme j'ai conté ailleurs'. For Chartier's remarks on Sorel see *Chronique*, ii. 181–6.
[146] See also iii, 6–7.

54156 clearly indicated that the unbound quires of Chastelain's archetype, BR, MS 15843, once contained a more complete narrative for the years 1454–61. More significantly, it is also clear that Chastelain's original copy was even fuller than these comparisons themselves suggest.

The first indication of this comes in Chastelain's chapter on the reception at the ducal court of a papal crusading banner in 1456. There he reminds 'vous autres qui avez vive mémoire' of an earlier digression on Calixtus III's crusading bull 'comme en un chapitre à part luy, le voeu a esté mis et déclaré icy dessus tout au long' (iii, 117–18).[147] Neither of our two manuscripts contains a reference to the promulgation of this bull, dated 15 May 1455. Nor do they mention a second putative passage from around the same time, revealed in a reminder to the reader of Philip the Good's confiscation of the lands held in Hainaut by Louis de Luxembourg 'comme il a esté dit icy-dessus' (iii, 344). Mathieu d'Escouchy, Jacques du Clercq and Olivier de La Marche situate the event in 1455, but again the account is nowhere in evidence in Chastelain's surviving work.[148] When we turn to BR, MS 15843, however, we find that there is indeed a lacuna in the text at precisely this point – not a blank, it should be noted, but an unquantifiable number of missing quires.[149] It is clear that although the London manuscript was based upon a fuller version of its Brussels counterpart, the latter had already begun to suffer depletions before it was ever copied in its seemingly more complete state. This point is confirmed by a pair of putative passages which crop up later in the text. Writing early in 1462 of events in the kingdom of Cyprus, the chronicler reminds us of how King James II 'avoit pris son retour au soudan pour parvenir à la couronne, comme par cy-devant a pu apparoir par lettres envoyées à la royne' (iv, 193). James II's usurpation of the crown with the assistance of the sultan of Cairo took place in September 1460.[150] One month earlier the count of Charolais had held a meeting at Ardres with Henry Beaufort, duke of Somerset. Chastelain also claimed to have described this event, 'comme avez oy en mon livre cinquiesme' (iv, 68). These two passages, so closely linked in time, strongly suggest the existence in the archetype of a fuller text for the events of the summer of 1460. We may assume that the apparently rapid disintegration of Chastelain's archetype had prevented the transcriptions of such passages in BL, Add. MS 54156. The observation clearly undermines the reliability of the Brussels manuscript (and thus how much more the others, all copied at a later date?) as a guide to what the chronicler thought his public would one day be able to consult. What was once thought to be a whole chunk of the archetype is itself a diminished version.

---

[147] *Ad summi apostolatus apicem*. For the date of this bull in the next sentence see S. H. Steinberg, *Historical tables 58 B.C.–A.D. 1965*, 8th edn, London 1967, 99.
[148] Cf. d'Escouchy, *Chronique*, ii. 306–7; du Clercq, *Mémoires*, xiv. 103–4; La Marche, *Mémoires*, ii. 394–5.
[149] See app. 1 below.
[150] Housley, *The later crusades*, 197.

The belief that certain passages were never written is challenged even more directly in the case of the lacuna detected between September 1462 and August 1463.[151] Jean de Nevers's plot against the count of Charolais was almost certainly recounted in the text for these months: Chastelain did not go into the topic at a later stage 'car il a esté ailleurs déclaré par la contrainte du cas' (v, 70).[152] Recounting the Anglo-Castilian alliance of 1468, Chastelain also thought to remind his reader that Henry IV of Castile had good reason to break with the king of France, his customary ally, 'car héoit de dure mort le roy Loys, pour causes passées, et lesquelles ont esté contées par moy en un autre volume' (v, 339). The events in question had their origins in Louis XI's intervention in Castilian affairs in the second half of 1462; in January 1463, Henry IV was openly encouraged by Pius II to ally himself to the house of York.[153] Finally, Chastelain explained the imprisonment of Philip of Savoy in 1464 by his royal brother-in-law in the following terms: 'L'offense de ce jeusne prince et l'exploit qu'il fit, de quoy le roy maintenant se voulut venger, est escript en ce mesme volume ici-dessus de l'année passée: sy ne besongne de le renouveller ici par récitation seconde' (v, 9). Philip's insurrection against his ineffectual father began in 1462 and continued in 1463. There can be no doubt that the chronicler had found time to write some account of events between August 1462 and September 1463.

A handful of references reveal that the remainder of Chastelain's archetype was rather more substantial than the manuscripts would suggest. The chronicler certainly considered the events of the war of the Public Weal (1465) as part of his archetype 'telle comme a esté conté cy en sus' (v, 217). In the same passage we learn that the first two campaigns against Liège, one in the winter of 1465–6, the other in the summer of 1466, may also have been described. An account of the death of Jacques de Bourbon in May 1468 was claimed as part of the text, 'comme je vous ay dit' (v, 381), as was the battle of Losecoat Field near Stamford in 1470, 'comme il a esté dit' (v, 499). According to Molinet (ii, 595), indeed, his master's account of events included some coverage of the siege of Neuss of 1474 by the time of his death.

The excavation of the archetype once kept in Chastelain's *comptoir* at Valenciennes is littered, as the preceding pages have attempted to show, with

---

[151] Delclos's chronology of the text's composition suggested that 'on peut se demander si la partie manquante . . . a jamais été écrite': *Le témoignage*, 71. As the evidence cited here shows, the chronicler thought otherwise.
[152] On this matter see B. de Mandrot, 'Jean de Bourgogne, duc de Brabant, comte de Nevers et le procès de sa succession', RH xciii (1907), 1–45 at pp. 9–11.
[153] P. M. Kendall, *Louis XI*, London 1974, 147–8; K. Bittmann, 'La question catalane et la politique générale au début du règne de Louis XI', *Annales du Midi* lvi–lx (1944–8), 80–90; J. Calmette, *Louis XI, Jean II et la révolution catalane (1461–73)*, Toulouse 1903, 116ff. It is also possible that Chastelain's putative passage on Joan de Copons, alluded to at iv, 425 ('de qui . . . a esté faite mention assez longue'), occurred around this point. On Copons see J. Calmette, 'Dom Pedro, roi des catalans et la cour de Bourgogne', AB xviii (1946), 7–15 at p. 13, and *Louis XI, Jean II*, passim.

finds of this nature. Together they indicate the existence of a greater whole; they throw light upon its constituent parts and even, in a few places, its sources. Two further categories of evidence may be adduced in support of the argument formulated here. The first concerns the division of Chastelain's work into distinct books.

The apparent confusion surrounding the numbering of the books of the Chronicle is usually taken as a sign of the work's incomplete state: how could Chastelain have formulated a clear idea of the whole when each of its parts was so fragmented? Yet there was some method here, and the chronicler's desire to force his will upon an unwieldy archetype deserves greater emphasis than it has received in the past. It seems to have been fairly clear in his mind that the first book would cover events from Philip the Good's accession up to and including those of 1429.[154] The second book is almost as straightforward, beginning with the duke's marriage and the foundation of the Order of the Golden Fleece in January 1430, and extending, through various putative accounts, at least as far as 1442.[155] The starting point of the third book, at some stage after 1442, is unknown.[156] It certainly came to an end with the return of Philip the Good from the congress of Regensburg late in 1454, since at that juncture Chastelain refers to the previous 'trois volumes . . . desquels le contenu, j'espoire, est demoré en bon recort des lisans' (iii, 5).[157] It may be that Chastelain, struck by the importance of the historical moment, intended to mark the beginning of Philip the Good's crusading venture with a new book in the official Burgundian chronicle.

The division of the work becomes more problematic with the fourth and fifth books. Chastelain certainly intended his sixth book to begin in 1461 with the coronation of Louis XI.[158] It is interesting to note that a great event in French royal history should have merited a clean sheet – in every sense – in the official Burgundian Chronicle. This left the fourth and fifth books to deal with events from 1454 to 1461. Chastelain had clearly begun in his own mind to divide up his material between the two.[159] For example, he considered an

---

[154] Writing of events in 1430, Chastelain refers back to his 'premier livre' on three separate occasions: ii, 14, 17–18, 72. Did 1429 seem a good year to interrupt the narrative because it witnessed the long overdue coronation of Charles VII?

[155] For Chastelain's references on the matter see Delclos, 122; iii, 214; iv, 7.

[156] The scribes who later copied Chastelain's work make a clear mistake on this point on at least one occasion. Shortly after a reference indicating that the events of 1430 belonged to the second book, it is noted that the offer of the Garter which was made to Philip in the same year was situated at the beginning of the third book: Delclos, 124. As Armstrong observed, Chastelain may have changed his mind more than once as to the ordering of the material into books: C. A. J. Armstrong, 'Le texte de la *Chronique* de Chastellain pour les années 1458–61 retrouvé dans un manuscrit jusqu'ici inconnu', PCEEBM x (1968), 73–8 (repr. in his *England, France and Burgundy*, 383–8).

[157] A point confirmed by a further reference at iii, 7.

[158] Louis's accession was described as the 'commencement de ce sixiesme volume': iv, 118.

[159] In this I disagree with Kondo's view that book five never existed: this seems too categorical a conclusion in view of the chronicler's loosely formulated thinking on the

event which had occurred in 1460 as part of his 'livre cincquiesme' (iv, 68). However, it is apparent that distinctions between the fourth and fifth books remained fluid. Writing of events in 1461, for example, Chastelain described the conflict between the count of St Pol and the Croy family, which had originated in the mid-1450s, as belonging to 'mon autre livre devant cestui' (iv, 130). There is a clear discrepancy here: the period in question was considered elsewhere as part of the fourth, not fifth, book.[160]

Paradoxically, such discrepancies may have arisen not from Chastelain's confusion over his scrappy, shapeless material, but from his desire to shape a fuller narrative into a form which reflected his own perception of its advanced state. By 1467 he had clearly decided that his work would be divided into seven books, even if that meant the division or reorganisation of his material for the years 1454–61 into books four and five. The decision was no doubt informed by the need to accommodate an obvious watershed in his narrative, the accession of Charles the Bold.[161] The desire to juggle the narrative in order to create *seven* books is of more than passing interest. In Christian numerology the number seven indicates perfection or completion.[162] It was consequently popular among medieval historians – Otto of Freising and Ranulf Higden being two examples – as the ideal number of books which should figure within a finished work of history.[163] By 1467 at the latest, Chastelain had thus alighted upon the form that his sustained, legitimating narrative would take. In the mind of the man best placed to know, the 'perpétuel chantier' had clearly reached an advanced stage of construction.

He was not alone in this view. The opinions of two well-informed contemporaries may be adduced here as one last strand in the argument. An isolated remark in Jean Molinet's Chronicle is often taken as proof that his mentor's work was left in a hopeless condition at the time of his death: 'grand planté de ses oeuvres sont demourez imperfaictes, qui donneront labeur intollerable à ceulx qui vouldront parattaindre la fin de ses conceptions' (ii, 594). When situated in its proper context, however, Molinet's testimony evokes a rather different picture. Further on in the same passage we learn that after his master's death he travelled to the siege of Neuss to petition Charles the Bold 'qu'il lui pleusist moy donner licence de parachever ce que mon très honoré seigneur et

---

matter: 'Le livre IV de la *Chronique* de Georges Chastelain', *Études de langue et de littérature françaises* l (1987), 1–18.

[160] For other references suggesting a lack of differentiation between the fourth and fifth books see Delclos, 323; iv, 133, 166.

[161] The existence of Book VII (in the chronicler's mind at least) is attested by the fact that early in the reign of Charles the Bold, he described the events of 1462–3 as having been 'contées par moy en un autre volume': v, 339.

[162] Cf. *Cruden's complete concordance to the Bible* (I have used an edition published by the Lutterworth Press: Cambridge 1977), p. 587 c.2.

[163] *The* most popular number, according to Guenée: *Histoire et culture historique*, 228–9. The model ultimately derived from St Augustine: A. Gransden, *Historical writing in England*, ii, London 1982, 46–7, 455, 476.

maistre, que Dieu pardoint, avoit encommencé; et iceluy . . . le m'accorda liberalement' (ii, 594). The remark is critical. Molinet's initial duty was to produce a recension of Chastelain's Chronicle. His reference to 'ceste grande charge' as a 'labeur intollerable' may thus have been an exaggeration made, consciously or unconsciously, to underscore the importance of his own post. It certainly contrasts with his later statement that 'mon intention est de rassembler plusieurs coyers escripts de la main de mondit seigneur et maistre, tous desemparéz, imparfaicts et sans ordre, pour les aduner en aucuns certains volumes par luy très grandement avancés' (ii, 594–5). Further evidence is to be found in the work of Jean Lefèvre. In a revealing passage following an explicit reference to Chastelain's 'nobles histoires et cronicques', Lefèvre wrote of the duke's 'notables orateurs et hystoriens' who, to his knowledge, had already written 'pluiseurs grans livres et volummes' by the time he had begun his own work.[164] The archetype of the Chronicle, although not complete, was thus thought to have evolved considerably by the later 1460s; it had been divided into several books and a smaller portion of it existed in the form of unbound quires. This material had to be brought together since, as Molinet put it, 'dommaige irrecuperable seroit . . . à ceste magnificque maison de Bourgogne, se tant de fières et merveilleuses emprinses, qui s'i forment continuellement de forts et vigoureux bras, se perissoient avecque le son des armes, sans les graver en solide memorial' (ii, 593). Just as the monks of St Denis had produced recensions of their predecessors' texts, so too would Molinet of Chastelain's – or so it seemed in 1475.[165] What happened after that point remains to be seen.

The provocative opening gambit of this chapter was clearly misplaced. Chastelain's achievement, although personal in terms of his creative ability, owed a great deal to the support he drew or received from other sources within the court environment. So far as its broad outlines are concerned, his archetype reflected many of the aspirations which were evinced in the patronage nexus and which came naturally to him through his experience at the centre: not the history of a Burgundian state severed from France, but one which set Burgundy within the wider kingdom and explored its political culture in that context. How Chastelain represented Burgundian history within that framework is the subject of the following chapter.

---

[164] Lefèvre, *Chronique*, i. 2, 4.
[165] Jean Castel's writings were assembled at the time of his death and placed in a box for safety's sake: Quicherat, 'Recherches', 471. Molinet's work was also gathered up after his death on the orders of Margaret of Austria: Dupire, *Jean Molinet*, 25 n. 3. Official chronicles were clearly too precious to throw away or to be exposed to risk.

5

Reading the Chronicle

It is clear that contemporaries would not have read the Chronicle with the same preconceptions and values as the modern reader, but assessing quite how they might have understood it is harder to say. We have no earlier readings to guide our own, or at least none before the first signs of audience response to the work late in the fifteenth century.[1] The Chronicle's fragmentary survival compounds our difficulties. Any attempt to solve the problem is, therefore, based on conjecture, and must work outwards from the assumptions and intentions of the author towards those passages which might have prompted a tut or a nod from an earlier reader immersed in that historical culture. At the outset certain clear points of reference help to chart a course through what remains of the work.

The first of these is the political and historical culture from which it emerged. The official Chronicle was written within a polity which had its own internal dynamic and its own concerns, but which also engaged with those of royal and princely France as a result of the politico-legal circumstances, personal or familial interests and historical traditions discussed in previous chapters. These centrifugal and centripetal forces within the Burgundian elite are difficult to ignore in any account of its history.

The second reference point is provided by Chastelain himself. Few have failed to notice that the Chronicle displays characteristics that are sometimes found wanting in aristocratic histories: a clear set of organising principles which dominate the narrative of events, even in its present state.[2] The work's central themes and sub-themes have been variously described as Chastelain's 'idée fondamentale', his 'grande préoccupation', the 'écheveau compliqué de ses idées' which he sought to '[faire] pénétrer . . . dans l'esprit du lecteur'.[3] Previous analyses, as we have seen, have identified the central tenet of this 'témoignage' as a simple but ultimately unattainable ideal of Franco-Burgundian unity.

This may seem a curiously passive and one-dimensional view for an official

---

[1] For later responses see ch. 6 below.
[2] On the supposed absence of this characteristic in aristocratic histories see W. J. Brandt, *The shape of medieval history*, New Haven–London 1966, 81–105.
[3] Hommel, *Chastellain*, 69; Urwin, *Georges Chastelain*, 39; Pérouse, *Georges Chastellain*, 29; Delclos, 'Le témoignage', i. 196. Chastelain's Chronicle is thought to offer remarkable examples of 'exposés ponctuels et systématiques sur un thème donné': H. Wolff, 'Traîtres et trahison d'après quelques oeuvres historiques de la fin du moyen âge', in *Exclus et système d'exclusion dans la littérature et la civilisation médiévales*, Aix-en-Provence 1978, 41–55 at p. 47.

Burgundian chronicler to espouse – particularly one so well-acquainted with the political realities of his day, and one who specifically demanded of his audience that they read meaning into his work.[4] It will be argued here that Chastelain produced a layered and, so far as it survives, coherent response to the circumstances which affected his ducal master and the elite surrounding him. In short, the Chronicle may be read as a work of propaganda; a work that reached out to the type of wider audience discussed in chapter three to propagate views which, without necessarily being contrived or insincerely held, would assist the Burgundian cause as the chronicler had reason to perceive it.[5] After a brief discussion of the controlling historical framework which Chastelain impressed upon his reader, we progress to his representation of the Chronicle's key protagonists. Second only to God, after all, it was the prince who made history. Philip the Good and his royal contemporaries occupy the greater part of what follows. This emphasis is justified by the fact that the passages devoted to Charles the Bold, although highly revealing in their own way of Burgundian court attitudes, constitute little more than one-eighth of the surviving text.

The historical framework

Chastelain's narrative was underpinned by models of historical development which naturally gave shape to his representation of events. Previous chapters have given some idea of where we might look for the models he would consciously deploy: among the emerging strands of a specifically Burgundian historical literature on the one hand, or within an older corpus of French traditions on the other. It should be clear by this stage that despite the emphasis which is often placed on the former, the latter provided a fecund source for the conceptual grid which Chastelain would superimpose upon events. The point remains to be proven with regard to the text itself; for, notwithstanding attempts to locate its direct sources and inspiration in previous chapters, it is clear that the wider literary substructure beneath the work cannot be gauged consistently.[6] If some of the models which follow seem familiar, even conven-

---

[4] See, most famously, the following passage: 'O vous humains coeurs des François, qui, par successives générations de père en fils, en temps advenir trouverez mes escripts . . . si faim vous peut prendre de visiter mes oeuvres, et que loisir vous puisse traire à l'advertence d'icelles, ne vueilliez doncques noter tant seulement le son des paroles, mais les causes et racines qui m'ont mu à les former telles': iv, 14–15.

[5] The term 'propaganda' is of course anachronistic: D. R. Kelley, *The beginning of ideology*, Cambridge 1981, 244–51. As this chapter seeks to show, however, Chastelain clearly set out to persuade his audience – an audience which he perceived to be both French and Burgundian: cf. i, 32, 336–7; ii, 115, 177; iii, 390; Delclos, 318; iv, 14–15, 22, 152; v, 201. For the use of the term 'propaganda' in the sense proposed here see B. Smalley, *Historians in the Middle Ages*, London 1974, 185.

[6] See ch. 4 above.

tional, we should not assume that they were the vehicles of a familiar or conventional interpretation of events.

The teleological slant of some court texts, where dominions, subjects and ruler united in a common destiny, is largely absent in the official Chronicle. Chastelain's distinctions between the subjects or lands of the duke and those of the king and other princes are hardly significant in this respect.[7] Contemporary Frenchmen were equally aware of the regional diversity of the kingdom itself.[8] On one occasion he does imply the existence of historical bonds between Philip's dominions 'qui ne peuvent l'un sans l'autre, et qui de tout temps ancien ont eu l'habitude l'un avecques l'autre' (iv, 124). Yet he can also write that Philip's 'multitude de . . . terres, seigneuries et puissances accouplées ensamble' (ii, 150) had never before been brought under the rule of one prince.[9] The most conspicuous historical arguments for a predestined sense of unity within and between the Burgundian lands – such as the Christian past of the kingdom of Burgundy, the unifying concept of Lotharingia or the legends attaching to the ancient kingdom of Friesia – receive little or no attention.[10] Instead, the history of the subjects and lands of the ducal dynasty are perceived in isolation from one another, as they often were in the historical literature of the court discussed in an earlier chapter. The courageous 'condition et nature ancienne' of the Burgundians (ii, 44) was singled out, for example, as was the 'constance et fermeté' of the Flemish, attested by 'anciennes histoires' (i, 268). Such distinct traditions could militate against the evolution of a sense of

[7] See iii, 287; iv, 274–5, 313, 392, 394; v, 83; or the employment of the terms 'par deça' and 'par delà' to distinguish between ducal and royal lands: iii, 308, 467; iv, 233; v, 43, 214, 309, 313, 338, 393, 411, 413, 422.

[8] Gilles le Bouvier, *Le livre de la description des pays*, ed. E.-T. Hamy, Paris 1908.

[9] A similar paradox occurs in the *Advertissement au duc Charles*, where 'mil ans' of history in the ducal dominions is referred to in almost the same breath as the different laws, privileges and customs which prevailed within them: vii, 306–7.

[10] He may refer to the negotiations of 1447 and 1463 in the empire for the raising to royal status of some or all of Philip's lands, but none of the historical arguments advanced on either occasion left an imprint upon his work: cf. ii, 150 and Delclos, 73; A. M. Bonenfant and P. Bonenfant, 'Le projet d'érection des états bourguignons en royaume en 1447', MA xlv (1935), 10–23; J. Schneider, 'Lotharingie, Bourgogne ou Provence?', in *Liège et Bourgogne*, Liège 1972, 15–44; A. G. Jongkees, 'Charles le Téméraire et la souveraineté', BMGN xcv (1980), 315–34 (repr. in *Burgundica et varia*, 191–211). Lacaze suggests that there are signs of a 'sentiment impérial' in some of the chronicler's comments, although whether the passages he cites can bear that interpretation is at least debatable: Lacaze, 'Le rôle des traditions', 375. Chastelain's description of Philip the Good's imperial courage or appearance suggest he is simply using the term 'empereur' as a superlative: vii, 220; i, 187. In his *Exposition* he does mention the 'vertus et richesses' which came to Philip, not from France, but 'de vraie naturelle succession légitime du trônc de l'Empire': vi, 336. It is interesting that Chastelain uses the word 'tronc' here, a term that has a genealogical connotation which the chronicler – as we shall see – uses far more regularly of the duke's connections to the French royal line. Finally, Chastelain's account of the campaigns in Friesland in 1456 does refer to Philip's 'royaume de Frise', but again he makes nothing of the mythology attaching to the royal title: iii, 158, 375. Philip was prepared to give up the conquest of this 'royaume' to honour his obligations to the dauphin of France: iii, 196.

historical homogeneity. The duke had to respect certain rights which the townsfolk of Valenciennes alone had enjoyed 'très-anciennement et de tout temps' (iii, 38). The inhabitants of the county of Burgundy had always sought to

> maintenir francise selon la nature du pays, qui à ceste cause se nomme France-Conté, comme celle entre toutes les autres du monde là où les nobles hommes vivent plus francs et plus aiant seigneurie sur leurs hommes ... avecques ce gardans les anciennes francises et libertés de leurs pères, dont ne veulent estre formenés par nulles occasions nouvelles. (iii, 13–14)

In cases such as these, Burgundian rule perched precariously upon a mass of diverse traditions. The problems posed by the multiple legacy of the past were more evident to the chronicler than any opportunities it might have offered.

Chastelain, the parvenu who reinterpreted his own lineage, was clearly aware of the value of genealogical argument.[11] It is therefore interesting to note that the pre-Valois dynastic history of Philip's dominions received little attention in his work. His few forays into the deep past produced only the vaguest of references: Philip the Good's 'devanciers ... de trois à quatre cens ans de devant luy' (ii, 143) are referred to indiscriminately, for example, as is 'l'ancien héritage des princes du pays' (iv, 223).[12] The chronicler is more specific with regard to the counts of Flanders, but even here there is no clear attempt to build bridges between past and present as some other court writers are thought to have done. Charles I (1119–27), described as a 'prince très-juste et très-dévot' (i, 26), was only mentioned to illustrate the theme that terrible misfortunes can befall great princes.[13] Baldwin IX (1195–1206), whose crusading exploits were a natural point of reference for some Burgundian writers, is described as Philip the Good's 'prédécesseur d'immortelle mémoire' (iii, 75). The value of the remark is diminished by the fact that it occurs in a passage of reported speech. Chastelain's treatment of Ferrand of Portugal (1212–33), husband of Countess Joan, reveals in fact a conscious rejection of any link between restive counts and the loyal duke. Among the former 'qui toujours n'ont pas été concordans avec les roys françois', Ferrand,

> non de sang si bon que de France, se monstra moult felle, et soy exposant contraire à la couronne, en confidence de sa haute fortune, fut humilié toutesvoies et vaincu par le pesché de son descongnoistre. Or n'est mie cestui [Philip the Good] un Ferrand de Portingal. Ce n'est mie celui qui descongnoit la sève dont il prend estre. Ce n'est mie celui qui, rebelle à la majesté glorieuse, se veulle eslever contre elle à main ennemie. Non! (vi, 406)

---

[11] For other examples of the deployment of genealogical argument see iii, 133; v, 67. Chastelain mentions the 'sang de Bourgogne', but not in an historical context: ii, 74; iii, 72; iv, 489; v, 27, 128.
[12] Cf. iii, 151. References as far back as the first Valois duke are relatively few and far between: see i, 11, 145; ii, 79; iv, 85, 392.
[13] A common topos: cf. Pisan, *Le Livre du corps de policie*, 54–60.

Indigenous dynastic traditions, like histories of the ducal dominions themselves, were not brought into play within the Chronicle's interpretive framework. Chastelain was not unaware of the real or imagined importance of figures like Girart de Roussillon or Ogier le Danois – he mentioned them elsewhere in his work.[14] He may simply have felt that it was not germane to his purpose to dwell on them in the Chronicle. To achieve his ends, an author has to assume a certain amount of preknowledge on the part of his reader; familiar models and forms draw the audience into his orbit and enable him to convey his message.[15] Perhaps the characters who figured in the nascent Burgundian historical consciousness discussed in chapter three were not yet sufficiently familiar to oust better established figures.[16]

Instead, Chastelain drew his exempla in dynastic matters from the deeds of French kings – the 'vaillans roys des François' whom Philippe de Mézières cited as role models for Charles VI and whose exploits were vaunted by the Dionysian tradition.[17] In his darkest hour occasioned by the appalling news from Montereau, Philip is counselled to take solace in the example set by John II after his personal nadir at Poitiers. Chastelain drew on Monstrelet for this section of the text, but the reference to John is of his own making.[18] The historical landscape is dotted with similar references to the reigns of monarchs whom royalist writers of the fifteenth century referred to constantly: Clovis, 'le premier chrestien' (iv, 89); Charlemagne, to whom Charles VII and Philip the Good, alone 'en ceste liliée région' (v, 246), could be compared; the Capetian Louis IX, 'prince d'une austère vie, relyé en divine amour' (i, 24); and finally the Valois Charles V, France's 'dernier conduiseur' and one of the 'glorieux pasteurs de jadis' (i, 38).[19] Some at the Burgundian court might use the transitions between the royal dynasties as an opportunity to question the legitimacy of the line.[20] Not so the official chronicler, who appears to have

---

[14] See ch. 4 above.

[15] R. Chartier, 'Texts, printing, readings', in L. Hunt (ed.), *The new cultural history*, Berkeley 1989, 154–75 at p. 165.

[16] Although, as we shall see in the following chapter, they were more familiar to the next generation.

[17] Philippe de Mézières, *Le songe du vieil pelerin*, ed. G. W. Coopland, Cambridge 1969, ii. 142.

[18] i, 46; cf. F. Fossier, 'Le règne de Jean le Bon dans les histoires françaises du XIVe au XIXe siècles', *PTSEC* (1975), 85–90; Monstrelet, *Chronique*, iii. 358–61.

[19] See also v, 91; vii, 325. These figures, by contrast with those of embryonic Burgundian traditions, were extremely familiar in the fifteenth century: C. Beaune, 'St Clovis', in B. Guenée (ed.), *Le métier d'historien au moyen âge*, Paris 1977, 139–56; F. Collard, 'Clovis dans quelques histoires de France de la fin du XVe siècle', *BEC* cliv (1996), 131–52; J. Monfrin, 'La figure de Charlemagne dans l'historiographie du XVe siècle', *ABSHF* (1964–5), 67–78; R. Lambrech, 'Charlemagne and his influence on late medieval French kings', *JMH* xiv (1988), 283–91; L. Carolus-Barré, 'St Louis dans l'histoire et la légende', *ABSHF* (1970–1), 37–49; C. R. Sherman, 'Representations of Charles V of France (1338–1380) as a wise ruler', *Medievalia et humanistica* ns ii (1971), 83–96; D. Byrne, 'Rex imago Dei', *JMH* vii (1981), 97–113.

[20] According to Philippe Wielant's *Recueil des antiquités de Flandre*, Charles the Bold

accepted the royalist myth of the *reditus regni ad stirpem Karoli*.[21] Acceptance of this myth, and some of the other historical models which follow, provided one of the pegs upon which his audience could hang an understanding of his work.

Dynastic references of this nature suggest that Chastelain, to an even greater extent than could be shown with certainty in previous chapters, was drawn to the ready-made models of royal and royalist history. In fact, these passages are the outer surface of a layered bedrock of French traditions in which his Chronicle was consciously grounded. The prologue, inevitably one of the more important passages of the work, is particularly instructive here. Chastelain broaches his subject matter with a conventional piece of universal history: conventional, that is, for any audience acquainted with an orthodox, royalist view of the *longue durée*. It is dominated by two strands, each of which can be related to a wider body of French historiography.

The first of these is biblical in origin. It traces the human past back to the Creation, the Fall and the later tribulations of the Jewish people. Chastelain equates the biblical history of the Jews with that of the French in his own lifetime. Both were permitted by God to suffer at the hands of tyrants (i, 3). The connection was a commonplace which, although it had originated in ecclesiastical circles, had reached a wider audience and gained in definition by the middle of the fifteenth century.[22] According to this tradition the French, like the Jews, were God's chosen people.[23] The land they inhabited was His country, 'ce très-glorieux royaume de France' (i, 10), the 'région françoise' which was 'le giron de toute loyauté chrestienne ... de toute vraye religion en Dieu' (i, 36). Chastelain did not establish as firm a connection between the French monarchy and the biblical past as some were inclined to do, but the key stages of that tradition are none the less in evidence: the descent of the Jews (and by extension the French) is traced back through Abraham, Noah, Abel and Adam. Once again, a fifteenth-century French reader would have found himself on entirely familiar ground.

In addition to this mainstream, biblical perception of the distant past, the prologue draws upon classically inspired traditions to launch and frame the narrative. These too were orthodox opinions.[24] The French were presented as

---

considered the Capetians (and by extension the Valois kings) to be usurpers, and himself, as duke of Brabant, to be 'descendu en directe lignie' from Charlemagne: *Recueil des chroniques de Flandre*, ed. J. J. de Smet, Brussels 1865, iv. 1–442 at p. 53.

[21] G. M. Spiegel, 'The *reditus regni ad stirpem Karoli Magni*', *French Historical Studies* vii (1971), 145–74; K. F. Werner, 'Die Legitimität der Kapetinger und die Entstehung des *Reditus regni Francorum ad stirpem Karoli*', *Die Welt als Geschichte* xii (1952), 203–25 (repr. in his *Structures politiques du monde franc*, London 1979).

[22] Beaune, *Naissance*, 35–6.

[23] J. R. Strayer, 'France: the holy land, the chosen people and the most Christian king', in T. K. Rabb and J. E. Seigel (eds), *Action and conviction in early modern Europe*, Princeton 1969, 3–16.

[24] For what follows see Guenée, *Histoire et culture historique*, 148–50; J. Krynen, *L'empire*

the latest in a series of great peoples who had dominated their lesser contemporaries. Before them there had been the Romans, 'les aigles du monde et dompteurs' (i, 5); before the Romans came the Greeks, who in turn had risen to prominence after subjugating 'la troyenne nation'.[25] The translation of the 'couronne impériale et thrône de souveraine sacrée majesté' (i, 6) to the French was divinely ordained. The classical tradition donned a Christian mantle. The dominance of the 'chrestien peuple françois' (i, 338) was assured so long as they remained the 'protecteurs . . . des bons, refuge aux désolés, vigoureux sustenteurs aux foibles, escu aux povres et innocens, miroir aux vertueux, règle aux vaillans, baston et fléaux des mauvais, de toutes tyrannies et exactions, et de toutes hérésies et toutes inhumaines crudélités, esmotions et fureurs populaires' (i, 7). 'Certes ainsi firent jadis les princes françois' (i, 7), noted Chastelain: they embraced and defended the true faith, 'aucunesfois en victoire sur les payens, autresfois, par divine permission, en ruine mesme de leur ost' (i, 8).

The origins of this influential idea of 'une alliance éternelle, bien que conditionnelle' between God and the French have been traced back to the ninth-century *Vita sancti Remigii* by Hincmar, archbishop of Rheims.[26] St Remigius is said to have predicted the perpetuation of French supremacy so long as they adhered to the path prescribed for God's chosen people. Deviation from it would incur divine retribution. This is precisely how Chastelain accounts elsewhere for the tribulations of the kingdom at the hands of the English in the reign of Charles VI, a mad king 'permis de Dieu estre tel pour nos péchés' (i, 163).[27] The French were afflicted by this misfortune 'pour en estre battus en temps de payement et punis de leur mésus, souverainement du péché d'envye et d'orgueil qui depuis leur a enveloppé les yeux et esteint la raison, et ingrats envers Dieu et descongnus en yvresse de voluptés et de biens trop abondans' (i, 8). The English, like some divine flail, behaved as though 'l'héritage des Francs estoit le leur, et que leur gouvernement et domination seroient désormais aboly par le nom des Anglois' (i, 202). This combination of the familiar theme of sin with a cyclical view of the historical process was also a commonplace by the time Chastelain was writing.[28] Understandably, the link seemed particularly prominent after the battle of Poitiers. It was

---

du roi, Paris 1993, 384–90; H. Hauser, 'Le transport des regnes et empires des Grecz ès François', *Revue des Études Rabelaisiennes* vi (1908), 182–9.

[25] It is interesting to note that Chastelain does not push his analysis further back in time to the matter of Troy, where there may have been room for conflict between ducal and royal traditions. He may have raised the matter in a chapter he announces – but which does not survive – on Jason and Gideon as patrons of the Order of the Golden Fleece: ii, 7. For relevant interpretations of the Trojan legends see A. Bayot, 'La légende de Troie à la cour de Bourgogne', *Société d'émulation de Bruges: mélanges* i (1908), 3–51; A. Bossuat, 'Les origines troyennes', *Annales de Normandie* viii (1958), 187–97.

[26] Beaune, *Naissance*, 215–16.

[27] The use of the first person plural deserves to be emphasised. It recurs at ii, 177 ('nos vicieuses passions') and v, 341 ('ce royaume-ici estoit perdu, et nous tous').

[28] See also i, 336–7.

perpetuated in the writings of Honoré Bouvet, Robert Gervais and Jean Gerson, all of whom lived through the worst years of the continuing French crisis.[29] In *Audite celi*, Jean Juvenal des Ursins later explained the English victories and occupation by the sins of the French, as did Alain Chartier in his *Quadrilogue invectif*.[30] The terms used in the latter are at times strikingly similar to those which would later fall from Chastelain's pen: 'l'orgueil de trop oultrecuidié povoir qui se descognoist est rabaissié par puissance ennemie, la superfluité des biens mondains, qui est nourrice de sedicions et de murmure, est chastiee par sa mesmes nourreture et l'ingratitude des dons de Dieu est punie sur les hommes par sustraction de sa grace'.[31] Here, as elsewhere in his prologue, Chastelain appropriated a tradition familiar to those articulate royalists of later medieval France who were led, by contemporary circumstances, to meditate upon the kingdom's past and present.

Beyond the prologue, the Chronicle was permeated by other strands which situated the deeper historical context of the work within an equally conventional context. This is best seen in his deployment of images which, by the fifteenth century, were the stock-in-trade of royalist writers. Again, the conventionality of Chastelain's historical framework is striking.

The misfortunes of France were frequently expressed through the personification of the kingdom as a princess neglected by her own children. Her laments served as a commentary upon France's recent history. This interpretive model, traced in embryonic form to the work of Eustace Deschamps and Nicolas de Clamanges, is present in several of Chastelain's lesser works.[32] It is also to be found in the Chronicle: 'O malheurée et très infortunée France pour cely temps! dame toutes-voies par avant spécieuse en beauté . . . princesse maintenant changée d'habit, muée de couleur, déclinée d'estat' (i, 37).[33] Among her children, the princes of the realm 'se sont plongés en profonde malédiction, et à la povre France leur mère ont procuré le fardeau dont elle s'est noyée en pleurs' (i, 22). Such images correspond closely to the most elaborate exposition of the theme in Alain Chartier's *Quadrilogue invectif*. There, France addresses 'ses enfans' (the people, the nobility and the clergy).[34] She is described as 'une dame dont le hault port et seigneury maintien signifioit sa tresexcellente extraction, mais tant fut dolente et esplouree que bien sembloit dame decheue de plus hault honneur'. Although it could not be shown in previous chapters that Chastelain had read Chartier, his recourse to a

---

[29] A. Vernet, 'Le *Tragicum argumentum de miserabili statu regni Francie* de François de Montebelluna (1357)', *ABSHF* (1962–3), 100–63; Beaune, *Naissance*, 215 and n. 61.
[30] Jean Juvenal des Ursins, *Écrits politiques*, ed. P. S. Lewis, Paris 1978, i. 196–7.
[31] Alain Chartier, *Le quadrilogue invectif*, ed. E. Droz, Paris 1950, 1–2.
[32] Cf. vi, 437–57; vii, 1–35. Eustache Deschamps, *Oeuvres complètes*, ed. A. Queux de St-Hilaire and G. Raynaud, Paris 1878–1903, ii. 93–4 (*Complainte du pays de France*); Nicolas de Clamanges, *Opera omnia*, I: *Epistolae*, Lyon 1613, 179–83 (ep. lxiii: 'Patria Franciae ad suos principes loquente').
[33] See also i, 40.
[34] *Quadrilogue invectif*, 7.

familiar symbolic mode in such passages leaves little doubt that he had.[35] So too, of course, had many among the governing classes of fifteenth-century France.

Two further, highly conventional images were deployed in the narrative framework: the kingdom as a garden and the Tree of France. In the first, the gardener-king was expected to maintain the hedges and to remove harmful growths and stones which obstructed the roses and lilies, the natural vegetation of a sacred place. This popular image was evoked in the work of Jean Gerson, Berry Herald and Robert Blondel among others.[36] God, who sought to 'faire florir et fructifier le jardin de sa foi' according to Chastelain, chose the French as his 'cultiveurs qui, en labeur et vertu de corps, sartissent et jetassent les espines et donnassent aux plantes eslevées lieu et aisance de verdoyer' (i, 7). The death of Charles VII and the accession of Louis XI in 1461 brought order and fertility to the Garden of France, the 'noble préau des lis' (i, 60) which constituted the chronicler's subject matter:

> (Fortune) m'a présenté landes pleines de joncs marins et de chardons, dont rien que venin et lésion ne se pouvoit traire, jusques à présent que, non pour le complaisement de ma povre personne, mais pour le bien universel du monde, elle m'a changé mon heur et m'a fait de vaucrage en longue annuyeuse bruyère poingnante, entrer en jardin plein d'arbres et fleurs sollacieuses, quant perchu me suis que terminé est le chief et le causeur des espines du monde et est sourse la plante qui produira les roses, si Dieu plaist, à la jocondité et salut de tout homme. (iv, 20-1)

It is interesting to note that Chastelain appends an openly Burgundian slant here to the interpretive model deployed by his predecessors and counterparts in the kingdom. Once on familiar ground, the reader was being pulled round to a less obvious perspective on events. This points to wider trends in Chastelain's work which will become clearer at a later stage. For the moment, it should be noted that his appropriation of the image of the Tree of France betrays similar inclinations.

By the later fourteenth century this biblical trope had come to encapsulate the dynasty (or genealogical tree) of France as well as the duty of the French to maintain and preserve it.[37] Chastelain uses it in both senses. He refers to Henry V as the 'ennemi ... du royal tronc' (i, 137), a king who inflicted misery upon France during the reign of Charles VI, that 'inutile rejeton, un rameau sans fruit qui gaste, qui diffâme, qui scandalise l'arbre' (i, 38). By contrast, during the reign of Charles VII, the 'tronc sec soubs une langoureuse escorce

---

[35] For copies of Chartier's work in the ducal library see Barrois, *Bibliothèque*, nos 986, 1003, 1084. Chartier's influence on Chastelain has not attracted much comment, but see J. M. Ferrier, *French prose writers of the fourteenth and fifteenth centuries*, Oxford 1966, 144.
[36] Jean Gerson, *Oeuvres complètes*, ed. P. Glorieux, Paris 1963, v. 151–68 ('In festo S. Ludovici Regis'); Gilles le Bouvier, *Description*, 38; Robert Blondel, *Oeuvres complètes*, ed. A. Héron, Rouen 1891-3, i. 86–8.
[37] Beaune, *Naissance*, 322–3.

tempestée et battue, devint un rameau flory précieusement et fueillu soubs un ryant soleil favorable' (ii, 180). Chastelain also uses the image in its genealogical sense to frame and explain the actions of members of the ducal family.[38] They were, by nature, scions of the Tree of France: Philip the Good 'demourroit joint avec le tronc de la Royale Majesté' (i, 85), 'le tronc de la racine de son extraction' (ii, 11); the tenacity of his cousin, Jacqueline of Bavaria, was to be explained by 'la très-haute prochaineté qu'avoit au royal tronc' (ii, 84); and if his only son 'déclinoit plus à l'amour des Englès', Chastelain did not forget that Charles was also 'du noble tronc des fleurs de lis' (iii, 426). Although the point is not substantiated by other sources, the chronicler believed that some in the kingdom had not forgotten Charles's connections either. Representatives of the Estates General of 1468 are said to have reminded him that 'il estoit du royal tronc, et que la couronne, par possible, pouvoit tourner sur luy' (v, 391).[39] It is interesting that Chastelain at least felt that he might attribute such sentiments to contemporary Frenchmen.

The Tree, the Garden and the personification of France were at times rolled into one within composite images, in Chastelain's work as in that of his predecessors from the royal domain. These might be amalgamated with others, such as the lily or the purity of the royal blood; these in turn could be identified with the 'royale sève' (iii, 488) of the Tree of France. It has been argued with some justification that we may detect the foundations of a specifically French historical consciousness in the combination of such images.[40] Individually and collectively, they enshrined the kingdom's ancient glories and its historical destiny. The official chronicler of the dukes of Burgundy clearly located his subject matter within the confines of that consciousness.

These conclusions are in keeping with the findings of previous chapters. To paraphrase Collinson, they suggest a mind so steeped in the cross-references and resonant concordances of French historiography that it was incapable of exercising itself in any other way.[41] Huizinga would agree.[42] For him, Chastelain epitomised 'la forme naturelle et inévitable que devait prendre l'opinion publique dans ce milieu français de sang, de droit et de langage'. Whether we should conclude from this that Chastelain was an idealist, 'un esprit simple' prey to 'une naïveté qu'on ne sauroit prendre pour sournoise habileté', is another matter. We would do well to remember that the act of writing is rarely

---

[38] For pictorial representations of the image see G. Spiegel and S. Hindman, 'The fleur de lys frontispieces to Guillaume de Nangis's *Chronique abrégée*: political iconography in late fifteenth-century France', *Viator* xii (1981), 381–407.

[39] The commission given to the plenipotentiaries of the Estates is obscure: N. Bulst, 'Louis XI et les états généraux de 1468', in *FFQS*, 91–104 at pp. 100–1.

[40] Beaune, *Naissance*, 323; cf. M. Zingel, *Frankreich, das Reich und Burgund*, Sigmaringen 1995, 135–56.

[41] P. Collinson, *The birthpangs of Protestant England*, London 1988, 124.

[42] Huizinga, 'L'état bourguignon'; cf. the similar conclusions of H. H. E. Wouters, 'Het nationaliteitsbesef in de Bourgondische Nederlanden bij de kroniekschrijvers der 15de eeuw', *Publications de la Société historique et archéologique dans le Limbourg* xxxv (1949), 751–87.

innocent. The one-time shipper had acculturated to the models of historical understanding which he found around him at the Burgundian court. His ready acceptance of them is even more suggestive of just how deep-rooted these models were within the consciousness of the elite in which he had established himself. However, the process of *acculturation* is but one side of the coin; on the other lies the *conscious appropriation* of models of historical understanding to specific ends. Huizinga does not consider this possibility. Yet if received opinion could constrain, it was also a resource to be exploited. As Burke observes in another context, 'taking over the forms of official culture did not necessarily involve taking over the meanings usually associated with them'.[43] It is possible to detect a Burgundian agenda at work in some of the passages cited above. When we turn to Chastelain's treatment of Philip the Good and his royal contemporaries, that agenda appears more clearly. Through these passages we may begin to see why one contemporary described Chastelain as a 'précepteur de totale escripture'.[44]

Philip the Good

Chastelain's depiction of Philip the Good is often seen as a function of his personal esteem for the duke.[45] His affection is said to have occasionally clouded an otherwise admirable sense of impartiality.[46] Once the flesh is stripped away, however, the representation of Philip – or, for that matter, his royal contemporaries – seems neither personal nor impartial in nature. This, by now, should not be surprising. As we saw at an early stage, Chastelain presented to his audience a reinvention of his own *persona* in the mould of the country squire. Although his themes had to be woven within a lengthy and complex fabric of events, he also reconstructed the image of the duke. Philip the Good was the ideal prince personified – albeit a particular type of ideal prince, as we shall see.[47] In this Chastelain displayed many of the instincts and techniques one would expect to find in the work of an official historian intent on representing his patron, and his patron's interests, in the best possible light.

Hélène Wolff has argued that this depiction of Philip served a primarily

---

[43] P. Burke, *Popular culture in early modern Europe*, London 1978, 123.
[44] The phrase is from Jean Robertet in the *Douze dames de rhétorique*: vii, 181.
[45] An esteem which he was not at pains to hide: cf. iii, 157, 231; v, 242; vi, 435; vii, 227. For similar comments on Charles VII, cf. vi, 431, 433.
[46] For Chastelain's self-proclaimed impartiality see ii, 177–8; iii, 325, 390; Delclos, 322–3; iv, 21, 91, 95, 129, 152–3, 393–4; v, 201–2, 457, 497–8. These protestations are accepted with few provisos by his modern commentators: Pérouse, *Georges Chastellain*, 40; Urwin, *Georges Chastelain*, 33–4; Hommel, *Chastellain*, 95ff.; Delclos, *Le témoignage*, 4ff.
[47] Delclos notes that 'c'est bien l'image du prince idéal qu'il veut ... dessiner sous nos yeux': *Le témoignage*, 131–2. At an earlier stage, however, we are told that 'nous sommes loin de l'apologie systématique': ibid. 12. At the outset it should be stated that the *Déclaration* presents a different picture of Philip: vii, 213–36. This is explained in app. 2 below.

pedagogic function.[48] She had no doubt that the work served political purposes, but omitted to describe them; they were simply subsumed within a wider 'enseignement moral, religieux et politique'. Here she displays the unease which historians often feel when confronted with mirrors for princes: works so conventional in nature as to have 'no visible relation to concrete political life'.[49] The problem, of course, is that the genre looks back to antiquity for its inspiration and models. It appears universal in its applications. At most, Chastelain's references might reveal a humanistic orientation.[50]

Yet it is clear that interpretations of the ideal prince varied according to time and place, political circumstance and need.[51] Graeco-Roman civilisation may have had a patent on most ideas concerning the deportment of rulers, but the medieval mirrors for princes which stemmed from them were not disengaged from contemporary political events or thought.[52] This was particularly true during the resurgence of the genre in the kingdom of France in the late fourteenth and early fifteenth centuries; in other words, in the two or three generations before Chastelain was writing.

It hardly needs to be emphasised here that these were years of considerable political crisis.[53] A long-lived king who thought himself to be made of glass was succeeded – but not without difficulties – by another who took what seemed an interminable time to impose himself.[54] All the while, the kingdom and the rights of the crown became the objects of English and princely ambitions.[55] In these circumstances it was perhaps inevitable that so many voices should have arisen to counsel the king: poets, like Chartier or Pisan;

[48] H. Wolff, 'Histoire et pédagogie princière au XVe siècle', in *Culture et pouvoir*, 37–49, at p. 40. For overt pedagogic statements see i, 12, 256; iv, 308–9.
[49] B. Guenée, *States and rulers in later medieval Europe*, trans. J. Vale, Oxford 1985, 70.
[50] Wolff, 'Histoire et pédagogie', 40. For descriptions of Philip in classical terms see i, 61, 284; ii, 151–2.
[51] Cf. G. Duby, 'L'image du prince en France au début du XIe siècle', *Cahiers d'histoire* xvii (1972), 211–16; J. Dickinson, 'The medieval conception of kingship and some of its limitations in the *Policraticus* of John of Salisbury', *Speculum* i (1926), 308–37; L. K. Born, 'The perfect prince', ibid. iii (1928), 470–504; D. Bornstein, 'Reflection of political theory and political fact in fifteenth-century mirrors for princes', in J. B. Bessinger and R. R. Raymo (eds), *Medieval studies in honor of H. Horstein*, New York 1976, 77–85.
[52] Cf. A. Black, *Political thought in Europe 1250–1450*, Cambridge 1992, 141. It has been observed that 'rares (sont) les auteurs de miroirs de prince qui ne (mêlent) à leurs leçons religieuses et morales l'écho des préoccupations sociales et politiques du moment. Longtemps considérées comme répétitives et conventionnelles, ... les miroirs enregistrent au contraire les transformations imposées par la marche nationale, étatique et même bureaucratique des grandes monarchies .... Ce fut particulièrement le cas en France': Krynen, *L'empire du roi*, 169. Cf. the views expressed in F. Chabaud, 'Les "Mémoires" de Philippe de Commynes: un "Miroir aux princes"?', *Francia* xix (1992), 95–114 at p. 100.
[53] Heightened, no doubt, by recent memories of Charles V's happier reign: F. Autrand, *Charles V*, Paris 1994.
[54] Famiglietti, *Royal intrigue*; F. Autrand, *Charles VI*, Paris 1986; Vale, *Charles VII*.
[55] J. d'Avout, *La querelle des Armagnacs et des Bourguignons*, Paris 1943; M. Nordberg, *Les ducs et la royauté*, Uppsala 1964; B. Schnerb, *Les Armagnacs et les Bourguignons*, Paris 1988; B. Guenée, *Un meurtre, une société*, Paris 1992.

secular clergy, like Gervais or Juvenal des Ursins; and academics, like Courtecuisse or Nicolas de Clamanges.[56] A certain commonality of purpose has been traced in the work of these writers and others, such as Bouvet, Philippe de Mézières or Jean de Montreuil.[57] In different ways and at different times, each advocated models of royal and princely behaviour to restore the Tree/ Garden/Princess which symbolised France to its proper state and place in history. If the crisis seemed over by the middle of the fifteenth century, it was not so very long since France had been plunged in 'l'abyme de tribulation' (i, 9). In its wake it left a heightened sensitivity to the ideals of a ruler's deportment. It might be said that French men of action and men of letters (and how many of the former did not aspire to at least some of the latters' qualities?) were imbued with the values of mirrors for princes; at the very least, they had good cause to acknowledge their importance. This, in part, was the audience which Chastelain addressed: 'vous qui cecy lisez *et sentez*' (i, 310).[58]

The duke, therefore, was not simply an ideal prince: he was the type of ideal prince which the intelligentsia of later medieval France had, with good reason, consistently foisted upon the consciousness – and conscience – of the political elite in recent years. The representation of Philip functioned on a common ground of shared and, at the time, cherished values. His more impulsive deeds did occasionally defy the interpretive straitjacket which Chastelain forced upon them. 'Comme le constructeur munist volentiers son edifice alencontre du feu' (Delclos, 321), however, the chronicler intervened again and again to point or shore up the construct.[59] By blunt affirmation, frequent repetition, carefully crafted vignettes, indirect eulogy and other techniques, the official historian maintained control of the composite, ideal image of his master. The main strands of this image may be delineated briefly.

The first duty of the 'homme princiant' (Delclos, 157) was to God, the Church and Christendom. The crusading agenda of the later fourteenth century and the Schism ensured that these themes were central to contemporary mirrors for princes and related literature. Chastelain duly emphasised Philip's status as the 'souverain et principal pilier et sousteneur' of the papacy (ii, 220). Despite Urwin's curious assertion, he also developed Philip's crusading zeal into a stock theme: 'sur tous les autres princes chrestiens avoit esté

---

[56] Krynen, *Idéal du prince*; D. M. Bell, *L'idéal éthique de la royauté au moyen âge*, Paris–Geneva 1962; J. Blanchard, 'Vox poetica, vox politica', *Actes du Ve colloque international sur le moyen français*, iii, Milan 1985, 39–51.
[57] N. Grévy-Pons, 'Propagande et sentiment national pendant le règne de Charles VI', *Francia* viii (1980), 127–45.
[58] Italics mine.
[59] For example see iii, 244–5: Philip's celebrated outburst of anger against his son in 1457. As Pisan noted, anger was natural. Hatred in a prince alone could be condemned: Christine de Pisan, *Le Livre de la paix*, ed. C. C. Willard, The Hague 1958, 93. As Chastelain noted elsewhere, Philip sought to 'fuir mérancolie et toutes occasions de courroux': iii, 442. For his interventions, cf. ii, 89, 140–1; iii, 244–5, 406; Delclos, 124, 156ff.; v, 60–4, 104–6, 202–12, 242–3.

continuel susciteur de ceste besogne' (iii, 10).[60] Peace within Christendom was closely linked to such ideals. The perfect prince was a pacifier of discord and a promoter of unity. Inevitably, the topos acquired a secular resonance in France during the troubled years after 1392. This, rather than any alleged 'pacifisme' on the chronicler's part, provides the context for his repeated depictions of Philip as a prince who 'amoit l'honneur et le salut du royaume comme de sa mère maison, et ploroit en coeur sa division et malheurté' (iii, 193).[61]

Secondly, the prince was expected to defend his people and govern them properly, to make himself both loved and feared for his justice and to be 'tres ameur et desireux du bien et proffit commun'.[62] Philip was liberally endowed with the martial qualities which Pisan thought necessary for the ideal prince who would protect his flock: his love of arms, temerity, constancy, loyalty, honour and caution made of him, in the eyes of his people, an 'escu de protection et arche de salut' (i, 276).[63] Like Charles V, he was only moved to pardon a felonious servant after third parties had pleaded him, at length, to do so.[64] His sense of justice was rigorous and exemplary.[65] Philip fulfilled the ideals of the pedagogues as a 'quéreur du bien publique' (ii, 6) in other ways.[66] A 'vray berger' (iii, 451), he was receptive to the 'clameur de son povre oppressé peuple' (ii, 123); so much so, it seemed, that 'en la terre n'avoit homme mieux aimé de luy' (iii, 442). If he was able to demand more money from his subjects than any of his predecessors, this was because of the 'amour et gratuité procédant de ferme dilection à luy, pour ce que begnin estoit, doux et humain' (ii, 143).

A third set of qualities related more directly to the person of the prince and those around him. Philip's private virtues – his humility, piety or abstinence – matched the counsels of perfection directed at princes by the likes of Pisan or Mézières.[67] Wisely, perhaps, his sexual mores are not mentioned in the Chronicle.[68] Confident in these personal attributes, Philip the Good 'ne craignoit mort, ne autre rien onques' (iii, 365).[69]

The ideal prince naturally surrounded himself with men of suitable quality

---

[60] Urwin, *Georges Chastelain*, 84: 'Chastelain n'a jamais montré d'enthousiasme pour les croisades'; cf. i, 334–5; iii, 118, 124, 386; v, 61.
[61] Hommel emphasises Chastelain's pacifism: *Chastellain*, 62–3. This may not be unrelated to the year of his book's publication (1946). For Philip as a prince of peace see i, 34; iii, 139, 232, 287; v, 199, 247.
[62] Christine de Pisan, *Le livre des fais et bonnes meurs du sage roy Charles V*, ed. S. Solente, Paris 1936–40, ii. 25; Honoré Bouvet, *The tree of battles*, ed. G. W. Coopland, Liverpool 1949, 210–13.
[63] Pisan, *Le livre du corps de policie*, 112–65; cf. i, 243, 241, 255, 265; ii, 36, 61, 133, 140, 144, 148; iii, 157; v, 246–7.
[64] Cf. iii, 105–7; *Livre de la paix*, 100.
[65] i, 79; iii, 86, 89, 137; v, 20, 68.
[66] Cf. ii, 85; iii, 98.
[67] Cf. i, 287, 293; ii, 11; iii, 134, 267; Delclos, 72; iv, 8; v, 209.
[68] Discussed in Vaughan, *PTG*, 132–5. A reference to his wife's jealousy provides the only hint of his appetites in the Chronicle: iii, 444. However see app. 2 below.
[69] Cf. iii, 411.

whom he chose, rewarded and employed appropriately.[70] Philip's observance of these maxims is emphasised almost instinctively. He behaved impeccably towards his servants.[71] With a few exceptions which Chastelain is inclined to excuse, the men he retained in his service conformed to a pattern encapsulated in a description of the prince of Orange: 'en luy avoit tout ce que un prince devoit quérir et convoitier en son serviteur: c'estoit la vaillance et hardement, grant conduite et grant sens' (iii, 189).[72] Before taking decisions he asked their opinion, since 'telles choses se font en ... mur conseil de sages preud'hommes ... que les princes ont emprès eux et doivent avoir' (ii, 81). 'Accompagné grandement de haulx nobles barons' (iii, 203) throughout the Chronicle, Philip ran a household which was a 'retraite et refuge d'honneur et de savoir', and where 'l'honneur et le sens de France y reposoit seul' (ii, 149).[73] It was important that 'la maison entre les crestiens la plus renommée' (iii, 264) should appear in this light. The writers of an earlier generation, when the crown had been so abased, considered the majesty of the prince as an expression of his divinely ordained superiority among men. Some commentators have suggested that Chastelain omitted or abridged accounts of ducal pomp and circumstance through a sense of probity and measure.[74] More importantly, he never failed to emphasise the majesty of the prince when it was appropriate to do so. Philip possessed 'la vertu de magnificence merveilleuse, et en toutes choses qui estoient grandes et scrutileuses en fruit, là veilloit-il' (v, 245). Accounts of ducal entries in the Chronicle thus correspond in structure and content to those we find described in Pisan's *Livre de la paix*, where it was the author's intention to show that Charles V 'bien sembloit estre prince'.[75]

Philip the Good may at times appear to clank through the Chronicle like some ungainly, lifeless construct. For contemporaries accustomed to such literary themes and devices, we may assume that he was, if not a more natural figure, then at least a more familiar one: in short, a 'miroir des princes chrestiens' (iv, 29).[76] By the same token, it is pointless to criticise the predilection for 'outer configurations' which these passages reveal.[77] Contemporaries were more sensitive than the modern reader to the historical culture from which such images were appropriated. They were, ineluctably, invested with meanings, and it is these we should attempt to locate.

Philip the Good naturally appeared in a similar light in some other Burgundian court texts. Where Fillastre or Germain took his qualities largely in

---

[70] Cf. Mézières, *Le songe*, ii. 326ff.
[71] iii, 332; v, 74.
[72] Cf. i, 178; ii, 19–20, 30, 70, 102.
[73] Chastelain uses the same terms in only two other passages. Interestingly, these concern the city of Paris and the French monarchy respectively: i, 194, 200.
[74] Pérouse, *Georges Chastellain*, 38; Delclos, *Le témoignage*, 10; cf. ii, 17; Delclos, 132, 275; iv, 63–4.
[75] *Livre de la paix*, 72; cf. iii, 32–5, 143–51, 301–6, 362–5, 412–16; iv, 44–6, 73–84.
[76] See also v, 230; vi, 234.
[77] See P. Archambault, *Seven French chroniclers*, Syracuse, NY 1974, 77.

isolation, however, Chastelain used them as a means to an end.[78] His intention was to make comparisons, implicit or explicit. Unlike Philip, for example, Louis I duke of Savoy was a bad prince, 'tout impotent et inutile quasi au monde'. His 'efféminée main' had ruined the affairs of state (v, 39, 42). The subjects of another of his cousins, Jean IV duke of Brabant, looked on with dismay while 'la chose publique se corrompoit toute et anéantissoit en leur pays' as a result of his 'féminin gouvernement' (i, 170). Chastelain's famous gallery of princely portraits was expressly written with the sole intention of proving Philip's superiority, 'comme les plus eslites et les plus précieuses pierres se jugent par autres emprès adjoustées' (ii, 151).[79]

It is difficult to see any grander meaning in such comparisons than the banal instinct to magnify the patron. This much has already been detected.[80] Yet when the work is set in its proper context – the historical culture from which it sprang, the audience to which it was addressed – it is possible to notice the formulation of more profound political statements. Above all, it was the kings of France who were judged, not simply by Chastelain's depiction of Philip's high standards (as Delclos suggests), but more specifically by the standards which – although present in Philip – had been set for kings in the past by their real or self-appointed preceptors. Herein lay the core of Chastelain's propagandistic intent. Where the tirades of the *Livre des trahisons* or *Le pastoralet* might be shrugged off by an unreceptive audience (if indeed they ever reached one), Chastelain's easy but conscious appropriation of stock themes was potentially much more damaging.[81]

The image of Charles VII was difficult to impugn. Although it had not always been so, the king's stock was as high as that of any previous French monarch by the time Chastelain began writing his Chronicle in 1455.[82] The grounds for this process of magnification had been present since Castillon two years earlier, but a sense of majesty and accomplishment was more clearly evinced in later historical representations of the king.[83] Royal officials such as Henri Baude or Berry Herald contributed to the making of this image, but its presence in the work of Jacques du Clercq, Mathieu d'Escouchy or Guillaume Leseur suggests that its impact extended to the far north and far south of the Francophone world.[84] 'Charles le Très Victorieux', as he was described at his

---

[78] Fillastre, *Toison d'Or*, fos 124–31v; Jean Germain, *Liber de virtutibus Philippi, Burgundiae et Brabantiae ducis*, in *Chroniques relatives à l'histoire de Belgique sous la domination des ducs de Bourgogne: textes latins*, ed. J. C. Kervyn de Lettenhove, Brussels 1876, 1–115.

[79] ii, 151–89. The passage was intended to culminate in a portrait of Philip the Good which is now lost but was certainly written – a scribal note concerning its location makes this clear: BM Arras, MS 256 (406), fo. 117v. See also ch. 6 and app. 1 below.

[80] Delclos, *Le témoignage*, 83–168.

[81] *Chroniques relatives à l'histoire de Belgique sous la domination des ducs de Bourgogne: textes français*, ed. J. C. Kervyn de Lettenhove, Brussels 1873, 1–258, 573–852.

[82] C. Beaune, 'L'historiographie de Charles VII', in *FFQS*, 265–81.

[83] For an early eulogy, probably written in the early 1450s, see Jacques Millet, *Le Mystère de la destruction de Troie la grant*, ed. E. Stengel, Marburg 1883, 390–1.

[84] Cf. Henri Baude, *Éloge ou portrait historique de Charles VII*, in *Chronique de Charles VII*

funeral and as he was thereafter most frequently known, had worked for the 'soulagement de son peuple' in matters of justice, finance and war.[85] In private he was pious, read 'anciennes histoires' and loved the ladies 'en toute honnesté'. In short, he had emerged as an example of ideal princely deportment by the third quarter of the fifteenth century.

The two passages of Chastelain's Chronicle which focus most closely on Charles's image pay lip service to these themes.[86] 'Dévot à Dieu' (ii, 179), 'historien grant, beau raconteur, bon latiniste et bien sage en conseil' (ii, 184), Charles was so blessed with the virtue of patience that he resembled 'ung second Job' (Delclos, 320). In the public sphere the king 'avoit l'oeil en guerre et en paix' and 'moult de cures en la chose publique' (Delclos, 321); he 'mist sus ordre et règle en son royaume, et tenant chascun en cremeur donna cours à justice' (ii, 184). Just as 'une petite lime consume un gros barreau de fer' (i, 312), however, the chronicler consistently filed away at this image elsewhere in his work. Indeed, his concessions to contemporary perceptions of Charles may well have been Fabian tactics; he too knew how to *reculer pour saillir plus loin* (to borrow one of Chastelain's images). This king fell far short of the precepts of the ideal prince as established by previous generations of French intellectuals.

The most Christian king was made to seem unequal to the title bestowed upon him by tradition. The Pragmatic Sanction of Bourges naturally contrasted with Philip's respect for Rome, but more telling is Chastelain's deeper criticism in the form of a comparison he makes with Charles's observant predecessors: 'il faisoit a increper et estre blamé, en contraire de ses peres devanciers, qui avoient esté les protecteurs de l'Eglise de Dieu, et li le desemparer' (Delclos, 286).[87] The same tactic is deployed in the context of his disregard for the crusade. Although God 'quéroit à faire son instrument de luy contre les infidèles, comme par le roy très-chrestien' (iv, 368), and although the king himself acknowledged as much in the correspondence cited in a previous chapter, Charles neglected the duties of his lineage.[88] Nor was he a prince of peace whose actions might have brought to fruition the *negotium Christi*. The affairs of Christendom 'requeroient plus paix et concorde entre les princes ... que guerres et tribulations hayneuses en avancement de privee querelle' (Delclos, 278). In a passage of scathing irony, Chastelain notes that this 'noble et digne roy françois, la fleur du monde en toute excellence' (iii,

---

roi de France par Jean Chartier, ed. A. Vallet de Viriville, Paris 1858, iii. 127–41; Gilles le Bouvier, *Chroniques*; d'Escouchy, *Chronique*, ii. 422; du Clercq, *Mémoires*, xiv. 127–32; Guillaume Leseur, *Histoire de Gaston IV, comte de Foix*, ed. H. Courteault, Paris 1893–6, ii. 99–101.

[85] M. G. A. Vale, 'Jean Fouquet's portrait of Charles VII', *Gazette des beaux-arts* lxxi (1968), 243–8; Henri Baude, *Éloge*, 129. For the next sentence see ibid., 128.

[86] ii, 178–9; Delclos, 311–23.

[87] Cf. A. G. Jongkees, 'Philippe le Bon et la Pragmatique Sanction de Bourges', AB xxxviii (1966), 161–71 (repr. in his *Burgundica et varia*, 94–103).

[88] See ch. 3 above.

389) preferred to pursue an illegal claim to Luxembourg rather than encourage peaceful relations with Philip the Good. Within his own household, indeed, discord and division were elevated to a system of government.[89]

Charles was no better as a pastor of his flock. He had certainly expelled the English, but less through his own martial qualities than through the efforts of others, for 'de sa personne luy-mesmes n'estoit pas homme belliqueux' (ii, 181). Nor were his victories a guarantee of the love which the ideal prince might expect from his people. Chastelain's blatant comparisons of the fortunes of Philip's subjects with Charles's may have been too crude to persuade, but at least some of his remarks found echoes within the kingdom itself.[90] Charles 'tailloit fort son royaume' (ii, 188). Although this was a common enough charge for a Burgundian sympathiser to lay against the king, others in the kingdom thought so too.[91] Charles's justice was equally flawed. In a less-than-innocent anecdote – describing an horrific murder that had occurred in the county of Boulogne, and which had resulted in a royal remission for the perpetrators – Chastelain prepares the ground for a typical jibe aimed at the king: 'jamais prince crestien bien informé ne l'eust fait' (iii, 438). To the charge of negligence was added repeated imputations of wilfulness. The king's men at the *Parlement*, targets of severe criticism throughout the Chronicle, revealed in their actions 'une hayne voluntaire entremelee d'envie . . . , esperans soubz tiltre de justice et de leur auctorité user de leur venin' (Delclos, 158).[92]

Charles, despite the eulogies elsewhere, had few of the personal qualities of the ideal prince. Where Philip's lubricity was passed over in silence, the king's was fully exposed.[93] More serious personal failings will be discussed below. With one or two notable exceptions, Charles chose servants in his own, rather shabby, image.[94] His entourage was certainly far inferior to Philip's.[95] The chronicler was prepared to accept that it was 'plus par aveugle fortune que par dignité de personne' that the king was surrounded by men like Rolin Renault, 'homme plein de vanité, de petit estocq et de sobre vertu' (iii, 389). Elsewhere, however, he reminds his audience of the view, recurrent in mirrors for princes, that the choice of servant reflected upon the ruler.[96] When he did display a sense of majesty, the king's choice of occasion is made to appear ludicrous. At Montbazon and Tours, where he coldly received Philip's ambassadors in 1459, Charles sat 'moult triumphament' upon his throne, 'ricement paré' in his finery,

---

[89] ii, 182; iii, 294, 306 ff.; Delclos, 312.
[90] ii, 145; iii, 363; iv, 105.
[91] P. S. Lewis, 'Jean Juvenal des Ursins and the common literary attitude towards tyranny in fifteenth-century France', *Medium Aevum* xxxiv (1965), 103–21 (repr. in his *Essays*, 169–87). See also K. A. Fowler, 'The attitude of some commentators to royal power in later medieval France', *Annali della Facoltà di Scienze Politiche, Perugia* xvii (1980–1), 169–79.
[92] Cf. iii, 82ff.; Delclos, 222; iv, 40–1.
[93] ii, 185; iv, 365–7.
[94] The exceptions included Foix: ii, 170; and of course Brézé: passim.
[95] As the king is made to admit himself: iii, 19.
[96] ii, 54.

'plus magnifiquement que oncques encoire n'avoit esté veu de tout le temps de son regne' (Delclos, 173).[97] Once again, irony verging on sarcasm bubbles to the surface of the text. Of the distinct characteristics which Charles displayed in each part of his 'double règne, advers et prospère', it was the shortcomings of his early years that Chastelain's representation impressed upon the reader.[98] The memory of a divisive, vacillating Charles was less than a generation old: recent enough to be revived and deployed to good effect.

If the chronicler sniped at Charles's image from well-covered positions in these cases, he was also prepared to raise his head above the parapet. Tyranny was not a charge to be levelled lightly against any prince, let alone a king of France. Tyrannical behaviour, like rebellion against the crown, was unnatural and broke the unwritten bond between ruler and ruled.[99] The tyrant placed his own interests above those of his subjects; unlike the good prince, who respected laws, took counsel and was loved by his people, his rule was arbitrary. He was a sower of discord in his household and realm.[100] Chastelain never describes Charles VII as a tyrant.[101] In places, however, the tenor of his criticism is indistinguishable from the unwritten charge itself.

Throughout the Chronicle, Chastelain repeatedly emphasises one characteristic of the king's personality: his irrational fear. We learn that Charles 'de sa propre ancienne nature ... estoit doubteux et plein de souppeçons' (iii, 218), that 'naturellement et de tout temps du monde il estoit plein de souppeçons et de diffidences' (Delclos, 123), that he had 'une imagination sauvage' (iii, 186), was prone to feeling 'grant peur' (iii, 22), and that were he to be surrounded by a hundred thousand or even a million men, 'se fust espovanté d'un homme seul non cognu' (ii, 181).[102] Irrational fear was in fact the cause of the king's death in Chastelain's account. Having received an anonymous warning that he was to be poisoned, Charles refused to eat. 'Sciamment et voluntairement se lessa perir sans mengier', notes Chastelain, repeating the comment twice in almost identical terms.[103] This startling account of an unnatural death is unique.[104] It is also peculiarly damning. The tyrant, by nature, lived in a

[97] In case we had missed the point, the chronicler uses almost identical words at pp. 189–90.
[98] The quote is from a variant in one of the manuscripts of the *Advertissement au duc Charles*: vii, 324 n. 1.
[99] Philip, of course, was no tyrant: ii, 81, 143.
[100] Cf. Black, *Political thought*, 148–54; Krynen, *Idéal du prince*, 335; W. Ullmann, *Principles of government and politics in the Middle Ages*, London 1961, 22, 153, 274.
[101] He seems to come close to it at vi, 346: in the context of his criticisms of French hostility towards the Burgundians at the end of Charles VII's reign, he points out that God often comes to the aid of 'gens traveillés et vexés par mains de tiran'. However, in his eulogy of the dead king – a eulogy which may have had ulterior motives, for the image of a glorious Charles helped to denigrate Louis XI – Chastelain writes that 'ce noble roy n'a portion nulle en tirannye': Delclos, 316; cf. ii, 184.
[102] Cf. iii, 307; Delclos, 312. In this, of course, Charles was the inverse of Philip the Good.
[103] Delclos, 309–10; iv, 369.
[104] A point noted in Delclos, *Le témoignage*, 97–100, attributed there to Chastelain's desire to portray 'un roi pusillanime'.

permanent state of fear. The monstrous acts to which he was inclined were likely to provoke a desire for revenge, divine or human, against him. Having firmly implanted but not explained the image of a fearful king throughout the Chronicle, Chastelain finally delivers the punchline. Charles's fears, in his own reported words, stemmed from the fact that

> celle main dont j'ay peur ne se peut resister par force. J'ay feru de glave en mes jennes jours; si ne fut oncques heure depuis que la main de Dieu [n']estoit devant mon front pour moy ferir du mesmes. Siques qui homme suis et en mon sang ay commis faute, je crains que par homme Dieu arriere ne me pugnisse.
> (Delclos, 312)

Little doubt is left in the reader's mind as to the precise nature of Charles's monstrous, tyrannical fault: his involvement in – and lack of reparation or apparent contrition for – the murder of John the Fearless. This was why 'la freeur du hault jugement de Dieu ... avoit esté par sy longs ans devant ses yeulx jour et nuit' (Delclos, 313). The image of this glorious king of France, underlined when necessary, undermined when possible, was seen to wither at the last.

Chastelain worked within certain constraints in his depiction of Charles VII. The distinct phases of his reign were becoming historically defined by 1455, and the king himself was emerging from the hands of the image-builders to take his place in a panoply of royal heroes. When dealing with the new monarch, however, the chronicler had much more room for manoeuvre.

From the very beginning Louis's image contradicts the precepts which the ideal prince was expected to observe.[105] As dauphin, he was not a peace-giver but an 'homme de division, un homme qui amaine les mauvaises aventures et les malédictions' in his wake (iii, 238).[106] Like his father, he was prone to bouts of irrational fear.[107] His impatience and inconstancy both before and after his coronation were emphasised and linked to his more unnatural acts, such as the compassing of his father's death or his sexual appetites.[108] These personal – but highly stylised – failings were rendered more alarming by Louis's tendency to take no counsel other than his own.[109] Hence his inability to recognise the value of servants and his low estimation of the type of counsellor which the ideal prince was expected to surround himself with.[110] His court was 'plus parée de chiens pour déduit que d'hommes pour vertu' (iv, 272). Louis was a hunter: not the convivial leader of the pack, but a curiously solitary, cunning soul.[111]

---

[105] A point which further undermines the use of Chastelain's attitude to the dauphin as a means of establishing the chronology of composition: see ch. 4 above.
[106] Cf. iii, 235, 248.
[107] iii, 69, 177–8, 191, 236, 303, 408–9; Delclos, 295.
[108] iii, 48; iv, 25, 27, 42, 57, 100, 115, 139.
[109] iii, 449; Delclos, 91; iv, 122, 196–7; v, 10, 12, 76.
[110] iii, 228, 464; Delclos, 122; iv, 26, 36, 180, 184; v, 127.
[111] Cf. iii, 301; iv, 342. There may indeed be some allegorical message with a deeper political meaning in the repeated depiction of Louis's excessive love of the hunt: J. Dufournet,

Inevitably, his rule was portrayed as oppressive, not just to the Burgundian duke, but more widely within the kingdom. His 'opérations volontaires' led to 'plaies et romptures en la chose publique' (v, 182). He governed according to one striking phrase 'par puissance absolue' (iv, 358), 'fit les coeurs froids contre luy, et acquit peu de grâce de ses subgets nobles et non nobles, et moins aussi des princes de son sang' (iv, 272–3).[112] For the mass of his subjects, it was (once again) the king's taxation which 'passoit règle et coutume, équité et bon usage' (iv, 341). The 'nobles du royaume, princes et barons' were alienated by 'nouvelletés' which broke with previous royal custom (iv, 342).[113] This was the language of the League of the Public Weal, and as such it was not unique to Chastelain.[114] Too great an emphasis upon the confrontations between king and duke can obscure the fact that it was not only Burgundian voices which objected to royal action. The reign of Charles VII had come to represent, for some at least, an age of peace and prosperity. Louis was aware of this himself, accusing the rebels (in a letter he sent to the towns of the Auvergne) of seeking even more than they had received from his predecessor.[115] Having conveniently deferred on occasion to an idealised image of Charles – particularly in that eulogy of the king which was written, as we have seen, in Louis's reign – the official chronicler was now able to note that Louis's morals were 'non semblables au père défunt' (iv, 357), that his people 'se trouvoit pis qu'avecques son père' (iv, 197), and that they 'commencèrent à regretter arrière le roy mort et souhaidier sa vie' (iv, 143).[116] In short, 'le roy Charles mourut et vint un nouveau monde' (v, 62).

By these means the new king was made vulnerable to the charge of tyranny. Although he could only imply it in Charles's case, Chastelain bluntly stated that Louis acted 'par volonté de tyran', 'par tyrannie' (v, 144–5). Tyrants were undeserving of royal office. This much is indicated more subtly in Chastelain's account of the coronation banquet at Rheims. Louis, who had already wearied of the day's ceremony, began the meal 'atout la couronne en chief'; 'pour cause qu'elle estoit un peu large et que ne tenoit close sur son bonnet', however, 'fut mise sur la table emprès luy ... pour son aise' (iv, 60–1). The crown did not fit this man, either physically or symbolically. The sentiment burst forth at a later stage in the narrative: 'est donc venu le temps maintenant que la royale dignité françoise est descendue sur homme bestial, et que la plus digne couronne et la plus sainte de la terre est assise sur cheveux d'un homme non homme' (v, 141).

'Retour à Georges Chastelain', MA lxxxviii (1982), 329–42 at p. 340. For parallels see J. Lemaire, *Les visions de la vie de cour dans la littérature française de la fin du moyen âge*, Brussels–Paris 1994, 147, 164, 331; and, on a royal ancestor, E. A. R. Brown, 'The case of Philip the Fair', *Viator* xix (1988), 219–46 at p. 137.

[112] Cf. iv, 116, 127, 144, 342, 416, 494; v, 12.
[113] See also v, 7.
[114] Beaune, 'L'historiographie', 266–76; cf. Thomas Basin, *Histoire de Louis XI*, ed. C. Samaran and M.-C. Garand, Paris 1963–72; Jean de Roye, *Journal*, passim.
[115] *Documents relatifs à la guerre du Bien Public*, ed. J. Quicherat, Paris 1843, 214.
[116] Cf. iv, 223, 229.

To compound matters, this unceremonial, unfettered and unworthy king seemed impervious to criticism, 'car portoit la couronne de millions d'or vaillant sous un chappelet de six gros' (iv, 360).

Chastelain's representation of both Louis and Charles was thus profoundly negative in essence. The difference in the degree of criticism between the portraits of each may have been dictated by perceptions of audience response and certainly had a textual function. The potential efficacy of the chronicler's comments lay in their repeated formulation in a variety of guises and, perhaps most importantly, in their markedly orthodox nature. After all, they were directed at two kings, not at the crown.[117] At this level the question of how a king should behave had always been 'discussed in terms of a return to the past'.[118] Literate Frenchmen were used to stereotypical representations of royal action, particularly in the wake of the literary developments discussed above.[119] They were well-placed to understand the chronicler's statement that it was the duty of the monarch to 'ajouster sur ses nobles vieux pères de jadis aucun nouvel acquest de clair titre' (v, 494).[120] By such statements Chastelain drew his subject matter, and with it his readers, onto familiar terrain, there to denigrate the images of Charles VII and Louis XI and magnify that of Philip the Good. Not coincidentally, he also raised searching questions as to the right-mindedness, and even the very legitimacy, of royal action.

In the light of this reading of the treatment of the key protagonists it becomes extremely difficult to sustain the view that Chastelain was impartial or that he was exclusively (or even partly) concerned with a mono-dimensional ideal of Franco-Burgundian union. This understanding of his work was based on a misconception of the formative experiences of his career and a related – and rather literal – reading of his claim to be a 'léal François avec mon prince' (i, 12). The chronicler had a profoundly realistic appreciation of Burgundian

---

[117] W. Paravicini rightly notes that Chastelain projects an almost mystical admiration for the crown: 'Sechs Neuerscheinungen', 671. On the distinction made in the text see E. Kantorowicz, *The king's two bodies*, Princeton 1957, 364–72, and Chastelain's references to the abstract concept of the crown, such as ii, 146; iii, 140; iv, 17, 387. The distinction is crystal clear at iv, 308: French kings might presume to be 'comme à demy divins en terres', but '(sont) hommes, et souvent moins que hommes'.

[118] J. Dunbabin, *France in the making 843–1180*, Oxford 1985, 265; G. Duby, *France in the Middle Ages*, trans. J. Vale, Oxford 1991, 251, 282–3; A. W. Lewis, *Royal succession in Capetian France: studies on familial order and the state*, Cambridge, Mass., 1981, 138–9.

[119] Spiegel, 'Political utility in medieval historiography'. Even in the royal chronicles written at St Denis, such was the concern for the king's behaviour towards the leading princes of his realm and the emphasis upon the authority of these men that the chronicles have been described, not only as 'le roman des rois, l'histoire du royaume, mais aussi l'épopée des barons du royaume': Guenée, 'Les Grandes chroniques de France', 195; cf. 198, 204.

[120] At the same time as Chastelain was writing, the royal secretary Noël de Fribois counselled Charles VII and the princes of France in his *Abrégé des chroniques* to take the 'haulx et vertueux faicts de leurs tres nobles predecesseurs' as a 'mirouer et exemple de bien vivre': cited in K. Daly, 'Histoire et politique à la fin de la guerre de cent ans: l'*Abrégé des chroniques* de Noël de Fribois', in *FA*, 91–101 at p. 92. For other examples of the king's duty to 'augmenter et accroître la couronne' see Krynen, *L'empire du roi*, 153–60.

interests in France – not just those of the master, but those of the servants he frequented himself. From this perspective the claim to be a loyal Frenchman may have had two, less disinterested and not mutually exclusive, functions. The chronicler's representation of Philip the Good and his royal contemporaries could play a role in both.

In the first instance, the contrasting images of flawed kings and a duke in the mould of the perfect French prince harked back to a period of greater Burgundian involvement in the kingdom during the reign of incompetent monarchs. That involvement had been curtailed and its revival was inconceivable, at least in the minds of Charles, Louis and royalists who shared their conception of the equilibrium of power in France. Whether this was true of others within the kingdom or at the Burgundian court is another matter.[121] The memory was long, and the reign of John the Fearless (in France as well as Burgundy) was not so distant in time.[122] As the Chronicle emphatically reminded the reader, Philip was the first peer (and a double peer) of the realm.[123] Chastelain's account of the duke's return to Paris in 1461 to place the crown on Louis's head inevitably revived many of the sentiments and themes of earlier years. Philip, like his father, was seen to be popular among the Parisians, particularly in that hotbed of Burgundian loyalties, the *quartier des halles*.[124] In a curious and seemingly unique passage, Chastelain has the sexagenarian duke hop on the back of the duchess of Orléans's horse, an act of familiarity which apparently led the Parisians to chorus 'Et velà un humain prince!' (and to add, of course, that 'n'est tel nostre roy').[125] It is surely no coincidence that the scene called to mind another, famously described by Monstrelet, in which John the Fearless and Charles d'Orléans rode on the same horse to public acclaim after the signing of the peace of Auxerre of 1412.[126] Precisely what the 'riche duc de Bourgongne' (iv, 45) hoped to gain from the coronation of Louis may never be known; he certainly acquired less than he would have liked. The key point is that Burgundian aspirations in France, despite some modern perceptions, were far from dead.[127] As long as

---

[121] Cf. the views expressed in Leguai, 'La "France bourguignonne"' and 'Royauté française'; M.-T. Caron, *Noblesse et pouvoir royal en France, XIIIe – XVIe siècle*, Paris 1994, 207–66.

[122] On memory see Guenée, *Histoire et culture historique*, 80–4. Cf. iv, 186–91: Bourges snubbed Charolais in 1461 because of their 'vieille hayne ... à l'encontre de la maison de Bourgongne, pour le siège de Bourges que le duc Jehan mit'. The siege had occurred a full half-century earlier. For John's rule in France see B.-A. Pocquet du Haut-Jussé, 'Jean sans Peur', AB xiv (1942), 181–96, and *La France gouvernée par Jean sans Peur*, Paris 1959.

[123] iii, 417, 477; iv, 57; v, 32.

[124] i, 68–9, 162, 188, 292; ii, 30; Delclos, 234ff.; iv, 42ff.; cf. G. L. Thompson, 'Le régime anglo-bourguignon à Paris', in FA, 53–60.

[125] iv, 136.

[126] Monstrelet, *Chronique*, ii. 294; Vaughan, *John the Fearless*, 97–8; d'Avout, *La querelle*, 157.

[127] Richard Vaughan, who is not generally inclined to admit continuing Burgundian aspirations in this regard, acknowledges their existence in 1461: Vaughan, PTG, 354–5; cf. P. Bonenfant, 'Les traits essentiels'.

this was the case, the representation of the duke and his royal contemporaries described above had clear potential. Chastelain reminded his reader that 'la maladie qui se meut du chief souverain fait plus a craindre que celle des autres membres' (Delclos, 260). Philip, a perfect French prince, was worthy of every confidence.

In the second instance, there was no denying the hard reality of royal rights and the ways in which they impinged upon ducal authority, particularly in lands that were held of the crown. Chastelain might pander to his patron's sense of glory and the clear awareness in court circles of the extent of his dominion and influence.[128] Yet he, like his colleagues, did not delude himself in the matter of the crown's right to interfere or, in the event of armed intervention, the king's recently proven might. This much is clear from Chastelain's political experience as discussed in chapters one and two. These facts were naturally a source of concern and/or frustration for a prince who had done well outside the kingdom in recent years but whose interests, like those of many of his supporters, were still linked to it. Like his Breton counterpart, the duke thus sought to 'jouyr du sien comme les autres' (v, 6) on the one hand, and to 'vivre en paix avecques luy [the king]' (iii, 445) on the other.[129] Chastelain had to contend with these realities. Effective propaganda, like the politics it served, was the art of the possible. Within the parameters set for him, Chastelain evolved a flexible way of representing the historical process. Undermining the moral authority of the king was one tactic here – a tactic made all the more effective by its sources and formulation. But this was not enough. Chastelain could well imagine that some in the kingdom believed that Philip, despite having recognised Charles as his 'souverain' at Arras, '[ne] recognoit . . . riens par desur luy, ne qu'il y ait roy, ne couronne, qui le doye faire humilier' (iii, 219).[130] The duke had to be exculpated before an imagined tribunal of royalist opinion. In turn, royalists had to be reminded of the possible consequences of their actions. These complementary strands may also be picked out in Chastelain's representation of events.

The chronicler's exculpation of the duke was based on one over-riding idea: Philip's loyalty to individual kings and to the crown. His 'parfonde léaulté' (iv, 149) was simply affirmed in many cases, but so frequent are the affirmations that the reader can be overwhelmed by them.[131] A conscious manipulation of historical events to this end can be seen in passages where his source was altered to incorporate the theme. Although he closely follows Monstrelet's account of

---

[128] For example, Chastelain's well-known description of Philip as 'point moindre d'un empereur, posé que non roy' (i, 138, 187; also i, 221; iii, 157; Delclos, 144); his repeated references to the kings who owed their crowns to the duke (iii, 122–3; iv, 37, 90, 156, 207, 297, 384; v, 26, 36); or his references to the 'divers pays' (iv, 392) which supported his 'querelle'.
[129] Cf. iii, 391–2.
[130] Cf. v, 439–42. For the use of the term 'souverain' see iii, 11, 14; Delclos, 268.
[131] See, for example, i, 41, 60; ii, 14; iii, 220, 225, 445; Delclos, 123, 125, 153, 305; iv, 6–10, 123–4, 454; v, 96, 125, 149.

the siege of Melun (1420), for example, Chastelain digresses on the care which Philip took throughout the campaign to visit the feckless Charles VI 'avec dues révérences, comme tousjours avoit fait par avant' (i, 160).[132] The Anglo-Burgundian alliance was effectively relegated to the background by this emphasis. Where Monstrelet limits himself to a factual account of the Burgundian defeat by Charles VII at Compiègne (1430), Chastelain adds that the duke 'n'y mist peine' because of his 'compassion du noble royal sang' (ii, 89).[133] This does not sit easily with Philip's recorded sentiments on the matter.[134] Verisimilitude within the context of his own work, rather than an exact reflection of sentiments felt more than thirty years earlier, was the chronicler's objective.

The one-time university man could also convey his theme with quodlibetical skill. He knew that Charles VII regarded the Order of the Golden Fleece with suspicion, 'pensant tousjours qu'en ycelle peust avoir quelque secrete conspiration en son contraire' (Delclos, 123).[135] As he observed elsewhere, however, 'oppinion n'a point de preuve apparue, n'a point de certaineté aussi qui soit maintenable' (Delclos, 261). Hence, no doubt, his unique and ultimately unverifiable explanation for the reasons behind the Order's foundation. Having envisaged the possibility 'par longtemps', Philip only acted after Bedford offered him the Garter.[136] He did not wish to remain the 'perpétuel allié' of the English 'en forlignant de ses pères' (ii, 12). Chastelain can thus inform those 'en temps advenir' that his master was motivated by 'la très-espéciale loyaulté qu'avoit envers sa mère-maison, la maison de France, de laquelle pour fortune ... n'avoit intention, ne nature, ne volenté qui l'en pust fourtraire' (ii, 13–14). The chronicler also turned the tables on imagined royalist opinion when describing Charles VII's provocative summons to Philip to attend the trial of Alençon in 1458. This clearly exasperated the duke: by the terms of Arras he was no longer at the king's beck and call. His men were mustered throughout the Low Countries.[137] Chastelain characteristically – and no doubt ironically – interprets this retaliation as the act of an observant vassal: the duke would enter France with 'quarante mille combattans pour servir le roy, si besoing en avoit, et jamais n'y entreroit à moins' (iii, 421). A Burgundian audience would no doubt have appreciated the sentiment of defiance beneath this dangerously literal interpretation of Philip's duties as a peer of the realm. However, if simple or complex expressions of Philip's loyalty were not enough, the chronicler might also appeal to common

---

[132] Cf. Monstrelet, *Chronique*, iii. 412. Similar depictions of Philip's loyalty to Charles VI are found at i, 199–201, 311.
[133] Cf. Monstrelet, *Chronique*, iv. 402–20.
[134] *Letters and papers illustrative of the wars of the English in France during the reign of Henry VI*, ed. J. Stevenson, London 1861–4, ii. 156–64.
[135] Cf. ii, 185.
[136] C. A. J. Armstrong, 'La double monarchie France–Angleterre et la maison de Bourgogne (1420–1435)', AB xxxvii (1965), 81–112 (repr. in his *England, France and Burgundy*, 343–74).
[137] ADN B2030, fos 228–30.

sense. How could Philip expect loyalty from his own men if he himself sought to 'refuser obeÿssance ailleurs a son plus grant'? To put it another way, 'seroit homme princiant injuste devant aultruy quant luy meismes requiert que raison se contourne et se paroffre envers sa personne?' (Delclos, 157). This was either a rational argument or a revealing comment on the limitations of Burgundian power. Perhaps it was both.

By these means the chronicler sought to build up a cast-iron case in favour of his master. Philip never acted 'par desobeÿssance au roy' (Delclos, 222); he was neither 'l'ennemy de la couronne' (iii, 445) nor 'le comprimeur du royal throsne par fierté' (iv, 387). The *quid pro quo* of his unimpeachable loyalty was, naturally enough, the king's fulfilment of his duties. Because this was not forthcoming, the historical record of events – or rather, the historian – gave the duke an advantage which any literate, politically aware contemporary could recognise and understand. This, quite simply, was a just cause.

The righteousness of Philip's cause is obviously emphasised where it was most needed in Chastelain's history: in his account of the Anglo-Burgundian alliance between 1420 and 1435.[138] He clearly alters Monstrelet's account of events to suggest that Philip was forced to sign the treaty of Troyes.[139] Loyal Frenchmen said the same of Charles VI.[140] Philip's 'juste défense de [s]on droit' was underlined thereafter by repeated emphasis upon his desire for vengeance. The recovery of John the Fearless's body from Montereau was embellished with an account of how its wounds, once disinterred, 'rendirent sang nouvel et tout frès, comme si hier eust esté tué' (i, 144).[141] Philip's first engagement with the dauphin's forces at Mons-en-Vimeu was transformed from Monstrelet's skirmish into a full-blown battle which quenched the duke's thirst for revenge.[142] Once peace was made, Philip continued to be in the right. Indeed, Chastelain's depiction of every significant confrontation between the king and the duke thereafter was hung around this simple theme. Charles VII's attempt to recover the Somme towns in 1455 could be resisted by Philip because of 'le beau droit qu'avoit de Dieu' (iii, 55). In the following year the French, 'non craignans de courcier Dieu' (iii, 325) once more, persisted in their unjust persecution of Philip over the matter of the dauphin's sojourn in the Low Countries. The duke could also take comfort in 'Dieu et [s]on bon droit' in the dispute over French claims to the duchy of Luxembourg in 1458 (iii, 391).

God was the ultimate arbiter between just and unjust causes. This, rather than his much-vaunted impartiality, may explain why Chastelain elevates the

---

138 Huizinga, 'L'état bourguignon', 188–9.
139 Cf. i, 130; Monstrelet, Chronique, iii, ch. ccxxiv.
140 *Response d'un bon et loyal françois au peuple de France de tous estats*, in Aubrée, *Mémoires*, i. 315–22.
141 Cf. Monstrelet, Chronique, iii. 404–5; Lefèvre, Chronique, ii. 11. One other source simply states that the body was in good condition: Pierre de Fenin, *Mémoires (1407–1422)*, in *Collection complète des mémoires relatifs à l'histoire de France*, ed. E. Petitot, Paris 1825, vii. 237–370 at pp. 330–1.
142 Cf. i, 256–78; Monstrelet, Chronique, iv. 60–6.

historiographer to the status of a divinely ordained office.¹⁴³ But the chronicler did not rely on God alone to 'justifiier l'innocent contre son malveullant a tort' (Delclos, 159). He sought signs of support for Philip's 'droite, juste et léale querelle' (iv, 292) in those circles where, in view of his perceived audience, it mattered most – within the political elite of the kingdom itself. The deathbed confession of the bishop of Meaux, whose conscience had been pricked by Charles VII's attempts to implicate the 'justes et innocens' Burgundians in the trial of Alençon, was seized upon to these ends.¹⁴⁴ Bourbon, Brittany, Orléans, Nevers and other princes of the realm were portrayed as being unconvinced of the righteousness of the king's cause.¹⁴⁵ Perhaps most revealingly, Philip's royal contemporaries were made to recognise this themselves. Louis XI publicly acknowledged the duke's irreproachable conduct.¹⁴⁶ In the case of Charles VII, Chastelain makes a more astonishing claim. There is no doubt that Burgundy and France were on the brink of open war in the last months of his reign.¹⁴⁷ Despite this, Chastelain affirms that the king's 'final intention longuement portee' was to draw back from the conflict and to announce to the duke that he 'desiroit et convoitoit son amour, son amistié et sa bonté envers ly comme de cel du monde seul lequel il voloit conforter et aydier, mesmes envers tous et encontre tous, lealement et de tout son pouoir' (Delclos, 303). This version of events, like Chastelain's account of the origins of the Order of the Golden Fleece, has yet to be corroborated by other sources.¹⁴⁸ What is certain, however, is that Charles VII's reported last wish fitted exactly with the main tenet of the chronicler's argument, the 'seule chose' that he had 'maintenue et escrite tousjours' (iv, 394): to show that the duke was in the right. By coming to his senses at the last – more specifically, 'a la congnoissance de [s]on tort' (Delclos, 304) – the king himself was made to vindicate Philip the Good's profoundly just cause.

Outflanking royalist opinion was one thing; reminding such an audience of the consequences of royal action was another matter. A literature of revolt would not do here, for with it came the loss of the moral advantage. Instead, Chastelain had recourse once again to the tried-and-tested formulae provided by a shared historical culture.

After the first turbulent decades of the fifteenth century, the promise of St Remigius – that the kingdom would flourish so long as its inhabitants adhered

---

¹⁴³ Cf. Delclos, 159, 261; iv, 14–15, 96; vi, 353, 416–17.
¹⁴⁴ iii, 430–1.
¹⁴⁵ iii, 438–41.
¹⁴⁶ iv, 39, 47, 150.
¹⁴⁷ Beaucourt, *Histoire*, vi. 310–45.
¹⁴⁸ The only comparable statement is Mathieu d'Escouchy's vague belief that despite the troubles in the kingdom and the wishes of some of his counsellors, Charles 'quant on lui parloit au prejudice d'icellui duc . . . estoit cellui qui en tout le supportoit et faisoit ses excuses': d'Escouchy, *Chronique*, ii. 415–16. Chastelain does attribute his story to a 'noble chevalier' who had been at the royal court at the time. The man in question remains curiously anonymous in the text, although it seems to have been Michel de Chaugy.

to the divine path of truth and faith – seemed once more to be in effect. This, at least, was how some royalist writers saw it; it was natural, perhaps even inevitable, that they should do so.[149] The official Burgundian chronicler partook of this orthodox literary response to the upturn in royal fortunes. The sins of the French, the ultimate cause of their afflictions at the hands of the English, had been purged. Charles VII had managed by his virtue to 'nettoyer son trosne plein de bruynes' (ii, 180). When the French had first risen to power in the world, as Chastelain observed at the very beginning of his work, they tamed 'toute la Germanie . . . ployèrent les Grecs, réduisirent les Espagnes, donnèrent règle aux terres maritimes, et tout l'enclos d'entre les deux mers haut et bas soumirent à leurs lois et obéissance' (i, 6–7). Those times had returned. He uses virtually the same terms to describe them at a later stage in the Chronicle: 'avoient les Italies qui les redoubtoient, Savoiens qui leur ploioient genoux, Allemans qui les quéroient avoir paisibles, et les Espaignes qui leur offrirent amministrations et services' (iii, 51). French force of arms – 'toutes les frontières [estoient] pourvues et garnies de gens d'armes' (iii, 348), 'les plus belles gens d'armes du monde' (iii, 50) – had achieved this. The *armées de l'ordonnance* had clearly made an impact, mentally as well as militarily.[150]

Thus far the chronicler follows contemporary interpretations of conventional wisdom – but no further. St Remigius' promise remained conditional. Charles VII's 'très-haute exaltation', achieved by virtue, could only be preserved by virtue, 'là où il y a plus de mistère à soy y parmaintenir sans décheoir que à y estre monté par labeur, ce que Dieu, j'espère, pour la félicité de son peuple ne souffrira pas, mais amodérera à tous lez les passions et superfluités vicieuses qui pourroient estre occasion de meschief' (ii, 188–9). The Romans served as a salutary reminder of the consequences of letting standards slip. In times of trouble, 'ils estoient les plus vertueux des autres; mais quant paix leur donna occasion de oysivetés et voluptés, nuls au monde plus vicieux. En quoy fait à entendre que les estroites fortunes clariffient les humaines vertus, et les comblées et voluptueuses les endorment' (ii, 181). Like the Romans, and like their own forefathers, the French were now in danger of bringing ruin upon themselves. Instead of learning to accommodate or at least live in peace with the duke, the triumphant king – Charles, invigorated by the reconquest, or Louis, at last on the throne – seemed unjustly determined to resolve the situation in his favour. Divine wrath would surely ensue. The unexpected death of Charles's ally, Ladislas of Hungary, was one in a series of warnings to the king:

comme en autres lieux ay parlé en termes samblables . . . ceste mort du jeusne roy ait esté faite par jugement de Dieu pour exempler le roy et reprendre en son

---

[149] Beaune, *Naissance*, 215–16.
[150] I agree that Chastelain was impressed by the standing army of Charles VII, but whether he was favourably impressed is another matter: D. Solon, 'Popular response to standing military forces in fifteenth-century France', *Studies in the Renaissance* xix (1972), 78–111 at pp. 102–3.

chemin, et pour lui oster hors des mains ce par quoy il avoit volenté peut-estre de donner moleste à la crestienté, traveil et inpugnation à ce bon duc, son tant léal serviteur et parent, son tant humble et révérend envers lui, son tant charitable pardonneur de mal oeuvre jadis. (iii, 384)

The stock literary response to France's misfortunes in an earlier age was subverted and revived in a new context. Spectres from the French past were conjured up to haunt a king who, because of his sinful conduct against the 'divin mand' (iv, 369), was now in danger of re-opening wounds which no right-minded Frenchmen, in the aftermath of war, could wish to see re-opened.[151] The warning might appear impartial and conventional; it was all the more effective for it.

For the surviving seven-eighths of his text which deal with the reign of Philip the Good, Chastelain thus had recourse to a set of related, simple themes for interpreting and representing the 'accidens' thrown up by the historical process. These inevitably derived from the historical culture of his milieu which, in turn, was linked to long-established traditions of history-writing within the kingdom of France. There was nothing new in his themes – that was their very strength. Nor was the chronicler their prisoner. Huizinga might emphasise the 'inertie mentale' of Chastelain's work, but we should remind ourselves that, in Weber's happy phrase, familiar arguments had the 'authority of the eternal yesterday'.[152] Public opinion in the principalities took different forms, but opinion borrowed from the centre did not have to be deployed in a centrist perspective. Chastelain, it seems, was not interested in an ideal of Franco-Burgundian union, at least not on the terms which an unreformed Charles VII or Louis XI might care to set. A princely conception of France was the limit of his ideals: one that gave an outwardly loyal duke and those who supported him optimum room for manoeuvre in a kingdom where, as we have seen throughout this study, they still had a stake. The royalist conception of France would eventually prevail. If Chastelain and other contemporaries sensed this, it had not yet come to pass.

Charles the Bold

By comparison with his father and his father's attitude to the kingdom, Charles the Bold was a man of a different stamp. Chastelain treated him differently too. The chronicler's equivocal attitude to Charles has often been remarked upon, but rarely attributed to anything more than personal sentiment.[153] Yet

---

[151] Lewis, 'Jean Juvenal des Ursins', 186. For the state of France in the aftermath of the conflict see C. T. Allmand, 'The aftermath of war in fifteenth-century France', *History* lxi (1976), 344–57.
[152] Huizinga, 'L'état bourguignon', 189; Weber cited in Spiegel, 'Political utility', 315.
[153] Urwin, *Georges Chastelain*, 44–5; Hommel, *Chastellain*, 85; Delclos, *Le témoignage*, 168–201.

Chastelain had welcomed Charles in his own hostel when he was count of Charolais, and had been well treated by him as duke.[154] This may explain why, in dealing with this prince, he still manifested the instincts of the official chronicler intent on presenting his master in the best possible light. Charles's motives and actions during his conflicts with Philip the Good were carefully distinguished from the unnatural behaviour of the dauphin Louis.[155] The familiar traits of the ideal prince resurface in the description of Charles both before and after his accession in 1467. A prince of justice whose word was his bond, he is presented as being constant in the face of adversity, vigorous in arms, majestic in his deportment and generous, in measure, to his servants.[156] Like his father before him, Charles could be depicted as a French prince – 'de sa vraie nature originale françoise' (v, 419), 'François et du sang' (v, 445) – who had been forced into an English alliance 'maugré luy et contre son coeur et contre sa nature' (v, 419) by the unreasonable actions of the monarch.[157] As a result, his resistance to Louis XI could be justified at times in the same way as his father's had been, 'non prenant titre pourtant contre le roy, ne contre sa couronne, par action qui regarde sa majesté, mais titre seulement sur son droit et sur le tort que le roy luy vouloit faire, ce que ne devoit, et lequel tort il ne vouloit tolérer' (v, 437–8).[158] If familiar arguments were still trotted out, it is also quite clear that Chastelain's support for the new duke and promotion of his cause were far from unconditional.

In detail that would be superfluous here, it has been shown that Charles the Bold, although presented as the moral superior of Louis XI, is none the less criticised in terms which are often remarkably similar.[159] Chastelain left his audience in no doubt that this 'nouveau jeusne duc' was not, at least in this early part of his reign, an ideal prince in his father's mould.[160] Of course, Chastelain's Chronicle was not the only narrative to present the duke as a hot-headed, proud and uncompromising ruler. Philippe de Commynes, Philippe Wielant, Jean Molinet and Olivier de La Marche confirm his perceptions.[161] Yet it is impossible to sustain close comparisons between these

---

154 See chs 2, 3 above.
155 iv, 344, 443–5.
156 iv, 135, 334–6, 345; v, 256, 262, 325, 360.
157 See also v, 312, 448.
158 However see v, 331, where, for the first time, the just cause of the French king is acknowledged over that of Charles; cf. v, 425, 438–45.
159 Delclos, Le témoignage, 186–201.
160 Chastelain repeatedly emphasises the duke's youth, despite the fact that he was thirty-three years old when Philip died: v, 249, 255, 267, 337, 341, 379. It is far from certain that such references were complimentary. Perhaps Charles always struck Chastelain as 'le petit', the baby whose birth at Dijon in November 1433 Chastelain may well have celebrated with the duke's men-at-arms, the boy who had been tutored by his own university master, or the youth who played 'aux barres' in the precinct of the Salle-le-Comte. An element of generational conflict cannot be ruled out when assessing the chronicler's attitude towards his new master.
161 J. Dufournet, 'Charles le Téméraire vu par les historiens bourguignons', in CCABN, 65–81.

depictions of the duke and Chastelain's. His criticisms were not grounded in the same concerns or experience: he did not feel he had to justify his own actions when writing of the duke, as Commynes is thought to have done, nor did he experience the political upheaval and personal misfortune which La Marche, Molinet and Wielant witnessed and suffered in the wake of Charles's demise at Nancy. What he had experienced, however, was the intricate legal and political relationship between the king and the duke, the interests and traditions of service among his contemporaries in court life and the historical culture with which these men were familiar. His Chronicle, as this chapter has sought to show, can be read as a flexible response to the factors which conditioned the outlook and concerns of certain Burgundian servants of his generation and experience. Under Charles the Bold, of course, the political climate changed, in some respects dramatically.[162] Two particular and, it may be argued, related, areas of change are highlighted in the official Chronicle. These, rather than the experience of later writers, form the basis of Chastelain's sharpest observations on his master.

The chronicler was concerned in the first instance by the harsh treatment meted out to the new duke's servants. Although Charles's ordinance of January 1469 instilled an appropriate level of magnificence in his household, Chastelain presented it as a considerable source of irritation for those who served under this new regime with its strict hierarchy, greater definition of function and range of financial penalties for the most minor of infringements.[163] There is a clear sense, here as elsewhere, that the nature of Burgundian government, a joint-stock enterprise involving the duke and his servants in pursuit of mutual interests, was being profoundly altered.[164] With the 'bon duc trespassé', 'le temps du présent' was 'tout autre, tout dur et estrange envers l'autre passé' (v, 473). Charles, unlike his father, is presented on several occasions as relying on 'son propre avis' rather than on the advice of his servants.[165] In his inflexible attitude towards the Bastard of Condé (whom several at court counselled the duke to pardon after he had failed to make reparation for an act of murder in 1468), Charles may have convinced everyone that he was a 'prince crému en face de toutes nations et de toute sa noblesse' (v, 405). In the process, however, he alienated the bastard's uncle, a knight of the Order of the Golden Fleece,

---

[162] In addition to the biographies of Bartier and Vaughan see, for further important comment, W. Paravicini, *Karl der Kühne*, Göttingen 1976; P. Contamine, 'Charles le Téméraire: fossoyeur et/ou fondateur de l'état bourguignon?', *Le Pays lorrain* lviii (1977), 123–34; H. Heimpel, 'Karl der Kühne und der burgundische Staat', in R. Nurnberger (ed.), *Festschrift Gerhard Ritter*, Tübingen 1950, 140–60; A. Leguai, 'Charles le Téméraire face au roi de France et au royaume de France', in CCABN, 269–89.
[163] v, 370–1, 469–70.
[164] 'Burgundian power... was something of a syndicate in which people took stakes so as to share in the fortunes of the house' – at least until Charles the Bold: Armstrong, 'The golden age of Burgundy' at p. 60.
[165] v, 317, 358, 379, 421.

and, according to the chronicler, 'toute la chevalerie de Haynau à qui cestui cas compétoit' (v, 400).

This sense of an emerging gap between the prince and at least some among his 'noblesse' becomes a recurrent theme. Louis de Bruges, another knight of the Order, is reported to have informed the duke during the Ghent riot of 1467 that he was not prepared to die on the market place because of Charles's obduracy.[166] A similar sentiment was expressed by the duke's captains when he refused to shift his camp during his campaign against Louis XI in the following year.[167] The 'nobles de Brabant', for their part, were affronted by Charles's attempt to deploy Hainaulters to quell rebellion in Mechelen in 1467.[168] The new duke did not carry his entourage as his father was seen to have done.

In view of his infrequent sojourns and declining role at court in these years, Chastelain's depiction of disenchanted elements within the household might be read as a projection of some personal sentiment of alienation after the death of his favourite duke. Once again, however, to personalise these sentiments, as commentators have often done with Chastelain, would be to marginalise them. The thoughts he expressed were not his alone. In the 1468 chapter of the Order of the Golden Fleece and again in that of 1473, the duke was petitioned by his most senior servants on the matter of his conduct.[169] The very first criticism they levelled concerned the heavy-handed treatment of his retinue and, in particular, the fact that he called some of them traitors. In keeping with their right to counsel the duke on matters of government, they also raised their concerns over Charles's willingness to resort to arms (at this time, against the king), and expressed doubts as to the ability of his subjects to withstand the pressures he was creating.[170] These, too, were views which Chastelain expressed in unequivocal terms. Charles, 'enfiéry' by his early success in arms against Louis XI, 'n'estoit à ployer, sinon à son singulier bon et à son plaisir' (v, 372). He was prepared to demand an 'horrible somme de deniers à prendre sur le peuple', including 400,000*l.t.* to be raised 'sur le *petit pays* de Hainaut' (v, 374–5).[171] The relative fragility of his dominion was apparent to some, if not to him.[172] Like Chastelain, the knights also thought that the duke worked 'too hard so that it is doubtful if he will live when he is older'. The prospect of the early death of a duke who 'n'avoit nuls enfans, fors une seule fille' (v, 474–5)

---

[166] v, 267–8.
[167] v, 435–6.
[168] v, 310–11.
[169] The original transcripts are preserved in the archive of the Order of the Golden Fleece in Vienna, register 3, fos 27–9v. I was unable to consult this source and have relied upon the translated version published in Vaughan, CTB, 172–8. Similar – but less complete – information is conveyed in the accounts of the relevant chapters of the Order in de Reiffenberg, *Histoire de la Toison d'Or*.
[170] Vaughan, CTB, 172–3.
[171] Italics mine.
[172] See v, 258, 279–80.

was a sobering one for all Burgundian servants. The limitations of ducal power and the dangers of confronting the king were thus as evident to the knights of the Order of the Golden Fleece as they were to the official chronicler. Chastelain voiced concerns which were shared at the very highest level in the Burgundian polity.

Equally prominent among the complaints of the knights of the Order was the view that the duke became 'emotional sometimes when talking about other princes'.[173] Although Louis XI (perhaps tactfully) was not mentioned by name on this occasion, there can be little doubt that Charles's attitude to his royal overlord figured prominently in their thoughts. According to the official chronicler, Charles stated in 1468 that in the matter of the rebellious city of Liège, 'ne me chault que le roy en fasse' (v, 357). In a celebrated outburst two years later, uttered in the presence of his entourage, the Italian prince Rodolfo Gonzaga and a French ambassador, he described himself as Portuguese (by dint of his mother's line) and commended the king of France to the hundred thousand devils of hell.[174] Chastelain's depiction of the reactions of the ducal entourage to this splenetic statement is highly revealing, and fits well with the criticisms made of the duke by the Golden Fleece knights. Murmurs ensued 'pour ce que tacitement contempnant le nom de France dont il estoit, ne se osa nommer Anglois, là où le coeur luy estoit' (v, 454). We are told that the manner of Charles's speech, so public and so irreverent, was 'durement mal pris entre ses propres gens'. The explanation for their discomfiture is important, 'car quoique le maistre fust, ne quel, ne comme fait, eux tous estoient en affection devers France, non pas vers Angleterre'. Charles's preference for an English alliance despite his French extraction – an alliance which was, unlike his father's, dynastic in nature – constituted Chastelain's second major criticism of the duke.[175] As this passage reveals, it was, once again, a sentiment which the official chronicler shared with some of his colleagues in court service.

One ducal servant in attendance that day, the chronicler's friend Philippe Pot, had particular reason to squirm upon hearing the duke's outburst.[176] The royal ambassador to whom the remark was addressed was none other than his own brother, Guyot, *bailli* of Vermandois.[177] For men like Pot, whose family traditions and interests in France pre-dated and unfortunately coincided with the reign of Charles the Bold, this authoritarian duke, who was 'Anglois et François, ainsi qu'il luy plaisoit' (v, 372), must have seemed a loose cannon. The cold warning which Charles gave to the count of St Pol – who held many

---

[173] Vaughan, *CTB*, 172.
[174] Cf. Plancher, *Histoire*, iv, pp. cclxxxv–vii. Charles's reference to his Portuguese connections may also have looked further back in time: cf. J. Paviot, 'Les relations diplomatiques et politiques entre la Bourgogne et le Portugal (1384–1482)', *PCEEB* xxxii (1992), 77–84 at p. 77.
[175] Cf. v, 448–9, 456.
[176] For Chastelain's relations with Pot see ch. 2 above.
[177] Gaussin, 'Les conseillers de Louis XI', 112.

of his lands from the duke, but his most significant office from the king – had a broader resonance for all those who had inherited such traditions and interests: 'pensez bien à vostre cas' (v, 356). A prince who was in the habit of labelling more loyal servants than St Pol as traitors could not look kindly upon those whose past – in his eyes, if not in his father's – may have seemed chequered.

Some justified Charles's suspicions of his entourage by taking the road to royal service. Chastelain's attitude towards these men is significant. Although the official chronicler condemns the base motive of personal gain behind some departures, he notes that Charles 'en estoit assez cause, par trop estre roide et dur à ses gens de diverses manières non apprises, par espécial aux nobles hommes, lesquels il maintint et voulut asservir en estroites servitudes' (v, 469). In the case of Guillaume Rolin, to which this quotation relates, Chastelain reports the incident in terms which are derogatory of the duke alone: 'beaucoup de gens de biens s'en tannèrent et en devinrent tous froids' (v, 470). Guillaume was not criticised for the fact that he kept himself safe in France 'où autres après le siévirent'. If Chastelain did express outrage at the entry into royal service in 1470 of Jean de Chassa, a ducal chamberlain, Jean d'Arson, a ducal equerry, and Baudouin de Lille, a half-brother of Charles himself, his sentiments related more to their reported plot on Charles's life than to their abandonment of the duke.[178] This nuanced judgement appears to stem from Chastelain's cognisance of the complex interests which these men, and others at the Burgundian court, had to bear in mind. Jean d'Arson had come to ducal service from France. Because he was a 'natif de Bourbonnois' (as was Michel de Chaugy, another of Chastelain's friends), Louis XI could remind him of the fact that 'il estoit de son royaume et son subjet' (v, 480). Add to this a financial incentive and it may well have seemed, as Chastelain put it in another case, that 'au monde n'avoit lieu là où mieux se pouvoit retraire qu'en France devers le roy' (v, 473). Guillaume Rolin, for his part, was a 'moult grant seigneur' in the duchy of Burgundy. Here, as other landholders in that region were aware, the king was the ultimate arbiter. The minds of these men were further concentrated by the reality of open war between France and Burgundy (v, 471) and by the fact that in the event of Charles's death, 'ses pays iroient tous estrangement' (v, 475).

It has been rightly stressed that Charles the Bold was 'well and loyally served' by the vast majority of men at his court.[179] Chastelain placed himself firmly in that category by criticising the cowardice and ingratitude of any man who went against 'son maistre et son nourrisseur' (v, 479). Although they stepped beyond the pale, however, it is clear that the official chronicler intended his reader to think that specific personal circumstances had led these men to act upon sentiments which were more widely felt within the Burgundian elite. 'Cestui jeusne prince' thought he had 'la faculté et le pouvoir d'en faire autant que le

---

[178] Cf. v, 471–2, 483.
[179] Vaughan, CTB, 234.

coeur luy en pouvoit dire' (v, 379). To a greater or lesser degree, others – including the official chronicler, the knights of the Order of the Golden Fleece and those who abandoned the duke – thought otherwise. Charles wished to lead where some were not prepared to follow; in his 'chaleur', he could not easily over-ride the complex web of legal realities, family or personal interests and historical traditions which combined in the outlook of some Burgundian courtiers. Chastelain, it now seems, intended to communicate that view. Most of his surviving work as official historian was geared, within a given political and historical framework, towards the promotion of the interests of the duke and his entourage. In its latter stages, however, the Chronicle spoke for elements of that entourage rather than for the last duke himself.

Writing of Charles the Bold's ordinance of Thionville in 1473, Vaughan suggested that 'by that time a distinctive Burgundian loyalty or sentiment had emerged to support and consolidate the dukes' admittedly somewhat incoherent attempts to unify their lands'.[180] Loyalties and sentiments are notoriously difficult to assess in the present; how much more so in the past.[181] The Francophone world of the fifteenth century is no exception; it may even be a particular case in point.[182] If historical cultures, legal realities, family traditions and personal interests form part of that wider picture, then Chastelain's Chronicle, the product of such factors, suggests that there was still a long way to go before Vaughan's claim would hold true for all of the court elite. In its own way, the Chronicle may reveal the point at which the judgement became more applicable. To demonstrate this we must turn to our final subject – the audience of the work.

---

[180] Idem, *Valois Burgundy*, 30–1; reinforced in his 'Five hundred years after the great battles', BMGN xcv (1980), 377–90 esp. pp. 387–9.
[181] For attempts to do so in the case of the Burgundian dominions see M. Chaume, *Le sentiment national en Bourgogne de Gondebaud à Charles le Téméraire*, Dijon 1922, 195–260; Y. Cazaux, 'L'idée de Bourgogne, fondement de la politique de Charles le Téméraire', PCEEBM x (1968), 85–91.
[182] See, for example, B. Guenée, 'État et nation en France au moyen âge', RH ccxxxvii (1967), 17–30; P. S. Lewis, 'La "France anglaise" vue de la "France française" ', in FA, 31–9.

6

The Audience of the Chronicle

So little is known of the work's audience before the editions of Buchon and Kervyn that one might be forgiven for wondering whether it had had one at all. It is certainly thought that the Chronicle made little impact upon historical culture in the fifteenth century or beyond. In crude quantitative terms, the total of ten surviving manuscripts compares favourably with two for Lefèvre's *Mémoires* or five for d'Escouchy's *Chroniques*.[1] However, unlike these (or the nine which survive for Monstrelet's work), the individual Chronicle manuscripts contain very little of the text. They are also considerably less numerous than the surviving copies of other histories, such as Commynes's *Mémoires* or Molinet's *Chroniques*.[2] Previous commentators have concluded that Chastelain's Chronicle quickly sank into obscurity; the writer himself became 'l'oublié'.[3]

These conclusions were reached without close reference to the manuscripts: the relationships – both textual and material – between them, their date and place of redaction or their subsequent history.[4] The codices will be exploited

---

[1] Lefèvre, *Chronique*, i, pp. i–viii; G. Halligan, 'La *Chronique* de Mathieu d'Escouchy', *Romania* xc (1969), 100–10. The ten manuscripts of Chastelain's Chronicle, and the sigla attributed to them for ease of reference in this chapter, are as follows (the dates, given for convenience, do not take account of the lacunae discussed in ch. 4 above): (a) 1419–22: Florence, BML, MS mediceo-palatino 177 (hereinafter F1); BM Arras, MS 516 (827) (hereinafter A1); (b) 1430–1: BM Arras, MS 256 (406) (hereinafter A2); Florence, BML, MS mediceo-palatino 176 (hereinafter F2); (c) 1454–8: Brussels, BR, MS 15843 (hereinafter B); London, BL, Add. MS 54156 (hereinafter L); (d) 1458–61: L only; (e) 1461–4: Château de Beloeil (Belgium), MS TA.V.D.17 (hereinafter Be); BM Arras, MS 578 (471) (hereinafter A3); (f) 1464–66: Paris, BN, MS fr. 2688 (hereinafter P1); (g) 1467–70: Paris, BN, MS fr. 2689 (hereinafter P2). Two further manuscripts of the Chronicle will be discussed below.

[2] Monstrelet, *Chronique*, i, pp. x–xxiii; Commynes, *Mémoires*, i, pp. xviii–xxv. The manuscripts of Molinet's Chronicle are discussed below.

[3] Hommel, *Chastellain*, 105–11; cf. Pérouse, *Georges Chastellain*, 156–7; Urwin, *Georges Chastelain*, 157.

[4] Cf. Muret, 'Chastelain parmi nous', 368. No published comment suggests that any previous commentator saw all of the manuscripts in the original – not even Kervyn de Lettenhove. In some instances (particularly the Florence manuscripts) he or his collaborators worked from transcripts. For this and other preparatory work for the edition, cf. B. Renard, 'Correspondance', *Bulletin de la Société de l'histoire de France* (hereinafter cited as BSHF) (1843), 37–9; A. Vallet de Viriville, 'Correspondance', *Bulletin du Comité de la langue* ii (1853–5), 207–8; J. C. Kervyn de Lettenhove, 'Note sur quelques fragments inédits des *Mémoires* de G. Chastelain', BSHF (1854), 132–3; B. Renard, 'Note relative à divers manuscrits des *Mémoires* de G. Chastelain', ibid. 165–6; Beaucourt, 'Le chroniqueur'. The

here as a means of locating and evaluating the extent of the Chronicle's diffusion.[5] If the work did not remain a 'private event', we might ask who its readers were and what they made of it.[6] To anticipate, the answers to some of these questions will provide a means of understanding the fragmentary survival of the text itself. Inextricably linked to this is the argument that changes detected in Burgundian historical culture under Philip the Good did not in fact enter the mainstream until much later.

The manuscript evidence

Several sections of the narrative survive in pairs of manuscripts. By comparing the texts they contain, their shared readings or significant variants, we may begin to assess the complexity of the manuscript tradition which stemmed from the lost archetype discussed in chapter four. Since the exercise may point to the existence (or absence) of intermediary manuscripts, it provides a useful preliminary guide to the extent of the work's diffusion.

F1 and A1 are closely connected in this regard. The Florence manuscript provides the more polished and complete of the two texts, incorporating a table of contents, chapter titles where appropriate and at least three short passages which are absent in its counterpart.[7] The scribes of the Arras volume were inclined to abridge the narrative and took less care when copying it out.[8] Setting aside those minor differences which inevitably occur in the scribal process (the substitution of synonyms, the occasional *bourdon* and so forth), the variants between the two texts are otherwise insignificant. Identical errors are made in both.[9] These close similarities indicate that A1 and F1 at least had

---

manuscripts have been studied in microform by at least twenty-seven students who worked between 1962 and 1972 under O. Jodogne and G. Muraille at the University of Louvain on parts of a new edition of the Chronicle. Their findings, now kept in the university library at Louvain-la-Neuve, are particularly useful regarding variants and shared readings and will be referred to below.

[5] I am indebted to the staff of the IRHT (Paris) for their initial guidance in this matter and for a copy of their detailed and unpublished 'Guide pour l'élaboration d'une notice de manuscrit', Paris 1977. Further relevant information is to be found in D. Muzerelle, *Vocabulaire codicologique*, Paris 1985; A. Foulet and M. B. Speer, *On editing old French texts*, Lawrence, Kans. 1979; J. Lemaire, *Introduction à la codicologie*, Louvain-la-Neuve 1989; J. Glénisson, *Le livre au moyen âge*, Turnhout 1988; G. Ouy, 'Histoire "visible" et histoire "cachée" d'un manuscrit', MA lxiv (1958), 115–38.

[6] A. Hauser, *Philosophy of art history*, New York 1958, 230.

[7] Cf. F1, fos 12–20v (table of contents). The additional material corresponds to short passages found at i, 135–6, 139, 141.

[8] For omissions and abridgements in A1, as well as the random inclusion of chapter titles and perfunctory annalistic observations see app. 1 below.

[9] See on this point the detailed analysis of variants and shared readings in the three relevant Louvain *mém. de licence*: J. Vanden Abeele, 'Chronique: prologue – livre I (chapitres i–xix)', 1962; J. Campion, 'Chronique: livre I (chapitres lxx–cviii)', 1963; H. Van Holm, 'Chronique: livre I (chapitres cix–cxxix)', 1963.

a common source; it is even possible that the Arras manuscript was an abbreviated copy of its Florentine counterpart.

A2 and F2, the second pair of manuscripts, seem at first glance to be less intimately linked to one another. The Florence volume presents a markedly fuller text for the years concerned and contains several chapter titles which are absent in its counterpart.[10] Although Kervyn used these differences to justify his choice of F2 as the base manuscript for his edition, he omitted to note that the lacunae in A2 resulted from the loss of quires rather than from any serious omission on the part of the scribes.[11] In fact, the two manuscripts are otherwise closely related, not least because they appear to have the same curious *terminus a quo* and *terminus ad quem* for the text of the second book.[12] Several emendations or corrections in the Arras volume find their way into F2, but it is impossible to prove that the Florence manuscript was a copy of its counterpart.[13] There is no reason to posit the existence of more than one manuscript between the pair that survives.

This last comment is even more justified in the case of the third pair, B and the recently edited L. It is almost certain that the London manuscript was a copy of the Brussels volume which, it will be recalled, was emended by Chastelain himself.[14] The differences in the contents of the two texts are readily explained by the loss of quires and the cancellation of folios in B before it reached the bindery.[15] L does present a few confused readings of the Brussels original, but it also faithfully reproduces corrected passages from the latter, the lacunae which the scribes left in the text and a few errors which escaped Chastelain's personal attention.[16] This would suggest that L was a copy of a

---

[10] For chapter titles in F2 see fos 36, 81, 114.

[11] The three lost quires in A2 were originally situated at the beginning, between fos 45v–6 and 101v–2: see app. I below. The manuscript also ends before its Florentine counterpart at ii, 216 of the printed text rather than ii, 220.

[12] This is the case if we allow for the missing quires in A2. On the contents of the fragment see ch. 4 above.

[13] See the relevant Louvain *mémoires*: J. Dujardin, 'Chronique: livre II (chapitres i–xxv)', 1963; J.-M. Mottart, 'Chronique: livre II (chapitres xxvi–liii)', 1963; M. L. De Vel, 'Chronique: livre II (chapitres liv–lxii)', 1964.

[14] Delclos compares the two in his edition, pp. 9–13. Most of the Brussels manuscript has been re-edited in the unpublished Louvain *mém. de licence*: A. Cornet, 'Chronique: livre IV (chapitres i–xiii)', 1963; E. Schenus, 'Chronique: livre IV (chapitres xiv–xxxii)', 1969; L. De Poorter, 'Chronique: livre IV (chapitres xxxiii–xlvi)', 1967; J.-M. Pereau, 'Chronique: livre IV (chapitres xlvii–lx)', 1972; P. Nélis, 'Chronique: livre IV (chapitres lxi–lxxvii)', 1967; W. Panis, 'Chronique: livre IV (chapitres lxxviii–xciv)', 1967.

[15] The table of contents present in L but absent in B may be explained by the loss of a quire or quires at the beginning of the latter. Cancelled folios in B explain the loss of several passages: the end of the judicial duel at Valenciennes; a short passage on the illness of Charles VII in 1457; and the beginnings of the vast lacunae made good by L between 1458 and 1461. One cancellation of folios precedes the loss of several quires. The material they contained is provided in L. On these matters see, respectively, Delclos, 325–7, 329–30, 121–327, 29–111.

[16] Cf. ibid. 9–13.

fuller, unbound version of B. The relationship between the two demonstrates most effectively the relatively simple manuscript tradition of the Chronicle. None of the texts in the first three pairs appears to have been at any great remove from its counterpart.

The only exception is the final pair, Be and A3. Although they share similar lacunae and cover the same section of the Chronicle, they do so in some passages in different ways. The greater number of variants here is indicated in Kervyn's edition, where thirty-one examples, ranging from single words to complete sentences, are noted.[17] Many more could be added.[18] The greater complexity of the manuscript tradition for these passages is confirmed by the evidence of P1. Although the latter does not contain the text for the years 1461 to 1463, a table of contents at the end of the volume indicates that it originally comprised the material now found only in the Beloeil and Arras codices.[19] For the first time we have an explicit indication of the existence of a third, lost manuscript to complement one of the pairs.

Textual comparisons thus suggest that the surviving manuscripts did not stray far from first copies based upon parts of Chastelain's working text. These fragments were themselves copied and passed into circulation while the more complete original, for reasons which have yet to be determined, was left behind. The apparently limited diffusion of the Chronicle is confirmed by clear physical connections between some of the codices. P1 and P2 were once part of the same volume: the materials, scribal hands and consecutive foliation of each prove this beyond all doubt.[20] We may suspect that the two were separated by the librarian of a former owner, Count Philippe de Béthune († 1649), who is known to have split volumes in order to increase the size of his master's

---

[17] Cf. iv, 79 n. 1, 260 n. 1, 267 n. 1, 268 n. 1, 273 n. 1, 274 n. 2, 276 n. 1, 285 n. 4, 294 n. 2, 299 n. 1, 307 n. 4, 313, nn. 1, 3, 318 n. 1, 320 n. 1, 321 nn. 1, 2, 322 n. 1, 324 n. 3, 333 n. 2 and 3, 336 n. 2, 338 n. 1, 344 n. 2, 345 n. 1, 395 n. 1, 396 n. 2, 403 n. 1, 406 n. 1, 437 n. 1, 442 n. 2.

[18] To appear in the new edition of the Chronicle which I have begun to prepare. Here, the findings of the Louvain students may be referred to once again: J. Verburg, 'Chronique: proesme – livre VI (chapitres i–xxii)', 1968; R. Billiet, 'Chronique: livre VI (chapitres xxiii–xxxix)', 1968; D. Bertrand, 'Chronique: livre VI (chapitres xl–lv)', 1969; G. Baudoux, 'Chronique: livre VI (chapitres lvi–lxxiv)', 1968; M. Demarcin, 'Chronique: livre VI (chapitres lxxv–lxxxvii)', 1969; D. Peltgen, 'Chronique: livre VI, 2e partie (chapitres i–xi)', 1969; C. Janssens, 'Chronique: livre VI, 2e partie (chapitres xii–xxvi)', 1969; C. Ruhl, 'Chronique: livre VI, 2e partie (chapitres xxvii–xliii)', 1971.

[19] Indicated, in a later hand, at the end of P1: 'les chapitres des quatre fueillets que dessus ne sont compris en ce volume'. The list of missing chapters and the folio numbers attached to them indicates that the manuscript in question contained at least 197 folios.

[20] The relevant Louvain mémoires for the Paris manuscripts are A. Fery, 'Chronique: livre VI, 2e partie (chapitres lxxx–xcv)', 1970; Y. Rollin, 'Chronique: livre VI, 2e partie (chapitres xcvi–cx)', 1972; P. Lambrechts, 'Chronique: livre VI, 2e partie (chapitres cxi–cxxii)', 1971; E. Matthijs, 'Chronique: livre VI, 2e partie (chapitres cxxiii–cxxxi)', 1971; J. Aspelagh, 'Chronique: livre VI, 2e partie (chapitres cxxxii–cxxxiii) et 3e partie', 1971; J.-P. Meurée, 'Chronique: livre VII (chapitres xvii–xxix)', 1972; J.-C. Kinon, 'Chronique: livre VII (chapitres xxx–xliv)', 1972.

collection.²¹ A2 and A3, although not originally part of a single volume, belong to the same recension. A large amount of the paper used in each is identical, and the same scribal hands are to be found in both.²² Once again, the evidence converges on the conclusion that the work's impact was not widespread. The chronological and geographical context of that impact may now be determined.

In the absence of colophons or other explicit inscriptions, the dating of manuscripts is an inexact science. We can at least be certain that B – the text, if not the binding – is the earliest of the ten, since it was emended in Chastelain's hand. The evidence of Chastelain's handwriting also enables us to reject the suggestion that the emendations found in A2 were also the chronicler's own work, and therefore the conclusion that this volume had been part of the archetype.²³ In reality, A2 and the remaining eight manuscripts all postdate Chastelain's death, some of them considerably.

The dating of the manuscripts composed of paper folios is suggested by the watermarks encountered throughout the volumes.²⁴ The single watermark in F1, a gothic P surmounted by a floret, corresponds to a Briquet analogy which is dated to 1509.²⁵ It can be suggested with the necessary provisos that the manuscript was made between the mid-1490s and the mid-1520s. The single watermark in A1 situates its fabrication at some point in the last three decades of the fifteenth century. If the Arras manuscript was copied from its Florentine counterpart, the latter should probably be dated earlier rather than later within the margins given above. The watermarks encountered in A2 and F2 suggest similar conclusions: the paper upon which they were written dates to the very end of the fifteenth century or the start of the sixteenth. A3, which was part of the Arras recension of the Chronicle, is clearly from the same period. Armstrong considers L to be earlier than any of these, but the evidence of four distinctive watermarks does not substantiate his conclusion that the volume

---

[21] Béthune's ownership is discussed in app. 1 below. For his librarian's practices see S. Solente, 'Les manuscrits des Béthune à la Bibliothèque nationale', unpubl. report, BN *Département des manuscrits*, Bureau casier 10, 1980 at p. 33.

[22] See app. 1 below.

[23] J. Quicherat, 'Fragments inédits de Georges Chastellain', BEC iv (1842-3), 62-78. Remarks on Chastelain's handwriting, here as earlier, are based upon close comparisons with his letters: ADN B17698.

[24] For watermark evidence I have used C. M. Briquet: *Briquet, Les Filigranes*, ed. A. Stevenson, Amsterdam 1968. Briquet analogies are given in app. 1 below. Although Briquet provides a surprising number of analogous or identical watermarks for those used in the paper of the manuscripts, we should bear in mind that analogies are not entirely safe. In addition, there may be a considerable discrepancy between the date of the paper's fabrication and the date of use. I therefore follow Laidlaw's practice of assigning dates with a margin of error of fifteen years on either side of the analogous or identical watermark: cf. Laidlaw, *Alain Chartier*, 59.

[25] For fuller indications on this case and the others see app. 1 below.

was made during Chastelain's lifetime.[26] The 'late fifteenth century' date ascribed to it by the British Library is more plausible.[27]

The clear pattern emerging from these manuscripts is confirmed by the three that remain to be discussed. One of the two watermarks encountered in Be, an unusual shield motif surmounted by a floret and bearing a superimposed R and a pendant C, is very close to Briquet no. 8992. This type of paper was in use in the Low Countries in the last decade of the fifteenth century and the first of the sixteenth.[28] Although P1 and P2 are composed on parchment and therefore cannot be dated by watermark evidence, the miniature in P2 suggests that the manuscript was made in the early sixteenth century.[29] Comparisons with other miniatures from this period, such as those found in Anne of Brittany's luxurious Book of Hours (1509), substantiate the view.[30] With the exception of B, the manuscripts of the Chronicle thus form a distinctive cluster around the years c. 1490 to c. 1520. Although the total of ten may be relatively unimpressive, the fact that they should all have emerged in such a relatively short period of time is worthy of note. The success of Froissart's Chronicles is attested well over one hundred manuscripts, yet the diffusion of the work took place over more than a century.[31] In its own way, Chastelain's text excited relatively intense, if short-lived, interest.

It is possible to locate where that interest lay.[32] According to Durrieu, the Paris manuscripts were the product of the Bruges or Ghent workshops which, at the turn of the fifteenth century, were producing miniatures of the style and quality evinced in P2.[33] Two other manuscripts bear indications of the scribes who produced them: F1 finishes with the colophon 'Et est finis. Rob. de Lile', and in a margin of A3 we find a reminder of a debt owed to one of the scribes for his work – 'Colin de Veyr. Il reste a paier xix foellet [sic] du petit'.[34] It would not be unreasonable to infer that these manuscripts were produced in the regions of Flanders and Artois, from where, to judge by their names, the scribes hailed.[35] Since A3 was part of a single recension incorporating A2, we can attribute the same origins to the latter.

---

[26] Armstrong, 'Le texte de la Chronique de Chastellain' (repr. in his England, France and Burgundy, 383–8).
[27] 'Aquisitions, January to June 1967', The British Museum Quarterly xxxii (1967–8), 149.
[28] See app. 1 below.
[29] P. Durrieu, La miniature flamande au temps de la cour de Bourgogne, Paris–Brussels 1921, plate lxxiv. Unfortunately the reproduction is inverted.
[30] E. Mâle and E. Pognon (eds), Les Heures d'Anne de Bretagne, Paris 1946. I am grateful to Jean-Pierre Aniel of the Département des manuscrits of the BN for his advice on the miniature.
[31] Jean Froissart, Chroniques, ed. S. Luce, G. Raynaud and A. Mirot, Paris 1869–1975, i, pp. vi–lxxxiii.
[32] B need not be discussed here; it clearly originated close to Chastelain in Valenciennes.
[33] On the dominance of these workshops see La miniature flamande, Brussels 1959, 184.
[34] See, respectively, fos 218, 73.
[35] Neither scribe is known to the Bénédictins du Bouveret, Colophons des manuscrits occidentaux des origines au XVIe siècle, Fribourg 1965–82.

We have no comparable indications for the remaining four manuscripts. The argument must pass through the textual evidence alone. Although Francien – originally from the Ile de France – was linguistically dominant in this period, scribes could still betray their geographical origins by the use in their texts of variant spellings and forms which reflected local peculiarities of speech.[36] The late fifteenth century saw a decline in the influence of Picard *scripta* after a revival under Burgundian court influence, but the forms associated with this region, now northern France and the Belgian Midi, were still employed in sixteenth-century texts.[37] To differing degrees, but without exception, the Chronicle manuscripts evince this continuity. Many of the characterisitic *scripta* of the northern and north-eastern regions of the Francophone area are to be found in these volumes: the frequent substitution of 'ch' for 'c' – and vice versa – when followed by a vowel (*francois* to *franchois*, *prince* to *prinche*, *merci* to *merchy*; or, in the other sense, *chasteau* to *casteau*, *chapitre* to *cappittre*, *chasteté* to *casteté*); the retention of an initial or intervocalic 'w' (*vuydant* to *wydant*, *veuglaire* to *wiglaire*, *eaue* to *eauwe*); or the inversion of vowels and consonants (*pourvu* to *prouveu*, *profit* to *pourfit*, *provision* to *pourvision*).[38] These common dialectal traits, when read in conjunction with the evidence of the miniatures, colophons and marginalia discussed above, all point to the conclusion that the diffusion of Chastelain's Chronicle was limited in space as well as time – possibly to the northern regions of the kingdom of France, but more probably to the regions ruled after the death of Charles the Bold by Mary of Burgundy and her Habsburg successors. Addressed in part to the ruling elites of France, the Chronicle apparently made little or no impact in these circles.

Before this conclusion can be accepted, we should also bear in mind that the work's diffusion might well have left some trace among later historians and antiquarians. Here we fortunately have access to the research of Jules Chifflet († 1676), counsellor, official historian and chancellor of the Order of the Golden Fleece under Philip IV of Spain. He was the son of Jean-Jacques († 1660), whose consuming passion for all things Burgundian he inherited.[39] Chastelain's work was naturally of some importance to Jules, and in 1634 he dutifully published an account of 'les auteurs qui ont faict mention de Georges Chastellain et de ses escrits' in the century and a half since the chronicler's death.[40] Chifflet clearly delved deeply; his list is impressive. It includes men who lived, not in the Habsburg Low Countries, but in the wider kingdom of

---

36 C. T. Gossen, *Französische Skriptastudien*, Vienna 1967. I am grateful to A.-F. Labie of the IRHT for her initial advice in this matter.
37 L.-F. Flûtre, *Le moyen picard d'après les textes littéraires du temps (1560–1660)*, Amiens 1970; R. Dubois, *Le domaine picard*, Arras 1957.
38 Cf. M. K. Pope, *From Latin to modern French*, Manchester 1934, 486–91.
39 Le père Nicéron, *Mémoires pour servir à l'histoire des hommes illustres dans la république des lettres*, Paris 1734, xxv. 255–73; E. Fourquet, *Les hommes célèbres et les personnalités marquantes de Franche-Comté*, Besançon 1929, 116.
40 Chifflet, *Histoire*, 8–16.

France: Guillaume Cretin, historiographer to Louis XII, for example, or Pierre Fabri, a curate and rhetorician from Rouen who lived during the reign of Charles VIII. Upon closer inspection, however, it is clear that Chastelain was known in these circles through his lesser works, not his Chronicle.[41] Even the antiquarians of the Low Countries remembered him first and foremost as a 'grand orateur'. Those who mention his *magnum opus* do so in passing, and almost without exception by paraphrasing the information contained in Pontus Heuterus' *Rerum Burgundicarum* (1583).[42] They had good reason to value the testimony of this canon from Gorinchem († 1602). Like Chifflet, he travelled widely in search of his material. At some stage in his research he unearthed and acquired a Chronicle manuscript containing a fuller version of the text conserved in A2 and F2.[43] The find was choice. For the indefatigable antiquarians of the sixteenth and seventeenth centuries it also seemed that the diffusion of Chastelain's Chronicle had been limited in scope.

Heuterus' reference to a manuscript, now lost, although not unique, is rare. A second, provided by a Habsburg source of 1524, will be examined at a later stage. A third from Jules Chifflet himself may be a reference to a manuscript which is still in existence.[44] The discovery of two seventeenth-century copies of fragments of the Chronicle – one in the municipal library at Besançon, another in the archives of the Ministry of Foreign Affairs in Paris – does little to alter our perceptions of the extent of the work's diffusion.[45] Both are based upon existing manuscripts. One of them is even thought to have been made for Cardinal Richelieu.[46] It is a pleasing (and slightly ironic) thought that Chastelain's Chronicle may have impinged, however briefly, upon the consciousness of one of the most influential men ever to have advised a French monarch. If so, the case was exceptional. As the rest of this section has shown, the initial reception of the Chronicle, in contrast to the reception of the

---

[41] The references Chifflet supplies (Geoffroy Tory, Pierre Fabri, Cretin and the abbot of St Cheron near Chartres) mention Chastelain as an orator or a poet.

[42] On Heuterus' life and work see J. N. Paquot, *Mémoires pour servir à l'histoire littéraire des dix-sept provinces des Pays-Bas*, Louvain 1765–70, i. 557–9, and S. de Wind, *Bibliotheek der Nederlandsche Geschiedschrijvers*, Middelburg 1831, i. 192–8. His writings were published in his *Opera historica omnia*, Louvain 1651. For those who draw on his work, cf. Valerius Andreas, *Bibliotheca Belgica*, Brussels 1973, 262–3; Antonius Sanderus, *Bibliotheca Belgica manuscripta*, Lille 1641–4; *Les bibliothèques françoises de La Croix du Maine et de Du Verdier*, ed. Rigoley de Juvigny, Paris 1772, i. 264; J. F. Foppens, *Bibliotheca Belgica*, Brussels 1739, i. 335–6.

[43] ii, 391–3.

[44] Chifflet, *Histoire*, 16: the reference is to a 'manuscrit original' in his father's possession which is discussed more fully in app. 1 below under the heading 'Later manuscripts'.

[45] BM Besançon, Collection Chifflet MS 202, fos 17–99: 'Fragment de l'histoire du bon duc Philippe de Bourgogne des annees M.CCCC.XXIX: XXX: et XXXI par messire Georges Chastellain son Indiciaire'; Paris, Archives du Ministère des affaires étrangères MSS 24–5: 'Histoire de Charles, dernier duc de Bourgogne, escripte par G. Chastelain, son historiographe'.

[46] See app. 1 below.

opuscula discussed in an earlier chapter, was a limited phenomenon closely focused on the Habsburg Low Countries and situated within the period from roughly 1490 to 1520.

The owners

One benefit of these findings is that they enable us to rule out earlier explanations for the Chronicle's seemingly rapid descent into obscurity. For Buchon, the problem lay with the text's potential audience. Chastelain's great work failed to attract attention because it was no longer relevant to the needs and aspirations of the post-Valois governing classes: 'Quel intérêt pouvait prendre des gouvernans [sic] autrichiens, puis espagnols, à des renommées littéraires étrangères à leur histoire, à leurs habitudes, à leur langue? George Chastellain subit le sort des provinces conquises: son nom périt avec celui de son pays.'[47] The notion that the Low Countries were 'conquises' after 1477 by an elite whose culture was wholly alien to that of the previous ruling dynasty is curious to say the least. Here we may detect the tendency of nineteenth-century historians to project the robust nationalisms of their own day upon a fragile past. This is even more apparent in the observations of Bruno Renard, 'aide de camp' in the recently-formed Belgian army and author of an unambiguously entitled *Histoire politique et militaire de la Belgique*. For this patriot, the disappearance of Chastelain's Chronicle was the result of 'un acte de spoliation historique'.[48] In support of his view he cited Jean Molinet's account of how, in 1505, certain passages of the *Mémoires* of Olivier de La Marche were excised at the request of the Lalaing family.[49] This example of censure is not unique in the sixteenth century.[50] For Renard, Chastelain's Chronicle must have experienced a similar fate. The culprits were perhaps to be found among the Croys, who may have felt that their new-found status as loyal servants of the Habsburg dynasty was compromised by Chastelain's account of their dual loyalties in France and Burgundy.

Between the views of Buchon and Renard there is clearly common ground. Chastelain's account of the Valois past was either a matter of indifference to the ruling elites of the Low Countries after 1477, or a potentially awkward subject best brushed under the carpet. Yet the Chronicle found its primary audience in precisely that place and time and, we might already suspect, among

---

[47] *Oeuvres historiques inédites de Sire Georges Chastellain*, ed. J. A. C. Buchon, Paris 1837, p. x.

[48] B. Renard, 'Nouvelles observations historiques à propos du IVe volume inédit de la Grande Chronique de Georges Chastellain', *Trésor national* iii (1842–3), 190–257 at pp. 199–202.

[49] Molinet, *Chroniques*, ii. 546–8.

[50] Several pages of the 1557 edition of the *Journal* of Jean de Roye († 1495) were suppressed to avoid insulting the descendants of certain families and the memory of Louis XI: Jean de Roye, *Journal*, i, pp. xi–xii.

the very groups mentioned by Buchon and Renard. In some cases this can only be a supposition. We are unable to adduce any documentary evidence to identify the 'haut personnage du début du seizième siècle' for whom P1–P2, the luxury manuscript copied at Bruges or Ghent, was made.[51] In other cases the evidence is much clearer.

The ownership of Be is a case in point. A contemporary inscription on the flyleaf notes that the volume belonged to Engelbert II († 1504), count of Nassau and lord of Diest after 1499.[52] This territorial acquisition was one of several which marked a highly successful career in the service of both the Valois dukes and their dynastic successors. Born in 1451, Engelbert first entered service under Charles the Bold during the Liège campaigns of 1468. In 1473 he replaced his father as lieutenant-general of Brabant and Limbourg and, while still only twenty-two, was elected as a member of the Order of the Golden Fleece. A survivor of the disaster at Nancy (albeit at the cost of an enormous ransom), Engelbert went on to serve and sustain the fragile new regime under Mary and her Habsburg husband, Maximilian I. The loyalty he displayed in 1479 at Guinegate against the French and in 1491 against the rebels of Bruges marked him out in the eyes of an insecure dynasty as a suitable candidate for high office. By 1498 he was president of the *Grand Conseil*. Three years later, Maximilian named him as lieutenant-general of the Low Countries. Between 1501 and his death in 1504, and in Philip the Fair's absence, Engelbert II was the principal representative and agent of the Habsburgs in the Low Countries.

Contrary to Buchon's view, it is clear that Chastelain was of some interest to the governing classes after 1477; outside the Habsburg family itself, indeed, Engelbert II was the single most influential figure within that ruling elite. On a superficial level this interest is to be explained by Engelbert II's evident and – for an aristocrat nurtured at the Burgundian court – entirely conventional love of letters. The impressive personal library of Engelbert 'le Vert', as he jauntily styled himself in his *ex-libris*, included copies of Xenophon, Virgil, Froissart and Monstrelet.[53] His interest in literary matters appears to have qualified him for the job of preparing an inventory of the archducal library in

---

[51] Durrieu, *La miniature flamande*, plate lxxiv; but see app. 1 below.

[52] For the following see P. De Win, 'Engelbert (Engelbrecht) II', in R. De Smedt (ed.), *De Orde van het Gulden Vlies te Mechelen in 1491*, Mechelen 1992, 85–115; W. Ossoba, 'Engelbert II de Nassau', in CTO, 154–5; *Nieuw Nederlandsch Biografisch Woordenboek*, Leiden 1911, xi. 819–21; BNB xv, Brussels 1899, 473–79; C.-A. Serrure, *Notice sur Engelbert II, comte de Nassau*, Ghent 1862. The acquisition of Diest is mentioned in J. Verbeemen, *Inventaris van het Archief der Heren en van het Stadsarchief van Diest*, Brussels 1961, p. xxii. A less complete version of the material that follows appeared as G. P. Small, 'Qui a lu la Chronique de George Chastelain?', PCEEB xxxi (1991), 101–11.

[53] A. S. Korteweg, 'De Bibliotheek van Willem van Oranje: de handschriften', in *Boeken van en rond Willem van Oranje*, The Hague 1984, 9–28 at pp. 21–6; F. Lyna. *Ex-libris de manuscrits conservés au Cabinet des manuscrits de la Bibliothèque royale*, Brussels 1921, 26; H. Knaus, 'Handschriften der Grafen von Nassau-Breda', *Archiv für Geschichte des Buchwesens* iii (1960), 567–80; *La miniature flamande*, 190–1; O. Pächt, *The master of Mary of Burgundy*, London 1948, 67.

1485.⁵⁴ He was a friend to Chastelain's court colleague and admirer, Olivier de La Marche, with whom he served on the regency council created by Maximilian I for his son.⁵⁵ He was also a friend to Chastelain's successor, Jean Molinet, who wrote a poem and an epitaph in his honour, and who used him as an intermediary to present a copy of his Chronicle to Philip the Fair.⁵⁶ Indeed, it is highly likely that Engelbert II was acquainted with Chastelain himself. He was made a member of the Golden Fleece in the same chapter in which Chastelain received his knighthood and the title of *indiciaire* from Charles the Bold at Valenciennes.⁵⁷ Whether Englebert II's interest in Chastelain's work stemmed from this occasion cannot now be proven. Even if it did, there is a more significant point to be made here.

The career of Engelbert II was deeply rooted in the Valois past. This, more than anything, explains the natural interest which he, and others like him, took in Chastelain's Chronicle in the period from c. 1490 to c. 1520. The views of Buchon and Renard are clearly informed by the belief that 1477 constituted an irreversible rupture in the political and historical culture of the former Burgundian dominions. In some respects it did, and in ways which, it might be reasonably argued, were far more significant than the effects of the death of John the Fearless earlier in the century.⁵⁸ The duchy of Burgundy, through which the dukes could claim their status as first peers of the realm, reverted to the king.⁵⁹ This symbolic and practical loss to the dynasty also damaged the personal fortunes of ducal supporters like Olivier de La Marche whose patrimonies lay there. In other respects, however, we should not over-emphasise the significance of Charles the Bold's death. With the notable exception of Burgundy, the territorial integrity of the Valois dominions remained largely intact. Ducal governmental institutions did not undergo dramatic change.⁶⁰ In religious, economic or monetary matters too, 1477 was no turning point.⁶¹ Most importantly of all, many of the families which had supported Philip the Good and Charles the Bold went on to support their successors. Commynes may once more have been working to a personal agenda when he weighed up

---

54 Barrois, *Bibliothèque*, 227.
55 BNB xv. 478.
56 Devaux, *Jean Molinet*, 144–6; Dupire, *Jean Molinet*, 20, 36; Jean Molinet, *Faictz et dictz*, i. 251–4.
57 See chs 2, 3 and the biographies of Englebert above.
58 For a narrative of events see C. A. J. Armstrong, 'The Burgundian Netherlands, 1477–1521', in G. R. Potter (ed.), *The New Cambridge Modern History, I: 1493–1520*, Cambridge 1957, 224–58.
59 J. Faussemagne, *L'apanage ducal de Bourgogne dans ses rapports avec la monarchie française (1363–1477)*, Lyon 1937, 283–7; A. Leguai, 'Dijon et Louis XI', AB xvii (1945), 26–37, 103–15, 145–69, 229–63; xix (1947), 40–1.
60 J. Richard, 'Le destin des institutions bourguignonnes avant et après Charles le Téméraire', CCABN, 291–304.
61 A. G. Jongkees, 'État et église dans les Pays-Bas bourguignons', CCABN, 237–47; H. Dubois, '1477', ibid. 147–74; P. Spufford, 'Dans l'espace bourguignon: 1477, un tournant monétaire?', ibid. 187–204.

the consequences of Charles's defeat at Nancy: 'en ceste derniere bataille, toute la puissance de son pays fut mise a néant a cause de la mort, destruction ou prise de tous les hommes qui voulaient ou pouvaient defendre la position et l'honneur de sa famille'.[62] Engelbert was one of several key men who escaped from the wreckage and who – unlike Chastelain's friend, Philippe Pot, among others – did not abandon Mary and throw in their lot with Louis XI.[63] Continuities such as these were an essential agent in the diffusion of Chastelain's Chronicle within the chronological and geographical parameters defined earlier.

One example will clearly not suffice to make this broad point. A second is provided by the owner of L, identified by a sixteenth-century inscription which indicates that the volume belonged to 'Monseigneur le Comte de Nassau, Marquiz de Cenettes, et est de sa librairie a Breda'. This was Henry III of Nassau-Dillenburg († 1538), son of Jean V, who inherited his father's lordship of Breda in 1516.[64] Henry's career was moulded by the changing interests of the Habsburg dynasty he served, and in particular by Emperor Charles V's acquisition of Spain, the patrimony of his maternal grandmother and grandfather, Ferdinand and Isabella. From 1517 onwards, when Charles's rule in Spain effectively commenced, members of the Flemish elite were able to attain high office under the new administration. Henry III, who had previously held the position of head of the *Conseil des Finances* in Flanders before accompanying the emperor to the Iberian peninsula, was appointed to the newly-formed *Consejo de Hacienda* in 1523.[65] He also contracted a lucrative and prestigious marriage around the same time to Doña Mencía de Mendoza († 1554), daughter of the first marqués del Cenete.[66] Here was a man born six years after the disaster at Nancy, who had spent much of his career between Spain and Flanders and who had known only the benefits of Habsburg, not Valois, rule. Yet he still possessed a copy of a Chronicle in which the memory of that rule was conserved. Indeed, the contents of his library reflect the continuing relevance of a residual historical culture to an individual who lived in a dramatically changed political environment. Henry III possessed such specifically Burgundian texts as the historical romance of *Gillion de Trazegnies*, Guillaume Fillastre's *Histoire de La Toison d'Or*, Jean de Wavrin's *Chronique d'Angleterre* and a manuscript containing works by Jean Molinet.[67] Political events moved on, and it is with these that historians are most often concerned; yet the men involved in these events conserved the legacy of a past which

---

[62] Commynes, *Mémoires*, ii. 156.
[63] The importance of some of these men is discussed in J. Devaux, 'Le rôle politique de Marie de Bourgogne au lendemain de Nancy', MA xcvii (1991), 389–405.
[64] Armstrong, 'Le texte de la *Chronique* de Chastellain', 384–5.
[65] J. H. Elliott, *Imperial Spain 1469–1716*, Harmondsworth 1970, 173. For his career in Spain see R. Carande, *Carlos V y sus banqueros*, Madrid 1949–65, i, 70–2, 76, 86–164.
[66] In addition to Armstong's references on this family see H. Nader, *The Mendoza family in the Spanish Renaissance*, New Brunswick 1979.
[67] Korteweg, 'De Bibliotheek van Willem van Oranje', 26–7.

could inform their understanding of the present. If the historical deposit of Valois Burgundy was still relevant to this Flemish grandee in Habsburg Spain, how much more so the historical deposit of Valois France to his Burgundian court predecessors of the fifteenth century, some of whom were still bound by ties of kinship and service to the French elite.

Henry III was the nephew of Engelbert II.[68] It can be suggested that the transmission of a Valois past to Habsburg posterity may have been channelled through family ties: how better to conserve the memory of one's lineage than by reading contemporary accounts such as Chastelain's? A third example lends weight to this view.

Claude Bouton († 1556) was the owner of the most complete manuscript in existence of the chronicler's lesser works. This is now to be found, along with F1 and F2, in Florence.[69] Bouton's career in Habsburg service was just as remarkable as Henry's.[70] He entered court service in 1488 at the customary age of fourteen or fifteen and later contracted a marriage alliance within the Lannoy family, which had also continued to prosper after the demise of Charles the Bold. His close relations with Margaret of Austria – who, as daughter of Maximilian I and Mary of Burgundy, became governess of the Low Countries from 1507 to 1519 – contributed to his rise.[71] Later, he would serve under Charles V as an ambassador to England, France and Spain, and would be rewarded with the posts of imperial counsellor and chamberlain.

Like Henry III, Bouton had no experience of Burgundian rule, but he did have personal connections to remind him of the interest and importance of the Valois past. His father, Philippe Bouton, was a godson of Philip the Good and a nephew of Philip's long-serving Francophile chancellor, Nicolas Rolin. *Bailli* of Dijon and an *écuyer tranchant* to Philip the Good at the same time as Chastelain, Philippe Bouton had also been something of a poet in his hours of leisure.[72] In one or other of these capacities he may well have associated with the official chronicler; at the very least it is difficult to believe that the two were not known to each other. If these connections were not enough to implant an interest in Chastelain's work in the mind of the Habsburg servant, another personal affiliation was of a nature to do so. Claude Bouton was introduced to court service in 1488 by his cousin, Chastelain's former friend and admirer, Olivier de La Marche. In the Habsburg Low Countries, as in the Valois Burgundian dominions, family ties, patronage bonds and personal friendships ensured the handing down from one generation to the next of

---

[68] W. K. von Isenburg, *Stammtafeln zur Geschichte der europäischen Staaten*, 2nd edn. Marburg 1960, i, no. 115.
[69] See Bliggenstorfer, 'Castellani Georgii'.
[70] See E. Beauvois, *Un agent politique de Charles-Quint*, Paris 1882.
[71] Ibid. pp. clxix–clxx: Margaret used Bouton's motto in her verse, and the two had at least a literary relationship.
[72] J. De la Croix Bouton, 'Un poème à Philippe le Bon sur la Toison d'Or', AB xlii (1970), 5–29; Caron, *La noblesse*, 143, 281–2, 293–4; A. Piaget, *Martin Le Franc, prévôt de Lausanne*, Lausanne 1888, 119.

selected elements of a shared historical culture. The past was never – could never be – entirely left behind.

A fourth example of a known reader of Chastelain's work provides a slightly different reason for the interest shown in the Chronicle. Although the identity of the original owner of the recension incorporating A2 and A3 is unknown, one individual was certainly instrumental in its making and may have intended it for himself. He is identified by a scribal note in A2 indicating that a missing fragment of the text, a description of the virtues and career of Philip the Good which formed part of Chastelain's gallery of princely portraits, was to be inserted by him at a later stage: 'Icy doit ensyeuvre celle [the description] que Messire Charles Le Clerc a es mains, laquelle il mettra ensuivant et viendra après.'[73] The editor passed over the question of this collaborator's identity. 'Messire Charles Le Clerc' was simply one of the scribes.[74] Unless we are dealing with a private joke among bored sixteenth-century copyists, it is highly unlikely that any scribe would have been designated with such deference. It seems much more likely that 'Messire Charles Le Clerc' was the man who bore exactly that title in the correspondence of Maximilian I and Margaret of Austria, and who served both of them in the highest echelons of their financial administration.[75]

The connection is justified on more than one count. As we shall see, Charles Le Clerc († 1533) gave his protection to Chastelain's illegitimate and only-known son, Gonthier. A bibliophile and something of a poet himself, he was an associate of Jean Lemaire de Belges, *indiciaire* and possibly the nephew of Jean Molinet, whose views on the post of official historian he was privy to.[76] In 1508 he offered to have engraved upon the tombs of Chastelain and Molinet a verse encomium 'en cuivre ou en marbre ou en tableau de paincture' in honour of both men. This had been written by his friend and their successor, Lemaire.[77] It was thus perfectly natural that Le Clerc should have sought to possess a copy of Chastelain's major work.

His interest in the Chronicle is particularly noteworthy because, unlike Engelbert II, Henry III or Bouton, he had no prestigious family history to connect him with the Valois past, still less any experience of Valois service himself.[78] Nor would Le Clerc's career suggest a natural predilection for

---

[73] A2, fo. 117v.
[74] ii, 189 n. 1.
[75] *Correspondance de l'Empereur Maximilien I et de Marguerite d'Autriche*, ed. M. Le Glay, Paris 1839, i. 47–8, 135–6; ii. 111–12, 250–1.
[76] 'Proverbe de Messire Charles Le Clerc, Sperans timeo, et rondelet sur le proverbe', in Brussels, BR, MS 7382, fo. 1; P. Jodogne, *Jean Lemaire de Belges, écrivain franco-bourguignon*, Brussels 1972, 103–5, 287; Jean Lemaire de Belges, *Oeuvres*, ed. J. Stecher, Louvain 1882–5, repr. 1969, iv. 321–3.
[77] See Jodogne, *Jean Lemaire de Belges*, 103; Lemaire de Belges, *Oeuvres*, iv. 318–20.
[78] His father was an *échevin* of Arras († 1516). This and – unless otherwise indicated – what follows is to be found in a short biographical note on Le Clerc in M. Jean, *La Chambre des comptes de Lille*, Paris 1992, 318–19.

Chastelain's 'nobles histoires'. He rose from relatively humble origins and appears to have attained his noble status – knight and lord of Bovekerke and Barlaere – on the strength of his valued service. His early career as a *watergrave*, responsible for the collection of river tolls and the inspection of dykes between 1499 and 1512, was relatively inauspicious.[79] By 1507 he had become Maximilian I's *trésorier des guerres* and counsellor, and was sponsored by Margaret of Austria in his attempts to enter the principal organ of the financial administration, the *Chambre des comptes* at Lille.[80] By 1512 he had entered the latter as a *maître extraordinaire* and continued to push for the first vacant post as a *maître ordinaire*. His involvement in several important commissions relating to taxation and ecclesiastical property appears to have enhanced his standing. Four years later this clearly ambitious man was finally appointed to the most influential financial post in the Habsburg administration of the Low Countries, the presidency of the *Chambre des comptes*. As in 1465, Chastelain's work had attracted the attention of the bureaucrats. Thereafter, Le Clerc was sent by Charles V to serve as his 'commissaire et controlleur général de tous les officiers de sa Majesté en son Royaume et païs de Naples', and returned to live out the remainder of his life in the Low Countries.

This was 'a man raised from the dust', a servant who had climbed to the top of the Habsburg administration and who, in the process, had acquired all the trappings of the courtier: wealth, noble status and those aristocratic affectations – such as dabbling in poetry and the company of men of letters – which complemented each.[81] Habsburg court interest in Chastelain's Chronicle, stimulated by the natural inclinations of a few old families, was sufficiently strong to communicate itself to an ambitious and possibly conformist bureaucrat. Of course, these remarks may be unfair on Le Clerc. His apparent affectations could just as easily have been, or have become, natural traits. The process of acculturation which is evident here finds a close parallel in the case of Chastelain himself. An ambitious man of humble origins, he too adapted, chameleon-like, to the natural colour of his surroundings.[82] He associated with court servants who had a stake in Valois Burgundy's real and historical associations with Valois France, just as Le Clerc associated with Habsburg servants for whom the Valois Burgundian past was part of their political and cultural patrimony. In both cases, the outsider had become an insider, a convert

---

[79] Ibid.; Gachard and others, *Inventaire des archives*, ii. 187–8.
[80] J. de Seur, *La Flandre illustrée par l'institution de la Chambre du roi à Lille*, Lille 1713, 80–2; L. P. Gachard, *Rapport sur les archives de Lille*, Brussels 1841, 363, 382; A. Henne, *Histoire du règne de Charles-Quint*, Brussels–Leipzig 1858–60, ii. 126–7; iii. 369; Gachard and others, *Inventaire des archives*, i. 18, 344; A. Walther, *Die burgundischen Zentralbehörden unter Maximilian I und Karl V*, Leipzig 1909, 62, 79–80; D. Hay and J. Law, *Italy in the age of the Renaissance 1380–1530*, London 1989, 99.
[81] The phrase is borrowed from Orderic Vitalis: R. V. Turner, *Men raised from the dust*, Philadelphia 1988, 1.
[82] See chs 1, 2 above.

to the values he detected and assimilated in the political elite through which he sought preferment.

To acculturation and family tradition we might add self-promotion as a further factor which helped to sustain a strong interest in Chastelain's Chronicle into the post-Valois period. This can be seen in the roles of two figures who played a significant part in the ultimate fate of the work: Jean Molinet, the chronicler's successor, and Gonthier, his illegitimate son.

Molinet acceded to the post of *indiciaire* on the strength of his ability to continue his master's work.[83] Chastelain's death was not an endpoint for his Chronicle, at least in the eyes of Charles the Bold or those 'hauts et puissants seigneurs' who intervened on Molinet's behalf at Neuss to get him the job.[84] It would be hard on the *indiciaire* to suggest that he did little or nothing for Chastelain's posthumous reputation. It was at his instigation that the *Chanchons georgines* first entered into print at Valenciennes.[85] His predecessor's work was in his thoughts as he composed his own Chronicle, for he included in it an account of 'les magnificences du duc Charles recoelliez par messire George Chastelain, chevalier, son indiciaire' (i, 170–2). However good his intentions, Molinet seems never to have fulfilled his promise to 'demener à conclusion finale' Chastelain's 'principes, dont les moyens sont de haulte recommendation' (ii, 594). The task of writing his own work was doubtless more gratifying. Those among the elite who remembered Chastelain's qualities had reason to believe that the completion and restoration of his great work were in hand. In reality, the opportunity seems to have been slipping away.

Gonthier Chastelain followed on from Molinet in his contribution to the ferment of interest which surrounded the Chronicle in the post-Valois period. Since Chastelain had died intestate, the issue of his inheritance was resolved by Mary of Burgundy. 'Non sachant que ledit messire George avoit filz', she divided the estate 'a la poursuite d'aucuns'.[86] Gonthier, the offspring of a liaison Chastelain had had as a bachelor with an unknown and unmarried woman, was then 'en minorité d'ans, esgaré de parents et amis'.[87] He received nothing. Shortly before Mary of Burgundy's untimely death in 1482, he sought recompense with the support of at least two well-placed courtiers who had reason to remember his father, or at least his father's work, fondly: the lord of Boussu, Pierre de Hennin, who had been one of the chronicler's personal contacts at Valenciennes; and Louis de Bruges, the bibliophile and knight of the Golden Fleece who had received a highly sympathetic treatment in Chastelain's

---

[83] See ch. 4 above.
[84] Molinet, *Chroniques*, ii. 594–5.
[85] H. Servant, 'Jehan de Liège, premier imprimeur valenciennois', *Valentiana* i (1988), 7–11. A copy survives as Chantilly, Musée Condé, IV E, 89/1.
[86] ADN B2160, no. 71.117.
[87] The facts relating to Gonthier's mother are to be found in the act of legitimisation issued to him in 1530: ibid. B1741, fos 201v–2.

history.[88] With the help of this patronage Gonthier was accorded a daily pension of five *sous* 'pour partie de sa recompense'.

Unfortunately for Gonthier, Mary's promise was not respected after her death. Molinet, who made far more careful provision for his own sons than Chastelain had for his, appears to have taken the young man under his wing.[89] One year after the failed attempt to secure a court pension, Gonthier was backed by Molinet and another canon, Amand Gourdin, in his efforts to become a brewer in Valenciennes.[90] The records of the brewers' guild in the town do not permit us to follow Gonthier's progress in this line of work, although it is of more than passing interest that he remained in contact with the *indiciaire* who was carrying on his father's great undertaking in the same town.[91] It is also interesting to note that the son, like his father before him, started out in life from a relatively humble position: upward social mobility in one generation was not always sustained in the next. Gonthier none the less continued to hope for compensation. Fourteen years after applying to become a brewer, and perhaps with the help of Charles de Rubempré (whose father tearfully recounted his family's misfortunes to the chronicler), Gonthier obtained the grant of a pension once more.[92] Philip the Fair's letter to this effect waxed lyrical on the subject of the achievements of Gonthier's father. Chastelain had served 'en l'estat d'orateur et historiographe, en exerçant lequel il a redigé et mis par escript en si beau et aorné stil et langaige les gestes et avenues de nostre maison de Bourgoingne que d'icelle sera memoire a perpetuité'. In addition to his pension, and on the strength of the sentiments his father's work could still arouse within the Habsburg family and among its servants, Gonthier was also promised a position in Philip the Fair's household.

It seems that once again he received neither, for we hear nothing more of Gonthier in the Habsburg accounts until 1513. In the interval his links to members of the court elite with roots in the Valois past developed still further.

---

[88] Mary acted 'a la poursuite et requeste de feuz les seigneurs de Boussu, de Gruthuuse et autres': ibid. B2160, no. 71.117. Pierre de Hennin was lord of Boussu until his death in 1491: A.-M. Legaré, 'L'héritage de Simon Marmion en Hainaut (1490–1520)', in Nys and Salamagne, *Valenciennes aux XIVe et XVe siècles*, 201–24 at p. 214 and nn. 63–4.

[89] In 1495 and 1502, Molinet's sons bought houses in their father's name which they inherited after his death: Servant, 'Culture, art et société', i. 273; E. Bouton, *Le testament de Jehan Molinet*, Valenciennes 1859.

[90] AMV J2/238, fo. 41: 'Sire Jehan Molinet et Amand Gourdin proposent cambier Gontier Castellain.' The act is undated, but falls between two others from Dec. 1483. Amand Gourdin is mentioned as Molinet's colleague as a canon in J2/239, fo. 15v and J2/240, fo. 8v.

[91] The series of documents for the brewers only begins in 1674: AMV Série HH. In the 'Ordonnance des métiers de Valenciennes promulgeé en 1403', a brief entry notes the sums the brewers were expected to pay to ply their trade: ibid. MS 748, fo. 28. Some published comment is to be found in Abbé Cappliez, *Histoire des métiers de Valenciennes et de leurs saints patrons*, Valenciennes 1893, 123 n. 1.

[92] ADN B2160, no. 71.117. This document also records the earlier grant discussed above. Rubempré was one of the five counsellors of Philip the Fair who were involved in the grant of 1497.

Sometime before 1505 the brewer appears to have followed Molinet into a career in the Church. In that year Gonthier, described as a former cleric of the diocese of Cambrai, became provost of the collegiate church of St Peter in Torhout, a small market town to the south-west of Bruges.[93] Nominations to this post were made by the lord of the nearby castle of Wijnendale, Philip of Cleves († 1528), also lord of Ravenstein.[94] The career of this powerful maverick is too well known to require much emphasis here.[95] Philip was the son of Adolf of Cleves and his Portuguese wife, Beatrice, herself the owner of one of Chastelain's works. The chronicler mourned her early death in 1462.[96] He became lieutenant-general to Maximilian I in 1483 and governed in conjunction with Engelbert II of Nassau in the archduke's absence three years later. Philip's acts of rebellion between 1488 and 1492 during the civil wars that afflicted Flanders did not irrevocably sever his connections with the Habsburg dynasty, but they almost certainly prevented him from attaining the sort of influence in the Low Countries that his landed wealth and talents would normally have guaranteed. With the accession in 1498 of his cousin, Louis XII, to the French throne, his career took a new direction. It would be fascinating to know whether Gonthier's connections with Philip of Cleves extended this far back, raising the possibility that Chastelain's son might have accompanied Cleves to Italy (where he served twice as the French governor of Genoa and acquired his Renaissance tastes) and to the East (where he went on crusade). Gonthier was certainly well-informed of his master's career and his exploits in the Italian peninsula, and wrote a brief summary of them on the flyleaf of the copy he made of Philip's *Briefve instruction de toutes manières de guerroyer*.[97] All we can be sure of is that by the time of Philip's return to the Low Countries, Gonthier was very much part of the Cleves circle. In 1510 we find him inspecting the accounts of the lordship of Wijnendale with Cleves's *maître d'hôtel*, secretary and receiver-general.[98] He is referred to as Philip's *conseiller* in this document, and in another described himself as Cleves's *argentier*.[99] This last reference also mentions Gonthier as a canon at the church of St Peter in

---

[93] A. Lowyck, 'Ledenlijsten van het kapittel van Sint-Pieter te Torhout', in *Archivaris Jos de Smet*, Bruges 1964, 241–58 at p. 247. Many of the documents of the deaconal archive at Torhout were destroyed in the last war, but a record of collations survives as Dekanaal Archief Torhout, no. 13 (formerly no. 106). Several acts in which Gonthier appears as provost are to be found here, including a number written and signed in his own hand (see fos 16–32), and one (fo. 16) mentioning that he came to Torhout from the diocese of Cambrai. Torhout itself was in the diocese of Tournai. I am grateful to the current dean for allowing me to see this document, and to M. Eric Lecomte and Daniel Lievois for arranging for me to see it.
[94] On the powers of the lord of Wijnendale see Lowyck, 'Ledenlijsten', 242.
[95] A. De Fouw, *Philips van Kleef*, Groningen 1937.
[96] See ch. 3 above.
[97] BN, MS fr. 1244, fo. 2r–v. I am grateful to Dr Jacques Paviot for suggesting that a Paris manuscript of this work by Cleves might contain a reference to Gonthier.
[98] Bruges, Rijksarchief, Heerlijkheid Wijnendale, no. 251 (1510–11), fo. 50.
[99] BN, MS fr. 1244, fo. 2.

Leuze, Hainaut. Appointments in this church lay in the gift of the lord of Enghien: in other words, Philip of Cleves, who held the lordship from 1485.[100] Gonthier eventually became *doyen* of Leuze, but seems to have left the chapter not long after his master lost the lordship of Enghien in 1523.[101]

Like his father before him, Gonthier was clearly adept at impressing patrons. We may suspect that it was through one of George Chastelain's former associates that he came to Cleves's attention, either Jean Molinet, who may have had access to Cleves's library and who certainly presented a *Roman de la Rose moralisé* to him, or perhaps even Olivier de La Marche, who was also an acquaintance.[102] For a bibliophile like Cleves, however, Gonthier must have been rather more than simply a useful servant. He was also a living connection with a great name from the past, his own and his family's. There is no evidence that Cleves ever acquired a copy of Chastelain's Chronicle, but the inventory of his books in Ghent in 1528 reveals that he did have some of the lesser works, including the *Temple de Bocace* and the *Douze dames de rhétorique*.[103] The sojourn in Italy gave Cleves an ultramontane outlook, but his library also reflected the continuing vitality of Burgundian historical culture in a Habsburg context, including – among many other things – Fillastre's *Histoire de la Toison d'Or*, the chronicles of Monstrelet, and histories of Brabant and France. It was perhaps fortunate for Gonthier that these strong traditions persisted, for it seems certain that they contributed to his advancement.

Although supported by Cleves, Chastelain's insistent son had still not been compensated for the loss of his father's estate. He was back once more before the council in 1513 to press for a resolution of the matter. Yet again he was promised a daily income and a place at court. This time he at least received the former and was paid until his death, which probably occurred in 1538.[104]

---

[100] E. Ouverleaux, *Notice historique et topographique sur Leuze*, Brussels 1886, 20; J. Nazet, *Les chapitres de chanoines séculiers en Hainaut du début du XIIe au début du XVe siècle*, Brussels 1993, 331–5.
[101] Most of the records of the chapter of Leuze were burned in a fire which destroyed the church in 1741. In an eighteenth-century *Cartulaire de rentes de St Pierre*, however, Gonthier Chastelain is mentioned in connection with a rent on lands in the village of Pipaix: Couvent des Capucins d'Enghien, boîte 25, reg. 31, fo. 453. I am grateful to Dr Ludovic Nys for discovering the reference. Gonthier is mentioned as 'doyen de Leuze' in a document discussed more fully below from Sept. 1424: ADN B2320, fo. 317v–18. The date of this reference is curious because a new deacon, Jean Masure du Portier, appears to have been appointed in 1523: L. A. J. Petit, 'Histoire de la ville de Leuze', *Société des sciences, des arts et des lettres du Hainaut: mémoires et publications* 4th ser. ix (1887), 29–466 at p. 255. It may be that Gonthier continued in the post for a short time before his successor took up his duties, or that the financial officers were referring to older documents in which this title was still attributed to Gonthier.
[102] Dupire, *Jean Molinet*, 90–101.
[103] ADN B3664, fos 69–71, edited in Le Glay and others, *Inventaire sommaire*, viii. 433–4. It has been pointed out that this list is not a complete record of all the books Cleves owned: De Fouw, *Philips van Kleef*, 361ff.
[104] Gonthier's pension is recorded in documents which also mention him as 'doyen de Thouroust'. The last of the payments was made in 1538. Since provision was to be made

Gonthier was also granted the substantial sum of 1,168*l.* as recompense for the previous sixteen years.[105] His success at the third time of asking is perhaps to be explained by the even stronger support he received on this occasion from men who, unlike Cleves, had the full confidence of the Habsburg dynasty. Maximilian I's letter to his 'conseillers, gouverneurs et trésorier général' was accompanied, unusually, by a stern and personally signed note from two highly-placed courtiers.[106] It read as follows: 'accomplissez le contenu ou blanc de ces presentes lettres selon sa forme et teneur et tout ainsi par la maniere que mesdits seigneurs le veullent et mandent estre faict. Escript soubz les seings manuels de deux de nous, le xij^e jour de juillet'. The first signatory was Charles de Croy († 1527), prince of Chimay, captain-general of Hainaut and knight of the Golden Fleece, whose own father, Philippe, had been Chastelain's friend and correspondent.[107] His support for Gonthier's cause confirms beyond any doubt that Chastelain's Chronicle was not suppressed, as Renard suggested, at the request of the Croys. On the contrary, Charles, like Philip of Cleves, Engelbert II or Claude Bouton, belonged to one of those families which had a stake in the Valois Burgundian past and in Chastelain's record of it. To judge from the impressive collection which he sold to Margaret of Austria in 1511, he was also a noted bibliophile with a more general interest in the promotion of letters.[108] The other signatory to the bluntly-worded note had similar interests: Charles Le Clerc, the admirer of Chastelain's work who played a role in the making of the Arras recension of the Chronicle. We may well imagine that the forceful intervention of the recently-appointed *maître extraordinaire de la Chambre des comptes* concentrated the minds of his penny-pinching subordinates in the financial administration.

These highly-placed men may not only have been thinking of Gonthier's welfare when they intervened so decisively in his favour. With the death of Molinet in 1507, the already slim prospect of the recension of Chastelain's work had diminished still further. Gonthier was the last surviving link with a text which continued to generate considerable interest (and which, of course, Le Clerc at some stage sought to possess). Although he had missed out on his father's inheritance – including, we may reasonably suppose, the archetype of

---

for him 'sa vie durant', we may assume that this was the date of his death. For the annual payments see ADN B8085, fo. 131; B8086, fo. 124; B8087. fo. 73v; B8088, fo. 121; B8089, fo. 129; B8090, fo. 102; B8091, fo. 107v; B8092, fo. 100v; B8093, fo. 96v; B8094, fo. 75v; B8095, unfoliated; B8096, fo. 134; B8097, fo. 168; B8098, fo. 159; B8099, fo. 123; B8100, fo. 200v; B8101, fo. 183; B8102, fo. 200v; B8103, fo. 324v. Gonthier left Torhout to take up a post in a church in Arras in 1532: Dekanaal archief Torhout, no. 13, fo. 32. I have been unable to trace him in the last years of his life, or to prove any connection between his presence in the town and the Arras recension of the Chronicle associated with Charles Le Clerc (who, it will be remembered, originally came from Arras). The possibility that Gonthier was involved in the recension cannot be ruled out.

[105] The 1513 grant is recorded in ADN B2232, no. 76.890.
[106] The note was written on the back of the document cited immediately above.
[107] *BNB* iv, Brussels 1873, 564–6; R. Wellens, 'Charles de Croy', in *CTO*, 203–4.
[108] M. Debae, *La librairie de Marguerite d'Autriche*, Brussels 1987, p. xvii.

the great work – there is good reason to believe that Gonthier had managed to recover at least some of his father's Chronicle. This, after all, must have seemed crucial to his personal prosperity.[109] Molinet was the one man most likely to have held on to it, and Gonthier's links with George's successor were, as we have seen, relatively close. Hence, perhaps, Gonthier's ability to offer a recension of his father's work to Margaret of Austria († 1530). Her interest in the Chronicle is the last and perhaps the most significant element in the story of the latter's public.

In 1524, Charles V ordered the payment of 120*l*. to be made to Gonthier Chastelain 'pour le recompenser des paines et despences qu'il avoit eu pour avoit [sic] fait grosser certaines cronicques faictes et composées par feu son pere a louenge des [sic] ses predicesseurs, desquelles il a faict recueil et les devoit baillier es mains de madicte dame [Margaret] pour en faire son plaisir'.[110] We have no proof that Margaret ever received Gonthier's copy, although why he should have been paid this large sum is otherwise difficult to explain. There is no record of any comparable manuscript in the inventory of Margaret's collection or in that of Mary of Hungary to whom her library was left.[111] If the ultimate fate of the volume(s) remains a mystery, one salient point should be emphasised. A full half-century after Chastelain's death, the leading figure in the Habsburg elite in the Low Countries still considered his work to be worthy of a costly – and, we may therefore assume, lavish and/or extensive – 'recueil'. Margaret of Austria's interest is no doubt to be explained in part by the influence of those prominent men around her who were involved, in different ways, in the diffusion of Chastelain's work: she furthered the career of Charles Le Clerc, pursued a literary relationship with Claude Bouton, bought Charles de Croy's library and was in regular contact with Philip of Cleves. Yet there is a parallel and more significant explanation to be considered here.

The 'gouvernans autrichiens' had good reason to be interested in texts which had been written in praise of their predecessors. The mastery of *terra* and *tempus* was a natural aim of lordship. Maximilian I, Margaret of Austria's father, was one such 'timelord' who marshalled the resources of the past in the most ingenious fashion. He took extreme care not only in the matter of his

---

[109] Gonthier may have continued to pursue some of his father's lost inheritance as late as 1530. His letters of legitimisation that year state (perhaps in a formulaic way, it must be admitted) that he would now be in a position 'comme personne ligitisme succed[a]nt tous les biens meubles et inmeubles esquelz de droit et selon la coustume et usaige du pays il debvroit et pourroit succeder sil estoit procree en leal mariaige et comme tel venir aux successions de sesdits pere et mere et autres que luy competent et competeront cy apres': ADN B1741, fos 201v–2.

[110] Ibid. B2320, fos 317v–18.

[111] Debae, *La librairie*, pp. xv–xvi; M. Michelant, 'Inventaire des manuscrits de Marguerite d'Autriche', BCRH (1871), 5–78; L. P. Gachard, 'Notice sur la librairie de la reine Marie de Hongrie, soeur de Charles-Quint, régente des Pays-Bas', ibid. (1845), 224–46. I have also checked the original copies of the inventories of Marie's collection, now AGR, MSS divers, nos 391, 3303.

own prestige and self-image, but in that of his dynasty.[112] Historical traditions derived from the Habsburg family's lands and those it later acquired were deployed in support of his not-inconsiderable pretensions.[113] In particular, Maximilian's patronage and close supervision of the work of Johannes Trithemius († 1516) secured a suitably prestigious Trojan ancestry for the family.[114] He associated himself with the genealogical research of Ladislaus Sunthaim and Jacob Mennel and the latter's efforts, in a rather fantastic piece of historical inquiry completed in 1507, to link the dynasty with the Merovingians.[115] In commissioning a copy of Chastelain's Chronicle, Margaret of Austria followed – albeit more modestly – in her father's footsteps. For the governess of the Low Countries, the Valois Burgundian past must have seemed a natural legitimation and an integral part of the Habsburg present. It is no less relevant to point out that Margaret was also following in the footsteps of her great-grandfather, Philip the Good. For the third duke, as we have seen, the historical identity of his dynasty was enmeshed in that of its French royal counterpart. His library, where the Dionysian tradition was strongly represented in historical matters, reflected this natural continuity, just as the libraries of Engelbert II, Henry III and Philip of Cleves reflected the associations of their families with the Valois Burgundian past. When Philip the Good appointed his own official chronicler, he found it natural to follow the tried and tested model adopted in France, just as his Habsburg successors, including Margaret of Austria, found it natural to maintain the office of *indiciaire* which they had inherited from Charles the Bold. Philip, like Maximilian, had a chronicler who marshalled the resources of the historical culture to which he had access in favour of his master.

Such continuities should not be under-estimated. The historical culture of an elite reflected and informed its political culture. 'L'idée de Bourgogne' has been identified as a dominant strand in the political thought of Emperor Charles V who was brought up at the court of his aunt, Margaret of Austria, and who, late in life, expressed a strong wish to be buried 'avecq les corps de feurent [ses] prédecesseurs Philippe dict le Hardy, Jean son filz et Philippe dict le Bon, en leurs vivans ducs dudict Bourgongne'.[116] Decades earlier, Philip the Good had attached great importance to his status as first peer of the French realm and had continued, long after 1419, to covet some role in its affairs.

---

[112] On his image see G. Benecke, *Maximilian I 1459–1519*, London 1982, 7–30.
[113] A. Wandruszka, *The house of Habsburg*, London 1964, 7, 9, 13, 14.
[114] K. Arnold, *Johannes Trithemius (1462–1516)*, Würzburg 1971, 167–79.
[115] G. Althoff, 'Studien zur habsburgischen Merowingersage', MIOG lxxxvii (1979), 71–100; A. Lhotsky, *Österreichische Historiographie*, Munich 1962, 61–3. Cf. W. Keesman, 'De Bourgondische invloed op de genealogische constructies van Maximilian van Oostenrijk', *Millennium* viii (1994), 162–72.
[116] Cited in P. Bonenfant, 'L'origine des surnoms de Philippe le Bon', AB xvi (1944), 100–3 at p. 103; cf. also H. Hauser, *Le traité de Madrid et la cession de Bourgogne à Charles-Quint*, Paris 1912. Philip was held up as a model for Charles V to follow: S. Anglo, *La tryumphante entrée de Charles, prince des Espagnes en Bruges, 1515*, Amsterdam–New York 1973, 14–16.

George Chastelain's Chronicle reflected this. By a circular process we have turned from the Habsburg audience of the Chronicle to the realities of the political development of Valois Burgundy which originally informed the work. Our knowledge of the former can be used to confirm the understanding of the latter which has been presented throughout this study.

Reception

A list of readers and a discussion of their interests only scratches at the surface of a deeper and often more obscure problem, namely the text's reception. Rhetoricians and courtiers thought highly of Chastelain's work, but they never say why, let alone how they used it or what its real influence might have been. That is not to say that answers to these important questions are beyond our reach. Reader reception might be classified as imitative or interpretive; in other words, attitudes to the work can be traced through its influence upon later texts, while interpretations of it might be pursued through a number of different sources. Among the latter, significant marginalia, textual glosses or revealing items of correspondence are conspicuous by their absence. Happily, the manuscripts are themselves a precious indicator of how the Chronicle was received by its Habsburg audience.

Although Molinet's work might be considered an imitation of Chastelain's, the Chronicle had a less obvious but perhaps more important influence on later historiography. It has been argued that in writing his *Mémoires* at the end of the fifteenth century, Commynes was the inventor of a new historiographical genre.[117] Some might argue that the emergence of the genre was also connected to contemporary interest in Caesar's *Commentaries*, or that Commynes was hardly the first layman to set down his reminiscences in historiographical form.[118] None the less, there is little doubt that memoirs-writing passed through a formative phase in Commynes's work and that the term gained in currency and definition as a result of his success in the sixteenth century and beyond.[119] Whether he was the original impetus behind the emergence of the genre is another matter.

---

[117] J. Dufournet, 'Commynes et l'inventiion d'un nouveau genre historique', MSHCW xviii (1988), 57–72, repr. in D. Buschinger (ed.), *Chroniques nationales et chroniques universelles*, Göppingen 1990, 59–77.

[118] R. Bossuat, 'Traductions françaises des *Commentaires* de César à la fin du XVe siècle', *Bibliothèque d'humanisme et renaissance* iii (1943), 253–411; J. Monfrin, 'La connaissance de l'antiquité et le problème de l'humanisme en langue vulgaire dans la France du XVe siècle', in M. G. Verbeke and I. J. Ijsewijn (eds), *The late Middle Ages and the dawn of humanism outside Italy*, Louvain–The Hague 1972, 131–70. It should be noted that this interest in Caesar's *Commentaries* was particularly keen at the Burgundian court.

[119] Commynes, along with Monstrelet and Froissart, was highly popular in the sixteenth century: H.-J. Martin, 'What Parisians read in the sixteenth century', in W. L. Gundersheimer, *French humanism 1470–1600*, London 1969, 131–45 at pp. 137–8; J. Dufournet, 'Les premiers lecteurs de Commynes, ou les *Mémoires* au XVIe siècle', MSHCW xiv (1984),

As Dufournet acknowledges, the writing of memoirs was a Burgundian court phenomenon which Commynes simply refined rather more than his predecessors. But he did have predecessors – La Marche, Lefèvre and Haynin in particular. Chastelain exercised a considerable influence over these men.[120] The first two claimed to have begun their *Mémoires* with the sole intention of providing information for the official chronicler.[121] Haynin did not say so explicitly, but it is interesting that the only items he deemed worthy of inclusion in his holograph were works by Chastelain.[122] These memorialists were naturally not quite as self-effacing as they make out. They were conscious of the value of their testimony in its own right, and may well have sought to improve, as much as assist, the official record of events. Commynes may even have sought to refute it, as later memorialists certainly did.[123] In his opinion, 'les croniqueurs n'escrivent communement que les choses qui sont a la louenge de ceulx de qui ilz parlent et laissent plusieurs choses ou ne les sçavent pas aucunes fois a la verité'.[124] This may be read as a barely disguised jab at Chastelain and his like.[125] Whatever the precise motivations of these early Burgundian memorialists, it is clear (by their own admission) that the existence of a strong tradition of official history was a common denominator in each case. The new genre emerged in Chastelain's shadow. Despite its limited success, his Chronicle thus spawned an historiographical progeny – even if that progeny was not in its own image.

Interpretive responses to the work are more difficult to fathom, but we can

---

51–94. He impressed the expert as well as the general reader: Jean Bodin, *Method for the easy comprehension of history*, ed. and trans. B. Reynolds, New York 1945, 374.

[120] To whom we might add Jean de Dadizeele, *Mémoires*, ed. J. C. Kervyn de Lettenhove, Bruges 1850. These predecessors were discussed in an insightful but as yet unpublished paper by D. A. L. Morgan, 'Burgundian *Mémoires*, their cultural milieu and political context', communication to the annual conference of the *Centre européen d'études bourguignonnes*, Middelburg 1990. Morgan provided the following résumé: 'The genre of "Mémoires", as it developed in and after the sixteenth century, emerged c. 1490 with Philippe de Commynes and La Marche. Politically they (together with contemporaries such as Haynin and Dadizeele) wrote in the context of, and with reference to, the crisis of the Burgundian state which had developed over the previous generation. Culturally, as writers as well as soldier-politicians, they were products of the household service of the "maison de Bourgogne" – service which entailed the writing of "mémoires"/memoranda as part of the process of the conduct of affairs and the formulation of policy. These memorialists' (selective) recording of their experiences may be seen as an extension and continuation, under the stimulus of political crisis, of the forms of political culture fostered by the Burgundian court.' What follows is a supplementary – not opposed – reading of the problem.

[121] La Marche, *Mémoires*, i. 185; Lefèvre, *Chronique*, i. 2.

[122] Van den Gheyn, 'Le manuscrit original'.

[123] See the seventeenth-century examples cited in M. Fumaroli, 'Les mémoires du XVIIe siècle au carrefour des genres en prose', *XVIIe siècle* xciv–v (1971), 7–37.

[124] Commynes, *Mémoires*, ii. 172–3.

[125] It has even been suggested that 'il se pourrait bien que Commynes ait eu connaissance d'une partie de l'oeuvre de son illustre devancier, et qu'il ait écrit la sienne d'après, et le plus souvent contre celle-là': Dufournet, *La destruction des mythes*, 87.

at least work towards them by examining the historical culture of the milieu in which the work was received. Although there were natural continuities in the post-Valois world, it is inevitable that there should also have been change. Later generations partook in the historical culture of their forefathers, but they did so in an altered political environment. The same was true, although no doubt to a lesser extent, of Valois Burgundy. Two related aspects of this divergence in the Habsburg period may be discussed here: the emergence of a more complex dynastic sense of the past on the one hand, and the increasing – although never complete – detachment of that sense of the past from its previously dominant Valois roots on the other. We may follow these linked developments through works written by, or attributed to, three Habsburg servants: Philippe Bartin, said to have been an *écuyer* in the service of Maximilian I; Olivier de La Marche, Maximilian's *premier maître d'hôtel* and the tutor of his son, Philip the Fair; and last but not least, Jean Molinet, Chastelain's successor and the leading creative figure in the historical culture of the Habsburg court in the Low Countries.

The ultimate fate of the research of Hugues de Tolins into the religious foundations and martyrs of the ancient kingdom of Burgundy is unknown.[126] If the work made little impact on the historical culture of the Valois Burgundian court, it does appear to have enjoyed some influence under the Habsburgs, and in particular upon a brief but significant *Chronique des roys, ducz et contes de Bourgogne depuis l'an quatorze apres la Ressurection*.[127] This curious work, described in some of the manuscripts as the abridgement of a larger text, is attributed to Philippe Bartin, although in reality the author cannot be identified with certainty. The most that can be said at present is that the text was first written during the reign of Charles the Bold and was frequently copied and revised thereafter.[128] The interest of the work lies first and foremost in its attempt to present an unbroken line of descent from the first kings of Burgundy down to the present time. This took considerable ingenuity on the author's part, and he only achieved his aim by deploying the most tenuous of arguments and genealogical connections. He sought to create the image of a prestigious dynasty by stressing the glorious Christian past of the kings of Burgundy and the symbols of power which derived from it, such as the cross of St Andrew,

---

[126] See ch. 3 above.
[127] The work, which I intend to deal with in a future publication, survives in at least five manuscripts: London, BL, MS Yates Thompson 32; Paris, BN, MSS fr. 4907, fos 109–11; 2200, fos 16–23; Vienna, Österreichische Nationalbibliothek HS 2579, fos 60–5; BM Metz, MS 855, fos 2–4v. There are also three early sixteenth-century editions: J. C. Brunet, *Manuel du libraire et de l'amateur des livres*, Paris 1860–5, i. 1875–6; G. Brunet, *La France littéraire au XVe siècle*, Paris 1865, 47. It is attributed to Philippe Bartin in Smith, 'The artistic patronage', app. IV; M. S. Hardy, 'Olivier de La Marche and chivalry and monarchy in the fifteenth century', unpubl. M.Phil. diss. London 1970, 126; Doutrepont, *Littérature*, 453–4. I am grateful to Alistair Millar for his comments on this subject.
[128] For an archducal copy in 1487, see Barrois, *Bibliothèque*, no. 2241. Different manuscript endings include the death of Charles the Bold or of his daughter and Charles V's birth. For a clear indication of its origins, however, see BN, MS fr. 4907, fo. 111.

first borne by the second Burgundian king, Stephen, as a sign of his allegiance to the faith.[129] By ending with a reference to Philip the Fair, the author sought to create the impression that the historical process had culminated naturally in Habsburg rule. Those aspects of Burgundian history which might detract from the image of a chosen dynasty ruling over a chosen land are studiously neglected. The French royal origins of the Valois Burgundian family are entirely omitted. Indeed, the French monarchy is portrayed throughout the work as a negative force in the history of Burgundy, in the wars fought by King Thierry in the seventh century and his resulting conquest of 'toute la terre entre Saine et Oize', or in the seventeen battles won by Girart de Roussillon and his recovery of the Burgundian kingdom 'que les roix de France avoient usurpé'. We also learn that the Capetian dukes of Burgundy had held their duchy 'en toute souveraineté'.[130] This, of course, stands in sharp contrast to the understanding of the Burgundian past which is presented in Chastelain's work (a contrast which may well stem from a sense of resentment at the recent French annexation of the duchy). Important changes, evinced in less concentrated form in some earlier historical romances, were now taking definite shape within the consciousness of the ruling elite.

The introduction to La Marche's *Mémoires*, once dismissed as a tendentious piece of historical fiction, provides further evidence for these developments.[131] The text was probably set down in the early 1490s and is addressed to Philip the Fair, La Marche's charge.[132] The history lesson takes the form of a more detailed and eclectic genealogical and heraldic account of Philip's family origins than that presented in the text discussed above. It begins not with a history of the French royal past as did Chastelain's, but with the history of the House of Austria, 'et comment Austrice fut royaulme'. Indeed, the conventional legendary version of the origins of the French monarchy is here subsumed within that of Philip the Fair's ancient predecessors, enabling La Marche proudly to inform his pupil that 'vous avez ceste honneur que de vostre nom d'Austrice sont yssus les premiers Roys de France'. After a brief digression on Philip's connections to the Portuguese crown through his great-grandmother, La Marche then moves on to deal with the history of Burgundy. This he does in much the same way as the *Chronique des roys*, but with a longer discussion of the original inhabitants of that region, the Allobrogians, and how they were later named the Burgundians at the instigation of their Roman conquerors. The history of a people is thus conflated with the history of a land, leading to a teleological perception of Burgundy's autonomous past. Only at this point is the history of the French monarchy deemed relevant to La Marche's purpose.

---

[129] 'Et fut celuy qui fist porter la croix saint andrieu ... et la prist et la voult porter pour son enseigne. Et ordonna estre portee a tous ceulx quy seroient chrestien en son royaume': BL, MS Yates Thompson 32, fo. 2v.
[130] Ibid. fos 5v–6, 7v–8, 8v, 10, 12.
[131] *Mémoires*, i. 7–181.
[132] The date is suggested by the fact that in his prologue La Marche states that he was sixty-six years old at the time of writing: ibid. i. 9.

The rise and demise of the Capetian dynasty is recounted in a neutral fashion, followed by the accession of the Valois dynasty 'dont vous [Philip the Fair] est yssu'. La Marche does not adopt the dismissive attitude towards the French crown which is evinced in the *Chronique des roys*. He tells Philip the Fair that

> je prie à Dieu que ceulx qui ont l'administracion de ce noble et très crestien royaulme de France se conduisent sy bien et si raisonnablement envers vous et voz pays, que vous ayez cause de demourer *bon et enthier François*, honnourant ce que devez honnourer, aymant ce que devez aimer, et que vous puissiez garder foi, hommaige et feaulté selon les bonnes et anciennes coustumes, et que chacun puist avoir son droit et le sien.[133]

This is the advice of a man brought up at the Valois Burgundian court, sensitive to the continuing concerns of the Habsburgs in the matter of Flanders and perhaps even mindful of the consuming preoccupations of his long-dead friend, George Chastelain. But where Chastelain made of these issues the central pillar of his work, La Marche does no more than raise them in passing. His prologue continues to build thereafter upon his main theme, the autonomous dynastic history of Philip the Fair, a ruler descended less from the French line than from four glorious dukes of Burgundy and their predecessors as counts of Flanders.[134] The change of dynasty had forced a notable change of perspective upon this Habsburg servant's sense of the past.

La Marche had strong personal reasons to think badly of the French monarchy: Louis XI's warrant for his arrest after the affair of the bastard of Rubempré, for example, or the loss in 1477 of his family lands in the duchy of Burgundy. Jean Molinet was surely in a better position to grasp and conserve his master's understanding of the dynastic history of the ruling elite.[135] The fact that he should have broken so clearly with Chastelain's thinking on this issue is therefore highly revealing of the changes which the accession of the new dynasty had effected.

This is best seen in his account of the 'confederation matrimoniale' between Mary of Burgundy and Maximilian.[136] Since the beginning of civilisation all men had owed 'fidelité, devotion et service' to the emperor 'comme à Dieu présent et corporel' (i, 224). Maximilian was the only man alive who could legitimately say that he was 'filz de empereur et de roy' (i, 228). All nations – England, Lombardy, France – had originated in 'le très saint empire d'Alemaingne' (i, 229). In the course of elaborating this theme of Habsburg supremacy, Molinet attacked the historical pretensions of the French who, like 'les mauvais angels', had been expelled and declared 'exemps de la coronne imperiale' (i, 225). If 'la maison de France' declared itself 'très cristienne', it

---

[133] Ibid. i. 100, italics mine.
[134] Ibid. i. 70–106, 121–47.
[135] It is also interesting to note that Molinet had studied in France for several years: Devaux, *Jean Molinet*, 120–2; Dupire, *Jean Molinet*, 8.
[136] Molinet, *Chroniques*, i. 224–35.

was only able to do so because Clotild, daughter of the king of Burgundy, had converted her French royal husband to the true faith (i, 231). In fact, the only 'exquise nobilité en son [France's] jardin' was Mary of Burgundy. Mary's Valois roots are grudgingly admitted in this remark, but Molinet does not allow his audience to leave with the impression that she was the descendant of French royal traditions. Her lineage went back instead to 'Bavo, roy de Frige... cousin germain du roy Priam', founder of 'le royaume de Belges' and ancestor of the counts of Hainaut, of whom Mary was the 'vraye heritière' (i, 229–31). The accuracy of this fantastic view of her dynastic past is irrelevant.[137] The point here was to establish an ancestry which made her a suitable bride for Maximilian. In the process, and not coincidentally, she was subtracted from her Valois background.

The French past of the Burgundian line was no longer apposite in the writing (or re-writing) of dynastic history, at least not in the work of men who, as we have seen, were by no means unimportant figures in the Habsburg elite. Alongside continuity there had been change – and the latter was more apparent now than it had ever been, as some believe it was, under Philip the Good. The *Chronique des roys* was no rarity; La Marche's *Mémoires* and Molinet's *Chronique* survive in varying forms in ten and twenty-seven manuscripts respectively. This type of success confirms the view that the historical culture which embraced Chastelain's Chronicle was recognisably different from its predecessor. On one level, it would seem, Huizinga was instinctively right in his assessment of Burgundian mentalities. On another, the observation has an important bearing upon the interpretive reception accorded to the Chronicle in the period from c. 1490 to c. 1520.

Contemporary reading habits should be borne in mind if we are to take the point any further. It may be argued that public interest in the Chronicle was diminished by the fact that it was incomplete, but then textual integrity is not always important to readers. Alongside the sequential and global reading of a work there existed discontinuous and selective readings, just as today we might use a book only partially – for pleasure, for edification or for gathering information.[138] Such reading habits are naturally reflected in the manuscripts of the period. Medieval audiences did not turn their noses up at incomplete codices or composite manuscripts consisting of excerpts.[139] Nine manuscripts of Molinet's Chronicle contain only part of his text.[140] They may originally have belonged to larger recensions, but the manuscript survival of Guillaume

---

[137] Many of Molinet's ideas can be traced back to the speculative writings of Jacques de Guise and others in the fourteenth century, and are related to Hainaut's nominal status as an imperial territory: see, for example, G. Doutrepont, *Jean Lemaire de Belges et la renaissance*, Brussels 1934, 34ff.

[138] Cf. P.-Y. Badel, *Le roman de la rose*, Geneva 1980, 65–6.

[139] An entire section of Philip the Good's library was given over to 'livres non parfaits': Barrois, *Bibliothèque*, nos 1595–612.

[140] *Chroniques*, iii. 102–56.

Fillastre's *Histoire de la Toison d'Or* confirms the readiness of some readers to acquire only part of an unfinished work.¹⁴¹

So ingrained were these reading habits that sensible authors and compilers took account of them. Aristocratic readers – 'hommes d'action' like Engelbert II and Charles Le Clerc or 'femmes d'action' like Margaret of Austria – were busy people who found time for history when they could: 'ils écoutent volontiers l'histoire, mais ils la veulent brève'.¹⁴² Big historical works like the chronicles of St Denis were excellent for reference purposes and for providing a coherent and sustained account of the past. They were also expensive to copy and sometimes indigestible as reading matter. Hence the greater popularity of historical anthologies based on Dionysian texts. Some authors provided edited versions of their work, perhaps in the hope of pre-empting the inevitable abridgements which others, less in tune with their intentions, might have been tempted to produce.¹⁴³

Contemporary reading habits and a changing historical culture were almost certainly decisive factors in the ultimate fate of the Chronicle. Chastelain's massive original, with its unbound quires, emended prose and various lacunae, was enough to make any scribe blanch. The original order of the archetype may have become confused and, to judge from the state of B, some of its contents lost or damaged as a result of its travels between the unknown beneficiaries of Chastelain's estate, Jean Molinet and the chronicler's son, Gonthier. The copying of extracts from the archetype would have appeared a more sensible and attractive proposition than any attempt to transcribe the original in its entirety. The survival of the text in a series of related fragments suggests that this is precisely what happened.

Margaret of Austria's commission in 1524 is sometimes taken as proof that a final copy of the Chronicle had once been made. In reality, she asked for no more than a 'recueil'. The term itself suggests that judgement was to be exercised in the transcription of the Chronicle. This is evinced elsewhere in the copying of the surviving manuscripts. The scribes of A1 abridged the text as we have seen, and substantive alterations were made to Chastelain's original narrative in A3. Apart from the clear desire to render a massive and unwieldy text more manageable, the interpretive criteria employed in these early readings of the Chronicle are sometimes difficult to fathom. In places there appears to have been no rhyme or reason to the process of excerption – we do not know

---

¹⁴¹ Fillastre only produced three of his intended six books. The work was none the less successful (eighteen surviving manuscripts and three sixteenth-century editions). Louis de Bruges contented himself with only the first two books of the history: A. Bayot, 'Observations sur les manuscrits de l'*Histoire de la Toison d'Or* de Guillaume Fillastre', *Revue des bibliothèques et archives de Belgique* (1907), 425–38.
¹⁴² Guenée, *Histoire et culture historique*, 280.
¹⁴³ Matthew Paris and Thomas Walsingham are two obvious examples. Guenée suggests that abridged versions of French royal chronicles were inspired by the need to cater for visitors who came to St Denis to visit the royal tombs: Guenée, 'Les Grandes chroniques de France', 196.

the particular interest which led to the transcription of Chastelain's text for 1470, for example. Elsewhere, it is possible to detect some logic in the choice of material. In several cases the beginnings of individual books provided a convenient *terminus a quo* for the scribal process.[144] One exception to this logic is to be found in the subject matter which was chosen as the starting point for the second fragment. Chastelain clearly indicates that the beginning of his second book was concerned with the marriage of Philip the Good to Isabella of Portugal. A2 and F2 pass over this event and begin instead with the founding of the Order of the Golden Fleece. This matter was close to the heart of those senior Habsburg servants who commissioned copies of Chastelain's Chronicle – several of them (although not Philip of Cleves) even belonged to the Order. The process of excerption may thus have been dictated not only by expediency, but by the interests of Chastelain's public. What seemed important to them did not necessarily coincide with what had interested the chronicler in the 1460s.

The collective memory took a selective view of the past. The Valois origins and connections of the Burgundian dukes were now of little relevance in the changed dynastic circumstances of the later fifteenth and early sixteenth centuries. Blood links, historic ties and political interests in France had been broken.[145] The chronicler's aim to write 'pour gloire et exaltation de ce très-chrestien royaume' (i, 11) would have rung a discordant note for Habsburg readers who had no great interest in a past they did not wish to claim for their own purposes. Chastelain's missing account for the years from 1431 to 1453 contained a good deal of French royal history (albeit, no doubt, from a Burgundian perspective). Why should a Habsburg audience have gone to the expense of transcribing (or the bother of reading) such material? Similarly, the reign of Charles the Bold, so ill-represented in the surviving fragments of the Chronicle, was a traumatic period which was remembered, at best, with a certain ambivalence. Molinet had worked with Chastelain and presumably knew how much his master had had to say on Charles. It is revealing that he was only interested in some of his predecessor's comments.[146]

By contrast, the reign of Philip the Good appeared in retrospect as a golden age.[147] For Commynes, famously, 'ses terres se povoient myeulx dire terres de

---

[144] As witnessed by the inclusion of the opening narratives for the first, fourth, sixth and seventh books in the surviving fragments.

[145] Interestingly, as we have seen, Philip of Cleves was an exception to this. We may legitimately wonder whether there is any connection between Cleves, his royal cousin Louis XII, his servant Gonthier Chastelain and the copy of an unidentified and curious 'Cronicques du duc Philippe' which was in Louis XII's library. For this work see P. Arnauldet, 'Catalogue de la bibliothèque du château de Blois en 1518', *Le bibliographe moderne* vi (1902), 145–74, 305–37 at p. 305 (no. 47). It is possible, therefore, that a copy of Chastelain's great work did reach a French royal audience, but we can say no more than that.

[146] Cf. J. Devaux, 'La fin du Téméraire, ou la mémoire d'un prince ternie par l'un des siens', MA xcv (1989), 105–28.

[147] J. Huizinga, 'La physionomie morale de Philippe le Bon', AB iv (1932), 101–39 at p.

promission que nulles autres seigneuries qui fussent sur la terre'.[148] Philip, described variously in his lifetime as 'l'Asseuré', 'le Vaillant' or even 'l'Auguste', was known after his death, quite simply, as 'le Bon'.[149] Mary of Burgundy and Maximilian I thought it natural to name their son, not after the boy's grandfather, but after his great-grandfather. For Philip the Fair, for those who succeeded him and for those who served the Habsburg dynasty, here was a man worth reading about. Where better to read of him than in the work of his official chronicler and greatest fan, George Chastelain? It seems no accident that most of the surviving fragments of Chastelain's history of the noble kingdom of France and its dependencies are concerned, first and foremost, with Philip the Good. The Chronicle, the product of one politico-historical culture, became both the victim and the accomplice of another.

125; Smith, 'The artistic patronage', app. iii ('The Golden Age: Burgundian mythology in the sixteenth century').
[148] Commynes, Mémoires, i. 13.
[149] H. Nélis, 'Origine de l'appellation: Philippe le "Bon" ', RBPH xii (1933), 145–54; Bonefant, 'L'origine', 101.

Conclusion

This study has situated Chastelain's Chronicle within the political and historical culture of the court of Burgundy as a means of understanding the representation of the historical process which it sought to impart. We have examined Chastelain's social origins and career, the nature of his appointment and the sources, redaction, archetype and audience – perceived and real – of his Chronicle. The degree of detail has been deliberate. These small facts, layered to form 'thick description', are vital if Chastelain is to be seen on his own terms rather than in relation to paradigms of historical understanding which were not of his making.[1] This inevitably leads us to reflect upon those paradigms themselves.

Huizinga's article did not dissuade Pirenne from his belief that a Burgundian state had existed. If we move away from the models of institutional history towards those advanced more recently, then it is indeed clear that the process of state formation was under way. The regime of the Three Members in Chastelain's home town of Ghent, the largest city of the Burgundian dominions, provided a framework for the communication and even the enforcement of the will of central authority. Within that regime the dukes found collaborators among the shippers, the group to which Chastelain's family belonged, and among urban elites, from which men like Jan van Culsbrouc, Chastelain's great-uncle, emerged to serve the duke. Chastelain too found his way to the centre. He came even closer to it than his great-uncle and business partner, and apparently without his help – although we have seen that other crisscrossing networks, entangled with the roots laid down in urban life by the Burgundian elite and incorporating members of his extended family, may well explain how the aspirant clambered to the top. Along the way Chastelain attended an institution which had its own role to play in the process of state formation. The University of Louvain employed and produced men who acquired a stake in Valois rule. Along the way too, Chastelain was himself an agent in that process. Although most of his work was aimed at a limited court audience at home and further afield, some of it was performed in the presence of townsmen in the Low Countries who were exposed to his official vision of Burgundian glory. A Burgundian state was taking shape – not quite in the terms of the debate which separated Huizinga and Pirenne, but certainly in the ways suggested by Prevenier, Blockmans, Boone and others. The mechanisms which help explain Chastelain's transition from urban background to courtly foreground are very often those which explain the durability of the ducal regime.

[1] Geertz, *Interpretation of cultures*, 3–30.

But clearly this was no *nation* state, nor the beginnings of one. Pirenne's view of the Low Countries in the fifteenth century may be likened to Robert Fawtier's depiction of Capetian France.[2] The grandeur of both lies in the fact that they were the products of momentous times. But the projection of modern sentiments upon the past, however laudable they might be in themselves, is always perilous. Huizinga detected as much and sought to show that the severance of Burgundy from France – which, as the work of Richard Vaughan shows, is still a theme in more recent historiography – did not occur in the ways Pirenne suggested. If Huizinga did not convince his Belgian friend, then this was perhaps because his thesis was not firmly rooted in empirical proof. Ideas and facts were not reconciled. In some ways this study may have filled out Huizinga's argument. Chastelain is an excellent source for commenting upon mentalities within the Burgundian elite. He came to it from a lowly background and acculturated, by necessity, to the values he perceived there. Few were better placed than he to grasp and understand the motivations and concerns of the men who mattered most in the Burgundian polity. His diplomatic experience, his contacts at court, the correspondence he received and his readings from the ducal library all contributed to an understanding of the political interests and historical culture of his patron, court superiors and peers. This understanding shaped his work.

Having found Huizinga's path by another route, however, this study must part from his interpretation of the text. Huizinga encourages us to abandon hindsight in attempting to understand the phenomenon of Valois Burgundy, and yet he also considers Chastelain to have been naive: essentially, it would seem, because the chronicler failed to see where the events of his day were leading. For Huizinga, as for many of Chastelain's later commentators, the Chronicle was reactive rather than proactive; a personal testimony more than an official account. Yet it clearly *was* an official account: without the duke's patronage it would not have existed. When viewed from this perspective and in the knowledge of the historical culture to which it was addressed, we might read the work in another way. Hence the view that the Chronicle, despite its fragmentary survival, drew upon the bank of consciousness and tradition to articulate a layered, structured response to the political and historical realities of its time.

If the conclusion is phrased cautiously, this is because our reading of the Chronicle, although grounded in contextual circumstance, is no less conjectural than any which has preceded it. Those who read the work in the later fifteenth and early sixteenth centuries had their own perspectives which, in

---

[2] Cf. Pirenne's introduction to the revised third edition of his *Histoire de Belgique*, ii, p. iv, where he writes of the previous edition of 1917 and, wise from the experience of his 'captivité en Allemagne', his attempts to 'dépister la censure allemande'; and Fawtier's famous account of how, in 1941, 'in a time of national tragedy I found a source of strength, for myself and my audience, in the study of the beginnings of the French nation and of the actions of its first leaders': *The Capetian kings of France*, trans. L. Butler and R. J. Adam, London 1960, p. vii.

turn, affected quite dramatically how we read it today. Without them Chastelain may well have sunk from sight, but because of them we do not see the Chronicle as the author himself intended it. The gap between their reading and Chastelain's writing is significant in itself. It suggests that the changes detected by some in the political and historical culture of the Burgundian court under Philip the Good did not enter the mainstream until the time of his great-grandson. But then Huizinga, once again, had marked out this terrain before us.

APPENDIX 1

The manuscripts: a codicological survey

F1 (Florence, BML, MS mediceo-palatino 177)[1]

Contents
Chronicle, 'Book I' (fragments). A modern hand has inscribed the title 'Histoire de george chastellain' on fo. 2, but no earlier title is given. The contents were divided by the scribe into three distinct sections: the 'prologhu de lacteur' (fos 3–11v), the 'table des rubrices de ce present volume' (fos 12v–20v), and the text of the Chronicle itself (fos 21–218). The chapter headings in the initial rubric are referenced by folio to the text and are repeated at the appropriate points in the latter.

Description
The original binding is lost, and the paper used in the volume reveals three watermarks (Briquet analogies: 9890, 8532, 12863/12866).[2] The volume consists of 218 written folios measuring 375 x 270 mm, plus three flyleaves at the front and three at the rear. Of the three foliations which appear in the volume, one is original and is given in roman numerals (xv to ccxi). Although almost all of the signatures and catchwords of the quires have been cut at the bindery, there is no reason to believe that there were any more quires than the twenty-eight which now make up the volume (1^4, $2-3^3$, $4-28^4$). The text itself is carefully presented in double columns, each normally consisting of twenty-seven lines, and is written throughout in one hand in *littera bastarda*. Black ink is supplemented by red for the foliation, the titles to the prologue and rubrics section, for paragraph marks and for the underlining of chapter titles within the main body of the text. The initial capitals of each chapter are written alternately in red and blue ink. Blanks appear before the prologue (fo. 3) and the first chapter (fo. 21), indicating that the volume may have been intended for illustration at these points. These decorative details indicate that this was one of the finer paper manuscripts of the Chronicle.

History
The watermark and scribal evidence indicate that the volume was made in the late fifteenth century. The high frequency of characteristic scripta in the text,

---

[1] A. M. Bandini, *Bibliotheca Leopoldina Laurentiana*, Florence 1791–3, iii. 414–15; first brought to wider attention in 1839 in P. Lacroix, *Dissertations sur quelques points curieux sur l'histoire de France*, Paris 1839, vii. 311.
[2] As stated in ch. 6 above, I have used a facsimile of C. M. Briquet's manual.

as well as the scribe's colophon – which gives his name as 'Rob. de Lile' (fo. 218) – locate the place of fabrication in northern France or in the southern Low Countries. Kervyn had reason to think that F1, like the other Florentine manuscripts containing Chastelain's work, belonged in the sixteenth century to Jean-Jacques Chifflet and passed thereafter into the collection of François de Lorraine, 'grand duc de Toscane et depuis empereur' (i, p. l). Although this would explain their current location, he did not provide evidence to substantiate the view. For reasons which are given below, the explanation is at least plausible.[3] The only other study of a Chastelain manuscript in this collection is unable to trace its history beyond its current location.[4]

A1 (Arras, BM, MS 516 [827])[5]

Contents

Chronicle, 'Book I' (fragments). A modern inscription indicates that the volume concerned 'Evenemens des guerres depuis 1419 a 1422', and a further inscription on fo. 1 states that it was 'par Georges Chastellain pannetier du duc Philippe de Bourgogne'. There is no original title. The contents are divided into two parts: the prologue, which is not entitled (fos 1–8), and the main body of the text (fos 8v–186v). There are two annalistic observations which divide the text chronologically (fo. 61: 'pour lan cccc xx'; fo. 117: 'pour lan xxi'), but chapter titles are given only infrequently (fos 20v, 77, 89, 114) and there is no rubric of chapter headings at the start of the volume. The scribe of A1 was more obviously abbreviating his source than that of F1: the treaty of Troyes, the introduction of which is given in F1, is omitted here with the remark that the source of A1 'contient quatre feulletz de papier'; the terms of the surrender of Meaux are absent in both, although the scribe of A1 indicates that 'icy fault avoir neuf articles'; and the speech of Nicolas Rolin to the *Parlement* of Paris in 1420 on the subject of John the Fearless's murder 'nest icy couchee pour cause de briefte'. This last item is included in F1.

Description

The binding is modern, and the paper contains a single watermark analogous to Briquet 12618.[6] The 189 folios, measuring 365 x 260 mm, have been foliated with roman numerals by the scribes (i–ix^{xx}vi). They are distributed in 12 large

---

[3] The argument is set out below under the heading 'Later manuscripts'.
[4] Bliggenstorfer, '*Castellani Georgii*', 149–51.
[5] 'Notice du MS Arras, Bibl. mun. 516 (827)', unpubl. report, IRHT 1961; and *Catalogue général des manuscrits des bibliothèques publiques des départements: Arras–Avranches–Boulogne*, Paris 1872, 205; first brought to wider attention in 1837 in *Oeuvres historiques*, but already cited and attributed in T. Phillipps, *Codices manuscripti in Bibliotheca Sancti Vedasti*, Paris 1828, 36.
[6] Here I disagree with the report cited above, which identifies the the watermark with the Briquet group 12519–20.

quires (1–11⁸, 12⁶), two of which have cancelled folios. Signatures and catchwords are not given, but since the narrative is consecutive throughout there is no reason to believe that any quires have been lost. The text, written in a single cursive hand and in one block of variable dimensions according to folio, bears little indication of decorative intent. Although spaces are left for ornate capitals, there is nothing to suggest that the volume was intended for illustration. The ink used throughout is black.

History

The watermark and scribal evidence indicate that the volume was made in the late fifteenth or early sixteenth century; that is to say, slightly later than its counterpart F1. The high frequency of characteristic scripta in the text again locates the place of fabrication in northern France or the southern Low Countries. The history of the manuscript is unknown until some point in the seventeenth century when it was in the possession of a certain 'Jan... [surname obliterated] du mont sainct Eloy, seigneur de Wendin' (fo. 2). The manuscript may later have been donated by this family to the nearby monastery of St Vaast d'Arras where it was to be found by 1748.[7]

A2 (Arras, BM, MS 256 [406])[8]

Contents

Chronicle, 'Book II' (fragments). There is no original title, but a later reader noted that the volume contained 'Mémoires sur ce qui s'est passé touchant la toison d'or' (fo. 4). The text is not preceded by any rubric, and only one chapter title is indicated throughout the volume (fos 132v–3). By comparison with F2, which also contains this section of the Chronicle, A2 has several lacunae which correspond to the following pages and lines in volume two of Kervyn's edition: 1–7 (l. 11); 67 (l. 17) to 83 (l. 18); 146 (l. 8) to 166 (l. 4); and 216 (l. 2) to the end. The first three lacunae can be explained by missing quires (see below), but the last is attributable to the scribes who left the final three folios blank. A further blank on fo. 117v is explained by the scribe who notes that Chastelain's pen portrait of Philip the Good was to be inserted at a later stage: 'icy doit ensyeuvre celle du duc phelippe que messire charles le clerc a es mains laquelle il mettra ensuivant et viendra apres'.

---

[7] 'Bibliothecae monasterii Sancti Vedasti Atrebatensis, 1748' (fo. 1).
[8] Cf. 'Notice du MS Arras, Bibl. mun. 256 (406)', unpubl. report, IRHT 1960; and *Catalogue général des manuscrits des bibliothèques publiques*, 110. For the first detailed indication of the manuscript's existence see Quicherat, 'Fragments inédits'. It had earlier been cited and attributed in Phillipps, *Codices manuscripti*, 21.

Description

As with most of the other volumes, the original binding is lost. The paper (295 x 212 mm) reveals four watermarks, the first three of which bear close comparison with Briquet 9185, 8622 and 12503. The fourth is a variant on the Briquet group 12517–12528.[9] The volume contains modern flyleaves at the front and rear plus 138 folios which, like those of A3, were not originally numbered by the scribes. The folios are organised into 17 quires of varying composition ($1-14^4, 15^5, 16-17^4$), although an examination of the catchwords at the end of each quire reveals that at least three were lost at some stage in the manuscript's life. The missing quires, whose contents are discussed above, were originally to be found before quire 1, between quires 6 and 7, and between quires 13 and 14. The text itself is written in a single block of variable dimensions and in two cursive hands. Like A3 and B (but unlike most of the other Chronicle manuscripts), this volume contains a significant number of contemporary emendations to the text. Quicherat believed that these were Chastelain's own corrections, but a comparison of the hands with that found in the chronicler's personal correspondence reveals this conclusion to be incorrect.[10] A2 was not, as Kervyn maintains, part of Chastelain's working copy of the Chronicle. Like A1, however, this was very much a basic text: there is no decoration or decorative intent in the volume and no ink other than black.

History

The scripta and watermark evidence situate the fabrication of this volume in the late fifteenth century and in northern France or the southern Low Countries. It was originally made for, or under the supervision of, Charles Le Clerc. The connection is indicated by the reference to him which is given above, and his career is discussed in chapter six. It should also be noted that the physical correspondences between this volume and A3, discussed below, indicate that the two were originally part of the same recension. As for the subsequent history of the volume, all that can be said with certainty is that it entered the collection of the monastery of St Vaast d'Arras some time before 1631.[11]

---

[9] The report cited above records the first and third of these watermarks.

[10] These comparisons are based on three letters from the chronicler to his correspondents at the *Chambre des comptes* at Lille: ADN B17698. Because the signature on each corresponds to the hand which wrote the contents, and because a contemporary note on the back of one letter describes the document as 'de george chastellain escript tremblant de la main baillees par son vallet le xii de juillet', these were undoubtedly the work of Chastelain rather than an amanuensis.

[11] 'Bibliothecae monasterii sancti Vedasti Atrebatensis, 1631. G. 34' (fo. 2).

F2 (Florence, BML, MS mediceo-palatino 176)[12]

Contents

Chronicle, 'Book II' (fragments). The only title in the volume is written on the flyleaf in a later hand: 'Fragment de l'Histoire de Philippe le Bon, Duc de Bourgongne, faicte par messire George Chastellain son Historiographe. Des annees MCCCCXXIX, XXX, et XXXI'. There is no rubric at the beginning of the volume, as with A2, and the text contains only three original chapter headings and two annalistic observations (fos 13, 36, 81, 102, 114). The absence of a rubric in these manuscripts is no doubt to be explained by the fact that neither began at the start of 'Book II' (which consisted of an account of Philip the Good's marriage to Isabella).[13] F2 provides the material missing in A2 due to the loss of quires, but has a blank folio where the pen portrait of Philip the Good, in the possession of Charles Le Clerc, should have figured (fo. 101v).

Description

The original binding of the codex is lost. The volume contains one modern flyleaf front and rear and 117 paper folios in which a single watermark, analogous to Briquet no. 8635, occurs. The folios measure 280 x 210 mm and are gathered into quires of regular composition ($1-6^{10}$). The last three folios of the final quire are cancelled, but otherwise the survival of catchwords (fos 40v, 60v, 80v, 100v) indicate that the volume is complete. The manuscript was not foliated by the scribes but by some later owner. The presentation of the text is not particularly elegant: there is no pricking or ruling to situate the single block consistently in the same place on the page, and the number of lines varies from 28 to 35. One scribe carried out the work. He occasionally used *littera bastarda* for the initial line of chapters but reverted thereafter to a more cursive style. The volume, written throughout in black ink, was not intended to be decorated in any way.

History

To judge from the scripta and watermark evidence, this volume originated in the late fifteenth or early sixteenth century in the north-eastern region of the francophone world. As with F1, there are no marginalia or other marks of ownership to help trace its history beyond that point. It is possible that the manuscript found its way to Florence by the same route suggested by Kervyn in the case of F1.

---

[12] Bandini, *Bibliotheca Leopoldina Laurentiana*, iii. 414; Lacroix, *Dissertations sur quelques points curieux*, vii. 310–11.
[13] See chs 4, 6 above.

APPENDIX 1

B (Brussels, Bibliothèque royale Albert 1er, MS 15843)[14]

Contents

Chronicle, 'Book IV' (fragments). The volume has no title, contemporary or modern, and no table of chapters. Chapter titles are to be found intermittently in the text before fo. 347 but have been added by a later hand (fos 20, 22v, 121, 167v). Towards the end of the volume they are inserted consistently by the scribe himself (fos 347–66). There are several blanks of significant length throughout the volume, few of which are indicated in Kervyn's edition. These correspond to iii, 12 (l. 14, blank on fo. 5 r–v); 49 (l. 15, blank on fo. 28v); 121 (l. 15, blank on fos 73v–4v); 124 (l. 9, blank on lower half of fo. 76v); 155 (l. 22, blank on fo. 98v); 160 (l. 8, followed by a blank, fos 102–7v);[15] 177 (l. 14, blank on fos 120r–v); 205 (l. 20, blank on fo. 140r–v); 229 (l. 5, blank on fos 156v–60v); 320 (l. 25, blank on lower half of fo. 232); 368 (l. 4, blank from second half of fo. 270v to 274v); 390 (l. 26, blank on fos 294–5v); 459 (l. 32, fo. 349 blank apart from first line); 490 (l. 16, blank from fo. 365v to end of volume). Many of these blanks indicate lacunae in the text, but several may be due to the fact that the volume was bound in an incomplete state (see below).

Description

The folios are bound between wooden boards (300 x 225 mm) covered by brown calf which originally had two clasps (now broken).[16] The interiors of the boards are covered in parchment bearing twelfth-century Latin script and musical notation. The water-damaged binding is decorated in the 'Netherlandish style' with fillets and stamping, elements of which are similar to motifs found in bindings of the late fifteenth and early sixteenth centuries.[17] The paper used in the volume is of earlier fabrication, as indicated by three of the four watermarks which find close Briquet analogies in nos 7546–9, 3820 and 8655. The paper has suffered considerable wear and some staining. Some folios had to be scarfed at an early stage, probably before or at the time of binding.[18] This would be in keeping with the early history of Chastelain's archetype which, it will be recalled, passed through several

---

[14] 'Notice du MS Bruxelles, Bibl. royale. 15843', unpubl. report, IRHT 1960; J. Marchal, *Catalogue des manuscrits de la Bibliothèque royale des ducs de Bourgogne*, Brussels 1842, i. 317; J. Van den Gheyn, *Catalogue des manuscrits de la Bibliothèque royale de Belgique*, Brussels 1900, vii. 335–6 (no. 5028). The manuscript was first commented upon in Renard, 'Nouvelles observations'.

[15] However, fo. 107 has a snippet of text, three lines in length, which is repeated from fo. 94: 'bel coursier et bon a ladvenant couvert richement/ dorfavrie dor la plus belle des aultres dont ny avoit/ page dariere ly'.

[16] For methods here see G. Pollard, 'Describing medieval bookbindings', in J. J. G. Alexander and M. T. Gibson (eds), *Medieval learning and literature*, Oxford 1976, 50–65; M. T. Roberts and D. Etherington, *Bookbinding and the conservation of books*, Washington 1982.

[17] Cf. J. B. Oldham, *English blind-stamped bindings*, Cambridge 1952, plates iv, xliii.

[18] For scarfed folios see in particular fos 320–49.

hands.[19] The volume comprises 368 folios which were not originally numbered by the scribes. These are gathered in twenty-seven quires of uneven composition (1–10⁸, 11⁵, 12–14⁸, 15–16⁷, 17⁸, 18⁷, 19¹, 20⁴, 21–6⁸, 27⁶), many of which have cancelled folios. Several of the quires have signatures and catchwords and were therefore in better order at some early stage in their history. The text is situated on the page in a single block of variable dimensions (23–8 lines) and is written in three cursive hands (fos 1–76v and 121–346v; 77–120v; 347–65v). The numerous corrections and emendations throughout the volume were occasionally carried out by the author himself, as comparisons with the letters conserved in ADN B17698 reveal. The ink used throughout is black, and blanks were left for the later addition of ornate initial capitals, some of which were inserted by the third scribe (fos 347–65).

History

The quires of the volume were clearly part of Chastelain's archetype and may well have been among the 'coyers . . . desemparéz, imparfaicts et sans ordre' described by Molinet (ii, 594–5). It is possible to suggest that the quires date to the 1460s, for some are written on the same paper used by Chastelain for his presentation copy of the *Exposition sur vérité mal prise* (now BR, MS 11101). The manuscript was in the possession of some unknown member of the Orville family in 1528.[20] Thereafter, it passed through the hands of the Lalaing family (fo. 1: 'Lalaing') before entering the collections of the countess of Yves, the Ghent bibliophile Joseph van Hulthem (1764–1832) and finally the Bibliothèque royale itself.[21]

L (London, BL, Add. MS 54156)[22]

Contents

Chronicle, 'Book IV' (fragments). The original title bears no indication of the author's identity, perhaps because B, almost certainly the source of L, has none

---

[19] See chs 4, 6 above.
[20] On the flyleaf we find the following inscription: '1528. Pour penser ensaigist. Suis d'Orville'. I have been unable to trace the individual in question: unfortunately, since the mark of ownership is important. It will be recalled that Gonthier Chastelain offered a 'recueil' of his father's work to Margaret of Austria in 1524, and that he was still alive in 1538. If 'Orville' owned B in 1528, it would seem that at least part of the archetype was already out of Gonthier's hands by that stage. It is also possible that 'Orville' was responsible for the binding of the volume.
[21] L. Gaudefroy, *Catalogue des livres rares et curieux provenant de la bibliothèque de Mademoiselle la Comtesse d'Yves*, Brussels 1820, ii. 245, no. 4670; A. Voisin, *Bibliotheca Hulthemiana*, Ghent 1836–7, vi. 76.
[22] Armstrong, 'Le texte de la *Chronique* de Chastellain' (repr. in his *England, France and Burgundy*, 383–8); Kondo, 'Étude de la *Chronique* de Georges Chastelain'; Delclos, 7–13. The discovery of the manuscript was first announced in 'Acquisitions. January–June, 1967', *British Museum Quarterly* xxxii (1967–8), 149.

either.[23] An initial rubric (fos 1–13) provides a list of chapter titles which correspond to the text itself as far as fo. 383. Although the manuscript contains much material which is no longer to be found in B (and which is now published in Delclos's edition), there are several blanks which correspond to iii, 49 (l. 15, blank on fo. 36r–v); 121 (l. 15, blank on fos 70–1v); 155 (l. 22, blank on fo. 89r–v); 160 (l. 8, blank on fos 92–4v); 177 (l. 14, blank on fos 103v–4v); 229 (l. 5, blank on fo. 130r–v); 368 (l. 4, blank on fo. 247r–v); 459 (l. 32, blank on fos 292v–4v); Delclos, 252 (l. 23, blank on fos 383–6v); Delclos 272 (l. 32, blank on fos 397v–8v). With the exception of the last two, these blanks correspond to those found in B.

Description

The original binding, dating to the late fifteenth or early sixteenth century, is preserved separately and is in poor condition.[24] It now consists of one complete wooden board (390 x 285 mm) which was originally decorated with five bosses. The first and second of the four watermarks found in the paper correspond closely to Briquet nos 4324–6 and 11417. The volume comprises 429 folios (380 x 285 mm), with modern flyleaves at the front and rear, and these were numbered (sometimes inaccurately) by the scribes from I to CCCIIII^{xx}III. The folios, some of which were cancelled, appear to be gathered in fifty-four quires.[25] If the composition of the latter is difficult to ascertain, the survival of catchwords and a few signatures indicate that the volume is as complete as it was when first made. The text is presented in a regular and elegant fashion in two columns (32 lines) which are situated on the page by pricking and ruling in faint red ink. There would appear to be three scribal hands (fos 1–13, 15–383, 387–426), each of which uses *littera bastarda*. Like F1, this was one of the finer paper volumes. Blanks appear to have been left for the insertion of miniatures (fos 29, 332), and yellow, red and blue ink is used throughout for initial capitals and paragraph marks.

History

The evidence of the binding, watermarks and scripta indicates that the volume was composed in the late fifteenth century in the same regions as the other manuscripts. At some point after 1523 it entered into the possession of Henry III count of Nassau, and it has been suggested (by Armstrong) that it may originally have been made for Henry's uncle, Engelbert II.[26] However, the volume did have some connection with the Croy family, for at fos 167 and 189 we find two contemporary (or near contemporary) inscriptions referring to

---

[23] 'Cy commence ung volume lequel traicte de pluseurs haultes gestes advenues en la triumphant maison de france et de bourgongne': fo. 1.
[24] Add. MS 54156, Old Binding. For this information I am grateful to Miss Janet Backhouse, curator, who originally secured the manuscript for the British Library in 1966.
[25] The recent binding of the volume makes the task of verifying the composition of the quires difficult. Most are composed of four sheets.
[26] See ch. 6 above.

'Monsieur' and 'Madame de Renty' (Renty being a Croy possession). The history of the codex is unknown from that point until 1919, when Miss Minnie Callard, who donated it to the British Library in 1966, was given it as a birthday present by her father ('who never bought rubbish').[27] It is possible that the manuscript found its way to England from France or Belgium in the wake of the First World War.

A3 (Arras, BM, MS 471 [578])[28]

Contents
Chronicle, 'Book VI' (fragments). There is no original title, and that added in a later hand is revealing of the anonymity which surrounded most of the Chronicle fragments until the nineteenth century. It reads 'Histoire de France par Georges Repreuve ou Lepreuve' (fo. 1) – an attribution based upon a misinterpretation of a chapter title at fo. 68v ('Comment george repreuve avoir faict lintroit de ce vi volume': cf. iv, 118). There is no rubric of chapter titles, but the latter are inserted throughout the text. Blank folios occur at fos 128r–v and 252r–v, although apparently without loss to the narrative. However, part of the text published by Kervyn from Be is absent in A3 due to the loss of a quire (cf. iv, 167–81). Because of the curious composition of the manuscript (see below), some material was repeated (fos 193–4) but was later scored out by one of the scribes.

Description
The binding is modern and the material used throughout is paper. The latter is in two formats: large folios (410 x 280 mm) from fos 1–192, and small folios (295 x 210 mm) from fos 193–314. The latter are of comparable size to those found in A2 – a first indication that the two manuscripts belonged to the same recension. Two of the three watermarks in the large folios find close Briquet analogies in nos 1826 and 9890, while two of the three found in the smaller folios are identical to those found in the paper of A2. The folios were not originally numbered by the scribes (as in A2), and are gathered into 40 quires of fairly even composition ($1-31^4, 32^2, 33-9^4, 40^3$). The presence of signatures until fo. 128v reveals the loss of a single quire between nos 12 and 13 (at fo. 96v). The consistent use of catchwords indicates that the volume is otherwise complete. The presentation of the page varies between the two formats. The text of the larger folios is written in double columns (33–24 lines) which are

---

[27] These were her words as kindly conveyed to me in a letter from Janet Backhouse (30 Nov. 1988).
[28] 'Notice du MS Arras, Bibl. mun. 471 (578)', unpubl. report, IRHT n.d.; *Catalogue général des manuscrits des bibliothèques publiques*, 186–7. The manuscript was first brought to wider attention in 1837 in *Oeuvres historiques*. It had earlier been cited and attributed in T. Phillipps, *Codices manuscripti*, 36.

situated on the page by pricking and ruling. *Littera bastarda* are used here, and it is possible to detect two scribal hands. The text of the smaller folios, as in A2, is written in a single block and in cursive style. The two hands here are indistinguishable from those we find in A2, indicating beyond doubt that the two manuscripts were part of the same recension. The volume was not intended for illustration, although the larger folios of the first section have blanks which were probably left for the inclusion of ornate initial capitals.

History

Since A3 is inextricably connected to A2, the remarks made above are applicable to this codex. An inscription on fo. 73 identifies one of the scribes as Colin de Veyr.[29]

Be (Château de Beloeil, Armoire des manuscrits, TA.V.D.17.)[30]

Contents

Chronicle, 'Book VI' (fragments). The original title of the volume is preserved on a flyleaf: 'Du koeronement du roy Loys XI quy fut sacre a reyns lan mil quatre cens LXI u estoit presens le noble duc Philippe de Bourgoingne son bel onckele et des estrange chose de son regne.' Once again, there is no indication that Chastelain was the author. There is no rubric of chapter titles, but the latter are inserted in the text from fo. 57 onwards (which corresponds to iv, 118). Although the text of this part of the Chronicle is particularly defective, the scribes of Be, like those of A3, show little awareness of lacunae in the form of significant blanks or other explicit indications of an incomplete source.

Description

The original binding is lost. The paper (275 x 210 mm) of the 226 folios has two watermarks which may be closely identified with Briquet nos 8992 and 8634. The folios were not numbered by the scribes and have been gathered in six large quires ($1-5^{20}$, 6^{15}). Four folios in the last quire have been cancelled. There are no catchwords, but signatures in the quires have occasionally escaped the binder's knife. This evidence, combined with the uninterrupted flow of the text, indicates that the volume is complete. The text is situated on the page in a single block of variable dimensions (38–32 lines) and is written

---

[29] 'Colin de Veyr. Il reste a paier XIX foellet du petit' (*sic*). This may be Vaire (near Corbie, Dépt. du Pas-de-Calais).

[30] 'Notice du MS Beloeil, Bibl. Bibl. du Château TA.V.D.17', unpubl. report, IRHT n.d.; A. Voisin, *Souvenirs de la bibliothèque des princes de Ligne à Beloeil*, Ghent 1839, 6; F. Leuridant, *La bibliothèque des princes de Ligne*, Brussels 1915, repr. Brussels–Paris 1923, 30. The manuscript includes a letter by Kervyn de Lettenhove (dated 19 Jan. 1862) who first brought it to wider attention in his edition. I am grateful to M. le Prince de Ligne for his permission to consult the volume, and to M. Pierre Mouriau de Meulenacker who showed me round the library.

in two cursive hands (fos 1–56; 56v–end). Apart from a few ornate capitals in black ink, there is no indication that the volume was intended to be illustrated or decorated in any way.

History

The scripta and watermark evidence situate the fabrication of the manuscript in northern France or in the southern Low Countries in the late fifteenth or early sixteenth century. It may have been made for Englelbert II count of Nassau, and certainly entered his possession at an early stage in its history.[31] Later in the sixteenth century the manuscript passed into the hands of two unidentified owners who are designated by their mottos on the flyleaf: 'Penser m'atriste. A. S' and '1555 A. L. G. suis Gottingnies'. An unknown hand of the same period added a reflective text with biblical references at the end of the volume (fos 218v–19). The manuscript appears to have been in the possession of its current owners, the Ligne family, by the seventeenth century.[32]

P1–P2 (Paris, BN, MSS fr. 2688 and 2689)[33]

Contents

Chronicle, 'Book VI' and 'Book VII' (fragments). A rubric of chapter titles and the folio references it contains, bound at the end of P1, indicate that the two manuscripts were originally one. Neither is entitled in a contemporary hand, but at some later stage P1 was described as an 'Histoire manuscrit dun duc de Bretagne', P2 as an 'Histoire manuscrit dun duc de Bourgogne avec une figure enluminé' (sic). The chapter titles are repeated throughout the text. The scribes were aware of the defective nature of their source and indicate lacunae by several blanks which Buchon took care to note.[34]

Description

The original binding is lost. P1–P2 is the only manuscript of the Chronicle to have been composed on parchment. The large folios (400 x 300 mm) are numbered consecutively from I to CII (P1) and from CIII to CCXXXII (P2).[35] In addition, P1 has eleven folios at the end of the volume which contain the rubric of chapter titles. These have an independent foliation, and we may assume that they were bound at a different location in the original volume.[36]

---

[31] Engelbert's ownership is attested by the inscription 'appartient a monseigneur de Diest' on the flyleaf. Engelbert became lord of Diest in 1499 and died in 1504: see ch. 6 above.
[32] Sanderus, Bibliotheca Belgica manuscripta, i. 1–2.
[33] Catalogue des manuscrits français de la Bibliothèque nationale: tome premier, ancien fonds, Paris 1868, 442; first brought to wider attention in Chronique des ducs de Bourgogne par Georges Chastellain, ed. J. A. C. Buchon, Paris 1827.
[34] Cf. ibid. i. 108, 209; ii. 66, 67.
[35] For the splitting of the manuscript into two volumes see ch. 6 above.
[36] The rubric also contains a list of chapter titles which do not correspond to the contents

The folios are gathered in quires of fairly even composition (P1: 1–12^4, 13^3, 14^2, 15^4; P2: 1^5, 2^6, 3^5, 4–7^4, 8^3, 9–15^4, 16^3). Catchwords and signatures are no longer in evidence, but the consecutive original foliation indicates that the manuscript has not suffered any loss of quires. The text is situated by pricking and ruling with considerable care on the page, and is written in double columns of 35 lines each. A single hand wrote the vast majority of P1–P2 in *littera bastarda*; another appears to have written the chapter titles in the fifteenth quire of the first volume. In terms of decoration, this manuscript is by far the most ornate. P2 has a fine miniature which Durrieu has commented upon, and a blank was left at fo. cxvii (original foliation) for another.[37] It is possible to detect an instruction to the miniaturist here: 'ce se fera au lieu'.[38] Red ink is used to differentiate chapter titles from the text itself, and initial capitals are painted in gold upon blue or red backgrounds.

History

The scripta and miniature indicate that this manuscript originated in the Low Countries early in the sixteenth century. It was clearly a luxury production, although there are no clues as to the identity of its original owner.[39] The date of the manuscript rules out Buchon's suggestion that it was a presentation copy destined for the duke. Kervyn thought it had been made for Louis de Bruges, whose collection later passed into the hands of Louis XII of France.[40] Louis de Bruges did not live into the sixteenth century, and Van Praet's research into his collection did not turn up a manuscript of the Chronicle.[41] The 1518 inventory of the royal collection at Blois does indeed mention a 'Cronicques du duc Philippe', but the modern editor of the inventory states that these are not to be confused with P1–P2.[42] In fact, the latter entered the royal library in 1658 along with the other manuscripts of Philip, count of Béthune (1561–1649). Béthune's arms are stamped on the binding of both P1 and P2, and he appears to have acquired them as a single volume in 1630.[43] Prior to

---

of P1–2. A later hand has noted that 'les chapitres des quatre fueillets que dessus ne sont compris en ce volume'. This indicates the existence of a sister manuscript which contained the material now to be found in A2 and Be. The rubric reveals that this lost codex had at least 197 folios.

[37] Durrieu, *La miniature flamande*, plate lxxiv. As noted in ch. 6 above, the reproduction is unfortunately inverted.

[38] On instructions to miniaturists see S. Berger and P. Durrieu, *Les notes pour les enlumineurs dans les manuscrits du moyen âge*, Paris 1893.

[39] Parchment manuscripts of this quality at this time were generally destined for 'un prince ou quelque grand personnage': M. Prou, *Manuel de paléographie*, 3rd edn, Paris 1910, 264.

[40] On the collection see L. Delisle, *Le cabinet des manuscrits de la Bibliothèque impériale*, Paris 1868–81, i. 140–6.

[41] Van Praet, *Louis de Bruges*.

[42] Arnauldet, 'Catalogue', 305 (no. 47).

[43] For Béthune's arms see J. Guigard, *Nouvel armorial du bibliophile*, Paris 1890, ii. 56–7. Béthune's purchase of the volume is indicated by an inscription in P2, fo. 232v (modern foliation): 'L'an 1630. le 30 janvier, J'ay achepté le present volume 243 livres... (line erased)

this, the single volume (and perhaps its sister volume, now lost) belonged to François Raphelengien (1539-97), nephew of the Antwerp printer and bibliophile Christophe Plantin.[44] If the luxury manuscript and its counterpart were to be found in the Low Countries in the middle of the sixteenth century, we may wonder whether its original owner was Margaret of Austria who, as was seen in chapter six, spent a small fortune on a 'recueil' of the Chronicle which she commissioned from Gonthier Chastelain. However, there is no evidence to substantiate the hypothesis.

Later manuscripts[45]

Despite the archivist's statement to the contrary, Kervyn's information that the Archives du Ministère des affaires étrangères contained manuscripts of the Chronicle was correct. MSS 24 and 25 of that collection are described as an 'Histoire de Charles, dernier duc de Bourgogne, escripte par G. CHASTELAIN, son historiographe'. These seventeenth-century manuscripts are associated in the catalogue with Cardinal Richelieu, although there is no *ex-libris* or marginal comment to substantiate the claim. Upon close inspection, the texts of the two manuscripts (243 folios and 242 folios respectively) reveal that they, like some others in the collection, were copied 'sur les manuscrits de Béthune': in other words, from P1 and P2. The texts correspond to one another – even in the inclusion of the remark which follows the rubric of the chapters of the now-lost sister volume in P1 ('Les chapitres des quatre feuillets que dessus ne sont compris en ce volume'). The copy would appear to have been made before Béthune's librarian had split the volume, for the rubric of chapter titles which is now bound at the end of P1 is here included at the beginning, its probable location in the original single volume. Béthune or his librarian thought the work to have been written by Lefèvre; the copyist of MSS 24 and 25 thought, equally erroneously, that the author was Guillaume Fillastre.[46]

... L'Autheur a este aux services et gages de Charles dernier Duc de Bourgongne, Memoires et Recueil des faicts par noble homme Jean Seigneur de Sainct Remy, de la Jaquerie, D'Avesnes et Morienne, premier Roy d'Armes du Toison. C'est l'Histoire des Ducs de Bourgongne jusques au chapitre V de l'ordre tenu à Bruges. Ce volume est cher Monsieur ... (line erased) ... comte d'Artois ...' (end cut by binder's knife). Once again Chastelain's text was of interest for his comments on the Golden Fleece; and once again the authorship of his work was not clear to later generations.

[44] This is indicated by an inscription on fo. 106 (modern foliation) of P1: 'Francisci Raphelengii'. On Raphelengien see L. Voet, *The golden compasses*, Amsterdam 1969-72, i. 147-51.

[45] These later manuscripts are less revealing of the Chronicle's *Nachleben* than those discussed above, and therefore do not need to be described in equivalent detail. For published descriptions see *Inventaire sommaire des archives du Département des affaires étrangères: mémoires et documents*, Paris 1883; *Catalogue général des manuscrits des bibliothèques publiques de France: Besançon*, Paris 1897-1904.

[46] MS 25, fo. 241v: 'L'Autheur a esté au service et gaiges de Charles dernier duc de

Another seventeenth-century copy is to be found in Besançon, Bibliothèque municipale, Collection Chifflet, MS 202, fos 17–99.[47] This is described as a 'FRAGMENT DE L'HISTOIRE DU BON DUC PHILIPPE DE BOURGONGNE des annees M.CCCC.XXIX.XXX. et XXXI. par messire Georges Chastellain son Indiciaire' (fo. 17). Close comparisons between this text and the surviving manuscripts for the relevant section of the Chronicle reveal that Coll. Chifflet MS 202 was copied directly from F2.[48] It is possible to identify the copyist as well as the source. The hand and even the paper in this seventeenth-century version are identical to those we find in other collections of Burgundian historical material which were made by Jean-Jacques Chifflet († 1660).[49]

This identification is of some significance in tracing the history of F2 and the other Florentine manuscripts of Chastelain's work. According to his son Jules, Jean-Jacques Chifflet possessed 'un manuscrit original' of Chastelain's Chronicle containing an 'Histoire, ou plutost Eloge, du Bon Duc Philippe'.[50] It is possible that Jean-Jacques copied F2 in order to supplement this 'manuscrit original' whose contents we are unable to verify. However, another possibility may be suggested. The second fragment of Chastelain's Chronicle fits Jules Chifflet's description of his father's 'manuscrit original' admirably. A significant part of it was given over to the famous gallery of princely portraits which were designed to show Philip's superiority among the princes of his day. The 'manuscrit original' in Chifflet's possession may thus have been F2 itself. It might seem curious that Jean-Jacques should have copied one of his own manuscripts, but then there may have been a number of good reasons for doing so. A spare copy of the text may have been useful, either for the owner's purposes, or for consultation by others. It would also preserve the text in the event of the sale or loss of the original. If so, Kervyn's otherwise unattested view that F2 and the other Chastelain manuscripts originally belonged to Chifflet before entering into the possession of François de Lorraine, grand duke of Tuscany, would be substantiated. It is otherwise difficult to explain why the Florentine library should possess one of the richest collections of Chastelain's work.

Bourgongne. Cette histoire finit en l'an 1470. Il semble que l'Autheur soit Guillaume Fillastre qui fut Abbé de St Bertin d'Arras, Evesque de Tournay et chancelier de l'ordre de la Toison Qui fut employé en diverses Ambassades et des principaux du conseil de Charles dernier duc de Bourgongne. Il decedda l'an 1473. Il se trouva au chapitre de l'ordre de la Toison qu'il descrit assez particulierement en cette histoire. En l'an 1472 il dedia au duc de Bourgongne son livre de l'ordre de la Toison.'

[47] The copy was made at some point after 1612: one of the other texts in this composite volume is described as a 'Mémoire des funérailles faites aux princes des Païs-Bas depuis l'an 1592 jusques à l'an 1612': ibid. fo. 120.

[48] These comparisons were carried out from microfilms of the three manuscripts which I obtained from the IRHT.

[49] Cf. BM Besançon, MS 1516; Florence, BML, MS mediceo-palatino 131.

[50] Chifflet, *Histoire*, 16.

APPENDIX 2

An anomalous work and its context

Chastelain's *Déclaration de tous les hauts faits du duc Philippe de Bourgongne, celuy qui se nomme le Grand Duc et le Grand Lyon* (vii, 213–36) is a curious piece.[1] Despite its title, it is divided into two more or less equal parts, one dealing with Philip's life, the other with the qualities of his son Charles. Chastelain speaks of the latter 'comme en temps passé, qui servira à tousjours' (228). The work is also remarkable, not for the eulogy of Philip which is to be found within it (for this was mirrored throughout the Chronicle, and was intended to present Philip as an ideal prince in the French mould), but rather for the criticism which Chastelain, 'afin toutefois que je ne semble flatteur' (223), levels against his dead master. The principal charges against Philip are as follows (223–6): he was negligent in the governance of his dominions; he was given to sexual excess and infidelity; he did not reward his noble supporters according to their merits, keeping instead the company of lesser varlets; and finally, that he was lax in matters of Christian observance. Some of these charges are tempered to a degree by the chronicler, but on no count is Philip entirely exculpated.

Some related observations lend significance to these charges. Not only are they without parallel in the rest of Chastelain's production, they are also of a nature to undermine fundamentally the image of Philip which Chastelain had promoted in this text and consistently throughout the rest of his *oeuvre*. As Krynen observes, 'on ne saurait déceler quelque faiblesse chez le prince parfait'.[2] In short (and to say the least), Philip was no longer presented unequivocally as an ideal prince. How is this to be explained?

The first stage of the explanation lies in the dating of the work. It was written after Philip's death but when Charles still found himself 'en nouvel estat' (234); in other words, not long after his accession on 15 June 1467. It was also written in the knowledge of 'l'alliance qu'il a faite' (233) with the English. Although Charles's alliances with Edward IV took root when he was still count of Charolais, his alliance as duke first emerged with the exchange of promises of friendship (July) and the formal agreement of his marriage to Margaret of York (1 October).[3] Clearly the work was written before this last date, but it is possible to be more precise. On 19 July, one of Chastelain's servants, a certain Jean Chenebaut, was paid for bringing to the new duke 'un livret . . . touchant le

---

[1] The work is to be edited and studied by H. M. Krol at the University of Utrecht under René Stuip. I am grateful to Anne Wanono of the IRHT in Paris for this information.
[2] Krynen, *Idéal du prince*, 118.
[3] C. Weightman, *Margaret of York*, Gloucester 1989, 39–41; J. Calmette, 'Le mariage de Charles le Téméraire et de Marguerite d'York', AB i (1929), 193–214.

trespas de feu de tres noble memoire monseigneur le duc Phelippe que dieu absoille'.[4] This could not be his *Advertissement au duc Charles* (which, despite Kervyn's view, did not concern Philip's 'trespas') or his mystery play on the subject of Philip's demise (which was performed at Mons early in 1468).[5] Chastelain describes the *Déclaration* as 'un livret' (v, 243), a term which corresponds to the physical description of the work which is found in the accounts. We may therefore conclude that the *Déclaration* was written within weeks, perhaps even days, of Chastelain hearing the news of Philip's death.

Charles's accession was a matter of immediate concern for the former servants of Philip the Good on at least two grounds. First, there was a natural concern for their own positions. New princes changed the personnel of the courts they inherited. Louis XI, as Chastelain himself had noted with more than passing interest, removed the office of historiographer from the monks of St Denis when he acceded to the throne in 1461 (iv, 100). Charles had his own men to reward, particularly those who had supported him loyally through the darkest hours of his frequent conflicts with Philip the Good.

Secondly, there was real concern at court that Charles was new to the practice of government and, more seriously, that he was a headstrong maverick capable of pursuing radically different policies from his father. These affected individual fortunes and the future of the house of Burgundy itself. Guillaume Fillastre, chancellor of the new duke, was one of several who counselled prudence and measure to his master and reminded him of the achievements of his lineage. In the first meeting of the Golden Fleece after Charles's accession, the knights of the Order petitioned the duke on the same point, and in the frank terms which counsellors believed themselves to be entitled to use.[6] Chastelain's *Déclaration* and the exceptional comments on Philip the Good which it contained may be read as a response to these two pressures. A close reading of the text will help to make this point.

Although Charles is portrayed as displaying the qualities of his father, he was clearly exempt from Philip's faults. He did not neglect his dominions but laboured 'soir et matin toudis en conseil, toudis en soin d'aucun grand cas, ou en finances ou en fait de guerre ou en provision du bien public' (229). Charles, unlike his father, 'vivoit plus chastement que communément les princes ne font' (231). Where his father appeared a distant figure to his noble servants, Charles 'entendoit à autruy raison et louoit les bonnes . . . aimoit fort ses serviteurs; estoit commun assez avec eux; bon à servir et de bonne nature' (229). By implied contrast (once again) with his less than devout father, Charles 'estoit dévot à la Vierge Marie; observoit jeusnes; donnoit largement aumones; crémoit la mort et la courte vie' (230). These elements of the ideal prince, found wanting in this one depiction of Philip the Good, were perceived to be present in Charles. Upon reflection, Chastelain now felt that his love of

---

[4] ADN B2064, fo. 202.
[5] On the date of the mystery play see ch. 3 above.
[6] Guillaume Fillastre, *Toison d'Or*, fo. 124ff. See also ch. 5 above.

the old duke 'me peut avoir . . . esté cause souvent de parler plus que à mesure' (227). He states that 'par temps cy-après, de sa clarté je feray à point; je retondray le superflu'. A remarkable change of heart – and a sense of contrition – had apparently emerged in July 1467.

But the new duke was not without his shortcomings either. His attention to detail in matters of government was, if anything, 'trop et plus qu'il ne séoit à tel prince' (229). He was a hard taskmaster to his own servants, 'aigre en son vouloir, et telle fois agu en ses mots', even if '[il] ne donna peine toutesfois à autruy que luy-mesme ne prit pareille'. He was a little too concerned with money, although this was said to reveal his solicitude 'en provision du bien public'. It is perhaps no coincidence that many of these frank observations were made not only by Chastelain, but also by the new duke's chancellor and by the knights of the Order of the Golden Fleece in the ways discussed above. In this respect the *Déclaration* was a timely set of counsels which should be seen in the context of the natural fears which arose within the governing elite when forced to deal with a new hand at the helm of the ship of state. Despite its title, then, the text was more concerned with the future of the house of Burgundy under Charles than it was with its past under Philip.

But the *Déclaration* was also about Chastelain's personal future. He had been a loyal servant of the old duke, but knew as well as anyone at court that Philip's disputes with Charles had led to the severance of the latter's pension and the threat of his exclusion from the succession. With the exception of Olivier de La Marche, those who had stuck with Charles in his hour of need did not figure in the chronicler's personal circle. Like every other creature of Philip the Good, Chastelain had his own position to consider in the days which followed his master's demise.[7] In the Chronicle we discern his doubts as he contemplates Philip's death and the prospect of Charles's accession: 'Or, en est le délit sensible passé en moy, et à tous autres ses bienveillants de jadis, fortrait; et en nouvel miroir et qui se présente à nos yeux, image du premier esvanouy, sommes à nouvelle délactation prendre en ce que le temps nous amène' (v, 242). The *Déclaration* was a response to these personal concerns.

Chastelain reasons in a crucial passage that just as the father had been close to his heart, so too should be the son: 'je [luy] dois le pareil' (227). He states that 'le désire à servir et à luy valoir, et de mon arbre et de mon temps luy apprester fruit'. His value to the new duke as a counsellor – a household office which Chastelain had held for over ten years by July 1467 – is highlighted by the *Déclaration* in its entirety. A reference to his Chronicle serves as a reminder of his abilities as official historian, as does an earnest mention of 'mes labeurs . . . [et] mes conceptions et spéculatives' (227). Chastelain had occupied this post since 1455. Having made these remarks, Chastelain then reveals the nub of the matter: Charles, he notes, 'encore me doit vie et entretenement, recongnoissance et provision pour mes vieux jours'. With the ink scarcely dry,

---

[7] Cf. the Chronicle's description of the rush for offices which a change of duke created: i, 68; v, 287–8.

one imagines, the *Déclaration des hauts faits et glorieuses advenues du duc Philippe de Bourgogne* was placed in the hands of one of the elderly chronicler's dependants, Jean Chenebaut, and was then dispatched to Brussels.

In the light of these comments, Chastelain's extraordinary treatment of Philip the Good in the *Déclaration* appears much less puzzling. Despite its title, the text has less to do with the old duke than with the problems presented by his demise: problems which the living – Charles, his entourage and his father's entourage – were left to deal with. In this rapidly written, relatively short and therefore quickly read work, Chastelain was taking certain initiatives: as a counsellor, as an official historian, but above all as a man eager to retain his standing in both capacities. If this meant reneging in part upon his depiction of the past, and there is no doubt that Chastelain did so, then perhaps that was not so serious. The *Déclaration* was destined for the new duke and his entourage, rather than for the wider audience which some of his lesser works addressed. The dynasty's dirty linen was not being washed in public. Moreover, within the *Déclaration* itself the classic eulogy of Philip the Good, which made up the first part of the work, was there to compensate. Those failings in Philip's character which Chastelain had suppressed in the Chronicle (but mentioned in the *Déclaration*) were hardly unknown at court. Charles more than anyone had good reason to be aware of them. Philip's flaws could be presented as an incentive for the new duke to do well and prosper. By exposing them, Chastelain showed himself to be something more than Philip the Good's creature. Here was a man who could and would – if given the chance – transfer his love for the father, his loyalty and his abilities, to the son.

By exposing Philip's failings Chastelain may also have been reminding his new master, who was not yet his patron, of something else. The well-turned phrase could castigate as well as praise its subject. The power of Chastelain's pen, revealed by degrees in the *Déclaration*, was wisely retained and cultivated by the new duke.

Bibliography

Archives and manuscript collections

Arras, Bibliothèque municipale (BM Arras)
MSS 256 [406], 516 [827], 256 [406], 578 [471], 926

Besançon, Bibliothèque municipale (BM Besançon)
Collection Chifflet 84, 164, 186, 202, 208; MSS 554, 1516

Bruges, Rijksarchief
Heerlijkheid Wijnendale, no. 251

Brussels, Archives générales du Royaume (AGR)
Acquits de Lille 1149, 1150; Chambre des comptes, CC1064, CC 1067 (Registres généraux: Flandres); CC1921, CC1923–5 (Recette générale des finances); CC3196 (Recette générale de Hainaut); CC 21797 (Conseils); MSS divers 273c, 391, 3303

Brussels, Bibliothèque Royale Albert 1er (BR)
MSS 2355, 7382, 10485, 11020–3, 11101, 15843, 16881, 18204–8, 19684, 21521–31, 21687–91, II 2545, II 6977, II 7828

Chantilly, Musée Condé
Cabinet des titres, carton 37; MS 687; IV E, 89/1 (Incunabula)

Dijon, Archives de la Côte d'Or (ACO)
B1706, B1712, B1713, B1728, B1729 (Recette générale de Bourgogne); B11805–6 (Montres d'armes); B11906, B11908 (Trésor des chartes)

Edinburgh, National Library of Scotland
ADV MS 19.1.4

Enghien, Couvent des Capucins
Boîte 25, reg. 31

Florence, Biblioteca Medicea-Laurenziana (BML)
MSS mediceo-palatino 120, 131, 176, 177

Ghent, Bijlokemuseum
HS 1101 (on permanent loan from the Stadsarchief)

Ghent, Rijksarchief
Fonds van het Sint-Veerlekapittel te Gent, no. 157

Ghent, Stadsarchief (SAG)
Fonds Lanchals, no. 693; Généalogie de la famille de Bracle (unnumbered series, heraldic and genealogical manuscripts); Jaerregisters van der Keure (Series 301), 16–43, 49, 54; Religieuze en caritatieve instellingen (Series LXXXIV), 1; Stadsrekeningen (Series 400), 12; Staten van goed (Series 330), 11–25; Vrije schippers (Series 180), 2

Ghent, Universiteitsbibliotheek (UBG)
HSS 567, 572, 2693, G6112, G11478

Lille, Archives départementales du Nord (ADN)
Chambre des comptes, B93 (Nécessités de la Chambre); B569, B570 (Trésor des chartes); B1607 (Registre des chartes); B1741 (Registre de l'Audience); B1938, B1942, B1945, B1951, B1954, B1957, B1982, B1988, B1991–6, B1998–2000, B2002, B2004, B2008–26, B2030, B2034, B2037–45 bis, B2048, B2050, B2051, B2054, B2058, B2061, B2064, B2083, B2096, B2160, B2232, B2320 (Recette générale des finances); B3411–3422 (États journaliers); B3659, B3664 (Comptes divers); B4092–5, B4101, B4105 (Recette générale de Flandre); B8043–5, B8085–8103, B8225 (Recette générale de Hainaut); B9879–99 (Recette de la Salle de Valenciennes); B10204 (Valenciennes. Compte des ouvrages); B17687, B17698 (Lettres reçues et dépêchées)

Lille, Bibliothèque municipale (BM Lille)
MS 336

London, British Library (BL)
Additional MS 54156; MS Yates Thompson 32

Metz, Bibliothèque municipale (BM Metz)
MS 855

Mons, Archives de l'État (AEM)
MS 89

Paris, Archives du ministère des affaires étrangères
MSS 24–5

Paris, Bibliothèque de l'Arsenal
MSS 3365, 3521, 4140, 4813, 5104 (Rés.), 5118 (Rés.)

Paris, Bibliothèque Nationale (BN)
Collection de Bourgogne 20, 22, 95; Collection Dupuy 724; Dossiers bleus

134; MSS fr. 1104, 1163, 1174, 1214, 1226, 1244, 1278, 1642, 1716–17, 1721, 2200, 2226, 2264, 2366, 2688–9, 2861, 3887, 4907, 5044, 5311, 5739, 12490, 12788, 24315, 25434; Nouv. Acq. fr. 4061; Pièces originales 509

Paris, Bibliothèque St-Geneviève
MSS 1999, 2444

Rouen, Bibliothèque municipale (BM Rouen)
MS 1234

Torhout, Dekanaal Archief
No. 13

Valenciennes, Archives municipales (AMV)
BB 202 (Administration communale); J2/238–40 (Bordereaux des Werps); J2/356, 358, 366–77 (Embriévures et criées); W.48–66 (Greffe des Werps)

Valenciennes, Bibliothèque municipale (BM Valenciennes)
MSS 670–1, 676, 748

Vienna, Österreichische Nationalbibliothek
HS 2579

Private collections
Dr Jean Cooreman, Hoogstraat 12, Lede, Belgium
M. le Prince de Ligne, Château de Beloeil, Belgium

Published primary sources

Catalogues and inventories
Arnauldet, P., 'Catalogue de la Bibliothèque du château de Blois en 1518', *Le bibliographe moderne* vi (1902), 145–74, 305–37
Bandini, A. M., *Bibliotheca Leopoldina Laurentiana, seu catalogus manuscriptorum*, 3 vols, Florence 1791–3
Barrois, J., *Bibliothèque protypographique, ou librairies des fils du roi Jehan, Charles V, Jean de Berri, Philippe de Bourgogne et les siens*, Paris 1830
Bautier, R.-H. and others (eds), *Les sources de l'histoire économique et sociale du moyen âge: les états de la maison de Bourgogne*, I: *Archives des principautés territoriales*, ii: *Les principautés du Nord*, Paris 1984
Caffiaux, M., 'Archives communales de Valenciennes', *Bulletin de la Commission historique du Département du Nord* x (1868), 175–91
Catalogue des livres composant la bibliothèque de feu Monsieur le Baron James de Rothschild, 5 vols, Paris 1884–1920

Catalogue général des manuscrits des bibliothèques publiques de France: Arras–Avranches–Boulogne (t. 4), Paris 1872

Catalogue général des manuscrits des bibliothèques publiques de France: Besançon (t. 32–3), Paris 1897–1904

Catalogue général des manuscrits des bibliothèques publiques de France: Lille–Dunkerque–Bergues–Roye–Péronne–Ham (t. 26), Paris 1894

Catalogue général des manuscrits des bibliothèques publiques de France: Poitiers–Valenciennes (t. 25), Paris 1894

Catalogue des manuscrits français de la Bibliothèque nationale: tome premier, ancien fonds, Paris 1868

Chantilly, les archives: le cabinet des titres, 4 vols, Paris 1926–9

Decavele, J. and J. Vannieuwenhuyse, *Stadsarchief van Gent. Archiefgids deel I: oud archief*, Ghent 1983

Delisle, L., *Le cabinet des manuscrits de la Bibliothèque impériale*, 4 vols, Paris 1868–81

Derolez, A., *Inventaris van de handschriften in de universiteitsbibliotheek te Gent*, Ghent 1977

De Smet, J., *Inventaris van het archief van het land van Wijnendale*, Tongeren 1934

Doutrepont, G., *Inventaire de la librairie de Philippe le Bon (1420)*, Brussels 1906

Gachard, L. P. and others, *Inventaire des archives des chambres des comptes*, 6 vols, Brussels 1837–1931

——— *Rapport sur les archives de Lille*, Brussels 1841

——— 'Notice sur la librairie de la reine Marie de Hongrie, soeur de Charles-Quint, régente des Pays-Bas', BCRH (1845), 224–46

——— *La Bibliothèque nationale à Paris: notices et extraits des manuscrits qui concernent l'histoire de Belgique*, 2 vols, Brussels 1875–7

——— *Études et notices historiques concernant les Pays-Bas*, 3 vols, Brussels 1890

Gaudefroy, L., *Catalogue des livres rares et curieux provenant de la bibliothèque de Mademoiselle la Comtesse d'Yves: vente, le 9 octobre 1820*, ii, Brussels 1820

Inventaire sommaire des archives du Département des affaires étrangères: mémoires et documents, Paris 1883

Kohler, C., *Catalogue des manuscrits de la Bibliothèque Sainte-Geneviève*, 2 vols, Paris 1893–6; *Supplément*, Paris 1913

Le Glay, A. and others, *Inventaire sommaire des archives départementales du Nord: série B*, 10 vols, Lille 1863–1906

Leuridant, F., *La bibliothèque des princes de Ligne*, Brussels 1915, repr. Brussels–Paris 1923

Marchal, J., *Catalogue des manuscrits de la Bibliothèque royale des ducs de Bourgogne*, i, Brussels 1842

Michelant, M., 'Inventaire des manuscrits de Marguerite d'Autriche', BCRH (1871), 5–78

Moreau, B., *Inventaire chronologique des éditions parisiennes du XVIe siècle*, II: *(1511–20)*, Paris 1977

Nélis, H., *Chambre des comptes de Lille: catalogue des chartes du sceau de l'audience*, Brussels 1915

Peignot, G., *Catalogue d'une partie des livres composant l'ancienne bibliothèque des ducs de Bourgogne de la dernière race*, Paris 1830
Phillipps, T., *Codices manuscripti in Bibliotheca Sancti Vedasti, apud Atrebatium*, Paris 1828
Rigault, J., *Guide des Archives de la Côte d'Or*, Dijon 1984
Rossignol, C. and others, *Inventaire sommaire des archives départementales de la Côte d'Or: série B*, 6 vols, Dijon 1863–94
Van den Gheyn, J., *Catalogue des manuscrits de la Bibliothèque royale de Belgique*, vii–x, Brussels 1900
Van Haegendoren, M., *Les Archives générales du royaume à Bruxelles: apeçu des fonds et des inventaires*, Brussels 1955
Verbeemen, J., *Inventaris van het Archief der Heren en van het Stadsarchief van Diest*, Brussels 1961
Vleeschouwers, C., *Het archief van de Abdij van Boudelo te Sinaai-Waas en te Gent*, ii, Brussels 1983
Vleeschouwers-Van Melkebeek, M., 'Het archief van de bisschoppen van Doornik: een inventaris uit 1477', BCRH cxlix (1983), 121–376
Voisin, A., *Bibliotheca Hulthemiana*, 6 vols, Ghent 1836–7
────── *Souvenirs de la bibliothèque des Princes de Ligne à Beloeil*, Ghent 1839

Editions and collections of documents
Aubrée, G., *Mémoires pour servir à l'histoire de France et de Bourgogne*, 2 vols, Paris 1729
Bewijsstukken betreffende den opstand van Gent tegen Philips den Goede, ed. V. Fris, Ghent 1914
Brom, G., *Archivalia in Italië belangrijk voor de Geschiedenis van Nederlanden*, 4 vols, The Hague 1908–14
Collection de documents inédits concernant l'histoire de la Belgique, ed. L. P. Gachard, 3 vols, Brussels 1833–5
Comptes généraux de l'état bourguignon entre 1416 et 1420, ed. M. Mollat and R. Favreau, 4 vols, Paris 1965–76
Correspondance de l'Empereur Maximilien I et de Marguerite d'Autriche, ed. M. Le Glay, Paris 1839
Cosneau, E., *Les grands traités de la guerre de cent ans*, Paris 1889
Coutume de la ville de Gand, ed. A. E. Gheldof and others, 2 vols, Brussels 1868–87
de Laborde, L., *Les ducs de Bourgogne: étude sur les lettres, les arts et l'industrie pendant le XVe siècle*, 3 vols, Paris 1849–52
de La Grange, A., 'Extraits des registres des consaulx de la ville de Tournai, 1431–76', published as *Mémoires de la Société historique de Tournai* xxiii (1893)
Dépêches des ambassadeurs milanais en France sous Louis XI et François Sforza, ed. B. de Mandrot, 4 vols, Paris 1916–23
Der Briefwechsel Karls des Kühnen (1433–1477), ed. W. Paravicini, 2 vols, Frankfurt am Main 1995

Dispatches with related documents of Milanese ambassadors in France, ed. V. Ilardi and F. Fata, Delkalb, Ill. 1981

Dispatches with related documents of Milanese ambassadors in France and Burgundy, 1450–1483, ed. P. M. Kendall and V. Ilardi, 2 vols, Athens, Oh. 1970–1

Documents relatifs à la guerre du Bien Public, ed. J. Quicherat, Paris 1843

Documents relatifs au Grand Schisme, V: Lettres de Benoît XIII (1394–1422), ed. M.-J. Tits-Dieuaide, ii, Brussels–Rome 1960

Documents relatifs au Grand Schisme, VI: Suppliques de Benoît XIII (1394–1422), ed. P. Briegleb and A. Laret-Kayser, i, Brussels–Rome 1973

Guerin, P., 'Recueil de documents concernant le Poitou dans les registres de la chancellerie de France', *Archives historiques du Poitou* xxix (1898)

Handelingen van de leden en van de staten van Vlaanderen (1384–1405), ed. W. Prevenier, Brussels 1959

Handelingen van de leden en van de staten van Vlaanderen (1405–1419), ed. A. Zoete, 2 vols, Brussels 1981–2

Les arrêts et jugés du Parlement de Paris sur appels flamands conservés dans les registres du Parlement 1320–1521, ed. R. C. Van Caeneghem, 2 vols, Brussels 1966–77

Letters and papers illustrative of the wars of the English in France during the reign of Henry VI, ed. J. Stevenson, 3 vols, London 1861–4

Lettres de Louis XI, roi de France, ed. J. Vaesen and E. Charavay, 12 vols, Paris 1883–1909

Leuridan, T., 'Épigraphie de Valenciennes', *Mémoires de la Société d'études de la province de Cambrai* xxv (1932); xxvi (1938); xxvii (1947); xxviii (1948)

Matricule de l'Université de Louvain, I: 1426 (origine) – 30 août 1453, ed. E. Reusens, Brussels 1903

Memorieboek der stadt Ghendt van 't jaar 1301 tot 1793, ed. P. Van Der Meersch, 4 vols, Ghent 1859–61

Morice, H., *Mémoires pour servir de preuves à l'histoire ecclésiastique et civile de Bretagne*, 3 vols, Paris 1742–6

Paravicini, W., 'Die Hofordnungen Herzog Philipps des Guten von Burgund: Edition', I, *Francia* x (1982), 131–66; II, ibid. xi (1983), 257–301; III, ibid. xiii (1985), 191–211; IV, ibid. xv (1987, publ. 1989), 183–231; V, ibid. xviii/1 (1991), 111–23

Promotions de la faculté des arts de l'Université de Louvain (1428–1797), ed. E. Reusens, Louvain 1869

Regesten op de Jaarregisters van de Keure: schepenjaar 1400–1401, ed. M. Houbrechts, Ghent, 1969–72

Scott, E. and L. Gilliodts van Severen, *Le Cotton manuscrit Galba B. I.*, Brussels 1896

Wils, J., 'Documents relatifs à l'histoire de l'Université de Louvain: les dépenses d'un étudiant à l'Université de Louvain (1448–1453)', *Analectes pour servir à l'histoire ecclésiastique de la Belgique* 3rd ser. ii (1906), 489–507

Chronicles and other narratives

Alain Bouchart, *Grandes croniques de Bretaigne*, ed. M.-L. Auger and G. Jeanneau, 2 vols, Paris 1986

Alain Chartier, *Le quadrilogue invectif*, ed. E. Droz, Paris 1950

Alienor de Poitiers, *Les honneurs de la cour*, ed. J. B. de Lacurne de St-Palaye, in *Mémoires sur l'ancienne chevalerie*, Paris 1759, ii. 169–282

Antoine de La Sale, *Jehan de Saintré*, ed. J. Misrahi and C. Knudson, Geneva 1978

Charles d'Orléans, *Poésies*, ed. P. Champion, 2 vols, Paris 1923–7

Christine de Pisan, *Le Livre de la paix*, ed. C. C. Willard, The Hague 1958

—— *Le Livre des fais et bonnes meurs du sage roy Charles V*, ed. S. Solente, Paris 1936–40

—— *Le Livre du corps de policie*, ed. R. H. Lucas, Geneva 1967

Chronique des Pays-Bas, de France, d'Angleterre et de Tournai, in *Recueil des chroniques de Flandre*, iii, ed. J. J. de Smet, Brussels 1856, 113–570

Chronique du Religieux de St Denis, ed. L. Bellaguet, 6 vols, Paris 1839–52

Coulon, A., 'Fragment d'une chronique du règne de Louis XI', *Mélanges d'archéologie et d'histoire de l'École française de Rome* xv (1895), 103–40

Cronicon Briocense, chronique de St-Brieuc, ed. G. Le Duc and C. Sterckx, Rennes–Paris 1972

Dagboek van Gent van 1447 tot 1470 met een vervolg van 1477 tot 1515, ed. V. Fris, 2 vols, Ghent 1901–4

Emond de Dynter, *Chronique des ducs de Brabant*, in *Chroniques belges inédites*, ed. P. F. X. de Ram, 3 vols, Brussels 1854–60

Enguerran de Monstrelet, *Chronique*, ed. L. Douët-d'Arcq, 6 vols, Paris 1857–62

Eustache Deschamps, *Oeuvres complètes*, ed. A. Queux de St Hilaire and G. Raynaud, 11 vols, Paris 1878–1903

Gilles le Bouvier, *Le livre de la description des pays*, ed. E.-T. Hamy, Paris 1908

—— *Les chroniques du roi Charles VII*, ed. H. Courteault, L. Celier and M.-H. Jullien de Pommerol, Paris 1979

Guillaume Fillastre, *Le premier volume de la Toison d'Or*, Paris 1516

Guillaume Gruel, *Chronique d'Arthur de Richemont, connétable de France, duc de Bretagne (1393–1458)*, ed. A. Le Vavasseur, Paris 1890

Guillaume Leseur, *Histoire de Gaston IV, comte de Foix*, 2 vols, Paris 1893–6

Henri Baude, *Éloge ou portrait historique de Charles VII*, in *Chronique de Charles VII roi de France par Jean Chartier*, ed. A. Vallet de Viriville, 3 vols, Paris 1858, iii. 127–41

Histoire des Seigneurs de Gavre, ed. R. Stuip, Paris 1993

Histoire du bon chevalier Jacques de Lalaing escrite par messire Georges Chastellain, ed. J. Chifflet, Brussels 1634

Honoré Bonet, *The tree of battles*, ed. G. W. Coopland, Liverpool 1949

Ijsewijn-Jacobs, J., 'Magistri Anthonii Haneron (ca. 1400–1490) opera grammatica et rhetorica', *Humanistica Lovaniensia* xxiv (1975), 29–59; xxv (1976), 1–83

Jacques du Clercq, *Mémoires*, ed. J. A. C. Buchon, in *Collection des chroniques nationales françaises écrites en langue vulgaire du treizième au quinzième siècle: Chroniques d'Enguerrand de Monstrelet*, xii–xv, Paris 1826–7

Jacques Millet, *Le Mystère de la destruction de Troie la grant*, ed. E. Stengel, Marburg 1883

Jean Bodin, *Method for the easy comprehension of history*, ed. and trans. B. Reynolds, New York 1945

Jean Chartier, *Chronique de Charles VII, roi de France*, ed. A. Vallet de Viriville, 3 vols, Paris 1858

Jean de Dadizeele, *Mémoires*, ed. J. C. Kervyn de Lettenhove, Bruges 1850

Jean de Haynin, *Mémoires 1465–77*, ed. D. D. Brouwers, 2 vols, Liège 1905–6

Jean de Roye, *Journal, connu sous le nom de Chronique scandaleuse*, ed. B. de Mandrot, 2 vols, Paris 1894–6

Jean de Wavrin, *Recueil des croniques et anchiennes histoires de la Grant Bretaigne*, ed. W. Hardy, 5 vols, London 1864–91

Jean Froissart, *Chroniques*, ed. S. Luce, G. Raynaud and A. Mirot, 15 vols, Paris 1869–1975

Jean Germain, *Liber de virtutibus Philippi, Burgundiae et Brabantiae ducis*, in *Chroniques relatives à l'histoire de Belgique sous la domination des ducs de Bourgogne: textes latins*, ed. J. C. Kervyn de Lettenhove, Brussels 1876, 1–115

Jean Gerson, *Oeuvres complètes*, ed. P. Glorieux, v, Paris 1963

Jean Juvenal des Ursins, *Écrits politiques*, ed. P. S. Lewis, i, Paris 1978

Jean Lefèvre de St Rémy, *Chronique*, ed. F. Morand, 2 vols, Paris 1876–81

Jean Lemaire de Belges, *Oeuvres*, ed. J. Stecher, 4 vols, Louvain 1882–5, repr. 1969

Jean Meschinot, *Lunettes des princes*, ed. C. Martineau-Genieys, Geneva 1972

Jean Molinet, *Chroniques*, ed. G. Doutrepont and O. Jodogne, 3 vols, Brussels 1935–7

—— *Faictz et dictz*, ed. N. Dupire, 3 vols, Paris 1936–9

Jean Robertet, *Oeuvres*, ed. M. Zsuppan, Geneva–Paris 1970

Le livre des trahisons de France envers la maison de Bourgogne, in *Chroniques relatives à l'histoire de Belgique sous la domination des ducs de Bourgogne: textes français*, ed. J. C. Kervyn de Lettenhove, Brussels 1873, 1–258

Le Pastoralet, in *Chroniques relatives à l'histoire de Belgique sous la domination des ducs de Bourgogne: textes français*, ed. J. C. Kervyn de Lettenhove, Brussels 1873, 573–852

Les Cent nouvelles nouvelles, ed. F. P. Sweetser, Geneva–Paris 1966

Les Grandes chroniques de France, ed. P. Paris, 6 vols, Paris 1836–8

Mathieu d'Escouchy, *Chronique*, ed. G. du Fresne de Beaucourt, 3 vols, Paris 1863–4

Nicolas de Clamanges, *Opera omnia*; I: *Epistolae*, Lyon 1613

Oeuvres complètes du roi René, duc d'Anjou, ed. T. de Quatrebarbes, 4 vols, Angers 1844–6

Oeuvres de Rigord et de Guillaume le Breton, ed. H.-F. Delaborde, 2 vols, Paris 1882–5

Olivier de La Marche, *Mémoires*, ed. H. Beaune and J. d'Arbaumont, 4 vols, Paris 1883–8
Philippe de Commynes, *Mémoires*, ed. D. Godefroy and Lenglet du Fresnoy, 4 vols, Paris 1747
—— *Mémoires*, ed. J. Calmette and G. Durville, 3 vols, Paris 1924–5, repr. 1981
—— *Memoirs*, ed. M. Jones, Harmondsworth 1972
Philippe de Mézières, *Le songe du vieil pelerin*, ed. G. W. Coopland, 2 vols, Cambridge 1969
Philippe Wielant, *Recueil des antiquités de Flandre*, in *Recueil des chroniques de Flandre*, ed. J. J. de Smet, iv, Brussels 1865, 1–442
Pierre de Fenin, *Mémoires (1407–1422)*, in E. Petitot (ed.), *Collection complète des mémoires relatifs à l'histoire de France*, vii, Paris 1825, 237–370
Pierre le Baud, *Histoire de Bretagne, avec les chroniques des maisons de Vitré et de Laval*, ed. C. d'Hozier, Paris 1638
Pontus Heuterus, *Opera historica omnia*, 3 vols, Louvain 1651
Recueil de farces françaises inédites du XVe siècle, ed. G. Cohen, Cambridge, Mass. 1949
Recueil général des sotties, ed. E. Picot, 3 vols, Paris 1902–12
'Response d'un bon et loyal françois au peuple de France de tous estats', ed. G. Aubrée, in *Mémoires pour servir à l'histoire de France et de Bourgogne*, Paris 1729, i. 315–22
Robert Blondel, *Oeuvres complètes*, ed. A. Héron, 2 vols, Rouen 1891–3
Rondeaux et autres poésies du XVe siècle, ed. G. Raynaud, Paris 1889
Thomas Basin, *Histoire de Charles VII*, ed. C. Samaran, 2 vols, Paris 1964–5
—— *Histoire de Louis XI*, ed. C. Samaran and M.-C. Garand, 3 vols, Paris 1963–72
Traités du duel judiciaire, ed. B. Prost, Paris 1872
Vernet, A., 'Le *Tragicum argumentum de miserabili statu regni Francie* de François de Montebelluna (1357)', ABSHF (1962–3), 101–63

Chastelain editions

Batissier, L. (ed.), *Les Douze dames de rhétorique*, Moulins 1838
Bliggenstorfer, S. (ed.), *Georges Chastelain, le Temple de Bocace: édition commentée*, Bern 1988
Buchon, J. A. C. (ed.), *Chronique des ducs de Bourgogne par Georges Chastellain*, 2 vols, Paris 1827
—— (ed.), *Oeuvres historiques inédites de Sire Georges Chastellain*, Paris 1837
Delclos, J.-C. (ed.), *Georges Chastellain, Chronique: les fragments du Livre IV révélés par l'Additional manuscript 54156 de la British Library*, Geneva 1991
Hommel, L. (ed.), *Pages choisies de Chastellain*, Paris 1949

Kervyn de Lettenhove, J. C. (ed.), *Oeuvres de Georges Chastellain*, 8 vols, Brussels 1863-6

Kondo, H, 'Le chapitre ix du Livre IV de la *Chronique* de Georges Chastellain dont la dernière partie est jusqu'ici inconnue', *ICU Comparative Culture* vi (1983), 24–31

—— 'Étude de la *Chronique* de Georges Chastelain: le texte inédit du IVe livre de *Chronique* d'après le manuscrit de la British Library Add. ms 54156 (folios 309–426)', unpubl. Ph.D. diss. International Christian University, Tokyo 1988

Lambert, C., 'Louenge à la trèsglorieuse Vierge de Georges Chastelain: étude et édition', unpubl. *mém. de licence*, Liège 1983

LOUVAIN EDITION: all *mémoires de licence* completed under the direction of O. Jodogne and G. Muraille, organised as follows in textual sequence:

Vanden Abeele, J., 'Georges Chastellain, Chronique: prologue – livre i (chapitres i–xix)' (1962)

Campion, J., 'Georges Chastellain, Chronique: livre i (chapitres lxx–cviii)' (1963)

Van Holm, H., 'Georges Chastellain, Chronique: livre i (chapitres cix–cxxix)' (1963)

Dujardin, J., 'Georges Chastellain, Chronique: livre ii (chapitres i–xxv)' (1963)

Mottart, J.-M., 'Georges Chastellain, Chronique: livre ii (chapitres xxvi–liii)' (1963)

De Vel, M. L., 'Georges Chastellain, Chronique: livre ii (chapitres liv–lxii)' (1964)

Cornet, A, 'Georges Chastellain, Chronique: livre iv (chapitres i–xiii)' (1963)

Schenus, E., 'Georges Chastellain, Chronique: livre iv (chapitres xiv–xxxii)' (1969)

De Poorter, L., 'Georges Chastellain, Chronique: livre iv (chapitres xxxiii–xlvi)' (1967)

Pereau, J.-M., 'Georges Chastellain, Chronique: livre iv (chapitres xlvii–lx)' (1972)

Nélis, P., 'Georges Chastellain, Chronique: livre iv (chapitres lxi–lxxvii)' (1967)

Panis, W., 'Georges Chastellain, Chronique: livre iv (chapitres lxxviii–xciv)' (1967)

Verburg, J., 'Georges Chastellain, Chronique: proesme – livre vi (chapitres i–xxii)' (1968)

Billiet, R., 'Georges Chastellain, Chronique: livre vi (chapitres xxiii–xxxix)' (1968)

Bertrand, D., 'Georges Chastellain, Chronique: livre vi (chapitres xl–lv)' (1969)

Baudoux, G., 'Georges Chastellain, Chronique: livre vi (chapitres lvi–lxxiv)' (1968)

Demarcin, M., 'Georges Chastellain, Chronique: livre vi (chapitres lxxv–lxxxvii)' (1969)
Peltgen, D., 'Georges Chastellain, Chronique: livre vi, 2e partie (chapitres i–xi)' (1969)
Janssens, C., 'Georges Chastellain, Chronique: livre vi, 2e partie (chapitres xii–xxvi)' (1969)
Ruhl, C., 'Georges Chastellain, Chronique: livre vi, 2e partie (chapitres xxvii–xliii)' (1971)
Fery, A., 'Georges Chastellain, Chronique: livre vi, 2e partie (chapitres lxxx–xcv)' (1970)
Rollin, Y., 'Georges Chastellain, Chronique: livre vi, 2e partie (chapitres xcvi–cx)' (1972)
Lambrechts, P., 'Georges Chastellain, Chronique: livre vi, 2e partie (chapitres cxi–cxxii)' (1971)
Matthijs, E., 'Georges Chastellain, Chronique: livre vi, 2e partie (chapitres cxxiii–cxxxi)' (1971)
Aspelagh, J., 'Georges Chastellain, Chronique: livre vi, 2e partie (chapitres cxxxii) et 3e partie' (1971)
Meurée, J.-P., 'Georges Chastellain, Chronique: livre vii (chapitres xvii–xxix)' (1972)
Kinon, J.-C., 'Georges Chastellain, Chronique: livre vii (chapitres xxx–xliv)' (1972)
I have been unable to trace three further *mémoires* which were said to have been in progress in 1974. The authors, who registered their work with the IRHT, were R. Lernould, M. E. Balazs and C. Quertimon.
Quicherat, J., 'Fragments inédits de Georges Chastellain', BEC iv (1842–3), 62–78
van Hemelryck, T., *George Chastelain, Le miroir de mort: édition critique*, Louvain-la-Neuve 1995

Chastelain studies

'Acquisitions, January to June 1967', *The British Museum Quarterly* xxxii (1967–8), 149
* Armstrong, C. A. J., 'Le texte de la *Chronique* de Chastellain pour les années 1458–61 retrouvé dans un manuscrit jusqu'ici inconnu', PCEEBM x (1968), 73–8
Ascher, H., 'Die Chronik des Georges Chastellain als literarisches Werk', unpubl. MA diss. Vienna 1933
Bambeck, M., 'Die Stadt Paris als 'Haus des Brotes' oder zur Verweltlichung der biblischen Allegorese bei Georges Chastellain', *Literaturwissenschaftliches Jahrbuch* xxiii (1982), 57–70
Bliggenstorfer, S., '*Castellani Georgii, Opera poetica gallice*: le recueil Chastelain

de la Bibliothèque Laurentienne à Florence: description du manuscrit mediceo-palatino 120', *Vox romanica* xliii (1984), 123–53

Bonenfant, P., 'Chastellain fut-il chevalier de la Toison d'or?', *RBPH* xxv (1946–7), 143–4

Bonté, D., 'Le règne de Charles VII (1403–1461) vu par Chastellain', unpubl. *mém. de licence*, Lille 1964

Brown, C. J., 'Du nouveau sur le "mistere" des *Douze dames de rhétorique*: le rôle de Georges Chastelain', *BCRH* cliii (1987), 181–221

Chavannes-Mazel, C. A., 'The twelve ladies of rhetoric in Cambridge', *Transactions of the Cambridge Bibliographical Society* x (1992), 139–45

Collard, G., 'Georges Chastellain (1415–1475): l'orateur bourguignon', unpubl. *mém. de licence*, Liège 1978

Cowling, D., 'Text and building: architectural fictions in the works of the *rhétoriqueurs*', in D. Maddox and S. Sturm-Maddox (eds), *Literary aspects of courtly culture*, Cambridge 1994, 123–32

Daunou, P., Review of Buchon, *Oeuvres historiques inédites de Sire Georges Chastellain, Journal des Savants* (1837), 332–40

Delclos, J.-C., 'Le témoignage de Georges Chastellain', partially publ. Ph.D. diss., 2 vols, Sorbonne 1977

——— *Le témoignage de Georges Chastellain*, Geneva 1980

——— '*Le prince* ou *les princes* de Georges Chastellain: un poème dirigé contre Louis XI', *Romania* cii (1981), 46–74

——— 'Le témoignage de Georges Chastellain', *Réforme, humanisme, renaissance* xiv (1981), 42–8

——— 'Jean Lefèvre: l'une des sources du Livre II de Georges Chastellain', *Rencontres médiévales en Bourgogne (XIVe–XVe siècles)* i (1991), 7–18

——— ' "Je doncques George Chastellain . . . ": de l'histoire commandée au jugement personnel', *Revue des langues romanes* xcvii (1993), 75–92

de Limburg-Stirum, T., 'Notes sur la famille de Georges Chastellain', *Annales de la Société d'émulation pour l'étude de l'histoire et des antiquités de la Flandre* 3rd ser. vi (1871), 1–6

de Rosanbo, C., 'Notice sur les *Douze dames de rhétorique*', *Bulletin de la Société française de reproduction de manuscrits à peintures* xii (1929), 5–16

Desmasures, J., 'Étude historique: Georges Chastellain', *Revue agricole, industrielle, littéraire et artistique. Société impériale d'agriculture, sciences et arts de l'arrondissement de Valenciennes (Nord)* xvi (1863), 184–91

Devaux, J., 'George Chastelain rhétoriqueur', *MA* xcix (1993), 516–32

Diverres, A. H., '*Le miroir de mort* by Georges Chastellain', *The National Library of Wales Journal* i (1940), 218–19

Droz, E. and C. Dalbanne, 'Le *Miroir de mort* de Georges Chastellain', *Gutenberg Jahrbuch* (1928), 89–92

Dufournet, J., 'Chastellain, Georges', *Dictionnaire des lettres françaises: le moyen âge*, Paris 1964, 173

——— 'Retour à Georges Chastelain', *MA* lxxxviii (1982), 329–42 du Fresne de Beaucourt, G., 'Le chroniqueur Georges Chastellain', *Revue bibliographique et littéraire* ii (1866), 57–65

Gros, G., '*Querant l'un oeil envers les cieulx estendre*: étude sur la *Louenge* mariale de George Chastelain', *MA* xcviii (1992), 429–45

Heilemann, C., *Der Wortschatz von Georges Chastellain nach seiner Chronik*, Leipzig 1937

Hemmer, K., *Georges Chastellain (1405–75): Dichter und Ratgeber seiner Fürsten, Lehrer seiner Zeit*, Münster 1937

Hommel, L., *Chastellain 1415–1474*, Brussels 1946

Jodogne, O., Review of Hommel, *Chastellain 1415–1474*, *Revue d'histoire ecclésiastique* xli (1946), 141–2

Jodogne, P., 'La rhétorique dans l'historiographie bourguigonne', in *Culture et pouvoir*, 51–69

Johnson, L. W., 'Prince or princes? Fifteenth-century politics and poetry', *The French Review* lxviii (1995), 421–30

Jung, M.-R., 'Les *Douze dames de rhétorique*', *Actes du IIIe colloque international sur le moyen français: du mot au texte*, Tübingen 1982, 229–40

Kervyn de Lettenhove, J. C., 'Note sur quelques fragments inédits des *Mémoires* de G. Chastelain', *Bulletin de la Société de l'histoire de France* (1854), 132–3

—————— 'Chastellain, Georges', *BNB*, iv, Brussels 1873, 40–50

Kondo, H., 'La transformation de la conscience de Georges Chastelain à travers sa *Chronique*', *Études de langue et de littérature françaises (Société japonnaise de langue et de littérature françaises)* xxxvii (1980), 5–15 (in Japanese)

—————— 'Le Livre IV de la *Chronique* de Georges Chastelain', *Études de langue et de littérature françaises (Société japonnaise de langue et de littérature françaises)* l (1987), 1–18

Krabusch, M., 'Georges Chastellain als Geschichtsschreiber und Betrachter des politischen Lebens seiner Zeit', unpubl. Ph.D. diss. Heidelberg 1950

Lemaire, J., '*L'oultré d'amour* de George Chastelain: un exemple ancien de construction en abyme', *Revue romane* xi (1976), 306–16

Maurin, M., 'La poétique de Chastellain et la *Grande rhétorique*', *Publications of the Modern Language Association of America* lxxiv (1959), 482–4

Mourin, L., 'Un manuscrit inconnu de l'*Advertissement au duc Charles* de Georges Chastellain', *Scriptorium* ii (1948), 119–21

Muhlethaler, J.-C., 'Un manifeste poétique de 1463: les *Enseignes des Douze dames de rhétorique*', in *Actes du Ve colloque international sur le moyen français, Milan, 4–6 mai 1985, I: Les grands rhétoriqueurs*, Milan 1985, 83–101

Muret, P., 'Chastelain parmi nous: à propos d'un livre récent', *RBPH* lxi (1983), 367–72

Pérouse, G., *Georges Chastellain: étude sur l'histoire politique et littéraire du XVe siècle*, Paris 1910

Piaget, A., 'Les *princes* de Georges Chastellain', *Romania* xlvii (1921), 161–206

Pinchart, A., 'Historiographes, indiciaires, écrivains: Chastellain (George)', in *Messager des sciences historiques* (1862), 301–21

Quicherat, J., Partial review of Kervyn, *Oeuvres de Georges Chastellain*, BEC xxiv (1863), 341–2; xxv (1864), 571–3

Renard, B., 'Quelques observations à propos de quatorze chapitres inédits de Georges Chastellain', *Trésor national* i (1842), 91–9

—— 'Nouvelles observations historiques à propos du IVe volume inédit de la *Grande Chronique* de Georges Chastellain', *Trésor national* iii (1842–3), 190–257

—— 'Correspondance', *Bulletin de la Société de l'histoire de France* (1843), 37–9

—— 'Note relative à divers manuscrits des *Mémoires* de G. Chastellain', *Bulletin de la Société de l'histoire de France* (1854), 165–6

Sankovitch, T., 'Death and the mole: two fifteenth-century dances of death', *Fifteenth century studies* ii (1978–80), 211–17

Saulnier, V. L., 'Sur George Chastelain poète et les rondeaux qu'on lui attribua', in *Mélanges de langue et de littérature du moyen âge et de la renaissance offerts à Jean Frappier*, ii, Geneva 1970, 987–1000

Small, G. P., 'George Chastelain à Valenciennes', *Valentiana* iv (1989), 26–31

—— 'Qui a lu la *Chronique* de George Chastelain?', PCEEB xxxi (1991), 101–11

—— and D. Lievois, 'Les origines gantoises du chroniqueur George Chastelain (ca. 1414–ca.1441)', HMGOG ns xlviii (1994), 121–77

—— 'Some aspects of Burgundian attitudes towards the English during the reign of Philip the Good: George Chastelain and his circle', PCEEB xxxv (1995), 15–26

Thiry, C., 'Un panégyrique pessimiste: la *Paix de Péronne* de Georges Chastelain', *Marche romane* xxvi (1976), 31–55

—— 'Le vieux renard et le jeune loup: l'évolution interne de la *Recollection des merveilleuses advenues*', MA xc (1984), 455–85

—— 'Stylistique et auto-critique: Georges Chastelain et l'*Exposition sur verité mal prise*', in *Actes du VIe colloque international sur le moyen français, Milan, 4–6 mai 1988*, III: *Recherches sur la littérature du XVe siècle*, Milan 1991, 101–35

—— 'Les Croy face aux indiciaires bourguignons: George Chastelain, Jean Molinet', in Aubailly and others, '*Et c'est la fin*', iii. 1363–80

Urwin, K., *Georges Chastellain, la vie, les oeuvres*, Paris 1937

Vallet de Viriville, A., 'Correspondance', *Bulletin du Comité de la langue* ii (1853–5), 207–8

—— 'Oeuvres de Georges Chastellain', *Journal des Savants* (1867), 49–63, 183–99, 385–93

—— 'Chastellain, Georges', *Nouvelle biographie générale*, x. 56–64

Vanden Bemden, F., 'Renseignements généalogiques inédits sur Georges Chastelain, historien gantois', BSHAG viii–ix (1901), 319–24

van Hemelryck, T., 'Villon, lecteur de Chastelain?', *Les lettres romanes* xlviii (1994), 1–13

Vosgien, B., 'Georges Chastellain, Chronique: étude critique du tome premier', unpubl. *mém. de licence*, Lille 1965

Wolff, H., 'Histoire et pédagogie princière au XVe siècle: Georges Chastelain', in *Culture et pouvoir*, 37–49

―――― 'Prose historique et rhétorique: les *Chroniques* de Chastelain et Molinet', in *Actes du VIe colloque international sur le moyen français, Milan, 4–6 mai 1988*, II: *Rhétorique et mise en prose au XVe siècle*, Milan 1991, 87–104

Secondary sources

Algemene Geschiedenis der Nederlanden, iv–v, Haarlem 1980

Allmand, C. T., 'The aftermath of war in fifteenth-century France', *History* lxi (1976), 344–57

Althoff, G., 'Studien zur habsburgischen Merowingersage', *Mitteilungen des Instituts für österreichische Geschichtsforschung* lxxxvii (1979), 71–100

Anglo, S., *La tryumphante entrée de Charles, prince des Espagnes en Bruges, 1515: a facsimile*, Amsterdam–New York 1973

Archambault, P., *Seven French chroniclers*, Syracuse, NY 1974

* Armstrong, C. A. J., 'Some examples of the distribution and speed of news at the time of the Wars of the Roses', in R. W. Hunt, W. A. Pantin and R. W. Southern (eds), *Studies in medieval history presented to F. M. Powicke*, Oxford 1948, 429–54

―――― 'The Burgundian Netherlands, 1477–1521', in G. R. Potter (ed.), *The New Cambridge Modern History*, I: *1493–1520*, Cambridge 1957, 224–58

* ―――― 'Politics and the battle of St Albans', *Bulletin of the Institute of Historical Research* xxxiii (1960), 1–72

* ―――― 'Had the Burgundian government a policy for the nobility?', in J. S. Bromley and E. H. Kossman (eds), *Britain and the Netherlands*, Groningen 1964, ii. 9–32

* ―――― 'La double monarchie France–Angleterre et la maison de Bourgogne (1420–1435): le déclin d'une alliance', AB xxxvii (1965), 81–112

* ―――― 'The language question in the Low Countries', in J. Hale, R. Highfield and B. Smalley (eds), *Europe in the late Middle Ages*, London 1965, 386–409

* ―――― 'La politique matrimoniale des ducs de Bourgogne de la maison de Valois', AB xl (1968), 5–58, 89–139

―――― 'The golden age of Burgundy: the dukes that outdid kings', in A. G. Dickens (ed.), *The courts of Europe: politics, patronage and royalty, 1400–1800*, London 1977, 55–75

―――― *England, France and Burgundy in the fifteenth century*, London 1983 (includes all titles by this author asterisked above)

Arnade, P. J., 'Secular charisma, sacred power: rites of rebellion in the Ghent entry of 1467', HMGOG ns xlv (1991), 69–94

Arnold, K., *Johannes Trithemius (1462–1516)*, Würzburg 1971, repr. 1991

Arnould, M.-A., *Historiographie de la Belgique: des origines à 1830*, Brussels 1947
Aubailly, J.-C. and others (eds), *'Et c'est la fin pour quoy sommes ensemble': hommage à Jean Dufournet*, 3 vols, Paris 1993
Autrand, F., *Charles VI*, Paris 1986
────── *Charles V*, Paris 1994
Badel, P.-Y., *Le roman de la rose: étude de la réception de l'oeuvre*, Geneva 1980
Balthau, E., 'Robert de Masmines', in CTO, 54-5
────── 'Robrecht van Massemen, heer van Massemen, Westrem, Hemelveerdegem, Beerlegem, Sint-Martens-Lierde, Sint-Maria-Lierde, Parike, Leeuwergem en Elene (1385/1390–september 1430)', *Handelingen der Zottegems Genootschap voor Geschiedenis en Oudheidkunde* vii (1995), 153-8
Barner, G., *Jacques Du Clercq und seine Mémoires: ein Sittengemälde des 15. Jahrhunderts*, Düsseldorf 1989 (not consulted)
Bartier, J., 'L'ascension d'un marchand bourguignon au XVe siècle: Odot Molain', *AB* xv (1943), 185-206
────── *Charles le Téméraire*, Brussels 1944, repr. 1970
────── *Légistes et gens de finance au XVe siècle*, Brussels 1952
────── 'De Bourgondische adel', *Flandria Nostria* iv (1959), 319-44
────── 'Une crise de l'état bourguignon: la réformation financière de 1457', in *Hommage au Professeur Paul Bonenfant (1899–1965)*, Brussels 1965, 501-11
Bauchond, M., *La justice criminelle du magistrat de Valenciennes au moyen âge*, Paris 1904
Bayot, A., 'Observations sur les manuscrits de l'*Histoire de la Toison d'Or* de Guillaume Fillastre', *Revue des bibliothèques et archives de Belgique* (1907), 425-38
────── 'La légende de Troie à la cour de Bourgogne: étude d'histoire littéraire et de bibliographie', *Société d'émulation de Bruges, Mélanges*, I, Bruges 1908, 3-51
────── 'Notice du manuscrit original des *Mémoires* de Jean de Haynin', *Revue des bibliothèques et archives de Belgique* (1908), 109-44
Beaulieu, M. and J. Baylé, *Le costume en Bourgogne de Philippe le Hardi à Charles le Téméraire*, Paris 1956
Beaune, C., 'St Clovis: histoire, religion royale et sentiment national en France à la fin du moyen âge', in B. Guenée (ed.), *Le métier d'historien au moyen âge*, Paris 1977, 139-56
────── 'L'historiographie de Charles VII: un thème de l'opposition à Louis XI', in *FFQS*, 265-81
────── *Naissance de la nation France*, Paris 1985
Beaussart, P. and L. Nys (eds), *Richesses des anciennes églises de Valenciennes*, Valenciennes 1987
Beauvois, E., *Un agent politique de Charles-Quint, le bourguignon Claude Bouton, seigneur de Corberon*, Paris 1882
Beck, J., *Le Concile de Basle (1434): les origines du théâtre réformiste et partisan en France*, Leiden 1979

Bell, D. M., *L'idéal éthique de la royauté au moyen âge*, Paris–Geneva 1962

Benecke, G., *Maximilian I 1459–1519*, London 1982

Bénédictins du Bouveret, *Colophons des manuscrits occidentaux des origines au XVIe siècle*, 7 vols, Fribourg 1965–82

Berger, R., *Nikolas Rolin: Kanzler der Zeitenwende im burgundisch-französischen Konflict, 1422–1461*, Fribourg 1971

Berger, S. and P. Durrieu, *Les notes pour les enlumineurs dans les manuscrits du moyen âge*, Paris 1893

Bernus, P., 'Essai sur la vie de Pierre de Brézé (vers 1410–65)', *PTSEC* (1906), 7–17

—— 'Le rôle politique de Pierre de Brézé au cours des dix dernières années du règne de Charles VII (1451–61)', *BEC* lxix (1908), 303–47

—— 'Louis XI et Pierre de Brézé (1440–65)', *Revue de l'Anjou* ns lxiii (1911), 241–89

Berriot, F., 'Images de l'Islam dans le *Débat* manuscrit de Jean Germain (1450)', *Réforme, humanisme et renaissance* xiii (1981), 1–14

Bigwood, G., 'Gand et la circulation des grains en Flandre, du XIVe siècle au XVIIIe siècle', *Vierteljahrsschrift für Sozial- und Wirtschaftsgeschichte* iv (1906), 397–460

—— *Le régime juridique et économique du commerce de l'argent dans la Belgique au moyen âge*, 2 vols, Brussels 1921–2

Bittmann, K., 'La question catalane et la politique générale au début du règne de Louis XI', *Annales du Midi* lvi–lx (1944–8), 80–90

—— *Ludwig XI. und Karl der Kühne: die Memorien des Philippe de Commynes als historische Quelle*, 2 vols, Göttingen 1964–70

Black, A., *Political thought in Europe 1250–1450*, Cambridge 1992

Blanchard, J., 'Vox poetica, vox politica: l'entrée du poète dans le champ politique au XVe siècle', *Actes du Ve colloque international sur le moyen français, Milan, 4–6 mai 1985*, III: *Etudes littéraires sur le XVe siècle*, Milan 1985, 39–51

Blockmans, W. P., 'La position du comté de Flandre dans le royaume à la fin du XVe siècle', in *FFQS*, 71–89

Boase, R., *The troubadour revival*, London 1978

Boeren, P. C., *Twee Maaslandse dichters in dienst van Karel de Stoute*, The Hague 1968

Boinet, A., 'Un bibliophile du XVe siècle: le grand bâtard de Bourgogne', *BEC* lxvii (1906), 252–69

Bonenfant, A. M. and P. Bonenfant, 'Le projet d'érection des états bourguignons en royaume en 1447', *MA* xlv (1935), 10–23

* Bonenfant, P., *Philippe-le-Bon*, Brussels 1943

—— 'L'origine des surnoms de Philippe le Bon', *AB* xvi (1944), 100–3

—— 'La persistance des souvenirs lotharingiens: à propos d'une supplique brabançonne au pape Martin V', *Bulletin de l'Institut historique belge de Rome* xxvii (1952), 53–64

* —— 'État bourguignon et Lotharingie', *Bulletin de l'Académie royale de Belgique* xli (1955), 266–82

────── 'Du *Belgium* de César à la Belgique de 1830: essai sur une évolution sémantique', *Annales de la Société royale d'archéologie de Bruxelles* l (1956–61), 31–58

* ────── *Du meurtre de Montereau au traité de Troyes*, Brussels 1958

* ────── 'Les traits essentiels du règne de Philippe le Bon', *Bijdragen en mededelingen van het historisch Genootschap te Utrecht* lxxiv (1960), 10–29

* ────── 'L'État bourguignon', in *La monocratie (Recueils J. Bodin*, xxi/2), Brussels 1969, 429–46

────── *Philippe le Bon: sa politique, son action*, Brussels 1996 (includes all titles by this author asterisked above)

────── and J. Stenghers, 'Le rôle de Charles le Téméraire dans le gouvernement de l'état bourguignon en 1465–1467', AB xxv (1953), 7–29, 118–33

Boone, M., 'De Gentse lening van 1436: bijdrage tot de studie der stedelijke elite', *Appeltjes van het Meetjesland* xxxix (1988), 87–99

────── 'Dons et pots-de-vin, aspects de la sociabilité urbaine au bas moyen âge: le cas gantois pendant la période bourguignonne', RN lxx (1988), 471–87

────── 'Diplomatie et violence d'état: la sentence rendue par les ambassadeurs et conseillers du roi de France, Charles VII, concernant le conflit entre Philippe le Bon, duc de Bourgogne, et Gand en 1452', BCRH clvi (1990), 1–54

────── *Gent en de Bourgondische hertogen, ca. 1384 – ca. 1453: een sociaal-politieke studie van een staatsvormingsproces*, Brussels 1990

────── 'Plus dueil que joie. Les ventes de rentes par la ville de Gand pendant la période bourguignonne: entre intérêts privés et finances publiques', *Bulletin trimestriel du Crédit communal de Belgique* clxxvi (1991–2), 3–25

────── 'Une famille au service de l'État bourguignon naissant: Roland et Jean d'Uutkerke, nobles flamands dans l'entourage de Philippe le Bon', RN lxxvii (1995), 233–55

────── and W. Prevenier, '1300–1500: the "city-state" dream', in J. Decavele (ed.), *Ghent: in defence of a rebellious city*, Antwerp 1989, 81–104

──────, M.-C. Laleman and D. Lievois, 'Van Simon sRijkensteen tot Hof van Ryhove: van erfachtige lieden tot dienaren van de centrale Bourgondische staat', HMGOG ns xliv (1990), 47–85

Born, L. K., 'The perfect prince: a study in thirteenth- and fourteenth-century ideals', *Speculum* iii (1928), 470–504

Born, R., *Les Croy: une grande lignée hennuyère d'hommes de guerre, de diplomates, de conseillers secrets, dans les coulisses du pouvoir, sous les ducs de Bourgogne et la maison d'Autriche (1390–1612)*, Brussels 1981

Bornstein, D., 'Reflection of political theory and political fact in fifteenth-century mirrors for princes', in J. B. Bessinger and R. R. Raymo (eds), *Medieval studies in honor of L. H. Horstein*, New York 1976, 77–85

────── 'William Caxton's chivalric romances and the Burgundian renaissance in England', *English Studies* lvii (1976), 1–10

Bossuat, A., *Perrinet Gressart et François de Surienne, agents de l'Angleterre:*

contributions à l'étude des relations de l'Angleterre et de la Bourgogne avec la France sous le règne de Charles VII, Paris 1936

—— 'Le rétablissement de la paix sociale sous le règne de Charles VII', MA lx (1954), 137–62

—— 'Jean Castel, chroniqueur de France', MA lxiv (1958), 285–304, 499–538

—— 'Les origines troyennes: leur rôle dans la littérature historique au XVe siècle', *Annales de Normandie* viii (1958), 187–97

Bossuat, R., 'Traductions françaises des *Commentaires* de César à la fin du XVe siècle', *Bibliothèque d'humanisme et renaissance* iii (1943), 253–411

Bouchard, H., 'Philippe Pot, grand-sénéchal de Bourgogne (1428–1493)', *PTSEC* (1949), 23–7

—— 'Philippe Pot et la démocratie aux États généraux de 1484', *AB* xxii (1950), 33–40

Boucquey, D., 'Enguerran de Monstrelet, historien trop longtemps oublié', *PCEEB* xxxi (1991), 113–25

Bouton, E., *Le testament de Jehan Molinet*, Valenciennes 1859

Brandt, W. J., *The shape of medieval history: studies in modes of perception*, New Haven–London 1966

Brown, C. J., *The shaping of history and poetry in late medieval France: propaganda and artistic expression in the works of the rhétoriqueurs*, Birmingham, Alabama 1985

Brown, E. A. R., 'The case of Philip the Fair', *Viator* xix (1988), 219–46, repr. in her *The monarchy of Capetian France and royal ceremonial*, Aldershot 1991

Brunelli, G. A., 'Jean Castel et le *Mirouer des dames*', MA lxii (1956), 93–117

Brunet, G., *La France littéraire au XVe siècle, ou catalogue raisonné des ouvrages en tout genre imprimés en langue française jusqu'à l'an 1500*, Paris 1865

Brunet, J. C., *Manuel du libraire et de l'amateur des livres*, 6 vols, Paris 1860–5

Bulst, N., 'Louis XI et les états généraux de 1468', in *FFQS*, 91–104

—— and J.-P. Genet (eds), *Medieval lives and the historian: studies in medieval prosopography*, Kalamazoo 1986

Burckhardt, J., *Judgements on history and historians*, trans. H. Zohn, London 1959

Burke, P., *Tradition and innovation in Renaissance Italy*, London 1974

—— *Popular culture in early modern Europe*, London 1978

—— and R. Porter (eds), *The social history of language*, Cambridge 1987

Byrne, D., '*Rex imago Dei*: Charles V of France and the *Livre des propriétés des choses*', *JMH* vii (1981), 97–113

Calmette, J., *Louis XI, Jean II et la révolution catalane (1461–73)*, Toulouse 1903

—— 'Le mariage de Charles le Téméraire et de Marguerite d'York', *AB* i (1929), 193–214

—— 'Dom Pedro, roi des catalans et la cour de Bourgogne', *AB* xviii (1946), 7–15

Campbell, L., 'The art market in the southern Netherlands in the fifteenth century', *Burlington Magazine* cxviii (1976), 188–98

Canivez, L.-A., 'Collégiale de Ste-Pharaïlde à Gand', *Annales de la Société royale des beaux-arts et de la littérature de Gand* iv (1851–2), 195–233

Cantor, N. F., *Inventing the Middle Ages*, Cambridge 1992

Cappliez, Abbé, *Histoire des métiers de Valenciennes et de leurs saints patrons*, Valenciennes 1893

Carande, R., *Carlos V y sus banqueros, la Hacienda real de Castilla*, Madrid 1949

Carolus-Barré, L., 'St Louis dans l'histoire et la légende', ABSHF (1970–1), 37–49

Caron, M.-T., *La noblesse dans le duché de Bourgogne 1315–1477*, Lille 1987

—— *Noblesse et pouvoir royal en France (XIIIe–XVIe siècles)*, Paris 1994

—— 'Pierre de Bauffremont', in CTO, 58–9

Cartellieri, O., 'Über eine burgundische Gesandtschaft an den kaiserlichen und päpstlichen Hof im Jahre 1460', *Mitteilungen des Instituts für Österreichische Geschichtsforchung* xxviii (1907), 448–64

—— 'Ein Zweikampf in Valenciennes im Jahre 1455', *Probleme der englischen Sprache und Kultur: Festschrift Johannes Hoops zum 60 Geburtstag*, Heidelberg 1925, 169–76

—— *The court of Burgundy: studies in the history of civilisation*, London 1929, repr. New York 1970

Cartier, N., 'The lost chronicle', *Speculum* xxxvi (1961), 424–34

Cauchies, J.-M., 'Liste chronologique provisoire des ordonnances de Philippe le Bon, duc de Bourgogne, pour le comté de Hainaut', *Bulletin de la Commission royale pour la publication des anciennes lois et ordonnances de Belgique* xxvi (1973–4), 35–146

—— *La législation princière pour le comté de Hainaut: ducs de Bourgogne et premiers Habsbourg (1427–1506)*, Brussels 1982

—— *Louis XI et Charles le Hardi: de Péronne à Nancy (1468–77): le conflit*, Brussels 1996

—— 'Valenciennes et les comtes de Hainaut (milieu XIIIe–milieu XVe siècle): des relations politiques mouvementées', in Nys and Salamagne, *Valenciennes aux XIVe et XVe siècles*, 67–88

Cazaux, Y., 'L'idée de Bourgogne, fondement de la politique de Charles le Téméraire', PCEEBM x (1968), 85–91

Cellier, L., 'Une commune flamande: recherches sur les institutions politiques de la ville de Valenciennes', *Mémoires historiques sur l'arrondissement de Valenciennes* iii (1873), 27–387

—— 'Les prévôts de Valenciennes: notes chronologiques', *Mémoires historiques sur l'arrondissement de Valenciennes* iv (1876), 129–347

Chabaud, F., 'Les "Mémoires" de Philippe de Commynes: un "Miroir aux princes"?', *Francia* xix (1992), 95–114

Champion, P., *La librairie de Charles d'Orléans*, Paris 1910

—— *Histoire poétique du XVe siècle*, 2 vols, Paris 1923

Chartier, R., 'Texts, printing, readings', in L. Hunt (ed.), *The new cultural history*, Berkeley 1989, 154–75

Chaume, M., *Le sentiment national en Bourgogne de Gondebaud à Charles le Téméraire*, Dijon 1922, 195–260

Chaytor, H. J., *From script to print: an introduction to medieval literature*, Cambridge 1945

Chevalier, B., 'The *bonnes villes* and the king's council in fifteenth-century France', in Highfield and Jeffs, *Crown and local communities*, 110–28

—— and P. Contamine (eds), *La France de la fin du XVe siècle*, Paris 1985

Cinq-centième anniversaire de la bataille de Nancy (1477), Nancy 1979

Cochrane, E., *Historians and historiography in the Italian Renaissance*, Chicago 1981

Cockshaw, P., 'Mentions d'auteurs, de copistes, d'enlumineurs et de librairies dans les comptes généraux de l'état bourguignon (1384–1419)', *Scriptorium* xxiii (1969), 122–44

—— *Le personnel de la chancellerie de Bourgogne-Flandre sous les ducs de Bourgogne de la maison de Valois (1384–1477)*, Courtrai–Heule 1982

Collard, F., 'Clovis dans quelques histoires de France de la fin du XVe siècle', *BEC* cliv (1996), 131–52

Collinson, P., *The birthpangs of Protestant England: religious and cultural change in the sixteenth and seventeenth centuries*, London 1988

Contamine, P., *Guerre, état et société à la fin du moyen âge: études sur les armées des rois de France 1337–1494*, Paris–The Hague 1972

—— 'Charles le Téméraire: fossoyeur et/ou fondateur de l'état bourguignon?', *Le Pays lorrain* lviii (1977), 123–34

Corryn, F., 'Het Schippersambacht te Gent (1302–1492)', *HMGOG* ns i (1944), 165–204

Cosneau, E., *Le connétable de Richemont, Artur de Bretagne (1393–1458)*, Paris 1886

Coulton, G., *The chronicler of European chivalry*, London 1930

Courteault, H., 'Un archiviste des comtes de Foix au XVe siècle', *Annales du Midi* vi (1894), 277–300

Coville, A., *Recherches sur quelques écrivains du XIVe et du XVe siècle*, Paris 1935

Cruden, A., *Complete concordance to the Bible* (Lutterworth Press), Cambridge 1977

Culture et pouvoir au temps de l'humanisme et de la renaissance: actes du congrès Marguerite de Savoie: Annecy, Chambéry, Turin, 29 avril–4 mai 1974, Paris–Geneva 1978

Cuttler, S., *The law of treason and treason trials in later medieval France*, Cambridge 1981

Daly, K., 'Some seigneurial archives and chronicles in fifteenth-century France', *Peritia* ii (1983), 59–73

—— 'Histoire et politique à la fin de la guerre de cent ans: l'*Abrégé des chroniques* de Noël de Fribois', in *FA*, 91–101

Dauzat, A., *Dictionnaire étymologique des noms de famille et des prénoms de France*, 3rd edn, Paris 1951

Davis, R. H. C., *The Normans and their myth*, London 1976

d'Avout, J., *La querelle des Armagnacs et des Bourguignons*, Paris 1943

Debae, M., *La librairie de Marguerite d'Autriche*, Brussels 1987

de Barante, A., *Histoire des ducs de Bourgogne de la maison de Valois 1364–1477*, 13 vols, 5th edn, Paris 1837–8

de Barthélemy, A., 'De la qualification d'écuyer', *Revue nobiliaire* iii (1865), 33–40

de Borchgrave, C., 'Diplomates et diplomatie sous le duc de Bourgogne Jean sans Peur', *PCEEB* xxxii (1992), 31–47

de Brouwer, J., *Geschiedenis van Lede*, Lede 1963

de Coussemaker, F., 'Thierry Gherbode, secrétaire et conseiller des ducs de Bourgogne et comtes de Flandre, Philippe le Hardi et Jean sans Peur, et premier garde des chartes de Flandre, 13 –1421: étude biographique', *Annales du Comité flamand de France* xxvi (1901–2), 175–385

De Fouw, A., *Philips van Kleef: een bijdrage tot de kennis van zijn leven en karakter*, Groningen 1937

de Herckenrode, J., *Nobiliaire des Pays-Bas et du comté de Bourgogne*, 2 vols, Ghent 1865

de Keyser, R., 'Chanoines séculiers et universités: le cas de St Donatien de Bruges (1350–1450)', in Ijsewijn and Paquet, *Universities in the late Middle Ages*, 584–95

Delaborde, H.-F., 'La vraie chronique du Religieux de St-Denis', *BEC* li (1890), 93–110

de La Borderie, A., 'Jean Meschinot, sa vie et ses oeuvres', *BEC* lvi (1895), 99–140, 274–317, 601–33

de La Croix Bouton, J., 'Un poème à Philippe le Bon sur la Toison d'Or', *AB* xlii (1970), 5–29

de La Fons Melicocq, A., 'Les rois de la fève, les fous en titre d'office et de la chapelle, les joueurs de farce et les mommeurs de l'hôtel de Philippe le Bon, duc de Bourgogne', *Messager des sciences historiques de Belgique* (1857), 393–400

De la lecture des livres françois, considérée comme amusement: première partie, Paris 1780

de Lannoy, B. and G. Dansaert, *Jean de Lannoy le bâtisseur, 1410–1492*, Paris 1937

de l'Espinoy, P., *Recherches des antiquitez et noblesse de Flandres*, Douai 1631

de Liedekerke, R., *La maison de Gavre et de Liedekerke*, ii, Brussels 1969

Delisle, L., 'L'oeuvre de Jean Mansel: la *Fleur des histoires*', *Journal des Savants* (1900), 16–26, 106–17, 196–7

Delsart, V., 'Les finances de la prévôté de Valenciennes sous les maisons de Bavière et de Bourgogne (1389–1477)', in Nys and Salamagne, *Valenciennes aux XIVe et XVe siècles*, 37–53

De Maesschalck, E., 'The relationship between the university and the city of Louvain in the fifteenth century', *History of Universities* ix (1990), 45–71

de Mandrot, B., 'Jean de Bourgogne, duc de Brabant, comte de Nevers et le procès de sa succession', *RH* xciii (1907), 1–45 de Moreau, E., 'Les familiers des ducs de Bourgogne dans les canonicats des anciens Pays-Bas', in *Miscellanea historica in honorem L. Van der Essen*, Brussels 1947, 429–37

de Potter, F., *Jaarboeken der Sint-Jorisgilde van Gent*, Ghent 1866

—— *Gent van den oudsten tijd tot heden: geschiedkundige beschrijving der stad*, 8 vols, Ghent 1883–1901

—— and J. Broeckaert, *Geschiedenis van de gemeenten der Provincie Oost-Vlaanderen: eerste reeks, arrondissment Gent*, v, Ghent 1864–70

de Reiffenberg, F., *Mémoire sur le séjour que Louis, dauphin de Viennois, depuis roi sous le nom de Louis XI, fit aux Pays-Bas de l'an 1456 à l'an 1461*, Brussels 1829

—— *Histoire de la Toison d'Or*, Brussels 1830

de Reilhac, A., *Jean de Reilhac: secrétaire, maître des comptes, général des finances et ambassadeur des rois Charles VII, Louis XI et Charles VIII: documents pour servir à l'histoire de ces règnes de 1455 à 1499*, 2 vols, Paris 1886–7

de Ridder-Symoens, H., 'Possibilités de carrière et de mobilité sociale des intellectuels-universitaires au moyen âge', in Bulst and Genet, *Medieval lives*, 343–57

Derville, A., 'Les étudiants morins à l'Université de Louvain au XVe siècle', *Bulletin de la Société des antiquaires de la Morinie* xviii (1955), 365–84

—— 'Pots-de-vin, cadeaux, racket, patronage: essai sur les mécanismes de décision dans l'état bourguignon', *RN* lvi (1974), 341–64

Deschaux, R., *Un poète bourguignon du XVe siècle, Michault Taillevent: édition et étude*, Geneva 1975

de Seur, J., *La Flandre illustrée par l'institution de la Chambre du roi à Lille*, Lille 1713

De Smedt, F., *Description de la ville et du comté d'Alost depuis ses origines jusqu'à l'entrée des armées françaises en Belgique, 1794*, Alost 1852

De Smedt, R., *Les chevaliers de la Toison d'Or*, Frankfurt am Main 1994

Desonay, F., 'Comment un écrivain se corrigeait au XVe siècle: étude sur les corrections du manuscrit d'auteur du *Petit Jehan de Saintré* d'Anthoine de La Sale', *RBPH* vi (1927), 81–121.

Devaux, J., 'La fin du Téméraire, ou la mémoire d'un prince ternie par l'un des siens', *MA* xcv (1989), 105–28

—— 'Le rôle politique de Marie de Bourgogne au lendemain de Nancy: vérité ou légende?', *MA* xcvii (1991), 389–405

—— *Jean Molinet, indiciaire bourguignon*, Paris 1996

Devillers, L., 'Les séjours des ducs de Bourgogne en Hainaut, 1427–1482', *BCRH* vi (1879), 323–468

de Vos, J., *Les dignités et les fonctions de l'ancien chapitre de Notre-Dame de Tournai*, ii, Bruges 1898

De Win, P., 'Queeste naar de rechtspositie van de edelman in de Bourgondische Nederlanden', *Tijdschrift voor Rechtsgeschiedenis* liii (1985), 223–74

—— 'The lesser nobility of the Burgundian Netherlands', in M. Jones (ed.), *Gentry and lesser nobility in late medieval Europe*, Gloucester 1986, 95–118

―――― 'Engelbert (Engelbrecht) II, Graaf van Nassau-Dillenburg en Vianden, Heer van Breda (1451–1504)', in R. De Smedt (ed.), *De Orde van het Gulden Vlies te Mechelen in 1491: Handelingen van de Koninklijke Kring voor Oudheidkunde, Letteren en Kunst van Mechelen*, Mechelen 1992, 85–115

―――― 'Anthoine de Croy', in CTO, 49–53

―――― 'Jean de Luxembourg', in CTO, 80–2

De Wind, S., *Bibliotheek der Nederlandsche Geschiedschrijvers (970–1566)*, Middelburg 1831

Dhanens, E., *Van Eyck: the Ghent altarpiece*, London 1973

Dickinson, J., 'The medieval conception of kingship and some of its limitations in the *Policraticus* of John of Salisbury', *Speculum* i (1926), 308–37

Dickinson, J. G., *The Congress of Arras 1435*, Oxford 1955

Diller, G., 'Robert d'Artois et l'historicité des *Chroniques* de Froissart', MA lxxxvi (1980), 217–31

Dogaer, G., 'Handschriften over de kruistochten in de librije der hertogen van Bourgondië', *Spiegel Historiael* ii (1967), 457–65

d'Oultreman, H., *Histoire de la ville et comté de Valenciennes*, Douai 1639

Doutrepont, G., 'À la cour de Bourgogne: le banquet du faisan et la littérature de Bourgogne', *Revue générale* (1899), 787–806; (1900), 99–118

―――― *La littérature française à la cour des ducs de Bourgogne*, Paris 1909

―――― *Jean Lemaire de Belges et la renaissance*, Brussels 1934

―――― *Les mises en proses des épopées et des romans chevaleresques du XIVe au XVIe siècle*, Brussels 1939

Dubled, H., 'L'écuyer en Alsace au moyen âge', *Revue d'Alsace* xcii (1953), 47–56

Dubois, H., '1477: une rupture dans la vie économique des pays bourguignons?', in CCABN, 147–74

Dubois, R., *Le domaine picard: délimitation et carte systématique*, Arras 1957

Duby, G., 'L'image du prince en France au début du XIe siècle', *Cahiers d'histoire* xvii (1972), 211–16

―――― *France in the Middle Ages*, trans. J. Vale, Oxford 1991

Duclos, C., *Histoire de Louis XI*, 3 vols, Paris 1745–6

Dufournet, J., *La destruction des mythes dans les* Mémoires *de Philippe de Commynes*, Geneva 1966

―――― *La vie de Philippe de Commynes*, Paris 1969

―――― 'Charles le Téméraire vu par les historiens bourguignons', in CCABN, 65–81

―――― 'Les premiers lecteurs de Commynes, ou les *Mémoires* au XVIe siècle', *Mémoires de la Société d'histoire de Comines-Warneton et de la région* xiv (1984), 51–94

―――― 'Commynes et l'invention d'un nouveau genre historique: les mémoires', *Mémoires de la Société d'histoire de Comines-Warneton et de la région* xviii (1988), 57–72, repr. in D. Buschinger (ed.), *Chroniques nationales et chroniques universelles: actes du colloque d'Amiens, 16–17 janvier 1988*, Göppingen 1990, 59–77 du Fresne de Beaucourt, G., 'Lettre de Jean de Capistran au duc de Bourgogne', *ABSHF* (1864), 160–6

—— *Histoire de Charles VII*, 6 vols, Paris 1881–91

Dunbabin, J., *France in the making 843–1180*, Oxford 1985

Dupic, J., 'Un bibliophile breton au XVe siècle, Jean de Derval', *Trésors des bibliothèques de France* xix (1935), 157–62

Dupire, N., *Jean Molinet: la vie, les oeuvres*, Paris 1932

Dupont-Ferrier, G., *Gallia Regia ou état des officiers royaux des bailliages et des sénéchaussées de 1328 à 1515*, 6 vols, Paris 1942–61

Durrieu, P., *La miniature flamande au temps de la cour de Bourgogne*, Paris–Brussels 1921

Du Teil, J., *Un amateur d'art au XVe siècle: Guillaume Fillastre, évêque de Tournai, abbé de St Bertin, chancelier de la Toison d'or*, Paris 1920

Duvosquel, J.-M., 'Bourgeoisie ou noblesse? À propos des origines familiales de Philippe de Commynes: perspectives de recherche', in Aubailly and others, *'Et c'est la fin'*, ii. 535–48

Elias, N., *The court society*, trans. E. Jephcott, Oxford 1983

Elliott, J. H., *Imperial Spain 1469–1716*, Harmondsworth 1970

Famiglietti, R. C., *Royal intrigue: crisis at the court of Charles VI 1392–1420*, New York 1986

Faussemagne, J., *L'apanage ducal de Bourgogne dans ses rapports avec la monarchie française (1363–1477)*, Lyon 1937

Favreau, R., 'Pierre de Brézé (vers 1410–1465)', *Société des lettres, sciences et arts du Saumurois* cxvii (Feb. 1968), 25–38

Fawtier, R., *The Capetian kings of France: monarchy and nation (987–1328)*, trans. L. Butler and R. J. Adam, London 1960

Febvre, L., 'Les ducs Valois de Bourgogne et les idées politiques de leur temps', *Revue bourguignonne* xxiii (1913), 27–50

Ferrier, J. M., *French prose writers of the fourteenth and fifteenth centuries*, Oxford 1966

Finot, J., 'Projet d'expédition contre les Turcs préparé par les conseillers du duc de Bourgogne Philippe le Bon', *Mémoires de la Société des sciences de Lille* xxi (1895), 161–206

Fitzsimons, M. A. and others (eds), *The development of historiography*, Harrisburg 1954

Flûtre, L.-F., *Le moyen picard d'après les textes littéraires du temps (1560–1660)*, Amiens 1970

Foppens, J. F., *Bibliotheca Belgica*, i, Brussels 1739

—— *Histoire du Conseil de Flandre*, ed. A. O'Kelly de Galway, Brussels 1869

Fossier, F., 'Le règne de Jean le Bon dans les histoires françaises du XIVe au XIXe siècles', *PTSEC* (1975), 85–90

—— 'La charge d'historiographe du 16e au 19e siècle', *RH* cclviii (1977), 73–92

Foulet, A. and M. B. Speer, *On editing old French texts*, Lawrence, Kans. 1979

Fourquet, E., *Les hommes célèbres et les personnalités marquantes de Franche-Comté du IVe siècle à nos jours*, Besançon 1929

Fourquin, G., 'La batellerie à Paris au temps des Anglo-Bourguignons (1418–1436)', MA lxix (1963), 707–25

Fowler, K. A., 'The attitude of some commentators to royal power in later medieval France', *Annali della Facoltà di Scienze Politiche, Perugia* xvii (1980–1), 169–79

—— 'News from the front: letters and despatches of the fourteenth century', in P. Contamine, C. Giry-Deloison and M. Keen (eds), *Guerre et société en France, Angleterre et en Bourgogne (XIVe–XVe siècles)*, Lille 1991, 63–92

Fris, V., 'La conspiration de Pierre Tyncke, à Gand, en 1451', BSHAG xiii (1905), 121–6

—— *Bibliographie de l'histoire de Gand depuis les origines jusqu'à la fin du XVe siècle*, Ghent 1907

—— *Histoire de Gand*, Brussels 1913

—— 'Philippe de Ternant', BNB xxiii, Brussels 1921–4, 705–8

—— 'La restriction de Gand (13 juillet 1468)', BSHAG xxx (1922), 57–142

Fumaroli, M., 'Les mémoires du XVIIe siècle au carrefour des genres en prose', *XVIIe siècle* xciv–v (1971), 7–37

Gabriel, A. L., 'Intellectual relations between the University of Louvain and the University of Paris in the fifteenth century', in Ijsewijn and Paquet, *Universities in the late Middle Ages*, 82–132

Gaier, C., 'Technique des combats singuliers d'après les auteurs bourguignons du XVe siècle', MA xci (1985), 415–57; xcii (1986), 5–40

Galbraith, V. H., *Historical research in medieval England*, London 1951

Gaussin, P.-R., *Louis XI: un roi entre deux mondes*, Paris 1976

—— 'Les conseillers de Charles VII (1418–1461): essai de politologie historique', *Francia* x (1982: publ. 1983), 67–130

—— 'Les conseillers de Louis XI (1461–1483)', in FFQS, 105–34

Gauvard, C., 'L'opinion publique aux confins des états et des principautés au début du XVe siècle', in *Les principautés au moyen âge: actes du IVe congrès de la Société des historiens médiévistes de l'enseignement supérieur public*, Bordeaux 1973, 127–52

Gauvin, A., *Petite histoire des rues de Valenciennes*, Valenciennes 1974

Geertz, C., 'Thick description: toward an interpretive theory of culture', in his *The interpretation of cultures*, New York 1973, repr. London 1993, 3–30

Gilbert, F., 'Biondo, Sabellico and the beginnings of Venetian official historiography', in J. G. Rowe and W. H. Stockdale (eds), *Florilegium Historiale: essays presented to Wallace K. Ferguson*, Toronto 1971, 275–93

Glénisson, J., *Le livre au moyen âge*, Turnhout 1988

Godding, P., *Le droit privé dans les Pays-Bas méridionaux du 12e au 18e siècle*, Brussels 1987

Gondry, G.-H., *Mémoire historique sur les grands baillis de Hainaut*, Mons 1888

Gorissen, P., 'De historiographie van het Gulden Vlies', *Bijdragen voor de geschiedenis der Nederlanden* vi (1951–2), 218–24

Gossen, C. T., *Französische Skriptastudien: Untersuchungen zu den nordfranzözosischen Urkundensprachen des Mittelalters*, Vienna 1967

Gransden, A., 'Propaganda in English medieval historiography', *JMH* i (1975), 363–81

—— *Historical writing in England*, II: c. 1307 to the early sixteenth century, London 1982

Green, R. F., *Poets and princepleasers: literature and the English court in the late Middle Ages*, Toronto 1980

Grévy-Pons, N., 'Propagande et sentiment national pendant le règne de Charles VI: l'exemple de Jean de Montreuil', *Francia* viii (1980), 127–45

—— and E. Ornato, 'Qui est l'auteur de la chronique latine de Charles VI dite du Religieux de St Denis?', *BEC* cxxxiv (1976), 85–102

Grunzweig, A., 'Namur et le début de la guerre du bien public', in *Études d'histoire et d'archéologie namuroises dédiées à Ferdinand Courtoy (Publication extra-ordinaire de la Société archéologique de Namur)*, Namur 1952, 531–64

—— 'Philippe le Bon et Constantinople', *Byzantion* xxiv (1954), 47–61

—— 'Le Grand duc du Ponant', *MA* lxii (1956), 119–65

* Guenée, B., 'État et nation en France au moyen âge', *RH* ccxxxvii (1967), 17–30

* —— 'Histoire, annales, chroniques: essai sur les genres historiques au moyen âge', *Annales ESC* (1973), 997–1016

* —— 'Y a-t-il une historiographie médiévale?', *RH* cclviii (1977), 261–75

—— *Histoire et culture historique dans l'Occident médiéval*, Paris 1980, repr. 1991

* —— '*Authentique at approuvé*: recherches sur les principes de la critique historique au moyen âge', in *La lexicographie du latin médiéval et ses rapports avec les recherches actuelles sur la civilisation du moyen âge: actes du colloque international, Paris, 18–21 octobre 1978*, Paris 1981, 215–29

—— *Politique et histoire au moyen âge: recueil d'articles sur l'histoire politique et l'historiographie médiévales (1956–1981)*, Paris 1981 (includes all titles by this author asterisked above)

—— 'Histoire et chronique: nouvelles réflexions sur les genres historiques au moyen âge', in Poirion, *La chronique et l'histoire*, 3–12

—— *States and rulers in later medieval Europe*, trans. J. Vale, Oxford 1985

—— 'Les *Grandes chroniques de France*: le *Roman aux roys* (1274–1518)', in P. Nora (ed.), *Les lieux de mémoire*, II: *La nation*, Paris 1986, i. 189–213

—— *Un meurtre, une société: l'assassinat du duc d'Orléans, 23 novembre 1407*, Paris 1992

—— and F. Lehoux, *Les entrées royales françaises de 1328 à 1515*, Paris 1968

Guiette, R., 'Chanson de geste, chronique et mise en prose', *Cahiers de civilisation médiévale* vi (1963), 423–40

Guigard, J., *Nouvel armorial du bibliophile*, 2 vols, Paris 1890

Haegeman, M., *De Anglofilie in het graafschap Vlaanderen tussen 1379 en 1435: politieke en economische aspecten*, Courtrai–Heule 1988

Hagopian-van Buren, A., 'Philip the Good's manuscripts as documents of his relations with the empire', *PCEEB* xxxvi (1996), 49–69

Halligan, G., 'La *Chronique* de Mathieu d'Escouchy', *Romania* xc (1969), 100–10

Harrison, A. T., 'Orléans and Burgundy: the literary relationship', *Stanford French Review* iv (1980), 475–84

Hauser, A., *Philosophy of art history*, New York 1958

Hauser, H., 'Le transport des regnes et empires des Grecz ès François', *Revue des Études Rabelaisiennes* vi (1908), 182–9

―――― *Le traité de Madrid et la cession de Bourgogne à Charles-Quint: études sur le sentiment national en Bourgogne en 1525–1526*, Paris 1912

Hay, D., 'The Historiographers Royal in England and Scotland', *Scottish Historical Review* xxx–xxxi (1951–2), 15–30

―――― 'History and historians in France and England during the fifteenth century', *Bulletin of the Institute of Historical Research* xxxv (1962), 111–27

―――― and J. Law, *Italy in the age of the Renaissance 1380–1530*, London 1989

Heimpel, H., 'Karl der Kühne und der burgundische Staat', in R. Nurnberger (ed.), *Festschrift für Gerhard Ritter zu seinem 60. Geburtstag*, Tübingen 1950, 140–60

Heins, M., *Les écoles au moyen âge à Gand*, Ghent 1885

―――― *Gand: sa vie et ses institutions*, 3 vols, Ghent 1912–15

Helmich, W., *Die Allegorie im französischen Theater des 15. und 16. Jahrhunderts*, Tübingen 1976

Henne, A., *Histoire du règne de Charles-Quint*, 10 vols, Brussels–Leipzig 1858–60

Henri Pirenne: hommages et souvenirs, i, Brussels 1938

Hexter, J., 'The education of the aristocracy in the Renaissance', in his *Reappraisals in history*, London 1961, 45–70

Highfield, J. R. L. and R. Jeffs (eds), *The crown and local communities in England and France in the fifteenth century*, Gloucester 1981

Hillard-Villard, D., 'Les relations diplomatiques entre Charles VII et Philippe le Bon de 1435 à 1445', *PTSEC* (1963), 81–5

Hintzen, J. D., *De kruistochtplannen van Philips den Goede*, Rotterdam 1918

Holzknecht, J., *Literary patronage in the Middle Ages*, Philadelphia 1923

Hommel, L., 'Les chroniqueurs bourguignons', in G. Charlier and J. Hanse (eds), *Histoire illustrée des lettres françaises de Belgique*, Brussels 1958, 105–18

Houdoy, J., *Études artistiques: artistes inconnus des XIVe, XVe et XVIe siècles*, Paris 1877

Housley, N., *The later crusades: from Lyons to Alcazar 1274–1580*, Oxford 1992

Hubert, J. R., *Chaucer's official life*, Menasha 1912

Hugenholtz, F. W. N., 'The fame of a masterwork', in W. R. H. Koops, E. H. Kossmann and G. van der Plaat (eds), *Johan Huizinga, 1872–1972: papers delivered to the Johan Huizinga conference, Groningen, 11–15 Dec. 1972*, The Hague 1973, 91–103

Hughes, M. J., 'The library of Philip the Bold and Margaret of Flanders, first Valois duke and duchess of Burgundy', *JMH* iv (1978), 145–88

Huizinga, J., *The waning of the Middle Ages*, London 1924

―――― *Tien Studiën*, Haarlem 1926

―――― 'L'état bourguignon, ses rapports avec la France et les origines d'une identité nationalité néerlandaise', *MA* xl (1930), 171–93; xli (1931), 11–35, 83–96

―――― 'La physionomie morale de Philippe le Bon', *AB* iv (1932), 101–39

―――― *Verzamelde Werken*, 9 vols, Haarlem 1948–53

Huydts, G., 'Le premier chambellan des ducs de Bourgogne', in *Mélanges d'histoire offerts à Henri Pirenne*, 2 vols, Brussels 1926, i. 263–70

Huyttens, J., *Recherches sur les corporations gantoises*, Ghent 1861

Ianziti, G., *Humanistic historiography under the Sforzas: politics and propaganda in fifteenth-century Milan*, Oxford 1988

Ijsewijn, J. and J. Paquet (eds), *The universities in the late Middle Ages*, Louvain 1978

Jean, M., *La Chambre des comptes de Lille: l'institution et les hommes (1477–1667)*, Paris 1992

Jodogne, P., *Jean Lemaire de Belges, écrivain franco-bourguignon*, Brussels 1972

Johanek, P., 'Hofhistoriograph und Stadtchronist', in W. Haug and B. Wachinger (eds), *Autorentypen*, Tübingen 1991, 50–68

Jollant, M., 'Philippe le Bon et les officiers ducaux', *AB* lv (1983), 137–9

* Jones, M., '*Bons Bretons et bons Françoys*: the language and meaning of treason in later medieval France', *Transactions of the Royal Historical Society* 5th ser. xxxii (1982), 91–112

―――― 'Brittany in the Middle Ages', in his *The creation of Brittany: a late medieval state*, London 1988, 1–12 (includes the title by this author asterisked above)

Jongkees, A. G., *Staat en kerk in Holland en Zeeland onder de Bourgondische hertogen, 1425–1477*, Groningen 1942

* ―――― 'Philippe le Bon et la Pragmatique Sanction de Bourges', *AB* xxxviii (1966), 161–71

* ―――― 'Une génération d'historiens devant le phénomène bourguignon', *BMGN* lxxxviii (1973), 215–32

* ―――― 'État et église dans les Pays-Bas bourguignons: avant et après 1477', *CCABN*, 237–47

* ―――― 'Charles le Téméraire et la souveraineté: quelques considerations', *BMGN* xcv (1980), 315–34

* ―――― 'Pie II et Philipe le Bon, deux protagonistes de l'union chrétienne', *PCEEBM* xx (1980), 103–15

―――― *Burgundica et varia*, Hilversum 1990 (includes all titles by this author asterisked above)

Kanao, T., 'L'organisation et l'enregistrement des messageries du duc de Bourgogne dans les années 1420', *RN* lxxvi (1994), 273–98

―――― 'Les messagers du duc de Bourgogne au début du XVe siècle', *JMH* xxi (1995), 195–226

Kantorowicz, E., *The king's two bodies: a study in medieval political theology*, Princeton 1957

Kauch, P., 'L'apparition d'un nouveau groupe social aux Pays-Bas bourguignons: celui des fonctionnaires', *Revue de l'Institut de sociologie Solvay* xv (1935), 122–9

Keen, M., 'Chivalry, nobility and the man-at-arms', in C. T. Allmand (ed.), *War, literature and politics in the late Middle Ages*, Liverpool 1976, 32–45

―――― 'Chivalry, heralds and history', in R. H .C. Davis and J. M. Wallace-Hadrill (eds), *The writing of history in the Middle Ages: essays presented to R. W. Southern*, Oxford 1981, 393–415

Keesman, W., 'De Bourgondische invloed op de genealogische constructies van Maximilian van Oostenrijk', *Millennium* viii (1994), 162–72

Kelley, D. R., *The beginning of ideology*, Cambridge 1981

Kendall, P. M., *Louis XI*, London 1974

Kerhervé, J., 'Aux origines d'un sentiment national: les chroniqueurs bretons de la fin du moyen âge', *Bulletin de la Société archéologique du Finistère* cviii (1980), 165–206

―――― 'Taxation and ducal power in late medieval Brittany', *French History* vi (1992), 1–23

Kervyn de Lettenhove, J. C., *Histoire de Flandre*, 6 vols, Brussels 1847–50

Knaus, H., 'Handschriften der Grafen von Nassau-Breda', *Archiv für Geschichte des Buchwesens* iii (1960), 567–80

Knight, A. E., *Aspects of genre in late medieval French drama*, Manchester 1983

Koller, F., *Au service de la Toison d'Or: les officiers*, Dison 1971

Korteweg, A. S., 'De Bibliotheek van Willem van Oranje: de handschriften', in *Boeken van en rond Willem van Oranje: catalogus van de tentoonstelling gehouden in de expositiezalen van de Koninklijke Bibliotheek, 8 juni– 26 juli 1984*, The Hague 1984, 9–28

Krynen, J., *Idéal du prince et pouvoir royal en France à la fin du moyen âge: étude de la littérature politique du temps*, Paris 1981

―――― *L'empire du roi: idées et croyances politiques en France, XIIIe–XVe siècle*, Paris 1993

Lacaze, Y., 'Philippe le Bon et les terres d'Empire: la diplomatie bourguignonne à l'oeuvre en 1454–1455', *AB* xxxvi (1964), 81–121

―――― 'Contribution à l'histoire économique et politique des pays de "pardeça": trois années de la négociation hanséato-bourguignonne ouverte en 1453', *MA* lxxv (1969), 95–119, 291–320

―――― 'Politique "méditerranéenne" et projets de croisade chez Philippe le Bon: de la chute de Byzance à la victoire chrétienne de Belgrade (mai 1453–juillet 1456)', *AB* xli (1969), 5–42, 81–132

―――― 'Le rôle des traditions dans la genèse d'un sentiment national au XVe siècle: la Bourgogne de Philippe le Bon', *BEC* cxxix (1971), 303–85

―――― 'Philippe le Bon et l'Empire: bilan d'un règne', *Francia* ix (1981), 133–75; x (1982), 167–227

Lacroix, B., *L'historien au moyen âge*, Montreal–Paris 1971

Lacroix, P., *Dissertations sur quelques points curieux sur l'histoire de France*, vii, Paris 1839

Lafortune-Martel, A., *Fête noble en Bourgogne au XVe siècle: le banquet du faisan: aspects politiques, sociaux et culturels*, Montreal–Paris 1984

La France anglaise au moyen âge: actes du 111e congrès national des sociétés savantes, Poitiers 1986: Section d'histoire médiévale et de philologie: I, Paris 1988

Laidlaw, J. C., *The poetical works of Alain Chartier*, Cambridge 1974

Lambrech, R., 'Charlemagne and his influence on late medieval French kings', *JMH* xiv (1988), 283–91

Lameere, E., 'La cour de Philippe le Bon', *Annales de la Société d'archéologie de Bruxelles* xiv (1900), 159–72

―――― *Le grand conseil des ducs de Bourgogne de la maison de Valois*, Brussels 1900

La miniature flamande: le mécénat de Philippe le Bon. Exposition organisée à l'occasion du 400e anniversaire de la fondation de la Bibliothèque royale de Philippe II, Brussels 1959

Lecoy de La Marche, A., *Le roi René*, 2 vols, Paris 1875

Lefrancq, P., 'Les Valenciennois devant leur histoire et devant leurs historiens', *Histoire des mentalités dans le nord de la France: actes du XVIIIe congrès de la Fédération des sociétés savantes du nord de la France*, Lille 1979, 29–35

Legaré, A.-M., 'L'héritage de Simon Marmion en Hainaut (1490–1520)', in Nys and Salamagne, *Valenciennes aux XIVe et XVe siècles*, 201–24

Leguai, A., 'Dijon et Louis XI: notes sur quelques aspects de la réunion de la Bourgogne (1461–1483)', *AB* xvii (1945), 26–37, 103–15, 145–69, 229–63; xix (1947), 40–1; repr. as *Dijon et Louis XI*, Dijon 1947

―――― *Les ducs de Bourbon pendant la crise monarchique du XVe siècle: contribution à l'étude des apanages*, Paris 1962

―――― 'Les "États" princiers en France à la fin du moyen âge', *Annali della Fondazione italiana per la storia amministrativa* iv (1967), 133–57

―――― 'Charles le Téméraire face au roi de France et au royaume de France', in *CCABN*, 269–89

―――― 'Charles le Téméraire et l'histoire', *PCEEBM* xxi (1981), 47–53

―――― 'La "France bourguignonne" dans le conflit entre la "France française" et la "France anglaise" (1420–1435)', in *FA*, 41–52

―――― 'Royauté française et État bourguignon de 1435 à 1477', *PCEEB* xxxii (1992), 65–75

―――― 'Royauté et principautés en France aux XIVe et XVe siècles: l'évolution de leurs rapports au cours de la guerre de Cent Ans', *MA* ci (1995), 121–36

Lemaire, J., *Introduction à la codicologie*, Louvain-la-Neuve 1989

―――― *Les visions de la vie de cour dans la littérature française de la fin du moyen âge*, Brussels–Paris 1994

Lesellier, J., 'Un historiographe de Louis XI demeuré inconnu, Guillaume

Danicot', *Mélanges d'archéologie et d'histoire de l'École française de Rome* xliii (1926), 1–42

Lewis, A. W., *Royal succession in Capetian France: studies on familial order and the state*, Cambridge, Mass. 1981

* Lewis, P. S., 'Jean Juvenal des Ursins and the common literary attitude towards tyranny in fifteenth-century France', *Medium Aevum* xxxiv (1965), 103–21

* ―― 'War propaganda and historiography in fifteenth-century France and England', *Transactions of the Royal Historical Society* 5th ser. xv (1965), 1–21

―― *Later medieval France: the polity*, London 1968

―― 'The centre, the periphery and the problem of power distribution in later medieval France', in Highfield and Jeffs, *Crown and local communities*, 33–50

―― *Essays in later medieval French history*, London 1985 (includes all titles by this author asterisked above)

―― 'La "France anglaise" vue de la "France française"', in FA, 31–9

Lhotsky, A., *Österreichische Historiographie*, Munich 1962

Lippert, W., 'La Bourgogne et la Saxe, 1451–4: nouvelles recherches et documents sur un projet de mariage du comte de Charolais et sur la question luxembourgeoise', *Mémoires de la Société Éduenne* ns xxv (1897), 1–44

Lloyd, T., *The English wool trade in the Middle Ages*, Cambridge 1977

Lough, J., *Writer and public in France*, Oxford 1978

Lowyck, A., 'Ledenlijsten van het kapittel van Sint-Pieter te Torhout', in *Archivaris Jos de Smet*, Bruges 1964, 241–58

Lyna, F., *Ex-libris de manuscrits conservés au Cabinet des manuscrits de la Bibliothèque royale de Belgique*, Brussels 1921

Lyon, B., *Henri Pirenne: a biographical and intellectual history*, Ghent 1974

McDonald, W. C. and U. Goebel, *German medieval literary patronage from Charlemagne to Maximilian I*, Amsterdam 1973

Mâle, E. and E. Pognon (eds), *Les Heures d'Anne de Bretagne: Bibliothèque nationale (ms lat. 9474)*, Paris 1946

Maliet, V., 'Valenciennes: La Salle-le-Comte', in P. Beaussart and A. Salamagne (eds), *Châteaux-chevaliers en Hainaut au moyen âge*, Brussels 1995, 134–7

Mályusz, E., 'La chancellerie royale et la rédaction des chroniques dans la Hongrie médiévale', *MA* lxxv (1969), 51–86, 219–54

Manetti, F., 'Giudizio di dio a Valenciennes nel 1455', *PCEEBM* xix (1978), 47–53

Marchello-Nizia, C., 'L'historien et son prologue: forme littéraire et stratégie discursive', in Poirion, *La Chronique et l'histoire*, 13–24

Marinesco, C., 'Philippe le Bon, duc de Bourgogne, et la croisade, ii. 1453–1467', *Bulletin des études portugaises* ns xiii (1949), 3–28

―― 'Philippe le Bon, duc de Bourgogne, et la croisade, i. 1419–1453', *Actes du VIe congrès international des études byzantines*, Paris 1950, 149–68

Marix, J., *Les musiciens de la cour de Bourgogne au XVe siècle*, Paris 1937

Martens, M., 'Bruxelles, capitale', in P. Bonenfant and others, *Bruxelles au XVe siècle*, Brussels 1953, 33–52

Martin, H.-J., 'What Parisians read in the sixteenth century', in W. L. Gundersheimer (ed.), *French humanism 1470–1600*, London 1969, 131–45

Martineau-Génieys, C., *Le thème de la mort dans la poésie française de 1450 à 1550*, Paris 1978

Matthieu, E., 'Un artiste picard à l'étranger: Jehan Wauquelin, traducteur, historien et littérateur, mort à Mons en 1452', *Mémoires de la Société des antiquaires de Picardie* xix (1889), 333–56

Méchineau, P., *Les chevaliers de la victoire: Pierre de Brézé, ministre de Charles VII*, Cholet 1986

Medeiros, M.-T., 'Le pacte encomiastique: Froissart, ses *Chroniques* et ses mécènes', MA xciv (1988), 237–55

Meyer, P., *Alexandre le Grand dans la littérature française du moyen âge*, 2 vols, Paris 1886

Mirot, A., 'Charles VII et ses conseillers assassins présumés de Jean sans Peur', AB xiv (1942), 197–210

Molinier, A., *Les sources de l'histoire de France des origines aux guerres d'Italie (1494), IV: Les Valois, 1328–1461*, Paris 1904

Monfrin, J., 'La figure de Charlemagne dans l'historiographie du XVe siècle', ABSHF (1964–5), 67–78

—— 'La connaissance de l'antiquité et le problème de l'humanisme en langue vulgaire dans la France du XVe siècle', in M. G. Verbeke and J. Ijsewijn (eds), *The late Middle Ages and the dawn of humanism outside Italy*, Louvain–The Hague 1972, 131–70

Morgan, D. A. L., 'The king's affinity in the polity of Yorkist England', *Transactions of the Royal Historical Society* 5th ser. xxiii (1973), 1–25

Morse, R., 'Historical fiction in fifteenth-century Burgundy', *Modern Language Review* lxxv (1980), 48–64

Moulin, L., *La vie des étudiants au moyen âge*, Paris 1991

Moulin-Coppens, J., *De geschiedenis van het oude Sint-Jorisgilde te Gent vanaf de vroegste tijden tot 1887*, Ghent 1982

Müller, H., *Kreuzzugspläne und Kreuzzugspolitik des Herzogs Philipp des Guten von Burgund*, Göttingen 1993

Munro, J. H. A., *Wool, cloth and gold: the struggle for bullion in Anglo-Burgundian trade, 1340–1478*, Brussels–Toronto 1972

Muzerelle, D., *Vocabulaire codicologique: répertoire méthodique des termes français relatifs aux manuscrits*, Paris 1985

Naber, A., 'Les manuscrits d'un bibliophile bourguignon du XVe siècle, Jean de Wavrin', RN lxxii (1990), 23–48

Nader, H., *The Mendoza family in the Spanish Renaissance*, New Brunswick 1979

Naïs, H., 'Grand temps et longs jours sont, monsieur l'indiciaire', in *Mélanges de linguistique française et de philologie et littérature médiévales offerts à Paul Imbs* (Travaux de linguistique et de littérature publiés par le Centre de philologie et de littérature romanes de l'Université de Strasbourg, xi), Strasbourg 1973, 207–18

Nazet, J., *Les chapitres de chanoines seculiers en Hainaut du début du XIIe au début du XVe siècle*, Brussels 1993

Nélis, H., 'Origine de l'appellation: Philippe le "Bon" ', *RBPH* xii (1933), 145–54

Nicéron, Le père, *Mémoires pour servir à l'histoire des hommes illustres dans la république des lettres*, xxv, Paris 1734

Nicholas, D., *Town and countryside: social, economic and political tensions in fourteenth-century Flanders*, Bruges 1971

—— 'Economic reorientation and social change in fourteenth-century Flanders', *Past and Present* lxx (1976), 3–29

—— *The domestic life of a medieval city: women, children and the family in fourteenth-century Ghent*, London–Lincoln, Nebraska 1983

—— *The metamorphosis of a medieval city: Ghent in the age of the Van Arteveldes, 1302–1390*, Lincoln, Nebraska–London 1987

—— *Medieval Flanders*, London–New York 1992

Noomen, W., *La traduction française de la Chronographia Johannis de Beka*, The Hague 1954

Nordberg, M., *Les ducs et la royauté: étude sur la rivalité des ducs d'Orléans et de Bourgogne (1392–1407)*, Uppsala 1964

Nys, L., 'La sculpture funéraire médiévale à Valenciennes: la part des ateliers valenciennois et des ateliers tournaisiens', in Beaussart and Nys, *Richesses des anciennes églises*, 31–65

—— and A. Salamagne (eds), *Valenciennes aux XIVe et XVe siècles: art et histoire*, Valenciennes 1996

Oldham, J. B., *English blind-stamped bindings*, Cambridge 1952

Ossoba, W., 'Engelbert II de Nassau', in *CTO*, 154–5

—— 'Philippe de Croy', in *CTO*, 149–50

Ouverleaux, E., *Notice historique et topographique sur Leuze*, Brussels 1886

Ouy, G., 'Histoire "visible" et histoire "cachée" d'un manuscrit', *MA* lxiv (1958), 115–38

Pächt, O., *The master of Mary of Burgundy*, London 1948

—— and D. Thoss, *Die illuminierten Handschriften und Inkunabeln der österrichischen Nationalbibliothek, französische Schule II*, Vienna 1977

Palmer, J. J. N. (ed.), *Froissart: historian*, Woodbridge 1981

—— 'Book I (1325–1378) and its sources', ibid. 7–24

—— 'Froissart et le héraut Chandos', *MA* lxxxviii (1982), 271–92

Paquet, J., 'Bourgeois et universitaires à la fin du moyen âge: à propos du cas de Louvain', *MA* lxvii (1961), 325–40

Paquot, J. N., *Mémoires pour servir à l'histoire littéraire des dix-sept provinces des Pays-Bas, de la principauté de Liège et de quelques contrées voisines*, 3 vols, Louvain 1765–70

Paravicini, W., 'Sechs Neuerscheinungen zur burgundisch-französischen Geschichte im 15. Jahrhunderts', *Francia* ii (1974), 665–91

—— *Guy de Brimeu: der burgundische Staat und seine adlige Führungsschicht unter Karl dem Kühnen*, Bonn 1975

―― *Karl der Kühne: das Ende des Hauses Burgund*, Göttingen 1976
―― 'Moers, Croy, Burgund: eine Studie über den Niedergang des Hauses Moers in der zweiten Hälfte des 15. Jahrhunderts', *Annalen des historischen Vereins für den Niederrhein* clxxix (1978), 7–113
―― 'Soziale Schichtung und soziale Mobilität am Hof der Herzöge von Burgund', *Francia* v (1977), 127–82
―― 'Administrateurs professionels et princes dilettantes: remarques sur un problème de sociologie administrative à la fin du Moyen Age', in W. Paravicini and K. F. Werner (eds), *Histoire comparée de l'administration (IVe–XVIIIe siècles)*, Munich 1980, 168–77
―― 'Expansion et intégration: la noblesse des Pays-Bas à la cour de Philippe le Bon', *BMGN* xcv (1980), 298–314
―― 'Peur, pratiques, intelligences: formes de l'opposition aristocratique à Louis XI d'après les interrogatoires du connétable de St Pol', in *FFQS*, 183–96
―― '*Ordonnances de l'hôtel* und *escroes des gaiges*: Wege zu einer prosopographischen Erforschung des burgundischen Staats im fünfzehnten Jahrhundert', in Bulst and Genet, *Medieval lives*, 243–66
―― 'The court of Burgundy: a model for Europe?', in R. G. Asch and A. M. Birke (eds), *Princes, patronage and the nobility: the court at the beginning of the modern age*, Oxford 1991, 70–102
Paris, G., 'Un poème inédit de Martin Le Franc', *Romania* xvi (1887), 383–437
Paviot, J., 'Les relations diplomatiques et politiques entre la Bourgogne et le Portugal (1384–1482), *PCEEB* xxxii (1992), 77–84
―― 'Jacques de Luxembourg', in *CTO*, 138–40
―― 'Jacques de Brégilles, garde-joyaux des ducs de Bourgogne Philippe le Bon et Charles le Téméraire', *RN* lxxvii (1995), 313–20
Perdrizet, P., 'Jean Miélot, l'un des traducteurs de Philippe le Bon', *Revue d'histoire littéraire de la France* xiv (1907), 472–82
Perret, A., 'Chroniqueurs et historiographes de la maison de Savoie aux XVe et XVIe siècles', in *Culture et pouvoir*, 123–34
Perroy, E., 'Social mobility among the French *noblesse* in the later Middle Ages', *Past and Present* xxi (1962), 25–38
Petit, L. A. J., 'Histoire de la ville de Leuze', *Société des sciences, des arts et des lettres du Hainaut: mémoires et publications* 4th ser. ix, Mons 1887, 29–466
Petri, F., 'Nordwestdeutschland in der Politik der Burgunderherzöge', *Westfälische Forschungen* vii (1953–4), 80–100
Philippeau, P., 'Froissart et Jean Le Bel', *RN* xxii (1936), 81–111
Piaget, A., *Martin Le Franc, prévôt de Lausanne*, Lausanne 1888
Pinchart, A., 'Miniaturistes, enlumineurs et calligraphes employés par Philippe le Bon et Charles le Téméraire et leurs oeuvres', *Bulletin des Commissions royales d'art et d'archéologie* iv (1865), 473–510
Pirenne, H., *Histoire de Belgique*, II: *Du commencement du XIVe siècle à la mort de Charles le Téméraire*, Brussels 1902, 3rd edn, 1922

────── 'The formation and constitution of the Burgundian state', *American Historical Review* xiv (1908–9), 477–502
Plancher, U., *Histoire générale et particulière de Bourgogne*, 4 vols, Dijon 1739–81
Platelle, H., 'La vie religieuse à Lille', in *Histoire de Lille, I: Des origines à Charles le Quint*, Lille 1970, 304–417
Pocock, J. G. A., 'The limits and divisions of British history', *American Historical Review* lxxxvii (1982), 311–36
Pocquet du Haut-Jussé, B.-A., *Deux féodaux: Bourgogne et Bretagne (1363–1491)*, Paris 1935
────── 'Jean sans Peur: son but et sa méthode', *AB* xiv (1942), 181–96
────── *La France gouvernée par Jean sans Peur*, Paris 1959
Poirion, D., *Le poète et le prince: l'évolution du lyrisme courtois de Guillaume de Machaut à Charles d'Orléans*, Paris 1965
────── (ed.), *Précis de littérature française au moyen âge*, Paris 1983
────── (ed.), *La chronique et l'histoire au moyen âge*, Paris 1984
Pollard, A. J., *The Wars of the Roses*, London 1988
Pollard, G., 'Describing medieval bookbindings', in J. J. G. Alexander and M. T. Gibson (eds), *Medieval learning and literature: essays presented to Richard William Hunt*, Oxford 1976, 50–65
Pope, M. K., *From Latin to modern French, with especial consideration of Anglo-Norman*, Manchester 1934
Populer, M., 'Le conflit de 1447 à 1453 entre Gand et Philippe le Bon: propagande et historiographie', *HMGOG* ns xliv (1990), 99–123
Pot, J., *Histoire de Regnier Pot, conseiller des ducs de Bourgogne, 1362–1432*, Paris 1929
Prevenier, W., 'Officials in town and countryside in the Low Countries: social and professional developments from the fourteenth to the sixteenth century', *Acta historiae Neerlandicae* vii (1974), 1–17
────── and W. P. Blockmans, *The Burgundian Netherlands*, trans. P. King and Y. Mead, Cambridge 1986
Prignet, A. (publ.), *Histoire ecclésiastique de la ville et comté de Valentienne par Simon Le Boucq, Prévost. 1650*, ed. A. Dinaux, Valenciennes 1844
Prou, M., *Manuel de paléographie*, 3rd edn, Paris 1910
Queller, D. E., *Early Venetian legislation on ambassadors*, Geneva 1966
────── *The office of ambassador in the Middle Ages*, Princeton 1967
Quicherat, J., 'Recherches sur le chroniqueur Jean Castel', *BEC* ii (1841), 461–77
Quicke, F., *Les chroniqueurs des fastes bourguignons*, Brussels 1943
Rapp, F., 'Universités et principautés: les états bourguignons', *PCEEB* xxviii (1988), 115–31
Richard, J., 'Les archives et les archivistes des ducs de Bourgogne dans le ressort de la Chambre des comptes de Dijon', *BEC* cv (1944), 123–69
────── ' "Enclaves" royales et limites des provinces: les élections bourguignonnes', *AB* xx (1948), 89–113

—— 'Les états de service d'un noble bourguignon au temps de Philippe le Bon', *AB* xxix (1957), 113–24

—— 'Les institutions ducales dans le duché de Bourgogne', in F. Lot and R. Fawtier (eds), *Histoire des institutions françaises au moyen âge, I: institutions seigneuriales*, Paris 1957, 209–48

—— 'Les débats entre le roi de France et le duc de Bourgogne sur la frontière du royaume à l'ouest de la Saône', *Bulletin historique et philologique du comité des travaux historiques* (1964), 113–132

—— 'La croisade bourguignonne dans la politique européenne', *PCEEBM* x (1968), 41–4

—— 'Un sentiment "national" bourguignon?', *AB* xlv (1973), 182–4

—— 'Le destin des institutions bourguignonnes avant et après Charles le Téméraire', *CCABN*, 291–304

—— *St Louis: crusader king of France*, ed. S. D. Lloyd, trans. J. Birrell, Cambridge 1992

Richmond, C. F., 'Hand and mouth: information gathering and use in England in the later Middle Ages', *Journal of Historical Sociology* i (1988), 233–52

Rigoley de Juvigny (ed.), *Les bibliothèques françoises de La Croix du Maine et de Du Verdier, sieur de Vauprivas*, i, Paris 1772

Riley-Smith, J., *The crusades: a short history*, London 1987

Roberts, M. T. and D. Etherington, *Bookbinding and the conservation of books: a dictionary of descriptive terminology*, Washington 1982

Rogghé, P., 'De Gentse klerken in de XIVe en XVe eeuw: trouw en verraad', *Appeltjes van het Meetjesland* xi (1960), 5–142

Root, R. K., 'Publication before printing', *Publications of the Modern Language Association of America* xxviii (1913), 417–31

Rousseaux, A., *Le monde classique*, 4 vols, Paris 1941–56

Saintenoy, P., *Les arts et les artistes à la cour de Bruxelles: le palais des ducs de Bourgogne sur le Coudenberg à Bruxelles du règne d'Anthoine à celui de Charles-Quint*, Brussels 1934

Salet, F., 'Mécénat royal et princier au moyen âge', *Comptes-rendus de l'Académie des inscriptions et belles-lettres* (1985), 620–9

Samaran, C., 'La chronique latine inédite de Jean Chartier (1422–1450) et les derniers livres du Religieux de St-Denis', *BEC* lxxxvii (1926), 142–63

—— 'La chronique latine de Jean Chartier (1422–1450)', *ABSHF* (1926), 183–273

—— 'Un ouvrage de Guillaume Danicot, historiographe de Louis XI', *Mélanges d'archéologie et d'histoire de l'École française de Rome* xlv (1928), 8–20

—— 'Mathieu Levrien, chroniqueur de St Denis à la fin du règne de Louis XI', *BEC* xcix (1938), 125–31

Sanderus, A., *Bibliotheca Belgica Manuscripta*, 2 vols, Lille 1641–4

Schefer, C., 'Le discours du voyage d'oultremer au très victorieux roi Charles VII, prononcé en 1452 [sic] par Jean Germain, évêque de Chalon', *Revue de l'Orient latin* iii (1895), 302–42

Schneider, J., 'Lotharingie, Bourgogne ou Provence?: l'idée d'un royaume d'entre-deux aux derniers siècles du moyen âge', in *Liège et Bourgogne: actes du colloque tenu à Liège, les 28, 29, 30 octobre 1968*, Liège 1972, 15–44

Schnerb, B., *Les armagnacs et les bourguignons: la maudite guerre*, Paris 1988

Schobben, J. M. G., *La part du Pseudo-Turpin dans les Croniques et conquestes de Charlemaine de David Aubert*, The Hague 1969

Schoonheere, A., 'Les premiers pas de Philippe de Commynes à la cour et sous les armes de Bourgogne', *Memoires de la Société d'histoire de Comines-Warneton et de la région* xxiii (1993), 51–84

Schwarzkopf, U., 'La cour de Bourgogne et la Toison d'Or', PCEEBM v (1963), 91–104

—— *Die Rechnungslegung des Humbert de Plaine über die Jahre 1448 bis 1452: eine Studie zur Amtsführung des burgundischen maître de la chambre aux deniers*, Göttingen 1970

—— 'Zum höfischen Dienstrecht im 15. Jahrhundert: das burgundische Beispiel', in *Festschrift für Hermann Heimpel zum 70. Geburtstag am 19. September 1971*, ii, Göttingen 1972, 422–42

Scufflaire, A., *Les fiefs directs des comtes de Hainaut de 1349 à 1504: essai d'inventaire statistique et géographique*, 4 vols, Brussels 1978–84

Seguin, P., 'L'information à la fin du XVe siècle en France: pièces d'actualité imprimées sous le règne de Charles VIII', *Arts et traditions populaires* (1956), 309–30; (1957), 46–74

Serrure, C.-A., *Notice sur Engelbert II, comte de Nassau, lieutenant-général de Maximilien et de Philippe-le-Beau aux Pays-Bas*, Ghent 1862

Servant, H., 'Jehan de Liège, premier imprimeur valenciennois', *Valentiana* i (1988), 7–11

Shears, F. S., *Froissart, chronicler and poet*, London 1930

Sherman, C. R., 'Representations of Charles V of France (1338–1380) as a wise ruler', *Medievalia et humanistica* ns ii (1971), 83–96

Sivéry, G., *Les comtes de Hainaut et le commerce de vin au XIVe siècle et au début du XVe siècle*, Lille 1969

—— 'Commerce et marchands à Valenciennes à la fin du moyen âge', in *Valenciennes et les anciens Pays-Bas: mélanges offerts à Paul Lefrancq* (Mémoires du Cercle archéologique et historique de Valenciennes, ix), Valenciennes 1976, 71–81

Small, G. P., 'Les origines de la ville de Tournai dans les chroniques légendaires du bas moyen âge', in *Les grands siècles de Tournai* (Tournai: art et histoire, vii), Tournai–Louvain-la-Neuve 1993, 81–113

—— 'Chroniqueurs et culture historique au bas moyen âge', in Nys and Salamagne, *Valenciennes aux XIVe et XVe siècles*, 271–96

Smalley, B., *Historians in the Middle Ages*, London 1974

Smith, J. C., 'Venit nobis pacificus Dominus: Philip the Good's triumphal entry into Ghent in 1458', in *'All the world's a stage': art and pageantry in the Renaissance and Baroque*, I: *triumphal celebrations and the rituals of statecraft*, Pennsylvania 1990, 259–90

Soldi Rondinini, G., 'Aspects de la vie des cours de France et de Bourgogne par les dépêches des ambassadeurs milanais (seconde moitié du XVe siècle)', in *Adelige Sachkultur des Spätmittelalters: kongress, Krems an der Donau, 1980*, published in *Österreichische Akademie der Wissenschaften*, cccclii, Vienna 1982, 195–214

Solon, D., 'Popular response to standing military forces in fifteenth-century France', *Studies in the Renaissance* xix (1972), 78–111

Sommé, M., 'Les déplacements d'Isabelle de Portugal et la circulation dans les Pays-Bas bourguignons au milieu du XVe siècle', *RN* lii (1970), 183–97

—— 'Étude comparative des mesures à vin dans les états bourguignons au XVe siècle', *RN* lviii (1976), 171–83

Spiegel, G. M., 'The *reditus regni ad stirpem Karoli Magni*: a new look', *French Historical Studies* vii (1971), 145–74

—— 'Political utility in medieval historiography: a sketch', *History and Theory* xiv (1975), 314–25

—— *The chronicle tradition of St Denis: a survey*, Brookline, Mass.–Leyden 1978

—— 'Pseudo-Turpin, the crisis of the aristocracy and the beginnings of vernacular historiography in France', *JMH* xii (1982), 207–23

—— *Romancing the past: the rise of vernacular prose historiography in thirteenth-century France*, Berkeley–Oxford 1993

—— and S. Hindman, 'The fleur de lys frontispieces to Guillaume de Nangis's *Chronique abrégée*: political iconography in late fifteenth-century France', *Viator* xii (1981), 381–407

Spufford, P., 'Dans l'espace bourguignon: 1477, un tournant monétaire?', *CCABN* 187–204

Stanger, M. D., 'Literary patronage at the medieval court of Flanders', *French Studies* xi (1957), 214–29

Stein, H., *Étude biographique, littéraire et bibliographique sur Olivier de La Marche*, Brussels 1888

—— 'Un diplomate bourguignon du XVe siècle: Antoine Haneron', *BEC* xcviii (1937), 283–348

Stein, R., *Politiek en historiografie: het onstaansmilieu van Brabantse kronieken in de eerste helft van de vijftiende eeuw*, Leuven 1994

Steinberg, S. H., *Historical tables 58 B.C. – A.D. 1965*, 8th edn, London 1967

Stenghers, J., 'Sur trois chroniqueurs: note sur les rapports entre la continuation anonyme de Monstrelet, les *Mémoires* de Jacques du Clercq et les *Chroniques d'Angleterre* de Jean de Wavrin', *AB* xviii (1946), 122–30

Stevenson, A. (ed.), *Briquet, Les Filigranes: a facsimile of the 1907 edition with supplementary material contributed by a number of scholars*, 4 vols, Amsterdam 1968

Strayer, J. R., 'France: the holy land, the chosen people and the most Christian king', in T. K. Rabb and J. E. Seigel (eds), *Action and conviction in early modern Europe: essays in memory of E. H. Harbison*, Princeton 1969, 3–16

Stuip, R., 'L'*Histoire des Seigneurs de Gavre*: sa popularité à la fin du moyen âge', in Q. Mok and others (eds), *Mélanges Smeets*, Leiden 1982, 281–92

―― 'Le public de l'*Histoire des Seigneurs de Gavre*', in K. Busby and E. Cooper (eds), *Courtly literature: culture and context*, Amsterdam–Philadelphia 1990, 531–7.

Thielemans, M.-R., 'Les Croÿ, conseillers des ducs de Bourgogne: documents extraits de leurs archives familiales, 1357–1487', BCRH cxxiv (1959), 1–141

―― *Bourgogne et Angleterre: relations politiques et économiques entre les Pays-bas bourguignons et l'Angleterre, 1435–1467*, Brussels 1966

Thiry, C., 'Une rédaction du XVIe siècle de l'*Histoire des Seigneurs de Gavre*', in *Mélanges offerts à Pierre Le Gentil*, Paris 1973, 839–50

Thompson, E. P., *The making of the English working classes*, Harmondsworth 1968

Thompson, G. L., 'Le régime anglo-bourguignon à Paris: facteurs idéologiques', in FA, 53–60

―― *Paris and its people under English rule: the Anglo-Burgundian regime 1420–1436*, Oxford 1991

Thompson, J. W., *The medieval library*, Chicago 1939

Tout, T. F., 'Literature and learning in the English civil service in the fourteenth century', *Speculum* iv (1929), 365–89

Tucoo-Chala, P., 'Froissart dans le Midi pyrénéen', in Palmer, *Froissart*, 118–31

Tuetey, A., *Les écorcheurs sous Charles VII*, 2 vols, Montbéliard 1874

Turlin, L., 'Notes sur Jean Robertet, grand rhétoriqueur, secrétaire de Jean II de Bourbon', *Bulletin de la Société d'émulation du Bourbonnais* lix (1976), 231–47

Turner, R. V., *Men raised from the dust: administrative service and upward mobility in Angevin England*, Philadelphia 1988

Tyson, D. B., 'Patronage of French vernacular history writers in the twelfth and thirteenth centuries', *Romania* c (1979), 180–222

―― 'French vernacular history writers and their patrons in the fourteenth century', *Medievalia et Humanistica* xiv (1986), 103–24

Ullmann, W., *Principles of government and politics in the Middle Ages*, London 1961

Urwin, K., 'Date of the *Mystère du Concile de Basle* attributed to Georges Chastelain', *Modern Language Review* xxx (1935), 508–10

Vale, J., *Edward III and chivalry*, Woodbridge 1982

Vale, M. G. A., 'Jean Fouquet's portrait of Charles VII', *Gazette des beaux-arts* lxxi (1968), 243–8

―― *Charles VII*, London 1974

―― *The Angevin legacy and the Hundred Years' War*, Oxford 1990

Valerius Andreas, *Bibliotheca Belgica: a facsimile of the edition of Louvain, 1643*, Brussels 1973

Vallet de Viriville, A., 'Duclercq, Jacques', in *Nouvelle biographie générale*, xv, Paris 1852, 16–7

Valois, N., *Le conseil du roi aux XIVe, XVe et XVIe siècles*, Paris 1888, repr. Geneva 1975

Van Belle, A., 'La faculté des arts de Louvain: quelques aspects de son organisation au XVe siècle', in Ijsewijn and Paquet, *Universities in the late Middle Ages*, 29–41

Van Calken, F., *Histoire de Belgique des origines à nos jours*, Brussels 1944

Van den Bruelle, J., *Geschiedenis van Haaltert*, n.p. 1975

Van den Gheyn, J., 'Le manuscrit original des Mémoires du sire de Haynin', BCRH lxx (1901), 44–59

Vanderjagt, A., *Qui sa vertu anoblist: the concepts of noblesse and chose publicque in Burgundian political thought*, Groningen 1981

Vander Linden, H., *Itinéraires de Charles, duc de Bourgogne, Marguerite d'York et Marie de Bourgogne*, Brussels 1936

────── *Itinéraires de Philippe le Bon, duc de Bourgogne (1419–1467) et de Charles, comte de Charolais (1433–1467)*, Brussels 1940

Van Dorsten, J., 'Literary patronage in the Elizabethan age: the early phase', in G. F. Lytle and S. Orgel (eds), *Patronage in the Renaissance*, Princeton 1981, 191–206

Van Houtte, J., *De voogdij over de minderjarigen in het Oud-Belgisch recht*, Gent 1930

Van Praet, J., *Recherches sur Louis de Bruges, seigneur de la Gruuthuse*, Paris 1881

Van Rompaey, J., *Het grafelijk baljuwsambt in Vlaanderen tijdens de Bourgondische periode*, Brussels 1967

────── *De Grote Raad van de hertogen van Bourgondië en het Parlement van Mechelen*, Brussels 1973

────── 'De Bourgondische staatsinstellingen', in *Algemene Geschiedenis der Nederlanden*, Haarlem 1980, iv. 136–55

Van Uytven, R., 'La Flandre et le Brabant, "terres de promission" sous les ducs de Bourgogne?', RN xliii (1961), 281–317

Vanwynsberghe, D., 'La miniature à Valenciennes: état des sources et aperçu chronologique de la production (fin XIVe–1480)', in Nys and Salamagne, *Valenciennes aux XIVe et XVe siècles*, 181–200

Varenbergh, E., *Histoire des relations diplomatiques entre le comté de Flandre et l'Angleterre au moyen âge*, Brussels 1874

Vaughan, R., *Matthew Paris*, London 1958, repr. 1979

────── *Philip the Bold: the formation of the Burgundian state*, London 1962

────── *The Valois dukes of Burgundy: sources of information*, Hull 1965

────── *John the Fearless: the growth of Burgundian power*, London 1966

────── *Philip the Good: the apogee of Burgundy*, London 1970

────── *Charles the Bold: the last Valois duke of Burgundy*, London 1973

────── *Valois Burgundy*, London 1975

────── 'Five hundred years after the great battles', BMGN xcv (1980), 377–90

────── 'Hue de Lannoy and the question of the Burgundian state', in R. Schneider (ed.), *Das spätmittelalterliche Königtum im Europäischen Vergleich*

(*Vorträge und Forschungen. Konstanzer Arbeitskreis für mittelalterliche Geschichte, Bd. 32*), Sigmaringen 1987, 335–45

Verger, J., 'The University of Paris at the end of the Hundred Years' War', in J. Baldwin and R. Goldthwaite (eds), *Universities in politics: case studies from the late Middle Ages and early modern period*, Baltimore–London 1973, 47–78

—— 'Noblesse et savoir: étudiants nobles aux universités d'Avignon, Cahors, Montpellier et Toulouse (fin XIVe siècle)', in P. Contamine (ed.), *La noblesse au moyen âge, XIe–XVe siècles: essais à la mémoire de Robert Boutruche*, Paris 1976, 289–313

—— *Histoire des universités de France*, Paris 1986

Vermaseren, B. A., 'Het ambt van historiograaf in de Bourgondische Nederlanden', *Tijdschrift voor Geschiedenis* lvi (1941), 258–73

Veronée-Verhaegen, N., *Les primitifs flamands: corpus de la peinture des anciens Pays-Bas méridionaux au XVe siècle, XIII: L'Hôtel-Dieu de Beaune*, Brussels 1973

Verwijs, E. and J. Verdam, *Middelnederlandsch Woordenboek*, iii, The Hague 1894

Voet, L., *The golden compasses: a history and evaluation of the printing and publishing activities of the* Officina Plantiniana *at Antwerp*, 2 vols, Amsterdam 1969–72

von Isenburg, W. K., *Stammtafeln zur Geschichte der europäischen Staaten*, i, 2nd edn, Marburg 1960

Vroonen, E., *Les noms de famille en Belgique*, 2 vols, Brussels n.d.

Walsh, R., 'The coming of humanism to the Low Countries: some Italian influences at the court of Charles the Bold', *Humanistica Lovaniensia* xxv (1976), 146–97

Walther, A., *Die burgundischen Zentralbehörden unter Maximilian I und Karl V*, Leipzig 1909

Walton, T., 'Amé de Montgesoie, poète bourguignon du XVe siècle', *AB* ii (1930), 134–58

—— 'Les poèmes d'Amé de Montgesoie', *Medium Aevum* ii (1933), 1–33

Wandruszka, A., *The house of Habsburg*, London 1964

Watkins, J. H., 'A note on the *Cent nouvelles nouvelles*', *Modern Language Review* xxxvi (1941), 396–7

Weale, W. H. J., *The Van Eycks and their art*, 2nd edn, London 1913

Weary, W. A., 'La maison de La Trémoille pendant la renaissance: une seigneurie agrandie', in *FFQS*, 197–212

Weightman, C., *Margaret of York, duchess of Burgundy, 1446–1503*, Gloucester 1989

Weiss, R., *Humanism in England in the fifteenth century*, Oxford 1951

Wellens, R., 'Charles de Croy', in *CTO*, 203–4

Werner, K. F., 'Die Legitimität der Kapetinger und die Entstehung des *Reditus regni Francorum ad stirpem Karoli*', *Die Welt als Geschichte* xii (1952), 203–25; repr. in his *Structures politiques du monde franc (VIe–XIIe siècles): études sur les origines de la France et de l'Allemagne*, London 1979

Whiting, B. J., 'Froissart as poet', *Medieval studies* viii (1946), 189–216
Willard, C. C., 'The concept of true nobility at the Burgundian court', *Studies in the Renaissance* xiv (1967), 33–48
—— 'Isabel of Portugal, patroness of humanism?', in *Miscellanea di studi e ricerche sul quattrocento Francese a cura di Franco Simone*, Turin 1967, 517–44
Wolff, H., 'Traîtres et trahison d'après quelques oeuvres historiques de la fin du moyen âge', in *Exclus et système d'exclusion dans la littérature et la civilisation médiévales: actes du colloque organisé par le C.U.E.R.M.A., Aix-en-Provence, 4–6 mars 1977*, Aix-en-Provence 1978, 41–55
Wouters, H. H. E., 'Het nationaliteitsbesef in de Bourgondische Nederlanden bij de kroniekschrijvers der 15de eeuw', *Publications de la Société historique et archéologique dans le Limbourg* xxxv (1949), 751–87
Yans, M., 'Jean de Wavrin', *BNB* xxvii–viii, Brussels 1938, 129–32
Zingel, M., *Frankreich, das Reich und Burgund im Urteil der burgundischen Historiographie des 15. Jahrhunderts*, Sigmaringen 1995
Zumthor, P., *Le masque et la lumière: la poétique des grands rhétoriqueurs*, Paris 1978

Unpublished material

Theses
Awerbuch, M., 'Über die Motivation der burgundischen Politik im 14. und 15. Jahrhundert', unpubl. Ph.D. diss. Berlin 1970
Farley, S. M., 'French historiography in the later Middle Ages, with special reference to the *Grandes chroniques de France*', unpubl. Ph.D. diss. Edinburgh 1969
Hardy, M. S., 'Olivier de La Marche and chivalry and monarchy in the fifteenth century', unpubl. M.Phil. diss. London 1970
Heron, A. G., '*Il fault faire guerre pour paix avoir*: crusading propaganda at the court of Duke Philippe le Bon of Burgundy (1419–1467)', unpubl. Ph.D. diss. Cambridge 1992
Régibeau, L., 'Le rôle politique des Croy à la fin du règne de Philippe le Bon, 1456–1465', unpubl. *mém. de licence*, Brussels 1956
Schwarzkopf, U., 'Studien zur Hoforganisation der Herzöge von Burgund aus dem Hause Valois', unpubl. Ph.D. diss. Göttingen 1955
Servant, H., 'Culture, art et société à Valenciennes dans la deuxième moitié du XVe siècle (vers 1440–1507)', unpubl. *École des chartes* diss. 2 vols, Paris 1989
Smith, J. C., 'The artistic patronage of Philip the Good, duke of Burgundy (1418–67)', unpubl. Ph.D. diss. Columbia 1979
Vander Stichele, M., 'De Hospitaalbroeders van St.-Jan van Jeruzalem in de balije en commanderij Vlaanderen tot 1550: een prosopografische benadering', unpubl. MA diss. Leuven 1982

Miscellaneous

'Guide pour l'élaboration d'une notice de manuscrit', unpubl. document, IRHT, 1977

Morgan, D. A. L., 'Burgundian Mémoires, their cultural milieu and political context', unpubl. communication, annual conference of the Centre européen d'études bourguignonnes, Middelburg 1990

'Notice du MS Arras Bibl. mun. 256 [406]', unpubl. report, IRHT (1960)

'Notice du MS Arras Bibl. mun. 471 [578]', unpubl. report, IRHT (n.d.)

'Notice du MS Arras Bibl. mun. 516 [827]', unpubl. report, IRHT (1961)

'Notice du MS Beloeil Bibl. du Château TA.V.D.17', unpubl. report, IRHT (n.d.)

'Notice du MS Bruxelles Bibl. royale. 15843', unpubl. report, IRHT (1960)

Prosser, G., 'Affinity and Ordonnances: the retinue of Pierre de Brézé, Grand Seneschal of Normandy, 1450–1465', paper delivered to the annual conference of the Society for the study of French History, 1994: not consulted

Solente, S., 'Les manuscrits des Béthune à la Bibliothèque nationale', unpubl. report, BN, Dépt. des manuscrits, Bureau casier 10, 1980

Thiry, C., 'Ville en fête, ville en feu: présences de la ville dans les Mémoires de Jean de Haynin', paper presented to the conference of the Centre de Recherches Francophones Belges, Edinburgh 1996

Index

Aalst, county of, 10–11, 15, 40
Abel, 167
Abraham, 167
Achilles, 99–100
Adam, 167
Advertissement au duc Charles soubs fiction de son propre entendement parlant a luy-mesme (wrongly a.k.a. *Miroer des vertus de l'auguste duc Philippe de Bourgoigne* in some MSS), 87n., 117n., 120, 131n., 146n., 164n., 246
Albergati, Nicolò, 32
Albret, Charles II, lord of, 155
Alençon, Jean II, duke of, 72, 123, 144n., 146n., 186, 188
Alexander the Great, 99–100
Amiens, 67, 68
Anjou, Isabelle d', duchess, 43n.
Anjou, Marguerite d', queen of England, 13, 14, 42n., 43, 122, 155
Anjou, Marie d', queen of France, 95
Anjou, René d', duke, 43, 44n., 47, 108, 123, 125
Anjou, Yolande d', duchess, 123
anonymous continuator of Monstrelet, 104, 134n.
anonymous of St Brieuc, 107
Antoing, Jean de Melun, lord of, 83
Arc, Joan of, 140, 148n.
Ardres, 157
Aristotle, 132n.
Armagnac, Isabelle d', 155
Armagnac, Jean IV, count of, 13
Armagnac, Jean V, count of, 13, 79n., 86n., 143n.
Arnolfini, Giovanni, 33n., 73
Arras, 34, 62, 68, 123, 210n.; jousts at, 49, 152
Arras, treaty of: 32, 47, 100; Burgundian servants and, 37–8, 58; copy made of, 139n.; Henry VI and, 99; historical record of, 104, 154; Philip the Good and, 53–4, 185, 186
Arson, Jean d', 195
Aubert, David, 103, 108, 109, 111
Austria, house of, 222. *See also* Margaret of; Maximilian I

Austria, Margaret of, 209, 210, 211, 216; commissions copy of Chronicle, 145n., 217–18, 225, 243; and Molinet, 161n
Auxerre, peace of (1412), 184
Avignon, 71

Barnard, Charles, 115n.
Barlaere, 211
Bartin, Philippe, 221
Basin, Thomas, 59n.
Baude, Henri, 177
Bauffremont, Pierre de, 48, 53, 58
Bavaria, Jacqueline of, 152, 171
Beaufort, Henry, 157
Bedford, John, duke of, 152, 186
Beerlegem, 27
Beka, Jean de, 103
Belgrade, 130
Bemden, Ferdinand van den, 17n., 42n.
Béthune, Philippe, count of, 200, 242, 243
Béthune, 23
Bierges, 28
Biévène, *see* Rubempré, Jean de
Bische, Guillaume, 149n.
Blaasveld, *see* Blaesvelt
Bladelin, Pierre, 33
Blaesvelt, Cornelius van, 28, 61n.
Blaesvelt, Louis van, 28
Blois, 226n., 242
Blondel, Robert, 170
Boccaccio, Giovanni, 131, 132n. *See also Le temple de Bocace*
Bordeaux, 94
Bouchart, Alain, 106, 113
Boulogne, county of, 179
Bourbon, Charles I, duke of, 65
Bourbon, Isabelle de, countess of Charolais, 65, 98, 121
Bourbon, Jacques de, 121, 158
Bourbon, Jean II, duke of, 73, 124, 125
Bourges, 184n.
Bourges, Pragmatic Sanction of, 178
Bourguignon, Auberi le, 105
Boursier, Jean le, 101, 130
Boussu, *see* Hennin, Pierre de
Bouton, Claude, 209–10
Bouton, Philippe, 121, 123, 209

293

Bouvet, Honoré, 169, 174
Bouvier, Gilles le, 155n., 170
Bovekerke, 211
Brabant, duchy of, 1n., 11, 77, 104, 139; histories of, 103, 108
Brabant, Jean de, student, 36n.
Brabant, Jean IV, duke of, 177
Breda, 208
Brederode family, 71n.
Brégilles, Jacques de, 132
Brézé, Jacques de, 43
Brézé, Pierre II de, 13, 44, 59, 134, 152, 179n.; career (1441–4), 42–4, 45, 154–5; relations with Philip the Good, 47–9, 52; captain of Rouen, 68, 155; banished and imprisoned, 144n., 147; eloquence of, 23n., 48n. See also *Déprécation pour messire Pierre de Brézé*, *Épitaphe de messire Pierre de Brézé*
Brittany, Anne of, 129, 202
Brittany, François II, duke of, 126, 185
Brittany, duchy of, 106–7, 151, 155n. See also Richemont
Broquière, Bertrandon de la, 52–3
Bruges, 93, 138, 147, 153, 202; court at, 56, 57, 60, 62, 101; rebellions of, 26, 206
Bruges, Galbert of, 131
Bruges, Louis de, 121, 193, 212, 242
Brussels, 31, 49, 62; court at, 47, 52n., 56, 68–9, 87
Buchon, J.A.C., 205, 206, 207, 242
Burckhardt, Jacob, 3n.
Burgundian court, 56–8, 70–1, 89–90; household offices, 32, 55–6, 61, 64–5, 66, 74–5, 76–7, 111, 115, 175–6, 192; library of, 107–8, 111, 120–1, 132; relationship of city and court, 22–42, 45–6, 49–50, 119–20, 228
Burgundy, Agnes of, duchess of Bourbon, 65n., 122
Burgundy, Anne of, duchess of Bedford, 152
Burgundy, Anthony, bastard of, 71
Burgundy, Anthony of, 16
Burgundy, Baudouin de Lille, bastard of, 195
Burgundy, Charles the Bold, duke of, 2, 3, 77, 138, 160; education and reading of, 35, 106n., 113, 118; marriages of, 65, 77, 98–100; entries, 26, 72, 193; relations with king, 139n., 171, 194; with courtiers, 80, 82, 84, 138, 158, 192–3, 195, 245–8; with Chastelain, 88, 90, 171, 190–6; posthumous reputation of, 226
Burgundy, Cornille, bastard of, 57n.
Burgundy, David, bastard of, 103
Burgundy, Hugh III, duke of, 97n.
Burgundy, Hugh IV, duke of, 97n.
Burgundy, Isabella of Portugal, duchess of, 11, 36n., 63, 98, 126, 194; marriage to Philip the Good, 153, 226
Burgundy, John the Fearless, duke of, 1, 31, 184, 187, 218; crusade of, 97, 101; murder of, 100n., 181, 232
Burgundy, Margaret of, countess of Hainaut, 133, 139n., 152
Burgundy, Mary of, 81, 206, 208, 209, 212, 223
Burgundy, Philip the Bold, duke of, 1, 2, 104, 107, 218
Burgundy, Philip the Fair of, see Philip I the Fair
Burgundy, Philip the Good, duke of, 1, 11, 26, 36n., 65, 138; accession of, 159; second marriage of, 153, 226; military campaigns of, 36–7; supposed apogee of reign, 2, 93–4; and crusade, 64, 98, 136; relations with king, 3, 185–6; with son and heir, 77; with servants, 52, 58, 82, 83; with Chastelain, 76, 172–7; epithets of, 135, 150n., 227; failings of, 245–8; posthumous reputation of, 218, 226–7
Burgundy, county of, 11, 165
Burgundy, duchy of, 36, 47, 77, 103, 195; reversion to French crown, 80–1, 207, 223; royal enclaves in, 47, 53
Burgundy, kingdom of, 164, 221–2

Caen, 59
Cairo, sultan of, 157
Calais, 26, 71
Calixtus III, pope, 94n., 157
Callen, Wouter, 20n.
Cambrai, 68n., 104, 214
Camogli, Prospero da, 149n.
Caron, Jean, 73
Castel, Jean, 116, 161n.; appointment as royal chronicler, 114n., 134; correspondence with Chastelain, 123, 125, 146n.
Castelain, Jan, chronicler's father, 10, 17–18, 19–22, 24, 38, 41
Castelain, Jan, chronicler's grandfather, 19–20
Castelain, Joris, see Chastelain, George

INDEX

Castelain, Lisbette, a.k.a. Van Erpe, chronicler's grandmother, 20–1, 23, 24n., 40
Castelain, Lisbette, chronicler's sister, 17, 22, 38, 39, 41n.
Castelain, Louis, chronicler's brother, 17, 39, 41, 42n., 46
Castelain, Marie, chronicler's mother, *see* Masmines, Marie van
Castelain, Mergriete, chronicler's sister, 17, 39, 41n., 42n.
Castelain, Pieter, chronicler's uncle, 20–1, 23, 24n., 42n.
Castile, herald of, 72, 130
Castillon, battle of (1453), 177
Caxton, William, 132
Cent nouvelles nouvelles, 73n., 74n., 111n.
Chalon, Charles de, 73
Chalon, Louis de, prince of Orange, 72, 176
Chalon family, 80
Châlons-sur-Marne, 47, 49
Chambre des comptes, *see* Lille
Chapperel, Oudart, 52n.
Charlemagne, 95, 166–7
Charles IV, Holy Roman Emperor, 135
Charles V, Holy Roman Emperor, 208, 209, 211, 217, 218
Charles V, king of France, 131, 166, 173n., 175
Charles VI, king of France, 30, 81, 166, 170, 186, 187; madness of, 168, 173
Charles VII, king of France, 1, 100, 155, 159n., 186, 188; and Burgundian servants, 58, 81; and Chastelain, 13, 135n., 177–81; and crusade, 95, 98, 101, 178–9; and historians, 92, 129, 182; correspondence of, 138, 141, 142; death of, 144n., 170, 180–1
Charles VIII, king of France, 204
Chartier, Alain, 124, 169–70, 173
Chartier, Jean, 72n., 92, 114–15, 134, 141, 156
Chassa, Jean de, 138, 195
Chasteaubelin, ducal herald, 56n.
Chastelain, Gonthier, chronicler's son, 61n., 210, 212–17, 225, 226n., 237n., 243n.
Chastelain, George: name, 3n., 19; date of birth of, 9n., 11n., 18n., 35n., 39; birthplace of, 10–11, 21, 40; childhood of, 11–12; immediate family of, 17–18; education and reading of, 9, 11–12, 22, 23, 31n., 33–6, 132; early military career of, 36–7; business career of, 27, 38–42; in royal service, 9, 13, 37–8, 39, 42–6; return to ducal service, 13, 46–9; diplomatic career of, 49, 52–4, 57–8, 60–1, 66–9; household service of, 54, 56, 62, 69–72, 147; personal circle of, 72–82; domestic circumstances of, 60–2, 63n., 87–8; marital status of, 61, 212; appointed official historian, 65–6, 109–16; working conditions of, 86–8; working practices of, 143–51; contemporary renown of, 113–14; salary of, 66, 84, 109, 112; relationship with Philip the Good, 76, 245–8; relationship with Charles the Bold, 191, 245–8; as *indiciaire*, 86, 113, 116–17; dies intestate, 16n., 90, 136, 212; tomb of, 9, 15, 210; heraldic arms of, 15–16; noble status of, 10, 12, 19, 24–5, 86; knighthood of, 86; correspondence of, 78, 84n., 87n., 136; handwriting of, 201, 234; lost works by, 63n., 111n., 145n.; language of, 11, 23, 57; and printing, 122, 212; early research on, 3n. *See also* Chronicle of George Chastelain
Chastellain, Pierre, 125
Chaucer, Geoffrey, 109
Chaugy, Michel de, 74–5, 80–1, 188n., 195
Chenebaut, Jean, 87, 245
Chevalier, Étienne, 47
Chifflet, Jean-Jacques, 203, 232, 244
Chifflet, Jules, 154n., 203–4, 244
Chin, Gilles de, 105
Chronicle of George Chastelain: status as official history, 91, 106, 113, 115, 129, 131, 229; sources of, 27n., 70–82, 89, 104, 129–42, 144n., 156, 163–4, 166, 169–70, 185–6, 187; chronology of composition of, 143–5, 147–50; subject matter of, 97, 102, 107, 128n., 156, 159–60, 171, 226; division into books, 159–60, 226; prologue of, 10, 93, 94–5, 167–9; missing passages of, 128, 144–5, 150–61, 225–7; passages wrongly attributed to, 154; claimed impartiality of, 142, 172; propaganda in, 163; relationship to *opuscula*, 116–17, 143, 145–7; editions of, 3n., 197n., 200n.; manuscripts of, 197–227. *See also* Austria, Margaret of
Chronique des roys, ducz et contes de Bourgogne, 221–2, 224

295

Clamanges, Nicolas de, 169, 174
Clercq, Jacques du, 123, 157, 177; access to sources, 104, 134n., 141, 142; family in kingdom, 80n.
Cleves, Adolf of, 46, 121, 214
Cleves, Beatrice of, 121, 214
Cleves, John, duke of, 57, 76, 137
Cleves, Mary of, 124
Cleves, Philip of, 214–16, 217, 218
Clerc, Gillis de, 20n.
Clobbaerts, Marie, 21n.
Clotild, queen of France, 224
Clovis, king of France, 166
Clugny, Jean de, 68
Clyte, Colart II de la, lord of Commynes, 31
Coeur, Jacques, 59
Cologne, archbishop of, 57
Commynes, Philippe de, 145, 219–20; career, 9, 33, 47, 82; family in royal service, 81n.; opinion of Philip the Good, 226–7; of Louis XI, 76; of Charles the Bold, 191–2, 207–8; of *clercs*, 12; of chroniclers, 113; of diplomatic practice, 68. *See also* Clyte, Colart II de la
Compiègne, 27, 186
Condé, bastard of, 192
Constantine XI, Byzantine emperor, 95
Constantinople, 73n., 94–5, 96n., 98, 137n., 156
Copons, Joan de, 158n.
Court, Dimanche de, 53–4
Courtecuisse, Jean, 174
Courtrai, 63
Coustain, Jean, 23n., 33n., 61n., 83
Coutances, bishop of, 68–9
Creil, 42n.
Cretin, Guillaume, 204
Crivelli, Lodrisio, 129n., 138
Croy, Antoine de, 56n., 58, 59, 78, 81–2, 101
Croy, Charles de, 216
Croy, Jean de, lord of Chimay and Tours-sur-Marne, 78, 82, 101, 126, 142; in Valenciennes, 85, 89
Croy, Jean de, lord of Croy and Renty, 81
Croy, Philippe de, lord of Sempy and Quiévrain, 66n., 78, 82, 89, 136, 216
Croy family, 77–9, 81–2, 138, 160, 205, 238–9
crusade, 71, 92, 178; Chastelain's appointment and, 94–102, 159; Philip the Good and, 64, 72, 76n., 174–5

Cueillette, Jean, 121
Culsbrouc, Jan van, chronicler's great-uncle, 30–2, 33, 35, 41–2, 228
Culsbrouc, Jan van, cousin of chronicler's mother, 35
Culsbrouc, Sophie van, chronicler's grandmother, 18, 28, 39–40
Culsbrouc family, 18–19, 40

Dadizeele, Jean de, 220n.
Danicot, Guillaume, 114n.
Danois, Ogier le, 132, 166
David, second king of the Hebrews, 95
Déclaration de tous les hauts faits du duc Philippe de Bourgongne, celuy qui se nomme le Grand Duc et le Grand Lyon, 117n., 147, 172n., 245–8
Déprécation pour messire Pierre de Brézé, 44, 146n., 147
Derval, Jean de, 123
Deschamps, Eustace, 169
Dhane, Lievin, 20n.
Diest, 206
Digoine, Chrestien de, 66n.
Dijon, 98n., 137, 209
Dionysian tradition, *see* St Denis
Doerne, Pieter van, 40n.
Dommessent, Louis, 52n.
Donct, Kateline van der, 22n.
Dordrecht, 153
Doucereau, Jean, 48n.
Douglas, William, earl of, 156
Doutrepont, Georges, 2, 92
Douzy, Guy de, 36n.
Driesche, Jean de la, 24n.
Dunois, Jean, bastard of Orléans, count of, 42n.
Dynter, Emond de, 103, 110

écorcheurs, 47
Edward III, king of England, 110
Edward IV, king of England, 110n., 130n., 137, 245
Eeken, Willem van, 19n.
Egmond, Arnold van, duke of Guelders, 149n.
Eke, 18
Enghien, Jean d', 132
Enghien, 215
Enseignements de vraie noblesse, 12
Épistre à Jehan Castel, *see* Castel, Jean
Épistre au bon duc Philippe de Bourgongne, *see* Le lyon bandé
Épitaphe de messire Pierre de Brézé, 44

Escouchy, Mathieu d', 10, 101, 157, 177, 188n., 197; sources of, 136, 141, 142
Étampes, Jean de Bourgogne, count of Nevers and of, 54n., 158
Eu, Charles, count of, 59
Everwijn, Roger, 26
Eyck, Jan van, 66, 73

Fabri, Pierre, 204
Fallerans, Jacques de, 79
Feast of the Pheasant (1454), 96, 98
Fenin, Pierre de, 187n.
Ferdinand II, king of Aragon, 208
Fillastre, Guillaume, 56n., 113n., 132, 138n., 243; in Angevin service, 83; and dukes of Burgundy, 76, 108, 175, 246; manuscripts of work, 208, 215, 224-5
Flanders, Baldwin IX, count of, 96, 97, 165
Flanders, Charles I, count of, 165
Flanders, Ferrand of Portugal, count of, 165
Flanders, Joan, countess of, 165
Flanders, county of, 30-1, 36, 47, 223; histories of, 102-3, 108, 164; Members of, 30, 60
Flechin, Maillart de, 63n.
Flémalle, Master of, 28n.
Flobecq, 28
Foix, Gaston IV, count of, 43, 179n.
Fontaines, lord of, 72
Fourmelles, Simon de, 31
France, Michelle de, 133n.
Frederick III, Holy Roman Emperor, 98
Freising, Otto of, 160
Fribois, Noël de, 183n.
Friesland, 103, 164
Froissart, Jean, 38, 78, 110, 116, 147-8; chronicle of, 70n., 73n., 104, 135, 141, 152, 202, 219n.

Gaffelkin, Jan, 39n., 41n.
Garter, order of the, 155, 186
Gaudoul, Guillaume, 125
Gavre family, 10, 15-17, 40
Gavre, Jean de, 16
Gavre, Marguerite de, 16
Georget, ducal kitchen-hand, 55
Germain, Jean, 95, 176-7
Gerson, Jean, 169, 170
Gervais, Robert, 174
Gestel, 28
Ghent, 23-4, 52n., 54, 56, 133n.; age of majority in, 39; archery contest (1440), 46; butchers' guild of, 26, 46; churches of, 19, 29, 30, 31n. 32, 66; conflicts with duke, 26, 29n., 60-1, 93, 137n., 154; ducal entries, 11, 26, 61, 63n., 64, 72, 120, 133n., 193; economy of, 22-3; guild of St George in, 46; incomes and cost of living in, 18n., 24n.; manuscript production in, 86, 202; parishes of, 38, 40; political alignments in, 25-6, 28, 228; potential base for ducal power, 60; rhetoricians of, 120; schooling in, 23, 31; shippers of, 22-3, 25-6, 33, 46, 228; *vinders* of, 38, 41
Ghent, Jan van, 38
Gherbode, Thierry, 30-1, 35
Ghinderop, 40-1, 88
Gistel, Margareta van, 37n.
Golden Fleece, order of the, 74-5, 140, 186; foundation of, 153, 159, 186, 188, 226; chapters of, 54, 62, 64, 86, 113, 140, 193, 207; members of, 28, 37, 58, 83, 192, 193-4, 196, 206, 212, 216, 246-7
Gonzaga, Rodolfo, 194
Gorinchem, 204
Gourdin, Amand, 213
Goux, Pierre de, 53
Greeks, 168
Gruuthuse, *see* Bruges, Louis de
Guinegate, battle of (1479), 206
Guise, Jacques de, 103, 224n.
Guyenne, reconquest of, 59, 62, 94-5, 155

Haaltert, 19
Hagenbach, Pierre de, 66n.
Haghen, Mergriete vander, 20n.
Hainaut, Philippa of, 38n.
Hainaut, county of, 1n., 11, 61, 139n., 193; histories of, 103, 104, 108, 224
Halluin, Josse de, 61n.
Haneron, Antoine, 34-5, 46, 57, 61n.
Hanseatic towns, 93
Harchies, Jacques de, 89
Haubourdin, *see* Luxembourg, Jean, bastard of
Haynin, Jean de, 113, 123, 140n., 220
Hector, 99-100
Hellen, Beatryce van der, 21n.
Hennin, Pierre de, lord of Boussu, 89, 212
Henry IV, king of Castile, 150n., 158
Henry V, king of England, 150n.
Henry VI, king of England, 42n., 99, 150n., 155

INDEX

Hesdin, 62, 68n., 71, 72, 77, 86
Hibert, Jean, 140
Higden, Ranulf, 160
Hincmar, archbishop of Rheims, 168
Histoire des Seigneurs de Gavre, 10
Holland, county of, 1n., 78, 103, 104, 152–3
Hollebeke, 27
Holy Roman Empire, 1, 11, 57. See also Charles IV, Sigismund, Frederick III, Maximilian I, Charles V
Huizinga, Johan, 1–7, 90, 171–2, 190, 224, 228–30
Hulthem, Joseph van, 237
Hundelgem, 18n.
Hungary, Ladislas, king of, 140, 189–90
Hungary, Mary of, 217
Hunyadi, John, 130
Hussites, 151

Iacopo, Emanuele de, 145n.
Idegem, 19
Isabella I, queen of Castile, 208
Italian Wars, 92

James II, king of Cyprus, 157
James II, king of Scotland, 156
Jaucourt, Philibert de, 57
Jerusalem, 96, 100
Jews, 167
John II, king of France, 166
Jonghe, Anthone de, 22n.
Julius Caesar, 219
Justus Lipsius, 2
Juvenal des Ursins, Jean, 129, 169

Kalken, 27, 39n.
Kerke, Perrin van der, 38
Knijf, Gillis de, 40n.
Küküllei, János, 129n.

La Barde, lord of, 154
La Charité, 101
La complainte d'Hector, 65, 74, 101, 116n., 122; analysis of, 99–100; MS of, 123
La Gazelle, Alardin de, 57
La Harpe, Robert de, 61n.
Lalaing, Simon de, 46, 89, 101
Lalaing family, 205, 237
La Marche, Olivier de, 61n., 120n., 125, 215; career of, 9, 33, 57, 74–5, 81n., 207, 209, 247; *Mémoires* of, 141, 157, 191–2, 205, 220, 221–3, 224; and Chastelain, 65, 74, 113, 136, 215.

Lambrechts, Gillis, 17n., 21n.
Lamet, Antoine de, 79–80
Lammins, Jan, 20n.
La mort du duc Philippe, mystère par manière de lamentation, 119–20
Lannoy, Guillebert de, 123
Lannoy, Jean de, 69, 78
Lannoy, Philippe de, 121
Lannoy family, 209
La paix de Péronne, 119
La Rière, André de, 125
La Sale, Antoine, 150. See also *Petit Jehan de Saintré*
La Trémoille, Georges de, 13
La Trémoille family, 80
Laval, Gui XIV, count of, 126, 127
Laval, Hélène de, 123, 126
Lay de Nostre Dame de Boulogne, 126
Le Baud, Pierre, 107
Le Bel, Jean, 135
Le Clerc, Charles, 210–12, 216, 233–4
Lede, 19, 39n., 40
Le dit de vérité, 14, 118, 124, 145n.
Leeuwergem, Elisabeth van, 37
Lefèvre, Jean de: origins and career, 25, 86; relations with Chastelain, 73–5, 113, 118n., 140–1, 152–3, 161, 242n.; family in royal service, 80; *Mémoires* of, 104, 109, 110n., 197, 220
Le Franc, Martin, 110n.
Le lyon bandé, 118–19, 125
Le lyon couronné, 123
Le lyon rampant, 123, 124
Lemaire de Belges, Jean, 117, 210
Le miroir de mort, 59n., 123, 124
Le miroir des nobles hommes de France, 125
Le miroir de vie, 146n.
Le mystère du Concile de Basle, 146n
Le mystère de la mort du roi Charles VII, 118n., 122, 124, 146n., 147
Le pastoralet, 177
Le prince, 126
Le Quesnoy, 139n.
Les douze dames de rhétorique, 125, 215
Leseur, Guillaume, 177
Les paroles de trois puissants princes, 123
Lessines, 28
Le temple de Bocace, 14, 122, 123, 132, 146, 215
Le throsne azuré, 59, 65, 116n., 125
Leuze, 215
Levrien, Mathieu, 114n.
L'exposition sur vérité mal prise, 14, 135n.,

145; autobiographical content of, 10, 13; presentation copy of, 86n., 120, 237
Liédet, Louis, 108n.
Liège, 72, 94, 158, 194, 206
Ligne family, 241
Lille, 66n., 78, 86; *Chambre des comptes* at, 51, 84, 87n., 88–9, 138–9, 147, 211, 216; court at, 36, 56, 59, 61, 62, 87
Lille, Alain de, 131
Lille, Robert de, 202, 232
Limbourg, duchy of, 1n., 206
Livre des faits de Jacques de Lalaing, 14
Livre des trahisons de France envers la maison de Bourgogne, 177
Lorraine, François I de, emperor, 232, 244
Losecoat Field, battle of (1470), 158
Lotharingia, 164
Louenge au duc Charles soubs forme de dyalogue, 120–1
Louis IX, king of France, 97, 166
Louis XI, king of France, 3n., 83–4, 108, 158, 182; and Chastelain, 148–9, 181–2, 188; sojourn in Burgundian dominions, 66–8, 97n., 141–2; coronation of, 159, 184
Louis XII, king of France, 214, 226n., 242
L'oultré d'amour, 44, 65, 118n., 123–4, 125
Louvain, university of, 34–5, 36n., 228
Luxembourg, Jacques de, 79–80
Luxembourg, Jean, bastard of, lord of Haubourdin, 79, 95, 101
Luxembourg, Louis de, count of St Pol, 79, 144n., 157, 160, 194–5; military career of, 45, 57n, 59
Luxembourg family, 46, 79, 80
Luxembourg, duchy of, 1n., 58, 94, 104, 179, 187

Machefoing, Jean, 121
Maine, Charles I, count of, 43n., 124
Mansel, Jean, 109, 132
Mantua, 137
manuscripts: BL, Add. MS 54156, 150, 156–7, 197n., 199–200, 201, 237–9; BM Arras MS 256 (406), 148n., 197n., 199, 201, 202, 204, 210, 216, 233–4; BM Arras, MS 516 (827), 197n., 198–9, 201, 232–3; BM Arras, MS 578 (471), 197n., 200, 201, 202, 210, 216, 239–40; BM Besançon, Coll. Chifflet MS 202, 204n., 244; BML, MS med. pal. 120, 121, 209; BML, MS med. pal. 176, 197n., 199, 201, 204, 235, 244; BML, MS med. pal. 177, 197n., 198–9, 201, 231–2; BM Rouen, MS 1234, 126; BN, MSS fr, 2688–9, 197n., 200, 202, 206, 241–2, 243; BN, MS fr. 12788, 123; BR, MS 11101, 86n.; BR, MS 15843, 86n., 148–50, 157, 197n., 199–200, 201, 225, 236–7; BR, MSS 21521–31, 123; Château de Beloeil, MS TA.V.D. 17, 197n., 200, 202, 206, 240–1; Paris, Ministère des affaires étrangères, MSS 24–5, 204n, 243
Map, Walter, 86
Mariette, Guillaume, 48–9, 52n.
Marliano, Raimondo de, 101
Marseilles, 71
Martin, Jean, 73n., 121, 132
Martin, Philippe, 73, 121
Martins, Ghiselbrecht, 17n.
Masmines, Gheerart van, chronicler's grandfather, 18, 19, 20n., 24
Masmines, Gillis van, chronicler's great-grandfather, 18, 20, 24, 27, 37
Masmines, Hector van, 27–8, 32, 37, 40n., 46, 61n.
Masmines, Jan van, 27
Masmines, Louis van, lord of Hollebeke, 27, 28n.
Masmines, Marie van, chronicler's mother, 17, 19–22
Masmines, Philip van, 18n., 27
Masmines, Robert van, 27–8, 37, 58, 61n.
Masmines, Waleran van, 27, 28n., 61n.
Masmines family, 10, 15n., 61
Maximilian I, Holy Roman Emperor, 206, 209, 217–18, 223; servants of, 210, 211, 214, 221
Mayence, Doon de, 132
Meaux, bishop of, 188
Mechelen, 31, 62n., 193
Mehmed II, 100n.
Melun, 134, 186
Mendoza family, 208
Menen, 35
Mennel, Jacob, 218
Meriadec, Hervé de, 79
Mérouvée, 131n.
Meschinot, Jean, 126
Meys, Jacop de, 20n.
Mézières, Philippe de, 166, 174, 175
Michault, Pierre, 113, 118n., 123
Miélot, Jean, 12, 97, 111, 112, 116n.
Milan, duchy of, 129
Miroer des vertus de l'auguste duc Philippe de Bourgoigne, see *Advertissement au duc Charles*

INDEX

mises en prose, 104–5
Moerbeke, 19
Moerkerke, Louis de, 31
Moers, 57
Molain, Odot, 33
Molinet, Jean, 210, 213, 216; as *indiciaire*, 115, 117n.; writings of, 116, 124, 191, 197, 205, 207, 208, 219, 221, 223–4; and Chastelain, 87, 113n., 118n., 122, 123, 160–1, 212, 213, 215, 217, 225, 226, 237
Molinier, Auguste, 102
Monmouth, Geoffrey of, 131
Mons, 62, 64, 119, 246
Mons-en-Vimeu, battle of (1421), 16, 27n., 135, 187
Monstrelet, Enguerran de, 104, 110, 197, 215, 219n.; as a source for Chastelain, 27n., 133–4, 135–6, 140, 152–4, 166, 185–6, 187
Montbazon, 142, 179
Montereau, 1, 50, 100, 166, 187
Montlhéry, battle of (1465), 44, 84
Montreuil, Jean de, 174
Munte, Jan van, chronicler's step-grandfather, 19, 28–30, 32
Munte, Johanne van, 29n.
Munte, Kateline van, 27
Munte, Willem van, 29
Munte family, 19, 29–30

Namur, county of, 1n.
Nancy, battle of (1477), 206, 208
Naples, 137, 211
Nassau-Dillenburg, Engelbert II of, 209, 218, 238, 241; career of, 206–7, 208, 214
Nassau-Dillenburg, Henry III of, 208–9, 218, 238
Nassau-Dillenburg, Jean V of, 208
Navagero, Andrea, 92
Neuss, 78, 136, 158, 160
Nevers, Charles, count of, 43, 155. See also Étampes
Nevers, 65, 99–100
Neville, George, 130
Neville, William, 151
Nicholas V, pope, 96
Nicopolis, 98
Nine worthies, 100
Nivelles, 69
Noah, 167
Normandy, duchy of, 68, 78, 127; reconquest of, 45, 59, 62, 81, 155

Nymhagen, Clais, 21n.

Oignies, Baudouin d', 68
Oordegem, 40
Orgemont, Pierre d', 135
Orléans, Charles, duke of, 52, 65, 81, 101, 108, 184; poetry of, 123, 125
Orléans, Louis, duke of, 100
Orléans, university of, 34
Ormes, Gilles des, 124
Orville family, 237
Ottergem, 21
Overmere, 27

Pale, Lisbette vander, 21n.
Pardiac, Bernard III, count of, 13
Paris, 47, 52, 67, 72, 135, 176n.; dukes of Burgundy in, 98n., 108, 122, 137n., 153, 184; *parlement* of, 47, 53–4, 80, 83, 179; recovery of, 45, 92; university of, 30, 34, 36n.
Paris, Matthew, 130, 225n.
Paternostre, Antoine, 36n.
Patroclus, 100
Péronne, 68n., 81
Petit Dare de Rouen, 124
Petit Jehan de Saintré, 14
Philip I the Fair, king of Castile, 213, 221, 222, 223, 227
Philip II, king of France, 135
Picardy, 36, 53–4, 203
Pillot, Jean, 122n.
Pinchart, Alexandre, 15–17, 51
Pintoin, Michel, 114, 134
Pipaix, 215n.
Pipe, Roland, 33n.
Pirenne, Henri, 1–7, 92, 93, 228–30
Pisan, Christine de, 123, 131, 132n.; advice to princes, 12, 173, 175, 176
Pius II, pope, 71, 158
Plantin, Christopher, 243
Poitiers, Alienor de, 33n.
Poitiers, battle of (1356), 166, 168
Poitiers, Philippe de, 66n.
Poitou, 154
Poncelet, Jean de Ponceau du, 111–12
Pons, Jacques, lord of, 43–4, 154
Pontiga, Rogerin de, 69n.
Pontoise, 42n., 45
Pontus Heuterus, 204
Postelles, Gilles de, 154
Pot, Guyot, 81, 194
Pot, Philippe, 23n., 80–1, 194, 208; and Chastelain, 67, 71n., 76–7

Pot, Regnier, 81
Public Weal, 84, 158, 182

Quillette, Willem, 29

Rabateau, Jean, 47
Raphelengien, François, 243
Rebremettes, Jean de, 130
Recollection des merveilleuses advenues, 120–1
Regensburg, 94, 98, 101, 156, 159
Reilhac family, 80
Renard, General Bruno, 205, 207, 216
Renault, Rolin, 52, 72, 179
Rennes, 80
Ressegem, Gheerart van, 27
Rheims, 47, 122, 147, 168, 182
Richard II, king of England, 132
Richelieu, Cardinal, 204, 243
Richemont, Arthur de, duke of Brittany and count of, 79–80
Robertet, Jean, 118n., 124, 125
Rochebaron, Claude de, 66n.
Rolin, Antoine, 89
Rolin, Guillaume, 195
Rolin, Nicolas, 58, 70n., 79, 101, 209, 232
Roman de Buscalus, 105
Romans, 168, 189
Rouen, 67–8, 156
Roussillon, Girart de, 105, 106n., 132, 166, 222
Roye, 134
Roye, Guy de, 37n.
Roye, Isabeau de, 37
Roye, Jean de, 113, 205n.
Rubempré, bastard of, 73, 81n., 151, 223
Rubempré, Charles de, 213
Rubempré, Jean de, lord of Biévène, 73, 89, 213
Ryolet, Jean, 25

St Amand, forest of, 89
St André, Guillaume de, 106
St Andrew, 59, 221
St Augustine, 160n.
St Cheron, abbot of, 204n.
St Denis, abbey of, 98n., 108, 129, 246; chronicles of, 105, 107, 108, 114–16, 128, 134–5, 161, 166–7, 183n., 218, 225
St George, guild of, *see* Ghent
St John of Jerusalem, order of, 29–30
St John the Evangelist, 30
St Omer, 140

St Pol, *see* Luxembourg, Louis de
St Quentin, 68n.
Saintrailles, Poton de, 152
St Remigius, 168, 188–9
St Vaast, abbey of, 233, 234
Salle-le-Comte, 16n., 62, 66, 85n., 87–8, 132
Sandwich, 68
Santiago de Compostela, 64
Saumur, 42n.
Savoy, Louis I, duke of, 158, 177
Savoy, Philip of, 158
Scaepdrivers, Mergriete, 20n.
Schendelbeke, 19
Scoenhove, Jean de, 137
Senlis, 153
Sigismund, Holy Roman Emperor, 151
Simonetta, Giovanni, 129n.
Soest, 57
Soissons, Waleran de, 62n.
Somme towns, 67, 72, 82, 187
Sorel, Agnès, 13, 43, 156
Steenberghe, Martin, 141
Sunthaim, Ladislaus, 218
Surienne, François de, 155–6
Surigonus, Stephanus, 113

Taillevent, Michel, 111–12
Tardif, René, 124
Ternant, Philippe de, 48, 49, 56–9, 63–4, 79; military career, 36–7, 45, 140
Thionville, ordinances of, 196
Tielt, 28
Tolins, Hugues de, 103, 110, 221
Tollin family, 15–17
Tollin, Philippe, 16
Tonnerre, county of, 53
Torhout, 214
Tory, Geoffroy, 204n.
Tournai, 23, 35, 79, 89, 138, 142n.
Tournai, peace of (1385), 26
Tours, 42n., 142, 144n., 179
Tours, Gregory of, 131
Tincke, Robert, 28n.
Towton, battle of (1461), 150n.
Traité par forme d'allégorie mystique sur l'entrée du roy Loys en nouveau règne, 146n., 147
Trazegnies, Gillion de, 208
Trithemius, Johannes, 218
Troyes, treaty of (1420), 1, 31, 50, 104, 187, 232

Uitbergen, 27, 39n.

universities, 33. *See also* Louvain, Orléans, Paris
Utenhove, Simon, 38
Utrecht, 94, 118–19, 149n.
Uutkerke, Roland d', 31

Valenciennes, 38, 85; Chastelain and, 16n., 62, 84–90, 119–20, 138, 140n., 207; books and manuscripts in, 86–7, 122, 132, 212; guilds of, 85, 213; judicial duel in, 85n., 165, 199n
Vallet de Viriville, Auguste, 7, 44
Valois, Marguerite de, 13, 44n.
Vandomme, Lyonnet de, 152
Venice, 71n., 92, 94
Vergy, Antoine de, a.k.a. de Montferrand, 121, 125
Vermandois, 81
Veyr, Colin de, 202, 240
Vijd, Joos, 66n.
Vilain family, 16–17
Vilain, Jean, 16
Vilain, Marie, 16
Villiers, Jean de, lord of l'Isle-Adam, 45, 46

Villon, François, 123
Virgil, 206
Vitalis, Orderic, 211n.
Voerde, Heinric van de, 19n.
Voeux du paon, 100
Vremde, Willem de, 20n.

Walsingham, Thomas, 225n.
Wauquelin, Jean, 103, 105, 111, 112
Wavrin, Jean de, 104, 109, 110n., 132, 134n., 208
Wendin, lord of, 233
Westrem, 27
Wetteren, 39
Weyden, Roger van der, 97
Wielant, Philippe, 166n., 191–2
Wijnendale, 214

Xenophon, 206

York, Margaret of, 245
York, house of, 158
Yves, countess of, 237

Zeeland, county of, 1n., 103, 104

www.ingramcontent.com/pod-product-compliance
Ingram Content Group UK Ltd.
Pitfield, Milton Keynes, MK11 3LW, UK
UKHW021317180426
11947UKWH00015B/1282